SQL Server 2008
Administration in Action

SQL Server 2008
Administration in Action

ROD COLLEDGE

MANNING
Greenwich
(74° w. long.)

For Jodster, Lachie, and Bella

For online information and ordering of this and other Manning books, please visit
www.manning.com. The publisher offers discounts on this book when ordered in quantity.
For more information, please contact:

>   Special Sales Department
>   Manning Publications Co.
>   Sound View Court 3B   fax: (609) 877-8256
>   Greenwick, CT 06830   email: orders@manning.com

Permissions: Figures 2.2, 2.3, 2.4 and 2.5—images provided courtesy of Advanced Computer and
Network Corp., www.raid.com. Figure 3.1—reproduced with permission from Rui Silva, "Disk
Geometry," MSExchange.org, http://www.msexchange.org/tutorials/Disk-Geometry.html.

⊗ Recognizing the importance of preserving what has been written, it is Manning's policy to have
the books we publish printed on acid-free paper, and we exert our best efforts to that end.
Recognizing also our responsibility to conserve the resources of our planet, Manning books
are printed on paper that is at least 15 percent recycled and processed without the use of
elemental chlorine.

Manning Publications Co.	Development editor: Tom Cirtin
Sound View Court 3B	Copyeditor: Linda Recktenwald
Greenwich, CT 06830	Typesetter: Marija Tudor
	Cover designer: Leslie Haimes

ISBN: 978-1-933988-72-6
Printed in the United States of America
1 2 3 4 5 6 7 8 9 10 – VHG – 15 14 13 12 11 10 09

contents

foreword   xiv
preface   xvii
acknowledgments   xix
about this book   xx
about the cover illustration   xxiii
about the author   xxiv

PART I PLANNING AND INSTALLATION 1

1 The SQL Server landscape   3

  1.1   SQL Server 2008: evolution or revolution?   4

  1.2   Editions and features   5

  *Enterprise   5 ▪ Standard   7 ▪ Workgroup   7 ▪ Other editions
  of SQL Server   8*

  1.3   SQL Server tools   8

  1.4   DBA responsibilities   10

2 Storage system sizing   12

  2.1   Characterizing I/O workload   13

  OLTP vs. OLAP/DSS   13 ▪ I/O metrics   14

v

2.2 Determining the required number of disks and
controllers 15

*Calculating the number of disks required 15 ▪ Bus
bandwidth 17 ▪ A note on capacity 18*

2.3 Selecting the appropriate RAID level 18

RAID 0 19 ▪ RAID 1 20 ▪ RAID 5 20 ▪ RAID 10 21

2.4 Selecting an appropriate storage system 22

*Direct-attached storage 22 ▪ Fibre Channel SANs 22
iSCSI 23 ▪ Recommendations 24*

2.5 SQL Server and SANs 25

*The SAN administrator 25 ▪ LUN configuration 26
Performance tuning 27 ▪ Disaster-recovery options 27*

2.6 Solid-state disks 28

*What is SSD? 28 ▪ Current limitations of SSD for enterprise
deployments 29 ▪ Potential advantages for SQL Server
deployments 29*

2.7 Best practice considerations: storage system sizing 30

3 Physical server design 31

3.1 Disk configuration 31

*Creating and aligning partitions 32 ▪ Distributing load over
multiple controllers 36 ▪ Configuring storage cache 37
Validating disk storage performance and integrity 38*

3.2 CPU architecture 42

*Hyperthreading and multicore 42 ▪ CPU cache and clock
speed 43 ▪ CPU platforms 44*

3.3 Memory configuration 45

Design for future RAM upgrades 46 ▪ NUMA 47

3.4 Networking components 50

*Gigabit switches 50 ▪ NIC teaming 50 ▪ Manually
configuring NIC settings 50*

3.5 Server consolidation and virtualization 51

*Goals of consolidation and virtualization 51
Consolidation 52 ▪ Virtualization 53*

3.6 Best practice considerations: physical server design 56

4 Installing and upgrading SQL Server 2008 58

4.1 Preparing for installation 59

Preinstallation checklist 59 ▪ Service accounts 59 ▪ Additional checks and considerations 60

4.2 Installing SQL Server 62

Default and named instances 62 ▪ GUI installation 62 Command prompt installations 67

4.3 Upgrading to SQL Server 2008 67

Upgrade Advisor 68 ▪ In-place upgrade 70 ▪ Side-by-side upgrade 71

4.4 Developing a service pack upgrade strategy 73

Installation considerations 74 ▪ Application outage 74 ▪ Recommended approach 75

4.5 Best practice considerations: installing and upgrading SQL Server 75

5 Failover clustering 78

5.1 Clustering overview 79

Clustering architecture 79 ▪ SQL Server clustering advantages and limitations 80 ▪ Clustering in Windows Server 2008 81 ▪ Quorum models 82

5.2 Clustering topologies and failover rules 83

Single-instance clusters 84 ▪ Multi-instance clusters 84 ▪ N+1/M clusters 85 ▪ Failover rules 85

5.3 Installing a clustered SQL Server instance 86

Integrated vs. advanced installation 86 ▪ Integrated installation steps 87

5.4 Best practice considerations: failover clustering 91

PART II CONFIGURATION 93

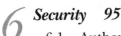
6 Security 95

6.1 Authentication mode 96

Windows Authentication mode 97 ▪ SQL Server and Windows Authentication mode (Mixed Mode) 98

6.2   Networking   98

    Protocol selection and configuration   99 ▪ *Static and dynamic TCP ports   100* ▪ *Windows Firewall   101* ▪ *Network encryption   102*

6.3   Implementing least privilege   103

    Windows and DBA privilege separation   103 ▪ *SQL Server service account permissions   104* ▪ *SQL Server Agent job permissions   105* ▪ *Role-based security   107*

6.4   Auditing   111

    SQL Server Audit   111 ▪ *DDL triggers   115* ▪ *Logon triggers   116* ▪ *Change Data Capture   117*

6.5   Data encryption   119

    Transparent Data Encryption   120 ▪ *Cell-level encryption   123*

6.6   SQL injection protection   123

6.7   Best practice considerations: security   124

7   Configuring SQL Server   128

7.1   Memory configuration   129

    32-bit memory management   129 ▪ *64-bit memory management   131* ▪ *Setting minimum and maximum memory values   132*

7.2   CPU configuration   134

    Boost SQL Server Priority option   135 ▪ *Maximum Worker Threads option   135* ▪ *Lightweight pooling   136* ▪ *CPU affinity   137* ▪ *Maximum Degree of Parallelism   137* ▪ *Cost Threshold for Parallelism   139*

7.3   Server configuration   139

    Recovery Interval   140 ▪ *Fill factor   141* ▪ *Locks   142* ▪ *Query Wait   142* ▪ *User Connections   143* ▪ *Query Governor Cost Limit   143*

7.4   Operating system configuration   144

    Running services   144 ▪ *Processor scheduling   144* ▪ *Network protocols   145* ▪ *Page file location   145*

7.5   Best practice considerations: configuring SQL Server   145

8   Policy-based management   147

8.1   Server management challenges   148

    Enterprise environments   148 ▪ *Enterprise DBA challenges   149* ▪ *The risks of mismanagement   150*

8.2   Policy-based management terms   151

Targets   151 ▪ Facets   151 ▪ Conditions   152
Policies   153

8.3   Policies in action   153

Importing policies from file   153 ▪ Evaluating
policies   155 ▪ Creating a database properties
policy   157 ▪ Exporting policies   158

8.4   Enterprise policy management   159

Central management servers   159 ▪ Policy-based management with
central management servers   161

8.5   Advanced policy-based management   162

ExecuteWql() and ExecuteSql()   162 ▪ PowerShell   164

8.6   Best practice considerations: policy-based
management   166

9   Data management   168

9.1   Database file configuration   169

Volume separation   169 ▪ Multiple data files   171 ▪ Sizing
database files   172 ▪ Instant initialization   174

9.2   Filegroups   175

Controlling object placement   175 ▪ Backup and restore
flexibility   175

9.3   BLOB storage with FileStream   177

BLOBS in the database   178 ▪ BLOBS in the file
system   179 ▪ FileStream data   180

9.4   Data compression   183

Data compression overview   183 ▪ Row compression   185 ▪ Page
compression   185 ▪ Data compression considerations   186

9.5   Best practice considerations: data management   190

PART III   OPERATIONS 193

10   Backup and recovery   195

10.1   Backup types   196

Full backup   196 ▪ Differential backup   199 ▪ Transaction log
backup   200 ▪ COPY_ONLY backups   203

10.2   Recovery models and data loss exposure   204

    Simple recovery model   204 ▪ *Full recovery*
    model   205 ▪ *Bulk_Logged recovery model   206*

10.3   Backup options   207

    Backup location and retention policy   207 ▪ *Backup*
    checksums   210 ▪ *Backup mirroring   210* ▪ *Transaction log*
    marks   211

10.4   Online piecemeal restores   212

10.5   Database snapshots   217

    Creating and restoring snapshots   218 ▪ *Snapshot usage*
    scenarios   219

10.6   Backup compression   221

10.7   Best practice considerations: backup and recovery   223

11   **High availability with database mirroring   226**

11.1   High-availability options   227

    Failover clustering   227 ▪ *Transaction log*
    shipping   227 ▪ *Database mirroring   228* ▪ *Comparing high-*
    availability options   229

11.2   Transaction log shipping   230

    Usage scenarios   231 ▪ *Setting up and monitoring log*
    shipping   232 ▪ *Failover and role reversal   237*

11.3   Database mirroring overview   238

    Terminology   238 ▪ *Mirroring restrictions   239*

11.4   Mirroring modes   240

    High performance (asynchronous)   241 ▪ *High safety*
    (synchronous)   242

11.5   Failover options   243

    Automatic failover with SNAC   243 ▪ *Manual*
    failover   245 ▪ *Forced service   245* ▪ *Failure scenarios   246*

11.6   Mirroring in action   246

    Mirroring setup   247 ▪ *Monitoring database*
    mirroring   250 ▪ *Suspending and resuming*
    mirroring   253 ▪ *Initiating failover   254* ▪ *Considerations for*
    mirroring multiple databases   255

11.7   Best practice considerations: high availability   256

12 *DBCC validation* 260

12.1 DBCC validation overview 261

*DBCC CHECKDB 262 ▪ Granular consistency
checking 265 ▪ Additional DBCC CHECK* commands 267*

12.2 Preventing and detecting corruption 268

SQLIOSIM 268 ▪ Page checksums 269

12.3 Controlling CHECKDB impact 270

*Running against backups 270 ▪ WITH
PHYSICAL_ONLY 271 ▪ Partitioned and granular
checks 272 ▪ User-defined snapshots 273*

12.4 Removing corruption 273

*Interpreting DBCC output 274 ▪ Determining the extent of data
loss with DBCC PAGE 275 ▪ Recovery options 275 ▪ Root
cause analysis 278*

12.5 Best practice considerations: DBCC validation 278

13 *Index design and maintenance* 280

13.1 An introduction to indexes 281

*Heaps 281 ▪ Clustered indexes 281 ▪ Nonclustered
indexes 283 ▪ Index structure 284 ▪ Key
lookup 286 ▪ Statistics 287*

13.2 Index design 287

*Selecting a clustered index 288 ▪ Improving nonclustered index
efficiency 291 ▪ Indexed views 299*

13.3 Index analysis 303

*Identifying indexes to drop/disable 304 ▪ Identifying indexes to
add 307 ▪ Identifying index fragmentation 314*

13.4 Index maintenance 316

*Dropping and disabling indexes 316 ▪ Removing
fragmentation 317*

13.5 Managing statistics 320

*Index statistics 320 ▪ Column statistics 322 ▪ Manually
creating/updating statistics 323 ▪ Inspecting statistics 324*

13.6 Best practice considerations: index design and
maintenance 325

14 **Monitoring and automation 330**

14.1 Activity Monitor 331

Processes 332 ▪ Resource Waits 332
Data File I/O 332 ▪ Recent Expensive Queries 333

14.2 SQL Server Profiler 334

Workload analysis 334 ▪ Server-side trace 337 ▪ Trace
replay 338 ▪ RML utilities 340 ▪ Deadlock
diagnosis 343 ▪ Blocked process report 345 ▪ Correlating traces
with performance logs 346

14.3 Performance Monitor 347

Viewing counters in real time 347 ▪ Baseline analysis 348

14.4 Task automation and alerts 350

Maintenance plans 350 ▪ SQL Server Agent 353 ▪ Event
alerts 354 ▪ Error logs 357

14.5 Best practice considerations: monitoring and
automation 358

15 **Data Collector and MDW 360**

15.1 Component overview 361

Data Collector 361 ▪ Data collection sets 361 ▪ Management
data warehouse 361

15.2 Setup and configuration 362

MDW selection or creation 362 ▪ Data collection setup 364

15.3 Data collection 365

Upload method and frequency 365 ▪ Backup
considerations 367 ▪ Retention period 368 ▪ Logging 368

15.4 Custom collection sets 368

15.5 Reporting 370

Disk Usage Summary 370 ▪ Query Statistics History 371
Server Activity History 372 ▪ Custom reports 374

15.6 Best practice considerations: Data Collector and MDW 374

16 **Resource Governor 375**

16.1 Resource Governor overview 376

Resource Governor benefits 376 ▪ Resource Governor
limitations 376 ▪ Resource Governor components 377

16.2 Classifier function 378

16.3 Workload groups 380

16.4 Resource pools 382

*Effective minimum: memory considerations 383 ▪ Effective
minimum: CPU considerations 383*

16.5 Resource Governor in action 384

16.6 Monitoring resource usage 387

*Performance Monitor 387 ▪ Events 387 ▪ DMVs 387
Establishing resource boundaries 388*

16.7 Best practice considerations: Resource Governor 388

17 **Waits and queues: a performance-tuning methodology 390**

17.1 SQLOS schedulers 391

17.2 Wait analysis 392

*sys.dm_os_wait_stats 393 ▪ Track/get
waitstats 394 ▪ sqlos.wait_info extended event 395*

17.3 Common performance problems 397

*Procedure cache bloating 398 ▪ CPU pressure 406 ▪ Index-
related memory pressure 408 ▪ Disk bottlenecks 409
Blocking 412*

17.4 Waits, queues, and DMV cross-reference 413

17.5 Best practice considerations: performance tuning 413

appendix A Top 25 DBA worst practices 417
appendix B Suggested DBA work plan 419
appendix C Common Performance Monitor counters 421
appendix D Top 10 Management Studio enhancements 423
appendix E Date/time data types in SQL Server 2008 425
index 427

foreword

One of the concepts that I've always been intrigued with is the idea of *institutional knowledge.* Institutional knowledge is the accumulated wisdom of many individual practitioners across many years, even generations, of practice and in a multitude of situations and scenarios. Those professions that have developed deep wells of institutional knowledge for their practitioners have become our most respected careers.

There are many examples of how the institutional knowledge of a certain profession, once it reached critical mass, resulted in enormous breakthroughs in productivity, creativity, and innovation. When the master merchants of medieval Genoa and northern Italy developed the concept of double-entry accounting (which they kept as a trade secret as long as they could), the new skills which enabled them to always know how many assets and liabilities they had at any given moment transformed their merchant houses into the wealth-generating powerhouses that financed the Renaissance. Double-entry accounting was a small change from the long-standing practice of single-entry running tallies (like in check book registers), but as is common with the law of unintended consequences, it proved to be so valuable that it served as the founding principle used by chartered and certified accountants today. When the master builders of medieval Europe incorporated the algebraic and geometric formulas of recently translated Arab-owned Greek manuscripts of Euclid and Pythagoras, they were able to transform the squat and ponderous churches of Christendom into the soaring and incredibly beautiful Gothic cathedrals that, for the first time in history, had more window than wall and stood more than a couple stories in height.

There are other more recent examples too. The physicians of England and Italy first argued in the 1850s that illness was not caused by bad-smelling air (the so-called *miasma theory* of disease propagation that had stood for centuries), but was instead caused by invisible agents too small to see. The medical profession, when complemented by the first anesthesias, soon ushered in a new phase of human health and longevity that is the basis of modern medicine. Here's another example many people may not know. Western civilization's first scientists where Christian monks who had devoted their lives to explaining divine creation. In this endeavor, they were called *natural philosophers* (that is, philosophers who explained the natural world and were exemplified by individuals such as Francis Bacon). They helped develop the foundational principles that would become the *scientific method* that is now so common as to be taken for granted in the Western world. Yet, in their day and in succeeding generations, these concepts and the accumulating institutional wisdom transformed the world.

Today, in the early 21st century, we have a host of new professions centered on information technology (IT) that didn't exist for earlier generations. Among the foremost of these careers is my own chosen profession, database administration. Database administration holds its prominent place because of the absolute value of data to the organization. If an application server experiences a catastrophic failure, management's first question is "How fast can we recover the database?" The hardware is inconsequential. The application, while not trivial, is not the first order of business. The database comes first because the hardware and application is the medium that hosts the part of the application that is valuable–the data. In this sense, database administrators are vital to organizations because they are the guardians of that most valuable corporate asset–its data.

As you read Rod's book, I hope you come away with two major impressions (in addition to the vast number of tips and tricks). The first is that, through Rod's collection of accumulated wisdom, you can see that our profession is maturing rapidly. Database administrators now must not only know the internals of the SQL Server relational engine, but must also have a good understanding of the underlying hardware, high availability, security, monitoring, performance tuning, troubleshooting, as well as the all important backup and recovery. Secondly, you begin to see, as you read Rod's book and its accompanying website at www.SQLCrunch.com, that good processes are often as valuable as understanding the underlying technology. Individuals that enact worst processes (or simply fail to implement best practices) run the risk of spending their time on redundant work and inefficient activities, as well as to put at risk the very assets (that is, the database) over which they are guardians.

My work at Quest Software since 2002 and my years on the board of directors for the Professional Association for SQL Server have enabled me to evangelize the message of rigorous processes and high quality standards for all activities undertaken by database administrators. In the following years, I've had the good fortune to meet many like-minded practitioners like Rod. In a word, we've been devoted students of institutional knowledge for the SQL Server professional.

While Rod's book is not an exceptionally big one, its information is highly concentrated and contains an exceptional wealth of actionable knowledge. Don't forget that many publishers equate the size of the book with its value and, consequently, attempt to manipulate its perceived value with lots of graphics, wide spacing, and large fonts. There's no need for that with this book, since it's simply *loaded* with excellent and immediately useful information. Whether you're a new and inexperienced database administrator or an old hand with decades of experience, I know that you'll find the collected institutional knowledge in this book to be extremely valuable. By applying the knowledge offered in the pages of this book, you'll design, configure, implement, and maintain databases that are as good as any in the world. This will lead to better applications and, in turn, better organizations built upon those organizations.

KEVIN KLINE
Technical Strategy Manager, Quest Software
Founding board member of PASS,
the Professional Association for SQL Server
http://sqlblog.com/kevin_kline/

preface

I love SQL Server. I often find myself defending its various shortcomings as I'd defend a good friend. In a relatively short period of time, it's developed from a good small-to-medium-size departmental database management system into a world class, enterprise-ready system capable of handling the most intense transaction workloads. That's a staggering achievement, and it's only getting better. SQL Server 2008 continues to build on the solid foundation provided by recent versions, and the future for SQL Server looks very bright indeed.

While I only began writing this book in January 2008, it's been a work in progress for about 15 years. Ever since I started working with SQL Server in the mid 1990s, I've been compiling notes on the best way to execute various DBA tasks. In the early years, as I fumbled my way around SQL Server 6.0, I made plenty of mistakes. Although frustrating, they were excellent learning experiences, and I committed to never repeating a previous mistake. A colleague of mine recently said, "Experience is realizing when you've just made the same mistake twice!"

Keen to share in the knowledge I'd collected, my colleagues and clients encouraged me to convert my *personal file* of SQL Server best practices into a format that others could access. In late 2007 I started the sqlCrunch.com website for that purpose. This book takes the concept further, and while all the information contained in these pages can be found in other locations, I believe *SQL Server 2008 Administration in Action* is valuable in that it presents a large collection of best practices in a single book. In short, it's the sort of book I wish I had had when I first started as a SQL Server DBA!

This book has two goals, and which of these applies to you depends on your background. For experienced DBAs, the goal is to introduce you to the new features of SQL Server 2008 that will improve your administration routines. For new DBAs, or for those who administer databases on a part-time basis, the goal is to fast-track your adherence to best practices by avoiding common mistakes. In either case, the intention is not to give you step-by-step instructions on how to do a particular task but to provide general directions on best practices. You'll need to do the hard yards yourself, but my hope is that this book will steer you in the right direction and save you a lot of time and energy by avoiding the mistakes that I've made myself—sometimes more than once!

acknowledgments

One of the great things about working with SQL Server is the incredible support community that has grown alongside the product. From local user groups to conferences and forum websites, these media offer a breadth and depth of knowledge that's possible only because many talented people are willing to share their valuable time in helping others.

In addition to my own experience, this book draws on the knowledge and experience of many others; in particular, I'd like to thank SQL Server MVPs Kevin Kline, Peter Ward, Paul Randal, and Microsoft's Michael Redman.

Thanks also to the reviewers who took time out of their busy schedules to read the manuscript at various stages during its development. Their feedback helped make this a better book: Andrew Siemer, Bettina Hamboeck, Berndt Hamboeck, Massimo Perga, Darren Neimke, Dave Corun, Peter Lee, Richard Siddaway, Sanchet Dighe, Tariq Ahmed, Amos Bannister, and Deepak Vohra. Special thanks to Kevin Kline for writing the foreword and to Peter Ward who reviewed the manuscript and also proofread it shortly before it went to press.

To the Manning team, in particular Michael Stephens, Tom Cirtin, Steven Hong, Katie Tennant, Linda Recktenwald, and Mary Piergies: thank you for your support, encouragement, and ideas. All of you have contributed to a product that I doubted I was capable of producing and will look back on with fond memories for many years to come.

Finally, to my amazing wife and children, Jodee, Lachlan, and Isabella: thanks for your unwavering support, love, and understanding over the last 18 months. I owe all of you plenty of one-on-one time!

about this book

It's getting harder and harder to define the role of a SQL Server DBA. Depending on the organization, a DBA may be involved in a huge number of tasks from data modeling and physical server design through operational tasks such as backup/restore, performance tuning, and security administration. And that's only scratching the surface; specialist development DBA roles are increasingly common, as are those that specialize in the business intelligence space.

While this book will appeal to a broad range of SQL Server professionals, it's primarily targeted at the production OLTP DBA whose role includes tasks such as installation, configuration, backup/restore, security, and performance tuning. In order to devote as many pages as possible to these topics, the following areas are *not* covered:

- Business intelligence tools: SQL Server Integration Services, Analysis Services, and Reporting Services
- Development topics: T-SQL programming, locking, and transaction isolation levels
- Replication and full-text search

In the areas that the book does cover, I've deliberately avoided using a step-by-step approach in favor of an emphasis on best practice. As a result, inexperienced readers may need to supplement their reading with other sources for more detailed coverage. SQL Server Books Online, included as part of a SQL Server installation, is the best resource for this purpose. Further, while many new SQL Server 2008 features are covered, the book's major themes are applicable to earlier versions of SQL Server.

How this book is organized

This book is presented in three parts.

- Part 1 "Planning and Installation" covers best practices for environment planning, hardware selection and configuration, installation, and clustering.
- Part 2 "Configuration" includes chapters covering security, SQL Server configuration, policy-based management, and data management.
- Part 3 "Operations" concentrates on the day-to-day operational tasks such as backups, DBCC checks, index maintenance, monitoring, and automation, and it introduces a number of new 2008 features including Resource Governor and Data Collector.

The final section of each chapter summarizes best practices in a list format. For the experienced DBA, the best way of reading this book is to start with the best practices, and if you require more information, you can read the chapter for the appropriate background.

In Appendix A, I offer my opinion on DBA *worst* practices. Sometimes, reading about inappropriate and/or downright bad practices is the best (and quickest) way to avoid common mistakes.

Companion website

Best practices of any sort, including those for SQL Server, tend to be controversial at times. A best practice in one environment may not be appropriate in another, or it may change over time. Further, internet forums are a great source of false best practices, and once "out there," they tend to take on a life of their own. This book is careful not to make definitive and broad-sweeping best-practice statements, particularly those in which environment-specific circumstances play an important role.

Like any technical book, this book cannot be all things to all people. Together with the diversity of the SQL Server product, different types of DBAs necessitate the exclusion of certain topics from its scope. I apologize in advance to those readers looking for topics that are either not covered or covered in insufficient depth. For this reason, I encourage you to visit the book's companion website, www.sqlCrunch.com.

In order to maximize the value of this book, each chapter has an accompanying website page (listed at the end of each chapter) providing links to white papers, scripts, blogs, and technical articles appropriate to the chapter's content. In order for you to make the best possible choices for your own environment, I encourage you to supplement the knowledge gained from this book with information from the provided website links.

Code conventions and downloads

All source code in listings or in text is in a `fixed-width font like this` to separate it from ordinary text. Code annotations accompany many of the listings, highlighting important concepts. In some cases, numbered bullets link to explanations that follow the listing.

The source code for the examples in this book is available online from the publisher's website at www.manning.com/SQLServer2008AdministrationinAction.

Author Online

The purchase of *SQL Server 2008 Administration in Action* includes free access to a private web forum run by Manning Publications, where you can make comments about the book, ask technical questions, and receive help from the author and from other users. To access the forum and subscribe to it, point your web browser to www.manning.com/SQLServer2008AdministrationinAction

This page provides information about how to get on the forum once you're registered, what kind of help is available, and the rules of conduct on the forum. Manning's commitment to our readers is to provide a venue where a meaningful dialogue between individual readers and between readers and the authors can take place. It's not a commitment to any specific amount of participation on the part of the author, whose contribution to the book's forum remains voluntary (and unpaid). We suggest you try asking him some challenging questions, lest his interest stray!

The Author Online forum and the archives of previous discussions will be accessible from the publisher's website as long as the book is in print.

About the title

By combining introductions, overviews, and how-to examples, *In Action* books are designed to help learning and remembering. According to research in cognitive science, the things people remember are things they discover during self-motivated exploration.

Although no one at Manning is a cognitive scientist, we are convinced that for learning to become permanent it must pass through stages of exploration, play, and, interestingly, retelling of what is being learned. People understand and remember new things, which is to say they master them, only after actively exploring them. Humans learn in action. An essential part of an *In Action* guide is that it is example-driven. It encourages the reader to try things out, to play with new code, and explore new ideas.

There is another, more mundane, reason for the title of this book: our readers are busy. They use books to do a job or to solve a problem. They need books that allow them to jump in and jump out easily and learn just what they want just when they want it. They need books that aid them in action. The books in this series are designed for such readers.

about the cover illustration

The illustration on the cover of *SQL Server 2008 Administration in Action* is taken from a French book of dress customs, *Encyclopédie des Voyages by J. G. St. Saveur,* published in 1796. Travel for pleasure was a relatively new phenomenon at the time and illustrated guides such as this one were popular, introducing both the tourist as well as the armchair traveler to the inhabitants of other far-off regions of the world, as well as to the more familiar regional costumes of France and Europe.

The diversity of the drawings in the *Encyclopédie des Voyages* speaks vividly of the uniqueness and individuality of the world's countries and peoples just 200 years ago. This was a time when the dress codes of two regions separated by a few dozen miles identified people uniquely as belonging to one or the other, and when members of a social class or a trade or a tribe could be easily distinguished by what they were wearing. This was also a time when people were fascinated by foreign lands and faraway places, even though they could not travel to these exotic destinations themselves.

Dress codes have changed since then and the diversity by region, so rich at the time, has faded away. It is now often hard to tell the inhabitant of one continent from another. Perhaps, trying to view it optimistically, we have traded a world of cultural and visual diversity for a more varied personal life. Or a more varied and interesting intellectual and technical life. We at Manning celebrate the inventiveness, the initiative, and the fun of the computer business with book covers based on native and tribal costumes from two centuries ago brought back to life by the pictures from this travel guide.

about the author

Rod Colledge was born in Brisbane, Australia, where he currently resides with his wife and two young children. After graduating with a degree in information technology in 1994, Rod worked in a variety of development and support roles before beginning to specialize in SQL Server development and administration in 1996. Since then, Rod has been involved in many large SQL Server development projects in industries including financial services, real estate, law enforcement, and gaming, as well as for state and federal government.

In 1999, Rod was the lead architect of a custom SQL Server replication solution for a Fijian organization, a challenging project involving bidirectional transactional replication of financial transactions over poor-quality communications lines linking Fijian islands.

Rod is currently the technical team leader of the Education Corporate Reporting and Business Intelligence project at the department of Education and Training in Queensland, Australia.

Through his own SQL Server development and consultancy business, Rod's recently completed projects include a SQL Server 2005 data warehouse and reporting services solution and a web-based license management/asset register system.

Rod has developed a specialty in both the development and administration of very large database systems based on SQL Server. He is an active participant in the Queensland SQL Server Users Group, is the founder and editor of www.sqlCrunch.com, and blogs at www.rodcolledge.com.

Part 1

Planning and installation

Laying the correct foundations is crucial for any project. In the context of SQL Server administration, this involves the correct selection and configuration of hardware components, and preparation and planning for good installation choices. Part 1 focuses on these tasks. You'll learn how attention to detail at this early stage lays the groundwork for a solid platform and allows you to avoid many common mistakes.

The SQL Server landscape

1

In this chapter, we'll cover

- An overview of SQL Server 2008
- SQL Server editions and features
- SQL Server tools overview
- DBA responsibilities

If there's one job where a lack of planning leads to a chaotic and reactive work environment, it's that of the database administrator (DBA). DBAs are often so consumed by the current crisis that the idea of planning for the future armed with appropriate budget resources seems like an impossible dream.

The aim of this book is to assist you in achieving that goal by laying out best practices for database administration with SQL Server. We'll cover hundreds of best practices across many categories, including hardware selection and configuration, installation and upgrades, security, index maintenance, backups, and a lot more.

Before we launch into the nuts and bolts of database administration, let's start with a broad overview of the SQL Server product itself. We begin this chapter with a brief look at the major new DBA features introduced in SQL Server 2008 before moving on to the various SQL Server editions and their corresponding features and

3

limitations. We then take a brief look at some of the SQL Server tools that we'll cover in more detail throughout the book, before closing the chapter with a summary of the key areas of DBA responsibility—areas that we'll spend the rest of the book exploring.

1.1   *SQL Server 2008: evolution or revolution?*

When Microsoft released SQL Server 2005, the general consensus was that SQL Server had finally *arrived* as an enterprise class database management system. With a host of new features, including Common Language Runtime (CLR) integration, dynamic management views/functions, and online index rebuilds, it was correctly considered a *revolutionary* release of the product, coming some 12 years after the first Microsoft release of SQL Server, as shown in figure 1.1.

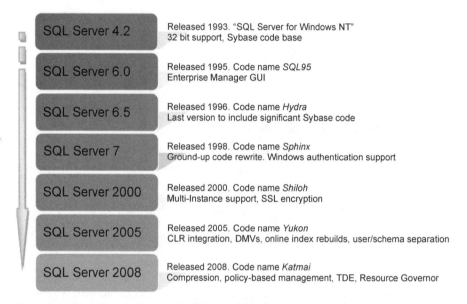

Figure 1.1   From there to here: a brief history of SQL Server from 1993 to today

While SQL Server 2008 improves many of the features first introduced in 2005, it too has an impressive collection of new features, many of which we'll cover throughout this book. From a DBA perspective, the standout new features include the following:

- *Policy-based management*—Arguably the most significant new SQL Server 2008 feature for the DBA, policy-based management dramatically simplifies the process of managing a large number of SQL Server instances through the ability to define and apply configuration policies. As you'll see in chapter 8, changes that violate policy can either be prevented or generate alerts, with groups of servers and instances remotely reconfigurable at the click of a button.
- *Resource Governor*—While SQL Server 2005 included coarse-grained control of server resource usage via instance memory caps, CPU affinity, and Query Governor Cost Limit, SQL Server 2008 permits the definition of *resource pools* into

which incoming connections are classified via group membership. As you'll see in chapter 16, each pool's memory and CPU usage can be constrained, therefore enabling more predictable performance, particularly for mixed-purpose SQL Server instances—for example, a data entry environment that's also used for reporting purposes.

- *Data Collector*—Covered in chapter 15, the new Data Collector feature enables the collection of performance and management-related information such as performance monitor counters, dynamic management view data, and query statistics. In addition to the automated collection, upload, and archival of such information, numerous reports are provided to enable the analysis of the collected data over time, making it a powerful and low-maintenance tool for baseline analysis and various other tasks.

- *Backup and data compression*—In SQL Server 2005 and earlier, third-party utilities were used to compress backups. SQL Server 2008 includes not only backup compression, but also the ability to compress data *within* the database, enabling significant disk space and cost savings, and in some cases, a significant performance boost. We'll cover data and backup compression in chapters 9 and 10.

- *Transparent Data Encryption*—SQL Server 2005 included the ability to encrypt individual columns within a table, but no way of encrypting the entire database and associated backup files. As such, anyone with access to the physical data files or backup files could potentially take the database offsite and have full access. SQL Server 2008 introduces the Transparent Data Encryption (TDE) feature for exactly this purpose; see chapter 6 for more.

In addition to these major new features are a whole range of others, including T-SQL enhancements, fine-grained auditing, support for geospatial data, NTFS-based FileStream binary large objects (BLOBs), and IntelliSense support. I believe that the release of SQL Server 2008 is as significant as the release of 2005.

A number of the new features introduced in SQL Server 2008 are only available in the Enterprise edition of the product. As we move through the book, I'll point out such features wherever possible, but now is a good time for a broad overview of the various SQL Server 2008 editions and their features.

1.2 Editions and features

Like earlier versions, the major editions of SQL Server are *Enterprise* and *Standard*, with a number of other specialized editions. Let's briefly walk through the editions, noting the significant features and limitations of each.

1.2.1 Enterprise

The edition of choice for mission-critical database systems, the *Enterprise* edition offers all the SQL Server features, including a number of features not available in any other edition, such as data and backup compression, Resource Governor, database snapshots,

Transparent Data Encryption, and online indexing. Table 1.1 summarizes the scalability and high availability features available in each edition of SQL Server.

Table 1.1   Scalability and high availability features in SQL Server editions

	Enterprise	Standard	Web	Workgroup	Express
Capacity and platform support					
Max RAM	OS Max[a]	OS Max	OS Max	OS Max[b]	1GB
Max CPU[c]	OS Max	4	4	2	1
X32 support	Yes	Yes	Yes	Yes	Yes
X64 support	Yes	Yes	Yes	Yes	Yes
Itanium support	Yes	No	No	No	No
Scalability and high availability features					
Partitioning	Yes	No	No	No	No
Data compression	Yes	No	No	No	No
Resource Governor	Yes	No	No	No	No
Max instances	50	16	16	16	16
Log shipping	Yes	Yes	Yes	Yes	No
DB mirroring	All[d]	Safety[e]	Witness[f]	Witness	Witness
—Auto Page Recovery	Yes	No	No	No	No
Clustering	Yes	2 nodes	No	No	No
Dynamic AWE	Yes	Yes	No	No	No
DB snapshots	Yes	No	No	No	No
Online indexing	Yes	No	No	No	No
Online restore	Yes	No	No	No	No
Mirrored backups	Yes	No	No	No	No
Hot Add RAM/CPU	Yes	No	No	No	No
Backup compression	Yes	No	No	No	No

a OS Max indicates that SQL Server will support the maximum memory supported by the operating system.
b The 64-bit version of the Workgroup edition is limited to 4GB.
c SQL Server uses socket licensing; for example, a quad-core CPU is considered a single CPU.
d Enterprise edition supports both High Safety and High Performance modes.
e High Performance mode isn't supported in Standard edition. See chapter 11 for more.
f "Witness" indicates this is the only role allowed with these editions. See chapter 11 for more.

1.2.2 Standard

Despite lacking some of the high-end features found in the Enterprise edition, the *Standard* edition of SQL Server includes support for clustering, AWE memory, 16 instances, and four CPUs, making it a powerful base from which to host high-performance database applications. Table 1.2 summarizes the security and manageability features available in each edition of SQL Server.

Table 1.2 Security and manageability features in SQL Server editions

	Enterprise	Standard	Web	Workgroup	Express
Security and auditing features					
C2 Trace	Yes	Yes	Yes	Yes	Yes
Auditing	Fine-grained	Basic	Basic	Basic	Basic
Change Data Capture	Yes	No	No	No	No
Transparent Data Encryption	Yes	No	No	No	No
Extensible key management	Yes	No	No	No	No
Manageability features					
Dedicated admin connection	Yes	Yes	Yes	Yes	Trace flag[a]
Policy-based management	Yes	Yes	Yes	Yes	Yes
—Supplied best practices	Yes	Yes	No	No	No
—Multiserver management	Yes	Yes	No	No	No
Data Collector	Yes	Yes	Yes	Yes	No
—Supplied reports	Yes	Yes	No	No	No
Plan guides/freezing	Yes	Yes	No	No	No
Distributed partitioned views	Yes	No	No	No	No
Parallel index operations	Yes	No	No	No	No
Auto-indexed view matching	Yes	No	No	No	No
Parallel backup checksum	Yes	No	No	No	No
Database Mail	Yes	Yes	Yes	Yes	No

a Trace flag 7806 is required for this feature in the Express version.

1.2.3 Workgroup

Including the core SQL Server features, the *Workgroup* edition of SQL Server is ideal for small and medium-sized branch/departmental applications, and can be upgraded to the Standard and Enterprise edition at any time. Table 1.3 summarizes the management tools available in each of the SQL Server editions.

Table 1.3 Management tools available in each edition of SQL Server

	Enterprise	Standard	Web	Workgroup	Express
SMO	Yes	Yes	Yes	Yes	Yes
Configuration Manager	Yes	Yes	Yes	Yes	Yes
SQL CMD	Yes	Yes	Yes	Yes	Yes
Management Studio	Yes	Yes	Basic[a]	Yes	Basic[a]
SQL Profiler	Yes	Yes	Yes	Yes	No
SQL Server Agent	Yes	Yes	Yes	Yes	No
Database Engine Tuning Advisor	Yes	Yes	Yes	Yes	No
MOM Pack	Yes	Yes	Yes	Yes	No

a Express Tools and Express Advanced only. Basic Express has no Management Studio tool.

1.2.4 *Other editions of SQL Server*

In addition to Enterprise, Standard, and Workgroup, a number of specialized SQL Server editions are available:

- *Web edition*—Designed primarily for hosting environments, the Web edition of SQL Server 2008 supports up to four CPUs, 16 instances, and unlimited RAM.
- *Express edition*—There are three editions of Express—*Express with Advanced Services, Express with Tools,* and *Express*—each available as a separate downloadable package. Express includes the core database engine only; the Advanced Services and Tools versions include a basic version of Management Studio. The Advanced Services version also includes support for full-text search and Reporting Services.
- *Compact edition*—As the name suggests, the Compact edition of SQL Server is designed for compact devices such as smart phones and pocket PCs, but can also be installed on desktops. It's primarily used for occasionally connected applications and, like Express, is free.
- *Developer edition*—The Developer edition of SQL Server contains the same features as the Enterprise edition, but it's available for development purposes only—that is, not for production use.

Throughout this book, we'll refer to a number of SQL Server tools. Let's briefly cover these now.

1.3 *SQL Server tools*

SQL Server includes a rich array of graphical user interface (GUI) and command-line tools. Here are the major ones discussed in this book:

- *SQL Server Management Studio (SSMS)*—The main GUI-based management tool used for conducting a broad range of tasks, such as executing T-SQL scripts, backing up and restoring databases, and checking logs. We'll use this tool extensively throughout the book.

- *SQL Server Configuration Manager*—Enables the configuration of network protocols, service accounts and startup status, and various other SQL Server components, including FileStream. We'll cover this tool in chapter 6 when we look at configuring TCP/IP for secure networking.
- *SQL Server Profiler*—Used for a variety of performance and troubleshooting tasks, such as detecting blocked/deadlocked processes and generating scripts for creating a server-side SQL trace. We'll cover this tool in detail in chapter 14.
- *Database Engine Tuning Advisor*—Covered in chapter 13, this tool can be used to analyze a captured workload file and recommend various tuning changes such as the addition of one or more indexes.

One very important tool we haven't mentioned yet is *SQL Server Books Online* (BOL), shown in figure 1.2. BOL is the definitive reference for all aspects of SQL Server and includes detailed coverage of all SQL Server features, a full command syntax, tutorials, and a host of other essential resources. Regardless of skill level, BOL is an essential companion for all SQL Server professionals and is referenced many times throughout this book.

Before we launch into the rest of the book, let's pause for a moment to consider the breadth and depth of the SQL Server product offering. With features spanning traditional online transaction processing (OLTP), online analytical processing (OLAP), data mining, and reporting, there are a wide variety of IT professionals who specialize in SQL Server. This book targets the DBA, but even that role has a loose definition depending on who you talk to.

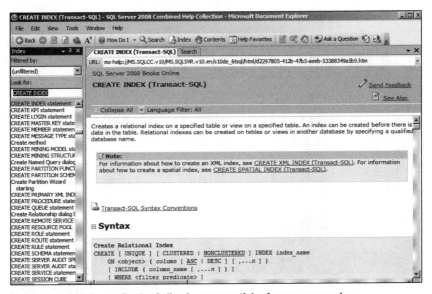

Figure 1.2 SQL Server Books Online is an essential reference companion.

1.4   *DBA responsibilities*

Most technology-focused IT professionals can be categorized as either developers or administrators. In contrast, categorizing a DBA is not as straightforward. In addition to administrative proficiency and product knowledge, successful DBAs must have a good understanding of both hardware design and application development. Further, given the number of organizational units that interface with the database group, good communication skills are essential. For these reasons, the role of a DBA is both challenging and diverse (and occasionally rewarding!).

Together with database components such as stored procedures, the integration of the CLR inside the database engine has blurred the lines between the database and the applications that access it. As such, in addition to what I call the *production DBA*, the *development DBA* is someone who specializes in database design, stored procedure development, and data migration using tools such as SQL Server Integration Services (SSIS). In contrast, the production DBA tends to focus more on day-to-day administration tasks, such as backups, integrity checks, and index maintenance. In between these two roles are a large number of common areas, such as index and security design.

For the most part, this book concentrates on the production DBA role. Broadly speaking, the typical responsibilities of this role can be categorized into four areas, or pillars, as shown in figure 1.3. This book will concentrate on best practices that fit into these categories.

Let's briefly cover each one of these equally important areas:

- *Security*—Securing an organization's systems and data is crucial, and in chapter 6 we'll cover a number of areas, including implementing least privilege, choosing an authentication mode, TCP port security, and SQL Server 2008's TDE and SQL Audit.

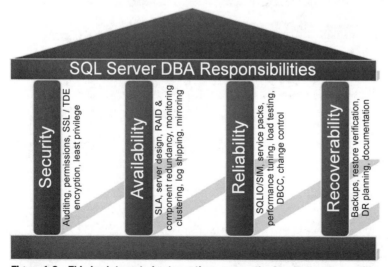

Figure 1.3   This book targets best practices across the four key areas, or pillars, of a DBA's responsibility: *security, availability, reliability,* and *recoverability.*

- *Availability*—Ensuring a database is available when required is a fundamental DBA responsibility, and in this regard, SQL Server 2008 includes a number of high-availability solutions, including failover clustering, database mirroring, and transaction log shipping, each of which we'll cover in this book. We'll also examine the importance of service level agreements in a high-availability plan, and learn how to design redundancy into server components.
- *Reliability*—Unexpected performance and corruption problems not only disappoint users, but they also lead to long, chaotic, and reactive working days for a DBA. Throughout this book, we'll cover a number of proactive maintenance and design practices, such as using the SQLIOSIM utility to validate a storage system, and using Database Console Commands (DBCC) to validate the integrity of a database.
- *Recoverability*—Of course, should disaster strike, a DBA needs to spring into action with a plan of attack for restoring a database as quickly as possible, and in chapter 10, we'll cover this process in detail.

Ensuring databases are *secure, available, reliable,* and *recoverable* are core DBA responsibilities. In subsequent chapters, we'll drill down into each of these responsibilities in more detail, beginning with the next chapter, in which we focus on the important topic of sizing a storage system.

Storage system sizing

Performance tuning SQL Server applications involves finding and addressing performance bottlenecks. While there will always be a bottleneck somewhere, the goal is to reduce the bottlenecks until application performance meets or exceeds the usage requirements, typically defined in a service level agreement (SLA).

Although it's undeniable that the largest performance gains usually come from good application design, inadequate hardware makes resolving performance problems much more difficult. Poorly designed storage systems account for arguably the largest percentage of hardware-based performance problems for SQL Server solutions, and fixing them is usually more complicated than a simple memory or CPU upgrade. It follows that a well-designed storage system removes the biggest hardware-based performance obstacle, and that storage design should therefore lead the way in sizing servers for use in SQL Server environments.

This chapter begins by covering the various I/O loads generated by the two major categories of database applications: online transaction processing (OLTP) and online analytical processing (OLAP). We'll look at the importance of striping data across multiple disks, the use of RAID technology to provide resilience against disk failure, and formulas for estimating the required number of disks to support the expected application load.

We conclude this chapter with a look at the various types of storage systems, including direct-attached storage (DAS) and Fibre/iSCSI storage area networks (SANs), and explore some of the challenges of using SANs with SQL Server. Finally, we cover the emergence of solid-state disks (SSDs) and the significant ramifications this technology will have on server sizing and performance tuning.

2.1 *Characterizing I/O workload*

To determine an application's ideal storage system and disk quantity, it's important to understand the type and volume of I/O the application will generate. This section focuses on the different types of I/O, the metrics used to classify workload, and methods used in measuring and estimating values for the I/O metrics.

In section 2.2, we'll take the information we've learned here and use it to derive the number of disks required to support an application's I/O workload.

2.1.1 *OLTP vs. OLAP/DSS*

When classifying the nature of I/O, two main terms are used: *OLTP* and *OLAP*. An example of an *OLTP* database is one that stores data for a point-of-sales application, typically consisting of a high percentage of simple, short transactions from a large number of users. Such transactions generate what's referred to as *random* I/O, where the physical disks spend a significant percentage of time *seeking* data from various parts of the disk for read and/or write purposes.

In contrast, as shown in figure 2.1, an *OLAP*, or *decision support system* (DSS), database is one that stores data for reporting applications that usually have a smaller number of users generating much larger queries. Such queries typically result in *sequential* I/O, where the physical disks spend most of their time scanning a range of data clustered together in the same part of the disk. Unlike OLTP databases, OLAP databases typically have a much higher percentage of read activity.

OLTP (online transaction processing)	**OLAP (online analytical processing)**
e.g.: point-of-sales system	e.g.: reporting system
Random I/O dominant	Sequential I/O dominant
Read/write intensive	Read intensive
Key metrics: IOPS, disk latency, transactions/sec	Key metrics: IO, throughput, parallel queries
Frequent & small transactions	Fewer but larger transactions compared to OLTP

Figure 2.1 Characterizing I/O workload is a crucial prerequisite in designing the appropriate storage system. Unlike OLTP, OLAP systems typically consist of fewer but larger sequential read dominant transactions.

Note that even for classic OLTP applications such as point-of-sales systems, actions like backups and database consistency checks will still generate large amounts of sequential I/O. For the purposes of I/O workload classification, we'll consider the main I/O pattern only.

As you'll see a little later, the difference between sequential and random I/O has an important bearing on the storage system design.

2.1.2   I/O metrics

To design a storage system for a database application, in addition to knowing the *type* of workload it produces (OLTP or OLAP), we need to know the *volume* of workload, typically measured by the number of disk reads and writes per second.

The process of obtaining or deriving these figures is determined by the state of the application. If the application is an existing production system, the figures can be easily obtained using Windows Performance Monitor. Alternatively, if the system is yet to be commissioned, estimates are derived using various methods. A common one is to use a test environment to profile the reads and writes per transaction type, and then multiply by the expected number of transactions per second per type.

EXISTING SYSTEMS

In chapter 17, we'll focus on the methods used to collect and analyze system bottlenecks, including disk I/O bottlenecks. For the purposes of this section, let's assume that disk I/O is determined to be a significant bottleneck and we need to redesign the storage system to correct it. The task, then, is to collect I/O metrics to assist in this process.

We can use the Windows Performance Monitor tool (covered in chapter 14) to collect the disk I/O metrics we need. For each logical disk volume—that is, the drive letter corresponding to a data or log drive—the following counters, among others, can be collected:

- *PhysicalDisk*—Disk reads per second
- *PhysicalDisk*—Disk writes per second

Note that the averages of these values should be collected during the database's *peak usage* period. Designing a system based on weekly averages that include long periods of very low usage may result in the system being overwhelmed during the most important period of the day.

In the next section, we'll use these values to approximate the number of physical disks required for optimal I/O performance.

NEW SYSTEMS

For a system not yet in production, application I/O is estimated per transaction type in an isolated test environment. Projections are then made based on the estimated maximum number of expected transactions per second, with an adjustment made for future growth.

Armed with these metrics, let's proceed to the next section, where we'll use them to project the estimated number of disks required to design a high-performance storage system capable of handling the application load.

2.2   *Determining the required number of disks and controllers*

In the previous section, we covered the process of measuring, or estimating, the number of database disk reads and writes generated by an application per second. In this section, we'll cover the formula used to estimate the number of disks required to design a storage system capable of handling the expected application I/O load.

Note that the calculations presented in this section are geared toward direct-attached storage (DAS) solutions using traditional RAID storage. Configuring SAN-based Virtualized RAID (V-RAID) storage is a specialist skill, and one that differs among various SAN solutions and vendors. Therefore, use the calculations presented here as a rough guideline only.

2.2.1   *Calculating the number of disks required*

In calculating the number of disks required to support a given workload, we must know two values: the required disk I/O per second (which is the sum of the reads and writes that we looked at in the previous section) and the I/O per second capacity (IOPS) of the individual disks involved.

The IOPS value of a given disk depends on many factors, such as the type of disk, spin speed, seek time, and I/O type. While tools such as SQLIO, covered in the next chapter, can be used to measure a disk's IOPS capacity, an often-used average is 125 IOPS per disk for random I/O. Despite the fact that commonly used server class 15,000 RPM SCSI disks are capable of higher speeds,[1] the 125 IOPS figure is a reasonable average for the purposes of estimation and enables the calculated disk number to include a comfortable margin for handling peak, or higher than expected, load.

> **Storage virtualization**
>
> The process of selecting RAID levels and calculating the required number of disks is significantly different in a SAN compared to a traditional direct-attached storage (DAS) solution. Configuring and monitoring virtualized SAN storage is a specialist skill. Unless already skilled in building SAN solutions, DBAs should insist on SAN vendor involvement in the setup and configuration of storage for SQL Server deployments. The big four SAN vendors (EMC, Hitachi, HP, and IBM) are all capable of providing their own consultants, usually well versed in SQL Server storage requirements, to set up and configure storage and related backup solutions to maximize SAN investment.

Here's a commonly used formula for calculating required disk numbers:

```
Required # Disks = (Reads/sec + (Writes/sec * RAID adjuster)) / Disk IOPS
```

Dividing the sum of the disk reads and writes per second by the disk's IOPS yields the number of disks required to support the workload. As an example, let's assume we

---

[1] Take the manufacturer's published specifications with a grain of salt.

need to design a RAID 10 storage system to support 1,200 reads per second and 400 writes per second. Using our formula, the number of required disks (assuming 125 IOPS per disk) can be calculated as follows:

```
Required # disks = (1200 + (400 * 2)) / 125 = 16 DISKS
```

Note the doubling of the writes per second figure (400 * 2); in this example, we're designing a RAID 10 volume, and as you'll see in a moment, two physical writes are required for each logical write—hence the adjustment to the writes per second figure. Also note that this assumes the disk volume will be dedicated to the application's database. Combining multiple databases on the one disk will obviously affect the calculations.

Although this is a simple example, it highlights the important relationship between the required throughput, the IOPS capacity of the disks, and the number of disks required to support the workload.

Finally, a crucial aspect of disk configuration, and one that we'll cover in more detail in chapter 9, is the separation of the transaction log and data files. Unlike random access within data files, transaction logs are written in a sequential manner, so storing them on the same disk as data files will result in reduced transaction throughput, with the disk heads moving between the conflicting requirements of random and sequential I/O. In contrast, storing the transaction log on a dedicated disk will enable the disk heads to stay in position, writing sequentially, and therefore increase the transaction throughput.

Once we've determined the number of disks required, we need to ensure the I/O bus has adequate bandwidth.

Storage formats

Here are some typical storage formats used by SQL Server systems:

ATA—Using a parallel interface, ATA is one of the original implementations of disk drive technologies for the personal computer. Also known as IDE or parallel ATA, it integrates the disk controller on the disk itself and uses ribbon-style cables for connection to the host.

SATA—In widespread use today, SATA, or serial ATA, drives are an evolution of the older parallel ATA drives. They offer numerous improvements such as faster data transfer, thinner cables for better air flow, and a feature known as Native Command Queuing (NCQ) whereby queued disk requests are reordered to maximize the throughput. Compared to SCSI drives, SATA drives offer much higher capacity per disk, with terabyte drives (or higher) available today. The downside of very large SATA disk sizes is the increased latency of disk requests, partially offset with NCQ.

SCSI—Generally offering higher performance than SATA drives, albeit for a higher cost, SCSI drives are commonly found in server-based RAID implementations and high-end workstations. Paired with a SCSI controller card, up to 15 disks (depending on the SCSI version) can be connected to a server for each channel on the controller card. Dual-channel cards enable 30 disks to be connected per card, and multiple controller cards can be installed in a server, allowing a large number of disks to be directly attached to a server. It's increasingly common for organizations to use a mixture of both SCSI drives for performance-sensitive applications and SATA drives for applications requiring high amounts of storage. An example of this for a database application is to use SCSI drives for storing the database and SATA drives for storing online disk backups.

SAS—Serial Attached SCSI (SAS) disks connect directly to a SAS port, unlike traditional SCSI disks, which share a common bus. Borrowing from aspects of Fibre Channel technology, SAS was designed to break past the current performance barrier of the existing Ultra320 SCSI technology, and offers numerous advantages owing to its smaller form factor and backward compatibility with SATA disks. As a result, SAS drives are growing in popularity as an alternative to SCSI.

Fibre Channel—Fibre Channel allows high-speed, serial duplex communications between storage systems and server hosts. Typically found on SANs, Fibre Channel offers more flexibility than a SCSI bus, with support for more physical disks, more connected servers, and longer cable lengths.

Solid-state disks—Used today primarily in laptops and consumer devices, solid-state disks (SSDs) are gaining momentum in the desktop and server space. As the name suggests, SSDs use solid-state memory to persist data in contrast to rotating platters in a conventional hard disk. With no moving parts, SSDs are more robust and promise near-zero seek time, high performance, and low power consumption. We'll cover SSDs in more depth later in this chapter.

2.2.2   *Bus bandwidth*

When designing a storage system with many physical disks to support a large number of reads and writes, we must consider the ability of the I/O bus to handle the throughput.

As you learned in the previous section, typical OLTP applications consist of random I/O with a moderate percentage of disk time *seeking* data, with disk *latency* (the time between disk request and response) an important factor. In contrast, OLAP applications spend a much higher percentage of time performing sequential I/O—thus the throughput is greater and bandwidth requirements are higher.

In a direct-attached SCSI disk enclosure, the typical bus used today is *Ultra320*, with a maximum throughput of 320MB/second per channel. Alternatively, a 2 Gigabit Fibre Channel system offers approximately 400MB/second throughput in full duplex mode.

In our example of 2,000 disk transfers per second, assuming these were for an OLTP application with random I/O and 8K I/O transfers (the SQL Server transfer size for random I/O), the bandwidth requirements can be calculated as 2,000 times 8K, which is a total of 16MB/second, well within the capabilities of either Ultra320 SCSI or 2 Gigabit Fibre Channel.

Should the bandwidth requirements exceed the maximum throughput, additional disk controllers and/or channels will be required to support the load. OLAP applications typically have much higher throughput requirements, and therefore have a lower disk to bus ratio, which means more controllers/channels for the same number of disks.

You'll note that we haven't addressed storage capacity requirements yet. This is a deliberate decision to ensure the storage system is designed for throughput and performance as the highest priority.

2.2.3 *A note on capacity*

A common mistake made when designing storage for SQL Server databases is to base the design on capacity requirements alone. A guiding principle in designing high-performance storage solutions for SQL Server is to stripe data across a large number of dedicated disks and multiple controllers. The resultant performance is much greater than what you'd achieve with fewer, higher-capacity disks. Storage solutions designed in this manner usually exceed the capacity requirements as a consequence of the performance-centric approach.

In our previous example (where we calculated the need for 16 disks), assuming we use 73GB disks, we have a total available capacity of 1.1TB. Usable space, after RAID 10 is implemented, would come down to around 500GB.

If the projected capacity requirements for our database only total 50GB, then *so be it*. We end up with 10 percent storage utilization as a consequence of a performance-centric design. In contrast, a design that was *capacity-centric* would probably choose a single 73GB disk, or two disks to provide redundancy. What are the consequences of this for our example? Assuming 125 IOPS per disk, we'd experience extreme disk bottlenecks with massive disk queues handling close to 2,000 required IOPS!

While low utilization levels will probably be frowned upon, this is the price of performance, and a much better outcome than constantly dealing with disk bottlenecks. A quick look at any of the server specifications used in setting performance records for the Transaction Processing Performance Council (tpc.org) tests will confirm a low-utilization, high-disk-stripe approach like the one I described.

Finally, placing capacity as a secondary priority behind performance doesn't mean we can ignore it. Sufficient work should be carried out to estimate both the initial and future storage requirements. Running out of disk space at 3 a.m. isn't something I recommend!

In this section, I've made a number of references to various RAID levels used to provide disk fault tolerance. In the next section, we'll take a closer look at the various RAID options and their pros and cons for use in a SQL Server environment.

2.3 *Selecting the appropriate RAID level*

In the previous section, we looked at a method for determining the number of disks we need in order to deliver the required I/O performance. This process included adjustments to take into account redundant disks used to provide protection against disk failure. Designing disk redundancy with RAID is the focus of this section.

A good server design is one that has no, or very few, single points of failure. Among the most common server components that fail are disks. Contributing factors include heat and vibration. A good data center design recognizes this and takes measures to reduce failure rates, such as locating servers in temperature-controlled positions with low vibration levels.

Despite environmental precautions, disks still fail, and the server design needs to take this fact into consideration. The commonly used method for providing protection against disk failure is *Redundant Array of Independent/Inexpensive Disks*, or *RAID*.

In addition to providing tolerance against disk failure, certain RAID levels increase performance by striping data across multiple disks and therefore distributing I/O load among the disks in the RAID volume. The stripe size, specified when building the RAID volume, can make a significant difference in I/O performance; you'll learn more about this in chapter 3.

This section will look at four RAID levels and their advantages and disadvantages from a cost, fault protection, and performance perspective. Note that there are more RAID levels than discussed here, but these are the common ones used for SQL Server implementations. As with the previous section, this section is geared toward RAID in DAS solutions. SAN-based V-RAID is quite different, although there's usually some correlation between V-RAID and traditional RAID, so the principles are still important.

2.3.1 *RAID 0*

Despite the name, RAID 0, as shown in figure 2.2, actually provides no redundancy at all. It involves striping data across all the disks in the RAID array, which improves performance, but if *any* of the disks in the array fail, then the *whole* array fails. In that sense, RAID 0 actually *increases* the chance of failure. Consider RAID 0 as the *zero redundancy RAID*.

Some have suggested that RAID 0 may be acceptable for the tempdb database, given that tempdb starts out empty every time SQL Server is restarted and therefore redundancy of tempdb isn't really important. Although this is true, it's also true that a failure in any of the tempdb disks will cause SQL Server to fail, and you're then faced with rebuilding the disks before SQL Server can be restarted. For most sites, this would lead to an unacceptable outage.

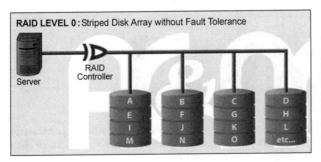

Figure 2.2 Providing zero disk failure tolerance, a RAID 0 partition is optimized for performance only, and is therefore not suitable for use with SQL Server. (Image provided courtesy of Advanced Computer and Network Corp., http://www.raid.com.)

While RAID 0 increases I/O performance through striping, due to the lack of redundancy it provides, I don't recommend you use it for any serious SQL Server implementation.

2.3.2   *RAID 1*

RAID 1, as shown in figure 2.3, is essentially disk mirroring. Each disk in a RAID 1 array has a mirror partner, and if one of the disks in a mirrored pair fails, then the other disk is still available and operations continue without any data loss.

Useful for a variety of SQL Server components, including backups and transaction logs, RAID 1 arrays provide good read performance, and write performance suffers little or no overhead.

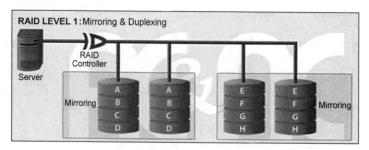

Figure 2.3   A RAID 1 partition mirrors each disk to a mirror pair, therefore allowing continued operation in the event of a disk failure. (Image provided courtesy of Advanced Computer and Network Corp.)

The downside to RAID 1 is the lower disk utilization. For every usable disk, two disks are required, resulting in a 50 percent utilization level.

2.3.3   *RAID 5*

RAID 5, as shown in figure 2.4, requires at least three disks. It addresses the low disk utilization inherent with RAID 1 by using parity to provide redundancy rather than storing a duplicate copy of the data on another disk. When a disk failure occurs in a RAID 5 array, the data stored on that disk is dynamically recovered using the parity information on the remaining disks.

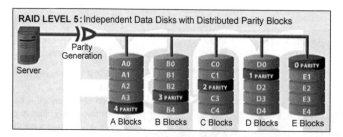

Figure 2.4   Each write to a RAID 5 partition involves multiple reads to calculate and store parity information. For SQL Server systems with substantial write activity, RAID 5 is often a poor choice. (Image provided courtesy of Advanced Computer and Network Corp.)

Disk utilization in RAID 5 is calculated as # of *drives-1/# of drives*. For three disk volumes, the utilization is 66 percent, for five disk volumes, 80 percent, and so forth. RAID 5's main advantage is higher disk utilization than RAID 1, and therefore a lower overall storage cost; however, the downsides are significant. Each write to a RAID 5 array involves multiple disk operations for parity calculation and storage; therefore, the write performance is much lower than other RAID solutions. Further, in the event of a disk failure, read performance is also degraded significantly.

Such overhead makes RAID 5 unsuitable for a lot of SQL Server implementations. Exceptions include installations with either predominantly read-only profiles or those with disk capacity or budgetary constraints that can handle the write overhead.

2.3.4   RAID 10

RAID 10 combines the best features of RAID 1 and 0, without any of the downsides of RAID 5. Also known as RAID 1+0, RAID 10 is the highest performance RAID option. As shown in figure 2.5, RAID 10 offers the high-performance striping of RAID 0 with the fault tolerance of RAID 1's disk mirroring without any of the write overhead of RAID 5.

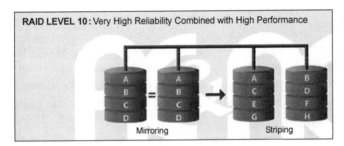

Figure 2.5   RAID 10 combines the benefits of mirroring and striping while avoiding the parity overhead of RAID 5. As such, a RAID 10 partition provides excellent performance and redundancy at the expense of higher cost. (Image provided courtesy of Advanced Computer and Network Corp.)

The downside of RAID 10 is the cost. Requiring at least four disks, RAID 10 arrays benefit from lots of disks to stripe across, each of which requires a mirror partner. In large deployments, the cost of RAID 10 may be prohibitive for some organizations, with the money perhaps better spent on other infrastructure components.

RAID 10 offers the most advantages to SQL Server and, despite the cost, should be seriously considered for environments requiring both high performance and fault tolerance. Table 2.1 compares RAID 10 with RAID 0, 1, and 5.

Table 2.1   RAID level comparisons

Attribute	RAID 0	RAID 1	RAID 5	RAID 10
Disk failure tolerance	0	>=1	1	>=1
Disk utilization %	100%	50%	66%+	50%
Read performance	High	High	High	High
Write performance	High	Medium	Low	Medium
SQL Server suitability	Bad	Good	Limited	Good

Finally, it's worth mentioning that RAID can be implemented at either the software level, via the Windows operating system, or the hardware level, using dedicated RAID controller cards. Software RAID shouldn't be used in server class implementations as doing so consumes operating system resources and doesn't offer the same feature set as hardware implementations. Hardware RAID requires no operating system resources and provides additional benefits, such as more RAID-level options, battery- backed disk cache (covered in chapter 3), and support for swapping out failed disks without bringing down the system.

Let's move on now and cover the different types of storage systems available today.

2.4   Selecting an appropriate storage system

In addition to DAS, recent years have seen the introduction of a number of other types of storage solutions. As well as DAS, this section will investigate Fibre Channel and iSCSI SANs. We'll explore their advantages and disadvantages for use in SQL Server systems from various perspectives, including performance, cost, manageability, and disaster recovery.

2.4.1   Direct-attached storage

Of the three storage options presented in this section, DAS is the most established and is used in a large percentage of SQL Server systems of varying size and usage profiles. As the name suggests, DAS systems connect disks directly to a server, either internally within the server itself or in external storage cabinets filled with disks connected to the server via controller cards.

Correctly configured DAS systems can rival or even exceed the I/O performance obtained with SANs. Using multiple external disk enclosures, you can build DAS systems containing hundreds of disks, and when these systems are connected to multiple controllers, the I/O performance that can be achieved is capable of servicing the most demanding workloads.

Unlike SANs, DAS systems don't rely on expensive storage infrastructure. As such, initial DAS costs tend to be much lower than SANs. On the downside, organizations with lots of DAS-configured servers may find that combined disk utilization levels and management overhead actually raise the cost above that of a SAN. Further, unlike SANs, DAS systems have limited disaster recovery options.

2.4.2   Fibre Channel SANs

Fibre Channel SANs are self-contained disk systems containing hundreds or even thousands of disks. Unlike DAS systems, which are connected to a single server, multiple servers can connect to a SAN, as shown in figure 2.6, via special host bus adapter (HBA) cards installed in each connected server. Disks within the SAN are grouped together into *logical unit numbers* (LUNs) and presented as required to connected servers. The server sees the LUN as a locally attached disk.

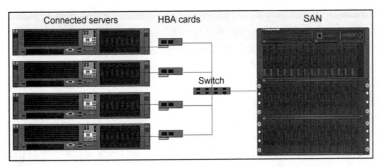

Figure 2.6 A typical storage area network. In this example, four servers connect to the SAN via their own internal HBA cards and a dedicated switch.

While expensive to set up initially, SANs provide increased disk usage efficiency, simplify storage management and allocation, and when configured correctly, can provide exceptional I/O performance for SQL Server platforms. Furthermore, SAN cache capacity, often running into hundreds of gigabytes, is far superior to that found in most DAS systems.

Depending on the vendor and model, SANs also offer superior disaster-recovery options. Examples of this include synchronously replicating LUN data to another SAN at a remote site and leveraging SQL Server's Virtual Device Interface (VDI) to enable near-instant database backup and restores by "snapping" locally mirrored LUNs.

On the downside, SANs are often configured for disk usage efficiency at the expense of maximizing performance. When you configure a SQL Server storage system for maximum performance, data is spread across as many dedicated physical disks as possible, often resulting in each disk having a low utilization percentage. One of the major benefits of a SAN is sharing disks among many servers to maximize usage. These are conflicting goals and, unless well understood, often lead to poor SQL Server performance. As a result, some organizations dedicate an entire SAN to a single, mission-critical database, thereby obtaining the best performance, while also benefiting from the scale and disaster-recovery options of SAN solutions.

Performance testing of SAN solutions needs to be conducted taking into account the impact from other connected servers, particularly if they're using LUNs sharing the same disks. As a result, performance testing in a SAN environment tends to be more complex compared to DAS.

These issues will be explained in further detail in the next section. For now, suffice to say that the correct configuration of a SAN is crucial in delivering high storage performance to SQL Server.

2.4.3 *iSCSI*

Apart from DAS, lower-cost alternatives to Fibre Channel SANs include network-attached storage (NAS) and iSCSI. NAS systems aren't recommended for use with SQL Server as some of them can't guarantee the write ordering that SQL Server requires in maintaining data integrity. Internet SCSI (iSCSI) SANs are recommended instead of NAS.

iSCSI is the name given to a network protocol that carries SCSI commands over a TCP/IP network. iSCSI SANs are similar to Fibre Channel SANs in that they're independent of the servers connected to them. Unlike a Fibre Channel SAN, servers connect to iSCSI systems over a standard TCP/IP infrastructure.

Best practice dictates connecting servers to the iSCSI SAN over a dedicated 1- or 10GB network physically separate from the main network. This involves dedicated switches and servers with multiple network cards, or separate iSCSI HBA cards, to connect to both the public network and the dedicated iSCSI network. The physical separation of networks enables the best I/O performance and reliability. Further, the connections to the iSCSI SAN should ideally be set up using dual network cards in a teaming arrangement. We'll cover NIC teaming in the next chapter.

Given the TCP/IP-centric nature of iSCSI, the components required to connect servers to iSCSI SANs are typically less expensive than the components used for Fibre Channel SANs. Standard network cards can be used to connect to the iSCSI SAN with software components (such as the Microsoft iSCSI Software Initiator), enabling the iSCSI support. Alternatively, dedicated iSCSI HBA cards can be used to offload iSCSI processing from the CPU and improve I/O throughput while reducing system overhead.

iSCSI SANs are becoming increasingly popular due to the lower cost of entry compared to the Fibre alternative, and the ease with which a storage network can be established. You'll see an example of this in chapter 5 when we take a look at the installation of a SQL Server failover cluster. The systems used for this installation are all virtualized, including a virtualized iSCSI host server. Both cluster nodes use the host for storage purposes via Rocket Division's StarWind iSCSI software.

Table 2.2 compares and contrasts the features and attributes of the three storage systems we've just covered. *TCO* (total cost of ownership) assumes a medium-to-large data center. *DR options* refers to the built-in ability of the storage system to offer block replication, snapshot backups, and other useful disaster-recovery features. *Scale* refers to the number of disks that can be stored within the system. *DBA control* refers to the ability of a DBA to quickly configure a storage system to precise requirements.

Table 2.2 Storage system attributes

System	Initial cost	TCO	DR options	Scale	DBA control
DAS	Low	Moderate	Poor	Moderate	High
iSCSI SAN	Moderate	Low	Good	Good	Low
Fibre SAN	High	Low	Good	Good	Low

2.4.4 Recommendations

Compared to DAS, commonly used SAN solutions offer superior disaster-recovery options, and TCO is typically lower with SAN solutions for medium-to-large enterprises.

In most cases, either DAS or Fibre/iSCSI SANs can be configured to deliver the required performance. One advantage DAS systems have over SANs is DBA control. It's much easier for a DBA to configure DAS to meet precise performance requirements than it is to request a specific configuration from the SAN administrator who has to take into account numerous other servers sharing the same SAN.

Perhaps the deciding factor in choosing a storage system is the required number of disks they must support. Earlier we focused on determining the number of disks required to support a specific workload. If the number runs into the hundreds or thousands, then SAN solutions are the clear choice, particularly considering the disaster-recovery options they provide. For smaller disk numbers, either DAS or SANs are valid options, but the overall cost, management, and disaster-recovery options should be considered before making a decision.

It's not uncommon for the storage system validation process to be skipped when SQL Server is installed on a SAN. This is often due to DBAs not having the same degree of control over the SAN as they would over DAS. The next section explores the importance of a good working relationship between the DBA and the SAN administrator in ensuring the required performance of SQL Server deployments involving SAN storage.

2.5   SQL Server and SANs

Don't make the mistake of thinking that because SANs are big and expensive you'll be guaranteed to get good I/O performance. SAN storage design goals are often in conflict with those of SQL Server. SANs are effective at maximizing disk utilization by sharing a large central store of disks between many servers. In contrast, SQL Server benefits from striping over dedicated disks, with an emphasis on disk quantity rather than utilization.

This section addresses some of the common issues that DBAs face in SAN-based environments, including the relationship with the SAN administrator, LUN configuration, performance tuning, and disaster-recovery options.

2.5.1   The SAN administrator

If you're like me, you like being in control. You like having operating system administrator privileges to all database servers, despite best practice, and you like having direct control over disk configuration. In environments with multiple servers and different applications sharing SAN storage, such control is unlikely, particularly when the DBA and SAN administration roles are separated. In such sites, it's not uncommon for the SAN administrator to be dismissive of the DBA's concerns about SAN configuration; often with a *let the SAN take care of it* attitude.

Like any other storage system, SAN disks that are presented to SQL Server need to be configured in line with the storage practices we've already covered. Given the complex, shared nature of SANs and the difficulty of changing a design after deployment, it's critical for you to become involved in the SAN configuration as early as possible and present storage requirements from a DBA's perspective.

I've been fortunate to work in environments with highly skilled SAN administrators who were receptive to the unique storage requirements of SQL Server. Through our good working relationship, we were able to combine our skill sets to deliver reliable, high-performance SAN storage for SQL Server. Unfortunately, such outcomes aren't always achieved; the most common problem is LUN configuration, which we'll look at next.

2.5.2   *LUN configuration*

A LUN is a logical unit of SAN disk created by the SAN administrator and presented to an attached server's operating system. The server is unaware of the physical makeup of the disks involved in the LUN, and sees it as a single locally attached disk.

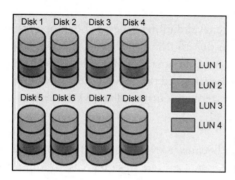

As shown in figure 2.7, each physical disk in the SAN can be carved up into parts and used in the creation of separate LUNs. As a result, LUNs from many servers can all be using different parts of the same physical disk.

Figure 2.7   A sample LUN composition. Physical disks are broken up into slices, or *hypers*. A LUN is constructed by combining hypers from several disks.

When troubleshooting performance problems involving SAN storage, I've found it useful to ask the SAN administrator a series of questions involving the makeup of the LUNs:

- *How many individual physical disks are included in the SQL Server LUNs?* Remembering the principle of striping across many physical disks, if a LUN consists of a small number of physical disks, then performance may be less than ideal.
- *What other servers are sharing the physical disks in the LUNs, and what is their I/O profile?* If many servers' LUNs share the same physical disks, performance may be reduced.[2] This is particularly important for transaction log LUNs. Transaction log I/O is sequential in nature, and dedicated physical disks mean the disk heads are able to stay in position, with writes proceeding in a sequential manner. This is obviously not possible if the transaction log LUNs are created on disks containing other LUNs. For SQL Server applications with high transaction log rates, this can have a large impact on transaction response time, leading to decreased performance and throughput.
- *What are the RAID levels of the LUNs?* Earlier in the chapter, we covered the various RAID levels, and noted that RAID 5 has a disk write overhead and is therefore not an ideal choice for SQL Server applications with a high percentage of disk writes. Given the SAN goal of increased disk utilization, RAID 5 is often chosen as the default RAID level. The SAN administrator should be able to tell you the current RAID level and the different levels supported in the SAN.

---

[2]   Some SAN solutions use a balancing mechanism whereby hypers are moved between physical disks for better I/O balancing.

- *Are my LUNs zoned?* Zoning is the process of matching disks and LUNs to particular servers via storage array ports, increasing security and I/O bandwidth as a result. In SANs with thousands of LUNs and attached servers, this is particularly important in guaranteeing minimum service levels.

The answers to these questions (or lack thereof in some cases) quickly establish the SAN administrator's degree of skill and knowledge of the SAN in regard to SQL Server's unique storage requirements. A correctly configured SAN is a vital component in any performance-tuning process, our next subject.

2.5.3 *Performance tuning*

Like any other storage system, performance testing a SAN before operational commissioning is critical in establishing a degree of confidence in the configuration. Unlike DAS, SANs have a number of specific (often vendor-specific) configuration settings that require specialist knowledge to derive maximum benefit.

Storage virtualization and large amounts of cache often obscure disk performance from tools such as Windows Performance Monitor. Therefore, it's wise to involve storage administrators and/or SAN vendors with vendor-supplied SAN monitoring tools and techniques to measure *actual* performance during any performance monitoring and baseline exercise.

Two commonly tuned SAN settings are the storage cache and the HBA queue depth setting. The SAN cache size is typically much larger than direct-attached cache, with more options for adjusting the read/write percentage. Take care when performance testing SANs containing large disk cache: make sure the tests are large enough, and run for long enough, to exhaust the disk cache and deliver real I/O performance metrics, not just those satisfied from cache. Like standard disk controller cache, SAN cache should be optimized for writes rather than reads. We'll discuss storage cache in greater detail in chapter 3.

HBA cards connecting the server to the SAN have a setting called *Queue Depth* that governs the number of I/O requests that can be queued at a given time. The default HBA queue depth setting is typically between 8 and 32. For SQL Server deployments, a queue depth value of 32 or greater often results in increased I/O performance, although changes to this setting should be confirmed with the storage vendor and validated with performance tests that confirm the effect of the change.

2.5.4 *Disaster-recovery options*

One of the main benefits of SAN storage from a DBA's perspective is the enhanced disaster-recovery options provided. SANs such as the EMC *Symmetrix* provide features such as block-level disk replication to a remote data center and near-instant, split mirror backup and recovery using SQL Server's VDI.

You should investigate such features as part of database disaster-recovery planning. While they may incur additional costs due to software licensing and increased storage requirements, they are important features to consider as part of realizing the full investment in the SAN.

SQL Server is capable of working with most modern SAN solutions from vendors such as EMC, Hitachi, IBM, and HP. Before purchasing, you should ensure the vendor guarantees the SAN's compatibility with SQL Server's specific I/O requirements such as write ordering. These I/O requirements are well known to SAN vendors and available for download from the Microsoft website. More information is available at http://support.microsoft.com/default.aspx/kb/967576.

In closing the chapter, let's examine an emerging storage technology that has the potential, among other benefits, of dramatically increasing I/O performance.

2.6   Solid-state disks

Solid-state disk (SSD) technology has been around for many years. When compared to traditional spindle-based hard drive storage, SSD storage, also referred to as *flash storage*, offers many crucial advantages, including reduced power consumption, smaller size, and reduced seek latency. It's used today in a broad range of consumer electronics devices, from USB memory sticks and MP3 players to recently released laptop hard drives.

In contrast, the implementation of SSDs in the enterprise space has been hampered by a number of key limitations, primarily the relatively poor random write performance and the increased cost. There's no denying that once these limitations are overcome (there's credible evidence to suggest we're almost there), enterprise-based deployments of flash storage are a real possibility, and 2009 may well be the tipping point.

Let's have a closer look at SSD, beginning with an overview of how it works and its key limitations, followed by the important ramifications it will have on SQL Server deployments in the not-too-distant future.

2.6.1   What is SSD?

In contrast to spindle-based hard drives where movable disk heads are positioned over spinning magnetized platters, SSD drives have no moving parts, storing data in an array of *cells*. SSD-based storage offers the following benefits over traditional spindle-based hard drives:

- Reduced seek latency
- Faster boot times
- Lower power consumption
- Shock resistance
- Reduced weight
- Lower heat generation

From a SQL Server perspective, arguably the greatest advantage of flash-based storage is its very low seek latency. In a traditional hard disk, accessing data requires spinning platters and moving heads in order to read data from the appropriate section of the disk. Therefore, seek time becomes the dominant cost of random I/O operations typical of OLTP applications. In contrast, seek latency in flash storage is constant (and low), regardless of the physical location of the required data on the flash device.

Where traditional hard drive seek latencies are measured in milliseconds and their IOPS in the hundreds, SSD latencies are measured in *microseconds* with IOPS in the *tens of thousands*. In summary, random read I/O operations are orders of magnitude faster.

Despite the very good random read performance, SSD-based storage faces a number of obstacles before it will see widespread use in the enterprise space, as you'll see next.

2.6.2 *Current limitations of SSD for enterprise deployments*

One of the key limitations of flash storage is the process used to overwrite existing data. Unlike spindle-based storage, which can simply overwrite data as required, flash storage must first *erase* cells before the new data can be stored. As a result, write performance, particularly *random* write performance, is (currently) lower than traditional spindle-based storage.

In addition to the erase operation slowing write performance, there's a limitation to the number of times a given cell can be erased and reused, therefore limiting the usable life of a given flash drive. Finally, the cost of flash storage makes its implementation in large database applications very expensive. While a single 320GB laptop drive may be affordable, the cost of a RAID-based storage array with terabytes of capacity is prohibitively expensive for most organizations.

Given the massive potential of flash storage for large-scale server use, manufacturers are coming up with various implementations to overcome its current weaknesses, with internal *write balancing* across cells to reduce wear and increase usage life, and several methods to increase write performance. Further, the increased production rates are seeing a corresponding decrease in cost.

It's the expectation of a lot of experts that flash-based storage will soon become a common server-based storage option, with SQL Server databases a prime beneficiary.

2.6.3 *Potential advantages for SQL Server deployments*

In almost all cases, the storage system is the slowest component of a server. It follows that a performance-tuning exercise, particularly for SQL Server deployments, will have a core goal of reducing the amount of data that needs to be read from and written to disk, therefore addressing the most likely performance bottleneck. Effective indexing strategies are front and center in this process, and we'll cover this topic in detail in chapter 13.

With the promise of a potentially massive increase in I/O performance, particularly in large-scale SSD-based arrays, one of the real implications of SSD storage is for the bottleneck to begin shifting away from disk I/O to the CPU and other server components. In turn, this has a number of interesting implications from a DBA perspective, not the least of which is for poor database design to be masked by improved I/O performance.

No one is seriously suggesting that database design will no longer be important, but there's no doubt that SSD technology is a potential game changer for the DBA, opening up new opportunities and forcing a reexamination of server-sizing and performance-tuning strategies in the years to come.

SSD disks have already started to appear in top-end SAN storage solutions; it won't be long before this technology filters down and becomes available as commodity server components.

2.7   *Best practice considerations: storage system sizing*

This chapter addressed server sizing from a storage performance perspective. Although there are some compute-constrained and network-constrained SQL Server implementations, they are reasonably rare, with the most common hardware problems related to poor storage design.

- Classify application workload as OLAP or OLTP and be aware of the difference in I/O patterns and bandwidth requirements between sequential and random I/O.
- Measure and implement the required number of disks to support the I/O workload. SQL Server performance is increased by striping data across many disks, thus having multiple spindles in action servicing I/O requests.
- SCSI or SAS disks (or Fibre in SAN-based solutions) typically offer higher performance than SATA disks, particularly ones with very high capacity. SATA disks, however, are a cost-effective option for smaller deployments of SQL Server or as online backup disks.
- Size storage for performance first, and then consider capacity requirements.
- Avoid RAID 0, and only use RAID 5 for applications with little write activity, or where budget is limited and the performance overhead is acceptable.
- When comparing and selecting a storage system, consider all aspects, including initial and total cost, DBA control, disaster-recovery options, scale, and performance.
- Develop a strong working relationship with the SAN administrator and present storage requirements from a DBA perspective (early in the design process) in order to avoid poorly configured SAN storage.
- If possible, create transaction log LUNs on dedicated SAN disks, particularly for databases with high transaction rates.
- When performance testing on a SAN, be mindful of how the production system LUNs will be configured, and take into account the load from other applications with LUNs on the same disks as the SQL Server LUNs.

Additional information on the best practices covered in this chapter can be found online at http://www.sqlCrunch.com/storage.

In the next chapter, we'll continue our look at storage, but from a broader, physical server design perspective.

Physical server design

In this chapter, we'll cover

- Disk allocation size and partition offset
- SQLIO and SQLIOSIM
- Benefits of a 64-bit platform
- NUMA architecture
- Server consolidation and virtualization

Chapter 2 addressed the important issue of determining I/O requirements and building a storage system to match. The selection of server components is directly related and will be the focus of this chapter.

In this chapter we look at various server components, including the CPU, memory, disk, and network. We explore the important properties of these components and their impact on SQL Server from both performance and fault tolerance perspectives. This chapter concludes by focusing on the ever-increasing march toward server consolidation and virtualization.

3.1   Disk configuration

As hardware components simultaneously increase in speed and capacity while falling in price, one of the consequences is a tendency to spend less time analyzing the precise performance requirements of a database application. Today's off-the-shelf/ commodity database servers from the major system vendors are both powerful and flexible enough for almost all database implementations. Given that, regardless of the available power, one of the fundamental truths of any computing system is that there will always be a bottleneck somewhere (and in most cases, particularly for SQL Server systems, the bottleneck is usually in the disk subsystem), making disk configuration an important DBA skill.

Multicore CPUs and higher-capacity (and cheaper) memory chips have made CPU and memory configuration reasonably straightforward. Disk configuration, on the other hand, is more involved, and for a disk-intensive server application such as SQL Server, correctly configuring disk storage components is critical in ensuring ongoing performance and stability.

As well as being the most complicated hardware bottleneck to fix once in production, incorrectly configured disks and poor data placement are arguably the most common cause of SQL Server performance problems. Chapter 9 will tackle disk management from a SQL Server data placement perspective. For now, let's focus on disk configuration from a hardware and operating system perspective. In this section, we'll take a look at disk drive anatomy, partition offsets, allocation unit size, using multipathing software, and configuring storage cache.

3.1.1 *Creating and aligning partitions*

Preparing disks for use by SQL Server involves configuring RAID arrays, creating partitions, and formatting volumes. We'll examine each of these tasks shortly, but first let's cover some of the terms used when discussing the anatomy of a disk drive:

- Each physical disk is made up of multiple magnetized *platters,* which are stacked on top of each other, with each platter storing data on both sides (top and bottom).
- A *track* is a ring of data storage on a disk platter. Tracks are numbered beginning with zero, starting from the outermost to the innermost ring.
- Each track consists of multiple *sectors,* which cut the track into portions similar to a pie slice. Sectors typically have a fixed size of 512 bytes, and represent the smallest accessible unit of data on the disk.
- Earlier disks had a fixed amount of sectors per track. Considering the smaller length of tracks toward the center of the disk platters, sectors on the outer tracks were padded with blank space to keep the sectors per track at a fixed ratio. Modern disks use various techniques[1] to utilize the blank space on the outer tracks to increase disk capacity.
- *Disk heads,* positioned above and below each platter, move in and out from the center of the disk. This motion, together with the spinning of the disk platters

---

[1] The most common technique is zoned-bit recording (ZBR), which uses more sectors on the outer track.

on their central axes, allows the disk heads to access the entire surface of each disk platter.

- An *allocation unit* is the smallest file allocation size used by Windows. The default allocation unit size is 4K, which equates to eight sectors. Smaller allocation units reduce the amount of wasted space for small files but increase fragmentation. Larger allocation units are useful for larger files and reducing fragmentation.

Figure 3.1 illustrates some of these terms.

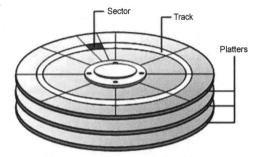

Figure 3.1 Anatomy of a hard disk. (Reproduced with permission: Rui Silva, "Disk Geometry," MSExchange.org, http://www.msexchange.org/ tutorials/Disk-Geometry.html.)

RAID ARRAY STRIPE SIZE

In chapter 2 we discussed commonly used RAID levels such as RAID 0 and RAID 10, both of which stripe data across multiple disks. Striping works by dividing data to be written to disk into chunks and spreading the chunks over the separate disks in the RAID array. When the data is read, the RAID controller reads the individual chunks from the required disks and reconstructs the data into the original format.

The RAID stripe size, not to be confused with the allocation unit size, determines the size of each chunk of data. Setting the stripe size too small will create additional work for the RAID controller in splitting and rejoining requested data. The *best* RAID stripe size is a contentious issue, and there's no single best answer.

Storage vendors, particularly for their enterprise SAN solutions, typically optimize the stripe size based on their expert knowledge of their systems. In almost all cases, the best option is to leave the existing default stripe size in place. Changes should be verified with the storage vendor and undergo thorough tests to measure the performance impact before making the change to a production system.

Once the RAID array is built, the next task is to create one or more partitions on the array that prepares the disk for use by Windows. As you'll see shortly, disk partitions should be built using the *diskpart.exe* tool, which provides a method to *offset*, or *align*, the partition.

TRACK-ALIGNED PARTITIONS WITH DISKPART

The first part of each disk partition is called the *master boot record* (MBR). The MBR is 63 sectors in length, meaning the data portion of the partition will start on the 64th sector. Assuming 64 sectors per track, the first allocation unit on the disk will start on the first track and complete on the next track. Subsequent allocation units will be split across tracks in a similar manner.

The most efficient disk layout is where allocation units are evenly divisible into the tracks—for example, eight 4K allocation units per 32K track. When a partition isn't track-aligned, allocation units start and finish on different tracks, leading to more disk activity than would be required in a track-aligned partition. For RAID arrays, similar alignment problems exist with the stripes, increasing disk activity and reducing cache efficiency. Some estimates suggest up to a 30 percent performance penalty—a significant amount, particularly for disk-bound systems. Figure 3.2 illustrates the before- and aftereffects of offsetting a partition.

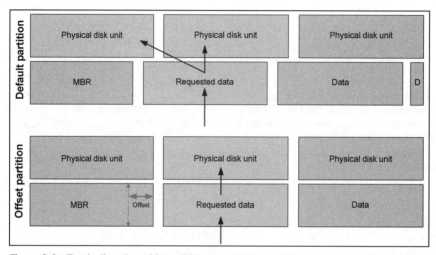

Figure 3.2 Track-aligned partitions. Without specifying an offset during partition creation, partitions incur I/O overhead. Using DiskPart with an offset allows partition alignment and more efficient I/O.

The task, then, is to offset the partition's starting position beyond the MBR. Starting in Windows Server 2008, all partitions are track-aligned by default. In Windows Server 2003 and earlier, partitions are track-aligned on creation using the diskpart.exe tool or diskpar.exe prior to Windows Server 2003 Service Pack 1. As shown in figure 3.3, the DiskPart tool can also be used to inspect an existing partition's offset.

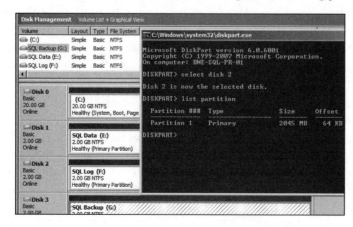

Figure 3.3 DiskPart can be used to track-align partitions and inspect the offset of existing partitions.

A common offset used for SQL Server partitions is 64K, or 128 sectors. Using Disk-Part, you achieve this by using the *Create Partition* command with an *align=64* option. Windows Server 2008 (and Vista) automatically use a 1024K offset, a value chosen to work with almost all storage systems. If unaligned partitions are used by these operating systems—for example, after an upgrade from Windows Server 2003—then the partition overhead remains until the partition is rebuilt.

As with the RAID stripe size, check the offset value with the storage vendor, and verify any changes from their recommended value with an appropriate performance test.

ALLOCATION UNIT SIZE

The final task in preparing a disk for use by SQL Server is to format the partition using the Windows Disk Management tool. By default, partitions are formatted using a 4K allocation unit size.

As discussed earlier, the smaller the allocation unit size, the less disk space is wasted for small files. For example, a 1K file created on a volume with a 4K allocation unit will waste 3K, as 4K is the minimum allocation unit size.

In contrast, large files benefit from a larger allocation unit. In fragmented disks with a small allocation unit size, a single large file will occupy many allocation units, which are probably spread over many different parts of the disk. If you use a larger allocation unit, a file will have a better chance of being located in consecutive disk sectors, making the read and writes to this file more efficient.

SQL Server allocates space within a database using *extents*, which are collections of eight 8K pages, making a total extent size of 64K. As you can see in figure 3.4, the recommended allocation unit size for a SQL Server volume is 64K, matching the extent size. Allocation unit sizes less than 8K (the default is 4K) aren't recommended, as this leads to split I/O, where parts of a single page are stored on separate allocation units—potentially on different parts of the disk—which leads to a reduction in disk performance.

Note that NTFS partitions created using allocation units of greater than 4K can't be compressed using NTFS compression. Such compression isn't recommended for SQL Server volumes, so this shouldn't be a determining factor. In later chapters, we'll examine various forms of native compression introduced in SQL Server 2008.

Let's turn our attention from the format of disks to the manner in which they're connected to the server: disk controller cards.

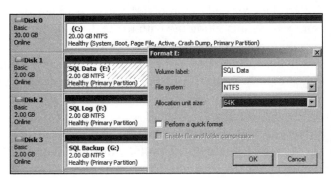

Figure 3.4   SQL Server volumes should be formatted with a 64K allocation unit size using the NTFS file system, after the underlying partition has been track-aligned.

3.1.2 *Distributing load over multiple controllers*

Storage controller cards, along with various other components, act as intermediaries between the physical disks and the software requesting the data on the disks. Like other storage components, disk controllers have a maximum throughput capacity and are subject to failure. When you design a storage system for SQL Server, storage controller cards play a pivotal role from both performance and fault tolerance perspectives.

A guiding principle in achieving the best possible storage performance for SQL Server is to stripe data across many disks. With multiple disks, or spindles, in action, the speed of a read or write operation is faster than what could be achieved with a single disk. Striping data across multiple disks also reduces the speed at which disk queues build. With more disks in action, the likelihood of a queue building for any single disk is reduced.

When large numbers of disks are used, the storage bottleneck begins to move from the disks to the storage controllers that coordinate the disk reads and writes. More disks require more storage controllers to avoid I/O bottlenecks. The ratio of disks to controllers is determined by various factors, including the nature of the I/O and the speed and bandwidth of the individual components. We discussed a technique for estimating disk and controller numbers in the previous chapter.

I/O PERFORMANCE

When choosing a server, pay attention to the server's I/O capacity, measured by the amount of supported PCI slots and bus type. Modern servers use the PCI Express (PCI-E) bus, which is capable of transmitting up to 250MB/second per *lane*. An x4 PCI Express slot has four lanes, x8 has eight lanes, and so forth. A good server selection for SQL Server systems is one that supports multiple PCI-E slots. As an example, the HP ProLiant DL585 G2 has seven PCI-E slots comprised of 3x8 slots and 4x4 slots for a total of 40 lanes. Such a server could support up to seven controller cards driving a very high number of disks.

MULTIPATH FOR PERFORMANCE AND TOLERANCE

Depending on the storage system, a large number of components are involved in the I/O path between the server and the disks. Disk controllers, cabling, and switches all play a part in connecting the disks to the server. Without redundancy built into each of these components, failure in any one component can cause a complete I/O failure.

Redundancy at the disk level is provided by way of RAID disks, as you learned in the previous chapter. To ensure redundancy along the path to the disks, multiple controller cards and *multipathing* software is used.

Multipathing software intelligently reroutes disk I/O across an alternate path when a component failure invalidates one of the paths. To do this, multiple disk controllers or HBA cards must be present and, ideally, connected to the storage system via separate switches and cabling.

Microsoft provides support for multipathing on the Windows Server platform (and therefore SQL Server) via Microsoft Multipath I/O (MPIO) drivers. Using MPIO, storage vendors provide reliable multipathing solutions for Windows Server platforms.

MPIO solutions are available for a variety of storage systems, including Fibre and iSCSI SANs and parallel SCSI.

The real value in multipathing software lies in the fact that when all disk paths are working, the multipathing software increases disk performance by balancing load across the available paths; thus, the solution services both fault tolerance and performance at the same time.

SEPARATE CONTROLLERS

Chapter 9 discusses separating data and transaction logs in more detail, but it's worth mentioning at this point that for SQL Server systems with very high transaction rates, it's important to ensure there are no bottlenecks while writing to the transaction log. Transaction log bottlenecks increase transaction duration, which has a flow-on effect that causes numerous other performance problems. One way of preventing this is to store the transaction log on dedicated, RAID-protected disks, optionally connected to a dedicated disk controller channel or separate controller card.

Using multiple controller cards and multipathing software helps to increase disk performance and therefore reduce the impact of the most common hardware bottleneck. Another means of improving disk performance is through the usage of storage cache.

3.1.3 Configuring storage cache

In chapter 2 we listed the benefits of hardware-based RAID, one of which was that the disk controllers usually include some degree of cache, which you can consider the disk controller's private RAM. Let's turn our attention to two important aspects of storage cache: protecting it during power failure and configuring a higher percentage of its use for disk writes compared to reads.

BATTERY-BACKED CACHE

Disk controller cache improves performance for both reads and writes. When data is read from the disk, if the requested data is stored in the controller cache, then physical reads of the disk aren't required. In a similar fashion, when data is written to disk, it can be written to cache and applied to disk at a later point, thus increasing write performance.

The most critical aspect of disk controller cache is that it must be battery backed. This will ensure that power failures don't cause data in the cache to be lost. Even if the server includes a UPS, which is recommended, disk controller cache must be battery backed.

READ VS. WRITE CACHE

It's important to make the distinction between read cache and write cache. SQL Server itself has a large cache stored in the server's RAM where, among other things, it caches data read from disk. In most cases, the server's RAM is likely to be much larger (and cheaper) than the disk controller cache; therefore, disk *read* performance increases attributed to storage cache are likely to be quite small, and in some cases can actually be worse due to the *double caching* involved.

The real value of disk controller cache is the write cache. Write cache is particularly useful for improving disk performance during bursts of write activity such as checkpoints (covered in chapter 7), during which large numbers of writes are sent to disk. In these circumstances, a large write cache can increase performance. The controller commits the writes to cache, which is much faster than disk, and *hardens* the writes to disk at a later point. As long as the controller cache is battery backed, this is a safe, high-performance technique.

Depending on the controller card or SAN, you may be able to configure the percentage of cache used for reads and writes. For SQL Server systems, reserving a larger percentage of cache for writes is likely to result in better I/O performance.

The quantity and read/write ratio of storage cache can make a significant difference to overall storage performance. One of the common methods of validating different settings prior to deploying SQL Server is to use the SQLIO tool, discussed next.

3.1.4   *Validating disk storage performance and integrity*

Before a system is production ready, you must conduct a number of performance tests to ensure the system will perform according to expectations. The primary test is to load the system with the expected transaction profile and measure the response times according to the service level agreements. We'll go into this process in more detail in chapter 14, when we'll focus on creating a *performance baseline.*

Prior to these tests, you'll need to carry out several system-level tests. One of the most important ones involves testing the storage system for capacity and integrity. This section focuses on two important tools, SQLIO and SQLIOSIM, both of which you can download for free from the Microsoft website. Links to both of these tools are available at sqlCrunch.com/storage.

SQLIO

SQLIO is a tool used to measure the I/O performance capacity of a storage system. Run from the command line, SQLIO takes a number of parameters that are used to generate I/O of a particular type. At the completion of the test, SQLIO returns various capacity statistics, including I/Os per second (IOPS), throughput MB/second, and latency: three key characteristics of a storage system, as you'll recall from chapter 2.

The real value in SQLIO is using it prior to the installation of SQL Server to measure the effectiveness of various storage configurations, such as stripe size, RAID levels, and so forth. In addition to identifying the optimal storage configuration, SQLIO often exposes various hardware and driver/firmware-related issues, which are much easier to fix before SQL Server is installed and in use. Further, the statistics returned by SQLIO provide real meaning when describing storage performance; what is perceived as *slow* can be put into context when comparing results between similar storage systems.

Despite the name, SQLIO doesn't simulate SQL Server I/O patterns; that's the role of SQLIOSIM, discussed in a moment. SQLIO is used purely to measure a system's I/O capacity. As shown in table 3.1, SQLIO takes several parameters used in determining the type of I/O generated.

Table 3.1 Commonly used SQLIO parameters

SQLIO option	Description
-t	Number of threads
-o	Number of outstanding I/O requests (queue depth)
-LS	Records disk latency information
-kR	Generates read activity
-kW	Generates write activity
-s	Duration of test in seconds
-b	I/O size in bytes
-frandom	Generates random I/O
-ssequential	Generates sequential I/O
-F	Config file containing test paths

The configuration file specified with the -F parameter option contains the file paths to be used by SQLIO for the test. For example, let's say we wanted to test a LUN exposed to Windows as T drive. The contents of the configuration file for this test would look something like this:

```
T:\sqlio_test_file.dat 8 0x0 1000
```

The additional parameters specified relate to the number of threads to use against the file (8 in this example), a mask value, and the file size.

Before we look at an example, let's run through some general recommendations:

- The file size and test duration should be sufficient to exhaust the cache of the storage system. Some systems, particularly SANs, have a very large storage cache, so a short test duration with small file sizes is likely to be fulfilled from the cache, obscuring the real I/O performance.
- Tests should be run multiple times, once for each file path. For instance, to test the capacity of four LUNs, run four tests, once for each LUN specified in the configuration file (using the -F parameter). Once each file path has been tested individually, consider additional tests with file path combinations specified in the configuration file.
- Ensure the tests run for a reasonable length of time (at least 10–15 minutes) and allow time between test runs to enable the storage system to return to an idle state.
- Record the SQLIO results with each change made to the storage configuration. This will enable the effectiveness of each change to be measured.

- Run tests with a variety of I/O types (sequential vs. random) and sizes. For systems used predominately for OLTP purposes, random I/O should be used for most tests, but sequential I/O testing is still important for backups, table scans, and so forth. In contrast, sequential I/O testing should form the main testing for OLAP systems.

- If possible, provide the results of the tests to the storage vendor for validation. Alternatively, have the vendor present during the tests. As the experts in their own products, they should be able to validate and interpret the results and offer guidance on configuration settings and/or driver and firmware versions that can be used to increase overall performance.

Let's look at an example of running SQLIO to simulate 8K sequential writes for 5 minutes:

```
sqlio -kW -t1 -s300 -o1 -fsequential -b8 -LS -Fconfig.txt
```

In this case, the config.txt file contains a path specification to a 1GB file located in e:\sqlio_test_file.dat. You can see the results of this test in figure 3.5.

As the results show, we achieved about 2,759 IOPS and 21.55 MB/second throughput with low average latency (2ms) but a high peak latency (1301ms). On their own, these results don't mean a lot. In a real-world case, the tests would be repeated several times for different I/O types and storage configurations, ideally in the presence of the storage vendor, who would assist in storage configuration and capacity validation.

Achieving good I/O capacity, throughput, and latency is all well and good, but that's not enough if the storage components don't honor the I/O requirements of SQL Server. The SQLIOSIM tool, discussed next, can be used to verify the integrity of the storage system and its suitability for SQL Server.

Figure 3.5   SQLIO results include IOPS, MB/second, and various latency metrics. Running several tests using different storage configurations helps to determine optimal storage configuration prior to SQL Server installation.

SQLIOSIM

Unlike SQLIO, *SQLIOSIM* is a storage verification tool that issues disk reads and writes using the same I/O patterns as SQL Server. SQLIOSIM uses checksums to verify the integrity of the written data pages.

Most SQL Server systems involve a large number of components in the I/O chain. The operating system, I/O drivers, virus scanners, storage controllers, read cache, write cache, switches, and various other items all pass data to and from SQL Server. SQLIOSIM is used to validate that none of these components alters the data in any adverse or unexpected way.

As you can see in figure 3.6, SQLIOSIM can be configured with various file locations and sizes along with test durations. The output and results of the tests are written to an XML file, which you specify in the Error Log (XML) text box.

During execution, the test progress is displayed to the screen, as shown in figure 3.7, with the final results captured in the XML log file you specified.

SQLIOSIM ensures that the SQL Server I/O patterns (covered in later chapters), such as random and sequential reads and writes, backups, checkpoints, lazy writer, bulk update, read ahead, and shrink/expand, all conform to SQL Server's I/O requirements. Together with SQLIO, this tool provides peace of mind that the storage system is both valid and will perform to expectations.

Let's turn our attention now from disk configuration to another major system component: CPU.

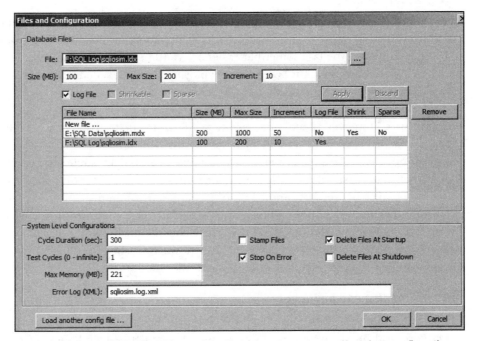

Figure 3.6   Use the SQLIOSIM Files and Configuration screen to specify various configuration options for I/O simulation tests.

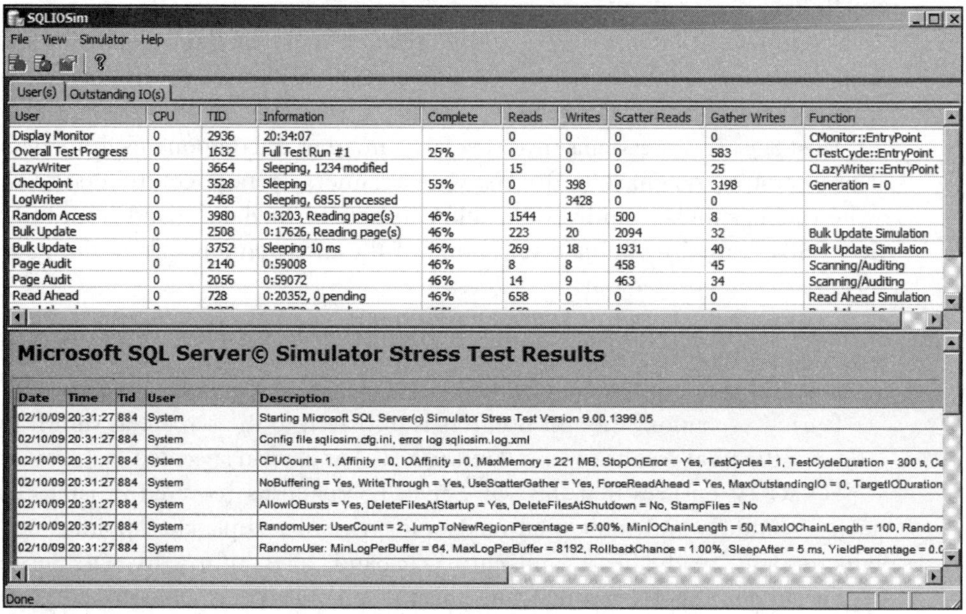

Figure 3.7   SQLIOSIM results are displayed to the screen as the simulation is in progress, and the final results are captured to the XML log file specified in the Files and Configuration screen.

3.2   *CPU architecture*

From multicores and hyperthreading, to clock speed, cache, and x86/x64/Itanium platforms, there are numerous aspects to consider when choosing a CPU platform for SQL Server. Making the task somewhat easier are vendors such as Dell and HP that pre-configure systems suitable for SQL Server deployments. Such systems typically support 2 or 4 dual- or quad-core x64 CPUs providing between 4 and 16 CPU cores per server. This level of processing power is usually plenty for most line-of-business SQL Server applications. Moreover, the x64 processing platform in such servers provides flexibility in choosing between 32- and 64-bit Windows and SQL Server.

Despite the processing power and flexibility provided by such servers, it's still important to understand the various CPU attributes and configuration options, particularly the choice between 32- and 64-bit processing environments.

In this section we'll address the various aspects of CPU platforms for SQL Server, including multicore systems, CPU cache, clock speed, and the advantages of a 64-bit processing platform. In chapter 7 we'll drill down into specific CPU configuration options such as max degree of parallelism and fiber mode.

3.2.1   *Hyperthreading and multicore*

In recent years, there's been a clear shift toward CPUs with multiple cores per die. Dual-core and quad-core chips are now common, and this trend should continue, with 8+-core CPUs not too far away.

Intel introduced its CPU *hyperthreading* technology in 2003. For each physical CPU, hyperthreading exposes a second virtual CPU to the operating system and is therefore able to provide support for multithreaded applications. SQL Server performance with hyperthreading enabled is often unpredictable, with mixed reports of performance increases, decreases, or no change at all. In contrast, today's multicore systems deliver two (or more) *real* CPU cores per die, and performance improvements are consistent.

The ability to pack multiple cores onto a single CPU die delivers two significant advantages: the processing capacity of servers is greatly increased, and perhaps more importantly, the overall server cost is reduced. Today's quad-core chips deliver similar performance to four single-core chips. In the single-core era, supporting eight CPUs required an expensive eight-way server. With today's quad-core chips, a much cheaper two-way server can be used that delivers similar processing performance.

Servers suitable for SQL Server deployments are typically ones with support for 2 or 4 dual- or quad-core chips. This delivers between 4 and 16 CPU cores in a relatively cheap two- or four-way server. Such CPU power is usually enough for most database server requirements, with the exception of compute-constrained or very high throughput SQL Server applications.

3.2.2 *CPU cache and clock speed*

With the advent of multicore technology, clock speed has become less important in determining overall CPU performance, with far more weight assigned to the number of cores and the amount of accessible cache.

CPU cache is implemented to speed up access to main system memory. Storing copies of the most frequently accessed memory, cache is typically implemented in three levels. As shown in figure 3.8, modern CPUs like those belonging to the Intel Core i7 family provide three levels of cache, two of which are private to each core, and one shared area.

The larger the cache, the better; however, much like a disk drive, larger caches have longer access latency. Multiple cache levels are implemented to reconcile between the size and latency goals; level 1 cache is checked before level 2, which in turn is checked before level 3. Finally, the main system memory is accessed if necessary. Such an arrangement results in the fastest overall memory access.

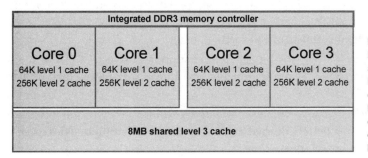

Figure 3.8 Intel CPUs based on the Nehalem architecture will support between two and eight cores, with each core having 64K of level 1 cache, 256K of level 2 cache, and 8MB of shared level 3 cache.

We'll cover memory access speed in more detail when we look at non-uniform memory access (NUMA) architecture a little later in this chapter. For now, let's focus on CPU platforms, and the advantages of 64-bit computing.

3.2.3   *CPU platforms*

The year 2001 saw the introduction of the first 64-bit CPU for the Microsoft Windows platform. The Intel Itanium CPU was designed from the ground up as a completely new architecture compared to the 32-bit x86 architecture that preceded it. Joint designers HP and Intel intended it for use in enterprise-class servers needing to expand beyond the constraints of the 32-bit platform, particularly in regard to addressable memory.

The original Itanium processor achieved only moderate success, primarily due to its incompatibility with all existing 32-bit software. In response to this, the x64 processors emerged, offering 64-bit processing capability, yet retaining backward compatibility with existing 32-bit software.

Led by AMD with its Opteron CPUs, x64 platforms became popular in large SQL Server deployments. Using the x64 versions of Microsoft Windows and SQL Server, these systems immediately benefited from the advantages of 64-bit computing, while avoiding the problems with 32-bit platforms.

PROBLEMS WITH 32-BIT PLATFORMS

The primary constraint with 32-bit platforms is addressable memory. Without using the AWE option (discussed shortly), 32-bit systems are limited to 4GB addressable memory, 2GB of which is used by the operating system, which leaves only 2GB for user applications like SQL Server.

The AWE option allows applications to acquire physical memory above 4GB as non-paged memory dynamically mapped in the 32-bit address space. Using this technique, SQL Server 2008 is able to address up to 64GB of memory.

Although the AWE option allows additional memory to be addressed by SQL Server, it's not without its problems. Overhead is involved in mapping memory in this manner, and the memory can only be used for SQL Server data buffers. Plan cache, sort space, and various other SQL Server resources are unable to use such memory. In contrast, 64-bit SQL Server has no such limitations, offering many advantages:

- *Large and directly addressable memory space*—Up to 2TB addressable memory can be used by all SQL Server resources, including data cache, plan cache, sort space, indexing, joins, and so forth.
- *Enhanced parallelism*—64-bit SQL Server supports up to 64 CPUs with enhanced parallelism for much more reliable and linear scalability compared to 32-bit systems.
- *Larger cache and improved bus architecture*—64-bit CPUs typically offer larger on-die cache and better internal architecture, allowing enhanced data movement between cache and processors.

Organizations that make the decision to move from 32- to 64-bit processing platforms are then faced with a further choice: which 64-bit platform?

WHICH 64-BIT PLATFORM?

Itanium CPUs are best used in delivering supercomputer-like performance in systems requiring the full benefits and scale of the 64-bit platform. An HP Integrity Superdome used in a TPC-C test[2] in November 2005 was configured with 1TB (1024GB) of memory and 64 Itanium2 CPUs running at 1.6GHz. Itanium-based systems such as these have exceptionally large memory and I/O bandwidths far exceeding the capacity of x64-based systems.

The vast bulk of 64-bit deployments in use today are based on Xeon or Opteron x64 CPUs. With the exception of all but the largest systems, the x64 platform represents the best choice from both a cost and a performance perspective.

Table 3.2 shows the number of CPUs supported by SQL Server 2008 running on Windows Server 2008.

Table 3.2   Maximum supported CPU sockets for each SQL Server version

SQL Server 2008 version	Maximum supported CPUs	
	32-bit	64-bit
Enterprise	OS max	OS max
Standard	4	4
Web	4	4
Workgroup	2	2
Express	1	1
Windows Server 2008	**32-bit**	**64-bit**
Data Center	32	64
Enterprise	8	8
Standard	4	4
Web Server	4	4
Itanium	N/A	64

With SQL Server's ability to support increasingly larger databases comes a need for larger amounts of RAM, an issue we'll focus on next.

3.3   *Memory configuration*

Insufficient RAM is a common problem in SQL Server systems experiencing performance problems. Fortunately, RAM is both reasonably inexpensive and relatively easy to upgrade.

---

[2]   http://www.tpc.org/results/individual_results/HP/hp_orca1tb_win64_ex.pdf

There are some important considerations when selecting and configuring server RAM, such as the module capacity and fault tolerance, and latency issues on large, multi-CPU systems. In this section, we'll look at configuring a server's RAM slots and take a brief look at the NUMA architecture, which is used to derive maximum performance in large, multi-CPU systems.

3.3.1   Design for future RAM upgrades

When selecting and configuring RAM for SQL Server, you must consider the amount, type, and capacity of the chosen RAM. If the server will be used for future system consolidation, or the exact RAM requirements can't be accurately predicted, then apart from loading the system up with the maximum possible memory, it's important to allow for future memory upgrades.

Virtualization, covered later in this chapter, addresses this issue nicely by being able to easily grant and revoke CPU/memory resources as the server's needs increase or decrease. On dedicated, nonvirtualized systems, this issue is typically addressed by using fewer higher-capacity memory chips, therefore leaving a number of free slots for future upgrades if required. This avoids the common problem of having to remove and replace lower-capacity RAM chips if the server's RAM slots are full and more memory is required. Although initially more expensive, this approach provides flexibility for future requirements.

> ### Hot-add CPU and memory
> The Enterprise edition of SQL Server 2008 supports hot-add memory and CPU, meaning that if the underlying hardware is capable of dynamically adding these resources, SQL Server can take advantage of them without requiring a restart. In both cases, there are a number of key restrictions on using this feature, fully described in Books Online.

Finally, in order to provide a system with a degree of resilience against memory errors, *error-correcting code* (ECC) RAM should be installed. Used by all the major system vendors, ECC forms an important part of configuring a fault-tolerant SQL Server system.

Table 3.3 shows the maximum memory supported by SQL Server 2008 running on Windows Server 2008.

Table 3.3   Maximum memory for SQL Server 2008 editions

SQL Server 2008 version	Maximum supported memory	
	32-bit	64-bit
Enterprise	OS max	OS max
Standard	OS max	OS max
Web	OS max	OS max

Table 3.3   Maximum memory for SQL Server 2008 editions *(continued)*

	Maximum supported memory	
SQL Server 2008 version	**32-bit**	**64-bit**
Workgroup	OS max	4GB
Express	1GB	1GB
Windows Server 2008	**32-bit**	**64-bit**
Data Center	64GB	2TB
Enterprise	64GB	2TB
Standard	4GB	32GB
Web Server	4GB	32GB
Itanium	N/A	2TB

Despite memory being significantly faster than disk, a large multi-CPU system may bottleneck on access to the memory, a situation addressed by the NUMA architecture.

3.3.2   NUMA

As we mentioned earlier, advances in CPU clock speed have given way to a trend toward multiple cores per CPU die. That's not to say clock speeds won't increase in the future—they most certainly will—but we're at the point now where it's become increasingly difficult to fully utilize CPU clock speed due to the latency involved in accessing system RAM. On large multiprocessor systems where all CPUs share a common bus to the RAM, the latency of RAM access becomes more and more of an issue, effectively throttling CPU speed and limiting system scalability. A simplified example of this is shown in figure 3.9.

As we covered earlier, higher amounts of CPU cache will reduce the frequency of trips out to system RAM, but there are obviously limits on the size of the CPU cache, so this only partially addresses the RAM latency issue.

The non-uniform memory access *(NUMA)* architecture, fully supported by SQL Server, addresses this issue by grouping CPUs together into NUMA *nodes*, each of which accesses its own RAM, and depending on the NUMA implementation, over its own I/O channel.

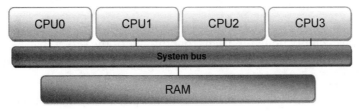

Figure 3.9   CPUs in a symmetric multiprocessing (SMP) system share access to system RAM via a single system bus, thus limiting scalability.

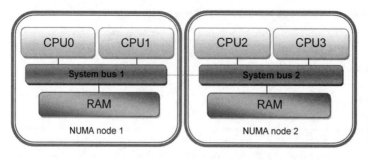

Figure 3.10   The NUMA architecture increases scalability by grouping CPUs and RAM into nodes.

In contrast, the symmetric multiprocessor architecture has no CPU/RAM segregation, with all CPUs accessing the same RAM over the same shared memory bus. As the number of CPUs and clock speeds increase, the symmetric multiprocessor architecture reaches scalability limits, limits that are overcome by the NUMA architecture; a simplified example appears in figure 3.10.

While the NUMA architecture localizes RAM to groups of CPUs (NUMA nodes) over their own I/O channels, RAM from other nodes is still accessible. Such memory is referred to as *remote memory*. In the NUMA architecture, accessing remote memory is more costly (slower) than local memory, and applications that aren't NUMA aware often perform poorly on NUMA systems. Fortunately, SQL Server is fully NUMA aware.[3]

On large multi-CPU systems running multiple SQL Server instances, each instance can be bound to a group of CPUs and configured with a maximum memory value. Both of these options are covered in chapter 7. In this way, SQL Server instances can be tailored for a particular NUMA node, increasing overall system performance by preventing remote memory access while benefiting from high-speed local memory access.

HARDWARE NUMA

The NUMA architecture just described is known as *hardware NUMA,* also referred to as *hard NUMA.* As the name suggests, servers using hardware NUMA are configured by the manufacturer with multiple system buses, each of which is dedicated to a group of CPUs that use the bus to access their own RAM allocation.

Some hardware vendors supply NUMA servers in *interleaved NUMA* mode, in which case the system will appear to Windows and SQL Server as an SMP box. Interleaved NUMA is suitable for applications that aren't NUMA optimized. For SQL Server systems, *pure NUMA* mode should be considered to take advantage of NUMA optimizations if appropriate. The sys.dm_os_memory_clerks Dynamic Management View (DMV) can be used to determine the NUMA mode:

```
-- TSQL to return the set of active memory clerks
SELECT DISTINCT memory_node_id
FROM sys.dm_os_memory_clerks
```

If node 0 is the only memory node returned from this query, the server may be configured in interleaved NUMA mode (or isn't NUMA hardware). Servers not configured

---

[3] SQL Server 2000 Service Pack 3 and earlier isn't NUMA aware and often performs poorly on NUMA systems.

for hardware NUMA (SMP servers) that contain lots of CPUs may benefit from software-based NUMA, or *soft NUMA*, which we'll look at next.

SOFT NUMA

Unlike hardware NUMA, soft NUMA isn't able to isolate, or affinitize, RAM to groups of CPUs over dedicated buses. However, in some cases system performance may increase by enabling soft NUMA.

On SMP systems without soft NUMA, each SQL Server instance has a single I/O thread and a single LazyWriter thread. Instances experiencing bottlenecks on these resources may benefit from configuring multiple NUMA nodes using soft NUMA, in which case each node will receive its own I/O and LazyWriter threads. We'll cover threads and the LazyWriter process in more detail in chapter 7.

SOFT NUMA IN SQL SERVER

Configuring a SQL Server instance for soft NUMA is a two-step process. First, the instance is configured with CPU affinity, as in this example, which configures an instance to use CPUs 0–3:

```
-- Configure an Instance to use CPUs 0-3
sp_configure 'show advanced options', 1;
RECONFIGURE;
GO
sp_configure 'affinity mask', 15;
RECONFIGURE;
GO
```

The next step is to configure the NUMA nodes, which is done at a server level—enabling all the defined NUMA nodes to be visible to all SQL instances on the server. A NUMA node is defined in the registry with its corresponding CPUs by adding node keys to HKEY_LOCAL_MACHINE\SOFTWARE\Microsoft\Microsoft SQL Server\100\Node-Configuration.

Suppose we want to create two NUMA nodes for a given SQL Server instance. In our previous example, we used the affinity mask option to affinitize CPUs 0, 1, 2, and 3. To create two NUMA nodes on those four CPUs, we'd add the registry keys, as shown in table 3.4.

Table 3.4 Registry entries used to define NUMA nodes

Key	Type	Name	Value
Node0	DWORD	CPUMask	0x03
Node1	DWORD	CPUMask	0x0c

In this case, CPUs 0 and 1 would be used by the first NUMA node (Node 0) and CPUs 2 and 3 would be used by NUMA Node 1. The hexadecimal equivalents of the binary bit masks are stored in the registry—that is, 0x03 (bit mask 00000011, hex equivalent of 3) for CPUs 0 and 1, and 0x0c (bit mask 00001100, hex equivalent of 12) for CPUs 2 and 3. In this example, the combination of CPU affinity and the registry modifications have provided a SQL Server instance with two soft NUMA nodes.

NUMA configuration is an advanced performance-tuning technique. It's beyond the scope of this book to give it more than a cursory glance, but it's certainly something that you should investigate to achieve maximum performance, particularly on large, multi-CPU systems. Before closing this chapter, let's take a look at one more system component: networking.

3.4 Networking components

Of the four main hardware components, network I/O isn't likely to contribute to SQL Server performance bottlenecks. Tuning disk I/O, memory, and CPU resources is far more likely to yield bigger performance increases. That being said, there are a number of important network-related settings that we need to take into account, such as maximizing switch speed, building fault tolerance into network cards, and manually configuring network card settings.

3.4.1 Gigabit switches

Almost all servers purchased today come preinstalled with one or more gigabit network connections offering roughly 10 to 100 times the bandwidth of previous generations.

The speed of the network card is only as good as the switch port it's connected to. It's common for SQL Servers with gigabit network cards to be connected to 100Mbps switch ports. Gigabit switches should be used where possible, particularly at the server level between database and application servers.

In smaller networks, it's not uncommon for hubs to be used instead of switches. Hubs broadcast traffic to all network nodes. In contrast, switches intelligently route traffic as required, and should be used to reduce overall network traffic.

3.4.2 NIC teaming

To increase network bandwidth and provide fault tolerance at the network level, a technique known as *NIC teaming* can be used. NIC teaming involves two or more physical network interface cards (NICs) used as a single logical NIC. Both cards operate at the same time to increase bandwidth, and if one fails, the other continues operating. For further fault tolerance, each card is ideally connected to a separate switch. As we covered in chapter 2, NIC teaming is recommended for connections to an iSCSI SAN.

Although NIC teaming is a useful technique from both a performance and a fault tolerance perspective, there are some known limitations and restrictions regarding its use in a clustered environment, which we'll discuss in chapter 5.

3.4.3 Manually configuring NIC settings

Finally, most network cards offer an *autosense* mode that permits self-configuration to match its speed with the connected switch port speed. It's not uncommon for autosense to get it wrong, artificially limiting throughput, so NIC settings (speed and duplex) should be manually configured.

Chapter 6 provides a number of other best practices relating to network configuration, including protocol selection, port bindings, firewall configuration, and encryption.

Let's move from individual server components to the server as a whole, focusing on the trend toward server consolidation and virtualization.

3.5   *Server consolidation and virtualization*

The arrival of personal computer networks marked a shift away from "big iron" main-frames and dumb terminals to a decentralized processing model comprised of many (relatively cheap) servers and lots of personal computers. In many ways, we've come full circle, with a shift back to a centralized model of SANs and virtualized servers running on fewer, more powerful servers.

In recent years, the shift toward server consolidation and virtualization has gained pace, and in the years ahead, the idea of a dedicated, *non*virtualized server may seem quite odd. From a SQL Server perspective, this has a number of important ramifications. Before we look at the considerations and differences, let's begin by taking a look at the goals of consolidation and virtualization.

3.5.1   *Goals of consolidation and virtualization*

The plummeting cost and increased power of today's server components has moved the real cost of modern computing from hardware to people, processes, power, and space. As such, in a never-ending quest to minimize operating costs, businesses have embraced consolidation and virtualization techniques. The major goals are to avoid server sprawl and minimize costs.

SERVER SPRAWL

The term *server sprawl* is used to describe the uncontrolled growth of servers through-out the enterprise, making administration very difficult. SQL Server sprawl is a particu-larly nasty problem; consider an example of a SQL Server instance running on a PC sitting under someone's desk, installed by a DBA who is no longer with the organiza-tion and who never documented its existence. Does this instance need backing up? Does it contain sensitive data? Do you even know that it exists?

Given the ease with which new SQL Server installations can be deployed, and the power of today's commodity PCs, SQL Server sprawl is an all-too-common problem. While there are tools for discovering the presence of SQL Server instances, and new SQL Server features such as policy-based management (discussed in chapter 8) that make administration much simpler, the sprawl issue remains a significant problem, and one of the prime reasons for consolidation and virtualization projects.

> #### Assessment and planning toolkit
> The *Microsoft Assessment and Planning Toolkit Solution Accelerator* is an excellent (free) tool that can be used in assessing existing infrastructure. From a SQL Server perspective, one of the great aspects of this tool is its ability to *discover* installed SQL Servers on the network, handy for planning upgrades and avoiding out-of-control sprawl situations.

OPERATING COSTS

Each physical server consumes space and power, the natural enemies of a data center. Once the data center is full, expanding or building a new one is a costly exercise, and one that makes little sense if the existing servers are running at 50 percent utilization.

As computing power increases and virtualization software improves, the march toward fewer, more powerful servers hosting multiple virtual servers and/or more database instances is an industry trend that shows no sign of slowing down. The real question for a DBA is often *how* to consolidate/virtualize rather than *whether* to consolidate/virtualize. In answering that question, let's look at each technique in turn, beginning with consolidation.

3.5.2   *Consolidation*

Although virtualization can be considered a form of consolidation, in this section we'll take consolidation to mean installing multiple SQL Server instances on the one server, or moving multiple databases to the one instance. Figure 3.11 shows an example of consolidating a number of database instances onto a failover cluster.

Support of NUMA hardware, the ability to install multiple instances and cap each one's memory and CPU, and the introduction of Resource Governor (covered in chapter 16) in SQL Server 2008 all contribute to the ability to effectively consolidate a large number of databases and/or database instances on the one server.

Just as creating a new virtual server is simple, installing a new SQL Server instance on an existing server is also easy, as is migrating a database from one instance to another. But just because these tasks are simple doesn't mean you should perform them without thought and planning. Let's take a look at a number of important consolidation considerations for SQL Server.

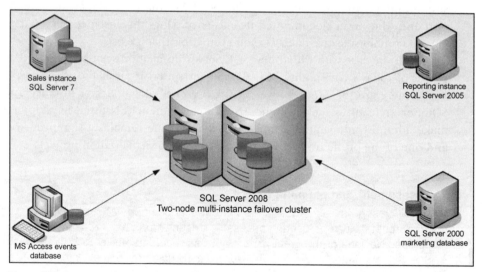

Figure 3.11   Among other benefits, SQL Server consolidation centralizes administration and combats server sprawl.

BASELINE ANALYSIS

In subsequent chapters we'll discuss the importance and value of collecting a number of performance monitor counters during periods of time in which performance is reported as being *normal*. From a consolidation perspective, having this data at hand helps you make sensible decisions on the placement of instances. For example, consolidating a number of CPU-starved servers on a single CPU core box doesn't make any sense. In contrast, consolidating servers that consume very little resources does make sense. Accurate baseline data is a crucial component in making the right choice as to which servers and/or databases should be consolidated.

When examining typical usage as part of a consolidation process, take care to ensure batch processes are considered. For example, two SQL Server instances may coexist on the one server perfectly well until the end of the month, at which point they both run a large end-of-month batch process, potentially causing each process to exceed the required execution window.

ADMINISTRATIVE CONSIDERATIONS

Consolidation brings with it an even mix of benefits and challenges. We've just covered the importance of consolidating complementary instances from a performance perspective. Equally important is considering a number of other administration aspects:

- *Maintenance windows*—How long is each server's maintenance window, and will the combination of their maintenance windows work together on a consolidated server?
- *Disk growth*—Is there enough disk space (and physical disk isolation) to ensure the database growth and backup requirements can be met?

TEMPDB

Apart from the ability to affinitize CPUs and cap memory usage, choosing to install multiple instances has one distinct advantage over placing multiple databases in the one instance: each instance has its own tempdb database. Depending on the databases being consolidated, installing multiple instances allows more than one tempdb database to be available, enabling the placement of databases with heavy tempdb requirements in the appropriate instance.

Let's turn our attention now to virtualization, a specialized form of consolidation.

3.5.3 Virtualization

Unlike the SQL Server instance/database consolidation techniques we've outlined so far, virtualization occurs at a lower level by enabling a single server to be logically carved up into multiple *virtual machines* (VMs), or *guests*. Each VM shares the physical server's hardware resources but is otherwise separate with its own operating system and applications.

Virtualization platforms, also known as *hypervisors*, are classified as either Type 1 or Type 2. Type 1 hypervisors, commonly referred to as *native* or *bare-metal hypervisors*, run directly on top of the server's hardware. VMware's ESX Server and Microsoft's Hyper-V (see figure 3.12) are recent examples of Type 1 hypervisors.

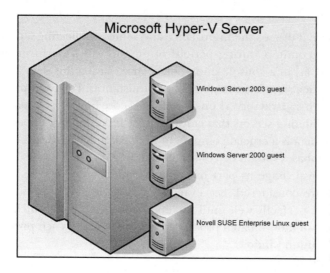

Figure 3.12   Hypervisors such as Microsoft's Hyper-V are used to virtualize multiple guest servers. Guests share the host's resources while appearing on the network as normal servers.

Type 2 hypervisors such as VMWare Workstation and Microsoft's Virtual Server run within an existing operating system. For example, a laptop running Windows Vista could have VMware Workstation installed in order to host one or more guest VMs running various operating systems, such as Windows Server 2008 or Novell SUSE Linux.

Type 1 hypervisors are typically used in server environments where maximum performance of guest virtual machines is the prime concern. In contrast, Type 2 hypervisors are typically used in development and testing situations, enabling a laptop, for example, to host many different guest operating systems for various purposes.

Let's take a look at some of the pros and cons of virtualization as compared with the consolidation techniques covered above.

ADVANTAGES OF VIRTUALIZATION

Virtualization offers many unique advantages:

- *Resource flexibility*—Unlike a dedicated physical server, resources (RAM, CPU, and so forth) in a VM can be easily increased or decreased, with spare capacity coming from or returned to the host server. Further, some virtualization solutions enable VMs to dynamically move to another physical server, thus enabling large numbers of virtual machines to be balanced across a pool of physical servers.

- *Guest operating systems*—A single physical server can host many different operating systems and/or different versions of the one operating system.

- *Ability to convert physical to virtual servers*—The major virtualization products include tools to create a VM based on an existing physical machine. One of the many advantages of such tools is the ability to preserve the state of an older legacy server that may not be required anymore. If required, the converted virtual server can be powered on, without having to maintain the physical server and the associated power, cooling, and space requirements while it's not being used.

- *Portability and disaster recovery*—A VM can be easily copied from one server to another, perhaps in a different physical location. Further, various products are available that specialize in the real-time replication of a VM, including its applications and data, from one location to another, thus enabling enhanced disaster-recovery options.

- *Snapshot/rollback capability*—A powerful aspect of some virtualization platforms is the ability to *snapshot* a VM for later rollback purposes. At the machine level, this feature can be considered as backup/restore. It enables you to make changes, safe in the knowledge that you can restore the snapshot if necessary. An example is performing an in-place upgrade of SQL Server 2005 to 2008. Should the upgrade fail, the snapshot can be restored, putting the system back to its pre-upgrade state.

Despite these clear advantages, there are a number of issues for consideration before you decide to virtualize SQL Server environments.

CONSIDERATIONS FOR VIRTUALIZING SQL SERVER

Arguably the single biggest issue for consideration when virtualizing SQL Server is that of *support,* particularly for mission-critical production systems. It's not uncommon to hear of organizations with virtualized SQL Server environments having difficulty during support incidents due to the presence of a virtualization platform. A common request during such incidents is to reproduce the problem in a nonvirtualized environment. Such a request is usually unrealistic when dealing with a critical 24/7 production SQL Server environment.

The support issue is commonly cited as the prime reason for avoiding virtualization in production environments (and associated volume/load test environments). Those who take this approach often use virtualization in other less critical environments, such as development and testing.

> ### Virtualization support policy
> Microsoft recently announced that both SQL Server 2005 and 2008 will be officially supported in Hyper-V environments, as well as those certified through the *Server Virtualization Validation Program* (SVVP). More information is available at http://support.microsoft.com/?id=956893.

Other considerations for SQL Server virtualization include the following:

- *Scalability*—The maximum resource limitations per VM (which varies depending on the virtualization platform and version) may present an issue for high-volume applications that require maximum scalability. In such cases, using physical servers, with scalability limited only by the hardware and operating system, may present a more flexible solution.
- *Performance overhead*—Depending on the hypervisor, a commonly cited figure in terms of the performance overhead of the virtualization platform is approximately 10 percent.

- *Baseline analysis*—As with the server consolidation techniques we discussed earlier, consideration should be given to the profiles of the individual virtual servers running on the same machine—for example, placing many CPU-intensive VMs together on a single CPU core host machine.
- *Licensing*—Licensing can be a tricky and complex area, so I'm not going to discuss the pros and cons of licensing virtualization. But I do recommend that before deciding on a server consolidation technique, understand the licensing implications fully.
- *Toolset*—One of the things that becomes apparent when troubleshooting a performance problem on a VM is that in order to get the full picture of what's happening on the server, you need access to the virtualization toolset in order to determine the impact from other VMs. Depending on the organization, access to such tools may or may not be granted to a DBA.

Virtualization and consolidation techniques are here to stay; it's vitally important that the pros and cons of each technique are well understood.

3.6   *Best practice considerations: physical server design*

Today's off-the-shelf database servers from one of the major system vendors are both powerful and flexible enough for most SQL Server implementations. However, a sound understanding of server design and configuration principles remains an important skill.

- The SQLIO and SQLIOSIM tools should be used to validate both the capacity and validity of a storage system before SQL Server is installed. Consider these tools an essential component in the commissioning process of a new production system.
- Track-align SQL Server partitions before formatting with a 64K allocation size using the NTFS file system.
- Use a switched gigabit network for maximum network performance, and ensure NIC speed and duplex settings are manually configured.
- Consider NIC teaming for performance and redundancy, particularly for connections to an iSCSI SAN, but be aware of the implications for use in a cluster (discussed in chapter 5).
- *Component redundancy* is a crucial aspect of a reliable database server. Build fault tolerance into as many server components as possible, including power supplies and fans, and protect servers from power failures with a UPS.
- To minimize costs and maximize performance, purchase servers and components within the framework of a server replacement policy. Taking into account falling prices and rapidly increasing component performance, servers should be purchased for a two- to three-year production lifecycle.
- Minimize support costs and fault correction time by developing standard database server builds, including standardizing hardware, software, bios and firmware versions, and so forth.

- Before consolidating or virtualizing SQL Servers on one host machine, consider the load profiles of each, best obtained through a baseline analysis process. Locating complementary instances together is of crucial importance in avoiding performance problems.

- In addition to the load profiles, give consideration to maintenance windows, disk usage, and tempdb usage when consolidating servers.

- Before virtualizing or consolidating SQL Server instances, understand the licensing impacts of both methods.

- To enable thorough performance analysis and tuning of a virtualized SQL Server, consider the need to access and learn the virtualization toolset. Such tools are required in order to understand the impact one virtual machine may be having on another.

- When virtualizing SQL Server instances, all of the other best practices we'll cover throughout this book hold true, such as using separate disks for data and logs, scheduling regular backups, preallocating space to avoid autogrowth operations, and so forth. Virtualization isn't an invitation to ignore the importance of these fundamental tasks.

- Most importantly, before virtualizing a critical SQL Server environment, ensure the support implications of doing so are well understood.

Additional information on the best practices covered in this chapter can be found online at http://www.sqlCrunch.com/server.

The last three chapters have been focused on planning and design. In the next chapter, we'll roll up our sleeves and install a SQL Server 2008 instance.

Installing and upgrading
SQL Server 2008

In this chapter, we'll cover

- Preparing for installation
- Installing SQL Server 2008
- Upgrading to SQL Server 2008
- Developing a service pack upgrade strategy

With SQL Server 2008's new and enhanced features, you can install and configure SQL Server instances that comply with best practices much easier than with earlier versions. Starting with the installation wizard, there are several new options, such as the ability to specify separate directories for backups, transaction logs, and the tempdb database. On the configuration side, policy-based management (which we'll discuss in detail in chapter 8) lets you store instance configuration settings in XML configuration files that can be applied to a server instance after installation.

The next chapter will focus on clustered installations of SQL Server. This chapter covers the installation and upgrade of nonclustered SQL Server instances. We'll start with some important preinstallation tasks, run through the installation process, and finish with upgrade techniques.

4.1 Preparing for installation

Adequate preinstallation planning is a crucial element in ensuring a successful SQL Server installation. A large percentage of problems with SQL Server environments can be traced back to poor installation choices, often performed by those with minimal SQL Server skills.

In this section, we'll cover the importance of a preinstallation checklist before looking at some additional preinstallation tasks, such as the creation of service accounts and directories.

4.1.1 Preinstallation checklist

Creating a preinstallation checklist is a great way to make sure appropriate attention is paid to the important elements of an installation. A checklist is particularly useful in environments where DBAs aren't involved in the installation of SQL Server. By creating and providing thorough checklists, you ensure that the chances of a successful deployment are significantly improved.

Figure 4.1 shows an example of a preinstallation checklist. The important point here isn't necessarily the contents of the checklist, but the fact that you create one and tailor it to the needs of your environment.

A lot of the items covered in the checklist shown in figure 4.1 are taken from the previous two chapters, and others will be covered in subsequent chapters. Let's move on now to look at some of these, beginning with the creation of service accounts.

SQL Server Preinstallation Checklist

Storage	RAID configuration	Misc	BIOS & firmware versions
	Battery backed write optimized cache		Physical security
	Partition offset		Antivirus configuration
	64K allocation unit size		WMI
	Multipathing		Pending reboots
	SQLIO/SIM checks		Windows service packs and hotfixes
	LUN configuration & zoning		No domain controller role
	Backup, tempdb, T-log, DB : volumes & directories		
CPU/Memory	PAE/3GB settings	Service Accounts	Separate, non-privileged accounts for each service
	NUMA configuration		Password expiration policy
	Page file configuration		Lock pages in memory
			Perform volume maintenance tasks
Clustering	IP addresses	Network	Manual configuration
	MSDTC in dedicated resource group		Switched gigabit connections
	Network priority & bindings		ISCSI NIC teaming
	Private LAN: connectivity & ping time		Windows & perimeter firewall configuration
	FCCP certification		Disable NETBIOS & SMB

Figure 4.1 Along with other strategies such as policy-based management, a preinstallation checklist enables a SQL Server installation to have the best chance of meeting best practice.

4.1.2 Service accounts

A SQL Server installation will create several new Windows services, each of which requires an account under which it will run. As we'll see shortly, these accounts are specified during installation, so they need to be created in advance.

Depending on which features are installed, SQL Server setup creates the following services for each installed instance:

- SQL Server
- SQL Server Agent
- SQL Server Analysis Services
- SQL Server Reporting Services
- SQL Server Integration Services

Prior to installation, you should create service accounts for each of these services with the following attributes:

- *Domain accounts*—While you can use local server accounts, domain accounts are a better choice as they enable the SQL instance to access other SQL Server instances and domain resources, as long as you grant the necessary privileges.
- *Nonprivileged accounts*—The service accounts do not, and should not, be members of the domain administrators or local administrator groups. The installation process will grant the service accounts the necessary permissions to the file system and registry as part of the installation. Additional permissions beyond those required to run SQL Server, such as access to a directory for data import/export purposes, should be manually granted for maximum security.
- *Additional account permissions*—Two recommended account permissions that SQL Server doesn't grant to the SQL Server service account are Perform Volume Maintenance Tasks, required for Instant Initialization (covered in chapter 9), and Lock Pages in Memory, required for 32-bit AWE-enabled systems and recommended for 64-bit systems (this setting is covered in more detail in chapter 7).
- *Password expiration and complexity*—Like any service account, the service accounts for SQL Server shouldn't have any password expiration policies in place, and the passwords should be of adequate complexity and known only to those responsible for service account administration.
- *Separate accounts for each service*—Each SQL Server service for each installed instance should be configured with a separate service account. This allows for the most granular security, a topic we'll examine further in chapter 6.

4.1.3   *Additional checks and considerations*

Before we launch into an installation, let's discuss a number of other important preinstallation checks and considerations:

- *Collation*—Like Windows, SQL Server uses collations to determine how characters are sorted and compared. As we'll see shortly, a collation is chosen during installation, and by default, SQL Server setup will select a collation to match the server's Windows collation. An inconsistent collation selection is a common cause of various administration problems, and a well-considered selection is therefore a crucial installation step. In almost all cases, you should accept the default collation during installation; if you choose a custom collation, take into account the potential collation conflicts when dealing with data from another instance with a different collation. SQL Server Books Online (BOL) covers this important topic in detail.

- *Storage configuration*—In previous chapters, we covered the importance of storage configuration. Prior to installation, you must ensure partitions are offset[1] and formatted with a 64K allocation unit size. Further, run SQLIO and SQLIO-SIM to validate storage performance/validity and driver/firmware versions are up to date. Additional checks include ensuring multipathing software is installed and working, and consider NIC teaming for maximum performance and redundancy for iSCSI installations.

- *Directory creation*—One of the installation steps is to specify locations for the database data and log files, backup files, and the tempdb data and log files. For maximum performance, create each of these directories on partitions that are physically separate from each other—that is, they don't share the same underlying disks. Directories for these objects should be created before installation. Chapter 9 discusses the importance of physical disk separation in more detail.

- *Network security*—SQL Server should be secured behind a firewall, and unnecessary network protocols such as NetBIOS and SMB should be disabled. Chapter 6 provides detailed coverage on this process.

- *Windows version*—SQL Server 2008 requires at least Windows Server 2003 Service Pack 2 as a prerequisite for installation; Windows Server 2008 is recommended for the best performance and security. Further, SQL Server shouldn't be installed on a primary or backup domain controller; the server should be dedicated to SQL Server.

- *Server reboot*—SQL Server won't install if there are any pending reboots;[2] therefore, reboot the server prior to installation if appropriate.

- *WMI*—The Windows Management Instrumentation (WMI) service must be installed and working properly before SQL Server can be installed. This service is installed and running by default on both Windows Server 2003 and 2008.

Windows Server 2008

The ideal underlying operating system for SQL Server is Windows Server 2008. Why? For starters, the networking stack in Windows 2008 is substantially faster, so there's an immediate boost in network transfer times. Second, the Enterprise and Data Center editions of Windows Server 2008 include Hyper-V, which provides virtualization opportunities for SQL Server instances. Other improvements over Windows Server 2003 include more clustering options, NUMA optimizations, and leaner installations that translate to less maintenance and smaller attack surfaces for better security.

---

[1] Windows Server 2008 does this automatically.
[2] Open the registry editor and navigate to HKLM\System\CurrentControlSet\Control\Session Manager. The existence of PendingFileRenameOperations is an indication of a pending reboot.

Now that we've covered the important preinstallation checks and planning, let's walk through an actual installation of SQL Server 2008.

4.2   Installing SQL Server

In this section, we'll walk through the installation of a SQL Server instance using a number of different techniques. Before we do that, let's cover an important installation selection: the choice between a default and a named instance.

4.2.1   Default and named instances

Since SQL Server 2000, multiple instances (copies) of SQL Server can be installed on one server, thus providing various benefits, such as the ability to control the amount of memory and CPU resources granted to each instance, and the option to maintain different collation and service pack levels per instance. Such benefits are crucial for server consolidation projects, and we'll spend more time on some of these benefits in chapter 7 when we cover the process of configuring memory usage on multi-instance servers.

As we'll see shortly, one of the choices during installation of SQL Server is the selection between a named instance and a default instance. While there can only be a single default instance per server, the Enterprise edition of SQL Server 2008 supports the installation of up to 50 named instances.[3]

When connecting to SQL Server, the instance name is specified in the connection string; for example, *BNE-SQL-PR-01\SALES* will connect to the SALES instance on the BNE-SQL-PR-01 server. In contrast, connecting to the default instance requires the server name only—that is, *BNE-SQL-PR-01*.

In addition to the instance name, SQL Server 2008 uses an *instance ID*, which by default has the same value as the instance name. The instance ID is used to identify registry keys and installation directories, particularly important on servers with multiple installed instances.

With this background in mind, let's install an instance of SQL Server using the GUI installation wizard.

4.2.2   GUI installation

Rather than bore you with every installation step, most of which are self-explanatory, I'll summarize the installation and include screen shots for the most important steps. Start the installation by running setup.exe from the SQL Server DVD. The setup process begins with a check on the installed versions of the Windows Installer and the .NET Framework. If the required versions are missing, the setup process offers the choice to install them. After these components are verified (or installed), setup begins with the SQL Server Installation Center, as shown in figure 4.2.

---

[3]   Other editions support up to 16 instances.

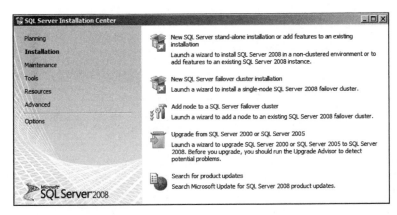

Figure 4.2 The Installation Center allows you to perform various installation-related tasks.

1 The Installation Center is the starting point for a wide variety of tasks. For our example, let's start by clicking the Installation tab and then selecting the "New SQL Server stand-alone installation or add features to an existing installation" option. Setup begins with a check for potential problems that may prevent an installation from completing successfully. You can view details of the checks by clicking Show Details. Address any problems preventing installation, or click OK to continue.

2 Click Install to install the required setup support files.

3 In the Setup Support Rules screen, additional checks are processed before installation continues; for example, the installer warns of the presence of Windows Firewall with a warning to unblock appropriate ports. Review the warnings/failures (if any) and click Next.

4 The Installation Type screen lets you choose between installing a new instance or adding features to an existing instance. For our example, let's choose the default (Perform a New Installation) and click Next.

5 The Product Key screen asks you to select between a free edition (Enterprise Evaluation or Express) or the option to enter a product key (supplied with the purchase of SQL Server). Make the appropriate choice and click Next.

6 At the license terms screen, review the terms, check the "I accept the license terms" box, and click Next.

7 On the Feature Selection screen shown in figure 4.3, select the appropriate features and choose an installation directory (or accept the default). You can display additional information on each feature by clicking on the feature name. Click Next.

8 In the Instance Configuration screen, shown in figure 4.4, choose between a default or a named instance, enter the instance ID and root directory (or accept the default settings), and click Next.

9 The Disk Space Requirements screen confirms the existence (or absence) of the necessary disk space for installation to proceed. Review the summary of required and available space and click Next to continue.

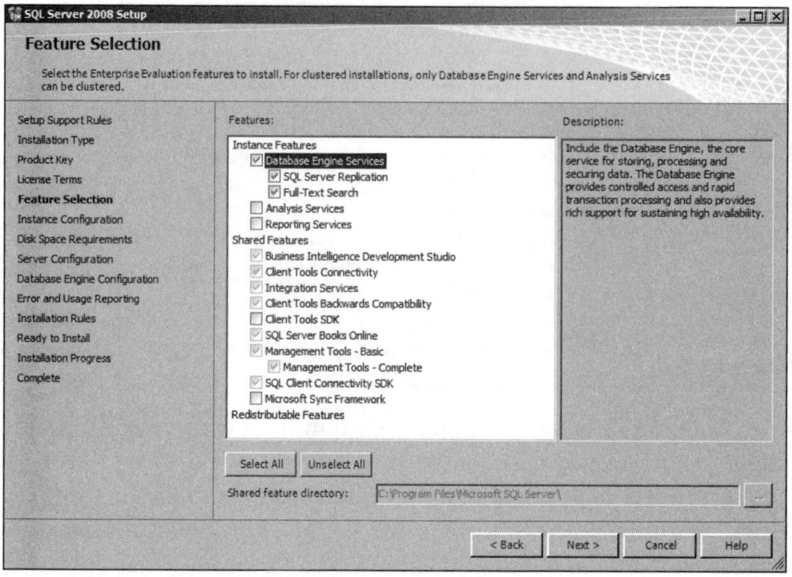

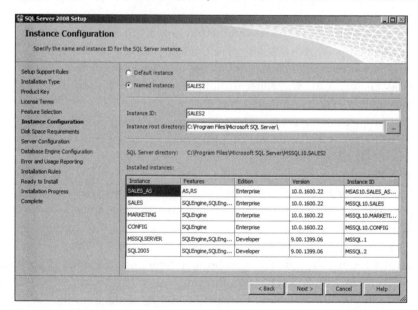

Figure 4.3   The Features screen enables you to select various features for installation.

Figure 4.4   This screen lets you select between a default and a named instance.

10 In the Server Configuration screen, shown in figure 4.5, enter the account names and passwords for the SQL services, and optionally change the startup type. As we discussed earlier in the chapter, these accounts should be created as standard privilege accounts prior to installation. Before clicking Next to continue, click the Collation tab to review (and optionally modify) the default collation. As we covered earlier, use caution when selecting a custom collation.

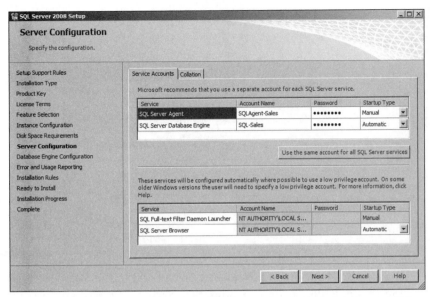

Figure 4.5   On this screen, you select a service account and startup type for each SQL service.

11 On the first tab of the Database Engine Configuration screen, shown in figure 4.6, you select the authentication mode for the instance: Windows or Mixed Mode. As we'll discuss in chapter 6, Windows authentication mode is the most secure option, and is therefore the default (and recommended) option. If you choose Mixed Mode, be sure to enter a strong system administration (SA) account password. Regardless of the selected authentication mode, click either

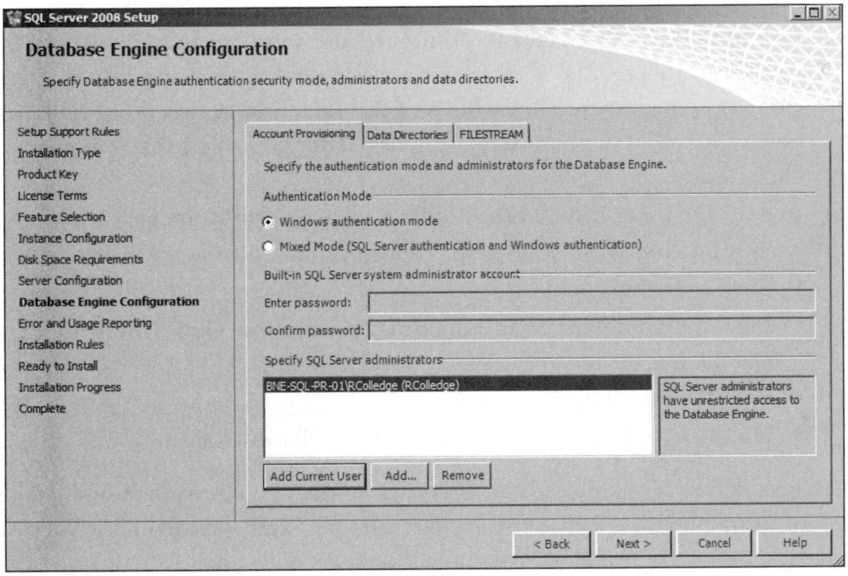

Figure 4.6   The Account Provisioning tab allows you to select the authentication mode and SQL Server administrators.

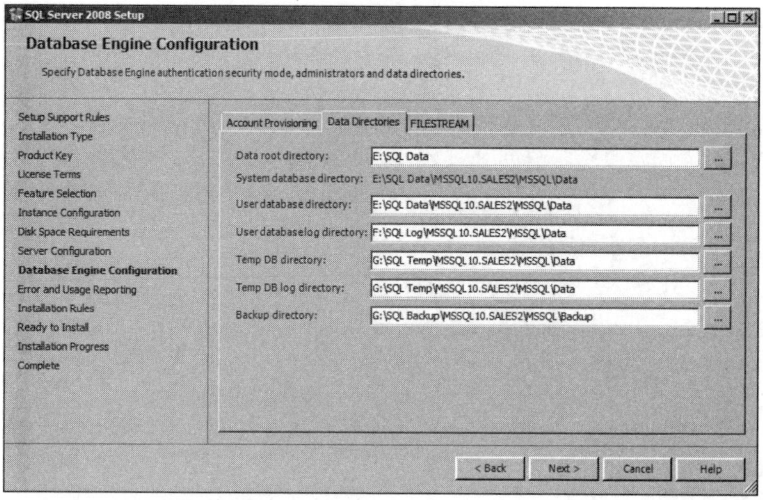

Figure 4.7   On the Data Directories tab, specify custom directories for data, logs, backup, and tempdb.

Add Current User or Add to select a user to add to the SQL Server administration group. Unlike earlier versions, SQL Server 2008 setup enforces this selection as a secure alternative to adding the BUILTIN\Administrators group to the SQL Server administration role. We'll explain this in more detail in chapter 6. To continue, click the Data Directories tab.

12   The Data Directories tab, as shown in figure 4.7, lets you specify default directories for data, log, tempdb, and backup directories. As covered earlier, physical disk separation of these directories is important, and we'll address this topic in greater detail in chapter 9. After entering the directory locations, click the FILESTREAM tab to continue.

13   Use the FILESTREAM tab to configure the instance for FileStream access. As you'll see in chapter 9, FileStream is a new option for binary large object (BLOB) management. Regardless of the selection at this point, FileStream can be configured as a postinstallation task. After reviewing the options on this tab, click Next.

14   In the remaining installation steps, you'll accomplish the following:

- Specify whether to send error reports and feature usage data to Microsoft
- Review final installation rules checks
- View the summary of installation choices, and click Install to execute the installation based on the previous selections
- View the installation progress
- On the Completion screen, view the installation log file

When installation is complete, SQL Server saves the choices you made during setup in ConfigurationFile.ini, which you'll find in the C:\Program Files\Microsoft SQL Server\100\Setup Bootstrap\Log*yyyymmdd_hhmmss* directory. You can use this file to confirm the installation proceeded with the required options, as well as use it as a base for subsequent unattended installations via the command prompt. We'll cover these options shortly.

After installation, you must perform a number of important configuration activities, such as sizing the tempdb database, setting minimum and maximum memory values, and creating SQL Agent alerts. We'll cover these tasks in subsequent chapters.

4.2.3   *Command prompt installations*

In addition to using the GUI installation wizard that we've just covered, you can install SQL Server 2008 from the command prompt, as you can see in figure 4.8. You can find the syntax and options in SQL Server BOL in the "How to: Install SQL Server 2008 from the Command Prompt" topic.

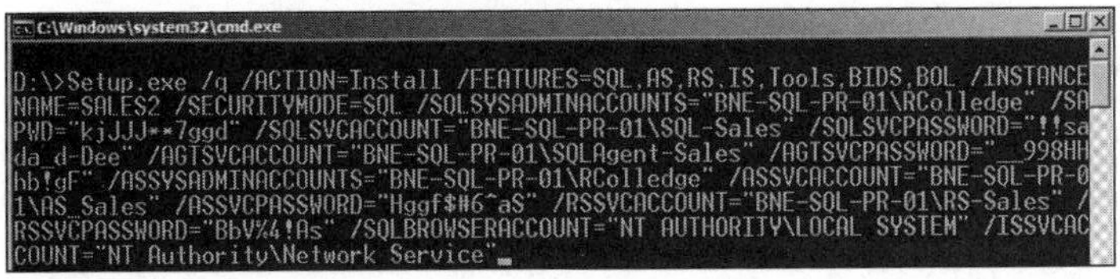

Figure 4.8   SQL Server 2008 command-line installation

As mentioned earlier, the ConfigurationFile.ini is created at the end[4] of a GUI-based installation. This file should be preserved in its original state for later analysis, but you can make a copy and use it for subsequent installations at the command prompt via the /Configurationfile parameter, as shown in figure 4.9.

Figure 4.9   Use the /Configurationfile option at the command line to direct SQL Server to install based on the contents of a ConfigurationFile.ini file.

Command prompt installations with configuration files are ideal in standardizing and streamlining installation, particularly when installations are performed by those without the appropriate SQL Server knowledge.

SQL Server 2008 can be installed alongside earlier versions of SQL Server. Doing so is a common technique in *migrating* databases, an alternative to an *in-place upgrade*, both of which we'll cover next.

4.3   *Upgrading to SQL Server 2008*

Depending on the environment, the upgrade to SQL Server 2008 can be complex, particularly when technologies such as replication and clustering are involved. In this section, rather than attempt to cover all of the possible upgrade issues, I've aimed for the more modest task of providing you with an insight into the various upgrade techniques.

---

[4]   The INI file can also be created by proceeding through the GUI installation, but cancel it at the very last step, on the Ready to Install page.

SQL Server 2008 Upgrade Technical Reference Guide

As with installation, upgrading to SQL Server 2008 requires considerable planning and preparation. Microsoft recently released the *SQL Server 2008 Upgrade Technical Reference Guide*. Weighing in at 490 pages and available for free download from the Microsoft website, this guide is essential reading as part of any upgrade project and contains important information on best practices and specific advice for various upgrade scenarios.

Depending on the availability of spare hardware and the allowed downtime, you can choose one of two upgrade techniques. The first is known as an *in-place* upgrade, in which an entire instance of SQL Server 2000 or 2005 along with all of its databases are upgraded in one action. Alternatively, you can use the *side-by-side* technique, in which individual databases can be migrated one at a time for more control. Both of these techniques have their advantages and disadvantages, as you'll see shortly.

Before we look at the details of in-place versus side-by-side, let's discuss the importance of analyzing the target database/instance before upgrading by using SQL Server's Upgrade Advisor tool.

4.3.1   *Upgrade Advisor*

Each new version of SQL Server contains behavioral changes, some major, some minor. In any case, even small, subtle changes can significantly impact application behavior. Regardless of the upgrade technique, a crucial step in preparing for an upgrade to SQL Server 2008 is to analyze the upgrade target and determine whether any issues require attention. Together with the appropriate upgrade technique, such analysis is essential in minimizing unexpected issues, making the upgrade process as smooth as possible.

SQL Server 2008, like 2005, includes an Upgrade Advisor tool, which you can use to examine existing 2000 and/or 2005 instances to determine whether any issues will prevent an upgrade from completing (blocking issues) or backward-compatibility issues that may lead to application failure after the upgrade. The Upgrade Advisor tool (which you access from the Planning menu of the SQL Server Installation Center as shown in figure 4.2) can be used to examine all SQL Server components, including Analysis Services, Reporting Services, Integration Services, and the core database engine itself.

The Upgrade Advisor has two main components: an analysis wizard and a report viewer. Use the wizard to select an upgrade target (SQL Server components, instances, and databases) and begin the analysis. Once complete, the report viewer can be used to view the details of the analysis, as shown in figure 4.10.

Like the 2005 version, the Upgrade Advisor tool can analyze trace files and Transact-SQL (T-SQL) scripts. You perform this analysis as a proactive measure to identify possible issues with application-generated data access code or T-SQL scripts, such as backup scripts used in scheduled maintenance plans.

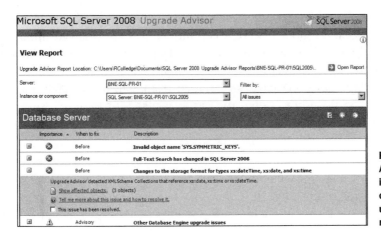

Figure 4.10 The Upgrade
Advisor wizard lets you
inspect a SQL Server 2000
or 2005 instance before
upgrading to detect issues
requiring attention.

Running the Upgrade Advisor produces a list of tasks that fall into two categories: those that must be completed before an upgrade can be performed, and those for attention once the upgrade is complete. Rather than list all of the possible post-upgrade tasks, here are the recommended ones for the core database engine:

- *Compatibility level check*—Post-upgrade, the *compatibility level* of the database is left at the pre-upgrade version. Although this is advantageous in minimizing the possibility of applications breaking due to the use of older language syntax that's no longer compatible with SQL Server 2008, some new functionality and performance optimizations won't be available until the new compatibility level is applied. Leaving an upgraded database at a previous compatibility level should be seen as an interim migration aid, with application code updated as soon as possible after installation. You can change the compatibility level of an upgraded database using the sp_dbcmptlevel stored procedure, or via the database properties in Management Studio, as shown in figure 4.11.

- *Max Worker Threads*—If you're upgrading from SQL Server 2000, the Max Worker Threads setting, covered in chapter 7, is kept at the default value of 255. After the upgrade, change this value to 0, which allows SQL Server to determine the appropriate value based on the number and type of CPUs available to the instance.

- *Statistics update*—Although SQL Server 2008 can work with statistics generated from earlier versions, I recommend you perform a full statistics update to take advantage of the query optimizer improvements in SQL Server 2008. Chapter 13 will discuss statistics in more detail.

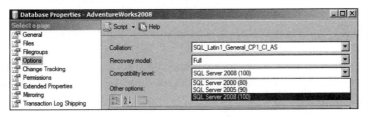

Figure 4.11 After you
upgrade, the compatibility
level of a database should
be set to SQL Server
2008, once testing has
confirmed the absence of
any unexpected problems.

- *Configuration check*—Like 2005, SQL Server 2008 complies with the *secure by default* installation mode, whereby certain features are disabled upon installation. We'll cover these issues in chapter 6. Depending on the installation, certain required features may need to be manually enabled postinstallation.

- `DBCC UPDATEUSAGE`—Databases upgraded from SQL Server 2000 may report incorrect results when using the `sp_spaceused` procedure. Running the `UPDATEUSAGE` command will update the catalog views used by this procedure, thus fixing this inaccuracy.

Before looking at the upgrade methods, note that regardless of the method you choose, performing a test upgrade is crucial in identifying possible issues. Test upgrades provide an opportunity to

- Determine the length of the upgrade process, crucial in planning downtime for the *real* upgrade.

- Determine application behavior after the upgrade. This will allow you to set the database compatibility level to SQL Server 2008 and ensure applications work as expected.

- Performance-test applications on the upgraded database. If performance is poor, a test upgrade provides a chance of investigating the reasons prior to the production upgrade.

- Last but not least, complex upgrades involving components such as replication are certainly not something you want to be doing the first time in production!

So, with these points in mind, let's take a look at the two upgrade methods, starting with the in-place method.

4.3.2   In-place upgrade

The *in-place* upgrade method upgrades an instance, and all of its databases, in a single irreversible action. For simple, small database instances, it provides the easiest and quickest upgrade method and has the following additional benefits:

- Applications connecting to any of the databases don't need modification. The instance name remains the same (if upgrading from a named instance), so no connection strings need to be changed.

- No additional hardware is required. The instance executables and data are changed in place.

Despite these benefits, there are some significant downsides to this method, making it unsuitable for a range of scenarios:

- All of the instance's databases have to be upgraded at once. There's no option to upgrade only some. If one of the databases (or its applications) needs modification before upgrading, then all of the other instance databases will have to wait before the upgrade can proceed.

- A failed upgrade, or one that produces unexpected results, can't be rolled back, short of running up new hardware and restoring old backup files, or using a virtualization snapshot rollback process.

Because the rollback options are limited with this method, it's critical that you complete a full backup and DBCC check on all databases before beginning the upgrade. If database activity occurs after the full backup, make transaction log backups immediately prior to the upgrade.

To begin the in-place upgrade, select Upgrade from SQL Server 2000 or SQL Server 2005 from the Installation menu of the SQL Server Installation Center.

For greater control of the upgrade process, you can choose one of several side-by-side upgrade methods.

4.3.3   *Side-by-side upgrade*

In contrast to an in-place upgrade, which upgrades all databases for a given instance, a side-by-side upgrade is a *per database* method:

1   A SQL Server 2008 instance is installed as a *new* installation (compared to an upgrade). The new instance can be installed on either the same server as the instance to be upgraded (legacy instance), or on a new server.

2   Each database to be upgraded is migrated from the legacy instance to the new 2008 instance, using one of several methods I'll describe shortly. Databases are migrated individually on their own schedule, and possibly to different destination servers.

3   Once the new 2008 instance is up and running, the legacy instance is decommissioned, or retained in an offline state for rollback purposes if required.

The side-by-side upgrade method offers several advantages over the in-place method. The major advantage is that if something goes wrong with the upgrade, or unexpected results render the upgrade a failure, the legacy instance is still available and unchanged for rollback purposes. Further, the upgrade is granular; individual databases can be migrated with others remaining on the original server, migrated to a different server, or migrated at a later point.

Disadvantages and complexities of this method when compared to the in-place method are as follows:

- Application connection strings will need to be modified to point to the new instance name.
- Security settings, maintenance plans, and SQL Server Agent jobs will need to be re-created on the new 2008 instance, either manually or from a script.
- If the new 2008 instance is on the same server as the legacy instance, the capacity of the server to run both instances in parallel must be taken into account. A possible workaround for this issue is to limit the resources of one of the instances, such as the maximum memory and CPU affinity, for the period of time that both are actively running.
- Downtime is typically longer than for an in-place method; there are several techniques used to limit this, as you'll learn in a moment.

Side-by-side upgrades are often scheduled for the same time as server replacements—that is, the new server is purchased, installed, configured, and loaded with a new instance of SQL Server 2008, and databases are migrated from the legacy instance. At the completion of this process, the legacy server is decommissioned, cycled back to lower environments, or used for other purposes.

The method used to migrate databases as part of a side-by-side upgrade is an important consideration in determining the rollback and downtime implications for the upgrade, particularly for larger databases. Let's walk through the major methods used, beginning with backup/restore.

BACKUP/RESTORE

The backup/restore method is straightforward and keeps the original database in place for rollback purposes. A full database backup is made on the legacy database and restored to the new SQL Server 2008 instance. As part of the restore process, SQL Server will upgrade the internal structures of the database as necessary.

A variation on this approach involves filegroup backups and piecemeal restores. These topics will be discussed in more detail in chapters 9 and 10, but essentially this involves backup and restore of the legacy database's primary filegroup to the new 2008 instance. After this, the database is online and available on the new 2008 instance, after which individual filegroups can be backed up and restored using a piecemeal approach in priority order.

ATTACH/DETACH

The attach/detach method involves detaching the legacy database and attaching to the new 2008 instance. Similar to a restore, SQL Server will upgrade the internal structure as part of the attach process. To keep the original database available for rollback, you can copy the database files to the new server before attaching them to the new 2008 instance. After the copy is complete, the database can be reattached to the legacy instance for rollback purposes if required.

TRANSACTION LOG BACKUP/RESTORE

Depending on the size of the database to be migrated, the time involved in copying either the data files or backup files in the previous two methods may exceed the downtime targets. For example, if the backup file was hundreds of gigabytes and had to be copied over a slow network link, the copy could take many hours to complete. To reduce downtime, a third method can be used involving transaction log backups. This method is similar to setting up log shipping (covered in chapter 11) and involves these steps:

1. A full database backup of the legacy database is taken and copied to the new SQL Server 2008 instance. The legacy database remains online and in use throughout the copy process.
2. The legacy database is restored on the new 2008 instance *WITH NORECOVERY* (full details provided in chapter 10).
3. Finally, at the moment of migration, users are disconnected from the legacy database, and a transaction log backup is made and copied to the 2008 instance.
4. The transaction log backup is restored *WITH RECOVERY.*
5. At this point, application connection strings are redirected to the 2008 instance and users are reconnected.

There are several variations of this method. If the transaction rate is very high, the size of the transaction log backup in step 3 may be very large; if so, regular transaction log backups can be made leading up to this step, reducing the size (and therefore copy time) of the final transaction log backup. If using this method, restore all but the last of the transaction log backups *WITH NORECOVERY.*

TRANSACTIONAL REPLICATION

This method is similar to the transaction log backup/restore but involves replication:

1　Transactional replication is set up from the legacy instance to the new 2008 instance.

2　At the moment of migration, replication is stopped and applications are redirected to the new 2008 instance.

3　Optionally, replication can then be set up in the reverse direction to support a rollback scenario—that is, data entered on the new 2008 instance post-migration is copied to the legacy database instance to prevent data loss in the event of a rollback.

OTHER TECHNIQUES

Other migration techniques include using the *Copy Database wizard* (in Management Studio, right-click a database and choose Tasks > Copy Database) and manually creating the database on the new 2008 instance from script and performing bulk copy operations.

Table 4.1 compares the attributes of the various upgrade techniques.

Table 4.1　Upgrade options compared

Upgrade technique	Complexity	Rollback options	App reconfig	Downtime
In-place	Lowest	No	No	Lowest
Side-by-side				
—Backup/restore	Medium	Yes	Yes	Highest
—Detach/copy/attach	Medium	Yes	Yes	Highest
—Filegroup restore	Medium	Yes	Yes	Moderate
—T-Log backup/restore	Medium	Yes	Yes	Lowest
—Transaction replication	Highest	Yes	Yes	Lowest

The side-by-side upgrade method offers much more flexibility and granularity than the all-or-nothing in-place approach. In all cases, regardless of the upgrade method, planning is crucial for a successful upgrade. The same is true for the installation of service packs, our next topic.

4.4　*Developing a service pack upgrade strategy*

If you were to develop a list of the top ten issues that a group of DBAs will argue about, one that's sure to appear is the approach to installing service packs. Let's take a look at the various considerations involved before looking at a recommended approach.

4.4.1   Installation considerations

You must consider a number of important factors before making the decision to install a service pack:

- *Third-party application vendor support*—Most application vendors include supported SQL Server versions and service pack levels in their support agreements. In such cases, a service pack upgrade is typically delayed until (at least) it becomes a supported platform.
- *Test environments*—The ability to measure the performance and functional impacts of a service pack in a test environment is crucial, and doing so counters a common argument against their installation—the fear that they'll break more things than they fix.
- *Support timeframes*—Microsoft publishes their support lifecycle at http://support.microsoft.com/lifecycle. While an application may continue to work perfectly well on SQL Server 6.5, it's no longer officially supported, and this risk needs to be considered in the same manner as the risk of an upgrade. It's not uncommon to hear of situations in which an emergency upgrade is performed as a result of a bug in a platform that's no longer supported. Clearly, a better option is to perform an upgrade in a calm and prepared manner.

Complicating the decision to apply a service pack is the inevitable discussion of the need for application outage.

4.4.2   Application outage

A common planning mistake is to fail to consider the need for scheduled maintenance; therefore, a request to apply a service pack is often met with a negative response in terms of the impact on users.

Very few organizations are prepared to invest in the infrastructure required for a zero outage environment, which is fine as long as they realize the importance of planning for scheduled outages on a monthly or quarterly basis. Such planning allows for the installation of service packs and other maintenance actions while enabling the management of downtime and user expectations.

> **Incremental servicing model**
>
> Microsoft has recently moved to an incremental servicing model (http://support.microsoft.com/default.aspx/kb/935897/en-us) whereby cumulative updates, consisting of all hotfixes since the last service pack, are released every 2 months. In addition to the bi-monthly release, critical on-demand hotfixes will be delivered as soon as possible, as agreed between Microsoft and the customer experiencing the critical issue.

So with these issues in mind, let's take a look at a recommended approach for installing SQL Server service packs.

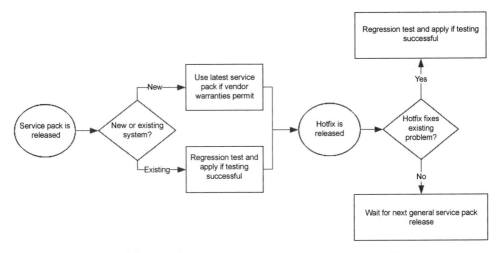

Figure 4.12   A recommended approach for implementing service packs and hotfixes

4.4.3   Recommended approach

Although each environment will have its own special circumstances, the following approach is generally accepted by most DBAs (see figure 4.12 for a summary):

- For a new deployment of SQL Server, use the latest service pack available, subject to application vendor support policies.
- For existing production systems, aim to apply service packs as soon as possible after their release—for example, at the next available/advertised maintenance window. This will require preparation and budget to ensure the availability of test environments for regression testing.
- Only apply hotfixes or cumulative updates if there's a particular need—that is, you're suffering from a bug or security vulnerability that's fixed in the release. If you're not in this category, wait for the next general service pack.
- If you're denied the chance to apply a service pack, for example, an objection to the required downtime or fear of the unknown consequences, ensure management is kept informed of the Microsoft support lifecycle for previous versions of SQL Server.

4.5   Best practice considerations: installing and upgrading SQL Server

Despite the ease with which SQL Server can be installed and upgraded, adequate preparation is essential in ensuring a stable and secure platform for later use:

- Review the best practices from the previous chapters to ensure hardware components are designed and configured appropriately.
- Prior to installation, create nonadministrator domain accounts for each instance/service combination, and ensure the accounts don't have any password expiration policies in place.

- Grant the SQL Server service account the Perform Volume Maintenance Tasks right; and for 32-bit AWE and 64-bit systems, also grant the Lock Pages in Memory right.
- Prior to installation of each SQL Server instance, prepare directories on separate physical disk volumes for the following database components:
  - Data files
  - Log files
  - Backup files
  - tempdb data and log
- Prior to installation, use the resources available in the Planning tab of the installation wizard. Included here (among others) are hardware and software requirements, security documentation, and online release notes.
- Only install the minimum set of SQL Server features required. This will increase security by reducing the attack surface area, and ensure unnecessary services aren't consuming system resources.
- Don't install SQL Server on a primary or secondary domain controller.
- Ensure consistency in the selection of collations across SQL Server instances, and unless compatibility is required with earlier SQL Server versions, select a Windows collation.
- Unless it's being used for applications that can't work with Windows authentication, don't choose the Mixed Mode option. If you do, make sure you choose a strong SA password and enforce strong password policies for all SQL Server logins.
- If you need to change any of the SQL Server service accounts after the installation, make changes using the SQL Server Configuration Manager tool. Changing in this manner ensures the appropriate permissions are granted to the new account.
- When installing SQL Server using the GUI wizard, take care to click and review each of the tabs before clicking Next. For example, the Database Engine Configuration screen lets you select the Authentication mode. Once you do this, clicking Next will skip the Data Directories and FILESTREAM tabs, which will enforce the default values. One of the ramifications of this is that data and log files will be created in the same directory, unless you manually change them after the installation.
- For a smoother installation process, particularly when a non-DBA is responsible for installation, use a tailored checklist. Alternatively (or as well as), copy and modify a ConfigurationFile.ini created from a successful installation and use the command-line method with the /Configurationfile option.
- Before upgrading, download and read the *SQL Server 2008 Upgrade Technical Reference Guide*. It contains important information on best practices and specific advice for various upgrade scenarios.

- Always run through a trial upgrade in a test environment using a recent copy of the production database (if possible). Doing so offers many benefits as well as circumvents potential problems. A trial upgrade will enable you to gather accurate timings for the actual production upgrade, determine the effect of the new compatibility level on application behavior, allow performance testing against a known baseline to determine the performance impact of the upgrade, and finally, develop a checklist to ensure the real upgrade runs as smoothly as possible.

- Use the Upgrade Advisor to analyze upgrade targets for issues that will prevent an upgrade or to gather a list of issues that will need to be addressed after the upgrade. If possible, feed SQL Server Profiler trace files into the Upgrade Advisor to examine any application code that may need to change before the upgrade.

- After the upgrade, attend to any issues identified by the Upgrade Advisor, including the following: setting the database compatibility level, updating statistics, checking configuration for features that need to be enabled, and if upgrading from SQL 2000, setting the Max Worker Threads option to 0 and running DBCC UPDATEUSAGE.

- The in-place upgrade method may be simple, but it exposes the possibility of having no rollback position if required. The various side-by-side upgrade methods offer more choices for rollbacks while also minimizing downtime.

- If using the in-place upgrade method, perform a full backup and DBCC check of each database prior to the upgrade.

- Using the Microsoft Assessment and Planning Toolkit Solution Accelerator tool is an effective means of discovering SQL Server instances and can be used as the starting point for consolidation and/or upgrade projects.

- Prior to any installation, upgrade, or service pack/hotfix install, always read the release notes for any late-breaking news and details on how certain components and features may be affected.

- Prepare for service packs. They're released for a good reason. Have both the time and environments ready for regression testing before applying in production, and consider any software vendor warranties before application.

- Only apply hotfixes and cumulative updates if there's a specific reason for doing so; otherwise, wait for the next service pack release.

- *Always* read the release notes that accompany service packs, hotfixes, and cumulative updates. Such notes often contain crucial information that may impact certain configurations.

Additional information on the best practices covered in this chapter can be found online at http://www.sqlCrunch.com/install.

In the next chapter, we'll discuss installing SQL Server on a failover cluster.

Failover clustering 5

In this chapter, we'll cover

- Clustering architecture
- Advantages and limitations of clustering
- Quorum models
- Clustering topologies
- Installing a clustered SQL Server 2008 instance

Although redundant component design, such as dual-power supplies, provides fault tolerance at a component level, failover clustering operates at the server level, enabling ongoing operations in the event of a complete server failure. Complementary to component redundancy, failover clustering is a commonly used high availability technique for SQL Server implementations and is the focus of this chapter.

In addition to the requisite SQL Server skills, successfully designing and administering a clustered SQL Server environment requires skills in a number of areas, including the configuration of cluster-compatible hardware components. While Windows Server 2008 has made clustering SQL Server somewhat easier, it's still a complex process requiring considerable planning and broad skills.

Rather than attempt to provide full coverage of the clustering design, creation, and administration process (such a goal would require at least an entire book!), this chapter focuses on installing a clustered SQL Server instance. Let's begin with a broad overview of clustering, exploring its benefits and limitations from a SQL Server perspective, and tackling important preinstallation configuration tasks.

5.1 Clustering overview

As a cluster-aware application, a SQL Server instance can be installed into an existing Windows cluster, creating what's referred to as a *failover clustering instance*. Once installed, the instance is accessed using a network name (aka *virtual server name*) without needing to know which of the underlying physical cluster servers the instance is currently running on.

The abstraction between a physical and a virtual server is a key component in providing continued database availability after a failure event. In the event of a server failure, the SQL Server instance automatically moves, or *fails over*, to another cluster server, while continuing to be accessed using the same virtual server name.

In this section, we'll take a high-level look at clustering architecture, including its benefits, limitations, and common usage scenarios.

5.1.1 Clustering architecture

Built on top of a Windows Server failover cluster, SQL Server clustering uses the *shared nothing* architecture, a term used to distinguish its clustering implementation from those of other database vendors, such as Oracle's *Real Application Cluster* (RAC). Under the shared nothing architecture, a SQL Server database instance is active on only one physical clustered server at any given time.

Unlike a network load-balanced solution, SQL Server failover clustering isn't a high-performance solution; in other words, the performance won't be any better, or worse, than a nonclustered implementation. SQL Server clustering is purely a high-availability solution and you should not choose it for any other reason.

Figure 5.1 illustrates a simple example of a two-node cluster with a single SQL Server failover clustering instance. Ordinarily, the instance resides on the *Sales1* server. In the event of a failure of this server, the SQL Server instance automatically fails over to the *Sales2* server. In either case, the SQL instance will continue to be accessed using the same virtual server name.

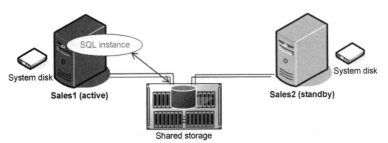

Figure 5.1   A simple failover clustering example in which a SQL Server instance can move from one cluster server to another in the event of failure

Key components of a Windows Server failover cluster solution are *shared storage* and *resource arbitration*. In figure 5.1, we can see both the Sales1 and Sales2 servers have access to shared storage. The databases contained in the SQL instance reside on the shared storage to enable either server to access them when required. But in order to prevent both servers from accessing them at the same time, and therefore causing data corruption, the Windows clustering service arbitrates ownership of the disk volumes based on the server's current role in the cluster.

Clusters consist of one or more *resource groups*, which are collections of resources required by a clustered application. In the case of a clustered SQL Server instance, its resource group would include the disks containing the database instance's data and transaction logs, an IP address and network name, and the three application services: SQL Server, SQL Agent, and full-text service. *Failover* is a term used to describe the transfer of ownership of resources from one server to another; it occurs at the resource group level, ensuring that all resources required for the application are moved and available on the failover server.

Given that a database instance can be owned by various servers in the cluster, applications are configured to connect to the virtual server name rather than the name of a physical cluster server. To avoid confusion with the Microsoft Virtual Server product, SQL Server 2005 and above refer to *failover clustering instances* rather than the virtual server name known in SQL Server 2000 and earlier.

As we move through this chapter, the terms and concepts we've covered thus far will become clearer, particularly when we walk through an installation of a clustered instance. For now, let's turn our attention to the major advantages and limitations of SQL Server clustering.

5.1.2   *SQL Server clustering advantages and limitations*

As a high-availability technology, clustering has a number of advantages and limitations when compared to other SQL Server high-availability options such as database mirroring and transaction log shipping (covered in chapter 11). Its primary advantage is that in the event of a server failure, the *entire instance and all of its databases* are moved to a failover server, a process that usually takes no more than about 90 seconds. This stands in contrast to mirroring or log shipping solutions, which are established on an individual database-by-database basis.

In addition to providing protection from unexpected server failure, the other major benefit of clustering is the ability to reduce downtime during planned outages. For example, consider a requirement to upgrade a server's RAM. Unless we have a server with hot-add RAM capabilities, we'd need to power off the server, upgrade the RAM, and power back on again, and during this time the database instance would be unavailable. In a clustering scenario, we could manually initiate failover, which would move the instance from one server to the other, enabling the upgrade to occur while the instance is available on another cluster server. Thus, the downtime is limited to the failover time, typically about 1 minute.

Unlike database mirroring and transaction log shipping, the major limitation of clustering, particularly in Windows Server 2003 and earlier, is that other than a RAID solution, there's no protection from failure of the disks containing the database files and/or the cluster quorum resource, discussed shortly. Further, typical clustering solutions don't offer protection from geographic disasters—that is, if all clustered servers exist in a single location, the destruction of that location will result in an outage. Although multisite clusters and the new Windows Server 2008 quorum models (discussed shortly) address these limitations, it's a common practice to combine multiple high-availability solutions to deliver the advantages of each while minimizing the individual limitations. For example, important databases within a clustered SQL Server instance can be mirrored to an offsite location for geographic (and disk) protection. We'll cover such combinations in more detail in chapter 11.

5.1.3 Clustering in Windows Server 2008

A SQL Server failover clustering instance is installed on, and in some ways is constrained by, the underlying Windows cluster. Although Windows Server 2003 and earlier had a solid and full-featured clustering solution, there were a number of limitations that constrained the configuration of the installed SQL Server failover clustering instances.

The SQL Server 2008 release was preceded by the release of Windows Server 2008, bringing with it a substantial improvement in the clustering options. In comparison to Windows Server 2003, the clustering improvements in Windows Server 2008 include the following:

- An enhanced *validation test*, as shown in figure 5.2, which can be used to ensure the validity of the hardware and software components in forming a cluster
- Support for IPv6 and up to 16 cluster servers (increased from 8)

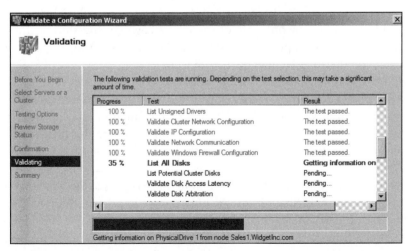

Figure 5.2 Use the Windows Server 2008 Validate a Configuration Wizard to ensure the validity of the cluster components.

- The ability of cluster servers to obtain IP addresses via DHCP
- Support for new *quorum* models, used to determine the number of failures a cluster can sustain while still operating

Apart from the enhanced validation and management tools, the increase in supported server nodes and relaxed networking restrictions enables the creation of much more flexible clustering solutions, making Windows Server 2008 the best server operating system for a clustered SQL Server 2008 deployment. Further enhancing its appeal are the improved quorum models.

> **Failover Cluster Configuration Program (FCCP)**
>
> Cluster hardware should be certified by both the hardware vendor and Microsoft as cluster compatible. With the release of Windows Server 2008, Microsoft announced the *Failover Cluster Configuration Program* (FCCP). Hardware vendors will certify complete cluster configurations against this program, making the process of choosing a cluster-compatible hardware solution much simpler than in the past.

5.1.4   *Quorum models*

A fundamental aspect of Windows Server clustering is the process whereby each node is assigned unambiguous ownership of a resource. For example, consider a two-node cluster like the one you saw in figure 5.1. If the network link between the two cluster nodes temporarily drops, what process prevents both servers from assuming that they're now the owner of the SQL instance? This process to resolve such an occurrence (commonly called the *split brain* problem) is referred to as the *cluster quorum*.

In earlier versions of Windows clustering (prior to Windows Server 2003), cluster quorum was maintained using a shared disk resource and a quorum database containing the resources and owners. In our previous example, a link failure between the two nodes would be resolved by only one of the nodes having ownership of the quorum disk. When the link is dropped, the node with quorum disk ownership continues its role and takes on the roles (if any) of the other node.

Despite the simplicity and effectiveness of this quorum model, the quorum disk was a single point of failure. Further, given the need for all cluster nodes to have access to the shared disk resource containing the quorum disk, the constraints of typical shared storage hardware prevented the creation of geographically dispersed clusters. Windows Server 2003 addressed this with the introduction of the Majority Node Set (MNS) quorum.

Nodes in an MNS quorum cluster operate with local copies of the quorum database, avoiding the limitations of shared storage, but in order to prevent the split brain problem, a majority of nodes must remain in contact for the cluster to be considered valid. One of the key attributes of an MNS cluster is the requirement for a minimum of three nodes to form a valid cluster, and in the case of a five-node cluster, a majority of the nodes (three) would need to remain in contact for the cluster to continue operating.

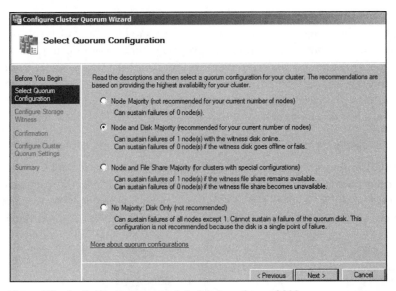

Figure 5.3   Available quorum models in Windows Server 2008

Windows Server 2008 further enhances the quorum model with a voting system. As you can see in figure 5.3, a number of options are available, with a recommended option based on the number of cluster nodes.

In summary, the following general recommendations apply to the selection of a quorum model in 2008:

- *Node Majority*—Used for clusters with an odd number of nodes
- *Node and Disk Majority*—Used for clusters with shared storage and an even number of cluster nodes
- *Node and File Share Majority*—Designed for multisite and Microsoft Exchange clusters
- *No Majority*—Compatible with earlier quorum models; isn't recommended given the single point of failure on the quorum disk

Before we look at some of the more important preinstallation configuration tasks, let's take a moment to dig a little deeper and review common clustering topologies.

5.2   *Clustering topologies and failover rules*

There are many aspects to consider when designing and planning high availability with SQL Server clustering. Chief among them is the number of dedicated *passive*, or *standby*, servers to include in the cluster for failover purposes.

In simple clusters with a 1:1 *working:standby* ratio, each working server is matched with a standby server that, during normal operations, isn't used for any purpose other than to simply wait for a failure (or planned failover). Alternatively, both (or all) servers can be active, but this introduces resource complications during failovers; for example, will a server be able to handle its own load plus that of the failed server?

In previous versions of clustering, *Active/Passive*, or *Active/Active* terminology was used to define the usage of two-node server clusters. The current terms are *single-instance* or *multi-instance* and are more appropriate terms considering the ability of today's clusters to contain up to 16 servers and many more SQL instances, with one or more standby servers available for failover from any number of other active servers.

This section will focus on the various clustering topologies commonly used and the resource considerations for each.

5.2.1   Single-instance clusters

The example earlier in figure 5.1 contained a single SQL Server instance in a two-node cluster. Under normal operating conditions, one node is in the standby status, existing purely to take on the load in the event of failure or a planned outage. When such action occurs, the instance moves between one server and the next, as shown in figure 5.4.

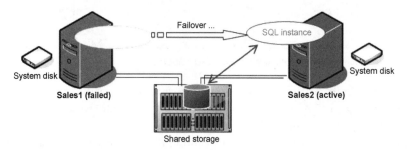

Figure 5.4   In the event of failure (or planned failover), single instance clusters such as this one have a simple failover process, with an instance moving from the active/failed node to the standby.

This clustering topology, known as a *single-instance cluster*, is the simplest to understand and administer, and also provides the highest availability while avoiding any performance impacts after failover. As such, it's commonly used to protect mission-critical SQL Server applications.

The major downside of this topology is the cost. During normal operation, one server isn't used in any capacity, and depending on the cost of the server, this can be an expensive approach. In addressing this, the multi-instance topology is frequently used.

5.2.2   Multi-instance clusters

As the name suggests, a *multi-instance* cluster contains multiple SQL Server instances. In a typical two-node multi-instance cluster, each cluster node runs one or more instances, and a failover situation causes an instance to assume another node's workload in addition to its own. In the example in figure 5.5, the *Sales* SQL instance resides on the Sales1 server, and the *Marketing* SQL Instance resides on the Sales2 server. In the event of failure of Sales1, Sales2 will run both the Sales and Marketing instances, potentially reducing the performance of both instances.

Because of the increase in server utilization, multi-instance clusters are typically used in budget-constrained environments, or in those valuing high availability much higher than reduced performance in a failed state.

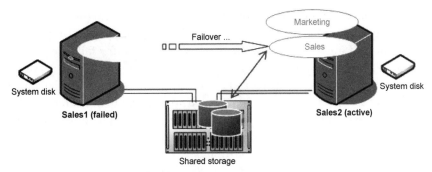

Figure 5.5   A two-node multi-instance cluster. Each node needs to be capable of handling the load of both instances during failover scenarios.

The multi-instance example in figure 5.5 achieves higher resource utilization than the single-instance example presented earlier; both servers are utilized in the normal working status.

Multi-instance clusters require careful consideration in terms of resource configuration. In our example, if the Sales1 and Sales2 servers each have 32GB of RAM, and both the Sales and Marketing SQL instances are using 28GB of RAM, a failover situation would see one (or both) instances with a potentially drastically reduced memory allocation after failover, a scenario I refer to as a *resource crunch*.

To avoid this issue, configure instances so that the sum total of maximum resource usage across both (or all) instances doesn't exceed the total resources of a *single* node that the instances could end up running on.

The two topologies we've covered so far represent the opposite ends of the scale; single-instance clusters with a 50 percent node utilization, and multi-instance clusters with 100 percent resource utilization. In between these two lies the N+1/M cluster.

5.2.3   *N+1/M clusters*

To avoid the cost of idle servers and limit the effects of a failover-induced resource crunch, a commonly used cluster configuration is an *N+1/M* cluster, whereby one or more standby servers exist for more than one working server. For example, in a three-node cluster, two nodes may be active, with a third existing as a failover node for both active nodes. Similarly, a five-node cluster with three active nodes and two failover nodes is a common cluster configuration.

As the number of cluster nodes and SQL Server instances increases, so too does the importance of considering the failover rules governing which node(s) a SQL Server instance can fail over to.

5.2.4   *Failover rules*

By regularly polling cluster nodes using a series of mechanisms called *LooksAlive* and *IsAlive* checks, a Windows cluster may conclude that a cluster node has failed. At that point the resources hosted by the node are failed over to another cluster node.

In a simple two-node cluster, the failover process is straightforward, as demonstrated in figure 5.4. But consider a five-node cluster containing two passive/standby nodes. Which (if any) of the standby nodes will be used for failover purposes when one of the active nodes fails? In large clusters containing many SQL Server instances, this is a particularly important consideration in maintaining a well-balanced cluster, ensuring that a single node doesn't carry a disproportionate burden of load.

Although beyond the scope of this book, there are several common strategies and techniques used in controlling failover, and central to them is the use of the *Preferred Owners*, *Possible Owners*, and *Failback* settings.

In figure 5.6, the properties of the SQL Server resource shows the Possible Owners property. This property lets you specify which nodes the instance is permitted to fail over to. In a similar manner, the Preferred Owner setting (not shown) is used to set the preferred failover node (this may not be chosen in some situations—for example, if the node is unavailable).

Finally, the Failback options (not shown) let you determine whether or not resources fail back to the original node if the failed node comes back online.

With this background in mind, let's continue by walking through the installation of a clustered SQL Server instance into a two-node Windows Server 2008 cluster.

5.3 Installing a clustered SQL Server instance

The process of installing a clustered SQL Server instance has changed since SQL Server 2005. There are now two installation options: Integrated and Advanced.

5.3.1 Integrated vs. advanced installation

An integrated installation creates a single-node failover cluster, from which additional nodes (nodes on which the instance can fail over to) are added via a separate installation. As shown in figure 5.7, the initial and subsequent node installations are started by choosing the New SQL Server Failover Cluster Installation and Add Node to a SQL Server Failover Cluster options on the Installation tab of the SQL Server Installation Center.

In contrast to the one-node-at-a-time approach of the integrated installation, the advanced installation prepares multiple-cluster nodes in one step, before completing the installation on the node chosen as the initial active node for the instance. As

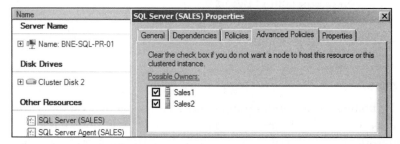

Figure 5.6   The Possible Owners setting gives you control over the cluster failover process.

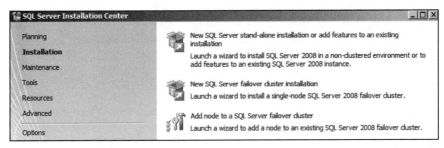

Figure 5.7   Choose the New SQL Server Failover Cluster Installation option to create a single-node failover cluster before adding additional nodes with the Add Node to a SQL Server Failover Cluster option.

shown in figure 5.8, you specify this installation type by selecting the Advanced Cluster Preparation and Advanced Cluster Completion options on the Advanced tab of the SQL Server Installation Center.

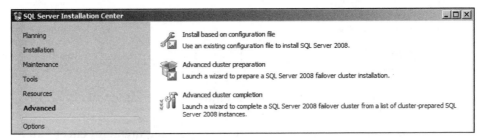

Figure 5.8   Choose the Advanced Cluster Preparation and Advanced Cluster Completion options to streamline the process of installing a clustered SQL Server instance on multiple-cluster nodes.

In the previous chapter, we discussed the installation of a nonclustered SQL Server instance. Clustered installations share some of the same installation screens and steps, so rather than repeat them, let's walk through the steps unique to a clustered installation using the integrated method.

5.3.2   *Integrated installation steps*

As with a nonclustered installation, you begin a failover clustering installation by running setup.exe from the installation DVD. Next, you go through a series of steps to install setup support files and check various setup rules. As shown in figure 5.9, the setup checks for a clustered installation are more detailed than for a nonclustered installation.

Installation continues with the usual prompts for a product key, acknowledgment of license terms, and feature selection, before arriving at the instance configuration step, as shown in figure 5.10.

The one difference between this step and the equivalent step in a nonclustered installation is the SQL Server Network Name field. The name you enter is used to identify an instance on the network. In our example, we'll use BNE-SQL-PR-02 as our network name, and together with the instance name (Marketing), we'll access this

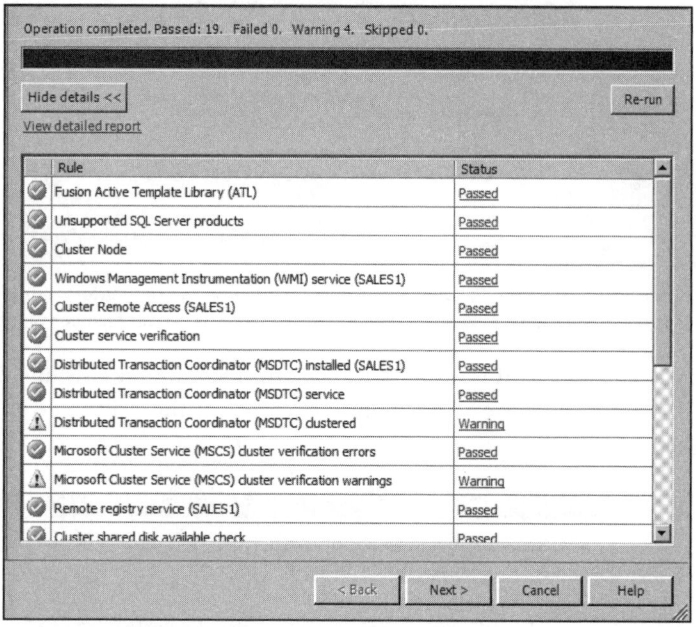

Figure 5.9   The Setup Support Rules for a clustered installation include cluster-specific checks such as the existence of a clustered Microsoft Distributed Transaction Coordinator (MSDTC) service.

instance as BNE-SQL-PR-02\Marketing without ever needing to know which of the two cluster nodes the instance is running on.

Installation continues through the disk space requirements check before prompting for a cluster resource group, as shown in figure 5.11. The resource group name is used as a container for holding the resources (disks, IP addresses, and services) for the installed instance. Later in this chapter, we'll see the resource group in the Cluster

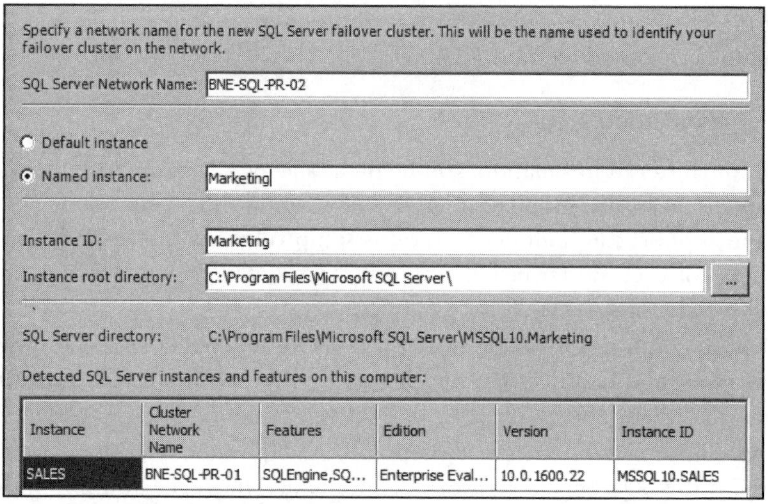

Figure 5.10   A clustered SQL Server installation is identified on the network with a unique network name you specify during installation.

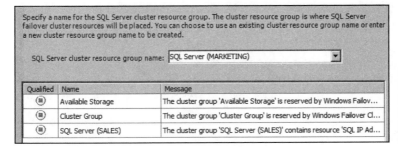

Figure 5.11 The cluster resource group name is used to both identify and group the instance's resources.

Management tool, and you'll see how to move the group to another cluster node to effect a planned failover.

In the next step, you'll identify available cluster disk resources that can be chosen for inclusion in the instance's resource group. As shown in figure 5.12, the quorum disk and cluster disks that have been previously assigned to another clustered instance are unavailable for selection.

As shown in figure 5.13, the next step lets you specify either a static or DHCP-based IP address for the SQL Server instance.

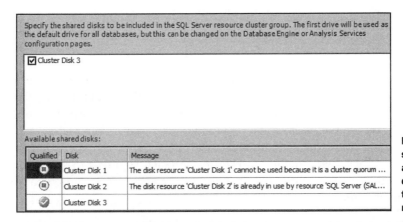

Figure 5.12 On this screen, you identify available cluster disks for assignment to the instance's resource group.

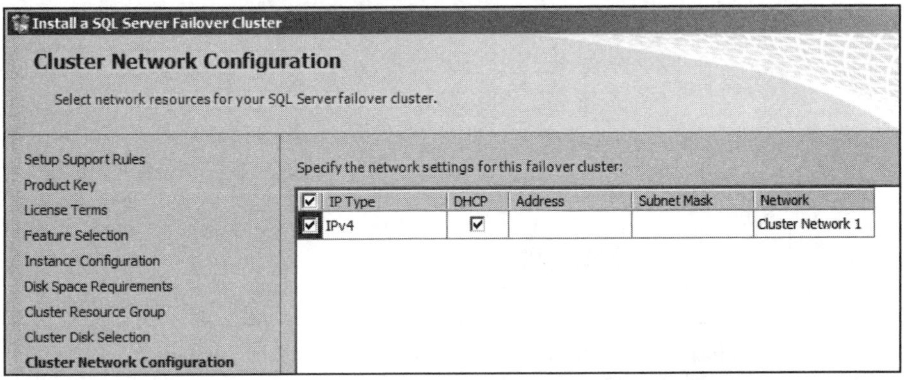

Figure 5.13 Unlike earlier versions, SQL Server 2008 permits DHCP-assigned IP addresses.

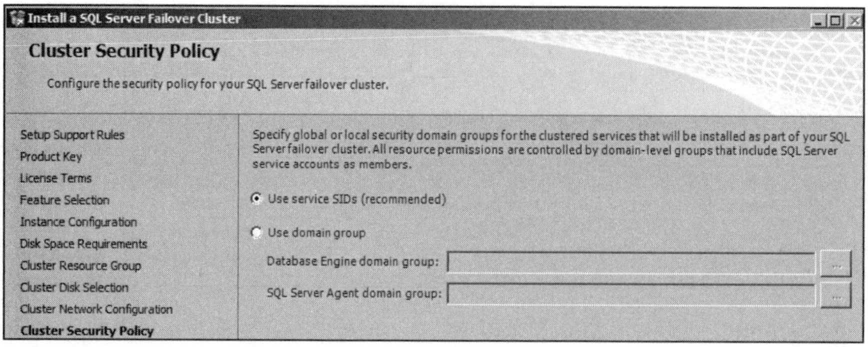

Figure 5.14 The Cluster Security Policy tab lets you select between the default service SIDs and custom domain membership.

The only remaining cluster-specific installation step is configuring the Cluster Security Policy. In previous versions of SQL Server, the service accounts had to be added to newly created domain groups prior to installation. Permissions for the service accounts were then managed at the domain group level. This requirement was often misunderstood, and introduced complexities when the domain groups needed to be changed. In response to this, SQL Server 2008 introduced an alternative method that uses service security identifiers (SIDs).

As you can see in figure 5.14, using SIDs is the recommended configuration, although support for the old domain group method remains.

The remaining steps in the installation process are the same as for the nonclustered installation described in the previous chapter. At the end of the installation, the clustered instance will be created and available, but can't fail over to other cluster nodes until you run the Add Node installation on the appropriate nodes. This installation option is used to enable additional cluster nodes to participate as failover nodes for an existing SQL Server failover clustering instance. Figure 5.15 shows one of the screens from this installation option, and in this case, we've chosen to allow the SALES2 server to host the MARKETING instance.

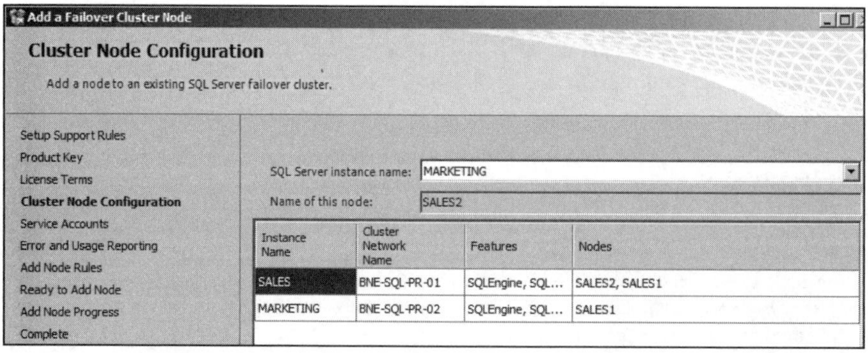

Figure 5.15 In this example, the Sales2 server is installed as a failover participant for the Sales instance installed on the Sales1 server.

Figure 5.16 Use the Cluster Management tool to view and manage a clustered SQL Server instance's resources and state.

When installation is complete, you can manage the clustered instance using the Failover Cluster Management tool in the Administrative Tools folder, or by running Cluadmin.msc from the Start menu. In the example in figure 5.16, you can manually move, or fail over, a clustered instance to another cluster node by right-clicking the resource group and selecting the "Move this service or application to another node" option.

Failover clustering is a complex area requiring a range of skills for a successful implementation. I encourage you to visit http://www.sqlCrunch.com/clustering for links to various clustering-related resources, including how clusters use public and private networks and how to use clustering over geographic distances.

5.4 *Best practice considerations: failover clustering*

Clustering SQL Server allows for the creation of highly available and reliable environments; however, failing to adequately prepare for a clustered installation can be counterproductive in that regard, with poorly planned and configured clusters actually *reducing* the availability of SQL Server.

- While multi-instance clusters are more cost-effective than single-instance clusters, give careful consideration to the possibility (and implications) of a resource crunch in the event of failover.
- N+1/M clusters offer both cost benefits and resource flexibility, but take into account the failover rules, particularly for clusters containing many servers and SQL Server instances.
- Before installing a SQL Server failover clustering instance, ensure the MSDTC service is created as a clustered resource in its own resource group with its own disk resource. In Windows Server 2003 and earlier clusters, it was common for the MSDTC resource to be configured as part of the quorum group. Certain applications, such as high-throughput BizTalk applications, make heavy use of the MSDTC resource. Insulating MSDTC from the quorum helps to prevent cluster failures due to quorum disk timeouts.
- Windows Server 2008 allows multiple clustered DTC instances to be installed. In such clusters, consider installing a clustered DTC instance *for each* SQL Server instance that requires DTC services. Such a configuration enhances the load balancing of DTC traffic.
- Like nonclustered SQL Servers, a clustered SQL Server node shouldn't be a domain controller, or run any other server applications such as Microsoft Exchange.

- Before installing a SQL Server failover clustering instance, run the Cluster Validation Wizard to ensure the validity of the cluster components.

- All aspects of cluster nodes should be configured identically, including hardware components and configuration, operating system versions and service packs, bios and firmware version, network card settings, directory names, and so forth. Such a configuration provides the best chance of continued smooth operations in the event of a failover.

- Antivirus (AV) software should either not be installed on clusters or configured to not scan any database or quorum disk files. A frequent cause of cluster failures is AV software scanning quorum files. If you're using such software, ensure it's cluster aware, and explicitly exclude all quorum files from all scan types, including on-access and scheduled scans.

- When installing a clustered SQL Server instance, set the service startup types to Manual (which is the default setting) to enable the cluster to stop and start services as required on the appropriate cluster node. The Control Panel Services applet should *not* be used in clusters for stopping or starting SQL Server services. If an instance needs to be taken offline (or moved to another node), use the Failover Cluster Management tool in the Administrative Tools folder or run Cluadmin.msc from the Start menu.

- When installing a clustered SQL Server instance, ensure the account used for the installation is a local administrator on all the cluster nodes the instance will be set up on and ensure any remote desktop connections are disconnected other than the node the installation is occurring on.

- Clustered servers should have at least two network cards, with at least one dedicated to the cluster's private network. Assign to the networks names like Public and Private.

- In the Control Panel, ensure the public LAN is bound first before the private LAN, and remove File/Print Sharing and Client for Microsoft Networks from the private LAN bindings.

- The private network should be physically separate from the public network using a cross-over cable (for two-node clusters), a dedicated hub, or a virtual LAN (VLAN).

- Define the private network at the highest level in the cluster network priority.

- The private network must not have any WINS, DNS, or NetBIOS settings enabled, and should use TCP/IP as the only protocol.

- Use NIC teaming in clusters with caution. There are documented cases of known issues with this approach, and Microsoft doesn't recommend or support NIC teaming for the private cluster network.

Additional information on the best practices covered in this chapter can be found online at http://www.sqlCrunch.com/clustering.

The last five chapters have been focused on planning and installation tasks. Let's move on now and look at post-installation configuration tasks, beginning with the next chapter, where we'll focus on security.

Part 2

Configuration

In part 1, we focused on preinstallation planning and the installation process itself. The next four chapters will focus on postinstallation configuration tasks, including securing an installation, configuring a SQL Server instance, using policy-based management, and configuring data.

6

Security

In this chapter, we'll cover

- Authentication modes
- Secure networking
- Least privilege
- Auditing and Change Data Capture
- Data encryption

As you learned in chapter 1, successful database administration involves designing and executing tasks that ensure that a database meets four key criteria: security, availability, reliability, and recoverability. This chapter is dedicated to the first of these criteria, security, and we'll address this topic from a range of perspectives.

Before we begin, it's important to note the difference between a *secure* environment and a *convenient* one. A convenient environment, in which developers, users, and database administrators are free to go about their business unhindered, is usually an insecure one that often ends in disaster, intentional or otherwise. In contrast, a secure environment is one in which complaints about "how long it takes to get stuff done" aren't uncommon. The key is striking the balance between security and productivity.

Designing and implementing a secure database environment is hard work. Trying to lock down an existing, insecure production environment almost always involves things breaking as part of the process. As a result, the job is often placed in the "too hard" basket, with systems left in an insecure state. The key to a good security model is prioritizing its development and implementation from the very beginning, and rolling out the model in all environments well before the production environment is installed.

Fortunately, there are some proven best practices in securing SQL Server, and they are the focus of this chapter. We begin with coverage of the various authentication models before looking at locking down network security and implementing least privilege. We then focus on some of the new security features in SQL Server 2008: Auditing, Change Data Capture, and Transparent Data Encryption. The chapter closes with a brief look at the dangers of SQL injection attacks.

6.1   *Authentication mode*

As you saw in chapter 4, installing SQL Server presents us with two options for login authentication: Windows Authentication Mode or SQL Server and Windows Authentication Mode (commonly called Mixed Mode). Regardless of the installation choice, you change this setting at any future point using `sp_configure`, or as shown in figure 6.1, by right-clicking on a registered server instance in SQL Server Management Studio, choosing Properties, and then clicking the Security page in the Properties dialog.

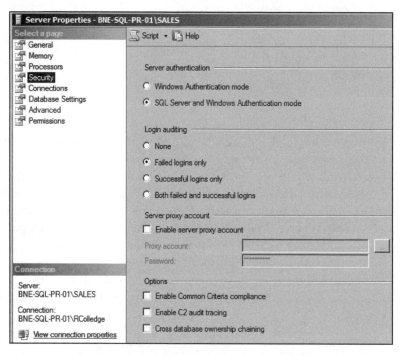

Figure 6.1   The Security page of a server's properties dialog lets you change a variety of security-related settings, including the authentication mode.

In Windows Authentication mode, SQL Server will only accept connections from sessions bearing a security token assigned during a successful Windows login. Not only does this simplify SQL Server login management (logins are already managed in Windows), Windows logins can be the subject of powerful password complexity and expiration policies, options that weren't available in SQL Server authentication in versions prior to 2005.

In SQL Server 2005, Microsoft significantly strengthened SQL Server authentication by providing a means to enforce password complexity and expiration policies to match the host Windows Server, as long as the server is running Windows Server 2003 or above. Despite this addition, Windows authentication remains the best choice.

6.1.1 Windows Authentication mode

Windows Authentication mode offers many advantages:

- It's the most secure. Passwords are never sent across the network, and expiration and complexity policies can be defined at a domain level.
- Account creation and management is centralized, and usually handled by specialist IT groups.
- Windows accounts can be placed into groups, with permissions assigned at a group level.

SQL Server, with its ability to accept Windows authenticated logins, can leverage all of these benefits, providing both a secure and simplified login and a permissions management environment.

Application vendors and the SA account

Unfortunately, many application vendors rely on SQL Server authentication, and in the worst examples, hard-code SA as the username in the connection properties (some with a blank password!). As DBAs, we should be exerting pressure on such vendors to ensure there's at least an option to use something other than the SA account, and ideally to use Windows Authentication mode.

If Windows Authentication mode is chosen during installation, the setup process still creates the SA account but disables it by default. Changing to Mixed Mode security, discussed next, requires this account to be reenabled before it can be used. If the authentication mode is changed, SQL Server will check for a blank SA password and prompt for a new one if appropriate. Given that brute-force attacks tend to target the SA account, having a nonblank, complex SA password is crucial in preventing unauthorized access.

In some cases, connections may originate from clients or applications unable to connect using Windows Authentication mode. To enable such connections, SQL Server also supports the SQL Server and Windows Authentication mode.

6.1.2   SQL Server and Windows Authentication mode (Mixed Mode)

Unlike Windows authentication, SQL Server authentication works by validating a username and password supplied by the connecting process. For example, in Windows Authentication mode, a process connecting from the WIDGETINC\JSmith account would be automatically accepted if the Windows account is defined as a SQL Server login with access to the appropriate database. No password needs to be supplied because Windows has already validated the login. In contrast, a SQL Server authentication session supplies a username and password for validation by SQL Server.

Despite welcome improvements to SQL Server authentication mode in 2005, some concerns with this login method remain:

- For applications using SQL Server authentication, SQL passwords are commonly included in connection strings stored in clear text in configuration files or registry entries. If you're using this authentication mode, store passwords in an encrypted form before unencrypting them for use in establishing a connection.
- Despite the login credentials being encrypted during the SQL Server login process, the encryption is typically performed using a self-signed certificate. While such encryption is better than nothing at all, it's susceptible to man-in-the-middle or identity spoofing attacks. In Windows authentication, passwords are never transmitted over the network as part of the SQL Server login process.
- While password expiration and complexity policies are available in SQL Server authentication, such policy enforcement isn't mandatory, and each SQL Server's policies could potentially have varying degrees of strength, compared to a policy defined and enforced at a domain level using Windows authentication.

For these reasons, Windows authentication remains the most secure choice for a SQL Server installation. If you do choose the SQL Server Authentication mode—for example, to support connections from non-Windows authenticated clients—ensure that passwords are adequately complex and you have an appropriate expiration policy in place.

Surface area configuration

Unlike SQL Server 2005, there's no Surface Area Configuration tool in SQL Server 2008; a variety of tools are used in its place, including policy-based management (covered in chapter 8), `sp_configure`, and Management Studio. Fortunately, the default installation and configuration settings are secure, so unless configuration settings are explicitly changed, the surface area of a SQL Server instance will remain secure.

A strong login authentication model is a crucial aspect of a secure SQL Server environment, as is locking down network access, as you'll see next.

6.2   Networking

Connections to SQL Server are established using a standard network protocol such as TCP/IP. Depending on the installed edition of SQL Server, certain protocols are disabled by default. In this section, we'll look at the process of enabling and configuring network protocols. You'll learn the importance of only enabling the required protocols, configuring TCP/IP settings, protecting SQL Server behind a firewall, and encrypting network communications. Let's begin with looking at enabling and configuring network protocols.

6.2.1 Protocol selection and configuration

The following network protocols are available for use with SQL Server 2008:

- *Shared Memory*—Enabled by default on all editions of SQL Server 2008, the Shared Memory protocol is used purely for local connections to an instance running on the same machine.
- *Named Pipes*—For all editions of SQL Server, Named Pipes is enabled by default for local connections only, with network connectivity over named pipes disabled.
- *TCP/IP*—The TCP/IP protocol is enabled by default for the Enterprise, Standard, and Workgroup editions of SQL Server, with the protocol disabled for the Developer, Express, and all other installations.
- *VIA*—A specialized protocol developed for use with specific hardware, the VIA protocol is disabled by default for all installations of SQL Server.

Note that an upgraded instance of SQL Server will preserve the pre-upgrade network configuration settings. Banyan VINES, Multiprotocol, AppleTalk, and NWLink IPX/SPX are no longer supported in SQL Server 2008. Looking at the protocols in the previous list, if we set aside VIA as a specialist choice and ignore Shared Memory as a local protocol only, the only two choices for a networked installation of SQL Server are TCP/IP and Named Pipes.

TCP/IP is the most widely used network protocol. Compared to Named Pipes, it provides better security and performance, particularly when used over a WAN or slower network.

From both performance and security perspectives, unused protocols should be disabled and, ideally, a single network protocol chosen for SQL Server communication. In almost all cases, TCP/IP should be used as the standard protocol for SQL Server instances, with all other protocols disabled. You enable and disable network protocols using the SQL Server Configuration Manager, as shown in figure 6.2.

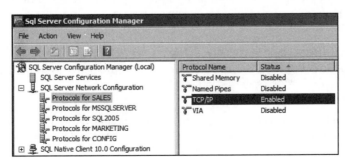

Figure 6.2 The SQL Server Configuration Manager is used to enable and disable network protocols.

Once it's enabled, you need to configure TCP/IP for maximum security by assigning a static TCP port along with appropriate firewall protection.

6.2.2 *Static and dynamic TCP ports*

Each SQL Server instance "listens" for client requests on a unique TCP/IP address/port number combination. In SQL Server 7 and earlier, we were restricted to installing a single instance per server, with the instance listening on port 1433. To support the installation of multiple named instances per server, SQL Server 2000 introduced *dynamic ports.*

Dynamic ports ease the configuration requirement for unique ports in a multi-instance installation. Rather than having to manually assign each named instance a unique port number, you can use *dynamic ports.* That way, SQL Server will automatically choose a free port number when an instance starts up.

By default, each named[1] SQL Server instance is configured to use dynamic TCP/IP ports. This means that each time a named instance of SQL Server is started, the TCP port used *may* be different. The SQL Server Browser service responds to client connection requests with the port number that the requested instance is running on, thus avoiding the need for client applications to be aware of the port number an instance is currently using. As we saw in chapter 4, the setup process sets the browser service's startup type to automatic.

Dynamic ports present a problem for firewall configuration. An attempt to secure a SQL Server instance behind a firewall by only opening a specific port number will obviously fail if the port number changes, courtesy of the dynamic port option. For this reason, static ports are the best (and most secure) choice when placing SQL Server behind a firewall. In return for the additional configuration required to assign each SQL Server instance a static port number, the appropriate ports can be opened on the firewall without running into the connection failures typical with dynamic ports.

When assigning a static TCP port, avoid using ports currently (and commonly) used by other services and applications. The IANA registration database, available at http://www.iana.org/assignments/port-numbers, is an excellent resource for this purpose; it lists registered port numbers for common applications, as well as "safe" ranges to use for SQL Server instances.

As you can see in figure 6.3, you can set an instance to use a static TCP port by using the SQL Server Configuration Manager tool. Simply delete the TCP Dynamic Ports entry for IPAll[2] and enter a port number in TCP Port. In our example, we've chosen port 49153.

The SQL Server Browser service runs on port 1434. If the browser service is stopped, or port 1434 is closed on the firewall, the port number needs to be included

---

[1] If installed, a default instance, that is, a non-named instance, will use port 1433 unless you change it manually.

[2] To configure SQL Server on a multihomed server, set the Active value to false for IP addresses that SQL should not listen on, and configure the TCP port for individual IP entries rather than the IPAll entry.

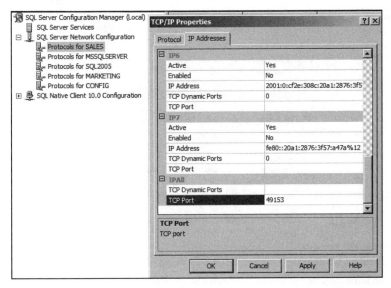

Figure 6.3   SQL Server Configuration Manager lets you configure SQL Server instances with a static TCP port.

in the connection request. For example, to connect to a SQL Server instance called SALES running on port 49153 on the BNE-SQL-PR-01 server, we'd connect using

```
BNE-SQL-PR-01\Sales,49153
```

An alternative to including the port number in the connection string is to create an alias on each connecting client using the SQL Server Configuration Manager tool. Full details of this process can be found in SQL Server Books Online (BOL) under the "New Alias (Alias Tab)" article.

We've spoken about firewalls a few times now. In addition to network firewalls, we also have the option of using the Windows Firewall. Since Windows XP SP2, the Windows Firewall has been enabled by default on client operating systems. For the first time in a server operating system, the firewall is also enabled by default in Windows Server 2008.

6.2.3   Windows Firewall

A 2007 survey[3] found approximately 368,000 SQL Server instances directly accessible on the internet. Of those, almost 15,000 were completely insecure and vulnerable to worms such as the infamous SQL Slammer, a worm that spread rapidly in 2003 by exploiting a buffer overflow bug in SQL Server (the patch for it was released six months before the worm struck).

In light of the proliferation of port scanners and widely accessible network firewall penetration techniques, having a solid host firewall strategy is crucial. Windows Server

---

[3]   The Database Exposure Survey 2007, David Litchfield, Next Generation Security Software.

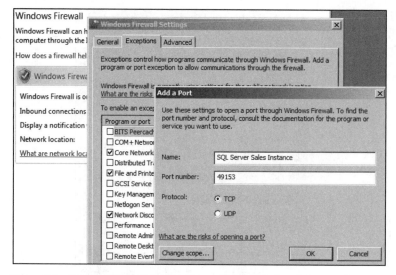

Figure 6.4   The Windows Firewall can be configured to allow communication on specific ports.

2008 enables the Windows Firewall by default. For the most secure SQL Server installation, the Windows Firewall should be left enabled, with the appropriate ports opened—that is, the port used by each installed SQL Server instance.

As we covered in chapter 4, the SQL Server installation process will detect the presence of the Windows Firewall and provide a warning to open the appropriate ports. This can be achieved using the Control Panel, as you can see in figure 6.4. You can find full details on this process in SQL Server BOL, under the "Configuring the Windows Firewall to Allow SQL Server Access" article.

In closing our section on network security, let's examine the process of encrypting network communications.

6.2.4   *Network encryption*

SQL Server 2008 introduces a feature called *Transparent Data Encryption* (TDE), which we'll discuss later in this chapter. When enabled, TDE automatically encrypts and decrypts data as it's read from and written to the database without the need for any application changes.

Even with TDE enabled, other than the initial login credentials, the network transmission of data is unencrypted, meaning *packet sniffers could be used to intercept data*. For maximum data security, the network transmission of SQL Server data can be encrypted using either Internet Protocol Security (IPSec) or Secure Sockets Layer (SSL).

Requiring no SQL Server configuration, IPSec encryption is configured at the operating system level on both the SQL Server and the connecting clients. SSL encryption can be enabled using a combination of an installed certificate and the SQL Server Configuration Manager tool.

SQL Server can use either self-signed or public certification authority certificates. As mentioned earlier in this chapter, self-signed certificates offer only limited security and are susceptible to man-in-the-middle attacks. For maximum SSL security, certificates from a public authority such as VeriSign can be used.

Once you've installed a certificate, you can use the SQL Server Configuration Manager tool to configure a SQL Server instance to use the certificate and to specify whether or not client connections are accepted that can't support an encrypted connection. In a similar manner, Configuration Manager lets you configure the client end of the connection, with the option to force encryption, and whether or not to trust a server with only a self-signed certificate.

SQL Server BOL contains a full description of the process for enabling SSL encryption for a SQL Server instance, including coverage of cluster-specific encryption processes. In addition to BOL, you'll find a number of links to articles containing step-by-step encryption setup instructions at the book's companion website, available at http://www.sqlcrunch.com/security.

As with any encryption, SQL Server network encryption involves processing overhead and therefore lowers performance to some degree. In environments with sensitive data, the performance impact of encryption is typically of less concern than protecting the data from unauthorized access. Before implementing encryption in a production environment, test and measure the process and overhead in a test environment.

Even with strong network security and authentication models in place, a SQL Server instance is far from secure if those with legitimate access to a SQL Server instance have *more* access than what they actually need. With a significant percentage of security breaches performed as inside jobs, the importance of least privilege is not to be underestimated.

6.3   *Implementing least privilege*

The ultimate goal of implementing least privilege is reducing the permissions of user and service accounts to the absolute minimum required. Doing this can be difficult and requires considerable planning. This section focuses on this goal from four perspectives:

- Separating Windows and database administrator privileges
- Reducing the permissions of the SQL Server service accounts
- Using proxies and credentials to limit the effective permissions of SQL Server Agent jobs
- Using role-based security to simplify and tighten permissions management

Let's begin with a contentious issue: separating and limiting the permissions of DBAs and Windows administrators.

6.3.1   *Windows and DBA privilege separation*

Removing the local admin group membership from a DBA is almost always likely to provoke a strong response. Most DBAs take it as a personal insult, akin to not being trusted with basic tasks. When questioned about whether Windows administrators should be SQL Server sysadmins, the response is typically as passionate, with the DBAs usually unaware of their own contradiction!

In most cases, DBAs don't need to be local administrators to do their job. Not only that, they shouldn't be. Equally true, Windows administrators shouldn't be SQL Server sysadmins.

Separation of powers in this manner is a basic security concept, but probably the most commonly abused one. The reasons for this are many and varied. First, in previous versions of SQL Server (2005 and earlier) the BUILTIN\Administrators group is automatically added to the SQL Server sysadmins server role, making Windows administrators effectively DBAs by default. Second, DBAs are often tasked (particularly in smaller environments) with being the Windows administrator as well as the DBA. And third, to avoid dealing with Windows administrators to get things done, some DBAs will come up with various reasons why they should be local administrators, often bamboozling management into submission.

Sysadmin lock-out

If all of the Windows logins and/or groups that are in the sysadmin server role be accidentally (or deliberately) removed and the SA password is unknown, system administrators can be effectively locked out from performing SQL Server sysadmin tasks. In such an event, the instance can be started in single-user mode using the −m or −f options by a user with membership in the local administrators group (rather than reinstalling SQL Server and reattaching databases). When started in this manner, the user connecting to SQL Server will connect as part of the sysadmin role and can add the necessary logins and/or groups back to the sysadmin role. Be careful when using this method to ensure the SQL Agent service is stopped so that it doesn't connect first and prevent further connections.

Why separate permissions? Well, a Windows administrator with very little DBA experience could accidentally delete critical data or entire databases without realizing it. Or a DBA, after accessing sensitive data, could cover his or her tracks by deleting audit files from the operating system.

There are obviously many more examples, all of which require separation of powers to protect against both deliberate and accidental destructive actions. As you saw in chapter 4, SQL Server 2008 helps out in this regard by not including the BUILTIN\ Administrators group in the sysadmin server role.

Continuing the theme of least privilege, the SQL Server service accounts shouldn't be members of the local administrators group.

6.3.2   *SQL Server service account permissions*

A common SQL Server myth is that the accounts used by the SQL Server services need to be members of the local administrators group. They don't, and in fact shouldn't be. During installation, SQL Server will assign the necessary file, registry, and system permissions to the accounts nominated for the services.

The need to avoid using local administrator accounts (or the localsystem account) is based on the possibility of the server being compromised and used to run OS-level commands using tools such as xp_cmdshell, which is disabled by default. While other protections should be in place to prevent such attacks, locking down all possible avenues of attack is best practice, and using nonprivileged service accounts is an important part of this process.

As you learned in chapter 4, separate accounts should be used for each SQL Server service to enable the most granular security permissions. Finally, should the security account be changed postinstallation, the SQL Server Configuration Manager tool should be used, rather than a direct assignment using the Control Panel services applet. When you use the Configuration Manager tool, SQL Server will assign the new account the necessary permissions as per the initial installation.

Like all items in this section, configuring nonadministrator accounts for SQL Server services is about assigning the minimal set of privileges possible. This is an important security concept not only for service accounts but for all aspects of SQL Server, including SQL Server Agent jobs.

6.3.3 SQL Server Agent job permissions

A common requirement for SQL Server deployments is for SQL Server Agent jobs (covered in more detail in chapter 14) to access resources outside of SQL Server. Among other tasks, such jobs are typically used for executing batch files and Integration Services packages.

To enable the minimum set of permissions to be in place, SQL Server Agent enables job steps to run under the security context of a *proxy*. One or more proxies are created as required, each of which uses a stored *credential*. The combination of credentials and proxies enables job steps to run using a Windows account whose permissions can be tailored (minimized) for the needs of the Agent job step.

In highlighting how proxies and credentials are used, let's walk through a simple example of setting minimal permissions for a SQL Agent job that executes an Integration Services package. We'll begin this process by creating a credential.

CREDENTIALS

When you create a SQL Agent proxy, one of the steps is to specify which credential the proxy will use. We'll see that shortly. It follows that before creating the proxy, the credential should be created. Figure 6.5 shows an example of the creation of a credential

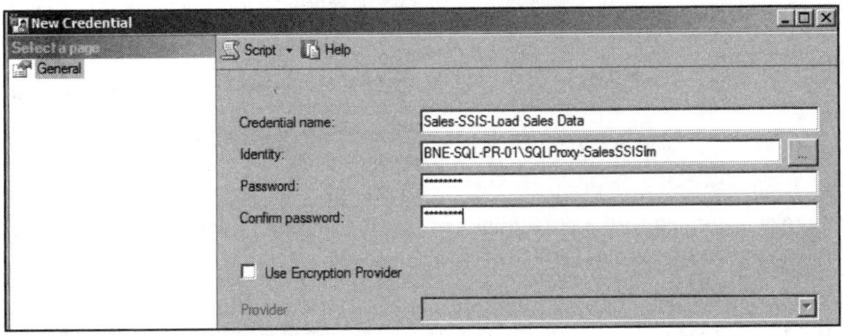

Figure 6.5 Create a credential in order to define the security context of a SQL Agent proxy.

in SQL Server Management Studio. You access this dialog by right-clicking Credentials under Security and choosing New Credential.

In figure 6.5, we've specified the SQLProxy-SalesSSISIm account, whose permissions[4] have been reduced to the minimum required for executing our Integration Services package. For example, we've granted the account read permissions to a directory containing files to import into the database. In addition to setting permissions at a domain/server level, we'd add this credential as a SQL login with the appropriate database permissions.

After creating the credential, we can now create the proxy.

PROXIES

You create a SQL Agent proxy in SQL Server Management Studio by right-clicking Proxies under SQL Server Agent and choosing New Proxy. The resulting screen, as shown in figure 6.6, allows you to specify the details of the proxy, including the name, the credential to use, and which subsystems the proxy can access. In our case, we'll use the credential we created earlier, and grant the proxy access to the SQL Server Integration Services (SSIS) Package subsystem.

Members of the sysadmin group have access to all proxies. The Principals page enables non-sysadmin logins or server roles to be granted access to the proxy, thereby

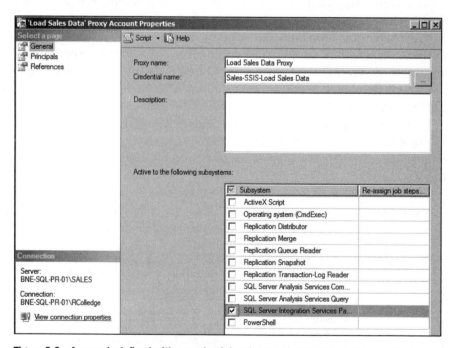

Figure 6.6   A proxy is defined with a credential and granted access to one or more subsystems. Once created, it can be used in SQL Agent jobs to limit permissions.

---

[4] The credential account must also have the "Log on as a batch job" permission on SQL Server.

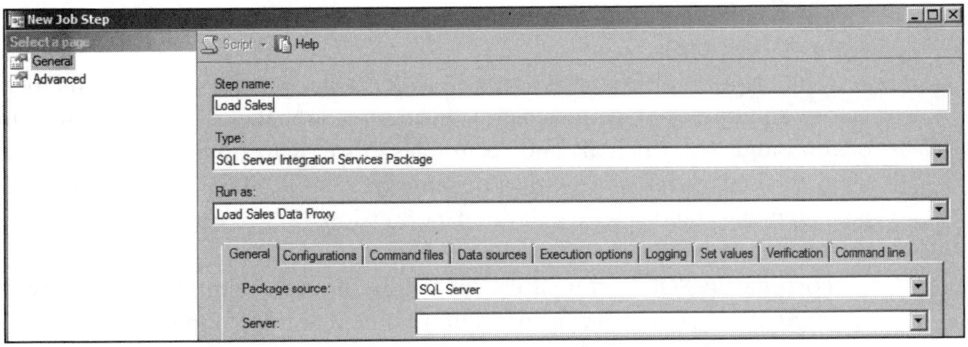

Figure 6.7   A SQL Agent job step can be run under the context of a proxy.

enabling such users to create and execute SQL Agent jobs in the context of the proxy's credential.

With the proxy created, we can now create a SQL Agent job that uses it.

SQL AGENT JOB STEPS

When you create a SQL Server Agent job, one of the selections available for each job step is choosing its execution context, or Run As mode. For job steps that perform actions at the operating system level, you have two options for the Run As mode: SQL Agent Service Account or Proxy. As shown in figure 6.7, we've created a SQL Agent job with a job step called Load Sales that uses the Load Sales Data Proxy that we created earlier.

The end result of such a configuration is that the effective permissions of the Load Sales job step are those of the proxy's credential, which is restricted to the requirements of the SSIS package and nothing more, and therefore meets the least privilege objective. Additional SQL Agent jobs and their associated steps can use the Load Sales Data proxy, or have specific proxies created for their unique permission requirements, all without needing to alter the permissions of the service account used for SQL Server Agent.

It's important to note that T-SQL job steps continue to run in the context of the SQL Agent job owner. The proxy/credential process I've described is specific to job steps accessing resources outside of SQL Server.

The ability to create multiple proxies for specific job types and with individual credentials and permissions allows you to implement a powerful and flexible permissions structure—one that conforms to the principles of least privilege.

In finalizing our coverage of least privilege, let's turn our attention to how user's permissions are secured within a server and database using role-based security.

6.3.4   *Role-based security*

When discussing security in SQL Server, the terms *principal* and *securable* are commonly used. A principal is an entity requesting access to SQL Server objects (securables). For example, a user (principal) connects to a database and runs a select command against a table (securable).

When a principal requests access to a securable, SQL Server checks the permissions before granting or denying access. Considering a database application with hundreds or thousands of principals and securables, it's easy to understand how the management of these permissions could become time consuming. Further, the difficulty in management could lead to elevated permissions in an attempt to reduce the time required to implement least privilege.

Fortunately, SQL Server offers several methods for simplifying permissions management. As a result, you can spend more time designing and deploying granular permissions to ensure the least privilege principle is applied all the way down to individual objects within a database.

While a full analysis of permissions management is beyond the scope of this book, it's important we spend some time looking at the means by which we can simplify and tighten permissions management using role-based security. Let's start with a look at database roles.

DATABASE ROLES

A database role, defined within a database, can be viewed in a similar fashion to an Active Directory group in a Windows domain: a database role contains users (Windows or SQL Server logins) and is assigned permissions to objects (schema, tables, views, stored procedures, and so forth) within a database.

Take our earlier example of the difficulty of managing the database permissions of thousands of users. Using database roles, we can define the permissions for a database role once, and grant multiple users access to the database role. As such, the user's permissions are inherited through the role, and we needn't define permissions on a user-by-user basis. Should different permissions be required for different users, we can create additional database roles with their own permissions.

Let's walk through an example of creating and assigning permissions via a database role. To begin, let's create a role called ViewSales in a database called SalesHistory using T-SQL, as shown in listing 6.1. We'll assign permissions to the role, select permissions on a view and table, and execute permissions on a stored procedure.

Listing 6.1   Creating a database role

```
-- Create the Role
USE [SalesHistory]
GO
CREATE ROLE [ViewSales]
GO

-- Assign permissions to the role
GRANT EXECUTE ON [dbo].[uspViewSalesHistory] TO [ViewSales]
GO
GRANT SELECT ON [dbo].[Store] TO [ViewSales]
GO
GRANT SELECT ON [dbo].[vwSalesRep] TO [ViewSales]
GO
```

With the database role in place, we can now assign logins to the role and have those logins inherit the role's permission. Consider the T-SQL code in listing 6.2.

Listing 6.2   Assigning logins to a database role

```
-- Create Logins from Windows Users
USE [MASTER]
GO

CREATE LOGIN [WIDGETINC\JSMith]
FROM WINDOWS WITH
    DEFAULT_DATABASE=[SalesHistory]
GO

CREATE LOGIN [WIDGETINC\KBrown]
FROM WINDOWS WITH
    DEFAULT_DATABASE=[SalesHistory]
GO

CREATE LOGIN [WIDGETINC\LTurner]
FROM WINDOWS WITH
    DEFAULT_DATABASE=[SalesHistory]
GO

-- Create Database Users mapped to the Logins
USE [SalesHistory]
GO

CREATE USER JSMith FOR LOGIN [WIDGETINC\JSMith]
GO

CREATE USER KBrown FOR LOGIN [WIDGETINC\KBrown]
GO

CREATE USER LTurner FOR LOGIN [WIDGETINC\LTurner]
GO

-- Assign the Users Role Membership
EXEC sp_addrolemember N'ViewSales', N'WIDGETINC\JSmith'
GO

EXEC sp_addrolemember N'ViewSales', N'WIDGETINC\KBrown'
GO

EXEC sp_addrolemember N'ViewSales', N'WIDGETINC\LTurner'
GO
```

The code in listing 6.2 has three sections. First, we create SQL Server logins based on existing Windows user accounts in the WIDGETINC domain. Second, we create users in the SalesHistory database for each of the three logins we just created. Finally, we assign the users to the ViewSales database role created earlier. The net effect is that the three Windows accounts have access to the SalesHistory database with their permissions defined through membership of the database role.

Apart from avoiding the need to define permissions for each user, the real power of database roles comes with changing permissions. If we need to create a new table and grant a number of users access to the table, we can grant the permissions against the database role once, with all members of the role automatically receiving the permissions. In a similar manner, reducing permissions is done at a role level.

Not only do roles simplify permissions management, they also make permissions consistent for all similar users. In our example, if we have a new class of users that require specific permissions beyond those of the ViewSales role, we can create a new database role with the required permissions and add users as appropriate.

User/schema separation

Beginning in SQL Server 2005, database schemas are a distinct namespace, without the tight user coupling that existed in SQL Server 2000 and earlier. Each database user is created with a *default schema* (dbo is the default if none is specified) and is used by SQL Server when no object owner is specified in T-SQL commands, such as select * from sales. Objects within a schema can be transferred to another schema, and the ability to grant or deny permissions at a schema level permits both powerful and flexible permissions structures. This means that sensitive tables could be placed in their own schema with only selected users granted access. Finally, schema permissions can be granted to database roles; for example, database role *users* can be granted select permissions on schema *standard* but denied select permission on schema *payroll*.

In cases where permissions are defined at an application level, application roles can be used.

APPLICATION ROLES

In some cases, access to database objects is provided and managed as part of an application rather than direct database permissions granted to users. In such cases, there's typically an application management function where users are defined and managed on an administration screen. In these cases, application roles can be used to simplify permissions. In effect, the application role is granted the superset of the permissions required, with the individual user permissions then managed within the application itself.

Application roles are invoked on connection to SQL Server by using the sp_setapprole stored procedure and supplying an application role name and password. As with a SQL Server login, you must ensure the password is stored in a secure location. Ideally, the password would be stored in an encrypted form, with the application decrypting it before supplying it to SQL Server.

The side benefit of application roles is that the only means through which users are able to access the database is via the application itself, meaning that direct user access using tools such as SQL Server Management Studio is prevented.

In closing this section, let's consider two additional types of roles: fixed server and database roles.

FIXED SERVER ROLES

In environments with lots of server instances and many DBAs, some sites prefer to avoid having all DBAs defined as members of the sysadmin role and lean toward a more granular approach whereby some DBAs are allocated a subset of responsibilities. In supporting this, SQL Server provides a number of fixed server roles in addition to the sysadmin role, which grants the highest level of access to the server instance.

An example of a fixed server role is the processadmin role, used to grant users permissions to view and kill running server processes, and the dbcreator role, used to enable users to create, drop, alter, and restore databases. SQL Server BOL contains a complete listing of the fixed server roles and their permissions.

Similar to fixed server roles, fixed database roles come with predefined permissions that enable a subset of database permissions to be allocated to a specific user.

FIXED DATABASE ROLES

In addition to the db_owner role, which is the highest level of permission in a database, SQL Server provides a number of fixed database roles. Again, all of these roles and descriptions are defined in BOL. Commonly used fixed database roles are the db_datareader and db_datawriter roles, used to grant read and add/delete/modify permissions respectively to all tables within a database.

One of the nice features of permissions management within SQL Server is that roles can include other roles. For example, the db_datareader role could contain the custom ViewSales database role that we created earlier, in effect granting select permissions on all tables to members of the ViewSales role, in addition to the other permissions granted with this role.

So far in this chapter, we've addressed techniques used to prevent unauthorized access. If such access be gained, it's important we have auditing in place, a topic we'll address next.

6.4   *Auditing*

Auditing solutions are built to enable retrospective analysis of user activity. SQL Server 2008 introduces a number of enhancements in this regard, which will be the focus of this section. We'll begin with coverage of the new SQL Server Audit feature before looking at DDL and logon triggers. We'll finish with a brief look at another new feature in SQL Server 2008, Change Data Capture.

6.4.1   *SQL Server Audit*

New in 2008

In SQL Server 2005 and earlier, auditing options consisted of simple server-level logon success/failure logging, custom audits using server-side traces or SQL Profiler, or the C2 trace option. What was missing was a more granular auditing option whereby a custom audit trace could be easily created that captured specific events such as executing DBCC commands.

In addition to all of the auditing options in 2005, SQL Server 2008 introduces a comprehensive new auditing model that addresses the need to easily create granular audit specifications. The new Audit feature in SQL Server 2008 consists of three main components:

- An *audit*, which specifies the location of the audit output (file, application, or security event log), an option to shut down SQL Server if the audit can't be written, and a queue delay setting that specifies the number of milliseconds that can pass before audit actions are processed
- *Server audit specifications*, which contain definitions of server-level audit events such as server logins
- *Database audit specifications*, which contain definitions of database level events such as schema modifications

Let's walk through an example of creating an audit solution using SQL Server Management Studio. The first step is to create an audit. First right-click on Audits under Security and choose New Audit. As shown in figure 6.8, the Create Audit screen lets you specify various properties, including the file path if the audit destination is file based. As with most other parts of Management Studio, use the Script button to save the creation script for later inspection.

Both server and database audit specifications are created in the context of a matching audit. The audit events collected are sent to the Audit object, and written to either file or the event log, as defined in the Audit object.

Known as *audit action groups*, both server- and database-level audit specifications have a wide variety of audit actions that can be captured. Let's continue by defining a server audit specification. SQL Server BOL contains a full list of all possible server-level audit actions that can be chosen. For this example, let's create a specification that will

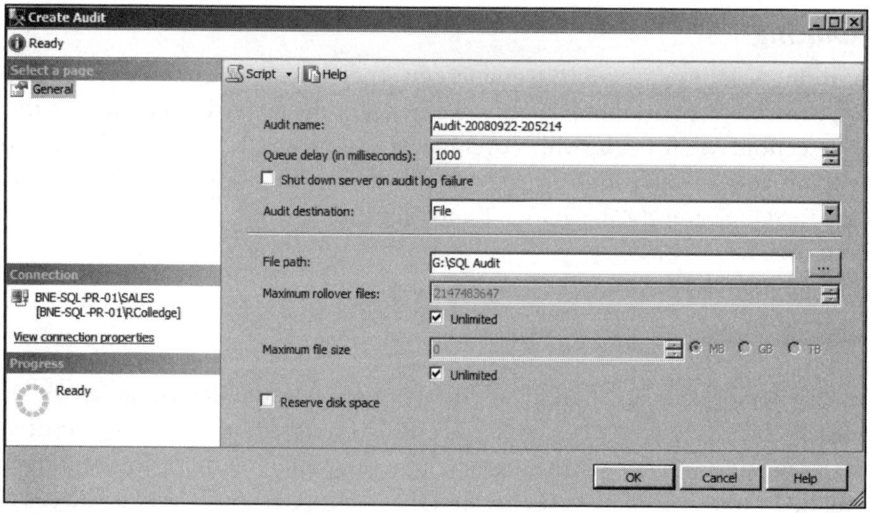

Figure 6.8   Define audits using Management Studio or with T-SQL code.

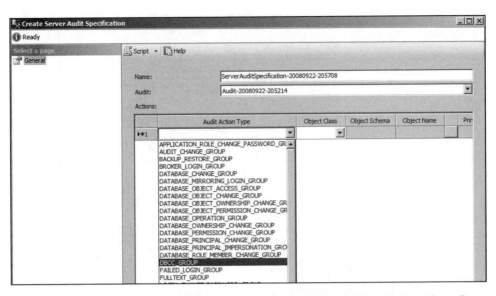

Figure 6.9 Once an audit has been defined, you can define audit specifications that use the audit. The specification can be at a server level (as shown here) or at a database level.

capture the execution of any DBCC command. We can do this in Management Studio by right-clicking Server Audit Specifications under Security and choosing New Server Audit Specification. In the Create Server Audit Specification screen, shown in figure 6.9, select the audit we created earlier, and then choose DBCC_GROUP from the Audit Action Type drop-down box. If necessary, we can choose multiple audit actions.

The nice thing about auditing in SQL Server 2008 is that the database-level audit specifications are defined within the database itself. What this means is that if the database is moved from one server to another, the database-level audit specification will move to the new server. When attached to the new server, the audit specification will be orphaned until you use the ALTER DATABASE AUDIT SPECIFICATION command to reassign it to the new server's Audit object.

Let's expand our audit by including a database-level audit specification. We'll do this for the AdventureWorks database by expanding it and right-clicking the Database Audit Specifications option under Security and choosing New Database Audit Specification. The Create Database Audit Specification screen is similar to the one for the server-level specification, as you can see in figure 6.10. Again, we'll select the audit created earlier and then select from the options in the Audit Action Type drop-down box. In this example, we'll select the DATABASE_ROLE_MEMBER_CHANGE_GROUP option, which will audit events involving logins being added to or removed from a database role.

Once our audit action groups are defined, we can start the audit by right-clicking on it and selecting Enable Audit. The next step is to select the Server and Database Audit specifications, again by right-clicking on them and choosing Enable. Viewing audit data is as simple as right-clicking the audit specification and choosing View

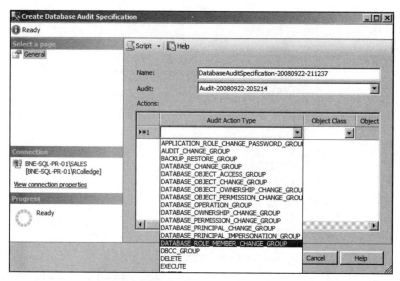

Figure 6.10   An audit specification at the database level

Audit Logs. Alternatively, if the audit events are directed to the Windows event logs, you can read them directly by using the event log viewing tools.

In our example, after running a DBCC command and adding a login to a database role, viewing the audit logs will reveal a screen like the one in figure 6.11. Although our example was a simple one, it reveals the ease with which granular auditing specifications can be created.

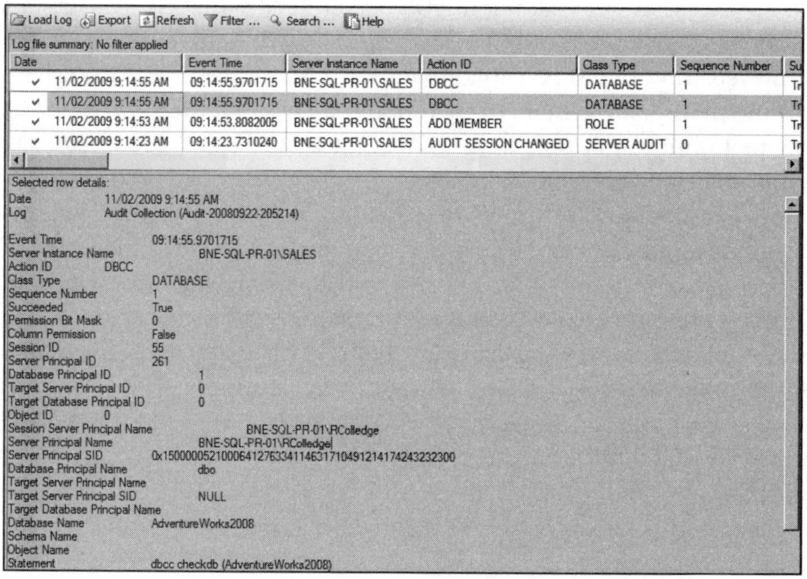

Figure 6.11   Viewing the audit logs is as simple as right-clicking the audit specification and choosing View Log.

You can use the new Audit feature to create granular audits at both a server and database level as needed to match your organization's custom auditing requirements. In comparison to other auditing options such as the C2 audit mode (described in SQL Server BOL), it offers a much more flexible option, while enabling powerful features such as portability of database audit specifications when transferred between servers.

Let's look at another feature that can be employed as part of a custom auditing solution: *DDL triggers.*

6.4.2   *DDL triggers*

DDL (Data Definition Language) triggers were introduced in SQL Server 2005 as a means of either auditing or preventing data definition statements. Not to be confused with DML (Data Manipulation Language) triggers, DDL triggers are defined on events such as CREATE TABLE. From an auditing perspective, they enable customized data to be collected for particular events.

Let's walk through a simple example to highlight the power and flexibility of DDL triggers. Suppose we want to capture the details related to the creation of new tables, including the T-SQL statement used to create the table, the user that executed the statement, and the date and time of the creation. Consider the T-SQL code in listing 6.3. We'll first create a table used to store the required details, before creating the DDL trigger that uses the EVENTDATA function to return the required details.

> **Listing 6.3   DDL trigger to capture table creation details**

```
-- create the table to store the audit details
CREATE TABLE dbo.CREATE_TABLE_LOG (
    eventTime datetime
    , eventOwner nvarchar(100)
    , eventTSQL nvarchar(3000)
)
GO


-- create the DDL trigger
CREATE TRIGGER DDLTrigger_CreateTable ON DATABASE FOR create_table
AS
    DECLARE @data XML
    SET @data = EVENTDATA()

    INSERT INTO CREATE_TABLE_LOG
    VALUES (
      GETDATE()
      , CURRENT_USER
      , @data.value('(/EVENT_INSTANCE/TSQLCommand/CommandText)[1]',
        'nvarchar(1000)')
    )
GO
```

Listing 6.3 obtains the T-SQL command from the EVENTDATA function, which returns information about server or database events. As such, it's ideal for use in the body of a DDL trigger.

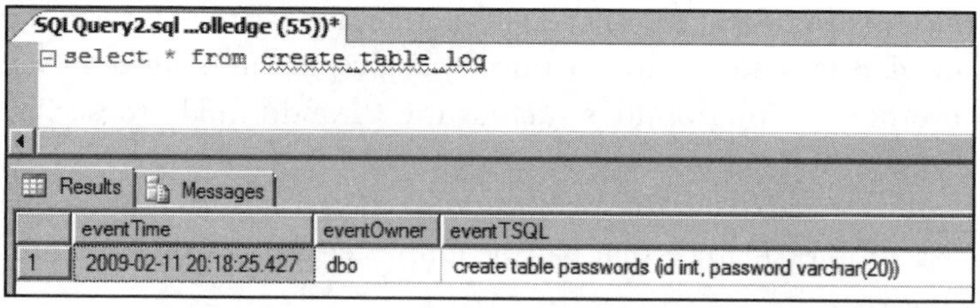

Figure 6.12 Querying the results of a create table command that fired a DDL trigger

With the table and trigger in place, a table creation command will fire the trigger and capture the associated event data. The results appear in figure 6.12.

Not only can DDL triggers audit actions, they can also actively prevent certain changes. Consider the example shown in listing 6.4, which rolls back any attempt to drop or alter a table definition.

Listing 6.4   DDL trigger to prevent table modifications

```
CREATE TRIGGER DDLTrigger_PreventTableChanges
ON DATABASE
FOR DROP_TABLE, ALTER_TABLE
AS
        PRINT 'Cannot drop or modify tables in this database'
ROLLBACK
```

As listing 6.4 shows, the ROLLBACK statement rolls back any attempt to drop or alter any table in the database in which the trigger is created, along with the error message "Cannot drop or modify tables in this database."

Similar to DDL triggers, logon triggers, discussed next, enable auditing and control of the logon process.

6.4.3   *Logon triggers*

In a manner similar to creating DDL triggers, you create a logon trigger to either roll back (deny) a logon or capture information surrounding the logon using the EVENT-DATA function.

Consider the example shown in listing 6.5, which prevents ReportUser from logging on between 11 p.m. and 11:30 p.m.

Listing 6.5   Logon trigger to prevent logon for a period of time

```
CREATE TRIGGER validateLogonTrigger
ON ALL SERVER WITH EXECUTE AS 'logonTrigger'
FOR LOGON
AS
BEGIN
    DECLARE @time time(0) = getdate()
    IF ORIGINAL_LOGIN() = 'ReportUser'
     AND @time BETWEEN '23:00:00' and '23:30:00'
    ROLLBACK
END
```

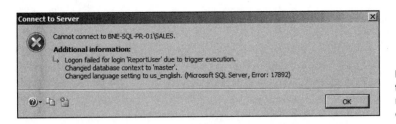

Figure 6.13 A logon failure message that results from the firing of a logon trigger

With the trigger in place, a logon attempt by ReportUser between 11 p.m. and 11:30 p.m. will be met with an error message similar to the one displayed in figure 6.13.

In our example, we used the ORIGINAL_LOGON function. There are a number of other functions that can be used, such as APP_NAME; however, as you'll see in chapter 16, careful consideration needs to be given to the function used, due to the possibility of function values being spoofed to circumvent the intention of logon triggers.

In closing our coverage of auditing features, let's consider another new feature in SQL Server 2008: *Change Data Capture*.

6.4.4 *Change Data Capture*

New in 2008

The Change Data Capture (CDC) feature, introduced in SQL Server 2008, is used to capture data modification activity in SQL Server tables and make the details of the activity available in a format that can be used for various purposes.

One of the main uses for CDC is for data warehousing solutions. The classic data warehouse load process involves identifying data that has been modified since the last load operation. Once identified, the data is the subject of an extract, transform, load (ETL) process.

The challenge for ETL processes is identifying which data has changed since the last load, and typically involves timestamp or GUID values along with a corresponding query to select all data with a timestamp/GUID value greater than the one used in the last load operation. CDC is perfect for this scenario, as all changes can be easily consumed, thus avoiding the need for expensive identification queries.

From an auditing perspective, CDC can be used to identify modifications to one or more tables. In versions of SQL Server prior to 2008, such auditing was typically performed using triggers or some other mechanism. CDC simplifies this process greatly while avoiding the expensive overhead of a trigger-based approach.

As a brief introduction to how CDC can be used from an auditing perspective, let's consider an example in which we want to track modifications to the Production.Product table in the AdventureWorks2008 database. To do so with CDC, we'll run the code shown in listing 6.6.

Listing 6.6 Setting up Change Data Capture

```
USE [AdventureWorks2008]
GO
```

```
-- enable change data capture
EXEC sys.sp_cdc_enable_db
GO

-- enable the Production.Product table for CDC
EXEC sys.sp_cdc_enable_table
    @source_schema = N'Production'
    , @source_name = N'Product'
    , @role_name = N'CDCRole'
GO
```

At this point the table is defined for CDC. A number of tables and functions are created in the AdventureWorks2008 database to support CDC, along with two SQL Server Agent jobs for capturing and cleaning up captured data. To simulate and view captured changes, let's run the script shown in listing 6.7.

Listing 6.7 Modifying data and viewing CDC changes

```
DECLARE @begin_time datetime
DECLARE @end_time datetime
DECLARE @from_lsn binary(10)
DECLARE @to_lsn binary(10)

-- Set the start time for the CDC query to 2 minutes ago
SET @begin_time = dateadd(MI, -2, GETDATE())              <--①

-- Make a change to the Production.Product table
UPDATE Production.Product                                 <--②
SET Name = 'AWC Logo Cap (XL)'
WHERE ProductID = 712

-- Get the end time for the CDC query
SET @end_time = GETDATE()                                 <--③

-- Wait for 10 seconds to allow the CDC process to record the change
WAITFOR DELAY '00:00:10'                                  <--④

-- Map the time intervals to log sequence numbers for CDC
SELECT @from_lsn = sys.fn_cdc_map_time_to_lsn(            <--⑤
    'smallest greater than or equal', @begin_time
)

SELECT @to_lsn = sys.fn_cdc_map_time_to_lsn(             <--⑤
    'largest less than or equal', @end_time
)

-- Return the Changes from CDC
SELECT *
FROM cdc.fn_cdc_get_all_changes_Production_Product(       <--⑥
    @from_lsn
    , @to_lsn
    , 'all');
GO
```

Let's walk through the code in listing 6.7 to understand the steps:

❶ First, after declaring variables, we initialize @begin_time to 2 minutes ago. CDC queries work by providing a transaction log sequence number (LSN) range in which to return changes. To derive the LSN numbers, we use date ranges and the sys.fn_cdc_map_time_to_lsn function discussed shortly.

❷ Next up, we run a modify statement on the Production.Product table. This is the change CDC will capture for us.

❸ We then capture the @end_time using the GETDATE() function.

❹ CDC captures changes using a SQL Agent job that reads the transaction log. The 10-second pause statement is inserted in order to give the Agent a chance to capture the change.

❺ The next two statements capture the starting and ending LSN numbers using the start and end date time values captured earlier.

❻ Finally, we select from the cdc.fn_cdc_get_all_changes_Production_Product function passing in the from/to LSN values as parameters. This function was automatically created for us when we enabled CDC on the Production.Product table in listing 6.6.

The output of the final select command in listing 6.7 is shown in figure 6.14.

After the required database and tables are defined, Change Data Capture enables a real-time, lightweight method of auditing changes to tables. SQL Server BOL contains a complete description of all of the functions we've used in this simple example, along with a range of other features of Change Data Capture.

The ability to easily define granular auditing solutions without the need for third-party tools or custom server-side traces is a powerful weapon in creating and managing secure SQL Server environments. In the next section, we'll take a look at another security feature that has been significantly enhanced in SQL Server 2008: encryption.

6.5 Data encryption

SQL Server 2005 introduced the ability to encrypt data *at rest*, meaning data stored within the database itself. Known as *cell-level encryption*, this was a welcome addition to the other encryption features in earlier versions that allowed encryption of data in transit, such as network encryption with SSL.

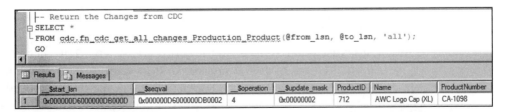

Figure 6.14 Output from the cdc.fn_cdc_get_all_changes_Production_Product Change Data Capture function

While cell-level encryption is a valuable enhancement, it requires changes to both applications and database schema to work. Most notably, the columns chosen for encryption have to be changed to the varbinary data type, and encrypted data is read and written with functions, requiring changes to application code, stored procedures, or both.

As a result, cell-level encryption in SQL Server 2005 is typically used in limited situations and for specific data, such as credit card details or passwords. What's missing is a way of encrypting *everything* without requiring *any* database schema or application changes. Enter SQL Server 2008 and Transparent Data Encryption.

6.5.1   *Transparent Data Encryption*

New in 2008

Transparent Data Encryption (TDE) allows us to encrypt the entire database without requiring any changes to the structure of the database or the applications that access it. It protects the database in situations where someone breaches physical and login security and obtains access to the .mdf (data) files or .bak (backup) files. Without TDE or another third-party encryption solution, the files could be taken offsite and attached or restored.

Later in this section we'll look at some of the restrictions of TDE that may limit its usefulness in certain situations. For the moment, though, let's take a look at implementing TDE with T-SQL scripts.

ENCRYPTING A DATABASE

The first step in implementing TDE is in creating a *master key*. Intended to protect the private keys of certificates and other keys, the master key is created as a symmetric key using the Triple DES algorithm along with a password supplied by the user creating it:

```
-- Create a Master Key
USE MASTER
GO
CREATE MASTER KEY ENCRYPTION BY PASSWORD = 'jGKhhg6647##tR';
GO
```

Next, we create a *certificate*, used to protect the database encryption key, which we'll create shortly:

```
-- Create a Certificate
USE MASTER
GO
CREATE CERTIFICATE tdeCertificate WITH SUBJECT = 'TDE Certificate';
GO
```

At this point, it's crucial that we back up the certificate. When a TDE-encrypted database is backed up, the backup itself is encrypted. If we want to restore an encrypted database to another server, the certificate used to encrypt the database needs to be loaded to the other server to enable the database to be restored. Further, should we suffer a catastrophic server failure, the newly installed server will also require the certificate in order to restore the database.

The certificate backup should be stored in a secure location, and ideally separated from both the database backups and private key backup. We can back up the certificate and private key as follows:

```
-- Backup the certificate
-- Required if restoring encrypted databases to another server
-- Also required for server rebuild scenarios
USE MASTER
GO
BACKUP CERTIFICATE tdeCertificate TO FILE = 'g:\cert\tdeCertificate.backup'
WITH PRIVATE KEY (FILE = 'e:\cert\tdeCertificatePrivateKey.backup',
ENCRYPTION BY PASSWORD = 'jjKiid_%%4-9')
GO
```

Now, let's change focus from the master database to the database we want to encrypt (AdventureWorks in this example) and create the *database encryption key* (DEK), used for encrypting the database with Transparent Data Encryption:

```
-- Create a Database Encryption Key
USE [AdventureWorks2008]
GO
CREATE DATABASE ENCRYPTION KEY
WITH ALGORITHM = AES_128
ENCRYPTION BY SERVER CERTIFICATE tdeCertificate
GO
```

In this example, we used the AES encryption algorithm with a 128-bit key. In addition, 192- and 256-bit keys are supported, as well as Triple DES. Now that we've created our DEK, we can encrypt the database:

```
-- Encrypt the database using Transparent Database Encryption (TDE)
-- Encryption will proceed as a background task
-- Use the sys.dm_database_encryption_keys DMV to check progress
ALTER DATABASE [AdventureWorks2008]
SET ENCRYPTION ON
GO
```

The encryption process will now start as a background task. During this time, some functions, such as modifying the database files and detaching the database, won't be available. The sys.dm_database_encryption_keys Dynamic Management View (DMV), fully described in BOL, can be used to inspect the progress of the encryption process.

Finally, earlier we discussed the need to back up the certificate for recovery purposes and to enable encrypted databases to be restored to another server. Attempting to restore a backup of a TDE-encrypted database to another server that doesn't have the appropriate certificate installed will result in failure of the restore process, resulting in an error like that shown in figure 6.15.

Let's take a quick look at the process of restoring a certificate on another server in preparation for restoring an encrypted database:

```
-- Create the Master Key if it doesn't already exist
USE MASTER
GO
```

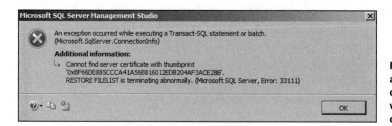

Figure 6.15   Restoring a TDE-encrypted database on a server without the appropriate certificate will fail.

```
CREATE MASTER KEY ENCRYPTION BY PASSWORD = 'jGK__g6647##tR';
GO


-- Restore the Certificate
CREATE CERTIFICATE tdeCertificate
FROM FILE = ' g:\cert\tdeCertificate.backup'
WITH PRIVATE KEY (FILE = 'e:\cert\tdeCertificatePrivateKey.backup'
, DECRYPTION BY PASSWORD = 'jjKiid_%%4-9');
GO
```

Now that the certificate is loaded on the new server, we can successfully restore backups of the TDE-encrypted database.

Despite the clear advantages of Transparent Data Encryption, there are a number of restrictions to be aware of.

TDE RESTRICTIONS

The key restrictions of TDE are summarized as follows:

- While data at rest is encrypted, data transmitted over the network is not, and as we saw earlier in the chapter, we can use SSL or IPSec to achieve this.
- TDE decrypts data as it's read into memory, meaning that if a person or process is able to access the memory contents of the server, the data could potentially be accessed in an unencrypted form.
- While the CPU overhead of TDE is moderate (Microsoft estimates a 3- to 5-percent overhead), it's a consideration nonetheless for systems close to CPU capacity. In large databases with only a small percentage of sensitive data, cell-level encryption (discussed shortly) may present a better alternative,
- The tempdb database will be automatically encrypted on a SQL Server instance in which *any* of the databases are encrypted with TDE. This is an important consideration in instances in which there are one or more databases that make heavy use of the tempdb database.
- FileStream data, covered in chapter 9, can't be encrypted with TDE. For a TDE-encrypted database containing sensitive FileStream data, consider alternate means of securing such data.
- The new backup compression feature in SQL Server 2008 (covered in chapter 10) has minimal effects on databases encrypted with TDE, with a very low compression yield. For this reason, enabling backup compression on TDE-encrypted databases isn't recommended.

With these restrictions in mind, cell-level encryption may prove to be a better alternative in particular cases.

6.5.2   *Cell-level encryption*

Typically, only certain parts of a database are sensitive enough to require encryption. Cell-level encryption, first introduced in SQL Server 2005, offers a more granular level of encryption compared to TDE, and for custom-written applications the additional work required in altering application code and database schema may be quite manageable.

Although data encrypted with cell-level encryption is still transmitted over the network in an unencrypted form, it avoids some of the restrictions of TDE, such as the impact on tempdb, and depending on the volume of data encrypted, may yield a much better backup compression ratio compared to that of a TDE-encrypted database. A further benefit of cell-level encryption is that the encrypted data remains encrypted until required and explicitly decrypted. As we mentioned earlier, one of the restrictions of TDE is that data is stored in an unencrypted form in memory, leaving it susceptible to inspection.

It's beyond the scope of this book to look at the process of establishing cell-level encryption, but the important thing to bear in mind is that depending on the database, it may present a better alternative to Transparent Data Encryption.

In the final section of this chapter, let's take a look at protecting the database from *SQL injection* attacks.

6.6   *SQL injection protection*

A SQL injection attack exposes unintended data to an application user by taking advantage of poor or missing application input parsing. As an example, consider the following code:

```
var city;
city = request.form ("shippingCity");
var sql = "select * from orders where ShipCity = '" + city + "'";
```

The *intention* of this code is that the city variable will be populated with something like Prague. However, what would happen if the following value was entered in the shippingCity form field?

```
Prague'; select * from creditCards--
```

The semicolon character marks the end of one command. The rest of the input will run as a separate query, and by adding the comments (--) characters to the end of the input, we ensure any code added to the end of the variable will be ignored, thus increasing the chances of running the injected code.

In our previous example, the command first selects orders from Prague, and then selects records from the CreditCards table, and the results of both queries are returned to the application. It's easy to imagine adding a range of other code such as dropping tables, deleting data, or running update commands. In most applications,

Injection vulnerability analysis

The *Microsoft Source Code Analyzer for SQL Injection* tool, described and download-able from http://support.microsoft.com/kb/954476, can be used to analyze and identify weaknesses in ASP pages that may be exploited as part of a SQL injection attack.

the code will execute with database owner privileges, so chances are the code will be able to run anything the hacker injects.

Although more in the domain of application development, protecting the database from SQL injection attacks is certainly something that a DBA should be well aware of. Fortunately, there are some well-established practices to prevent injection attacks. The implementation of these best practices are probably outside the domain of DBA responsibilities, but DBAs should ensure that development and test staff are aware of the potential threat and encourage both development and testing strategies to mitigate this risk.

- All user input should be validated by the application before being submitted to SQL Server to ensure it doesn't contain any escape or comment characters. The application should either reject the input or strip out such characters. In our example, the following characters should be removed or rejected: ', ;, and --.
- Transact SQL statements shouldn't be dynamically built with user input appended. Stored procedures should be used that accept input parameters.
- Application testing strategies should be developed that test applications with a variety of input values.
- Applications should anticipate not only injection attacks but also attacks that try to crash the system—for example, a user supplying a large binary file (MPEG, JPEG, and so forth) to a form field designed to accept a username or city.
- Input should be validated at multiple levels. For example, it's not enough to only validate input at the application if the user is able to execute a stored procedure with a malformed parameter.

As the gatekeepers of an organization's data, DBAs have a crucial role to play in ensuring data is protected from unauthorized access. The next section examines best practices for doing so.

6.7   *Best practice considerations: security*

Since 2002, Microsoft's Trustworthy Computing Initiative has been an integral component in the design of each of their products. As a result, the default settings in SQL Server are designed for maximum security. Together with these defaults, the following best practices should be considered as part of achieving the most secure SQL Server environment.

- Where possible, use Windows Authentication mode. Where SQL Server login authentication is required, ensure the SA password is strong, password policies are in effect, and passwords aren't stored in plain text in any connection strings or registry entries.

- Install only the features you need. If you think you may need a feature like Reporting Services in the future, don't install it until you need it.
- Surface Area Configuration (SAC) settings such as xp_cmdshell and Database Mail are secure by default in SQL Server 2005 and above. Before enabling any SAC option, make sure you're aware of the security risks of doing so.
- Perhaps the most dangerous SAC option, xp_cmdshell should remain disabled wherever possible. If you enable it, ensure the Server Proxy account is configured to limit permissions. SQL Server BOL contains a description of both the dangers of xp_cmdshell and the procedures for limiting the potential adverse effects if enabled.
- If mail functionality is required, use Database Mail in place of the older SQL Mail. Among other benefits, Database Mail doesn't require an Outlook client to be installed on the SQL Server, and it provides more stability by running in its own process space. Also consider the possibility of someone with access to Database Mail emailing sensitive data to someone not authorized to view it. We'll cover Database Mail in chapter 14.
- To reduce the need for mail solutions such as Database Mail being enabled on the database server, consider using tools such as Systems Center Operations Manager (SCOM/MOM) as part of an integrated monitoring solution. We'll discuss this further in chapter 14.
- Disable network protocols that aren't required. In almost all cases, TCP/IP should be the only enabled network protocol.
- Configure SQL Server instances with static TCP ports, and place them behind firewalls with only the required ports opened.
- Ensure SQL Servers are never directly accessible on the internet without an appropriate perimeter firewall strategy.
- Enable the Windows Firewall on all SQL Servers and add the appropriate port exclusions.
- Consider stopping the SQL Server Browser Service. In such a configuration, client applications need to include the appropriate TCP port as part of the connection details, either in the connection string or using an alias.
- Use IPSec or SSL to encrypt network connections for applications containing sensitive data. Even if the database is encrypted with TDE or cell-level encryption, the network transmission of data is not, leaving it exposed to network packet sniffers.
- For maximum security, use certificates from public certification authorities such as VeriSign in place of self-signed SQL Server certificates.
- Separate the permissions of system administrators and DBAs. For almost all tasks, DBAs don't need to be local administrators, and system administrators shouldn't be members of the SQL Server sysadmin server role.

- Ensure SQL Server service accounts aren't localsystem or local administrator accounts and use separate accounts for each service.

- If the SQL Server service accounts are changed, make the changes using the SQL Server Configuration Manager tool, which ensures the appropriate permissions are assigned to the new account.

- For SQL Agent jobs requiring access to operating system resources, run the jobs using proxies and credentials rather than using the SQL Agent service account.

- Utilize schema and server/database roles to simplify management and reduce permissions.

- While a Windows group can be added as a SQL Server login (therefore allowing simplified management of groups of logins), take into account the limitations with this technique, including the inability to assign the group a default schema, and complications with object creation requiring implicit ownership.

- Application roles can be effective in cases where user permissions are managed internally within an application. Similar to database roles, permissions are assigned to the application role, and have the added benefit of ensuring the only way users can access the database is via the application.

- Consider using the fixed server roles to avoid adding all DBAs to the sysadmin role. In environments where some DBAs have limited responsibilities, the fixed server roles provide a means of implementing least privilege. In a similar manner, fixed database roles provide the same function, but at a database level.

- Despite the availability of advanced auditing options such as audit action groups, Change Data Capture, and logon triggers, don't overlook the need for basic auditing of login failures, which is enabled by default.

- Take care when using the APP_NAME function in logon triggers. This value can be spoofed by someone with access to a connection string, therefore circumventing the intended logic of the trigger. We'll cover this in more detail when we look at Resource Governor in chapter 16.

- If enabling Change Data Capture, reduce the performance overhead by only capturing the tables and columns required. The `sys.sp_cdc_enable_table` command takes an optional parameter for specifying a table's columns to capture.

- Consider the new Transparent Data Encryption feature to prevent databases from being attached or restored to unauthorized servers, but be aware of its limitations before implementing it.

- Cell-level encryption, also available in SQL Server 2005, is suitable in cases where only a small amount of data needs to be encrypted and the application and database schema changes required for cell encryption are manageable. With cell encryption, the possibility of unauthorized attach or restore should still be considered.

- Back up all encryption certificates in a secure location, ideally separate from the database backup files. The certificate backup will be required when restoring encrypted databases to another server.

- For maximum encryption strength, consider using encryption keys stored on hardware security modules (HSM) via Extensible Key Management (EKM).

- Keep in mind that alternate encryption methods such as EFS and BitLocker aren't suitable for SQL Server implementations.

- To prevent SQL injection attacks, ensure applications validate all user input for both data type adherence and for the presence of escape characters such as ', ;, and --. Ensure the testing processes are aware of the risks of SQL injection attacks and test accordingly. Finally, validate user input at multiple levels, not just at the initial application layer.

- Consider using the Microsoft Source Code Analyzer for SQL Injection tool to assess the vulnerability of code to a SQL injection attack.

- When disposing of tape or disk media containing sensitive data (backups, database, extract files, and so forth), destroy the media before disposal by using magnetic erase tools.

- Secure disk backup directories appropriately, particularly backups made from unencrypted databases.

- If virus-scanning software is installed on the SQL Server, exclude database files (MDF, NDF, LDF, and BAK files) from the scan, and if running on a cluster, ensure the quorum disk (usually Q:) is completely excluded.

- Ensure the stability and performance impact of any virus-scanning software is measured in a load test environment before introduction into a production environment, and ensure the software is cluster aware before use in a cluster.

- Secure SQL Servers in locations that prevent physical access to the general public and unauthorized staff.

- Delete FTP utility executables from SQL Servers unless required.

- Database ownership chaining should be disabled (which is the default setting) to prevent cases in which a user can create an object with a specific owner in a database in which he is the database owner for the explicit purpose of accessing objects in another database with the same owner. Without the ownership chain in effect, the user would be denied access to those objects in the other database.

- Stay up to date with security notification, service packs, and hotfixes. The Microsoft website provides links to various resources for this purpose, including an RSS feed, email, instant messaging, and mobile device notification.

- Where possible, create linked servers that preserve the calling user's security context. Do so by selecting the "Be made using the logins current security context" option in the Security page of the Linked Server properties dialog. For servers not supporting this option, consider the security ramifications of a user's privileges being potentially elevated when made in another security context.

Additional information on the best practices covered in this chapter can be found online at http://www.sqlCrunch.com/security.

The focus of this chapter was configuration from a security perspective. In the next chapter, we'll examine configuration from a performance and stability perspective.

Configuring SQL Server

7

In this chapter, we'll cover

- Memory configuration
- CPU configuration
- Server configuration
- Operating system configuration

As with security configuration, you should make server and database configuration changes with care. Most of the configurable settings in SQL Server work best when left at their default values. You should measure any changes from the defaults for performance and stability impacts in a controlled testing environment before introducing those changes into production.

Like any change, configuration changes should be accompanied by a detailed change log. It's often tempting to *flick the switch* on a configuration setting on the assumption that it may improve performance. Without an adequate change log and a controlled process to measure the effect of the change, uncontrolled configuration changes make future troubleshooting complex. For example, as part of investigating a performance problem, you may notice an odd configuration setting. Was this change made for a reason? Did the change help or hinder performance? Without a change log including the recorded impact, such questions are difficult to answer, particularly in large environments with many SQL Server instances.

In this chapter we drill down into some of the configurable settings and look at situations in which alternate configurations may lead to performance and administrative advantages. We begin the chapter by looking at memory configuration options, including the differences between 32- and 64-bit environments. We then look at other configuration categories: CPU, SQL Server settings, and operating system configuration.

7.1 Memory configuration

As we saw in chapter 3, most versions of SQL Server 2008 can address the amount of memory supported by the underlying operating system. However, like previous versions, 32-bit editions of SQL Server 2008 are constrained to 2GB of RAM unless configured with special settings. Let's begin our coverage of memory configuration with a look at 32-bit memory management.

7.1.1 32-bit memory management

All 32-bit systems can natively address a maximum of 4GB of memory (2^{32} = 4,294,967,296 bytes). Until recent times, this limitation wasn't an issue; a quick scan of older documentation reveals terms such as *very large* when referring to memory beyond 4GB. In today's terms, systems with 8 or 16GB of RAM are considered *normal*, making correct memory configuration in 32-bit systems very important in order to derive the maximum performance benefit.

Apart from installing 64-bit versions of Windows and SQL Server, there are two ways of providing SQL Server with more than 2GB of memory; using the /3GB option or using Address Windowing Extensions (AWE) with the /PAE option.

/3GB
Of the 4GB of RAM that a 32-bit system can natively address, 2GB is reserved by Windows, leaving applications such as SQL Server with a maximum of 2GB. In Windows Server 2003, we used the /3GB option in the boot.ini file to limit Windows to 1GB of memory, enabling SQL Server to access up to 3GB. In Windows Server 2008, we use the BCDEdit command with the increaseuserva option with an optional parameter that determines the size of the available user space, such as 3072 for 3GB.

For 32-bit systems with 4GB of RAM, these options are a good way of squeezing more memory out of Windows for use by SQL Server, but limiting Windows to 1GB of RAM isn't always trouble free, particularly on systems with a large number of drivers and/or drivers that use a large amount of memory. Depending on the server configuration, these options may actually reduce performance and reliability, so use them with care.

For 32-bit systems with more than 4GB of RAM, we can use the /PAE option.

PAE AND AWE
Intel first introduced 36-bit *Physical Address Extensions* (PAEs) in the Pentium Pro in the late 1990s. The extra 4 bits enable applications to acquire physical memory above 4GB (up to 64GB) as nonpaged memory dynamically mapped in the 32-bit address space.

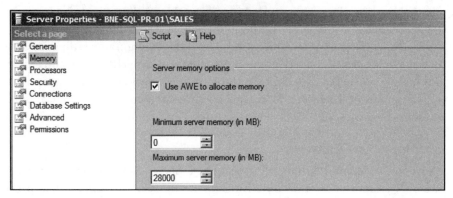

Figure 7.1   The Memory page of a server's properties window contains the Use AWE to Allocate Memory option.

You enable the /PAE option in Windows Server 2003 in the boot.ini in the same way as the /3GB option. In Windows Server 2008, use the BCDEdit command with the /PAE option. After enabling PAE, you configure SQL Server with AWE to enable it to access the increased memory. You enable AWE either by using the sp_configure command or via the Server Properties window in SQL Server Management Studio (see figure 7.1).

Despite the increased memory that can be accessed with PAE/AWE, there are some limitations when used by SQL Server in 32-bit environments:

- Memory above 4GB accessed using PAE/AWE can only be used by the SQL Server data cache. The procedure cache, used for query compilation plans, isn't able to take advantage of this memory. We'll cover the procedure cache in more detail in chapter 17, along with a number of related settings, such as forced parameterization.
- Analysis Services and Integration Services components aren't able to utilize memory accessed using PAE/AWE.
- Unlike a *flat* 64-bit environment, there's some overhead in mapping into the AWE memory space in 32-bit systems.

On 32-bit AWE-enabled systems, the service account running the SQL Server service must be given the Lock Pages in Memory right. As a consequence, AWE memory isn't paged out to disk by the operating system. As you can see in figure 7.2, you assign this right to an account by using the Windows Group Policy Editor.

So if the /PAE option allows us to address memory above 4GB and /3GB allows us to get an extra 1GB from Windows below 4GB, then to obtain the maximum amount of memory for SQL Server we should use both, right? Well, maybe not...

/3GB AND /PAE

When using PAE, Windows uses memory *below* 4GB to map to memory *above* 4GB. The more memory above 4GB to map to, the more memory below 4GB is required for the mapping. The magic number is 16GB. As shown in table 7.1, for systems with more than 16GB of memory, you must not use /3GB (or increaseuserva in Windows Server

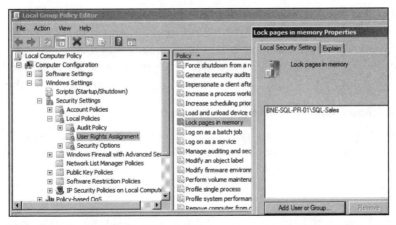

Figure 7.2   The Group Policy Editor can be used to assign the Lock Pages in Memory right to the SQL Server service account.

2008) with /PAE. If you do, only 16GB will be addressable, and any additional memory beyond that is wasted.

Table 7.1   Recommended memory configuration options

Startup option	Use if system RAM is...
Default settings	<4GB
/3GB (or increaseuserva)	4GB
/3GB and /PAE	5–16GB
/PAE	>16GB

As I mentioned earlier, the /3GB option is known to cause stability issues in some circumstances, so even with systems containing between 5GB and 16GB of RAM, you must use this setting with caution.

One of the nice things about 64-bit systems is that all of the configuration issues we've just covered are no longer of concern.

7.1.2   *64-bit memory management*

Unlike 32-bit systems, 64-bit systems don't require the memory configuration just described. The full complement of system RAM can be accessed by all SQL Server components without any additional configuration.

The one optional memory configuration for 64-bit systems is setting the Lock Pages in Memory right, as covered earlier. While this setting is optional for a 64-bit system, locking pages in memory is beneficial in order to prevent Windows from paging out SQL Server's memory. If you don't enable this setting, certain actions such as large file copies can lead to memory pressure with Windows paging, or *trimming*, SQL Server's memory. This sometimes leads to a sudden and dramatic reduction in SQL Server performance, usually accompanied by the "A significant part of sql server process memory has been paged out..." message. Setting the Lock Pages in Memory option prevents such incidents from occurring, and is therefore a recommended setting. Note that Windows Server 2008 handles memory trimming a lot better than 2003.

Regardless of the processor platform (32- or 64-bit), one of the important memory configuration tasks is to set the minimum and maximum server memory values.

7.1.3   *Setting minimum and maximum memory values*

When SQL Server starts, it acquires enough memory to initialize, beyond which it acquires and releases memory as required. The minimum and maximum memory values control the upper limit to which SQL Server will acquire memory (maximum), and the point at which it will stop releasing memory back to the operating system (minimum).

As you saw earlier in figure 7.1, the minimum and maximum memory values for an instance can be set in SQL Server Management Studio or by using the sp_configure command. By default, SQL Server's minimum and maximum memory values are 0 and 2,147,483,647, respectively. The default min/max settings essentially allow SQL Server to cooperate with Windows and other applications by acquiring and releasing memory in conjunction with the memory requirements of other applications.

On small systems with a single SQL Server instance, the default memory values will probably work fine in most cases, but on larger systems we need to give this a bit more thought. Let's consider a number of cases where setting min/max values is required, beginning with systems that lock pages in memory.

LOCK PAGES IN MEMORY

As you know, when the Lock Pages in Memory setting is enabled, SQL Server's memory will not be paged out to disk. This is clearly good from a SQL Server performance point of view, but consider a case where the maximum memory value isn't set, and SQL Server is placed under significant load. The default memory settings don't enforce an upper limit to the memory usage, so SQL Server will continue to consume as much memory as it can get access to, all of which will be locked and therefore will potentially starve other applications (including Windows) of memory. In some cases, this memory starvation effect can lead to system stability issues.

In SQL Server 2005 and above, even with the Lock Pages in Memory option enabled, SQL Server will respond to memory pressure by releasing some of its memory back to the operating system. However, depending on the state of the server, it may not be able to release memory quickly enough, again leading to possible stability issues.

For the reasons just outlined, systems that use the Lock Pages in Memory option should also set a maximum memory value, leaving enough memory for Windows. We'll cover how much to leave shortly.

MULTIPLE INSTANCES

A server containing multiple SQL Server instances needs special consideration when setting min/max memory values. Consider a server with three instances, each of which is configured with the default memory settings. If one of the instances starts up and begins receiving a heavy workload, it will potentially consume all of the available memory. When one of the other instances starts, it will find itself with very little physical memory, and performance will obviously suffer.

In such cases, I recommend setting the maximum memory value of each instance to an appropriate level (based on the load profile of each).

SHARED SERVERS

On servers in which SQL Server is sharing resources with other applications, setting the minimum memory value helps to prevent situations in which SQL Server struggles to receive adequate memory. Of course, the ideal configuration is one in which the server is dedicated to SQL Server, but this is not always the case, unfortunately.

A commonly misunderstood aspect of the minimum memory value is whether or not SQL Server reserves that amount of memory when the instance starts. It doesn't.

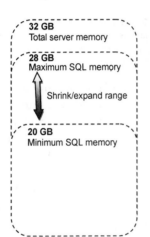

When started, an instance consumes memory dynamically up to the level specified in the maximum memory setting. Depending on the load, the consumed memory may never reach the minimum value. If it does, memory will be released back to the operating system if required, but will never drop *below* the value specified in the minimum setting. Figure 7.3 shows the relationship between a server's memory capacity and SQL Server's minimum and maximum memory values.

Figure 7.3   A SQL Server instance will consume memory up to the level specified by the maximum. Once past the minimum level, it will not release memory below the minimum level.

CLUSTERS

As you learned in chapter 5, configuring memory maximums in a multi-instance cluster is important in ensuring stability during failover situations. You must ensure that the total maximum memory values across all instances in the cluster is less than the total available memory on any one cluster node that the instances may end up running on during node outage.

Setting the maximum memory values in such a manner is important to ensure adequate and consistent performance during failover scenarios.

AMOUNT OF MEMORY TO LEAVE WINDOWS

One of the important memory configuration considerations, particularly for 32-bit AWE systems and 64-bit systems that lock pages in memory, is the amount of memory to leave Windows. For example, in a dedicated SQL Server system with 32GB of memory, we'll obviously want to give SQL Server as much memory as possible, but how much can be safely allocated? Put another way, what should the maximum memory value be set to? Let's consider what other possible components require RAM:

- Windows
- Drivers for host bus adapter (HBA) cards, tape drives, and so forth

- Antivirus software
- Backup software
- Microsoft Operations Manager (MOM) agents, or other monitoring software

As shown in figure 7.4, in addition to the above non–SQL Server components, there are a number of SQL Server objects that use memory from outside of the buffer pool—that is, the memory area defined by the maximum memory setting. Memory for objects such as linked servers, extended stored procedures, and object linking and embedding (OLE) automation objects is allocated from an area commonly called the *MemToLeave* area.

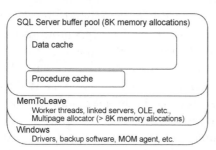

Figure 7.4   The SQL Server buffer pool, as defined by the Max Server Memory setting, must share the server's physical memory with other memory consumers such as Windows and MemToLeave.

As you can see, even on a dedicated server, there's a potentially large number of components vying for memory access, all of which comes from outside the buffer pool, so leaving enough memory is crucial for a smooth-running server. The basic rule of thumb when allocating maximum memory is that the total of each instance's maximum memory values should be *at least* 2GB less than the total physical memory installed in the server; however, for some systems, leaving 2GB of memory may not be enough. For systems with 32GB of memory, a commonly used value for Max Server Memory (totaled across all installed instances) is 28GB, leaving 4GB for the operating system and other components that we discussed earlier.

Given the wide variety of possible system configuration and usage, it's not possible to come up a single best figure for the Max Server Memory value. Determining the best maximum value for an environment is another example of the importance of a load-testing environment configured identically to production, and an accurate test plan that loads the system as per the expected production load. Load testing in such an environment will satisfy expectations of likely production performance, and offers the opportunity to test various settings and observe the resulting performance.

One of the great things about SQL Server, particularly the recent releases, is its self-tuning nature. Its default settings, together with its ability to *sense and adjust*, make the job of a DBA somewhat easier. In the next section, we'll see how these attributes apply to CPU configuration.

7.2   *CPU configuration*

When an instance of SQL server starts, it's created as an operating system *process*. Unlike a simple application that performs a series of serial tasks on a single CPU, SQL Server is a complex application that must support hundreds or even thousands of simultaneous requests. In order to do this, the SQL Server process creates *threads*.

A multithreaded operating system such as Windows allows applications like SQL Server to create multiple threads in order to maximize CPU efficiency and application throughput. Threads are assigned and balanced across the available CPUs in a server. If a thread is waiting on the completion of a task such as a disk request, SQL Server can schedule the execution of other threads in the meantime. The combination of a multithreaded architecture and support for multi-CPU servers allows applications such as SQL Server to support a large number of simultaneous requests.

With this background in mind, let's take a look at some of the configuration options that can be set to control the manner in which SQL Server threads are executed.

7.2.1 *Boost SQL Server Priority option*

Threads created in Windows are assigned a priority from 1 to 31, with thread priority 0 reserved for operating system use. Waiting threads are assigned to CPUs in priority order—that is, higher-priority threads are assigned for execution ahead of lower-priority threads.

By default, SQL Server threads are created with a "normal" priority level of 7. This priority ensures SQL Server threads are assigned and executed in a timely manner without causing any stability issues for anything else running on the server.

The Boost SQL Server Priority option runs SQL Server threads at a priority level of 13, higher than most other applications. Although this sounds like a setting that should always be enabled, much like the "turbo" button on old PCs, it should only be used in rare circumstances.

Enabling this option has resulted in problems, such as not being able to shut down the server and various other stability issues. In almost all cases, on well-configured dedicated servers, the performance difference is likely to be negligible at best. Unless you have a very accurate load-testing environment in which you can prove this option results in a measurable performance boost *and* doesn't cause any other stability and performance issues, use the default setting.

7.2.2 *Maximum Worker Threads option*

Despite each thread being *light* in terms of resource consumption, they consume resources nonetheless. In systems with thousands of concurrent tasks, creating a dedicated thread per task would consume a significant amount of resources. To counter this, SQL Server implements thread pooling, whereby threads are assigned to tasks from a pool as required.

SQL Server will size the thread pool automatically based on the number of CPUs in the server and whether the system is 32- or 64-bit. As table 7.2 shows, this ranges from 256 to 960. Optionally, you can define the number of threads for greater control.

Table 7.2 Default worker threads created by SQL Server based on the CPU number and type

Number of CPUs	32-bit	64-bit
1–4	256	512
8	288	576
16	352	704
32	480	960

In situations where the number of running tasks is less than the defined number of threads, each task will have its own dedicated thread. If the number of concurrent tasks rises beyond the number of threads, threads are pooled, and pending tasks are granted threads from the pool when available.

When system load is very high and all available threads are assigned to running tasks, the system may become unresponsive until a thread becomes available. In such situations, the dedicated administrator connection (DAC) can be used to connect to the server and perform troubleshooting tasks, possibly involving terminating some processes.

> **Dedicated administrator connection (DAC)**
> When a SQL Server instance has become unresponsive, troubleshooting can be difficult. To assist with these situations, SQL Server reserves resources for a dedicated administrator connection (DAC), enabling a DBA to connect to the instance and take appropriate actions, such as terminate a process. A connection to the DAC is made using either the SQLCMD command prompt utility or SQL Server Management Studio. Books Online describes how to use these tools to establish a DAC connection.

One of the common recommendations for systems supporting a large number of connections is to increase the number of worker threads in an attempt to increase throughput. Although this *may* improve performance, it can also lead to a performance reduction.

When SQL Server starts up, it reserves a quantity of memory for each configured thread. The higher the number of threads, the more memory needs to be reserved. Further, this memory comes from the MemToLeave area, so the configured worker thread count is directly linked to the maximum memory value that can be safely configured.

The recommended maximum value for worker threads is 1024 in a 32-bit environment and 2048 in a 64-bit environment. As with all other configuration settings, the best value in almost all cases is the default (0). If you change the value, first verify it for stability in an accurate load-testing environment.

Finally, if you're upgrading from SQL Server 2000, the Maximum Worker Threads setting is kept at the SQL 2000 default value of 255. After the upgrade, change this value to 0, which allows SQL Server to determine the appropriate value based on the number and type of CPUs available to the instance.

7.2.3 *Lightweight pooling*

On servers with a large number of CPUs close to capacity, performance may benefit from enabling *fiber mode*, also known as lightweight pooling. With this setting in place, SQL Server creates *fibers* instead of threads. A fiber is a lightweight version of a thread that's able to switch context in user mode rather than kernel mode.

Systems experiencing a very high level of *context switches per second* (>20,000), a value measured using the Windows Performance tool, may experience some performance increase with this option enabled. In chapter 17, we'll cover the measurement and threshold value for this setting in more detail. Like all configuration options, the Use Windows Fibers (Lightweight Pooling) setting should only be changed from the default value after careful analysis in a testing environment capable of accurately simulating production load.

7.2.4 CPU affinity

SQL Server can be configured so that threads will only be assigned to particular CPUs. This setting is typically used in NUMA-enabled systems, or on systems used for environments where a certain level of CPU resource needs to be reserved for other purposes, for example, other SQL Server instances or applications, to prevent one SQL Server instance from dominating CPU usage.

On single instance servers dedicated to SQL Server, this setting is best left at the default, in which case threads will be balanced across all available CPUs.

The Processor Affinity option, along with the Fiber Mode, Maximum Worker Threads, and Boost SQL Server Priority settings, can be modified using `sp_configure` or via the Processors page of the Server Properties window in SQL Server Management Studio, as you can see in figure 7.5.

7.2.5 Maximum Degree of Parallelism

A commonly altered setting is *Maximum Degree of Parallelism* (MAXDOP), which controls the maximum number of CPUs that can be used in executing a single task. For example, a large query may be broken up into different parts, with each part executing threads on separate CPUs. Such a query is known as a *parallel query*.

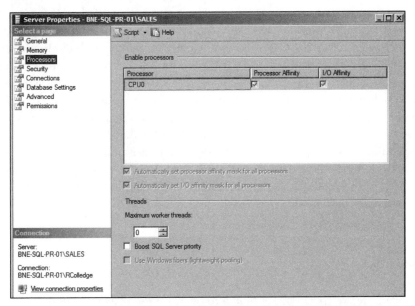

Figure 7.5   The Processors page of the Server Properties window allows changes to CPU configuration settings: CPU Affinity, Maximum Worker Threads, Boost SQL Server Priority, and Use Windows Fibers (Lightweight Pooling).

In a typical OLTP system consisting of lots of short, simple transactions, multiple CPUs are valuable in their ability to service lots of simultaneous threads from multiple users. In contrast, a typical OLAP (reporting/data warehouse) application consists of a smaller number of much larger queries. It follows that splitting up a query into multiple chunks, with each chunk running on a separate CPU, is more suited to an OLAP system whereby large amounts of resources can be used to speed up the execution time of large queries.

During query compilation, SQL Server will decide whether to use a parallel query if the MAXDOP setting allows and if the estimated cost of executing the query in a serial manner on a single CPU exceeds a cost threshold. By default, MAXDOP is 0, meaning that SQL Server is left to decide the appropriate number of CPUs to use. You can set this value to 1, effectively disabling parallel queries, or to a specific number that limits the number of CPUs that can be used.

Max MAXDOP?

In OLTP systems, use a maximum MAXDOP setting of 8, including systems with access to more than 8 CPU cores. The effort to split and rejoin a query across more than 8 CPUs often outweighs the benefits of parallelism.

In some cases, parallel queries in an OLTP environment are chosen by SQL Server to circumvent poor design and maintenance practices, most often as a result of missing indexes or out-of-date statistics. For example, SQL Server may decide to perform an index scan rather than a lookup, in which case it may parallelize the query. A high incidence of parallel queries is typically accompanied by a large number of CXPACKET waits. In chapter 17, we'll spend more time analyzing wait types, including CXPACKET.

In typical OLTP environments, MAXDOP is often set to 1 to limit the CPU and memory impact from parallel queries. In such cases, the question needs to be asked as to *why* SQL Server is choosing parallel queries—that is, are the indexes being designed and maintained appropriately? We'll cover index design and maintenance in chapter 13.

One of the downsides from setting MAXDOP to 1 is that certain operations, such as index rebuilds, benefit greatly from parallelism but are unable to do so with a MAXDOP 1 setting. In such cases, you can specify the MAXDOP setting at a statement level. For example, the CREATE INDEX command, an example of which is shown here, accepts a MAXDOP parameter:

```
-- Use a MAXDOP hint to override the default server MAXDOP setting
CREATE NONCLUSTERED INDEX [IX_Address_StateProvinceID]
    ON [Person].[Address] ([StateProvinceID] ASC)
WITH (MAXDOP=0)
GO
```

In this example, we specify MAXDOP = 0 to override the instance default MAXDOP setting, and thereby permit the index creation to be parallelized if SQL Server decides that's the best approach.

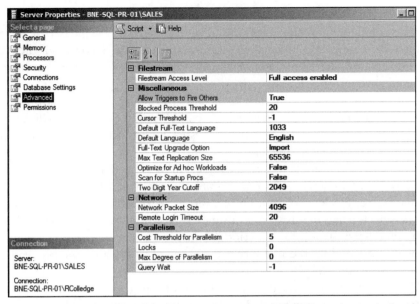

Figure 7.6   The Advanced tab of the Server Properties window allows changes to Server configuration settings, such as Max Degree of Parallelism and Cost Threshold for Parallelism.

Like all configuration options, Max Degree of Parallelism can be set using sp_configure, or via the Advanced page of a server's properties window in SQL Server Management Studio, as shown in figure 7.6.

7.2.6   *Cost Threshold for Parallelism*

If MAXDOP is left at the default value, or set to a number higher than 1, the threshold at which SQL Server will consider a parallel plan can be set through the *Cost Threshold for Parallelism* option. This value, specified in seconds, represents the estimated time the query would take if executed serially on a single CPU. Queries estimated to take longer than this will be considered for parallelism. The default value for this setting is 5.

In some cases, increasing this value is a better alternative to setting MAXDOP to 1 when dealing with a large number of (unwanted) parallel queries.

With these CPU configuration options covered, let's turn our attention now to some other general server settings. Like most of the CPU settings, these settings are also best left at their default values.

7.3   *Server configuration*

The name of this section, *Server configuration*, refers to a range of additional SQL Server settings that can be tuned for particular behavior. While the list is by no means exhaustive, it covers some common settings that are often changed to alter server operation.

As with CPU and memory settings, the settings we'll cover in this section can be adjusted with either sp_configure or by using SQL Server Management Studio.

7.3.1   *Recovery Interval*

A *page* is the fundamental storage unit in SQL Server, with each database divided into multiple 8K pages. When a database page is required, SQL Server reads the page from disk into memory (if it's not already there) and stores it in the data cache. Pages are modified as required and marked as *dirty*.

Pages are modified in the data cache along with a corresponding transaction log entry. At some point, the modified (dirty) pages need to be written to disk, a task handled by the *LazyWriter* and *Checkpoint* processes, both of which are fundamental components of SQL Server architecture.

The LazyWriter process periodically examines the data cache and writes dirty pages to disk. Once written, the pages are then returned to the *free list* in order to maintain a certain level of free buffers required for other threads. The LazyWriter process selects pages to flush to disk using an algorithm that targets pages that haven't been referenced (read) for a period of time. In essence, LazyWriter balances the needs of maintaining free memory with the need to keep frequently read pages in memory to avoid disk I/O.

The Checkpoint process also writes dirty buffer pages to disk, but unlike the LazyWriter process, pages aren't added to the free list. The primary purpose of the Checkpoint process is to reduce the database recovery time. When SQL Server starts, it examines the transaction log and *rolls forward* (writes changes to disk) committed transactions since the last checkpoint, and *rolls back* uncommitted transactions. The recovery process ensures that no committed changes are lost or half-written changes are persisted in the event of an unexpected shutdown, thus maintaining data integrity and avoiding corruption.

The *Recovery Interval* setting determines the frequency of Checkpoint operations. The default recovery interval is 0, meaning SQL Server aims to run checkpoints frequently enough to recover databases on startup within approximately 1 minute—that is, complete the roll forward and rollback process from the transaction log when SQL Server starts up.

The rate of database change will determine the checkpoint frequency. Databases with very little write activity will go for long periods without a checkpoint. In contrast, databases with high write activity will have frequent checkpoints in order to keep the recovery interval to 1 minute.

The Recovery Interval value can be changed to a numeric value representing the target number of minutes for the recovery to complete within. A frequently documented suggestion is to increase the recovery interval in an attempt to decrease the impact of the checkpoint operation, but doing so increases the recovery time and the impact of each checkpoint. Better alternatives include ensuring the write cache of the storage controller is large enough to withstand bursts of write activity associated with checkpoint operations, and separating transaction logs onto a dedicated disk, a topic we'll cover in more detail in chapter 9.

Like all other configuration settings, the default value for the recovery interval is the best value in almost all cases.

7.3.2 Fill factor

When an index is created or rebuilt, the *fill factor*, a numeric value between 0 and 100, determines how *full* each index page will be. A fill factor of 100 (or 0) will fill each page completely, with 50 resulting in pages half full. The specified value is interpreted as the percentage full to make each page.

The benefits of full pages are that less I/O is required to fulfill an index scan/seek as each page contains more data. The downside comes when data is inserted, in which case a full page needs to be split in order to allow the new data to be inserted in index order. The best fill factor is determined by the rate of data modification.

A database with a high volume of updates may benefit from a lower fill factor as each page contains some free space for new records to be inserted and therefore avoids the page split process. As a consequence, though, the index will be larger, increasing database size and the amount of I/O required to satisfy query requests.

Note that the fill factor value is only used when the index is first created or rebuilt; after that, the page will fill/split as a natural consequence of the data inserts and updates.

In a similar manner to the MAXDOP setting that we covered earlier, the default server fill factor of 0 (equivalent to 100) can be overridden on a per command basis. We'll cover fill factor in more detail in chapter 13 when we cover indexes.

Both the Recovery Interval and Default Index Fill Factor values can be set using sp_configure or the Database Settings page of the Server Properties window in SQL Server Management Studio, as shown in figure 7.7.

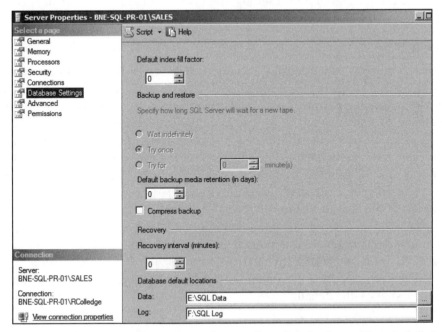

Figure 7.7   The Database Settings page allows configuration of various settings, including Recovery Interval and Default Index Fill Factor.

7.3.3   Locks

Locks are a fundamental component of any relational database management system and are used, among other purposes, to prevent access to data that's in the middle of being modified. Doing so avoids many different problems caused by inconsistent, or *dirty*, reads.

By default, SQL Server reserves sufficient memory for a lock pool consisting of 2,500 locks. If required, and additional buffer space is available, the lock pool will grow using additional memory from the buffer pool.

When the number of used locks reaches 40 percent of the size of the (non-AWE) buffer pool, SQL Server will consider lock escalation; for example, it will convert a number of row locks to a single page or table lock, therefore reducing the memory impact of lots of locks. When 60 percent of the buffer pool is used for locks, new lock requests will be denied, resulting in an error. SQL Server will also consider lock escalation at a statement level if the number of locks acquired by the statement on a single object exceeds approximately 5,000.

A common (frequently misguided) suggestion is to enable trace flags[1] to prevent lock escalation (trace flag 1211 and 1224). Such suggestions are often given in an attempt at avoiding blocking and deadlock scenarios. Such advice is normally a poor alternative to investigating and resolving database design and/or maintenance problems. Further, the large number of resulting locks often leads to significant memory pressure and overall stability issues.

Like the Recovery Interval setting, the Locks value can be manually specified, but again, I don't recommend that for almost all cases.

7.3.4   Query Wait

When a query is submitted for execution, SQL Server first checks to see if there's already a cached query plan it can reuse. If no such plan exists, a new plan needs to be created. Avoiding this process through query parameterization is a key performance-tuning goal, and one that we'll spend more time on in chapter 17.

Regardless of whether the plan was selected from cache or re-created, it can't be executed until enough memory is obtained for the execution process. In systems with poor plan reuse, or those starved of memory (or both), a common occurrence is for queries to time out with the "A time out occurred while waiting for memory resources to execute the query..." error.

The estimated cost of the plan determines the length of time that SQL Server will wait for resources before the query times out. By default, SQL Server will wait for 25 times the estimated cost of the query. You can use the Query Wait option to override this default by specifying the amount of time to wait in seconds. The best value to use? You guessed it—the default.

---

[1]   Through the ALTER TABLE command, SQL Server 2008 enables lock escalation to be disabled for an individual table.

Both the Locks and Query Wait values can be set using `sp_configure` or the Advanced page of the Server Properties window in SQL Server Management Studio, as shown earlier in figure 7.6.

7.3.5 User Connections

By default, SQL Server will allow an unlimited number of user connections, within the constraints of its available resources. Setting a non-zero value allows control over the number of concurrent connections.

Once the number of connections is exceeded (bearing in mind a user or application can have multiple connections), new connections will be denied with the exception of the dedicated administrator connection.

7.3.6 Query Governor Cost Limit

As part of the query compilation and execution process, SQL Server estimates the cost of the query. As we saw earlier, this value is used in determining the query timeout value. The other use for this value is comparing it to the *Query Governor Cost Limit*.

If enabled, the Query Governor Cost Limit option is used to prevent queries from running whose estimated cost exceeds the configured value, specified in seconds. By default, this option is disabled. Note that the new Resource Governor feature in SQL Server 2008 is a far more effective way of controlling resource usage, and will be covered in detail in chapter 16.

Both the User Connections and Query Governor Cost Limit values can be set using `sp_configure` or the Connections page of the Server Properties window in SQL Server Management Studio. As shown in figure 7.8, User Connections are set

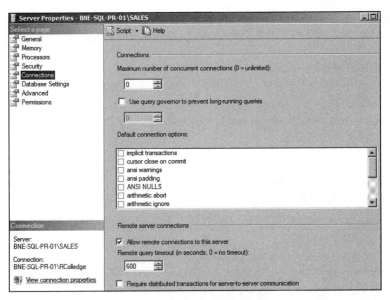

Figure 7.8 The Connections page allows configuration of various settings, including Maximum Number of Concurrent Connections and Use Query Governor to Prevent

using the Maximum Number of Concurrent Connections option, and the Query Governor Cost Limit is set using the Use Query Governor to Prevent Long-running Queries" option.

In the final section of this chapter, let's turn our attention to configuration of the Server operating system.

7.4   *Operating system configuration*

An often overlooked configuration area for SQL Server is configuration of the operating system itself. In this section, we'll take a look at configuration from a Windows perspective, focusing on items that can have a measurable impact on SQL Server performance and stability.

7.4.1   *Running services*

In chapters 4 and 6 we covered the importance of only installing the required SQL Server features. It's very easy during installation to select all features on the off chance that they may be required in the future. As a result, people often end up with Analysis Services, Reporting Services, Integration Services, and full-text search, all of which create Windows Services that run on startup.

In addition to these SQL Services, there are a host of other Windows Services such as IIS that may be running that are possibly not required. It's outside the scope of this book to list and describe which ones are candidates for disabling, but IIS is worth a special mention. In SQL Server 2005, IIS was required for Reporting Services. Fortunately, this is no longer the case in SQL Server 2008. If you installed IIS solely for the purpose of supporting Reporting Services, you won't need it if you're running SQL Server 2008.

Disabling nonessential services is good from a performance perspective as well as an effective security practice in reducing the attack surface area.

7.4.2   *Processor scheduling*

Accessed via the Control Panel, the advanced options of System Properties let you choose between adjusting processor resources to favor foreground applications or background services. As a background service, SQL Server obviously benefits from this option being set to Background Services, as shown in figure 7.9.

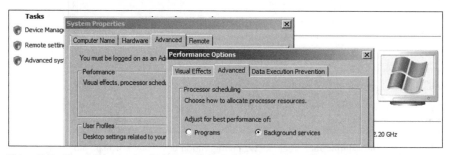

Figure 7.9   The options under Processor Scheduling should be adjusted for the best performance of background services.

7.4.3 *Network protocols*

As you saw in chapter 6, disabling unnecessary network protocols is important from both a security and performance optimization perspective.

7.4.4 *Page file location*

By default, Windows will create a page file that is 1.5 times the size of the physical memory up to a maximum of 4GB (on 32-bit systems). On a server dedicated to SQL Server with sufficient memory, particularly those with the Lock Pages in Memory option, the amount of paging should be negligible. As a result, page file configuration isn't a task that most DBAs spend a lot of time considering.

That being said, for systems with large amounts of memory, one of the benefits of configuring a larger than normal page file is to assist in advanced troubleshooting scenarios. For example, if SQL Server crashes, the memory dump can be inspected for later diagnosis. Configuring a page file large enough for such a memory dump is worth considering for such cases.

7.5 *Best practice considerations: configuring SQL Server*

In almost all cases, the best configuration setting is the default. Any change should be based on sound advice, and tested for performance and stability in an accurate load-testing environment before implementation in production.

- The reason for a configuration change is sometimes easy to forget. To assist in future troubleshooting, each configuration change should be recorded in a change log with *at least* the following details: date and time of the change, person executing the change, script location (if change was script based), and the results of the change (observed performance, any errors, etc.).
- In a 32-bit platform, the /3GB switch (or BCDEdit/increaseuserva) can be used to enable an extra 1GB of RAM for SQL Server, but only for systems containing up to 16GB of RAM. Before using this option, ensure the impacts are fully understood and measured in an accurate load-testing environment.
- The Lock Pages in Memory right should be assigned to the SQL Server service account for both 32-bit AWE systems and 64-bit systems.
- The Maximum Server Memory value should be specified, particularly for multi-instance servers, clustered servers, shared servers, and those using the Lock Pages in Memory setting.
- When setting the value for Maximum Server Memory, consider the other system components such as drivers, backup software, and the MemToLeave area. Even on dedicated servers, their memory requirements need to be considered in creating a stable environment for SQL Server.
- In OLTP systems with more than eight CPUs, using a maximum MAXDOP setting of 8 is recommended in most cases. The effort to split and rejoin a query across more than eight CPUs often outweighs the benefits of parallelism.

- On NUMA systems, the MAXDOP setting shouldn't exceed the number of CPUs available to the NUMA node(s) used by the SQL Server instance.
- Only the applications, services, and network protocols required should be installed and running. Performance and security improves as a result of disabling items not required.
- Ensure the Windows Server is configured for Background Services in System Properties.
- Although paging shouldn't be present in any significant volume on a well-configured SQL Server, consider placing the page file on a separate disk from the operating system and SQL data files.

Additional information on the best practices covered in this chapter can be found online at http://www.sqlCrunch.com/config.

Until SQL Server 2008, one of the challenges with server configuration was maintaining good configuration settings across a large number of servers, particularly in enterprise environments with lots of instances and many DBAs of varying skill levels. Policy-based management, covered in the next chapter, has made this task significantly easier.

Policy-based management *8*

In this chapter, we'll cover

- Enterprise DBA challenges
- Policy-based management
- Central management servers
- PowerShell and `ExecuteWQL()`

The major goal of this book is to list and describe best practices for the administration of SQL Server systems. *Knowing* best practices is one thing, but ensuring they're implemented, and *remain* implemented, is an entirely different matter.

Suppose you've accepted a position as the new DBA for a company with thousands of server instances spread across production, test, and development environments, each of which were installed and configured by various DBAs and developers with different preferences and knowledge of best practices. If you're asked to perform an audit of all servers for compliance with best practices, how will you go about it? If you're handy with scripting technologies such as *SQL Server Management Objects* (SMOs) and *PowerShell*, that will certainly help, but other than that, you're facing a significant and time-consuming challenge. When you finally complete the exercise, how can you be confident that none of the servers have changed configuration since you started inspecting them? Like painting a bridge, by the time you finished you'd be due to start all over again!

Recent versions of SQL Server ship with good out-of-the-box settings and self-managing features, and together with well-documented and well-managed policies, ensuring enterprise-wide consistency in SQL Server configuration is somewhat easier, but it's still a challenge.

SQL Server 2008 introduces a new feature called *policy-based management,* and it's arguably the single most significant new feature for the DBA. In this chapter, we'll discuss some of the challenges facing DBAs in enterprise environments and how policy-based management can be used in assisting with such challenges. We'll also take a look at combining the power of policy-based management with central management servers and PowerShell.

8.1   Server management challenges

Enterprise DBAs—those who manage complex environments with a mix of database products and versions—face a number of challenges. In addition to keeping many systems up and running, they need to provide a smooth path for the implementation of changes to production databases. Before looking at policy-based management in depth, let's spend some time covering the typical enterprise environment and the tasks faced by an enterprise DBA.

8.1.1   Enterprise environments

In a typical enterprise environment (see figure 8.1 for a simple example), one of the first things that comes to mind is the number of production server instances requiring support. A large number of servers are usually accompanied by a mix of product versions, and possibly even other DBMS products such as Oracle or MySQL. In such environments, some degree of specialization usually exists, and DBAs are often grouped into areas of product expertise.

In addition to the production server instances, test and development servers, some or all of which may be provided using virtualization products, exist for the purposes of developing and testing new databases or making changes to existing production systems. Accompanying such systems are various development tools and change management processes to ensure changes are version controlled and implemented in accordance with an appropriate deployment process.

In environments with critical systems, dedicated operations staff are usually on hand 24/7, with DBAs typically on call on a rotation basis. Products such as *Systems Center Operations Manager* (SCOM) are typically used for monitoring disk space and event logs in an attempt to identify and solve problems before they manifest themselves as production outages.

In complex environments such as these, successful database administration must overcome a range of challenges, some of which are presented next.

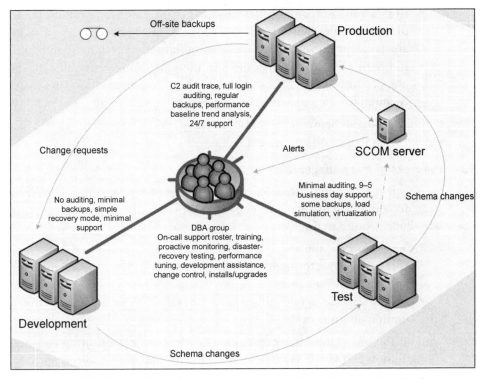

Off-site backups

Production

C2 audit trace, full login auditing, regular backups, performance baseline trend analysis, 24/7 support

Change requests

Alerts

SCOM server

No auditing, minimal backups, simple recovery mode, minimal support

Minimal auditing, 9–5 business day support, some backups, load simulation, virtualization

Schema changes

DBA group
On-call support roster, training, proactive monitoring, disaster-recovery testing, performance tuning, development assistance, change control, installs/upgrades

Development

Test

Schema changes

Figure 8.1 A typical enterprise environment consists of development, test, and production servers

8.1.2 Enterprise DBA challenges

Let's take a look at some of the tasks facing DBAs in administering an enterprise environment:

- Production systems should be secured with the *least privilege* principle. This is often in contrast with development environments in which changes originate. When developed code reaches test and production systems, certain functions often fail as a result of the security differences between environments. DBAs must therefore coordinate environment configuration across the enterprise, particularly settings that may cause certain functions to fail.

- Databases in production environments (should) use the *full recovery* model along with regular transaction log backups. In development and test environments that don't perform transaction log backups, the full recovery model may cause the transaction log to consume all available disk space. DBAs must match environments with backup profiles and recovery model settings.

- In sites where different DBAs manage different environments—for example, development, test, and production—systems must be in place to ensure that both common and environment-specific settings are applied where appropriate. Where many DBAs are involved, each of whom has his or her own preferences and skills, this becomes a difficult and time-consuming process.

- In sites with a range of DBMS products that require support, it's often the case that the requirement for a broad range of skills prevents expertise in any one area, making correct and consistent configuration even more difficult.
- In poorly configured environments, the time taken to troubleshoot highly visible production problems often prevents important proactive maintenance required for ongoing environment performance, security, and stability.

Without strong proactive maintenance routines, mismanagement is a real danger, presenting a number of organizational risks.

8.1.3 *The risks of mismanagement*

Even with the best intentions and a good grasp of best practices, the sheer size of some deployments creates a challenging environment for even the most experienced DBA. Poorly configured servers pose a number of risks:

- Security weak points
- Unexpected performance problems due to different configuration settings between environments
- Scripts working in one environment but failing in another, again due to configuration differences

Without the use of third-party or custom-developed tools, ensuring consistent server configuration across the enterprise is a difficult and time-consuming process. This process often requires manual inspection or development of PowerShell and/or SMO scripts, a skill possessed by only a small percentage of DBAs.

Discovering incorrect configurations is more often than not a result of investigating script failures, poor performance, or worse, a security breach. Such a process is commonly known as *exception-based management*. What's needed is a way of defining and applying standard configurations to groups of server instances, and either preventing or alerting on deviations from the standard. This is typically called *intent-based management*, and as you've probably guessed, that's exactly what we can now achieve using the new policy-based management feature in SQL Server 2008.

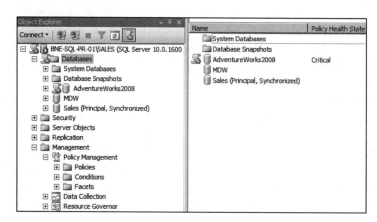

Figure 8.2 Policy-based management is found in SQL Server Management Studio under the Management node.

Figure 8.2 shows the location of policy-based management in SQL Server Management Studio along with the new *Data Collection* and *Resource Governor* features we'll cover in later chapters.

Before looking at the details of policy-based management, let's cover some of the terms used.

8.2 Policy-based management terms

New in 2008

You can think of policy-based management as Active Directory for SQL Server. Active Directory is used in simplifying the process of administering thousands of domain users and computers. In a similar manner, policy-based management is the tool of choice in ensuring consistent SQL Server configuration, and like Active Directory, its value is magnified in environments with large numbers of server instances.

There are several new terms used when discussing policy-based management: targets, facets, conditions, and policies. Let's look at each in turn.

8.2.1 Targets

A *target* is the entity managed by a policy. Depending on the policy, targets may be SQL Server instances, databases, tables, and so forth. In the example in figure 8.3, the target chosen for a table name policy is *every table in every database*.

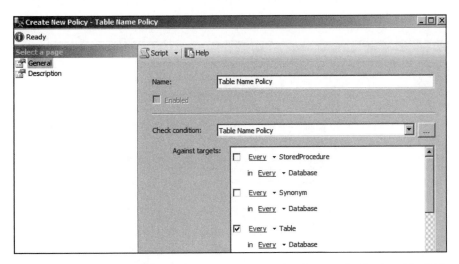

Figure 8.3   When creating a policy, you choose a target. In this example, the target for Table Name Policy is "Every Table in Every Database."

8.2.2 Facets

A *facet* is the name given to a group of configurable properties that are appropriate for a certain number of targets. For example, as shown in figure 8.4, the *Surface Area*

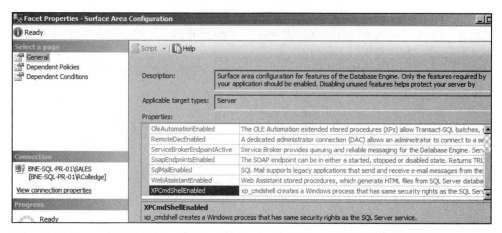

Figure 8.4   Facets, such as Surface Area Configuration, contain a number of properties that can be used in defining policy conditions.

Configuration facet, applicable to the *Server* target, contains properties such as Data-baseMailEnabled, CLRIntegrationEnabled, and XPCmdShellEnabled.

8.2.3 *Conditions*

A *condition* is created to specify the required state of one or more facet properties. Continuing our surface area configuration example, the condition shown in figure 8.5 contains the required state of ten properties belonging to the Surface Area Configuration facet.

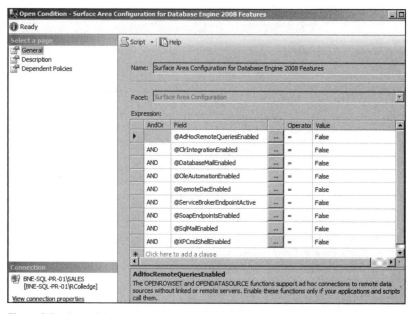

Figure 8.5   A condition contains the required value of one or more facet properties.

8.2.4 Policies

Putting it all together, a policy contains a condition, a target, and an evaluation mode, which defines how the policy conditions will be enforced. Evaluation modes, some of which are only available for certain facets, are as follows:

- *On Change–Prevent*—This mode ensures policy violations are prevented through the use of DDL triggers that roll back changes that violate policy. The mechanism used for the rollback (DDL trigger) limits the situations in which this evaluation mode can be used.
- *On Change – Log Only*—This mode logs violations when a change occurs that violates an enabled policy. Corresponding alerts can then be set up as appropriate.
- *On Schedule*—Using SQL Agent jobs, the On Schedule evaluation mode will periodically check policy compliance, and log violations if appropriate. This mode is useful in reducing the performance impact of a large number of enabled policies.
- *On Demand*—This evaluation mode is used when creating ad hoc checks. The policies are created as disabled and, as such, have no performance impact on a running instance.

With these terms in mind, let's take a look at the process of importing, creating, and evaluating policies.

8.3 Policies in action

SQL Server 2008 ships with a number of predefined policies that can be imported and evaluated. These policies encapsulate best practices such as those for securing the surface area of a SQL instance. In addition to importing these policies, new policies can be created and exported to file for later use on other server instances.

In this section, we'll start off by importing an existing policy and looking at the various evaluation options. We'll then walk through the process of creating a new policy from scratch and exporting it to file.

8.3.1 Importing policies from file

In SQL Server 2005 and earlier, tools such as Best Practices Analyzer and Baseline Security Analyzer were used to periodically check a SQL Server instance for adherence to various best practices. In SQL Server 2008, policy-based management can be used to import predefined policies that encapsulate best practice settings.

Once imported, depending on the evaluation mode, the policies remain in place, actively checking, preventing, and/or logging violations. As such, they're a stronger, more active version of previous-generation tools such as Best Practices Analyzer, and can be customized to suit a particular environment's requirements.

Importing an existing policy is straightforward. In SQL Server Management Studio simply right-click the Policies menu under Policy Management, choose Import Policy, and specify the location of the policy definition file. SQL Server 2008 ships with a number of predefined policies that can be imported. These policies are located in C:\Program Files\Microsoft SQL Server\100\Tools\Policies.

In this directory (or the equivalent installation directory) are three subdirectories containing polices for the Database Engine, together with Reporting Services and Analysis Services. The policies for Reporting and Analysis Services are limited to surface area configuration checks, and the Database Engine directory contains approximately 50 policies covering a wide variety of best practices. Here are some examples of best practices addressed by the supplied policies:

- Backup files must be on separate devices from the database files.
- Data and log files should be on separate drives.
- The default trace should be enabled.
- Max Degree of Parallelism should be less than 8.
- No unexpected system failures should be detected.
- Backups should be performed frequently.
- No I/O delay messages should be detected.

One of the nice things about the supplied policies is that some of them can be used with previous versions of SQL Server. For example, the File Growth for SQL Server 2000 policy can be used to check for the existence of SQL Server 2000 databases larger than 1GB whose AutoGrowth property is percentage based rather than a fixed size. Although policies can be defined and executed against versions of SQL Server prior to 2008, there are some restrictions, and we'll cover these (and some workarounds) later in this chapter.

In the example shown in figure 8.6, we'll import the supplied Surface Area Configuration for Database Engine 2008 Features.

Once the file is selected, the only other option we need to specify is Policy State. By default, the policy state is preserved on import—that is, if the policy is enabled in the

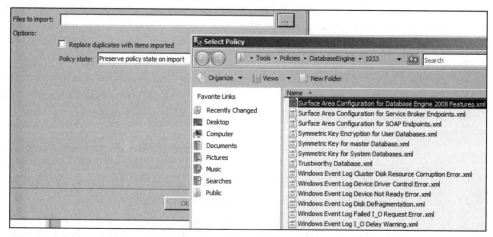

Figure 8.6   You can import existing policies to check SQL instances for compliance based on predefined configuration files.

definition file, it will be enabled on import. Alternatively, we can explicitly enable or disable the policy as part of the import process.

Now that we've imported a policy, let's look at the process of evaluating it.

8.3.2 Evaluating policies

One of the most powerful features of policy-based management is the variety of ways in which checks and violations can be defined and managed at an individual policy level.

In the previous section we covered the four evaluation modes: On Change – Prevent, On Change – Log Only, On Schedule, and On Demand. Let's take a look at an example of each of these methods, starting with On Demand.

ON DEMAND

When you create a policy using the On Demand evaluation mode, the policy is created in a disabled state. You can then use it in an ad hoc manner as required by right-clicking the policy and choosing Evaluate. Let's do this for the Surface Area Configuration policy we imported earlier. Figure 8.7 shows the evaluation results of this policy. In this example, the evaluation failed because the target server has Database Mail enabled.

In addition to clicking View to see the details of the evaluation, you can click Apply, which will reconfigure the server to be compliant with the policy.

ON CHANGE – PREVENT

You may wish to enforce certain policies so that violations are prevented from occurring. Unfortunately, this is only possible for a certain class of conditions, specifically those able to be rolled back with DDL triggers.

As an example, figure 8.8 contains the error message returned when a table create statement violates a table name condition specifying that tables must be created with a *tbl_* prefix.

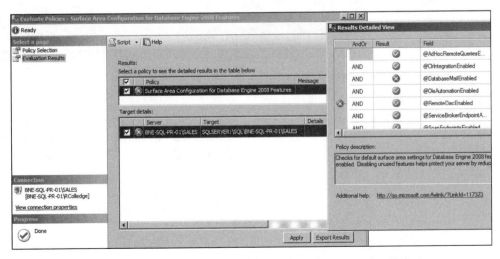

Figure 8.7   You can manually evaluate a policy by right-clicking it and choosing Evaluate.

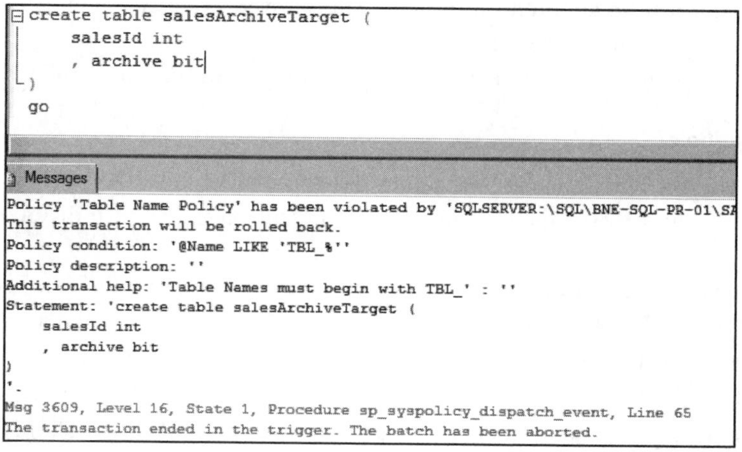

```
create table salesArchiveTarget (
    salesId int
    , archive bit
)
go
```

Messages

```
Policy 'Table Name Policy' has been violated by 'SQLSERVER:\SQL\BNE-SQL-PR-01\SA
This transaction will be rolled back.
Policy condition: '@Name LIKE 'TBL_%''
Policy description: ''
Additional help: 'Table Names must begin with TBL_' : ''
Statement: 'create table salesArchiveTarget (
    salesId int
    , archive bit
)
'.
Msg 3609, Level 16, State 1, Procedure sp_syspolicy_dispatch_event, Line 65
The transaction ended in the trigger. The batch has been aborted.
```

Figure 8.8   The On Change – Prevent evaluation mode will actively prevent changes that violate policy conditions.

ON CHANGE – LOG ONLY

Like On Change – Prevent, On Change – Log Only actively monitors for policy violations, but rather than roll back the violation, it logs the violation to the SQL Server log. Regardless of the evaluation mode, all policy failures are logged,[1] enabling custom policy failure alerts to be set up, a process we'll cover in chapter 14. Figure 8.9 shows such a policy failure error in the SQL Server log.

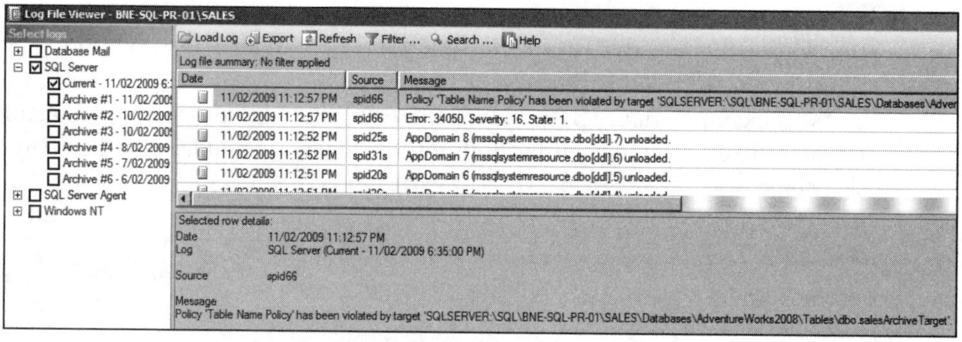

Figure 8.9   All policy violations are recorded in the SQL Server log.

ON SCHEDULE

The On Schedule evaluation mode lets you enable policies to be checked on a scheduled basis. This mode ensures that the overhead of active policy checking doesn't impact performance. When you choose this mode, the policy creator selects a schedule, which creates SQL Agent jobs to run the scheduled policy checks.

Now that we've looked at the process of importing policies and covered the evaluation modes, let's walk through the process of creating a new policy to check database properties such as AutoClose and AutoShrink.

---

[1]   Error numbers 34050 through 34053 are reserved for policy failures.

8.3.3 Creating a database properties policy

The first step in creating a new policy is to right-click Policies under Policy Management and choose New Policy. You then enter a policy name and either choose an existing condition or create a new condition.

In the example shown in figure 8.10, we'll create a policy called Database Properties Policy and create a new condition. We'll use the Database facet and specify that both AutoClose and AutoShrink should be false.

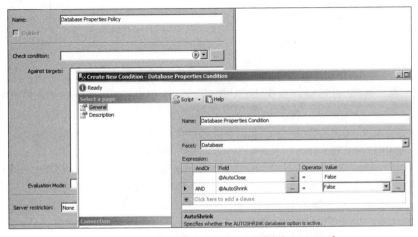

Figure 8.10   After selecting a condition's facet, we build the expression.

After clicking OK, we're returned to the policy definition screen shown in figure 8.11. Here we select Every Database for the condition's target. For the evaluation mode, we'll choose On Schedule and create a new schedule for Nightly 11PM.

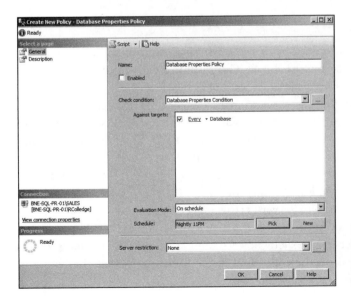

Figure 8.11   When you're creating a policy, after choosing a condition, you select the condition target and evaluation mode.

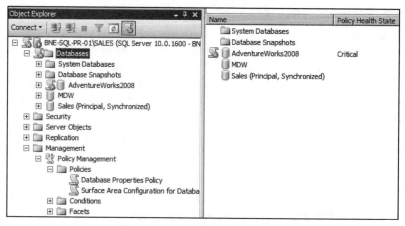

Figure 8.12   SQL Server Management Studio includes visual aids to make policy violations stand out. In this case, the AdventureWorks2008 database has failed a policy.

At this point, the policy is created and will run according to the defined schedule. One of the really useful features of the new SQL Server Management Studio is that it's aware of policy failures. As shown in figure 8.12, any server and/or database that has failed a policy will be marked with a red cross icon. In this example, the AdventureWorks2008 database is set to AutoShrink and AutoClose, contrary to the policy we just created.

To correct the policy failure, rather than manually setting these two database properties we can simply right-click the database and choose Polices > Evaluate to view the policy failure, and then click Apply to force the server's properties to comply with the policy conditions.

Once created, policies can be easily exported, and doing so enables a number of important management functions.

8.3.4   *Exporting policies*

Policies can be exported in one of two ways. First, you can simply right-click an existing policy and choose Export Policy. The resulting dialog box allows you to select a location in which to save the XML-based policy file.

The other method is based on an instance facet. By right-clicking on a registered SQL Server instance, you can choose Facets. The View Facets window allows you to view the instance properties on a facet-by-facet basis, but more important, you can choose the option Export Current State as Policy.

Figure 8.13 shows the Server Performance facet of the BNE-SQL-PR-01\SALES instance. By clicking the Export Current State as Policy button, we're able to create a new policy file based on the Server Performance properties of this server.

The importance of this function can't be overstated; essentially, we're able to configure a single server to be exactly how we want all servers to be configured, and then create policies based on the individual facets. Doing so makes the configuration of multiple servers very simple, a process we'll cover next.

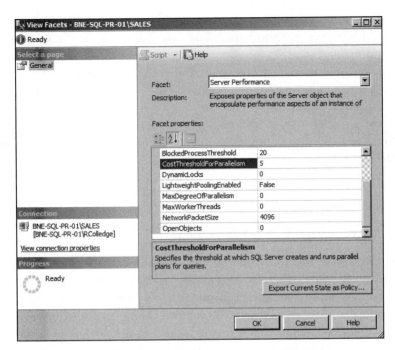

Figure 8.13 The Export Current State as Policy button allows us to create a policy file based on an instance's facet configuration.

8.4 Enterprise policy management

In opening this chapter, we discussed the challenges faced by a DBA in maintaining consistent best practice configuration across many SQL Server instances. We've looked at the new policy-based management feature and how it can be used to create, import, and evaluate policies.

Although the new feature is unquestionably useful, there still remains a significant challenge in being able to deal with instances running into the hundreds or thousands, particularly when the instances are spread across a number of categories such as production, test, and development, each of which may have individual configuration requirements.

What's really needed is a way of defining a template server for each environment, and then applying the configuration of that server to all other servers in that category, for example, *make all those production servers just like this one*. Using policy-based management in conjunction with *central management servers* allows us to do exactly that.

Before we look at combining these two features, let's start with a look at central management servers.

8.4.1 Central management servers

In SQL Server 2005 we could use the *registered servers* feature to register and group frequently managed servers. For example, we could create a production group, containing multiple production servers, and a test group containing multiple test servers. By exporting the registration information to file, DBAs could import it and quickly see the same groups and servers in their copy of SQL Server Management Studio.

In SQL Server 2008, this facility still exists, and it's referred to as *local server groups*. In addition to this feature, we now have *central management servers*. Unlike local server groups, central management servers store the group and server registration details within the server itself, thereby avoiding the import/export process. This way, DBAs can simply register an existing central management server and automatically see its groups and registered servers.

Unlike local server groups, central management servers only support the registration of servers using Windows authentication mode. As such, even though multiple DBAs can register the central management server, they'll only have access to the registered servers if permitted via Windows authentication.

Along with the ability to share a central repository of registration information, configuration servers enable two additional features: the ability to run a query against multiple servers simultaneously, and the ability to evaluate a policy against multiple servers.

In the example in figure 8.14, BNE-SQL-PR-01\CONFIG has been registered as a central management server with a production servers group containing the BNE-SQL-PR-01\Marketing and BNE-SQL-PR-01\Sales instances. By clicking Production Servers and then New Query, we can execute a query against all servers in the group. The result set includes an extra column to enable us to distinguish results from the different servers.

One of the things to note about figure 8.14 is the red/pink status bar at the bottom of the screen denoting that this is a multiserver query. *Production Servers* is included in the status bar to help us easily determine which group of servers the query was executed against. In fact, when registering a server (including through the central management servers feature) we can use the Connection Properties page to associate a custom color with the registration. That way, all subsequent queries against the registered server will display this color in the status bar. Such a feature comes in handy for those who accidentally run queries in the wrong environment!

From a policy perspective, central management servers provide a huge benefit, as we'll see next.

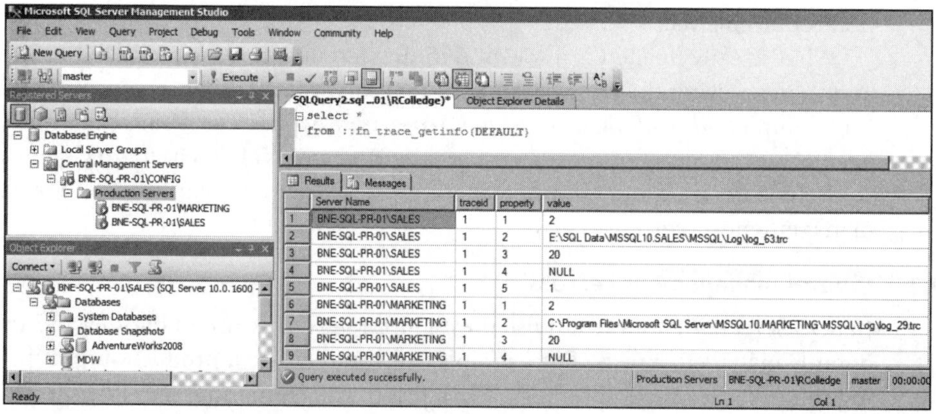

Figure 8.14 You can run multiserver queries against central management server groups. The result set includes an extra column for the server name.

8.4.2   *Policy-based management with central management servers*

Earlier in the chapter we covered the process of importing and evaluating a policy against a single server. Using central management servers, we're able to do that against all of the registered servers in one action. Further, each server that fails policy validation can then be configured at the click of a button.

To demonstrate, let's use the central management server from figure 8.14. Under the Production Servers group, we have two registered servers. In a real-world enterprise environment, we'd obviously have more servers and more groups. Let's right-click on the Production Servers group and select Evaluate Policies.

In the window that opens (shown in figure 8.15), we can select the location of a policy file. This can be either one of the predefined policies or one that we've exported from an existing instance. Let's select the predefined Surface Area Configuration policy.

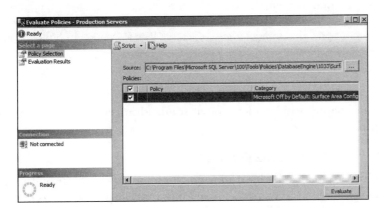

Figure 8.15   After right-clicking a central management server group and choosing Evaluate Policies, we can choose the policy source and click Evaluate.

By clicking Evaluate, we're evaluating the policy across all of the servers in the configuration group. In our example, as shown in figure 8.16, one of the servers passed validation and one failed. The great thing about evaluating policies in this manner is that you can reconfigure servers that fail validation by simply selecting the check box next to that server name and clicking Apply.

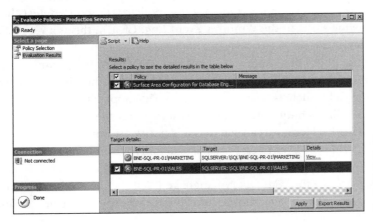

Figure 8.16   Evaluating a policy against a central management server group lets you evaluate and reconfigure groups of servers in a single step.

In the introduction to this chapter we spoke about the problem of coming into a poorly managed environment and being presented with the task of assessing a large number of servers for best practice. By grouping the servers with central management servers, you can validate policies across groups of servers, and you can easily reconfigure those that fail validation by clicking the Apply button.

Once they're configured, you can import policies into each of the servers with a scheduled evaluation mode to ensure their ongoing compliance. To make this even easier, import the policies against a central management server group, which will perform the import against each of the servers in the group.

Documentation

At best, documenting server configuration produces an historical snapshot of how a server looked at a given moment. At worst, it's a monumental waste of time, particularly if the configuration changes in an uncontrolled manner. In contrast, policy-based management provides a much more efficient "living" document of server configuration. Better still, its Apply function enables simple reconfiguration should the server deviate from the desired state.

Let's wrap up this chapter with a brief look at some advanced policy-based management techniques.

8.5   *Advanced policy-based management*

The policies we've looked at so far have all been based on *static* server properties, such as checking the value of various surface area configuration properties to determine whether xp_cmdshell is enabled. In this section, we'll look at ways of enabling more advanced, or *dynamic*, policy checks. We'll also cover the benefits of combining policy-based management with PowerShell.

8.5.1   *ExecuteWql() and ExecuteSql()*

Earlier in the chapter we covered some of the policies included with SQL Server 2008 that can be imported for evaluation. One of these policies is used to detect the presence of I/O delay messages in the Windows Event Log. Clearly, this is a very different type of policy from those we've covered so far.

Let's import the policy file Windows Event Log I_O Delay Warning.xml and have a look at its condition. As shown in figure 8.17, we can see that rather than use one of the familiar condition fields such as @AutoClose, it uses what appears to be a function call.

By clicking the ellipsis button next to the field, we enter the Advanced Edit mode, as shown in figure 8.18. Here, we can see that this policy uses the ExecuteWql() function to query the Windows Event Log for a particular error event code.

The ExecuteWql() function permits you to use Windows Management Instrumentation (WMI), specifically the WMI Query Language (WQL), to query the operating system for information. The usage shown here is one example of a nearly limitless number of possible uses.

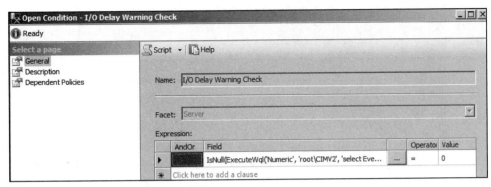

Figure 8.17 The condition definition of the Windows Event Log I/O Delay Warning Check policy uses the ExecuteWql function.

Note in figure 8.18 the other functions available. Directly above `ExecuteWql()` is `Exe-cuteSql()`, which you can use to run a traditional T-SQL query. In a similar manner to `ExecuteWql()`, this function can run any T-SQL code, and can therefore be used to create flexible and powerful policies.

When using the `ExecuteSql()` function, you must keep in mind a few things. First, the value returned needs to be something that can be evaluated in the condition editor. For example, you can use a case statement to return a single numeric value and compare that to an expected value in the condition editor.

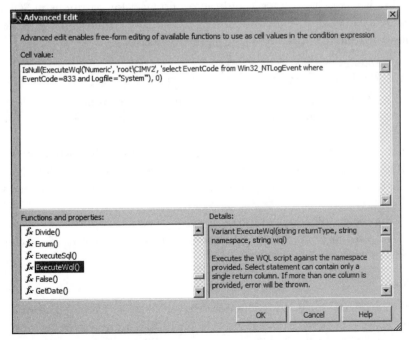

Figure 8.18 The Advanced Edit mode lets you use functions such as ExecuteWql() and ExecuteSql() to create advanced policies.

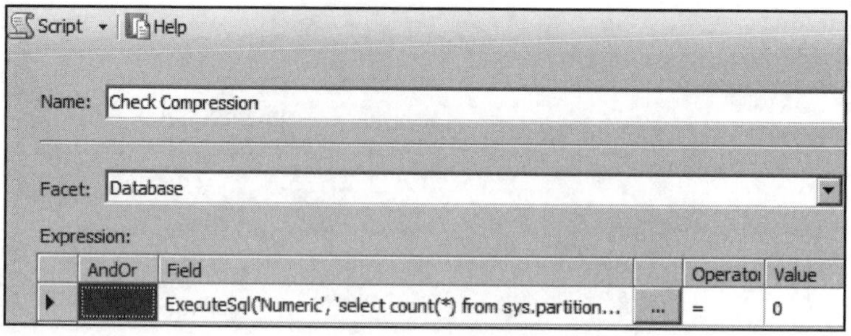

Figure 8.19   **Use a custom expression to check for the existence of uncompressed tables.**

Second, given the fact that ExecuteSql() accepts and runs *any* SQL (including delete statements), take into account the security implications. One of the new fixed database roles in the MSDB database is called PolicyAdministratorRole. Members of this role are able to execute policy checks. To prevent such users from executing ExecuteSql()-based policies that elevate their privileges, the ##MS_PolicyTsqlExecutionLogin## SQL Server login is used as a proxy account for the execution of this function. As such, not only does this login have to be enabled, the appropriate permissions need to granted on the objects referenced in the ExecuteSql() function.

Despite the wide range of facets and included policies, certain aspects of SQL Server instances and databases can't be checked in SQL Server 2008. An example is checking that all tables use data compression (covered in the next chapter). Data compression is a *partition* property, and there's no facet for partitions in SQL Server 2008. As such, you could use the ExecuteSql() function to query for the existence of any tables that aren't compressed, using a function like this:

```
Executesql('Numeric', 'select count(*)
from sys.partitions p where p.data_compression=0')
```

If the results of this query return a nonzero value, that means tables are present that aren't compressed. You'd use such a function in a condition like the one shown in figure 8.19.

Both the ExecuteSql() and ExecuteWql() functions, fully documented in SQL Server BOL, enable you to create policies with almost limitless flexibility, and could potentially be used to check policy compliance of items completely unrelated to SQL Server.

In closing the chapter, let's examine how SQL Server's support of PowerShell can be used to overcome some of the limitations with using policy-based management against earlier versions of SQL Server.

8.5.2   *PowerShell*

Released in 2006 and included in Windows Server 2008, *Windows PowerShell* is a command line–based scripting language used to perform administrative tasks using *cmdlets*. SQL Server 2008 is PowerShell aware and exposes its management interface via its own cmdlets.

Earlier in the chapter we briefly covered the ability to evaluate policies against earlier versions of SQL Server. For example, by registering a SQL Server 2005 instance with the 2008 Management Studio tool, you can right-click 2005 objects and manually evaluate policies. What you *can't* do (without using PowerShell) is store policies *within* a 2005 instance for scheduled evaluation as you can with a 2008 instance.

Enter PowerShell. Using the Invoke-PolicyEvaluation cmdlet, you can evaluate policies against SQL Server instances (2000, 2005, or 2008) as a PowerShell script. SQL Server 2008 also includes the ability to run PowerShell-based SQL Agent job steps, so the combination of these two features enables you to schedule policy evaluation against a variety of SQL Server versions.

Right-click a SQL Server 2008 instance in Management Studio and click Start PowerShell, to open a PowerShell interface from which you can (among other things) evaluate a policy. In the example shown in figure 8.20, after using the `sl` command to change directory to the location containing the policy files, we've used the Invoke-PolicyEvaluation cmdlet to evaluate a policy against a SQL Server 2005 instance using the PowerShell interface.

As you can see in the Result column, the server failed evaluation. One of the nice things about the Invoke-PolicyEvaluation cmdlet is the variety of parameters it takes, a few of which are as follows:

- The `-Policy` option is used to specify the required policy to execute. An alternate use of this option is to supply a comma-separated list of policies, allowing multiple policies to be executed as part of the one command.
- The `gci` option allows Invoke-PolicyEvaluation to receive input from a pipe. For example, `gci | Invoke-PolicyEvaluation -TargetServer "BNE-SQL-PR-01\SQL2005"` will evaluate every policy in the current directory against the specified server.
- `-OutputXml` allows you to direct the output of the evaluation to a file for later inspection. This option is particularly useful when running scheduled evaluations.
- `-AdHocPolicyExecutionMode "Configure"` implements the policy conditions. Should the evaluation fail, the server will be reconfigured according to the policy.

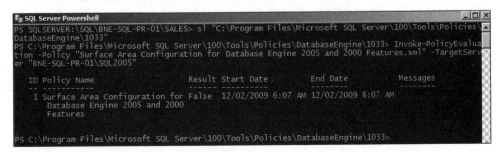

Figure 8.20   Using the Invoke-PolicyEvaluation cmdlet to evaluate a policy using the PowerShell interface

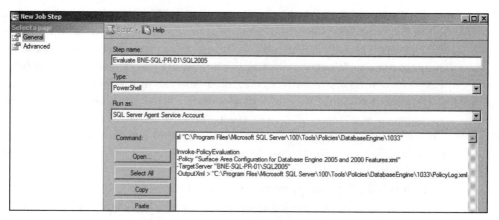

Figure 8.21   Creating a SQL Agent Job step to execute a PowerShell script enables the scheduled evaluation of policies against a SQL Server 2000/2005 instance.

So in order to schedule policy checks against earlier SQL Server versions, we can take our policy script and create a PowerShell-based SQL Server Agent job step, as shown in figure 8.21. Note that we formatted the script for visibility by adding extra line breaks.

We can optionally enhance the job step using the additional parameters described earlier to reconfigure the server in case it fails evaluation and/or to evaluate multiple policies at once.

In summary, the combination of policy-based management, central management servers, and PowerShell cmdlets enables a whole new level of powerful management possibilities for the enterprise DBA.

8.6   *Best practice considerations: policy-based management*

As an enterprise DBA who struggles with best practice implementation on a daily basis, I'm excited about the potential of policy-based management:

- Policies (and their evaluation history) are stored in the MSDB database. You should back up this database on a regular basis, or at least each time a policy definition changes.

- Implement proactive DBA checks as automated policies where possible. As well as saving time that can be spent on other tasks such as performance baselining, creating policies enables you to configure new servers faster and more reliably than with manual methods.

- Create central management servers to maximize the power of policy-based management. Where classes of servers exist, such as production, test, and development, use individual central management server groups to check groups of servers in a single action.

- If using the On Change - Prevent mode, ensure the policies are tested in a load-testing environment for their potential performance impact. If a measurable impact is detected, implement policies as On Schedule.

- Consider creating alerts for policy violations. All policy failures are logged to the SQL Server error log with an error code of 34050 through 34053.
- If you use the `ExecuteSQL()` function to create custom policy conditions, ensure the permissions of the ##MS_PolicyTsqlExecutionLogin## account are set to the minimum required, particularly if you're using the MSDB PolicyAdministratorRole.

Additional information on the best practices covered in this chapter can be found online at http://www.sqlCrunch.com/policy.

Throughout this chapter, we've touched on a number of database properties such as AutoClose and AutoShrink. In the next chapter, we'll expand on these properties further when we look at the topic of data management.

Data management

In this chapter, we'll cover

- Database files
- Filegroups
- FileStream data
- Data compression

A significant percentage of SQL Server performance and administration problems stem from poor choices in laying out and sizing database files. By default, a database has a single data and log file, both of which are located in the same directory and set to automatically grow by small amounts. With the exception of the smallest databases, such a configuration is almost guaranteed to constrain performance, increase disk fragmentation, and lead to various other administration challenges, particularly with large databases and/or those with high usage rates.

Successful database administration requires a solid understanding of database file layout, sizing, and management strategies. In this chapter, we'll begin by exploring database file configuration, including volume separation and initial size. We'll then take a look at using secondary filegroups and their performance and administration benefits.

We'll conclude the chapter with coverage of two significant new data management features introduced in SQL Server 2008: FileStream and data compression.

9.1 Database file configuration

In previous chapters, we've seen how default SQL Server installations come with good out-of-the-box settings that lessen administration requirements, strengthen security, and maximize performance. When it comes to individual databases, there are a number of recommended configuration steps that SQL Server doesn't perform, in large part due to dependencies on disk configuration and unknown future usage of the databases.

Before covering specific file configuration recommendations, let's address some of the terms used when discussing database files:

- *Primary data file*—The primary data file, and by default the *only* data file, contains system tables and information on all files within a database. By default, this file has an .mdf extension. If there are no other files in the database, the primary file also contains user objects such as tables and indexes.
- *Secondary data file*—Secondary files, which usually have an .ndf extension, are optional files that can be added to a database for performance and/or administrative benefits, both of which we'll cover shortly. A database can contain one or more secondary files.
- *Filegroups*—Every database contains a primary filegroup, containing at least the primary data file, and possibly all secondary data files unless other filegroups are created and used. Filegroups are logical containers that group together one or more data files, and as we'll see later in the chapter, provide several benefits.
- *Transaction log file*—Typically using the .ldf extension, the transaction log file records details of each database modification and is used for various purposes, including transaction log shipping, replication, database mirroring, and recovery of a database to a consistent state.

With these terms in mind, let's cover some of the major file configuration recommendations, starting with separating a database's different storage objects across separate physical disk volumes.

9.1.1 Volume separation

By default, a database is created with a single data and transaction log file. Unless specified during installation or modified during database creation, both of these files will be created in the same directory, with the default size and growth rates inherited from the model database.

As shown in figure 9.1, an important database file configuration task, particularly for databases with direct-attached storage, is to provide separate physical RAID-protected disk volumes for data, transaction log, tempdb, and backup files.

As we covered in chapter 2, designing SAN-based virtualized storage is quite different from designing direct-attached storage; that being said, the principles of high performance and fault tolerance remain. In both cases, a good understanding of SQL Server's various storage objects is crucial in designing an appropriate storage system. Let's walk through these now, beginning with the transaction log file.

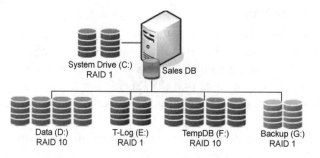

Figure 9.1   An example physical disk design with separate RAID volumes for data, log, tempdb, and backup files

TRANSACTION LOG FILE

Unlike random access to data files, transaction logs are written sequentially. If a disk is dedicated to a single database's transaction log, the disk heads can stay in position writing sequentially, thus increasing transaction throughput. In contrast, a disk that stores a combination of data and transaction logs won't achieve the same levels of throughput given that the disk heads will be moving between the conflicting requirements of random data access/updates and sequential transaction log entries. For database applications with high transaction rates, separation of data and transaction logs in this manner is crucial.

BACKUP FILES

A common (and recommended) backup technique, covered in detail in the next chapter, is to back up databases to disk files and archive the disk backup files to tape at a later point in the day. The most optimal method for doing this is to have dedicated disk(s) for the purpose of storing backups. Dedicated backup disks provide several benefits:

- *Disk protection*—Consider a case where the database files and the backup files are on the same disk. Should the disk fail, both the database *and* the backups are lost, a disastrous situation! Storing backups on separate disk(s) prevents this situation from occurring—either the database or the backups will be available.

- *Increased throughput*—Substantial performance gains come from multiple disks working in unison. During backup, the disks storing the database data files are dedicated to reading the files, and the backup disks are dedicated to writing backup file(s). In contrast, having both the data and backup files on the same disk will substantially slow the backup process.

- *Cost-effective*—The backup disks may be lower-cost, higher-capacity SATA disks, with the data disks being more expensive, RAID-protected SCSI or SAS disks.

- *Containing growth*—The last thing you want is a situation where a backup consumes all the space on the data disk, effectively stopping the database from being used. Having dedicated backup disks prevents this problem from occurring.

TEMPDB DATABASE

Depending on the database usage profile, the tempdb database may come in for intense and sustained usage. By providing dedicated disks for tempdb, the impact on other databases will be reduced while increasing performance for databases heavily reliant on it.

WINDOWS SYSTEM AND PROGRAM FILES

SQL data files shouldn't be located on the same disks as Windows system and program files. The best way of ensuring this is to provide dedicated disks for SQL Server data, log, backups and tempdb.

> ### Mount points
>
> A frequently cited reason for not creating dedicated disk volumes for the objects we've covered so far is the lack of available drive letters, particularly in clustered servers used for consolidating a large number of databases and/or database instances. *Mount points* address this problem by allowing a physically separate disk volume to be grafted onto an existing volume, therefore enabling a single drive letter to contain multiple physically separate volumes. Mount points are fully supported in Windows Server 2003 and 2008.

For small databases with low usage, storing everything on a single disk may work perfectly fine, but as the usage and database size increases, file separation is a crucial configuration step in ensuring the ongoing performance and stability of database servers.

In addition to increasing throughput, creating physically separate storage volumes enables I/O bottlenecks to be spotted much more easily, particularly with the introduction of the new Activity Monitor, covered in chapter 14, which breaks down response time per disk volume.

As with object separation across physically separate disk volumes, using multiple data files isn't a default setting, yet deserves consideration given its various advantages.

9.1.2   *Multiple data files*

A common discussion point on database file configuration is based on the number of data files that should be created for a database. For example, should a 100GB database contain a single file, four 25GB files, or some other combination? In answering this question, we need to consider both performance and manageability.

PERFORMANCE

A common performance-tuning recommendation is to create one file per CPU core available to the database instance. For example, a SQL Server instance with access to two quad-core CPUs should create eight database files. While having multiple data files is certainly recommended for the tempdb database, it isn't necessarily required for user databases.

The one file per CPU core suggestion is useful in avoiding *allocation contention* issues. As we'll see in chapter 12, each database file holds an allocation bitmap used for allocating space to objects within the file. The tempdb database, by its very nature, is used for the creation of short-term objects used for various purposes. Given tempdb is used by all databases within a SQL Server instance, there's potentially a very large number of objects being allocated each second; therefore, using multiple files enables contention on a single allocation bitmap to be reduced, resulting in higher throughput.

It's very rare for a user database to have allocation contention. Therefore, splitting a database into multiple files is primarily done to enable the use of filegroups (covered later in the chapter) and/or for manageability reasons.

MANAGEABILITY

Consider a database configured with a single file stored on a 1TB disk partition with the database file currently 900GB. A migration project requires the database to be moved to a new server that has been allocated three 500GB drives. Obviously the 900GB file won't fit into any of the three new drives. There are various ways of addressing this problem, but avoiding it by using multiple smaller files is arguably the easiest.

In a similar manner, multiple smaller files enable additional flexibility in overcoming a number of other storage-related issues. For example, if a disk drive is approaching capacity, it's much easier (and quicker) to detach a database and move one or two smaller files than it is to move a single large file.

TRANSACTION LOG

As we've covered earlier, transaction log files are written to in a sequential manner. Although it's possible to create more than one transaction log file per database, there's no benefit in doing so.

Some DBAs create multiple transaction log files in a futile attempt at increasing performance. Transaction log performance is obtained through other strategies we've already covered, such as using dedicated disk volumes, implementing faster disks, using a RAID 10 volume, and ensuring the disk controller has sufficient write cache.

For both transaction logs and data files, sizing the files correctly is crucial in avoiding disk fragmentation and poor performance.

9.1.3   *Sizing database files*

One of the major benefits of SQL Server is that it offers multiple features that enable databases to continue running with very little administrative effort, but such features often come with downsides. One such feature, as shown in figure 9.2, is the *Enable Autogrowth* option, which enables a database file to automatically expand when full.

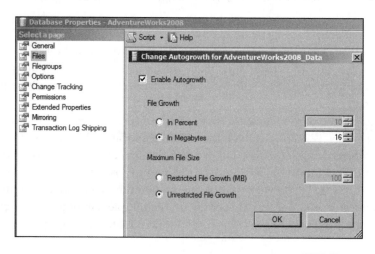

Figure 9.2   Despite the lower administration overhead, the Enable Autogrowth option should not be used in place of database presizing and proactive maintenance routines.

The problem with the autogrowth feature is that every time the file grows, all activity on the file is suspended until the growth operation is complete. If enabled, instant initialization (covered shortly) reduces the time required for such actions, but clearly the better alternative is to initialize the database files with an appropriate size before the database begins to be used. Doing so not only avoids autogrowth operations but also reduces disk fragmentation.

Consider a worst case scenario: a database is created with all of the default settings. The file size and autogrowth properties will be inherited from the model database, which by default has a 3MB data file set to autogrow in 1MB increments and a 1MB log file with 10 percent autogrowth increments. If the database is subjected to a heavy workload, autogrowth increments will occur every time the file is increased by 1MB, which could be *many* times per second. Worse, the transaction log increases by 10 percent per autogrowth; after many autogrowth operations, the transaction log will be increasing by large amounts for each autogrowth, a problem exacerbated by the fact that transaction logs can't use instant initialization.

In addition to appropriate presizing, part of a proactive database maintenance routine should be regular inspections of space usage within a database and transaction log. By observing growth patterns, the files can be manually expanded by an appropriate size ahead of autogrowth operations.

Despite the negative aspects of autogrowth, it's useful in handling unexpected surges in growth that can otherwise result in out-of-space errors and subsequent downtime. The best use of this feature is for emergencies only, and not as a replacement for adequate presizing and proactive maintenance. Further, the autogrowth amounts should be set to appropriate amounts; for example, setting a database to autogrow in 1MB increments isn't appropriate for a database that grows by 10GB per day.

Given its unique nature, presizing database files is of particular importance for the tempdb database.

TEMPDB

The tempdb database, used for the temporary storage of various objects, is unique in that it's re-created each time SQL Server starts. Unless tempdb's file sizes are manually altered, the database will be re-created with default (very small) file sizes each time SQL Server is restarted. For databases that make heavy use of tempdb, this often manifests itself as very sluggish performance for quite some time after a SQL Server restart, with many autogrowth operations required before an appropriate tempdb size is reached.

To obtain the ideal starting size of tempdb files, pay attention to the size of tempdb once the server has been up and running for enough time to cover the full range of database usage scenarios, such as index rebuilds, DBCC operations, and user activity. Ideally these observations come from load simulation in volume-testing environments before a server is commissioned for production. Bear in mind that any given SQL Server instance has a single tempdb database shared by all user databases, so use across all databases must be taken into account during any load simulation.

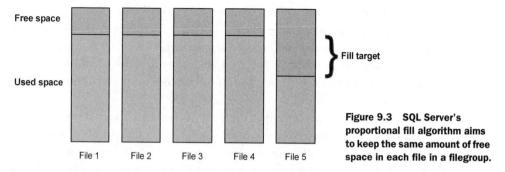

Figure 9.3 SQL Server's proportional fill algorithm aims to keep the same amount of free space in each file in a filegroup.

One other aspect you should consider when sizing database files, particularly when using multiple files, is SQL Server's *proportional fill* algorithm.

PROPORTIONAL FILL

When a database filegroup (covered shortly) uses multiple data files, SQL Server fills each file evenly using a technique called *proportional fill*, as shown in figure 9.3.

If one file has significantly more free space than others, SQL Server will use that file until the free space is roughly the same as the other files. If using multiple database files in order to overcome allocation contention, this is particularly important and care should be taken to size each database file the same and grow each database file by the same amount.

We've mentioned instant initialization a number of times in this chapter. In closing this section, let's take a closer look at this important feature.

9.1.4 *Instant initialization*

In versions of SQL Server prior to 2005, files were *zero padded* on creation and during manual or autogrowth operations. In SQL Server 2005 and above, the instant initialization feature avoids the need for this process, resulting in faster database initialization, growth, and restore operations.

Other than reducing the impact of autogrowth operations, a particularly beneficial aspect of instant initialization is in disaster-recovery situations. Assuming a database is being restored as a new database, the files must first be created before the data can be restored; for recovering very large databases, creating and zero padding files can take a significant amount of time, therefore increasing downtime. In contrast, instant initialization avoids the zero pad process and therefore reduces downtime, the benefits of which increase linearly with the size of the database being restored.

The instant initialization feature, available only for data files (not transaction log files), requires the SQL Server service account to have the Perform Volume Maintenance Tasks privilege. Local Admin accounts automatically have this privilege, but as we discussed in chapter 6, this isn't recommended from a least privilege perspective; therefore, you have to manually grant the service account this permission to take advantage of the instant initialization feature.

Earlier in the section we explored the various reasons for using multiple data files for a database. A common reason for doing so is to enable us to use *filegroups*.

Figure 9.4 The default filegroup structure consists of a single filegroup called *primary* with a single file containing all system and user-created objects.

9.2 Filegroups

As we covered earlier, you can think of filegroups as logical containers for database disk files. As shown in figure 9.4, the default configuration for a new database is a single filegroup called *primary*, which contains one data file in which all database objects are stored.

Before we cover recommended filegroup configurations, let's look at some of the ways in which filegroups are used (and abused), beginning with controlling object placement.

9.2.1 Controlling object placement

A common performance-tuning recommendation is to create tables on one filegroup and indexes on another (or some other combination), with each filegroup containing files on dedicated disks. For example, Filegroup 1 (tables) contains files on a RAID volume containing 10 disks with Filegroup 2 (indexes) containing files on a separate RAID volume, also containing 10 disks.

The theory behind such configurations is that groups of disks will operate in parallel to improve throughput. For example, disks 1–10 will be dedicated to table scans and seeks while index scans and seeks can operate in parallel on another dedicated group of disks.

Although it's true that this can improve performance in *some* cases, it's also true that in most cases it's a much better option to have simpler filegroup structures containing more disks. In the previous example, the alternative to two filegroups each containing 10 disks is to have one filegroup containing 20. In simpler configurations such as this, each database object has more disk spindles to be striped across.

Generally speaking, unless the data access patterns are very well known, simpler filegroup structures are almost always a better alternative, unless alternate configurations can be proven in load-testing environments.

Another common use for filegroups is for backup and restore flexibility.

9.2.2 Backup and restore flexibility

As we'll cover in the next chapter, filegroups offer a way of bringing a database online before the full database restore operation is complete. Known as *piecemeal restore*, this feature is invaluable in reducing downtime in recovery situations.

Without going into too much detail (full coverage in the next chapter), piecemeal restores enable the restore process to be prioritized by filegroup. For example, after

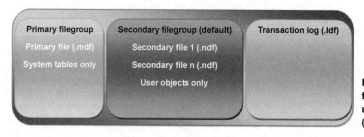

Figure 9.5   A recommended filegroup structure with all user objects stored in a (default) secondary filegroup

you restore a filegroup containing objects required for data entry, you can make a database available to users, after which you can restore an *archive* filegroup in the background. As long as the users don't require access to any of the data in the archive filegroup, they won't be affected. Therefore, the user impact is reduced by bringing the database online much faster than waiting for the full database to be restored.

In the next chapter, we'll see how the first part of a piecemeal restore is to restore the primary filegroup, after which individual filegroups can be restored in priority order. To speed up this process, best practice dictates avoiding the use of the primary filegroup for storing user objects. The best way of enabling this is to create a secondary filegroup immediately after creating a database and marking it as the *default* filegroup. Such a configuration, as shown in figure 9.5, ensures that the only objects stored in the primary filegroup are system objects, therefore making this very small, and in turn providing the fastest piecemeal restore path.

Listing 9.1 contains the T-SQL code to create a Sales database using the filegroup structure just covered. We'll create two additional filegroups: one called POS (which we'll mark as the default) and the other called Archive. The POS filegroup will contain two files and the Archive filegroup a single file.

Listing 9.1   Create a multi-filegroup database

```
CREATE DATABASE [SALES] ON PRIMARY
( NAME = N'Sales'
  , FILENAME = N'E:\SQL Data\MSSQL10.SALES\MSSQL\DATA\SalesDb.mdf'
  , SIZE = 51200KB
  , FILEGROWTH = 1024KB
)
, FILEGROUP [POS]
( NAME = N'Sales1'
  , FILENAME = N'E:\SQL Data\MSSQL10.SALES\MSSQL\DATA\SalesDb1.mdf'
  , SIZE = 51200KB
  , FILEGROWTH = 1024KB
)
,( NAME = N'Sales2'
  , FILENAME = N'E:\SQL Data\MSSQL10.SALES\MSSQL\DATA\SalesDb2.mdf'
  , SIZE = 51200KB
  , FILEGROWTH = 1024KB
)
, FILEGROUP [ARCHIVE]
( NAME = N'Sales3'
  , FILENAME = N'E:\SQL Data\MSSQL10.SALES\MSSQL\DATA\SalesDb3.mdf'
```

```
  , SIZE = 51200KB
  , FILEGROWTH = 1024KB
)
LOG ON
(
  NAME = N'SalesLog'
  , FILENAME = N'F:\SQL Log\SalesDbLog.ldf'
  , SIZE = 51200KB
  , FILEGROWTH = 1024KB
)
GO

ALTER DATABASE [SALES]
MODIFY FILEGROUP [POS] DEFAULT
GO
```

By specifying POS as the default filegroup, we'll avoid storing user objects in the primary filegroup and thus enable the fastest piecemeal restore process. Any object creation statement (such as a CREATE TABLE command) will create the object in the POS filegroup unless another filegroup is explicitly specified as part of the creation statement.

Partitioned tables

Filegroups are a fundamental component of *partitioned tables*. Although beyond the scope of this book, partitioned tables can be used in the creation of sophisticated sliding window scenarios whereby large chunks of data can be moved into (and out of) a table with little or no user impact. As such, they're ideal in archiving and data warehouse solutions.

Next up, you'll learn about a special type of filegroup in SQL Server 2008 that's used for storing FileStream data.

9.3   *BLOB storage with FileStream*

Prior to 2008, SQL Server–based applications used one of two methods for storing binary large objects (BLOBs) such as video, images, or documents (PDFs, docs, and so forth). The first method was to store the object within the database in an *image* or *varbinary(max)* column. Alternatively, BLOBs were stored in file system files, with a link to the file (hyperlink/path) stored in a table column.

Both of these methods have their pros and cons. SQL Server 2008 introduces a third method known as *FileStream*. This method lets you combine the benefits of both of the previous methods while avoiding their drawbacks.

Before we continue, keep in mind that character-based BLOBs are often referred to as *CLOBs*, or *character large objects*. In some texts, BLOBs and CLOBs are referred to collectively as *LOBs*, or *large objects*. For the purposes of this section, we'll use the term BLOBs to refer to either binary large objects or character large objects.

Before we cover the new FileStream option, let's briefly cover the details of the previous methods of BLOB storage, both of which are still supported in SQL Server 2008.

9.3.1   *BLOBS in the database*

SQL Server's storage engine is designed and optimized for storage of normal relational data such as integer and character-based data. A fundamental design component of the SQL Server engine is the 8K page size, which limits the maximum size of each record. All but the smallest BLOBs exceed this size, so SQL Server can't store them *in row* like the rest of the record's data.

To get around the 8K limitation, SQL Server breaks the BLOB up into 8K chunks and stores them in a B-tree structure, as shown in figure 9.6, with a pointer to the root of the tree stored in the record's BLOB column.

Prior to SQL Server 2005, the primary data type for in-database BLOB storage was the image data type. SQL Server 2005 introduced the varbinary(max) data type to overcome some of the image limitations, discussed next.

IMAGE AND TEXT DATA TYPES

The primary data type used for binary-based BLOB storage prior to SQL Server 2005 is the image data type, and the text data type supports character-based BLOBs (CLOBs). Both data types provide support for BLOBs up to 2GB.[1] Still supported in SQL Server 2008, these data types have a number of drawbacks that limit their usefulness, chiefly the inability to declare image or text variables in T-SQL batches. As such, accessing and importing BLOB data required a combination of programming techniques, reducing the appeal of in-database BLOB storage somewhat.

VARBINARY(MAX) AND VARCHAR(MAX)

Introduced in SQL Server 2005, the *varbinary(max)* data type, and its text equivalents *varchar(max)* and *nvarchar(max)*, overcome the limitations of the image and text data types by providing support for variable declaration and a range of other operations.

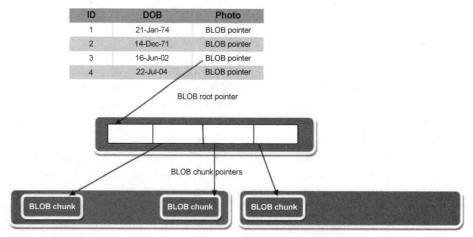

Figure 9.6   SQL Server implements support for BLOB storage by using a pointer to a B-tree structure in which BLOBs are broken up into 8K chunks and linked using pointers.

---

[1]   The NTEXT data type, used for Unicode, supports up to 1GB of data.

Such support makes BLOB access and importing much simpler than the equivalent process in SQL Server 2000 with image and text data types. Here's an example:

```
-- Insert a jpg file into a table using OPENROWSET
INSERT INTO clients (ID, DOB, Photo)
SELECT 1, '21 Jan 1974', BulkColumn
FROM OPENROWSET (Bulk 'F:\photos\client_1.jpg', SINGLE_BLOB) AS blob
```

As a BLOB storage strategy, in-database storage allows BLOBS to be tightly coupled with the related data. The BLOBS are transactionally consistent—that is, updates on the BLOB are rolled forward or back in line with the rest of the record, and included in backup and restore operations. All good so far. The downside, however, is significant. For databases with large numbers of BLOBs, or even moderate amounts of very large BLOBs, the database size can become massive and difficult to manage. In turn, performance can suffer.

In addressing these concerns, a common design is to store BLOBs in the file system with an appropriate reference or hyperlink stored in the column.

9.3.2 *BLOBS in the file system*

The alternative to storing BLOBs in the database is to store them in their native format as normal files in the file system. Windows NTFS is much better at file storage than SQL Server, so it makes sense to store them there and include a simple link in the database. Further, this approach lets you store BLOBs on lower-cost storage, driving down overall costs.

An example of this approach is shown in figure 9.7. Here, the table contains a photolink column storing the path to a file system–based file.

	id	dob	photolink
1	1	1977-01-18	f:\photos\client1.jpg
2	2	1905-12-01	f:\photos\client2.jpg
3	3	1967-03-22	f:\photos\client3.jpg
4	4	1991-09-30	f:\photos\client4.jpg

Figure 9.7 Rather than store the BLOB in the database, an alternate approach is to simply store the link to the file in the database.

The problem with this approach is twofold; the data in the database is no longer transactionally consistent with the BLOB files, and database backups aren't guaranteed to be synchronized with the BLOBs (unless the database is shut down for the period of the backup, which isn't an option for any 24/7 system).

So on one hand we have transactional consistency and strongly coupled data at the expense of increased database size and possible performance impacts. On the other hand, we have storage simplicity and good performance at the expense of transactional consistency and backup synchronization issues. Clearly, both options have significant advantages and disadvantages; DBAs and developers often passionately argue in favor of one option over another. Enter FileStream, King of the BLOBs...

9.3.3 *FileStream data*

New in 2008

Offering the advantages of both file system and in-database storage is the *FileStream* data type, introduced in SQL Server 2008.

OVERVIEW

FileStream provides these advantages:

- BLOBs can be stored in the file system. The size of each BLOB is limited only by the NTFS volume size limitations. This overcomes the 2GB limit of previous in-database BLOB storage techniques, which prevented SQL Server from storing certain BLOB types such as large video files.
- Full transactional consistency exists between the BLOB and the database record to which it's attached.
- BLOBs are included in backup and restore operations.
- BLOB objects are accessible via both T-SQL and NTFS streaming APIs.
- Superior streaming performance is provided for large BLOB types such as MPEG video.
- The Windows system cache is used for caching the BLOB data, thus freeing up the SQL Server buffer cache required for previous in-database BLOB storage techniques.

FileStream data combines the transactional strength of SQL Server with the file management and streaming performance strengths of NTFS. Further, the ability to place FileStream BLOBs on separate, NTFS-compressed volumes provides opportunities to significantly lower overall storage costs.

Unfortunately, there are some limitations with FileStream data, which we'll come to shortly. In the meantime, let's run through the process of enabling and using FileStream.

ENABLING FILESTREAM

In chapter 4, we discussed installing SQL Server 2008. One of the steps involved choosing to enable FileStream data. Once it's installed, you can enable or disable FileStream using SQL Server Configuration Manager. Just right-click the SQL Server service for a selected instance and choose Properties, and then select the FILESTREAM tab (as shown in figure 9.8). Here you can enable FileStream for T-SQL access and optionally for file I/O streaming access.

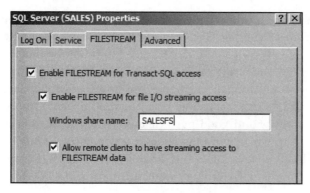

Figure 9.8 You can enable FileStream using the SQL Server Configuration Manager tool.

Once enabled through Configuration Manager (or as part of the initial installation), the SQL Server instance must then be configured as a secondary step using the sp_configure command. For example, to configure an instance for both T-SQL and Windows streaming access:

```
-- Enable FileStream Access for both T-SQL and Windows Streaming
EXEC sp_configure 'filestream access level', 2
GO
RECONFIGURE
GO
```

Here, we used 2 as the parameter value. 1 will enable FileStream access for T-SQL only, and 0 will disable FileStream for the instance. Let's take a look now at the process of creating a table containing FileStream data.

USING FILESTREAM

When creating a database containing FileStream data, the first thing we need to do is ensure there is a FileStream filegroup. In our next example, we'll create the database with a *SalesFileStreamFG* filegroup by specifying CONTAINS FILESTREAM. We also use a directory name (G:\FSDATA\SALES in this example) to specify the location of the FileStream data. For optimal performance and minimal fragmentation, disks storing FileStream data should be formatted with a 64K allocation unit size, and be placed on disk(s) separate from both data and transaction log files.

```
-- Create a database with a FILESTREAM filegroup
CREATE DATABASE [SALES] ON PRIMARY
(  NAME = Sales1
    , FILENAME = 'M:\MSSQL\Data\salesData.mdf'
)
,  FILEGROUP [SalesFileStreamFG] CONTAINS FILESTREAM
(  NAME = Sales2
    , FILENAME = 'G:\FSDATA\SALES'
)
LOG ON
(  NAME = SalesLog
    , FILENAME = 'L:\MSSQL\Data\salesLog.ldf'
)
GO
```

Next up, we'll create a table containing a column that will store FileStream data. In this example, the Photo column contains the FILESTREAM attribute with the varbinary(max) data type. Note that we're adding a UNIQUEIDENTIFIER column to the table with the ROWGUIDCOL attribute and marking it as UNIQUE. Such columns are mandatory for tables containing FileStream data. Also note the use of the FILESTREAM_ON clause, which specifies the filegroup to use for FileStream data.

```
-- Create a table with a FILESTREAM column
CREATE TABLE Sales.dbo.Customer
(
    [CustomerId] INT IDENTITY(1,1) PRIMARY KEY
    , [DOB] DATETIME NULL
    , [Photo] VARBINARY(MAX) FILESTREAM NULL
```

```
    , [CGUID] UNIQUEIDENTIFIER NOT NULL ROWGUIDCOL UNIQUE DEFAULT NEWID()
) FILESTREAM_ON [SalesFileStreamFG];
GO
```

At this point, we're ready to insert data into the column. For the purposes of this example, we'll insert a simple text fragment. A more realistic example (but beyond the scope of this book) would be an application that allows a user to specify a local JPEG image that would be streamed into the column:

```
INSERT INTO Sales.dbo.Customer (DOB, Photo)
VALUES ('21 Jan 1975', CAST ('{Photo}' as varbinary(max)));
GO
```

After inserting this record, inspection of the file system directory specified for the FileStream filegroup will reveal something similar to that shown in figure 9.9.

As you can see in figure 9.9, there is no obvious correlation between database records and FileStream file or directory names. It's not the intention of FileStream to enable direct access to the resulting FileStream data using Windows Explorer. The important thing is that SQL Server maintains transactional consistency with the data and includes it in backup and restore commands.

As mentioned earlier, there are some limitations with the FileStream data type that you should consider before implementing it.

FILESTREAM LIMITATIONS

Despite the obvious advantages covered earlier, FileStream has some restrictions that limit its use as a BLOB storage technique:

- Database mirroring, which we'll cover in chapter 11, can't be enabled on databases containing FileStream data.
- Database snapshots, covered in the next chapter, aren't capable of including FileStream data. You can create a snapshot of a database containing FileStream data, but only if you exclude the FileStream filegroup.
- FileStream data can't be encrypted; a database that uses transparent data encryption won't encrypt the FileStream data.
- Depending on the BLOB size and update pattern, you may achieve better performance by storing the BLOB inside the database, particularly for BLOBs smaller than 1MB and when partial updates are required (for example, when you're updating a small section of a large document).

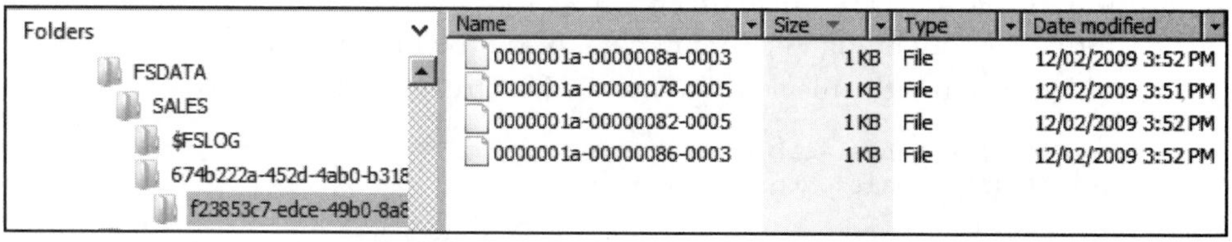

Figure 9.9 FileStream directories and files. As shown here, there is nothing obvious about FileStream directory and filenames to enable individual BLOB objects to be identified.

Of these limitations, perhaps the biggest is the inability to use database mirroring on databases containing FileStream data. In such cases, alternate BLOB storage techniques such as those covered earlier in this section are required. SQL Server Books Online (BOL) contains a number of other limitations, guidelines, and best practices for using the FileStream feature.

Despite its limitations, FileStream is a powerful new feature introduced in SQL Server 2008. The same can be said for data compression, our next topic.

9.4 Data compression

New in 2008

Predicting the future is a risky business, but if there's one thing that's guaranteed in future databases, it's an ever-growing volume of data to store, manage, and back up. Growing regulatory requirements, the plummeting cost of disk storage, and new types of information such as digitized video are converging to create what some call an *information storage explosion*. Managing this information while making it readily accessible to a wide variety of client applications is a challenge for all involved, particularly the DBA. Fortunately, SQL Server 2008 delivers a number of new features and enhancements to assist DBAs in this regard.

In the previous section we looked at the FileStream data type, which enhances the storage options for BLOB data. One of the great things about FileStream is the ability to have BLOBs stored *outside* the database on compressed NTFS volumes. Until SQL Server 2008, compressing data *inside* the database was limited to basic options such as variable-length columns, or complex options such as custom-developed compression routines.

In this section, we'll focus on a new feature in SQL Server 2008, data compression, which enables us to natively compress data inside the database without requiring any application changes. We'll begin with an overview of data compression and its advantages before looking at the two main ways in which SQL Server implements it. We'll finish with a number of important considerations in designing and implementing a compressed database.

9.4.1 Data compression overview

Data compression, available only in the Enterprise edition of SQL Server 2008, allows you to compress individual tables and indexes using either page compression or row compression, both of which we'll cover shortly. Due to its potentially adverse impact on performance, there's no option to compress the entire database in one action.

As you can see in figure 9.10, you can manage a table's compression by right-clicking it and choosing Storage > Manage Compression.

When considering compression in a broad sense, *lossy* and *lossless* are terms used to categorize the compression method used. Lossy compression techniques are used in situations where a certain level of data loss between the compressed and uncompressed file is accepted as a consequence of gaining higher and faster compression

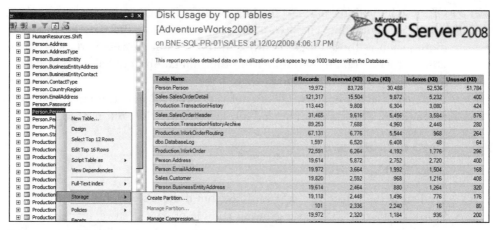

Figure 9.10   Individual tables can be selected for compression using SQL Server Management Studio.

rates. JPEG images are a good example of lossy compression, where a reduction in data quality between the original image and the compressed JPEG is acceptable. Video and audio streaming are other common applications for lossy compression. It goes without saying that lossy compression is unacceptable in a database environment.

SQL Server implements its own custom lossless compression algorithm and attempts to strike a balance between high compression rates and low CPU overhead. Compression rates and overhead will vary, and are dependent on a number of factors that we'll discuss, including fragmentation levels, the compression method chosen, and the nature of the data being compressed.

Arguably the most powerful aspect of SQL Server's implementation of data compression is the fact that the compressed data remains compressed, on disk *and* in the buffer cache, until it's actually required, at which point only the individual columns that are required are uncompressed. Compared to a file system–based compression solution, this results in the lowest CPU overhead while maximizing cache efficiency, and is clearly tailored toward the unique needs of a database management system.

Let's consider some of the benefits of data compression:

- *Lower storage costs*—Despite the rapidly decreasing cost of retail storage, storage found in high-end SANs, typically used by SQL Server implementations, is certainly *not* cheap, particularly when considering actual:usable RAID ratios and duplication of data for various purposes, as figure 9.11 shows.
- *Lower administration costs*—As databases grow in size, disk I/O–bound administration tasks such as backups, DBCC checks, and index maintenance take longer and longer. By compressing certain parts of the database, we're able to reduce the administration impact. For example, a database that's compressed to half its size will take roughly half the time to back up.[2]

---

[2] In addition to data compression, SQL Server 2008 introduces backup compression, covered in detail in the next chapter.

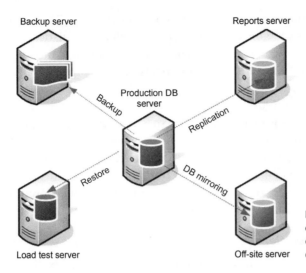

Figure 9.11 Compared to retail disk, enterprise SAN storage is expensive, a cost magnified by RAID protection and data duplication such as that shown here.

- *RAM and disk efficiency*—As mentioned earlier, compressed data read into the buffer cache will remain compressed until required, effectively boosting the buffer size. Further, as the data is compressed on disk, the same quantity of disk time will effectively read more data, thus boosting disk performance as well.

SQL Server 2008 implements two different methods of data compression: page compression and row compression. The makeup of the data in the table or index determines which of these two will yield the best outcome. As we'll see shortly, we can use supplied tools to estimate the effectiveness of each method before proceeding.

9.4.2 Row compression

Row compression extends the variable-length storage format found in previous versions of SQL Server to all fixed-length data types. For example, in the same manner that the varchar data type is used to reduce the storage footprint of variable length strings, SQL Server 2008 can compress integer, char, and float data in the same manner. Crucially, the compression of fixed-length data doesn't expose the data type any differently to applications, so the benefits of compression are gained without requiring any application changes.

As an example, consider a table with millions of rows containing an integer column with a maximum value of 19. We could convert the column to tinyint, but not if we need to support the possibility of much larger values. In this example, significant disk savings could be derived through row compression, without requiring any application changes.

An alternative to row compression is page compression, our next topic.

9.4.3 Page compression

In contrast to row compression, page compression, as the name suggests, operates at the page level and uses techniques known as *page-dictionary* and *column-prefix* to identify common data patterns in rows on each page of the compressed object. When common patterns are found, they're stored once on the page, with references made to the common storage in place of the original data pattern. In addition to these methods, page compression includes row compression, therefore delivering the highest compression rate of the two options.

Page compression removes redundant storage of data. Consider an example of a large table containing columns with a default value specification. If a large percentage of the table's rows have the default value, there's obviously a good opportunity to store this value once on each page and refer all instances of that value to the common store.

Compressing a table, using either the page or row technique, involves a considerable amount of work by the SQL Server engine. To ensure the benefits outweigh the costs, you must take a number of factors into account.

9.4.4   *Data compression considerations*

In considering the merits of data compression for a given table or index, the first and most straightforward consideration is the potential compression rate.

COMPRESSION RATE

The compression rate achieved depends on the underlying data and the compression method you choose. SQL Server 2008 includes two tools for estimating disk savings: a Management Studio GUI-based wizard (shown in figure 9.12) and the `sp_estimate_ data_compression_savings` procedure. Let's look at the wizard first.

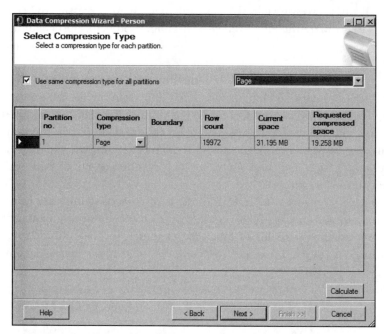

Figure 9.12   Using SQL Server Management Studio, you can estimate the effectiveness of both row and page compression for a particular table.

```
exec sp_estimate_data_compression_savings 'Sales', 'Customer', NULL, NULL, 'PAGE';
```

Results | Messages

object_name	schema_name	index_id	partition_number	size_with_current_compression_setting(KB)	size_with_requested_compression_setting(KB)
Customer	Sales	1	1	984	672
Customer	Sales	2	1	472	568
Customer	Sales	5	1	296	160
Customer	Sales	3	1	432	264

Figure 9.13 Use the `sp_estimate_data_compression_savings` procedure to estimate the disk savings for a table and optionally all its indexes using both page and row compression.

You can access the wizard by right-clicking a table and choosing Storage > Manage Compression. The wizard can be used to estimate, script, and compress the table using the selected compression technique.

The second tool, the `sp_estimate_data_compression_savings` procedure, as shown in figure 9.13, lists, for a given table and optionally all its indexes, the estimated size before and after compression. Like the Management Studio wizard, you can produce estimates for both row and page compression.

Using the estimate tools as we discussed earlier is an important step in evaluating the benefits of compression before implementing it. Once you complete the evaluation, you can implement compression using the same Management Studio wizard used for estimating the savings. Alternatively, use the ALTER TABLE statement as shown here:

```
-- Compress a table using 4 CPUs Only
ALTER TABLE [Sales].[SalesPerson]
REBUILD WITH (DATA_COMPRESSION = PAGE, MAXDOP=4)
```

One of the nice things about the ALTER TABLE[3] method of implementing compression is its ability to accept a MAXDOP value for controlling CPU usage during the initial compression process. Depending on the size of the table and/or indexes being compressed, CPU usage may be very high for an extended length of time, so the MAXDOP setting allows some degree of control in this regard.

Finally, you should consider the tables and indexes proposed for compression. Compressing a table that represents a very small percentage of the overall database size will not yield much of a space gain. Further, if that same table is used frequently, then the performance overhead may outweigh the small gain in disk savings. In contrast, a very large table representing a significant portion of the total database size may yield a large percentage gain, and if the table is used infrequently, the gain comes with little performance overhead.

PERFORMANCE OVERHEAD

As with any compression technique, space savings and increased CPU usage go hand in hand. On systems close to CPU capacity, the additional overhead may preclude data compression from being an option. For other systems, measuring the level of overhead is an important consideration.

---

[3] The ALTER INDEX statement also contains the DATA_COMPRESSION option.

The ideal targets for compression are tables and indexes that are used infrequently yet represent a significant percentage of the database size. Targeting such tables minimizes the performance impact while maximizing disk space savings.

Dynamic management functions and views such as sys.dm_db_index_operational_stats and sys.dm_db_index_usage_stats assist in the process of identifying the least frequently used objects, and we'll cover these in detail in chapter 13. For frequently used objects, the performance impact of data compression needs to be carefully measured in a volume-testing environment capable of simulating production load.

Despite the CPU overhead, certain operations such as table scans can actually receive a performance boost with data compression enabled. Let's have a look at two examples of both the positive and negative performance impacts of data compression. In viewing these examples, keep in mind that the results of any tests such as these are very much dependent on the makeup of the underlying data. These tests were conducted on modified versions of the tables in the AdventureWorks sample database. Results from real-world customer databases will obviously vary.

The first example tests the time taken to insert the contents of a modified version of the AdventureWorks SalesOrder_Detail table containing 1.6 million records into a blank table with the same structure. The insert was repeated multiple times to observe the insert time and resultant table size with both page and row compression enabled. For comparison purposes, we also ran the test against an uncompressed table.

```
-- Measure the size and execution time of various compression settings
TRUNCATE TABLE [Sales].[SalesOrder_Detail_Copy];
GO

ALTER TABLE [Sales].[SalesOrder_Detail_Copy]
REBUILD WITH (DATA_COMPRESSION = PAGE) -- repeat for ROW, NONE
GO

INSERT [Sales].[SalesOrder_Detail_Copy]
SELECT *
FROM [Sales].[SalesOrder_Detail];
GO
```

Rather than execute DBCC DROPCLEANBUFFERS between executions to clear the buffer cache, each test was run multiple times to ensure the data to insert was cached in memory for all three tests. This method lets you more accurately compare the relative performance differences between the compression methods by narrowing the focus to the time taken to write the new rows to disk.

The results of the three tests, shown in figure 9.14, clearly indicate higher compression rates for page compression over row compression, but at a correspondingly higher cost in terms of execution time.

PERFORMANCE INCREASE

Despite the CPU overhead required to compress and uncompress data, in certain cases compressed data can actually boost performance. This is particularly evident in disk I/O bound range scans. If the data is compressed on disk, it follows that fewer

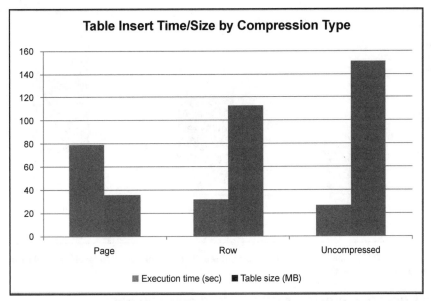

Figure 9.14 Inserting 1.6 million rows into a destination table with three different compression settings. Actual results will differ based on various factors.

pages will need to be read from disk into memory—which translates to a performance boost. Let's use another example to demonstrate.

In this example, we'll select the average unit price from the Sales.SalesOrder_Detail_Copy table. Again, this table was modified for the purposes of the test. For this example, the table was increased in size to 6.7 million rows. Given that the UnitPrice field isn't indexed, a full table scan will result, which is ideal for our test. We'll run this three times, on an uncompressed table, and with both forms of compression enabled. For this test, we'll clear the buffer cache with DBCC DROPCLEANBUFFERS before each test to ensure the query reads from disk each time. The script used for this test looks like this:

```
-- Measure the table scan time of various compression settings
ALTER TABLE [Sales].[SalesOrder_Detail_Copy]
REBUILD WITH (DATA_COMPRESSION = ROW) -- repeat for PAGE, NONE
GO

DBCC DROPCLEANBUFFERS;
GO

SELECT AVG(UnitPrice)
FROM Sales.SalesOrder_Detail_Copy;
GO
```

The results of the three tests, shown in figure 9.15, clearly indicate that page compression enables the fastest execution time for this particular example—almost three times quicker than the query against the uncompressed table.

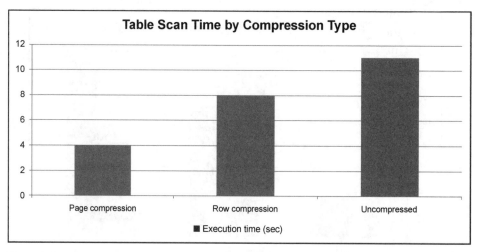

Figure 9.15   Table scan execution time using three different compression levels. Actual results will differ based on various factors.

9.5   *Best practice considerations: data management*

Despite SQL Server 2008's inclusion of advanced data management features such as FileStream and data compression, the importance of basic best practices such as presizing files is not to be overlooked.

- To avoid transaction throughput bottlenecks, ensure the transaction log is stored on a dedicated RAID-protected (ideally RAID 1 or 10) disk volume. Combining data and transaction logs on the same disk won't achieve the same levels of throughput given the disk heads will be moving between the conflicting requirements of random data access/updates and sequential transaction log entries. For database applications with high transaction rates, separation of data and transaction logs in this manner is crucial.

- Defragging a transaction log disk may improve performance if the transaction log has had significant growth/shrink activity and/or is shared with other files undergoing frequent modification. Ensure SQL Server is shut down before defragging, and make sure frequent growth/shrink operations are addressed through adequate log file sizing and the absence of manual shrink operations.

- For maximum performance, ensure backups and the tempdb database are stored on physically separate volumes from data, transaction log, and Windows system files.

- To avoid data loss in the event of disk failure, never store backups on the same disk(s) as the database files, and ensure all volumes are RAID protected.

- Designing SAN-based virtualized storage is quite different from that of direct-attached storage; that being said, the principles of high performance and fault tolerance remain. For transaction log files in particular, consider creating LUNs on dedicated disks that aren't shared by any other server or application.

- Consider using mount points as a means to maintain physical disk volume separation within the confines of the 26-letter drive limitation.

- Unless supported by solid load-test evidence and a very good understanding of data access patterns, creating additional filegroups should be considered for administrative benefits such as piecemeal backup restores rather than as an attempt to maximize performance through control over object placement. In almost all cases, it's a far better option to create simpler filegroup structures spread across more physical disk spindles.

- To support the fastest piecemeal restore process, avoid using the primary filegroup for any user objects. Create a secondary filegroup and mark it as the default.

- Given its unique usage, the tempdb database *does* benefit from multiple files, typically 0.25–0.5 times the number of CPU cores available to the SQL Server instance. For example, an instance with access to four quad-core CPUs (16 cores) would benefit from a tempdb database with between four and eight data files. Hyperthreaded CPUs should be considered as a single core. There are some rare examples of user databases with allocation bitmap contention that may derive a performance benefit from multiple data files, but in almost all cases, multiple data files are used for filegroup and administrative benefits.

- Compared to one large data file, multiple smaller data files provide administrative benefits and should be considered from that perspective rather than as a performance optimization technique. The benefits of smaller files include the ability to restore backups to another server with smaller disk drives and to detach a database and rearrange files to balance drive space usage.

- There's no benefit in multiple transaction log files. Better transaction log performance comes through fast and dedicated RAID-protected disks with an adequate write cache.

- For maximum performance and minimum disk fragmentation, database files should be presized appropriately based on historical usage and growth expectations. In particular, the tempdb database should be manually sized to prevent it from returning to its initial small size when SQL Server restarts. The Enable Autogrowth option should be enabled for emergency situations only, and shouldn't be used as a substitute for good capacity planning and proactive database maintenance.

- Similarly, disable the AutoShrink and AutoClose options (which they are by default) to avoid poor performance and disk fragmentation.

- In order for SQL Server's proportional fill algorithm to operate with maximum efficiency, when multiple files are added to a filegroup, they should be set to the same size, with the same autogrowth values. Further, manual growth increments should be the same across all files.

- The Perform Volume Maintenance Tasks right should be granted to the SQL Server service account in order to take full advantage of the Instant Initialization feature, which reduces the time taken in initializing files during database creation, restores, and autogrowth events.

- Despite the obvious strengths of FileStream, consider database mirroring as a high-availability option before implementing it in place of other BLOB storage techniques. SQL Server 2008 is unable to mirror a database containing FileStream data.

- The best FileStream performance is gained with large BLOBs (>1MB) which are either read only or updated in whole—that is, no partial updates—where the data is accessed via streaming APIs (as opposed to T-SQL access). A database containing BLOBs with an average size of less than 1MB may perform better with the objects stored within the database.

- For the best performance and minimal fragmentation, ensure disk volumes storing FileStream data are formatted with a 64K allocation unit size (the default NTFS allocation unit size is 4K). Further, the volume should ideally be dedicated to the FileStream data with no other SQL Server database files or paging files.

- Data compression yields the biggest gains at the lowest costs when used to compress infrequently used tables and indexes representing a significant portion of the total database size.

- Together with dynamic management views such as `sys.dm_db_index_usage_stats`, the provided compression estimate tools can be used to target compression candidates. For example, a table containing many large indexes that are used infrequently represents a good opportunity to reduce database size while minimizing the performance impact.

- In most cases, particularly for heavily used OLTP systems, row compression will usually have a smaller performance impact compared to page compression, but page compression can result in big performance increases for certain operations such as large table scans.

- As with all other configuration changes, measuring the performance impact of data compression in a load-testing environment is crucial before production implementation. This obviously requires an up-to-date copy of the production database, production-configured hardware, and load-testing tools and strategies.

Additional information on the best practices covered in this chapter can be found online at http://www.sqlCrunch.com/data.

One of the things we covered in this chapter was data compression. SQL Server 2008 also introduces backup compression, and we'll discuss that in the next chapter. We'll also expand on this chapter's introduction to piecemeal restores.

Part 3

Operations

In parts 1 and 2, we covered preinstallation planning, installation, and postinstallation configuration. The remainder of the book will be dedicated to day-to-day operational tasks such as backups, index maintenance, and performance tuning. Let's begin with perhaps the most important of these tasks, backups.

Backup and recovery

10

In this chapter, we'll cover

- Backup types
- Recovery models
- Online piecemeal restore
- Database snapshots
- Backup compression

The importance of backups can't be overstated. During normal activity, it's easy to view backing up databases as an administrative chore that complicates the day and offers little benefit. However, when required in an emergency, the presence of valid backups could make all the difference to an organization's ongoing survival. As DBAs, we have a vital role to play in that process.

Successful backup strategies are those that are designed from a restore perspective—that is, they begin with service level agreements covering data loss and restoration times, and work backwards to derive the backup design. Second only to not performing backups, the biggest backup-related mistake a DBA can make is failing to verify backups. There are countless stories of backup tapes being recalled for recovery before finding out that the backups have been failing for the past few months (or years!). While the backup may *appear* to have succeeded, how can you be sure until you actually restore it?

In this chapter, we begin with an overview of the various types of backups that can be performed with SQL Server before we look at database recovery models. We then move on to cover online piecemeal restores, expanding on the previous chapter's coverage of filegroups. We then explore the benefits of database snapshots, and we conclude with a new backup feature introduced in SQL Server 2008: backup compression.

10.1   Backup types

Unless you're a DBA, you'd probably define a database backup as a complete copy of a database at a given point in time. While that's *one* type of database backup, there are many others. Consider a multi-terabyte database that's used 24/7:

- How long does the backup take, and what impact does it have on users?
- Where are the backups stored, and what is the media cost?
- How much of the database changes each day?
- If the database failed partway through the day, how much data would be lost if the only recovery point was the previous night's backup?

In considering these questions, particularly for large databases with high transaction rates, we soon realize that simplistic backup strategies limited to full nightly backups are insufficient for a number of reasons, not the least of which is the potential for data loss. Let's consider the different types of backups in SQL Server.

> ### Backup methods
> There are many tools and techniques for performing database backups, including various third-party products and database maintenance plans (covered in chapter 14). For the purposes of the examples throughout this chapter, we'll use a T-SQL script approach.

10.1.1   Full backup

Full backups are the simplest, most well understood type of database backup. Like standard file backups (documents, spreadsheets, and so forth), a full backup is a complete copy of the database at a given time. But unlike with a normal file backup, you can't back up a database by simply backing up the underlying .mdf and .ldf files.

One of the classic mistakes made by organizations without appropriate DBA knowledge is using a backup program to back up all files on a database server based on the assumption that the inclusion of the underlying database files (.mdf and .ldf) in the backup will be sufficient for a restore scenario. Not only will this backup strategy be unsuccessful, but those who use such an approach usually fail to realize that fact until they try to perform a restore.

For a database backup to be valid, you must use the BACKUP DATABASE command or one of its GUI equivalents. Let's look at a simple example in which we'll back up the AdventureWorks database. Check Books Online (BOL) for the full description of the backup command with all of its various options.

```
-- Full Backup to Disk
BACKUP DATABASE [AdventureWorks2008]
TO DISK = N'G:\SQL Backup\AdventureWorks.bak'
WITH INIT
```

You can perform backups in SQL Server while the database is in use and is being modified by users. Such backups are known as online backups. In order for the resultant backup to be restored as a transactionally consistent database, SQL Server includes *part* of the transaction log in the full database backup. Before we cover the transaction log in more detail, let's consider an example of a full backup that's executed against a database that's being actively modified.

Figure 10.1 shows a hypothetical example of a transaction that starts and completes during a full backup, and modifies a page *after* the backup process has read it from disk. In order for the backup to be transactionally consistent, how will the backup process ensure this modified page is included in the backup file? In answering this question, let's walk through the backup step by step. The step numbers in the following list correspond to the steps in figure 10.1.

1. When the backup commences, a checkpoint is issued that flushes dirty buffer cache pages to disk.
2. After the checkpoint completes, the backup process begins reading pages from the database for inclusion in the backup file(s), including page X.
3. Transaction A begins.
4. Transaction A modifies page X. The backup has already included page X in the backup file, so this page is now out of date in the backup file.
5. Transaction B begins, but won't complete until after the backup finishes. At the point of backup completion, this transaction is the oldest active (uncommitted/incomplete) transaction.

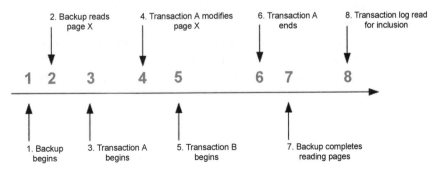

Figure 10.1 Timeline of an online full backup. Based on an example used with permission from Paul S. Randal, managing director of SQLskills.com.

6 Transaction A completes successfully.

7 The backup completes reading pages from the database.

8 As described shortly, the backup process includes *part* of the transaction log in the backup.

If the full backup process didn't include any of the transaction log, the restore would produce a backup that wasn't transactionally consistent. Transaction A's committed changes to page X wouldn't be in the restored database, and because transaction B hasn't completed, its changes would have to be rolled back. By including parts of the transaction log, the restore process is able to roll forward committed changes and roll back uncommitted changes as appropriate.

In our example, once SQL Server completes reading database pages at step 7, it will include all entries in the transaction log since the *oldest* log sequence number (LSN) of one of the following:

- The checkpoint (step 1 in our example)
- The oldest active transaction (step 5)
- The LSN of the last replicated transaction (not applicable in our example)

In our example, transaction log entries since step 1 will be included because that's the oldest of these items. However, consider a case where a transaction starts *before* the backup begins and is still active at the end of the backup. In such a case, the LSN of that transaction will be used as the start point.

This example was based on a blog post from Paul Randal of SQLskills.com. The full post, titled "More on How Much Transaction Log a Full Backup Includes" is available at http://www.sqlskills.com/BLOGS/PAUL/post/More-on-how-much-transaction-log-a-full-backup-includes.aspx.

It's important to point out here that even though parts of the transaction log are *included* in a full backup, this doesn't constitute a transaction log *backup*. Another classic mistake made by inexperienced SQL Server DBAs is never performing transaction log backups because they think a full backup will take care of it. A database in full recovery mode (discussed shortly) will maintain entries in the transaction log until it's backed up. If explicit transaction log backups are never performed, the transaction log will continue growing forever (until it fills the disk). It's not unusual to see a 2GB database with a 200GB transaction log!

Finally, when a full backup is restored as shown in our next example, changes since the full backup are lost. In later examples, we'll look at combining a full backup with differential and transaction log backups to restore changes made after the full backup was taken.

```
-- Restore from Disk
RESTORE DATABASE [AdventureWorks2008]
FROM DISK = N'G:\SQL Backup\AdventureWorks.bak'
WITH REPLACE
```

To reduce the user impact and storage costs of nightly full backups, we can use differential backups.

Multi-file backups

Backing up a database to multiple files can lead to a significant reduction in backup time, particularly for large databases. When you use the T-SQL BACKUP DATABASE command, the DISK = clause can be repeated multiple times (separated by commas), once for each backup file, as per this example:

```
BACKUP DATABASE [ADVENTUREWORKS2008]
    TO
      DISK = 'G:\SQL BACKUP\ADVENTUREWORKS_1.BAK'
      , DISK = 'G:\SQL BACKUP\ADVENTUREWORKS_2.BAK'
      , DISK = 'G:\SQL BACKUP\ADVENTUREWORKS_3.BAK'
```

10.1.2 *Differential backup*

While a full backup represents the most complete version of the database, performing full backups on a nightly basis may not be possible (or desirable) for a variety of reasons. Earlier in this chapter we used an example of a multi-terabyte database. If only a small percentage of this database changes on a daily basis, the merits of performing a full nightly backup are questionable, particularly considering the storage costs and the impact on users during the backup.

A differential backup, an example of which is shown here, is one that includes all database changes since the last full backup:

```
-- Differential Backup to Disk
BACKUP DATABASE [AdventureWorks2008]
TO DISK = N'G:\SQL Backup\AdventureWorks-Diff.bak'
WITH DIFFERENTIAL, INIT
```

A classic backup design is one in which a full backup is performed weekly, with nightly differential backups. Figure 10.2 illustrates a weekly full/nightly differential backup design.

Figure 10.2   Differential backups grow in size and duration the further they are from their corresponding full backup (base).

Day	Backup Type	Includes ...	Contents
Sunday	Full	Everything	
Monday	Differential	Changes since Sunday	
Tuesday	Differential	Changes since Sunday	
Wednesday	Differential	Changes since Sunday	
Thursday	Differential	Changes since Sunday	
Friday	Differential	Changes since Sunday	
Saturday	Differential	Changes since Sunday	

Compared to nightly full backups, a nightly differential with a weekly full backup offers a number of advantages, primarily the speed and reduced size (and therefore storage cost) of each nightly differential backup. However, there comes a point at which differential backups become counterproductive; the further from the full backup, the larger the differential, and depending on the rate of change, it may be quicker to perform a full backup. It follows that in a differential backup design, the frequency of the full backup needs to be assessed on the basis of the rate of database change.

When restoring a differential backup, the corresponding full backup, known as the *base* backup, needs to be restored with it. In the previous example, if we needed to restore the database on Friday morning, the full backup from Sunday, along with the differential backup from Thursday night, would be restored, as in this example:

```
-- Restore from Disk. Leave in NORECOVERY state for subsequent restores
RESTORE DATABASE [AdventureWorks2008]
FROM DISK = N'G:\SQL Backup\AdventureWorks.bak'
WITH NORECOVERY, REPLACE
GO

-- Complete the restore process with a Differential Restore
RESTORE DATABASE [AdventureWorks2008]
FROM DISK = N'G:\SQL Backup\AdventureWorks-Diff.bak'
GO
```

Here, we can see the full backup is restored using the WITH NORECOVERY option. This leaves the database in a *recovering* state, and thus able to restore additional backups. We follow the restore of the full backup with the differential restore.

As you'll recall from the restore of the full backup shown earlier, without transaction log backups, changes made to the database since the differential backup will be lost.

10.1.3 *Transaction log backup*

A fundamental component of database management systems like SQL Server is the transaction log. Each database has its own transaction log, which SQL Server uses for several purposes, including the following:

- The log records each database transaction, as well as the individual database modifications made within each transaction.
- If a transaction is canceled before it completes, either at the request of an application or due to a system error, the transaction log is used to undo, or *roll back*, the transaction's modifications.
- A transaction log is used during a database restore to roll forward completed transactions and roll back incomplete ones. This process also takes place for each database when SQL Server starts up.
- The transaction log plays a key role in log shipping and database mirroring, both of which will be covered in the next chapter.

Regular transaction log backups, as shown here, are crucial in retaining the ability to recover a database to a point in time:

```
-- Transaction Log Backup to Disk
BACKUP LOG [AdventureWorks2008]
TO DISK = N'G:\SQL Backup\AdventureWorks-Trn.bak'
WITH INIT
```

As you can see in figure 10.3, each transaction log backup forms part of what's called a *log chain*. The head of a log chain is a full database backup, performed after the

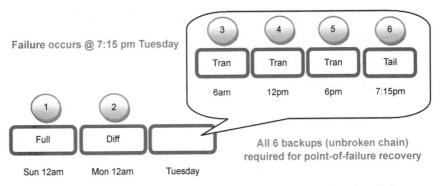

Failure occurs @ 7:15 pm Tuesday

All 6 backups (unbroken chain)
required for point-of-failure recovery

Figure 10.3   An unbroken chain of backups is required to recover to the point of failure.

database is first created, or when the database's recovery model, discussed shortly, is changed. After this, each transaction log backup forms a part of the chain. To restore a database to a point in time, an unbroken chain of transaction logs is required, from a full backup to the required point of recovery.

Consider figure 10.3. Starting at point 1, we perform a full database backup, after which differential and transaction log backups occur. Each of the backups serves as part of the chain. When restoring to a point in time, an unbroken sequence of log backups is required. For example, if we lost backup 4, we wouldn't be able to restore past the end of backup 3 at 6 a.m. Tuesday. Attempting to restore the transaction log from log backup 5 would result in an error message similar to that shown in figure 10.4.

In addition to protecting against potential data loss, regular log backups limit the growth of the log file. With each transaction log backup, certain log records, discussed in more detail shortly, are removed, freeing up space for new log entries. As covered earlier, the transaction log in a database in full recovery mode will continuing growing indefinitely until a transaction log backup occurs.

The frequency of transaction log backups is an important consideration. The two main determining factors are the rate of database change and the sensitivity to data loss.

TRANSACTION LOG BACKUP FREQUENCY

Frequent transaction log backups reduce the exposure to data loss. If the transaction log disk is completely destroyed, then all changes since the last log backup will be lost.

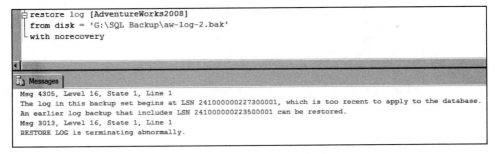

Figure 10.4   Attempting to restore an out-of-sequence transaction log

Assuming a transaction log backup was performed 15 minutes before the disk destruction, the maximum data loss would be 15 minutes (assuming the log backup file isn't contained on the backup disk!). In contrast, if transaction log backups are only performed once a day (or longer), the potential for data loss is large, particularly for databases with a high rate of change.

The more frequent the log backups, the more restores will be required in a recovery situation. In order to recover up to a given point, we need to restore each transaction log backup between the last full (or differential) backup and the required recovery point. If transaction log backups were taken every minute, and the last full or differential backup was 24 hours ago, there would be 1,440 transaction log backups to restore! Clearly, we need to get the balance right between potential data loss and the complexity of the restore. Again, the determining factors are the rate of database change and the maximum allowed data loss, usually defined in a service level agreement.

In a moment we'll run through a point-in-time restore, which will illustrate the three backup types working together. Before we do that, we need to cover tail log backups.

TAIL LOG BACKUPS

When restoring a database that's currently attached to a server instance, SQL Server will generate an error[1] unless the *tail* of the transaction log is first backed up. The tail refers to the section of log that hasn't been backed up yet—that is, new transactions since the last log backup.

A tail log backup is performed using the WITH NORECOVERY option, which immediately places the database in the restoring mode, guaranteeing that the database won't change after the tail log backup and thus ensuring that all changes are captured in the backup.

> WITH NO_TRUNCATE
> Backing up the tail of a transaction log using the WITH NO_TRUNCATE option should be limited to situations in which the database is damaged and inaccessible. The COPY_ONLY option, covered shortly, should be used in its place.

When restoring up to the point of failure, the tail log backup represents the very last transaction log backup, with all restores preceding it performed using the WITH NORECOVERY option. The tail log is then restored using the WITH RECOVERY option to recover the database up to the point of failure, or a time before failure using the STOPAT command.

So let's put all this together with an example. In listing 10.1, we first back up the tail of the log before restoring the database to a point in time. We begin with restoring the full and differential backups using the WITH NORECOVERY option, and then roll forward the transaction logs to a required point in time.

---

[1]   Unless the WITH REPLACE option is used.

Listing 10.1 Recovering a database to a point in time

```
-- Backup the tail of the transaction log
BACKUP LOG [AdventureWorks2008]
TO DISK = N'G:\SQL Backup\AdventureWorks-Tail.bak'
WITH INIT, NORECOVERY

-- Restore the full backup
RESTORE DATABASE [AdventureWorks2008]
FROM DISK = N'G:\SQL Backup\AdventureWorks.bak'
WITH NORECOVERY
GO

-- Restore the differential backup
RESTORE DATABASE [AdventureWorks2008]
FROM DISK = N'G:\SQL Backup\AdventureWorks-Diff.bak'
WITH NORECOVERY
GO

-- Restore the transaction logs
RESTORE LOG [AdventureWorks2008]
FROM DISK = N'G:\SQL Backup\AdventureWorks-Trn.bak'
WITH NORECOVERY
GO

-- Restore the final tail backup, stopping at 11.05AM
RESTORE LOG [AdventureWorks2008]
FROM DISK = N'G:\SQL Backup\AdventureWorks-Tail.bak'
WITH RECOVERY, STOPAT = 'June 24, 2008 11:05 AM'
GO
```

As we covered earlier, the NO_TRUNCATE option of a transaction log backup, used to perform a backup without removing log entries, should be limited to situations in which
the database is damaged and inaccessible. Otherwise, use the COPY_ONLY option.

10.1.4 *COPY_ONLY backups*

Earlier in this chapter we defined a log chain as the sequence of transaction log backups from a given *base*. The base for a transaction log chain, as with differential backups, is a full backup. In other words, before restoring a transaction log or differential
backup, we first restore a full backup that preceded the log or differential backup.

Take the example presented earlier in figure 10.3, where we perform a full backup
on Sunday night, nightly differential backups, and six hourly transaction log backups.
In a similar manner to the code in listing 10.1, to recover to 6 p.m. on Tuesday, we'd
recover Sunday's full backup, followed by Tuesday's differential and the three transaction log backups leading up to 6 p.m.

Now let's assume that a developer, on Monday morning, made an additional full
backup, and moved the backup file to their workstation. The differential restore from
Tuesday would now fail. Why? A differential backup uses a Differential Changed Map
(DCM) to track which extents have changed since the last full backup. The DCM in
the differential backup from Tuesday now relates to the full backup made by the

developer on Monday morning. In our restore code, we're not using the full backup from Monday—hence the failure.

Now, there are a few ways around this problem. First, we have an unbroken transaction log backup sequence, so we can always restore the full backup, followed by *all* of the log backups since Sunday. Second, we can track down the developer and ask him for the full backup and hope that he hasn't deleted it!

To address the broken chain problem as outlined here, COPY_ONLY backups were introduced in SQL Server 2005 and fully supported in 2008.[2] A COPY_ONLY backup, supported for both full and transaction log backups, is used in situations in which the backup sequence shouldn't be affected. In our example, if the developer performed the Monday morning full backup as a COPY_ONLY backup, the DCM for the Tuesday differential would still be based on our Sunday full backup. In a similar vein, a COPY_ONLY transaction log backup, as in this example, will back up the log without truncation, meaning that the log backup chain will remain intact without needing the additional log backup file:

```
-- Perform a COPY ONLY Transaction Log Backup
BACKUP LOG [AdventureWorks2008]
TO DISK = N'G:\SQL Backup\AdventureWorks-Trn_copy.bak'
WITH COPY_ONLY
```

When discussing the different backup types earlier in the chapter, we made several references to the database recovery models. The recovery model of a database is an important setting that determines the usage of the transaction log and the exposure to data loss during a database restore.

10.2   *Recovery models and data loss exposure*

When a database is created, the recovery model is inherited from the *model* database. You can modify the recovery model in Management Studio or use the ALTER DATABASE statement, as shown here:

```
-- Set the Recovery Model to BULK_LOGGED
ALTER DATABASE [ADVENTUREWORKS2008]
SET RECOVERY BULK_LOGGED
```

There are three different recovery models: *simple, full,* and *bulk logged.*

10.2.1   *Simple recovery model*

A database in the simple recovery model will automatically truncate (remove) committed transactions from the log at each checkpoint operation. As a result, no transaction log backups are required in limiting the growth of the log, so maintenance operations are simplified.

---

[2] Management Studio in SQL Server 2008 includes enhanced support for COPY_ONLY backups with GUI options available for this backup type. Such options were absent in SQL Server 2005, which required a T-SQL script approach.

Despite the reduction in maintenance overhead, the major downside of the simple recovery model is the inability to recover a database to a point in time. As such, the only recovery options are to recover to the previous full or differential backup. This strategy may lead to significant data loss depending on the amount of change since the last full/differential backup.

The simple recovery model is typically used in development and test environments where recovering to the last full or differential backup is acceptable. In such environments, the potential for some data loss is accepted in return for reduced maintenance requirements by avoiding the need to execute and store transaction log backups.

> **Simple logging vs. no logging**
>
> Don't confuse the simple recovery model for the (nonexistent) *no* logging model. Regardless of the recovery model, transactions are logged by SQL Server in order to maintain database integrity in the event of a transaction rollback or sudden server shutdown.

Finally, long-running transactions can still cause significant growth in the transaction log of databases in the simple recovery model. Log records generated by an incomplete transaction can't be removed, nor can any completed transactions that started *after* the oldest open transaction. For example, in figure 10.5, even though transaction D has completed, it can't be removed as it started *after* the incomplete transaction C.

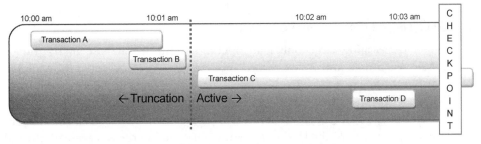

Figure 10.5   Log truncation can't remove log records for active transactions or records from completed transactions that began after the oldest active transaction.

The simple recovery model has further downsides: features such as transaction log shipping, covered in the next chapter, can't be used with this recovery model. For compatibility with SQL Server's full feature set and to minimize data loss, we use the full recovery model.

10.2.2   *Full recovery model*

A database in the full recovery model will log and retain *all* transactions in the transaction log until the log is backed up, at which point committed transactions will be removed from the log, subject to the same rule that we saw in figure 10.5. Regular transaction log backups are crucial in limiting the growth of the transaction log in a database in the full recovery model.

As well as recording update, insert, and delete statements, the full recovery model will record index creation and maintenance operations, Bulk Copy Process (BCP) commands, and bulk inserts. As a result, the size of transaction logs (and therefore the backup time) can grow very quickly with the full recovery model, and is therefore an important consideration when using log shipping and/or mirroring. We'll cover this in more detail in later chapters when we address index maintenance techniques.

> ### Disaster recovery plan
>
> A good disaster recovery (DR) plan considers a wide variety of potential disasters, from small events such as corrupted log files and accidentally dropping a table, right through to large environmental disasters such as fires and earthquakes. A crucial component of any DR plan is a well-documented and well-understood backup and re-store plan. Perhaps the best way to validate a DR plan is to simulate various disas-ters on a random/unannounced basis, similar to a fire drill, with each DBA talking it in turns to practice the recovery process. Not only will this ensure documentation is up to date and well understood by all team members, it will liven up the day, and add some competitive spark to the DBA team!

A common technique used when bulk-loading data into a database in the full recov-ery model is to switch the database to the Bulk_Logged model, discussed next, prior to the load.

10.2.3 *Bulk_Logged recovery model*

When performing large bulk-load operations into a database in the full recovery model, each data and index record modified by the bulk-load process is logged by SQL Server. For very large loads, this can have a significant impact on the load perfor-mance.

Under the Bulk_Logged model, SQL Server uses a *Bulk Changed Map* (BCM) to record which *extents*[3] the load modified. Unlike the full recovery model, the individual records affected by the bulk load aren't logged. As a result, bulk loads can be signifi-cantly quicker than under the full recovery model.

The trade-offs of the Bulk_Logged model are significant: when a transaction log backup occurs after a bulk-load operation, SQL Server includes the entire contents of each extent touched by the bulk-load process, even if only a small portion of the extent was actually modified. As a result, the transaction log backup size can be mas-sive, potentially almost as big as the entire database, depending on the amount of modified extents.

---

[3] An *extent* is a collection of eight 8K pages.

The other downside to this recovery model is the inability to restore a transaction log containing bulk-load operations to a point in time. Given these limitations, it's generally recommended that the Bulk_Logged model be used as a temporary setting for the period of the bulk load before switching back to the full recovery model. Making a transaction log backup before and after entering and leaving the Bulk_Logged model will ensure maximum data protection for point-in-time restores while also benefiting from increased performance during the bulk-load operation(s).

Before looking at the backup recovery process in more detail, let's consider some additional backup options at our disposal.

10.3 Backup options

SQL Server 2008 includes a rich array of options that can be employed as parts of a customized backup and recovery strategy. In this section, we'll consider three such options: *checksums, backup mirroring,* and *transaction log marks.* But before we cover these options, let's have a look at an important part of any backup strategy: the backup location and retention policy.

10.3.1 Backup location and retention policy

A key component of a well-designed backup strategy is the location of the backups: disk or tape (or both). Let's consider each of these in turn before looking at a commonly used backup retention policy.

TAPE

Historically, organizations have chosen tape media as a backup destination in order to reduce the cost of online storage while retaining backups for long periods of time. However, a *tape-only* approach to backups presents a number of challenges:

- Tape systems typically have a higher failure rate when compared to disk.
- Typically, tapes are rotated offsite after a predefined period, sometimes as soon as the morning after the backup. Should the backup be required for restore, there may be a time delay involved in retrieving the tape for restore.
- Depending on the tape system, it may be difficult/cumbersome to restore a tape backup to a different server for restoration verification, or to use it as a source for DBCC checks or other purposes.

In addressing these concerns, disk backups are frequently used, although they too have some challenges to overcome.

DISK

Due to some of the limitations with the tape-only approach, backup verification, whereby backups are restored on a regular basis to ensure their validity, are often skipped. As a result, problems are often discovered for the first time when a *real* restore is required.

In contrast to tape, disk-based backups offer the following advantages:

- When required for a restore, they are immediately available.
- Disk media is typically more reliable than tape, particularly when RAID protected.

- Disk-based backups can be easily copied to other servers when required, making the verification process much simpler compared with a typical tape-based system.

Despite its advantages, a disk-based backup approach has some drawbacks. The main one is the extra disk space (and associated cost) required for the backup files. Further, the cost advantage of tape is fully realized when considering the need to store a history of backups—for example, daily backups for the last 30 days, monthly backups for the past 12 months, and yearly backups for the last 7 years. Storing all of these backups on disk is usually more expensive compared to a tape-based system, not to mention the risk of losing all of the disk backups in an environmental disaster.

With the introduction of third-party backup compression tools and the inclusion of backup compression as a standard feature of SQL Server 2008 (Enterprise edition), the cost of disk storage for backups is significantly reduced, but the overall cost is still typically higher than a tape-based system.

In addressing the negative aspects of both tape and disk, a common approach is to combine both methods in what's known as a *disk then tape* approach.

DISK THEN TAPE

As shown in figure 10.6, the ideal backup solution is to combine both disk and tape backups in the following manner:

1 Database backups are performed to disk.
2 Later in the day/night, the disk backup files are archived to tape in the same manner as other files would be backed up (documents, images and so forth).
3 Typical restore scenarios use the most recent backup files on disk. After a number of days, the oldest disk-based backup files are removed in order to maintain a sliding window; for example, the past 5 days of backups are stored on disk.
4 If older backups are required, they can be sourced from tape.

The advantages of such a system are numerous:

- Backups are stored in two locations (disk and tape), thus providing an additional safety net against media failure.

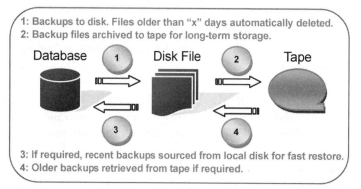

Figure 10.6 The disk then tape backup methodology provides fast restore, dual backup protection, and long-term archive at a moderate cost.

- The most common restore scenario, typically that of the previous night's backup, is available on disk for fast restore without requiring tapes to be requested from offsite.
- A full history of backups is available for restore from tape.
- The cost of the overall system is reduced, while still providing all of the advantages of disk-based backups for the most common restore scenarios.

A variation on this approach is using SAN-based backup solutions. In chapter 3 we covered the benefits that SANs provide in disaster recovery scenarios. Most of the enterprise-class SANs available today provide several methods of *snapping*, or *cloning*, LUNs in order to provide near instant backup/restore solutions. Once snapped, the cloned LUN can be archived to tape, thereby providing long-term storage like the disk then tape approach. If using these backup types, take care to ensure the backup method used is SQL Server compatible and enables transaction log roll forwards for point-in-time recovery.

Regardless of the backup destination, an important consideration is how long to retain the backups before deleting or overwriting them.

BACKUP RETENTION

Assuming the disk then tape backup method is used, the retention period for each location needs to be considered separately. For the disk backups, the retention period is dependent on the backup model. For example, if a weekly full, nightly differential system is in place, then the weekly backup would need to be retained on disk for the whole week for use with the previous night's differential backup. If disk space allows, then additional backups can be retained on disk as appropriate.

In considering the tape rotation policy (how long to keep a tape before overwriting it), the classic rotation policy typically used is the *grandfather–father–son* (GFS) system, whereby 22 tapes are used per year.

The GFS tape rotation policy, as shown in table 10.1, uses 6 sons, 3 fathers, and 13 grandfathers (52 weeks per year divided by 4-week periods) for a total of 22 tapes per year. Optionally, one of the grandfather tapes can be retained as a yearly backup tape for a period of years.

Table 10.1 Grandfather–father–son tape rotation policy

Week	Mon	Tue	Wed	Thu	Fri	Sat	Sun
1	Son1	Son2	Son3	Son4	Son5	Son6	Father1
2	Son1	Son2	Son3	Son4	Son5	Son6	Father2
3	Son1	Son2	Son3	Son4	Son5	Son6	Father3
4	Son1	Son2	Son3	Son4	Son5	Son6	Grandfather-x

Regardless of the disk location and retention period, ensuring backups are valid is an important consideration. Short of actually restoring each backup, one of the options available for detecting media failure is to use *backup checksums*.

10.3.2 *Backup checksums*

One of the features introduced in SQL Server 2005 was the ability for backups to verify the validity of pages as part of the backup process, and for the backup itself to include a checksum.

When using the optional[4] WITH CHECKSUM option of the BACKUP command as shown here, the backup process verifies the checksum of each page as the backup is performed, assuming the PAGE_VERIFY database option, covered in more detail in chapter 12, is set to CHECKSUM (which is the default).

```
-- Verify Page Validity during backup with CHECKSUM
BACKUP DATABASE [AdventureWorks2008]
TO DISK = N'G:\SQL Backup\AdventureWorks.bak'
WITH CHECKSUM
```

The PAGE_VERIFY option calculates and stores a checksum value for each database page written to disk. When read from disk, the checksum is verified against the page read and used to alert the presence of suspect pages.

The WITH CHECKSUM option of the BACKUP command calculates and verifies the checksum value of each page as it's read by the backup process. If a checksum error occurs, the backup fails, unless the CONTINUE_AFTER_ERROR option is used. In that case, the backup is flagged as containing errors and the suspect page(s) are marked in the suspect_pages table in the msdb database.

In addition to verifying the checksum of each page, the WITH CHECKSUM option calculates a checksum for the entire backup process. When a database is restored from a backup created with the checksum option, the restore process verifies the checksums as part of the restore process, unless the NO_CHECKSUM option is used. If a checksum error is found as part of the restore, the restore will fail, unless the CONTINUE_AFTER_ERROR option is used.

Although backup checksums provide additional confidence in the validity of the backups, they do introduce additional CPU overhead during the backup process. Before enabling this option, ensure the overhead is measured on a test system, particularly in cases where the additional overhead may extend the backup window beyond the desired time frame. That being said, the additional confidence this option provides is well worth the typically small CPU overhead.

Another technique commonly used for backup assurance is the mirroring option.

10.3.3 *Backup mirroring*

There is no such thing as too many backups. One of the optional backup clauses is MIRROR TO. Here's an example:

```
-- Mirror the backup to a separate backup server using a UNC path
BACKUP DATABASE [AdventureWorks2008]
TO DISK = N'G:\SQL Backup\AdventureWorks-20080701.bak'
MIRROR TO DISK = '\\BACKUP-SERVER\SQL-Backups\AdventureWorks-20080701.bak'
WITH FORMAT
```

---

[4] Enabled by default on compressed backups.

The MIRROR TO clause allows a backup to be streamed to multiple destinations. The typical use of this option is for making a duplicate backup on a file server using a Universal Naming Convention (UNC) path to a file share (in the previous example, \\BACKUP-SERVER\SQL-Backups). This option provides multiple advantages:

- Additional backups for protection against media failure.
- Different retention periods for different locations; for example, the file server backups can be retained for a longer period on disk when compared to the backup file on the database server.
- The tape archive process can archive from the file share rather than the database server. Not only does this reduce the additional load the tape archive process places on the database server, it also avoids the need for tape drivers and associated software to be installed on the database server.

In concluding this section, let's take a look at the challenge of coordinating backups across multiple databases.

10.3.4 Transaction log marks

A common backup requirement is for coordinated backups across multiple databases. This is usually a requirement for the restore process rather than the backup—when a database is restored, all associated databases must be restored to exactly the same point.

Synchronized restores are enabled using *transaction log marks*. Before we take a look at using them in a restore scenario, let's see how they're used in recovering from an unintended action. Consider the following statement, which increases product prices by 2 percent:

```
-- Update all prices by 2%
BEGIN TRANSACTION updatePrices WITH MARK 'Updating Prices Now';
    UPDATE Products
    SET Price = Price * 1.02
COMMIT TRANSACTION updatePrices
```

Let's imagine we only intended to update *some* products, not *all* of them, as shown in the previous statement. Short of running additional commands to roll back the price increase (and other flow-on effects), we'd be looking at a database restore, but if we can't remember the time of the update, a transaction log recovery using the STOPAT option won't help.

One of the optional clauses we used in the update price transaction was WITH MARK, and we can use that in a restore command. After performing a restore of a full backup in NORECOVERY mode, we can then restore a transaction log backup made after the transaction to the point immediately before the mark, using the STOPBEFOREMARK option:

```
-- After restoring the full backup, roll forward the transaction log
-- Use the STOPBEFOREMARK option to stop before the marked transaction
RESTORE LOG [AdventureWorks2008]
FROM DISK = N'G:\SQL Backup\AdventureWorks-log.bak'
WITH RECOVERY, STOPBEFOREMARK = 'updatePrices'
GO
```

Now that's all well and good (and very handy), but how does that help us with coordinating backups and restores across multiple databases? Well, by encapsulating statements that update multiple databases within a single marked transaction, we can achieve the desired result (see listing 10.2).

Listing 10.2   Marking multiple transaction logs for coordinated restores

```
-- Use a dummy transaction to mark multiple databases
-- If required, each database can be restored to the same point in time
BEGIN TRANSACTION backupMark WITH MARK
    UPDATE db1.dbo.dummytable set col1 = 1
    UPDATE db2.dbo.dummytable set col1 = 1
    -- other databases here ...
COMMIT TRANSACTION backupMark
```

By executing a simple update statement in multiple databases *within one transaction*, we're marking the transaction log of each database at the same time. Such an update statement could be executed immediately before transaction log backups are performed, thus enabling the backups to be restored to the same point in time using the STOPBEFOREMARK that we saw earlier. Bear in mind, however, that data entered in the databases *after* this transaction will be lost, and this is an important consideration in a coordinated restore scenario.

Using transaction marks to enable synchronized restores across multiple databases is one example of using backup/restore features beyond the basics. While a basic backup/restore approach may suffice for small databases, it's insufficient for very large databases (VLDBs). In the previous chapter, we covered the use of filegroups as a mechanism for enabling enhanced administration options. We also explored a best practice whereby user objects are placed on secondary filegroups so that the only objects in the primary filegroup are system objects. Let's take a look at that process in more detail, and see how it can be used to minimize the user impact of a restoration process.

10.4   *Online piecemeal restores*

Consider a very large, multi-terabyte database in use 24/7. One of the challenges with databases of this size is the length of time taken for various administration tasks such as backups and the effect such operations have on database users.

One of the advantages of using multiple filegroups is that we're able to back up individual filegroups instead of (or as well as) the entire database. Such an approach not only minimizes the user impact of the backup operation, but it also enables *online piecemeal restores*, whereby parts of the database can be brought online and available for user access while other parts are still being restored.[5] In contrast, a traditional restore process would require users to wait for the entire database to restore before being able to access it, which for a VLDB could be quite a long time.

In this section we'll walk through the process of an online piecemeal restore using filegroups. Online restores can also be performed at the individual page level, and we'll take a look at that in chapter 12 when we cover the DBCC tool.

---

[5]   Online restores are available in the Enterprise version of SQL Server 2005 and 2008 only.

The database used for our examples is structured as shown in listing 10.3. This code creates a database with three filegroups.

Listing 10.3 Creating a database with multiple filegroups for online restore

```
-- Create "Sales" database with 3 secondary filegroups
-- Each filegroup has 2 files and 1 table
CREATE DATABASE [Sales] ON PRIMARY (
    NAME = N'Sales'
    , FILENAME = N'E:\SQL Data\Sales.mdf'
    , SIZE = 51200KB
    , FILEGROWTH = 1024KB
)

, FILEGROUP [FG1] (
    NAME = N'Sales1'
    , FILENAME = N'E:\SQL Data\Sales1.ndf'
    , SIZE = 51200KB
    , FILEGROWTH = 10240KB
), (
    NAME = N'Sales2'
    , FILENAME = N'E:\SQL Data\Sales2.ndf'
    , SIZE = 51200KB
    , FILEGROWTH = 10240KB
)

, FILEGROUP [FG2] (
    NAME = N'Sales3'
    , FILENAME = N'E:\SQL Data\Sales3.ndf'
    , SIZE = 51200KB
    , FILEGROWTH = 10240KB
), (
    NAME = N'Sales4'
    , FILENAME = N'E:\SQL Data\Sales4.ndf'
    , SIZE = 51200KB
    , FILEGROWTH = 10240KB
)

, FILEGROUP [FG3] (
    NAME = N'Sales5'
    , FILENAME = N'E:\SQL Data\Sales5.ndf'
    , SIZE = 51200KB
    , FILEGROWTH = 10240KB
), (
    NAME = N'Sales6'
    , FILENAME = N'E:\SQL Data\Sales6.ndf'
    , SIZE = 51200KB
    , FILEGROWTH = 10240KB
)
LOG ON (
    NAME = N'Sales_log'
    , FILENAME = N'F:\SQL Log\Sales_log.ldf'
    , SIZE = 10240KB
    , FILEGROWTH = 10%
)
GO
```

```
-- Set FG1 to be the default filegroup
ALTER DATABASE [Sales]
MODIFY FILEGROUP [FG1] DEFAULT
GO

USE [SALES]
GO

-- Create a table on each filegroup
CREATE TABLE dbo.Table_1 (
    Col1 nchar(10) NULL
) ON FG1
GO

CREATE TABLE dbo.Table_2 (
    Col1 nchar(10) NULL
) ON FG2
GO

CREATE TABLE dbo.Table_3 (
    Col1 nchar(10) NULL
) ON FG3
GO
```

As you can see in listing 10.3, we've created a database with three filegroups and one table on each. We've also ensured that user objects won't be created in the primary filegroup by marking the secondary filegroup, FG1, as the default. Listing 10.4 sets up the basis for our restore by seeding the tables and making a filegroup backup of the primary and secondary filegroups. For this example, all of the filegroup backups occur in sequence, but in a real example, we'd perform the filegroup backups over a number of nights to reduce the nightly backup impact. Once the filegroup backups are complete, we'll modify some data for a transaction log backup in a later step.

Listing 10.4   Filegroup backups

```
-- Seed tables
INSERT table_1
VALUES ('one')
GO

INSERT table_2
VALUES ('two')
GO

INSERT table_3
VALUES ('three')
GO

-- Take FileGroup Backups
BACKUP DATABASE [Sales]
FILEGROUP = N'PRIMARY'
TO DISK = N'G:\SQL Backup\Sales_Primary_FG.bak'
WITH INIT
GO
```

```
BACKUP DATABASE [Sales]
FILEGROUP = N'FG1'
TO DISK = N'G:\SQL Backup\Sales_FG1_FG.bak'
WITH INIT
GO

BACKUP DATABASE [Sales]
FILEGROUP = N'FG2'
TO DISK = N'G:\SQL Backup\Sales_FG2_FG.bak'
WITH INIT
GO

BACKUP DATABASE [Sales]
FILEGROUP = N'FG3'
TO DISK = N'G:\SQL Backup\Sales_FG3_FG.bak'
WITH INIT
GO

-- Modify data on FG2
INSERT table_2
VALUES ('two - two')
GO
```

At this point, let's imagine that the disk(s) containing the filegroups is completely destroyed, but the transaction log disk is okay. Restoring a multi-terabyte database as a single unit would take a fair amount of time, during which the entire database would be unavailable. With filegroup restores, what we can do is prioritize the restores in order to make the most important data available as soon as possible. So for this example, let's imagine that filegroup 2 was the most important filegroup from a user perspective. Let's get filegroup 2 back up and running first (see listing 10.5).

> **Listing 10.5   Online piecemeal restore: restoring the most important filegroup first**

```
-- Disaster at this point. Prioritize Restore of Filegroup 2
USE MASTER
GO

-- Start by performing a tail backup
BACKUP LOG [Sales]
TO DISK = N'G:\SQL Backup\Sales_log_tail.bak'
WITH NORECOVERY, NO_TRUNCATE
GO

-- recover Primary and FG2
RESTORE DATABASE [Sales]
FILEGROUP='Primary'
FROM DISK = N'G:\SQL Backup\Sales_Primary_FG.bak'
WITH PARTIAL, NORECOVERY

RESTORE DATABASE [Sales]
FILEGROUP='FG2'
FROM DISK = N'G:\SQL Backup\Sales_FG2_FG.bak'
WITH NORECOVERY

RESTORE LOG [Sales]
```

```
FROM DISK = N'G:\SQL Backup\Sales_log_tail.bak'
WITH RECOVERY
GO


-- At this point the database is up and running for Filegroup 2 only
-- Other filegroups can now be restored in the order required
```

As shown in listing 10.5, the first step in performing a piecemeal restore is to back up the tail of the transaction log. This will enable us to restore up to the point of failure. Once this backup is completed, we can then start the restore process by restoring the primary filegroup. According to our best practice, this is very small as it contains system objects only. As a result, the primary filegroup restore is quick, and as soon as it completes, the database is online and available for us to prioritize the remainder of the filegroup restores.

In line with our priorities, we proceed with a restore of the FG2 filegroup. The last statement restores the transaction log tail backup, which rolls forward transactions for FG2. At this point, FG2 is online and available for users to query. Attempting to query tables 1 and 3 at this moment will fail as these filegroups are offline pending restore. An error message will appear when you attempt to access these tables:

```
Msg 8653, Level 16, State 1, Line 1
The query processor is unable to produce a plan for the table or view
    'table_3' because the table resides in a filegroup which is not online.
```

Let's recover the remaining filegroups now, as shown in listing 10.6.

Listing 10.6 Online piecemeal restore for remaining filegroups

```
-- restore FG1
RESTORE DATABASE [Sales]
FILEGROUP='FG1'
FROM DISK = N'G:\SQL Backup\Sales_FG1_FG.bak'
WITH NORECOVERY

RESTORE LOG [Sales]
FROM DISK = N'G:\SQL Backup\Sales_log_tail.bak'
WITH RECOVERY
GO

-- restore FG3
RESTORE DATABASE [Sales]
FILEGROUP='FG3'
FROM DISK = N'G:\SQL Backup\Sales_FG3_FG.bak'
WITH NORECOVERY

RESTORE LOG [Sales]
FROM DISK = N'G:\SQL Backup\Sales_log_tail.bak'
WITH RECOVERY
GO
```

Listing 10.6 assumed *all* the filegroups were damaged and needed to be restored. Should some of the filegroups be undamaged, then a restore for those filegroups is unnecessary. Let's imagine that filegroups 1 and 3 were undamaged. After FG2 is restored, we can bring the remaining filegroups online with a simple recovery statement such as this:

```
RESTORE DATABASE [Sales] FILEGROUP='FG1', FILEGROUP='FG3' WITH RECOVERY
```

While normal full backup/restores on single filegroup databases may be acceptable for small to medium databases, very large databases require more thought to reduce the backup impact and minimize user downtime during recovery scenarios. By placing user objects on secondary filegroups, filegroup backups and the online piecemeal restore process enable both of these goals to be met.

As we covered earlier, online restores are available only in the Enterprise edition of SQL Server 2005 and 2008. Another Enterprise-only feature is the *database snapshot*, which we explore next.

10.5 *Database snapshots*

A common step in deploying changes to a database is to take a backup of the database prior to the change. The backup can then be used as a rollback point if the change/release is deemed a failure. On small and medium databases, such an approach is acceptable; however, consider a multi-terabyte database: how long would the backup and restore take either side of the change? Rolling back a simple change on such a large database would take the database out of action for a considerable period of time.

Database snapshots, not to be confused with snapshot backups,[6] can be used to address this type of problem, as well as provide additional functionality for reporting purposes.

First introduced in SQL Server 2005, and only available in the Enterprise editions of SQL Server, snapshots use a combination of Windows *sparse files* and a process known as *copy on write* to provide a point-in-time copy of a database. After the snapshot has been created, a process typically taking only a few seconds, modifications to pages in the database are delayed to allow a copy of the affected page to be posted to the snapshot. After that, the modification can proceed. Subsequent modifications to the same page proceed without delay. Initially empty, the snapshot grows with each database modification.

> **Sparse files**
>
> Database snapshots are created on the NTFS file system, which provides the necessary *sparse file* support. Unlike traditional files, sparse files only occupy space on disk when data is actually written to them, with the size of the file growing as more data is added. As a result, very large files can be created quickly, even on file systems with limited free space.

---

[6] Snapshot backups are specialized backup solutions commonly used in SANs to create near-instant backups using split-mirror (or similar) technology.

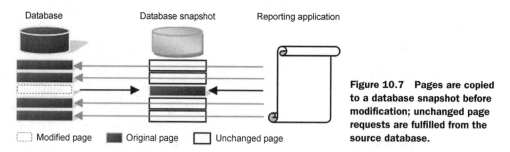

Figure 10.7   Pages are copied to a database snapshot before modification; unchanged page requests are fulfilled from the source database.

As figure 10.7 shows, when a page in a database snapshot is read, if the page hasn't been modified since the snapshot was taken, the read is redirected to the source database. Conversely, modified pages will be read from the snapshot, thus allowing consistent, point-in-time results to be returned.

Let's take a look now at the process of creating a snapshot.

10.5.1   *Creating and restoring snapshots*

A database snapshot can be created using T-SQL, as shown here:

```
-- Create a snapshot of the AdventureWorks database
CREATE DATABASE AdventureWorks2008_Snapshot_20080624 ON (
    NAME = AdventureWorks2008_Data
    , FILENAME = 'E:\SQL Data\AdventureWorks_Data.ss'
)
AS SNAPSHOT OF [AdventureWorks2008];
GO
```

As you can see in figure 10.8, a snapshot is visible after creation in SQL Server Management Studio under the Database Snapshots folder. You can select it for querying as you would any other database.

Given its read-only nature, a snapshot has no transaction log file, and when created, each of the data files in the source database must be specified in the snapshot creation statement along with a corresponding filename and directory. The only exceptions are files used for FileStream data, which aren't supported in snapshots.

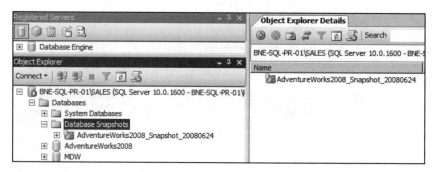

Figure 10.8   A database snapshot is visible in SQL Server Management Studio under the Database Snapshots folder.

You can create multiple snapshots of the same database. The only limitations are the performance overhead and the potential for the snapshots to fill the available disk space. The disk space used by a snapshot is directly determined by the amount of change in the source database. After the snapshot is first created, its footprint, or used space, is effectively zero, owing to the sparse file technology. With each change, the snapshot grows. It follows that if half of the database is modified since the snapshot was created, the snapshot would be roughly half the size of the database it was created from.

Once created, a database can be reverted to its snapshot through the RESTORE DATABASE T-SQL command using the FROM DATABASE_SNAPSHOT clause as shown here (this example will fail if the AdventureWorks database contains FileStream data). During the restore process, both the source and snapshot databases are unavailable and marked *In Restore.*

```
-- Restore the AdventureWorks database from the snapshot
USE master
GO
RESTORE DATABASE AdventureWorks2008
FROM DATABASE_SNAPSHOT = 'AdventureWorks2008_Snapshot_20080624';
GO
```

There are a number of restrictions with reverting to snapshots, all of which are covered in Books Online. The major ones are as follows:

- A database can't revert to a snapshot if more than one snapshot exists. In such a case, all snapshots should be removed except the one to revert to.
- Despite the obvious advantages of snapshots, they're no substitute for a good backup strategy. Unlike a database restore with point-in-time roll-forward capabilities, a database reverted to a snapshot loses all data modifications made after the snapshot was taken.
- Restoring a snapshot breaks the transaction log backup chain; therefore, after the restore, a full backup of the database should be taken.
- Databases with FileStream data can't be reverted.

Given the copy-on-write nature of snapshots, there's a performance overhead in using them, and their unique nature means update and delete modifications aren't permitted against them—that is, they're effectively read-only databases for the duration of their existence. To reduce the performance overhead, older snapshots that are no longer required should be dropped using a DROP DATABASE command such as this one:

```
-- Drop the snapshot
DROP DATABASE AdventureWorks2008_Snapshot_20080624
```

To fully understand the power of database snapshots, let's cover some of the many different ways they can be used.

10.5.2 *Snapshot usage scenarios*

Database snapshots are useful in a variety of situations. Let's cover the most common uses, beginning with reporting.

REPORTING

Given a snapshot is a read-only view of a database at a given moment, it's ideal for reporting solutions that require data accurate as at a particular moment, such as at the end of a financial period.

The major consideration for using snapshots in this manner is the potential performance impact on the source database. In addition to the copy-on-write impact, the read impact needs to be taken into account: in the absence of a snapshot, would you run reports against the source database? If the requested data for reporting hasn't changed since the snapshot was taken, data requested from the snapshot will be read from the source database.

A common snapshot scenario for reporting solutions is to take scheduled snapshots, for example, once a day. Given each snapshot is exposed as a new database with its own name, reporting applications should ideally be configured so that they are aware of the name change and be capable of dynamically reconnecting to the new snapshot. To assist in this process, name new snapshots consistently to enable a programmatic reconnection solution. Alternatively, *synonyms* (not covered in this book) can be created and updated to point to the appropriate snapshot objects.

READING A DATABASE MIRROR

We'll cover database mirroring in the next chapter, but one of the restrictions with the mirror copy of a database is that it can't be read.

When you take a snapshot of the database mirror, you can use it for reporting purposes, but the performance impact of a snapshot may lead to an unacceptable transaction response time in a synchronous mirroring solution, a topic we'll cover in the next chapter.

ROLLING BACK DATABASE CHANGES

A common use for snapshots is protecting against database changes that don't go according to plan, such as a schema change as part of an application deployment that causes unexpected errors. Taking a snapshot before the change allows a quick rollback without requiring a full database backup and restore.

The major issue with rolling back to a snapshot in this manner is that all data entered after the snapshot was created is lost. If there's a delay after the change and the decision to roll back, there may be an unacceptable level of data changes that can't be lost.

For changes made during database downtime, when change can be verified while users aren't connected to the database, snapshots can provide an excellent means of reducing the time to deploy the change while also providing a safe rollback point.

TESTING

Consider a database used in a testing environment where a given set of tests needs to be performed multiple times against the same data set. Traditionally, a database backup is restored between each test to provide a repeatable baseline. If the database is very large, the restore delay may be unacceptably long. Snapshots provide an excellent solution to this type of problem.

DBCC SOURCE
Finally, as you'll see in chapter 12, a DBCC check can be performed against a database snapshot, providing more control over disk space usage during the check.

In closing the chapter, let's focus on a very welcome addition to SQL Server 2008: backup compression.

10.6 *Backup compression*

New in 2008

To reduce the time and space required for backups, some organizations choose to purchase third-party backup tools capable of compressing SQL Server backups. While such products are widely used and proven, other organizations are reluctant to use them for a variety of reasons, such as the following:

- *Cost*—Despite the decreased disk usage (and therefore cost) enabled by such products, some organizations are reluctant to provide the up-front expenditure for new software licenses.
- *Portability*—Depending on the product, compressed backups performed on one licensed server may not be able to be restored on an unlicensed server.
- *Non-Microsoft software*—Some organizations feel uncomfortable with using non-Microsoft software to control such a critical operational process.

In avoiding backup compression products for these reasons, many organizations choose suboptimal backup designs, such as tape only, in order to reduce storage costs. Such designs are often in conflict with their service level agreements for restoration times and acceptable data loss, and often the limitations of such designs are realized for the first time after an actual data loss event.

Introduced in the Enterprise edition of SQL Server 2008, backup compression allows native SQL Server backups to be compressed, which for many organizations will introduce a whole range of benefits and cost savings. No doubt some companies will upgrade to SQL Server 2008 for this reason alone. Although compressed backups can only be *created* using the Enterprise edition of SQL Server 2008, they can be *restored* to any edition of SQL Server 2008.

As with data compression, covered in the previous chapter, there is some CPU overhead involved in backup compression (about 5 percent is typical). To control whether a backup is compressed, you have a number of options, beginning with a server-level default setting called Backup Compression Default, which you can set using sp_configure or SQL Server Management Studio, as shown in figure 10.9.

For individual backups, you can override the default compression setting using options in SQL Server Management Studio, or by using the WITH COMPRESSION/ NO_COMPRESSION T-SQL options as shown here:

```
-- Backup the AdventureWorks database using compression
BACKUP DATABASE AdventureWorks2008
TO DISK = 'G:\SQL Backup\AdventureWorks-Compressed.bak'
WITH INIT, COMPRESSION
```

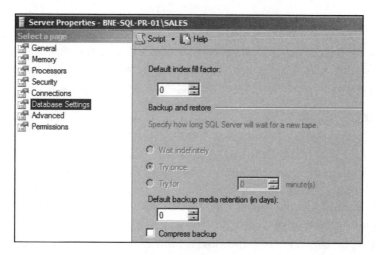

As with data compression, the actual compression rates achieved depend largely on the makeup of the data within the database. Similar to data compression, the goal of backup compression is *not* to achieve the maximum possible compression, but to strike a balance between CPU usage and compression rates.

Given that, the observed compression rates are quite impressive considering the moderate CPU overhead. For example, as you can see in figure 10.10, the observed size of a native AdventureWorks2008 database backup was 188MB compared with the compressed backup size of 45MB. Further, the time taken to back up the database in uncompressed form was 10 seconds compared to 7 seconds for a compressed backup.

Although the actual results will differ depending on the scenario, extrapolating out the compression and duration figures to a very large database scenario promises significant savings in disk space (and therefore money) as well as time.

For those organizations with a tape-only backup approach, backup compression presents an excellent argument to move to a disk then tape approach. For those

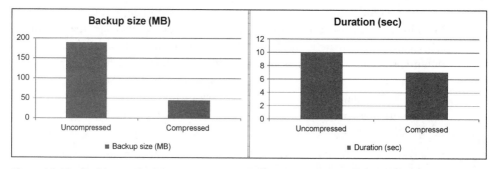

Figure 10.10   Backing up the AdventureWorks2008 database with and without compression. For a moderate CPU overhead, compressed backups yield significant space and duration savings.

already using disk-based backups, the opportunities for storage savings and greater backup availability are compelling reasons for an upgrade to SQL Server 2008.

Finally, as you saw in chapter 6, a backup produced from a database that's protected with Transparent Data Encryption (TDE) will also be encrypted and can't be restored to another server unless that server has the appropriate certificate restored. From a compression perspective, the space savings of a compressed backup on a TDE-encrypted database will be minimal. As such, I don't recommend compressing backups of TDE-encrypted databases.

10.7 *Best practice considerations: backup and recovery*

Developing a reliable backup strategy is arguably the most fundamental and important of all DBA tasks. Fortunately, there are a number of well-established best practices to assist in this process.

- Design a backup strategy for the speed and ease of restoration, not the convenience of the backup. The design should be centered around the service level agreements for restoration time and acceptable data loss.
- Thoroughly document the backup and restore process and include actual code for various restore scenarios. Anyone with moderate DBA skills should be able to follow the documentation to ensure the correct restore process is executed in the shortest possible time.
- When developing disaster recovery plans, consider smaller events as potential disasters in addition to complete site failure. "Small" disasters such as the accidental deletion of a production table can have just as much impact as big ones.
- Simulate and practice recovering from disasters on a regular basis to ensure that documentation is up to date and that all appropriate support staff are comfortable with, and trained in, the recovery process. Consider implementing random "fire drills" to more accurately simulate disaster.
- To minimize the performance impact, schedule full backups for periods of low-usage times.
- Ensure system databases (with the exception of tempdb) are backed up on a regular basis, and immediately after the installation of any service packs, hotfixes, or cumulative updates. System databases store important instance-level data such as login information, maintenance plans, SQL Agent job definitions, and execution history. Restoring a master database backup that was taken when an earlier service pack version was installed is not an experience I recommend!
- Use COPY_ONLY backups to avoid breaking backup chains when additional backups are required.
- Backing up the tail of a transaction log using the WITH NO_TRUNCATE option should be limited to situations in which the database is damaged and inaccessible; otherwise, the COPY_ONLY option should be used in its place.
- After first creating a database or changing the recovery model, take a full backup to initialize the log chain.

- To provide point-in-time restore capabilities and manage transaction log growth, production databases should be in the full recovery mode with regular transaction log backups.

- Development and test databases that don't require point-in-time restoration capabilities should be placed in the simple recovery mode to limit administration overhead and disk space usage.

- Use the Bulk_Logged model on a temporary basis only during bulk-load operations. Take transaction log backups immediately before and after using the bulk logged model for maximum point-in-time protection.

- Consider the disk then tape backup technique whereby backups are written to disk before being archived to tape and removed from disk after a number of days. As well as enabling two copies of recent backups for resilience against media failure, the local disk copies provide fast restoration if needed, and you maintain offsite tape copies for long-term archival purposes.

- Assuming the CPU overhead is measured and within the available headroom, consider backup checksums (along with page checksums) as a means of enabling constant and ongoing I/O verification.

- Consider the MIRROR TO DISK option when performing disk backups to create an *off-server* disk backup for tape archive. With this approach, you avoid the need for tape backup software and drivers on the SQL Server, and you create an additional disk backup with independent retention periods.

- If using the MIRROR TO DISK option to back up to a secondary backup file over the network, consider a private LAN connection to the backup server to maximize network performance and minimize the effect on the public LAN.

- Streaming a backup to multiple backup files can produce a significant performance increase compared to single file backups, particularly for very large databases.

- For small databases, full nightly backups with regular transaction log backups through the day are ideal. For larger databases, consider a weekly full, daily differential, and hourly transaction log model. For very large databases running on the Enterprise edition of SQL Server, consider a filegroup backup/restore design centered around online piecemeal restores.

- Keep in mind the diminishing returns of differential backups. The frequency of the full backup needs to be assessed on the basis of the rate of database change.

- Restore backups on purpose-built backup verification servers or as part of an infrastructure solution, such as a reporting server with automated restores. Log shipping (covered in the next chapter) is an excellent way of verifying transaction log backup validity as well as providing a mechanism to enable reporting databases to be refreshed with current data.

- An alternate means of verification is the RESTORE WITH VERIFYONLY operation, which will read the contents of the backup file to ensure its validity without actually restoring it. In the absence of an automated restore process, this is a good method for verifying that backups are valid.

- Consider the use of backup devices (not covered in this book) for more flexibility when scripting backup jobs. Rather than creating script jobs containing hard-coded directory paths and filenames, using backup devices enables portability of backup scripts; each environment's backup devices can be configured for the appropriate drive letters, directory paths, and filenames.

- If using database snapshots for reporting purposes, ensure they're consistently named to assist with programmatically redirecting access to new snapshots, and make sure old snapshots are removed to reduce disk space requirements and the performance overhead of copy-on-write.

- If using the Enterprise edition of SQL Server, consider backup compression as a means of reducing backup disk cost. Alternatively, consider keeping more backups on disk for longer periods (or use both strategies).

- Compressing backups of databases that use Transparent Data Encryption isn't recommended because the compression rate is likely to be low while still incurring CPU overhead.

Additional information on the best practices covered in this chapter can be found online at http://www.sqlCrunch.com/backup.

As we've covered in this chapter, transaction logs form a fundamental part of a backup and recovery plan. In the next chapter, we'll take a look at log shipping, an excellent mechanism for ongoing verification of the validity of the transaction log backups.

High availability with database mirroring

11

In this chapter, we'll cover

- High-availability options
- Transaction log shipping
- Database mirroring
- Automatic and manual failover
- Setup and administration tasks

When the term *high availability* is used in the context of a SQL Server deployment, features such as database mirroring and failover clustering are almost always the focus of attention. While their contribution to a highly available SQL Server environment is beyond question, they should be seen as a single, albeit important, component of a much broader solution.

Every topic in this book can be viewed in the context of high availability. Security breaches, corrupt backups, and poor maintenance practices can all contribute to unexpected outages and missed availability targets. In many ways, high availability is as much a state of mind as it is a feature or installation option.

This chapter begins with a broad overview of a number of high-availability options and compares their relative strengths and weaknesses. We then cover transaction log shipping, which in many ways can be considered an extension of the previous chapter. Our focus then shifts to database mirroring and how it can be used in contributing to a highly available SQL Server environment.

11.1 High-availability options

Broadly defined, a high-availability solution refers to any system or mechanism put in place to ensure the ongoing availability of a SQL Server instance in the event of a planned or unplanned outage. We've already covered the importance of a well-designed and tested backup and recovery strategy, so the major high-availability options we'll examine here are clustering, log shipping, and database mirroring. While replication can (and is) used by many as part of a high-availability solution, we won't consider it here on the basis of its major purpose as a *data distribution* technology.

11.1.1 Failover clustering

As you learned in chapter 5, failover clustering's major advantage is that it protects the entire server and all of its components from failure. From a SQL Server perspective, the benefits of this are numerous:

- All databases for a given failover clustering instance are *failed over* in a single action.
- SQL Agent jobs, logins, system configuration, and all other items are automatically moved.
- No client redirection logic is required; a failover clustering instance is accessed over the network using a virtual server name which automatically maps to the new server should failover occur.

The major limitation of failover clustering, particularly in Windows Server 2003 and earlier, is that other than a RAID solution, there's no protection from failure of the disks containing the database files and/or the cluster quorum resource. As we saw in chapter 5, Windows Server 2008 brings with it a number of enhanced quorum models that eliminate the problem of a single shared storage quorum resource, but that still leaves the issue of the potential failure of the disks containing the database files. Both log shipping and database mirroring address this by maintaining a hot/warm copy of the database, often in a physically separate location. Let's consider log shipping first.

11.1.2 Transaction log shipping

In the previous chapter we covered the importance of the transaction log in providing the ability to recover a database to a point in time. We also highlighted the need to perform regular restores of backups to ensure their validity, which is a frequently skipped proactive maintenance task amid the chaos of reactive work environments. Transaction log shipping takes care of both of these goals while enabling additional reporting options.

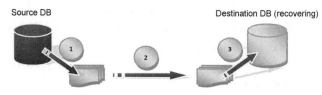

Source DB   Destination DB (recovering)

Figure 11.1   Transaction log shipping automates the process of backing up, copying, and restoring transaction logs from a source database to a destination database on another server.

1) Transaction log backup 2) Logs copied to destination server 3) Logs restored

As illustrated in figure 11.1, a log shipped database sends its transaction log backups to a copy of the database on one or more secondary servers for regular restoration. As we'll see shortly, the log shipping configuration screens provided in SQL Server Management Studio enable the frequency of the transaction log backup, copy, and restore jobs to be set, along with the option to leave the database copy in a read-only state in between log restores, thus enabling the database to be used for reporting purposes.

Unlike clustering, log shipping has no shared storage and therefore no central point of failure. Each server in the log shipping pair is completely independent: it has its own storage and could theoretically be located anywhere in the world.

The major disadvantage of log shipping is that each database must be log shipped independently. For a SQL Server instance containing multiple databases, all of which require protection, the administrative effort required to set up and administer log shipping for each database is substantial when compared to a clustering solution.

Log shipping has no automatic failover process. If one server fails, manual intervention is required to bring the log ship partner online and redirect clients to the new server. Database mirroring, discussed next, addresses this issue nicely.

11.1.3 *Database mirroring*

In a manner similar to log shipping, servers in a database mirroring session use the transaction log to move transactions between a *principal* server and a *mirror* server. The main advantage of database mirroring is that the movement of transactions can be performed synchronously, guaranteeing that the mirror is an exact copy of the principal at any given moment. In contrast, a log shipping destination is typically at least 15 minutes behind the source (which can actually be an advantage in some situations, as we'll see shortly).

Like log shipping, database mirroring needs to be set up on a database-by-database basis, therefore limiting its appeal for instances containing many critical databases. Unlike log shipping, however, it can optionally be configured with a *witness* instance to initiate automatic failover to the mirror server. Further, with the correct configuration, client connections can be automatically redirected to the mirror server on failure of the principal.

A typical database mirroring session is illustrated in figure 11.2. Covered in detail later in the chapter, database mirroring also overcomes the shared storage limitation of clustering, therefore enabling mirroring partners to be located large distances from one another.

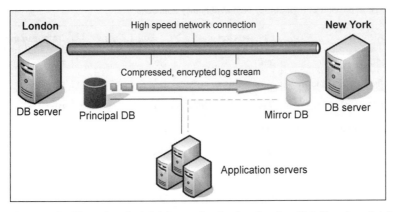

Figure 11.2   Figure A typical database mirroring topology in which the mirror database is receiving and applying transactions from the principal server over a high-speed network link

When compared with log shipping, the major disadvantages of database mirroring are the fact that only a single mirror can exist for each principal (log shipping allows multiple destinations for the one source) and the inability to read the mirror database (unless using a database snapshot), thus limiting the use of mirroring in providing a reporting solution.

Service level agreements

A critical component of *any* SQL Server solution (but particularly a high-availability solution) is a *service level agreement* (SLA), which defines a number of system attributes such as the acceptable data loss, disaster-recovery time, and transaction performance targets. A common SLA entry is the availability target, usually expressed as a percentage; for example, a 99 percent availability target allows approximately 3.5 days of downtime per year. In contrast, a 99.999 percent target allows 5 minutes! Each "9" added to the availability target exponentially increases the cost of building an appropriate solution. As such, agreeing on an availability target *before* designing and building a solution is a critical step in both minimizing costs and meeting customer expectations.

To more easily highlight the strengths and weaknesses of each solution, let's compare them side by side.

11.1.4 Comparing high-availability options

Table 11.1 compares clustering, log shipping, and mirroring from various perspectives. Note that combinations of these solutions are frequently deployed for mission-critical databases, therefore minimizing the weaknesses of any one option. For example, using a failover cluster in combination with database mirroring enables local failover support for all databases with mission-critical databases mirrored to an off-site location.

Table 11.1   A comparison of SQL Server high-availability solutions

Attribute	Clustering	Log shipping	Database mirroring
Multiple database failover	Yes	No	No
Logins, config, and job failover	Yes	No	No
Automatic failover support	Yes	No	Yes[a]
Automatic client redirection	Yes	No	Yes[b]
Provides a reporting solution	No	Yes[c]	Yes[d]
Central point of failure	Disk	No	No
Multiple standby destinations	No	Yes	No
Geographical distance support	Yes[e]	Yes	Yes
Data latency	Nil	15mins+[f]	Nil[g]

[a] Optional
[b] If using SNAC or custom application logic
[c] Assuming standby restore mode
[d] If using database snapshots
[e] Typically with high-end custom solutions
[f] Configurable; defaults to 15 minute backup/copy/restore frequency
[g] If using synchronous (high safety) mode

Regardless of which of the high-availability solutions you choose (if any), the importance of a solid backup strategy together with adherence to other best practices covered throughout this book can't be overstated; all of them contribute to a highly available SQL Server environment in their own way.

Before we get to the main focus of this chapter, database mirroring, let's delve a little deeper into transaction log shipping.

11.2   *Transaction log shipping*

Log shipping was first introduced in SQL Server 2000, although many DBAs implemented it before then using a series of custom jobs. Put simply, log shipping automates the backup, copy, and restore of a source database's transaction logs to one or more secondary server instances seeded with a full backup of the source database restored in recovering mode.

A commonly referenced backup best practice is to restore backups on a regular basis to ensure they're valid. Until they're restored you can't be 100 percent sure that they'll work in an emergency restore scenario. The problem a lot of organizations have with this recommendation is the time and equipment required to carry it out. Manually copying and restoring backup files on the off chance that something may be wrong isn't the most rewarding of tasks, and as a result, it's often shelved as a good idea for implementation at a later point, once everything else is done—which of course never happens.

The best way of implementing this recommendation is to automate it as part of an infrastructure solution. For example, in the next chapter we'll look at automating a full backup and restore together with DBCC checks in providing a reporting database that's automatically refreshed on a regular basis while also taking care of the recommendation to run backup verification and DBCC checks.

As we covered earlier, transaction logs are a crucial component in the ability to recover a database to a point in time, and a broken log chain destroys this ability. Perhaps the best method for automating the restore of transaction logs, and therefore validating the log chain, is through the use of transaction log shipping.

Later in this section we'll walk through the process of establishing a log shipping session, which will highlight its various components and advantages. Before we do that, let's examine some of the common log shipping usage scenarios.

11.2.1 Usage scenarios

In addition to the major benefit of constant, automatic log chain validation, log shipping provides a number of other benefits, making it a commonly used solution for a variety of scenarios.

OFFSITE RECOVERY POINT

Log shipping can be used to provide an offsite, up-to-date copy of a mission-critical database. In the event of total environment destruction, the offsite copy can quickly restore any remaining logs and be brought online and available for application usage.

Compared to database mirroring, discussed in detail later in the chapter, log shipping has a much greater transaction latency. The default frequency of the log backup, copy, and restore jobs is 15 minutes, so the secondary database will typically be between 30 and 45 minutes behind the primary. While at first this may appear to be a weakness of log shipping, in some instances it presents a stronger solution than database mirroring.

Consider a situation in which a table is accidentally (or maliciously) dropped. In the case of database mirroring, by the time the error was realized, the change would probably already exist on the mirror. With log shipping, the restore containing the error can be canceled, or restored just prior to the error. Think of this as a 7-second broadcast delay.

REPORTING SOLUTION

As we'll see shortly, when restoring the transaction logs on the secondary database, the *standby* option can be invoked. This option enables the secondary database to be used for read purposes in between log restores. Together with the ability to schedule the restores, this can enable the database to be used for reporting purposes for certain periods of the day.

The major benefit of log shipping when compared to database mirroring is that a log shipping source can be shipped to multiple destinations. For example, one destination could be used as a reporting source and another destination set up as a dedicated failover point. Each can have its own copy and restore schedules. Further, each destination can be in different physical locations from the source for further geographical failure resilience.

UPGRADE SOLUTION

As we covered in chapter 4, log shipping can be set up between one version of SQL Server and the next. For example, a SQL Server 2005 source database can log ship to a 2008 destination. Such a configuration could be used to minimize the upgrade time in the following way:

1   A new server can be installed, configured, and tested as required with SQL Server 2008 loaded and configured.
2   A full backup of the source 2005 database is made and copied to the new server.
3   The 2005 database is restored to the new 2008 instance on the new server in recovering mode.
4   Log shipping is set up between the old and new server instances with transaction logs shipping on a regular basis.
5   When the upgrade time arrives, users are disconnected from the 2005 instance, remaining logs shipped to the 2008 instance, and the database is then recovered with applications reconfigured to point at the new instance.

Until step 5, the original 2005 instance continues to run with no user interruption. The only downtime comes in step 5, which will typically be very short given the small number of transactions to ship across. The other benefit of this approach is that the original 2005 server still exists as a rollback point with its data still accurate as at the time of the last transaction log ship.

This solution could also be used when upgrading or decommissioning server hardware, but like database mirroring, log shipping is implemented on a database-by-database basis, so if a given server has many databases, it may not be the best approach.

To further highlight the options and benefits of log shipping, let's walk through an implementation using the SQL Server Management Studio tool.

11.2.2 Setting up and monitoring log shipping

You establish a log shipping session in SQL Server Management Studio by right-clicking a database and choosing Tasks > Ship Transaction Logs. Note that the selected database must be using either the Full or Bulk_Logged recovery model. As shown in figure 11.3, the resulting screen provides the option "Enable this as a primary database in a log shipping configuration." If the database is already log shipped, you can deselect this option to remove log shipping from the database.

After choosing the option to enable the database for log shipping, click the Backup Settings button. In the resulting screen, shown in figure 11.4, you can set a number of properties, such as the transaction log backup destination (including a file share accessible from the log shipping destination server), the log backup retention period, the backup frequency, and whether to use backup compression.

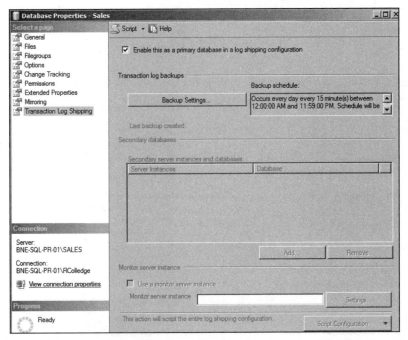

Figure 11.3 **The initial log shipping configuration screen permits access to the various configuration components, including backup settings and secondary servers.**

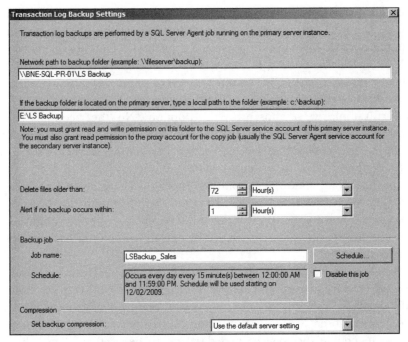

Figure 11.4 **The Transaction Log Backup Settings screen enables the configuration of log backup frequency, destination, and retention period.**

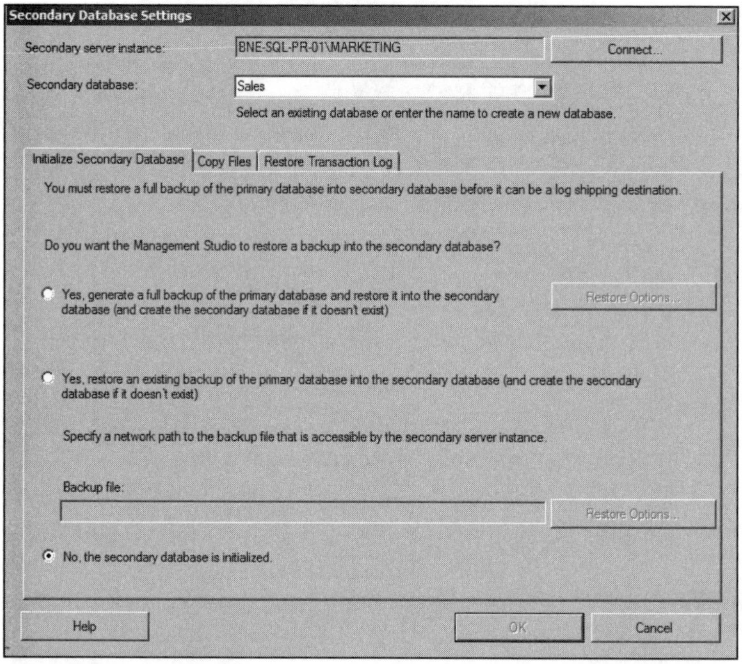

Figure 11.5   On the Initialize Secondary Database tab you can specify how the log shipped database will be created on the destination server.

Once you complete these settings, click OK to return to the screen shown earlier in figure 11.3. The next step is repeated for each required log shipping destination. In our example, we'll do this once for a simple 1:1 primary:secondary relationship.

Click Add under Secondary databases to specify a log shipping destination. In the resulting screen, you can specify a secondary server instance. On the Initialize Secondary Database tab, you're given three options, as you can see in figure 11.5.

For our example, we've chosen the third option, "No, the secondary database is initialized." We've done this because a full backup of the source database has already been restored in NORECOVERY mode on the destination server. Alternatively, we could choose the first option, which will automate the full backup, copy, and restore process, or the second option, if we want to restore a preexisting backup.

Next, click the Copy Files tab, where you can specify where the log backup files will be copied to and how frequently the copy will take place. As shown in figure 11.6, this tab also contains the option to automatically remove copied log backup files after a certain time period.

Finally, click the Restore Transaction Log tab, shown in figure 11.7, and select a restore mode and frequency. The default restore mode is No Recovery Mode, which leaves the database in the recovering status, and therefore unable to be used. For our example, we've chosen Standby Mode, along with the option to disconnect users. These options enable the log shipped database to be used in read-only mode in between log restores for reporting purposes.

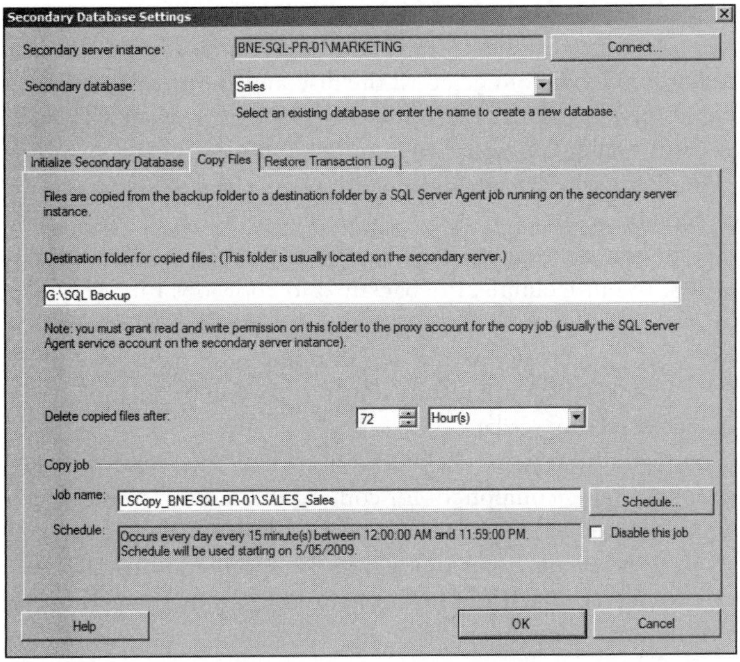

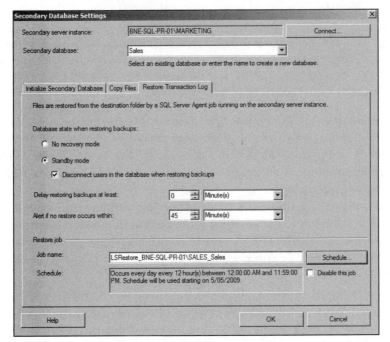

Figure 11.6   The Copy Files tab lets you specify the log backup copy location, frequency, and retention period.

Figure 11.7   Figure The Restore Transaction Log tab allows you to set the restore frequency along with the database state between restores.

Note that when using standby mode, you must take into account the restore frequency. The default restore frequency of 15 minutes is inappropriate for a reporting solution, as users would be disconnected (if the disconnect option is chosen) every 15 minutes to enable the log restore. For our example, we've chosen a 12-hour restore frequency. This will enable 12 hours of uninterrupted reporting before the next restore, and assuming users are advised on the restore times, such a configuration may be quite acceptable.

Regardless of the restore frequency, the backup and copy jobs have their own independent schedules. In our example, the backup and copy jobs run every 15 minutes. If the secondary database is required in an emergency, the restore process—accessible via a SQL Server Agent job created by the log shipping setup process—can be manually executed at any time, which will restore any outstanding transaction logs and thus bring the secondary server up to date.

Once you complete these steps, click OK to return to the screen shown in figure 11.3. The other log shipping component for consideration is the monitoring instance, which will actively monitor (via SQL Server Agent jobs) the backup, copy, and restore progress. If any of these events don't run within the specified intervals, the monitoring server generates alerts, which can be configured to notify the appropriate DBAs. We'll cover alerts in more detail in chapter 14.

Monitoring instance

Although the primary or secondary log shipping instance can also be the monitoring instance, using an independent instance for monitoring is recommended. In such a configuration, the load on the primary and secondary instances is reduced, and monitoring continues in the event of failure on either the primary or secondary instance. Further, a monitoring instance can monitor more than one log shipping configuration.

After deciding whether to use a monitoring instance, save the log shipping configuration for later use by clicking the Script Configuration button. SQL Server implements the backup, copy, restore, and monitoring steps as SQL Server Agent jobs, requiring this service to be running on all instances (primary, secondary, and monitoring) to enable log shipping to function.

Finally, in order to determine the status of the log shipping session, SQL Server includes a number of options, one of which is the built-in transaction log shipping status report, as shown in figure 11.8. Access this report by right-clicking on a server involved in a log shipping role (primary, secondary, or monitor) and select Reports > Standard Reports > Transaction Log Shipping Status.

Note that this report contains additional information not shown in figure 11.8, including the filename of the last file backed up, copied, and restored.

If you're using log shipping to maintain a warm standby server for failover purposes (as opposed to a pure reporting server solution), then one of the important tasks is the failover and role reversal process.

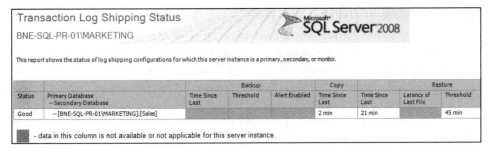

Figure 11.8 The built-in transaction log shipping status report allows you to view status information easily.

11.2.3 *Failover and role reversal*

If the primary instance in a log shipping solution fails (or a manual failover is required for planned maintenance), the failover process is largely a manual effort, requiring you to back up, copy, and restore outstanding logs to the secondary instance before configuring log shipping in the reverse direction. This process can be summarized as follows:

1 Disable the log shipping backup, copy, and restore SQL Server Agent jobs.
2 Manually run the backup, copy, and restore SQL Server Agent jobs to push across any outstanding transaction log backups.
3 Back up the transaction log on the primary instance using the WITH NORECOVERY option. This will place the database in the recovering mode, enabling it to receive logs from the secondary server once the roles are swapped.
4 Restore the backup from step 3 on the secondary instance using the WITH RECOVERY option. This will place the secondary database in read/write mode and make it available for use. At this point, you will need to manually redirect client connections to the secondary instance.
5 Set up log shipping in the reverse direction, ensuring that the "No, the secondary database is initialized" option is selected, as shown in figure 11.5 earlier. At this point, there will be a set of SQL Agent jobs for the new configuration as well as disabled jobs for the old configuration. Leaving the old disabled jobs in place makes future role changes easier—you simply disable one set, enable another, and ensure tail log backups are applied in the appropriate direction. At this point, the log shipping roles are reversed.

One of the real benefits of log shipping is its simplicity. The core components of log shipping are fundamental SQL Server tasks: transaction log backups and restores. Other than running out of disk space, there isn't a lot that can go wrong, unless someone makes (and removes) an additional transaction log backup without the COPY_ONLY option that we covered in the previous chapter. That being said, it's not without its limitations; the primary one is the manual effort required to change roles and reconnect clients. In that regard, database mirroring offers a superior solution.

11.3   *Database mirroring overview*

Available in the Standard and Enterprise editions of SQL Server, database mirroring is used to maintain a *hot standby* copy of a database. Transactions generated on the source (principal) database are sent to the mirror over an encrypted, compressed log stream and applied in either a synchronous or asynchronous manner. You can choose between the two modes to prioritize transaction safety or performance.

If the principal instance fails, an optional witness server can be used to automatically bring the mirror database online with zero data loss. With the necessary connection logic, applications can automatically reconnect to the mirrored database. The combination of synchronous mirroring with automatic failover and application reconnection logic delivers a truly *hands-free* high-availability solution for mission-critical SQL Server databases.

Unlike log shipping (which applies transactions to the database copy using scheduled transaction log backups and restores), database mirroring streams transactions directly to the mirror database in real time. If you're using the synchronous mode, transactions won't commit at the principal until they're received and written to the transaction log at the mirror. As such, databases in a mirroring solution are either an exact mirror, or seconds apart, which explains why we use the term *hot standby* rather than *warm standby*.

Like log shipping, database mirroring is established on an individual database-by-database basis. This is in contrast to failover clustering, which provides protection for an entire instance, and all the databases contained within. But unlike clustering, mirrored databases are typically located on servers in different geographical locations connected via high-speed communication links. Such configurations assist in the creation of disaster-recovery designs for mission-critical databases.

Before we go too much further, let's define a number of database mirroring terms that we'll be using throughout the remainder of this chapter.

11.3.1   *Terminology*

Like failover clustering, database mirroring comes with a healthy dose of new terminology:

- *Principal and mirror database*—In a database mirroring solution, there's a single source database that applications connect to. This is known as the *principal* database. The *mirror* database is the copy being maintained for failover purposes. If failover occurs, the roles of principal and mirror are swapped.
- *Principal and mirror instance*—The SQL Server instance containing the principal database is the *principal instance*. The *mirror instance* is the instance containing the mirror database. These instances are frequently located in different locations as part of a disaster-recovery design. A SQL Server instance can't be both a mirror and a principal instance *for the same database*, but can have different roles for different databases—for example, an instance can be a mirror instance for database A and a principal instance for database B.

- *Failover*—A *failover* is the process of moving the principal role to the mirror. This can be an automatic process using a *witness*, or can be initiated manually.
- *Witness*—A *witness* is an optional role in a mirroring solution that enables an independent SQL Server instance to observe the mirroring process and provide automatic failover where required.
- *High-performance mode*—In *high-performance* mode, transactions are sent from the principal to the mirror database *asynchronously*; therefore, depending on the transaction rate and network bandwidth/congestion, the mirror database may fall behind the principal by longer than expected.
- *High-safety mode*—In *high-safety* mode, transactions are sent from the principal to the mirror database *synchronously*. For mission-critical databases connected over high-speed network interfaces, this is the option used for achieving zero data loss automatic failover with a witness instance.
- *Forced service*—In high-performance mode, or high-safety mode without automatic failover, *forced service* forces the principal role to move to the mirror database, which may result in data loss.
- *Endpoint*—Principal and mirror databases communicate over dedicated mirroring *endpoints* using the TCP/IP protocol and unique port numbers.
- *Send and redo queues*—In some situations, the transaction rate on the principal database may exceed the rate at which transactions can be sent to the mirror. Equally so, on the mirror they may be received faster than they can be applied. In each case, the transaction logs are used at the principal and mirror to *catch up*. The section of the transaction log that's yet to be sent or applied is referred to as the *send queue* and *redo queue*, respectively.

As with all high-availability technologies, database mirroring has a number of important restrictions.

11.3.2 *Mirroring restrictions*

Before we continue, let's cover some of the restrictions of database mirroring:

- Unlike transaction log shipping, which supports the Bulk_Logged recovery model, database mirroring only works for databases using the full recovery model.
- The mirror database can't be read unless you create a database snapshot against it. We covered database snapshots in the previous chapter. Depending on the environment and mirroring mode, a snapshot may introduce an unacceptable performance overhead.
- Mirroring is set up for individual databases—in other words, you can't mirror at an instance level. While you can individually mirror more than one database within an instance, there are special considerations when mirroring databases with interdependencies, a topic we'll cover later in this chapter.
- System databases (master, model, msdb, and tempdb) can't be mirrored.

- You can have only one mirror database for each principal, unlike log shipping where logs from a source database can be shipped to multiple destinations. However, the one database can be both log shipped *and* mirrored.
- Databases involved in cross-database or distributed transactions aren't supported in database mirroring. We'll explore this restriction in more detail later in the chapter.
- As covered in chapter 9, database mirroring can't be enabled on databases containing FileStream data.

With that brief introduction in mind, let's move on and discuss the two major types of database mirroring modes: asynchronous (high performance) and synchronous (high safety).

11.4 *Mirroring modes*

Later in the chapter we'll go through the process of preparing for and setting up a mirroring session. For now, let's concentrate on the process behind the delivery of transactions from the principal to the mirror during a mirroring *session*, and how this process is performed based on the mirroring mode.

A database mirroring session begins with the mirror instance identifying the log sequence number (LSN) of the last transaction applied to the mirror database. The mirror instance then obtains any outstanding transactions from the transaction log of the principal database. The outstanding transactions received from the principal instance are written to the transaction log of the mirror database and rolled forward. The outstanding transactions to roll forward are known as the *redo queue*, and the depth of this queue determines the catch-up time and therefore the minimum time to fail over the principal role to the mirror database.

The mirroring process for a synchronous mirroring session is summarized in figure 11.9.

Synchronous Database Mirroring (High Safety)

Principal DB   **Mirroring DB**

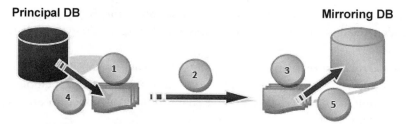

1) Transaction written to log **2)** Log record streamed to mirror
3) Log record hardened to transaction log **4)** Transaction commits on the principal
5) Transaction rolled forward on the mirror DB

Figure 11.9 Synchronous database mirroring. In asynchronous mirroring, the transaction commits on the principal database after step 2.

As updates on the principal database continue, the transactions are streamed from the principal's transaction log to the mirror's transaction log and rolled forward on the mirror database. The mirroring mode, asynchronous (high performance) or synchronous (high safety), determines how the principal's transactions are sent and received.

11.4.1 High performance (asynchronous)

Asynchronous mirroring is only available in the Enterprise edition of SQL Server. Under asynchronous mode, a transaction is committed on the principal as soon as it's *sent* to the mirror; it doesn't wait for an acknowledgment from the mirror that the transaction has been written to the mirror's transaction log, nor is the principal affected in any way by a failure at the mirror (other than a loss of failover capabilities). As such, asynchronous mirroring is used when transaction performance at the principal is of prime concern.

The high-performance nature of asynchronous mode comes with a reduction in high availability. In cases where the transaction load at the principal is very high, or the mirror server is overloaded (or both), the redo queue on the mirror may become very deep, increasing failover time. Further, given the transaction delivery method, there's no guarantee that the mirror partner receives and applies each transaction.

> **Database mirroring in SQL Server 2008**
>
> First introduced in SQL Server 2005, database mirroring is improved in 2008 through automatic recovery from certain types of data corruption (Enterprise edition only) and log stream compression. Upon detection of a corrupted page, the principal and mirror databases can request fresh copies of the page from each other and overwrite the corrupted page with a good copy. Log stream compression improves the performance of database mirroring by compressing the transaction log stream between the principal and mirror and therefore reducing the network bandwidth requirements while increasing transaction throughput.

The only failover option for asynchronous mirroring is forced service, which is only available if the principal instance is disconnected from the mirror. When this option is invoked (we'll cover this feature later in this chapter), the mirroring database assumes the role of principal.

Given the possibility of data loss, the forced service failover option should be used as a last resort. If you're considering using this option due to failure of the principal, consider these alternatives:

- You can wait for the principal server to recover.
- If the downtime is unacceptable and service needs to be resumed immediately, attempt to back up the tail of the transaction log on the principal. If this succeeds, mirroring can be removed and the tail of the log restored to the mirror database and brought online.

Asynchronous mode mirroring is typically used in disaster-recovery designs where the principal and mirror servers are in different physical locations and the network connectivity between them may lead to unacceptably large transaction latency under the synchronous mode. If the possibility of some data loss is accepted as a consequence of the highest performance, asynchronous mirroring presents a good disaster-recovery option, but for situations in which zero data loss is the target, consider high-safety synchronous mirroring.

11.4.2 High safety (synchronous)

Synchronous mirroring is available in both the Standard and Enterprise editions of SQL Server. In synchronous mode, transactions aren't committed on the principal database until written, or *hardened*, to the transaction log on the mirror database. While this increases transaction latency, synchronous mirroring ensures each transaction is recoverable on the mirror database, and is therefore an excellent solution for protecting mission-critical data.

When running in high-safety mode, special consideration needs to be given to long-running or intensive operations (or both) such as index rebuilds and bulk loads. The load from these types of operations often leads to a measurable reduction in the performance throughput. While the suspend option, discussed later in the chapter, can assist here, such impact should be carefully measured in a testing environment before production implementation.

A crucial consideration when choosing high-safety mirroring is the network latency between the principal and mirror instances. The excellent Microsoft whitepaper[1] "Database Mirroring Best Practices and Performance Considerations" highlights a connection between network latency, transactions per second, and transaction response time. One of the things that stands out, as shown in figure 11.10, is that once

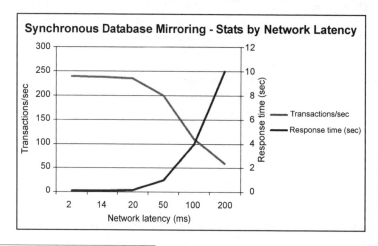

Figure 11.10 As network latency increases, the impact on transaction response time and throughput increases.

---

[1] *Database Mirroring Best Practices and Performance Considerations,* Sanjay Mishra, Microsoft Corporation, February 2006. Links and further details available at http://www.sqlCrunch.com/HA.

the network latency increases beyond 50ms, the effect on transaction throughput and response time is dramatic.

The average local area network (LAN) typically has a latency of less than 5ms with metropolitan area networks (MANs) and wide area networks (WANs) anywhere up to 200ms or more. Before selecting synchronous mirroring, perform thorough testing with actual or simulated network latencies to measure the performance impact on the expected workload.

When the principal and mirror instances are separated over large distances using a WAN, asynchronous mirroring is typically used as part of a disaster-recovery solution. In LANs or low-latency MANs, synchronous mirroring is often deployed in preventing/reducing downtime for both planned and unplanned outages.

Based on the mirroring mode, and the presence or absence of a witness instance, there is a variety of failover options.

11.5   Failover options

The three types of failover options are *automatic, manual,* and *forced service.* Table 11.2 summarizes the availability of these options based on the mirroring mode and presence of a witness instance.

Table 11.2   Supported failover modes by mirroring type

Mirroring mode	Witness	Supported failover modes
High performance	No	Forced service
High safety	No	Manual or forced service
High safety	Yes	Automatic, manual, or forced service

Let's begin this section with a look at automatic failover.

11.5.1   Automatic failover with SNAC

If the principal instance fails, automatic failover brings the mirror database online as the new principal database. For this to occur, all of the following conditions must be true:

- Mirroring must be operating in the high-safety (synchronous) mode.
- A witness instance must be present.
- The mirror database must be *synchronized*—that is, all outstanding transactions from the principal should be written to the transaction log on the mirror database.
- The principal instance must lose communication with the witness and mirror.
- The witness and mirror instance must remain in contact.
- The mirror instance must detect the loss of the principal instance.

The last bullet is a crucial item and requires more explanation. There are various types of failure conditions that may lead to the loss of the principal and are broadly categorized into *hard* and *soft* errors. An example of a hard error is a power failure; a TCP/IP timeout is regarded as a soft error.

Unlike soft errors, hard errors are typically reported immediately. In either case, database mirroring uses a timeout setting in combination with a *heartbeat* between the mirroring partners in order to detect failure. The default timeout value is 10 seconds. If a mirroring partner doesn't receive a response within that time, a failure is assumed. For synchronous mirroring, you can adjust this value, although you shouldn't use a value of less than 10 seconds to prevent unwanted failovers due to temporary network issues.

With these conditions in mind, let's walk through the process of an automatic failover, starting from the point of assumed failure:

1 The principal database, if still available, sets its status to *disconnected*, and drops any client connections.
2 The witness and mirror instances register the principal instance as unavailable.
3 The mirror database rolls forward any outstanding transactions in its redo queue.
4 The mirror database comes online as the new principal.
5 When the original principal database comes online, it's registered as the mirror, and synchronizes missing transactions.

Let's consider step 1 in more detail. Imagine a case where a private network connection to the mirror and witness instances breaks but the public network used for client connections is still available. In this case, the database is still up and running and available to clients, but a mirroring failure is assumed. By actively disconnecting the client connections, a situation is prevented whereby both databases may temporarily receive updates to the database, resulting in a loss of data.

Mirroring quorum

Enabling a witness role in a mirroring session introduces the concept of *quorum*. A mirroring session is said to *have quorum* when at least two of the three instances (principal, mirror, and witness) in the mirroring relationship are connected. For a mirroring database to be available, quorum must exist. When all three instances are connected, *full quorum* exists. If the principal instance fails, the mirror instance has quorum with the witness and coordinates with it to take on the role of principal. If the new principal then loses the connection to the witness, no quorum exists, and the database is taken offline.

To fully benefit from automatic failover, you should consider how clients can be automatically reconnected to the mirror database. One of the great things about database mirroring is that client connections using *SQL Server Native Client* (SNAC) can benefit from its understanding and awareness of database mirroring. A SNAC connection string includes the Failover Partner option, as shown in this example:

```
Data Source=SV1\Sales; Failover Partner=SV2\Sales; Initial Catalog=Sales;
```

Using the SNAC's failover partner option automates a lot of the hard work in application reconnection logic required for other high-availability options. However, even with database mirroring in place, client connections originating from non-SNAC sources won't be able to take advantage of automatic reconnection, unless the reconnection logic is coded into the application. This is an important high-availability consideration; while the database may fail over immediately and without any data loss, if the clients can't automatically reconnect to the mirror, it can hardly be considered a success, thus devaluing part of the appeal of automatic failover.

High-safety mirroring sessions can also use the manual failover method.

11.5.2 *Manual failover*

The manual failover method, available only in high-safety (synchronous) mode, is typically used when preparing for a planned outage such as a hardware or service pack upgrade. We'll see an example of a manual failover later in the chapter, but a summary follows:

1 The DBA enacts the manual failover, which swaps the mirroring roles between the principal and mirror.
2 Applications are reconnected to the new principal database once it completes the processing of its redo queue and comes online.
3 Mirroring is suspended and the mirror instance is taken offline for upgrade, during which time the principal database runs exposed—that is, failover of any type isn't possible, so if the new principal instance fails, an outage will result.
4 Once the upgrade is complete, the mirror database rejoins the mirroring session and synchronizes outstanding transactions (catches up).

At this point, the mirroring roles can be reversed to return the instances to their original state, although assuming both servers are configured with the same processing capacity and load, this step shouldn't be required, so the current roles could remain in place.

Of course, if there are multiple databases on the server being taken offline for a planned outage, and some of them aren't mirrored, then this approach obviously needs to be reconsidered.

The final failover mode is *forced service*.

11.5.3 *Forced service*

Typically used in disaster-recovery scenarios with high-performance (asynchronous) mirroring, this option brings the mirror database online and makes it available for client connections only if the link between the principal and mirror instances is lost.

The critical consideration before enacting this failover mode is the possibility of data loss. If a network connection drops and the principal database continues processing transactions before failover, these transactions won't be available for recovery on the mirror database. As such, forced service is typically only used when service must be resumed as soon as possible and the possibility of data loss is accepted.

In closing our section on failover modes, let's walk through a number of failover scenarios.

11.5.4 Failure scenarios

To understand how failure is handled based on the mirroring mode and which instance fails, consider table 11.3. Read the notes that follow the table in conjunction with each example.

Table 11.3   Failure scenarios by mirroring topology and transaction safety

Failure	Mirroring mode	Witness	Action
Principal	Synchronous	Yes	Automatic failover (see note 1)
Principal	Synchronous	No	Manual failover (see note 2)
Principal	Asynchronous	No	Force service to make mirror available (see note 3)
Mirror	Both	Both	Principal runs exposed and transactions retained (see note 4)
Witness	Synchronous	Yes	Automatic failover not possible

Action Notes:

1   Assuming the mirror and witness are in contact, automatic failover occurs after the nominated timeout.

2   Mirroring is stopped on the mirror database using `ALTER DATABASE <dbname> SET PARTNER OFF`. The mirroring database is then recovered using `RESTORE DATABASE <dbname> WITH RECOVERY`. When the principal server becomes available, mirroring would need to be reestablished, this time in the reverse direction.

3   Service is forced by running this command on the mirror database: `ALTER DATABASE <dbname> SET PARTNER FORCE_SERVICE_ALLOW_DATA_LOSS`.

4   For as long as database mirroring exists, transactions generated on the principal must remain in the transaction log, so disk space usage would need to be closely monitored while the mirror instance is unavailable.

Armed with an overview of database mirroring principals and options, let's roll up our sleeves and get into the details of the implementation.

11.6   Mirroring in action

In this section we'll walk through an example of setting up, failing over, and monitoring database mirroring. Before we start the setup process, let's review a number of important design considerations and preparatory steps:

- *SQL version*—The principal and mirror instances must be running the same version and edition of SQL Server. If the database fails over, the same feature set needs to be available to ensure application behavior continues as normal.

- *Collation*—Ensure the principal and mirror instances are using the same collations.

- *Network latency*—As covered earlier, this can have a significant impact on transaction throughput and response time for high-safety (synchronous) mode. There are a number of tools and techniques for simulating varying levels of network latency, and the impact on load should be measured with the highest expected latency before proceeding with the high-safety mode.

- *Network quality*—Consider the possibility of small network problems causing unwanted automatic failovers. If using synchronous mirroring, you can avoid unwanted failovers by removing the witness server from the mirroring topology.

- *Capacity*—The capacity of the mirror server should be at least as great as that of the principal. In the event of failover, if the mirror server is unable to handle the load, the benefits of mirroring are obviously reduced. Capacity includes enough free disk space and processing power. Ideally, both the mirror and principal instances are configured identically, with load on the mirroring instance able to sustain the additional load from the principal in a failover event.

- *Application failover*—To fully capitalize on the automatic failure mode, consider the ability of the application to automatically reconnect to the mirror database when failover occurs—for example, using SNAC with a failover partner specified in the connection string.

- *Recovery model*—The principal database must be using the full recovery model.

- *SQL logins*—To enable applications to continue working after a mirroring failover, ensure that the same logins are created on both the principal and mirror instance and that they're created with the same security identifier (SID) values (using the `SID =` clause of the `CREATE LOGIN` statement).

So let's get started. Like most tasks, the setup of database mirroring can be performed using either a T-SQL script or SQL Server Management Studio. For our example, we'll use Management Studio.

11.6.1 Mirroring setup

The first step in setting up database mirroring is to initialize the mirror database. This is achieved by restoring a full backup of the principal database and at least one transaction log backup using the `WITH NORECOVERY` option. A transaction log backup must be restored in order to obtain the latest log sequence number (LSN) to determine the starting point for the redo queue when mirroring starts.

If any additional transaction log backups are made on the principal database before mirroring setup is started, these backups need to be restored using the `WITH NORECOVERY` option on the mirror database. If any scheduled transaction log backup jobs exist, such as maintenance plans or log shipping jobs, disabling them until mirroring is initialized will simplify the mirroring setup process.

In the previous chapter we covered the process of restoring database backups and transaction logs without recovery; here's an example of doing this on the mirror server:

```
-- Restore the Sales DB and roll forward using a transaction log restore
RESTORE DATABASE [Sales]
FROM DISK = N'G:\SQL Backup\Sales.bak'
WITH NORECOVERY
GO

RESTORE LOG [Sales]
FROM DISK = N'G:\SQL Backup\Sales-Trn-1.bak'
WITH NORECOVERY
GO
```

Once the mirrored database is initialized, begin the mirroring setup process by right-clicking on the database to be mirrored and choosing Tasks > Mirror. The resulting screen, shown in figure 11.11, is the starting point for mirroring configuration.

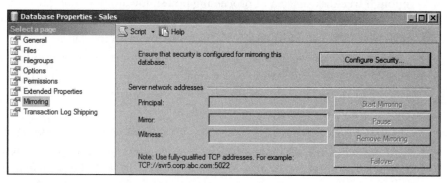

Figure 11.11   The mirroring tab of a database's properties allows mirroring to be established, or if already established, paused, resumed, removed, or failed over.

At this point, click the Configure Security button, which will take you to the screen shown in figure 11.12. You can choose whether or not you'd like to include a witness server in the mirroring setup. For our example, we'll choose Yes and click Next.

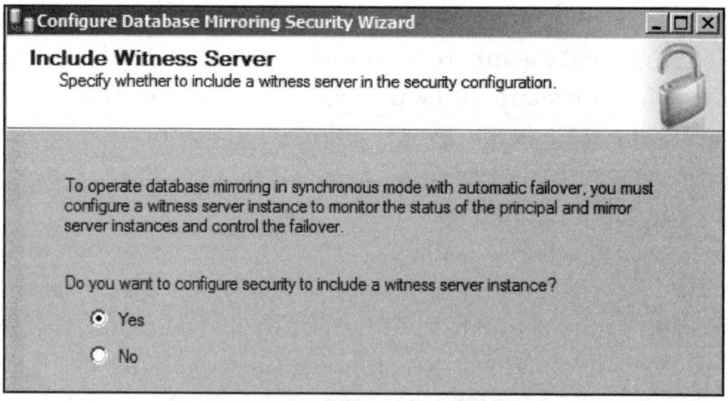

Figure 11.12   Selection of a witness server is optional.

After choosing to save the security configuration in the witness instance, the next three steps are to configure the principal (see figure 11.13), mirror, and witness instances. In each case, we select the instance to use, the TCP port, the endpoint name, and the encryption choice. Other than the instance name, all other options are supplied with default values, as shown in figure 11.13.

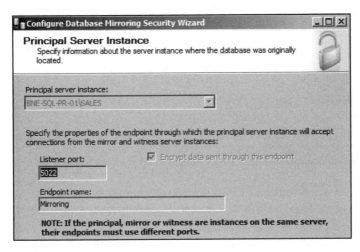

Figure 11.13 The Mirroring Security Wizard allows each instance in the mirroring configuration to be configured with a TCP port, endpoint, and encryption option.

The next screen, shown in figure 11.14, lets you specify the service account for each instance in the mirroring configuration. If you leave these fields blank, you'll have to manually add each service account to each instance, in addition to granting each account access to the mirroring endpoint. For example, in our example after adding the service account as a SQL login, we'd run the following command on each instance:

```
-- Grant the service account access to the mirroring endpoint
GRANT CONNECT on ENDPOINT::Mirroring TO [BNE-SQL-PR-01\SQL-Sales];
```

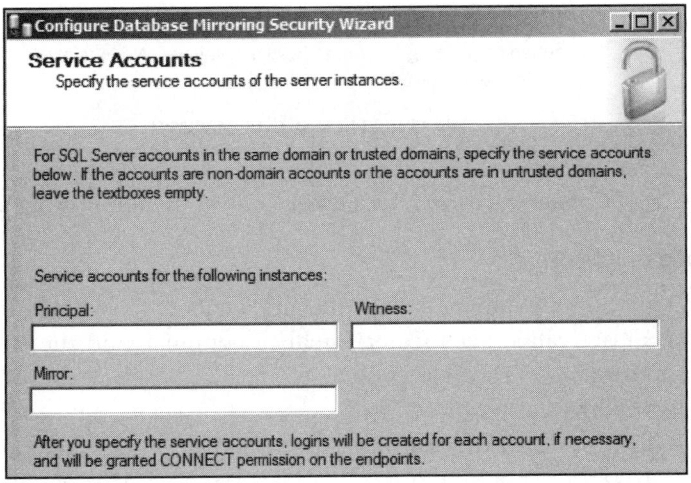

Configure Database Mirroring Security Wizard

Service Accounts
Specify the service accounts of the server instances.

For SQL Server accounts in the same domain or trusted domains, specify the service accounts below. If the accounts are non-domain accounts or the accounts are in untrusted domains, leave the textboxes empty.

Service accounts for the following instances:

Principal: Witness:

Mirror:

After you specify the service accounts, logins will be created for each account, if necessary, and will be granted CONNECT permission on the endpoints.

Figure 11.14 For each instance in the mirroring configuration, service accounts are provided.

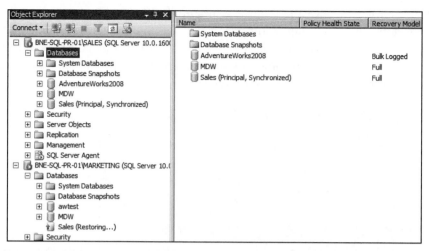

Figure 11.15   SQL Server Management Studio marks the role and status of the mirrored database.

Once you've provided this information, the wizard completes and offers to start the mirroring session. At this point, the databases will synchronize and then appear in SQL Server Management Studio, as shown in figure 11.15.

In our case, the Sales database is now in the Principal, Synchronized state, with the mirror remaining in the Restoring state. The list of possible statuses for the principal database appears in table 11.4.

Table 11.4   Mirroring session states

Mirroring state	Description
Synchronizing	The mirror DB is catching up on outstanding transactions.
Synchronized	The mirror DB has caught up.
Disconnected	The mirror partners have lost contact.
Suspended	Caused by pausing (covered shortly) or failover. No logs are sent to the mirror DB.
Pending failover	Temporary state at the principal during failover.

Now that we've set up database mirroring, let's take a look at the monitoring process.

11.6.2   *Monitoring database mirroring*

There are several tools and techniques for monitoring database mirroring, including system stored procedures, catalog views, performance counters, and the GUI-based Database Mirroring Monitor.

DATABASE MIRRORING MONITOR

You can access the Database Mirroring Monitor in SQL Server Management Studio by right-clicking a database and choosing Tasks > Launch Database Mirroring Monitor.

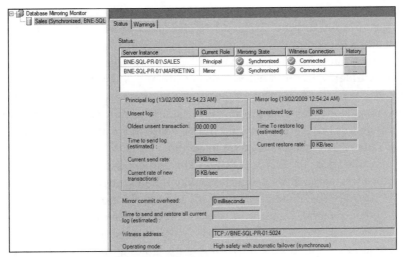

Figure 11.16   Database Mirroring Monitor

This tool, as you can see in figure 11.16, displays the mirroring status and related information for all mirrored databases on the SQL Server instance.

Information displayed by the Database Mirroring Monitor includes the following:

- Mirroring state
- Role of the server instance (principal or mirror)
- Status of the witness instance if present
- Amount of log in the principal's send queue and the mirror's redo queue
- Oldest unsent transaction
- Current rate of new transactions entering the principal database (kb/sec)
- Current rate at which transactions are being sent to the mirror (kb/sec)
- Current rate at which transactions are being processed at the mirror's redo queue (kb/sec)
- Average delay per transaction in waiting for confirmation of transaction hardening on the mirror (this is specific to high-safety [synchronous] mirroring only, and indicates the overhead of this mode in comparison to high performance [asynchronous] mirroring)

Information displayed by the Database Mirroring Monitor is captured on a regular basis (1 minute by default) by a SQL Server Agent job that updates mirroring information stored in msdb tables. If a mirroring session is created using SQL Server Management Studio, the SQL Server Agent job is created automatically.

SYSTEM STORED PROCEDURES

In addition to the Database Mirroring Monitor job, several system stored procedures exist that you can use to view and configure monitoring:

- *sp_dbmmonitorupdate*—This procedure is called by both the SQL Agent job and Database Mirroring Monitor to perform the updates on the mirroring status table in the msdb database. This database is used by both the Database Mirroring Monitor and the sp_dbmmonitorresults procedure (discussed shortly). When first executed, this procedure will create the msdb table to store database mirroring status information. Then it will insert new status records and purge records older than the retention period (default: 7 days).

- sp_dbmmonitoraddmonitoring—This procedure creates the SQL Server Agent jobs to periodically update the msdb tables containing the mirroring status. Running this procedure is required if database mirroring is established using T-SQL rather than using Management Studio.
- sp_dbmmonitorchangemonitoring — This procedure is used to change the update interval for the SQL Agent job that updates mirroring status information.
- sp_dbmmonitorhelpmonitoring—This procedure returns the current value for the update interval, set using sp_dbmmonitorchangemonitoring.
- sp_dbmmonitordropmonitoring—This procedure stops and removes the SQL Agent job that updates the mirroring status tables in the msdb database.
- sp_dbmmonitorresults—This procedure can be used as an alternative to the Database Mirroring Monitor. It returns the same information but in a text-based format. It takes three parameter values: a value specifying the mirrored database name to return results for, a value indicating the quantity of rows to return, and a value indicating whether you want to update mirroring status as part of the execution.

CATALOG VIEWS

SQL Server exposes database mirroring metadata through a number of catalog views:

- sys.database_mirroring—This view returns one row for each database on the instance in which the view is queried. Columns returned include the mirroring status, role, safety level, and witness status.
- sys.database_mirroring_endpoints — Returns information about each database mirroring endpoint enabled on the instance.
- sys.database_mirroring_witnesses — Returns a row for each witness role played by the instance containing information, such as the safety level, principal, and mirror server names and synchronization state of the mirroring partners.

PERFORMANCE COUNTERS

On either the principal or mirror server, Windows System Monitor can be used to view database mirroring information, including redo and send queue depth, and log data throughput per second. The counters are exposed using the SQLServer:Database Mirroring performance object.

WARNING THRESHOLDS

Finally, one important aspect of monitoring of any type is being able to specify threshold values for important metrics and be alerted when such thresholds are exceeded. For database mirroring, thresholds can be set for the following metrics:

- *Oldest unsent transaction* —This metric is used to alert on the existence of old transactions in the send queue. If transactions exist that exceed the specified age in minutes, an alert is raised using event ID 32040.

- *Unsent log*—This metric is used to set the maximum allowable size (in kb) of transactions in the send queue. This threshold uses event ID 32042.
- *Unrestored log*—Similar to the unsent log, this metric applies to the allowable size of the redo queue on the mirror database. This threshold uses event ID 32043.
- *Mirror commit overhead*—Used for high-safety (synchronous) mirroring, this metric allows an alert to be generated when the average transaction delay to harden log records to the mirror log exceeds a specified number of milliseconds. This threshold uses event ID 32044.

You can set threshold values through the Set Warning Thresholds tab, as shown in figure 11.17, accessible by clicking the Set Thresholds button on the Warnings tab of the Database Mirroring Monitor tool, or by using the system stored procedures `sp_dbmmonitorchangealert`, `sp_dbmmonitorhelpalert`, or `sp_dbmmonitordropalert`.

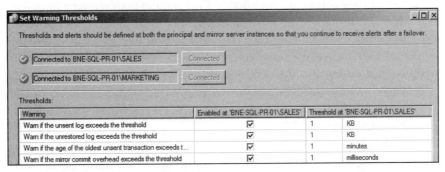

Figure 11.17 Set warning thresholds for various mirroring delay conditions in the Set Warnings Thresholds tab accessible through the Database Mirroring Monitor.

When a threshold value is exceeded, an informational entry is written to the Windows event log, and as we'll see in chapter 14, alerts on these messages can be created very easily.

At some point in the mirroring session, we may need to suspend mirroring. Let's take a look at that process now.

11.6.3 Suspending and resuming mirroring

A running mirroring session can be suspended using either SQL Server Management Studio or T-SQL as shown here:

```
-- Suspend Mirroring
ALTER DATABASE Sales
SET PARTNER SUSPEND
```

When suspended, the mirroring session remains in place for later resumption with the principal database available for use. While suspended, transactions aren't copied to the mirror database. During this time, the principal runs *exposed*—that is, no failover to the mirror database is possible. Further, transactions can't be truncated from the principal's transaction log until they're copied to the mirror's log, which means transactions will build up in the principals log for the duration of suspension. It follows that the longer the suspension, the larger the transaction log will grow. Further, when resumed, the redo log on the mirror database may be quite large, increasing the failover time if the principal database fails.

So why would you *choose* to suspend mirroring? Let's imagine we're running in high-safety mode (synchronous mirroring) and we're about to bulk load a very large data file and/or rebuild a large index. We want to complete this process as soon as possible to reduce the impact on users, or within a defined maintenance window. As we explained earlier, transactions won't commit in synchronous mode until they're hardened to the transaction log on the mirror database. For long-running operations such as large bulk loads or maintenance on large indexes, the performance overhead of synchronous mode is magnified, potentially extending the completion time of certain operations to an unacceptable level.

By suspending mirroring, we're able to complete maintenance operations in the time taken in a nonmirrored environment. Once resumed, the transactions will *catch up* on the mirror. If we accept the possibility of running exposed for the duration of the suspension and ensure adequate transaction log space is available, we're able to maximize performance and transaction throughput during periods of high activity.

A mirroring session can be resumed using T-SQL:

```
-- Resume Mirroring
ALTER DATABASE Sales
SET PARTNER RESUME
```

Once resumed, the mirroring session will enter the synchronizing state, with the mirroring database catching up on transactions that have occurred since mirroring was suspended.

In addition to pausing and resuming the mirroring session, we can also initiate failover.

11.6.4 *Initiating failover*

Manually initiating failover is possible in either high-safety mode (synchronous mirroring) through manual failover, or in high-performance mode (asynchronous mirroring) using forced service.

When the mirroring databases are in the synchronized state, manual failover is specified by running the `ALTER DATABASE SET PARTNER FAILOVER` command on the principal database, as in this example:

```
-- Initiate Manual Failover
ALTER DATABASE Sales
SET PARTNER FAILOVER
```

At this point, clients are disconnected, active transactions are rolled back, and the roles of principal and mirror are swapped. As mentioned earlier, the only failover mode supported for databases mirrored in high-performance mode is the forced service option, which may result in data loss. The forced service option is executed on the mirror database as shown in the following example, and is only available when the principal instance is disconnected:

```
-- Force Failover - run on mirror instance - data loss possible
ALTER DATABASE Sales
SET PARTNER FORCE_SERVICE_ALLOW_DATA_LOSS
```

In addition to the T-SQL methods, we can use Management Studio to implement failover mirroring using the Mirroring page of a database's properties window, as shown earlier in figure 11.11.

Before concluding the chapter, let's cover some important considerations when mirroring multiple databases on the same SQL Server instance.

11.6.5 *Considerations for mirroring multiple databases*

One of the limitations with a database mirroring session is that it's used to mirror a *single* database with other mirrored databases on the server operating on different mirroring sessions and therefore failing over independently. One of the implications of this for connected databases is that if there are interdependencies between two or more mirrored databases, there's no way of ensuring that they fail over as a group.

Take, for example, an application that uses two or more databases. If each of the databases can fail over independently of the other, and the application uses a single connection string for the server and instance name, problems will result when only one database fails over.

In most cases, a failure will occur at an instance level, causing all mirrored databases to fail over at once, but individual disk failures or temporary network problems may cause single database failovers. To reduce the problems associated with multiple mirrored databases on the same instance, consider these practices:

- Configure all principal databases to fail to the same mirror instance. This ensures shared connection settings can use the one failover instance for multiple databases.
- Set up alerts, covered in chapter 14, for failover events. Such alerts can be used to ensure all databases fail together, and potentially can be used to automate the manual failover of remaining databases.
- Consider alternate high-availability strategies. Depending on the situation, failover clustering may present a better alternative to database mirroring.

There's one final thing to consider for mirroring multiple databases on the same instance: additional worker threads, memory, and other resources are used for each mirroring session. The more mirrored databases, the greater the load on the instance, and the higher the network saturation. It follows that each session won't perform as well as the load increases, and in the worst case, may lead to session failovers. There's no maximum number of mirrored databases per instance.[2] The load characteristics of each database should be considered in line with the overall server capacity.

---

[2] Books Online suggests a maximum of 10 mirrored databases for a 32-bit server instance.

11.7   *Best practice considerations: high availability*

As with performance tuning where there will always be a bottleneck *somewhere*, each high-availability plan typically has its own weak points. On its own, database mirroring won't protect against poor maintenance practices and corrupted backups; it should therefore be seen as one component of a much broader high-availability plan.

- Service level agreements should be considered your binding contract. You wouldn't pay a builder to build your house without specific instructions and contract conditions; likewise, you can't effectively design and administer a highly available database system without a set of service level agreements in place. Know what they are and have confidence that they're achievable through well-thought-out and simulated disaster-recovery plans.

- During the process of developing service level agreements, prepare option papers that clearly list alternate options, costs, and corresponding service levels that can be achieved. Such papers assist the decision-making and budgeting process, and set expectations at the appropriate level for both customers and management.

- To prevent unexpected problems leading to system outages (therefore impacting availability targets), ensure appropriate development and test systems exist to assess the impact of database changes before they reach production; by the time a change makes its way to production, everyone responsible for the change should have complete confidence that it won't have any adverse effects.

- Database object definition and modification scripts should be stored in a source control tool in order to support reproducing a database at a defined version with options to roll forward changes as required to achieve a desired state.

- Aside from resource capacity such as the amount of RAM or CPU power, development, test, and production environments should be as identical as possible to minimize unexpected problems. Items that should be the same include collation, CPU platform, SQL version/edition, and service pack/hotfix level.

- For each production environment, a corresponding load-testing environment should be available and ideally configured identically to production, or at a scale such that the performance differences are well understood. Such environments, in combination with a load-testing tool, are critical in ensuring changes will work under production load.

- Consider the importance of accurate test data in development/test environments. If possible, provide complete copies of production data, or obfuscate where appropriate for security. Consider cloning a database's histograms and statistics to enable more accurate query execution plans for development databases if production-sized databases can't be used.

- Use a schema comparison tool such as Visual Studio Team System Database Edition (aka Data Dude) or a third-party tool. These tools are invaluable in troubleshooting schema difference problems.

- Document each database change, including details such as the date and time of the action, the location of the script, who performed the change, change output or log files, and so forth, and where possible, have undo scripts for each change. Use database backups or snapshots before significant changes if undo scripts aren't feasible.

- Unless the organization has invested in infrastructure capable of achieving five nines (99.999%) availability, it's crucial that planned outages be scheduled on a regular basis in order to manage user (and management) expectations and plan for critical maintenance operations such as service pack upgrades.

- Consider combining high-availability solutions to minimize the limitations of each. For example, use clustering to protect instances and databases as a group together with mirroring or log shipping critical databases offsite for geographical protection.

- Use an independent monitoring instance in a log shipping configuration—that is, don't use the primary or secondary instance as the monitor.

- If using transaction log shipping on a cluster, set up the file share for the transaction logs as a clustered resource. This will ensure the file share survives a cluster node failover, enabling log shipping to continue running.

- The default mirroring configuration is high safety with automatic failover (if a witness server is included). Prior to production implementation, simulate various network latencies in a test lab to measure the impact on transaction performance and the chances of unwanted failovers. Starting with high performance (asynchronous) mirroring is perhaps the best approach until the environment-specific nuances of mirroring are well understood.

- Allow plenty of free disk space for transaction logs; in situations where the mirror database is unavailable, transactions can't be removed from the principal's transaction log until delivered to the mirror.

- Like a clustering implementation, ensure both mirroring partners are configured identically (hardware capacity, SQL Server edition and version, collation, and so forth), and make sure the additional load from a failover condition can be handled by the mirror partner.

- To enable applications to continue working after a mirroring failover, create the same logins on both the principal and mirror instance and use the same SID values (via the SID = clause of the create login statement).

- Avoid using a witness instance for high performance (asynchronous) mirroring. Unlike high-safety (synchronous) mirroring, the witness instance can't initiate automatic failure in high-performance mode, which means the major benefit of using a witness is unavailable. On the downside, a witness can introduce a "false positive," whereby the database is taken offline if the principal loses network contact with the mirror and witness. In essence, you get no benefit while keeping the downside.

- Before commissioning a production database mirroring solution, observe application connection behavior with test failovers to ensure logins (and other aspects of system behavior) continue working on the mirror instance.
- Avoid reconfiguring mirroring endpoints while in use. Doing so may introduce an unwanted failover.
- Consider pausing high-safety (synchronous) mirroring during periods of high activity such as large bulk loads and index maintenance. Doing so will speed up the processing time of these actions (at the price of running exposed). Before doing so, ensure enough transaction log disk space is available on the partner servers.
- In a two-site high-safety (synchronous) mirroring solution used for disaster-recovery purposes, place the witness instance on the side of the principal instance. This avoids a common situation whereby the link between the sites goes down, and the principal instance loses quorum (in other words, loses contact with both the mirror and witness). In this case, the principal instance will take its database offline. By placing the witness with the principal, losing the network link will enable the principal to continue running, albeit in an exposed mode.
- On a server containing multiple mirrored databases, ensuring all of the databases fail to the same mirror server will simplify application connection processes. Further, ensuring all mirrored databases on a server are either mirrors or principals will enable rolling upgrades (manual failovers) to proceed in a smooth manner.
- Carefully monitor the CPU usage on servers participating in high safety with automatic failover mirroring. Servers with very high CPU usage may fail to respond to ping requests within the nominated timeout period, and may be subjected to unwanted failover events.
- The minimum timeout period for a mirroring session should be 10 seconds or greater. A value less than this may lead to false positive failover conditions during temporary network or server conditions.
- If a mirroring principal is set up as a clustered instance, consider adjusting the mirroring session timeout value to greater than the default 10 seconds. Doing so will prevent mirroring failover during a clustering failover. Typical cluster failovers take up to 90 seconds to complete, so adjusting the mirroring timeout to at least this value is recommended. Use `ALTER DATABASE x SET PARTNER TIMEOUT 90` or something similar.
- If combining mirroring and log shipping together in one solution, set up mirroring first, and make sure both mirror servers are configured to use the same share for transaction log backups.
- Review the index maintenance strategy when using database mirroring. Given the requirement for a mirrored database to be in full recovery mode, running unnecessary full index rebuilds may saturate the network link between the mirroring partners for little overall performance gain. While log stream compression helps

alleviate the transaction load, using a lighter index maintenance technique, covered in chapter 13, will reduce the network usage in a mirrored solution.

- Use snapshots on the mirror database with caution. The additional load of the copy on write process may lead to a significant redo queue, lengthening failover time. If the mirror database needs to be available for queries, consider other high-availability solutions such as transaction log shipping with standby restore mode, peer-to-peer transactional replication, or shared scalable databases.

- Finally, if using synchronous mirroring with automatic failover, consider the ability of the client connections to reconnect to the mirror. If you're not using the SQL Server Native Client (SNAC), custom reconnection logic is required. If the client can't detect connection failure and reconnect, the value of mirroring as a high-availability solution is significantly diminished.

Additional information on the best practices covered in this chapter can be found online at http://www.sqlCrunch.com/HA.

One of the benefits of database mirroring in SQL Server 2008 is the ability of mirror partners to exchange pages to recover from corruption, a topic we'll focus on in the next chapter.

DBCC validation

12

In this chapter, we'll cover

- Using the DBCC validation commands
- Preventing and detecting corruption
- Controlling CHECKDB impact
- Repairing corruption with DBCC

The DBCC group of commands, of which there are more than 20, are grouped into four categories: informational, validation, maintenance, and miscellaneous. In versions of SQL Server prior to 2000, DBCC stood for Database Consistency Check and consisted of a smaller set of commands (which are included in the current validation category). Over time, the DBCC command set grew to include more and more functionality, and the acronym was updated to Database Console Commands, reflecting these commands' ability to do more than just validation.

This chapter's focus will be on the commands found in the validation category, sometimes referred to as the DBCC CHECK* commands. Used to report on the integrity of objects in a given database, these commands provide peace of mind that the database is free from corruption, usually caused by faulty disk I/O hardware or software. In combination with a good backup/restore design, regular DBCC validation checks form a crucial part of a database maintenance strategy.

We begin this chapter with an overview of the various DBCC commands before concentrating on the validation group. We then move on to look at the causes of database corruption and techniques for preventing and detecting corruption.

In closing the chapter, we concentrate on techniques for reducing the impact of running CHECKDB on production databases and some important considerations (and alternatives) for repairing corruption with DBCC.

12.1　*DBCC validation overview*

Table 12.1 shows the full set of DBCC commands by category. Note that there are a number of undocumented commands not found in this list, such as DBCC PAGE, which we'll cover later in the chapter.

Table 12.1　DBCC commands by category

DBCC category	DBCC statement
Informational	DBCC INPUTBUFFER
	DBCC SHOWCONTIG
	DBCC OPENTRAN
	DBCC SQLPERF
	DBCC OUTPUTBUFFER
	DBCC TRACESTATUS
	DBCC PROCCACHE
	DBCC USEROPTIONS
	DBCC SHOW_STATISTICS
Validation	DBCC CHECKALLOC
	DBCC CHECKFILEGROUP
	DBCC CHECKCATALOG
	DBCC CHECKIDENT
	DBCC CHECKDB
Maintenance	DBCC CLEANTABLE
	DBCC INDEXDEFRAG
	DBCC DBREINDEX
	DBCC SHRINKDATABASE
	DBCC DROPCLEANBUFFERS
	DBCC SHRINKFILE
	DBCC FREEPROCCACHE
	DBCC UPDATEUSAGE

Table 12.1   DBCC commands by category *(continued)*

DBCC category	DBCC statement
Miscellaneous	DBCC DLLNAME
	DBCC HELP
	DBCC TRACEON
	DBCC TRACEOFF

You can find the full description of each of these commands in SQL Server Books Online (BOL). In the next chapter we'll cover some of the maintenance and informational commands along with their preferred replacements. For now, our focus is on the validation commands.

The DBCC validation commands are primarily concerned with checking the logical and physical integrity of database objects. Figure 12.1 highlights the relationships among these commands.

We'll cover what each of these commands do shortly, but for now it's important to point out that running DBCC CHECKDB automatically runs CHECKALLOC, CHECKTABLE, and CHECKCATALOG. Running these commands individually (instead of DBCC CHECKDB) is useful in some situations, such as when you want to reduce the runtime on large databases, an important technique we'll cover later in the section "Controlling CHECKDB impact."

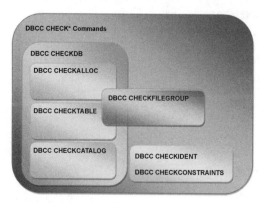

Figure 12.1   The DBCC validation commands. Running DBCC CHECKDB **also executes** CHECKALLOC, CHECKTABLE, **and** CHECKCATALOG.

Let's walk through these commands now, beginning with DBCC CHECKDB.

12.1.1 *DBCC CHECKDB*

DBCC CHECKDB is the most commonly used validation command for checking the logical and physical integrity of the entire database. Among other things, DBCC CHECKDB

- Runs DBCC CHECKALLOC on the specified database. CHECKALLOC validates the correct allocation of each page within the database.
- Runs DBCC CHECKTABLE on each table and indexed view in the specified database. CHECKTABLE runs a comprehensive series of tests, including checking that each row in the base table has a corresponding row in each nonclustered index.

- Runs DBCC CHECKCATALOG. In SQL Server 2000 and earlier, this command had to be run in addition to DBCC CHECKDB. Now included as part of CHECKDB, CHECK-CATALOG checks database metadata consistency.
- If you're using FileStream, CHECKDB validates the links between table metadata and the appropriate files and directories containing the FileStream data.
- Validates indexed views and service broker data.

Looking through these actions, you'll note that one of the things CHECKDB does is confirm that all base table rows have matching nonclustered index rows (covered in more detail in the next chapter). DBCC CHECKDB is an online operation, so one of the challenges for CHECKDB is running against a transactionally consistent view of the database.

TRANSACTIONAL CONSISTENCY

In prior versions of SQL Server, a number of techniques were used by DBCC to obtain a transactionally consistent view of the database—approaches such as including table locks and using the transaction log to catch up with transactions that occurred during the check. In some cases, these techniques resulted in substantial blocking, and therefore performance reduction, or complex checking logic that sometimes led to false positives, requiring additional CHECKDB runs to confirm any reported inconsistencies. Such limitations caused some sites to either exclude CHECKDB from their maintenance routines, or run it infrequently, a particularly dangerous move for large, mission-critical databases.

In SQL Server 2005, a significant breakthrough was made in obtaining a transactionally consistent view of the database without the performance impact of table locks or false positives. By leveraging the database snapshot technology (covered in chapter 10), CHECKDB runs without requiring table locks or transaction log analysis. The database is read through a special system-generated hidden snapshot ensuring that the before image of any concurrent activity is made available to CHECKDB.

One of the downsides of using a system snapshot is the lack of control over its placement. If CHECKDB is run during periods of high activity, the snapshot may grow very large, and in some cases, potentially consume all available disk space. We'll cover this case a little later when we look at running CHECKDB against a user-defined snapshot, which gives you control over the placement of the snapshot in a specific disk location.

Despite the significant advances made with snapshots, the performance impact of running CHECKDB operations may still exceed the desired level, particularly for large, 24/7 databases with a high transaction load. Given the importance of what CHECKDB delivers, there are a number of techniques that can be used to reduce the impact, and we'll cover these later in the chapter. For now, let's look at the syntax and options of the CHECKDB command.

SYNTAX AND OPTIONS

The full syntax of the DBCC CHECKDB command is as follows:

```
DBCC CHECKDB
[
    [ ( database_name | database_id | 0
        [ , NOINDEX
```

```
      [ , { REPAIR_ALLOW_DATA_LOSS | REPAIR_FAST | REPAIR_REBUILD } ]
      ) ]
  [ WITH
      {
          [ ALL_ERRORMSGS ]
          [ , EXTENDED_LOGICAL_CHECKS ]
          [ , NO_INFOMSGS ]
          [ , TABLOCK ]
          [ , ESTIMATEONLY ]
          [ , { PHYSICAL_ONLY | DATA_PURITY } ]
      }
  ]
]
```

Despite the large amount of options, DBCC CHECKDB can be run on its own as well. Here's a brief description of these options:

- *database_name/id*—Providing no value for this option runs the check against the current database; otherwise, the checks are run against the specified database.

- *NOINDEX*—When specified, nonclustered indexes aren't checked, reducing overall execution time. We'll cover clustered and nonclustered indexes in the next chapter.

- *REPAIR options*—If corruption is found, and no appropriate backups exist (a worst-case scenario), the repair options can be used as a last resort in removing database corruption. We'll cover the implications and details of these options later in the chapter.

- *ALL_ERRORMSGS*—If this option is excluded, CHECKDB displays only the first 200 errors for each object. Even if this option is included, SQL Server Management Studio displays the first 1,000 errors only. So for a complete list of errors, run CHECKDB with this option using either the sqlCmd utility or as a SQL Agent job with output directed to a file for later analysis.

- *EXTENDED_LOGICAL_CHECKS*—When run against SQL Server 2008 databases (compatibility level 100), this option will perform logical consistency checks against spatial and XML indexes as well as indexed views.

- *NO_INFOMSGS*—This option excludes informational messages from the output. When executed with this option, a successful CHECKDB will simply return *Command(s) completed successfully*; otherwise, messages will be returned for each object such as *There are 19118 rows in 187 pages for object "Sales.CreditCard"*.

- *TABLOCK*—When executed with this option, CHECKDB will use table locks rather than an internal snapshot. For databases under heavy transaction load, this option usually results in a faster execution time at the expense of lower concurrency. Note that this option will preclude service broker and CHECKCATALOG checks from being run.

- *ESTIMATE_ONLY*—This option estimates the amount of tempdb space required to run the DBCC command (without actually running it) and can be used to ensure the tempdb database is large enough and/or has access to enough free disk space for the CHECKDB operation.

- *PHYSICAL_ONLY*—A full execution of CHECKDB, including all logical checks, may take a considerable amount of time, given the extensive checks involved. Using this option reduces the execution time while still checking important aspects of the database integrity. We'll cover this option in more detail later in the chapter.
- *DATA_PURITY*—When a database is upgraded from SQL Server 2000 or earlier, DBCC CHECKDB won't check column value integrity until CHECKDB is successfully executed with this option.

So with these options in mind, let's take a look at running CHECKDB against the AdventureWorks database:

```
DBCC CHECKDB (AdventureWorks2008)
```

The abbreviated output of this command is as follows:

```
DBCC results for 'AdventureWorks'.
Service Broker Msg 9675, State 1: Message Types analyzed: 14.
Service Broker Msg 9676, State 1: Service Contracts analyzed: 6.
DBCC results for 'sys.sysrowsetcolumns'.
There are 1331 rows in 10 pages for object "sys.sysrowsetcolumns".
DBCC results for 'sys.sysrowsets'.
There are 255 rows in 2 pages for object "sys.sysrowsets".
DBCC results for 'Sales.SpecialOfferProduct'.
There are 538 rows in 3 pages for object "Sales.SpecialOfferProduct".
DBCC results for 'Production.ProductModel'.
There are 128 rows in 12 pages for object "Production.ProductModel".
CHECKDB found 0 allocation errors and 0 consistency errors in database
➥ 'AdventureWorks'.
DBCC execution completed. If DBCC printed error messages, contact your
➥ system administrator.
```

In this example, CHECKDB was executed without the NO_INFOMSGS option; therefore, we receive messages such as those shown here (the output has been truncated for brevity). The most important part of the output is toward the end: 0 allocation errors and 0 consistency errors. Later in the chapter we'll look at an example where DBCC returns errors and use that to discuss the recovery options.

Earlier in the chapter we discussed the fact that DBCC CHECKDB is a *superset* command that actually runs CHECKALLOC, CHECKTABLE, and CHECKCATALOG. To understand what CHECKDB is doing under the covers, let's examine these commands a little further.

12.1.2 *Granular consistency checking*

As mentioned earlier, CHECKALLOC is included as part of CHECKDB, but can be run separately. CHECKALLOC validates that each page in the database has been allocated correctly. To understand how allocation works (and how it's verified by CHECKALLOC), we need to look at the space allocation process used in a database.

SPACE ALLOCATION WITH GAM AND SGAM PAGES

As covered earlier in the book, tables and indexes in a database are stored on one or more 8K pages. Pages are allocated to objects from *extents*, which are collections of eight pages, making each extent 64K. To reduce wasted space for small tables or indexes, the first eight pages of an object are allocated from *mixed extents*—that is, eight tables may be using one page each from a single mixed extent. Once a table or index reaches eight pages, additional space is allocated one extent (64K) at a time from *uniform extents*.

To keep track of what mixed and uniform extents are available for allocation, SQL Server uses special allocation maps: the *global allocation map* (GAM) and the *shared global allocation map* (SGAM). Both the GAM and SGAM map to database extents using one bit to represent each extent. The GAM maps to all extents, and the SGAM maps to mixed extents only. In both cases, a bit value of 1 represents an available extent, and a 0 value represents an allocated (unavailable) extent.

As shown in figure 12.2, the first two pages of each database file are reserved for the file header and page free space pages, which we'll discuss shortly. The GAM and SGAM are located on the third and fourth pages (pages 2 and 3), respectively. With each page containing some 64,000 bits (8,000 bytes) and each bit representing an extent (64K), it follows that each GAM and SGAM page can therefore map to about 4GB of space. For database files larger than this size, additional allocation maps are used in the file.

When SQL Server needs to allocate a uniform extent to an object, it searches the GAM for a bit value of 1 and sets it to 0. It then has an extent for allocation. To allocate a mixed extent, SQL Server finds a GAM bit of 0 with the corresponding SGAM bit of 1 (allocated extent with free pages available). Table 12.2 illustrates the bit map used by GAM and SGAM pages.

Table 12.2   GAM and SGAM bit settings

Extent status	GAM bit setting	SGAM bit setting
Free	1	
Uniform extent (allocated)	0	
Mixed extent with free pages	0	1
Full mixed extent	0	0

As you learned in chapter 9, one of the advantages of creating multiple files for a database is getting multiple allocation maps. This is particularly useful for the tempdb database, which typically spends a large percentage of time allocating and deallocating tables. With multiple files, multiple GAMs and SGAMs reduce the contention to

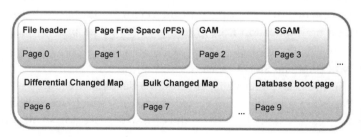

Figure 12.2   Pages within each database file

these resources, which, for a single file database (less than 4GB) would contain only a single GAM and SGAM.

Page Free Space (PFS) pages record information about each page in the database file, including its allocation status and the amount of free space in the page. After an object is allocated an extent, PFS pages are used to record which pages within the extent are available for allocation in the object—for example, when inserting a row into a table.

Let's take a look now at the commands executed by CHECKDB that can also be executed individually.

DBCC CHECKALLOC

When CHECKALLOC runs, it checks the validity of page and extent allocation in the database as recorded by the GAMs and SGAMs. Like CHECKDB, the CHECKALLOC command takes options for suppressing informational messages, ignoring indexes, and estimating tempdb usage.

DBCC CHECKTABLE

Like CHECKALLOC, CHECKTABLE is included as part of CHECKDB but can be executed separately for an individual table. It also contains options for suppressing informational messages, ignoring indexes, and other options, as documented for CHECKDB earlier.

CHECKTABLE runs a series of checks for a specified table, including the following:

- Page linkage for all pages within the table
- Index sorting
- Pointer consistency
- Correct values for computed columns
- Matches between index and base table records
- Correct placement of records in a partitioned table
- Correct linkage for FileStream data

The command also checks that indexed view contents match the appropriate view definition.

DBCC CHECKCATALOG

Also run as part of CHECKDB (since SQL Server 2005), CHECKCATALOG checks the consistency of metadata between system tables.

Unlike inconsistencies reported from CHECKTABLE, there are no repair options for errors resulting from CHECKCATALOG; a database restore is the only option. If run separately from CHECKDB, the only option CHECKCATALOG takes is NO_INFOMSGS.

Before completing our overview of DBCC validation commands, let's take a look at three more we haven't covered yet.

12.1.3 *Additional DBCC CHECK* commands*

The following three CHECK* commands round out the DBCC validation category:

- CHECKFILEGROUP is similar to CHECKDB but is limited to objects in the specified filegroup. We'll cover this option in more detail a little later.

- CHECKIDENT is used to validate, correct, or re-seed the identity value for a table containing an identity column.
- CHECKCONSTRAINTS validates the integrity of a given table's foreign key and check constraints, and is useful for validating data entered while the constraint(s) were disabled.

While DBCC commands are unmistakably valuable in identifying (and in the worst-case scenario, removing) database corruption, what's equally important is ensuring databases remain corruption free. In the next section, we'll address some of the techniques useful in avoiding corruption.

12.2 *Preventing and detecting corruption*

Before we go too much further, it's important to define *corruption* as it relates to a SQL Server database. There are essentially two different types of corruption: logical and physical. Logical corruption refers to situations in which people (or applications) remove data they shouldn't—for example, deleting one half of an Order:OrderDetail relationship. In contrast, physical corruption is almost always caused by faulty I/O subsystem components; examples include crashed hard drives and faulty RAID controllers.

Making the distinction between logical and physical corruption is important. A statement from a DBA to the effect of "The database is corrupt!" usually means something much more sinister than the same statement made from an application support person. Throughout the rest of this chapter, our definition of corruption will be of the physical kind, which is the target of the DBCC CHECK* commands.

This section will focus on tools and options used to validate an I/O subsystem and detect the presence of physical corruption. Let's begin by revisiting a tool we covered in chapter 3: SQLIOSIM.

12.2.1 *SQLIOSIM*

While a reliable and well-configured I/O system should rarely cause any database corruption, it can, and does, happen. As we'll see later in this chapter, relying on DBCC to remove corruption is a poor alternative to a good design and maintenance strategy aimed at preventing corruption and implementing early detection mechanisms.

In chapter 3, we covered the importance of running SQLIOSIM to validate the I/O subsystem prior to production implementation. To briefly recap, SQLIOSIM simulates SQL Server I/O workload, without SQL Server needing to be installed. The primary benefit of this tool is being able to detect issues in any part of the I/O chain (hardware, software, OS, drivers, firmware, and so forth) that may lead to database corruption at a later point.

The most likely cause of database corruption is an issue somewhere in the I/O subsystem. If and when corruption appears, it's often difficult to come up with conclusive proof as to the cause, and as a result, DBAs, hardware vendors, and administrators often end up in a heated blame game. SQLIOSIM offers a powerful method for validating each component of the I/O chain. When used as part of the validation and commissioning process for new hardware, it offers a tremendously valuable clean bill of health, offering peace of mind that corruption caused by the I/O subsystem, while possible, is unlikely.

In addition to using SQLIOSIM to validate the health of an I/O subsystem, enabling the page checksums feature offers a nice method of ongoing page validation outside explicit DBCC checks.

12.2.2 Page checksums

Page checksums, enabled by default as a database property as shown in figure 12.3, ensure ongoing validation of pages written to and read from the file system. When a page is *written to* disk, SQL Server calculates a checksum value based on the page contents and writes the value to the page. When a page containing a checksum value is read from disk,[1] the checksum is recalculated and compared.

The process of writing a page checksum is performed by SQL Server as the last action before the page leaves its control (flushed from the buffer pool). In a similar manner, the checksum is recalculated and compared as the first action when read from disk. If when recalculated the checksum value is different from the checksum stored on the page, that's a fairly solid indication some part of the I/O system has corrupted the page.

The performance overhead of calculating, writing, and comparing checksums has been estimated at approximately 2 percent, a small price to pay for ongoing validation of I/O integrity. In addition to validating pages as they're read from disk, the DBCC CHECK* commands will validate each page's checksum value as part of their operation. Further, as we saw in chapter 10, the backup and restore process can also validate

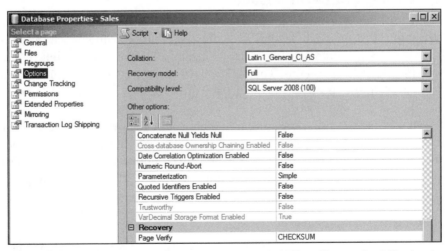

Figure 12.3   The default page verification level of CHECKSUM enables ongoing I/O subsystem verification.

---

[1] Databases upgraded from SQL Server 2000 won't contain a checksum value until the page is modified.

checksums using the optional WITH CHECKSUM clause. Assuming regular backups are in place that use this option, page checksums enable constant and ongoing validation of I/O integrity.

If a page checksum is detected as being incorrect, messages are written to the SQL Server log and Windows event logs. Assuming these are being actively monitored, this presents a mechanism for early detection and investigation.

Auto corruption recovery with database mirroring

Prior to SQL Server 2008, aside from restoring a backup or risking data loss with the DBCC repair options, there was no way of *safely* overcoming a corrupted page without the potential for data loss. In the Enterprise edition of SQL Server 2008, database mirroring partners can exchange pages to automatically overcome certain types of page corruption.

While SQLIOSIM and page checksums are excellent tools for initial and ongoing I/O validation, there's no substitute for regular DBCC checks. In chapter 14, we'll cover a number of SQL Server tools used to incorporate DBCC checks into a regular database maintenance plan. That being said, running regular checks on large, heavily loaded databases in use 24/7 presents a number of challenges, not the least of which is the performance impact such checks may have on user access. In the next section, we'll investigate a number of techniques that can be used in minimizing the impact of DBCC checks when running against production databases.

12.3   *Controlling CHECKDB impact*

Along with index maintenance and backups, executing regular DBCC checks are very straightforward for small databases, or those with large maintenance windows. In an ideal world, every night would see a full backup, all indexes completely rebuilt, along with full CHECKDB operations. The reality, however, is quite different. Large databases, particularly those in use 24/7, don't have the luxury of a nightly maintenance plan like the one just described.

In chapter 10, we examined differential and filegroup backups, options that enable large database backups to be staggered throughout the week. In the next chapter, we'll look at efficient index maintenance techniques. In this section, let's explore some of the options for reducing the impact of DBCC checks, beginning with using backups as the source.

12.3.1   *Running against backups*

One of the ways of offloading the overhead of a DBCC check is running the check on a restored copy of a production database in a test environment. If a page is corrupted on the source database, it will be corrupted on the restored copy. Not only is this a valid approach in offloading the impact of the DBCC check operation, *automating* this

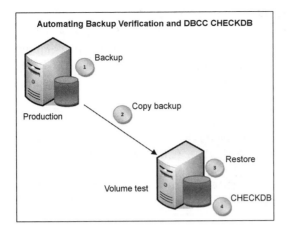

process, as shown in figure 12.4, enables a number of best practices to be handled in one process; verifying backups, performing DBCC checks, and maintaining a recent database copy for disaster recovery and/or reporting purposes.

Figure 12.4   Adding DBCC checks to automated backup verification enables a number of best practices to be handled at the same time.

The one (minor) downside of this method is when corruption is actually found in the restored copy. At this point, the DBCC check would need to be performed on the production database to confirm that the corruption exists and that it wasn't introduced by the copy or restore process.

Assuming no test environment exists for the purposes of offloading CHECKDB impact from production, one of the other options is using the WITH PHYSICAL_ONLY option, discussed next.

12.3.2 *WITH PHYSICAL_ONLY*

As we covered earlier in the chapter, DBCC CHECKDB performs a number of logical and physical checks. By specifying the WITH PHYSICAL_ONLY option, you can reduce the runtime substantially by performing a reduced set of checks that excludes the extensive logical checks.

As the example in figure 12.5 shows, running DBCC CHECKDB against the AdventureWorks2008 database with and without the PHYSICAL_ONLY option highlights a significant difference in the execution time. Performing the full check takes roughly double the amount of time compared to running CHECKDB using the WITH PHYSICAL_ONLY option (SQL Server was restarted before each test). Although this was a simple test against a small database, it's easy to see how such time savings would be considerable against a much larger database.

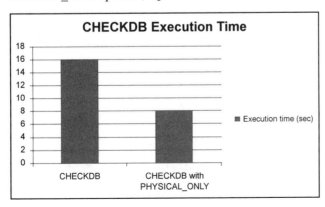

Figure 12.5 DBCC CHECKDB execution time against the AdventureWorks2008 database with and without the PHYSICAL_ONLY option

When executed with the PHYSICAL_ONLY option, CHECKDB reads each database page and checks the allocation consistency via CHECKALLOC. Further, if page checksums are present, it will validate those as well. Using page checksums in conjunction with PHYSICAL_ONLY reduces the production impact of CHECKDB while giving reasonable assurance that the I/O system is behaving itself and not causing any corruption.

Last successful CHECKDB

Need to know when CHECKDB last completed without finding any corruption? After enabling trace flag 3604 with DBCC TRACEON (3604); run DBCC PAGE (*dbname*, 1, 9, 3); replacing *dbname* with the required database name. The date and time of the last successful corruption-free CHECKDB will be listed in the dbi_dbccLastKnownGood field.

Despite the suitability of this option for production use, I recommended that you run a full CHECKDB when possible. A common maintenance design is for nightly PHYSICAL_ONLY checks with a full CHECKDB scheduled weekly, or alternatively, a nightly PHYSICAL_ONLY check combined with a weekly restore and CHECKDB verification in a load-testing or backup verification environment.

Another option for reducing the impact of DBCC is implementing a more granular verification approach, covered next.

12.3.3 *Partitioned and granular checks*

Earlier in the chapter we explained that executing CHECKDB also executes CHECKALLOC, CHECKCATALOG, and CHECKTABLE for each table in the database. As you saw, you can run each of these commands individually.

One of the alternatives to running CHECKDB is to run CHECKTABLE for a subset of tables, spreading the load over a number of nights—for example, running CHECKTABLE on three tables per night over seven nights rather than 21 tables in one night. On one (or more) of these nights, CHECKALLOC and CHECKCATALOG can also be run. Like CHECKDB, the CHECKTABLE command also takes the PHYSICAL_ONLY option, so the impact can be reduced further.

The DBCC CHECKFILEGROUP command also presents opportunities for granular checking by enabling checks on large databases to occur one filegroup at a time. In some cases, particular filegroups may be infrequently modified, or may be read only. In such cases, excluding these filegroups from the checks, or running them less frequently, may enable the runtime to be cut substantially.

MAXDOP and DBCC

By default, if multiple CPUs are available to a SQL Server instance and the MAXDOP setting allows, DBCC CHECKDB, CHECKTABLE, and CHECKFILEGROUP will use parallel checking. To disable parallel checking, use trace flag 2528, or manually adjust the MAXDOP setting for the period of the DBCC operation.

In closing this section, let's consider one final technique for controlling DBCC activity: user-defined snapshots.

12.3.4 *User-defined snapshots*

As you learned in chapter 10, a database snapshot uses sparse file technology to create a near-instant, read-only copy of a database. The snapshot is initially empty with all page reads redirected to the base database. When the original database is modified, the page to be modified is copied to the snapshot before the modification occurs. The snapshot therefore represents the database at the time of the snapshot. Over time, as more and more of the database is modified, the snapshot becomes larger and larger; the maximum size is the size of the database at the time of the snapshot.

DBCC CHECK* commands use a special hidden database snapshot[2] to ensure the operation runs against a transactionally consistent copy of the database that is accurate as at the time of the DBCC execution. This process is an improvement over earlier DBCC checks that used either table locks or complex transaction log operations that sometimes led to false positives.

When running a DBCC check against a database that's receiving updates, each of the pages to be modified must be copied to the snapshot to ensure DBCC views the page in its pre-update form. The more updates that occur during the DBCC check, the larger the snapshot will be. By default, the snapshot files are created in the same disk location as the database files. If the number of updates causes the snapshot to grow to the point where there isn't enough disk space for the snapshot files, the DBCC check will fail after running out of disk space.

Apart from running DBCC checks during periods of low activity or using the TABLOCK option (which will block user activity), running DBCC checks against a user-defined snapshot allows the snapshot files to be placed in a location with the appropriate amount of free disk space. This ensures that concurrent updates won't grow the snapshot to consume all the available disk space on the disk(s) storing the database files. Further, placing the snapshot on a physically separate disk may assist in isolating the snapshot-related disk overhead, therefore reducing the performance impact to users.

In the final section of this chapter, let's look at the options available when DBCC discovers corruption during its check.

12.4 *Removing corruption*

Despite the existence of DBCC options for repairing corruption, certain repairs occur at the expense of data loss; hence, the inclusion of ALLOW_DATA_LOSS as part of the name of one of the repair options. As such, using this option should be considered a last resort. In this section, let's look at an example in which DBCC discovers corruption and investigate the scope of potential data loss as well as the options available for recovery.

---

[2] Snapshots aren't used when the DBCC check is run against the master or tempdb database, a read-only database, a database in single-user or emergency mode, or when using the TABLOCK option.

12.4.1   *Interpreting DBCC output*

Consider the following (abbreviated) output from a CHECKDB operation:

```
DBCC results for 'AdventureWorks'.
Msg 8909, Level 16, State 1, Line 1
Table error: Object ID 0, index ID -1, partition ID 0, alloc unit ID 0
➥ (type Unknown), page ID (1:676) contains an incorrect page ID in its
➥ page header. The PageId in the page header = (0:0).
CHECKDB found 0 allocation errors and 1 consistency errors not associated
➥ with any single object.
DBCC results for 'sys.sysrscols'.
DBCC results for 'Person.Address'.
There are 19614 rows in 280 pages for object "Person.Address".
DBCC results for 'testtable'.
Msg 8928, Level 16, State 1, Line 1
Object ID 87671360, index ID 0, partition ID 72057594058244096, alloc unit
➥ ID 72057594062635008 (type In-row data): Page (1:676) could not be
➥ processed.  See other errors for details.
Msg 8928, Level 16, State 1, Line 1
Object ID 87671360, index ID 2, partition ID 72057594058309632, alloc unit
➥ ID 72057594062700544 (type In-row data): Page (1:800) could not be
➥ processed.  See other errors for details.
Msg 8939, Level 16, State 98, Line 1
Table error: Object ID 87671360, index ID 2, partition ID 72057594058309632,
➥ alloc unit ID 72057594062700544 (type In-row data), page
➥ (1:800). Test (IS_OFF (BUF_IOERR, pBUF->bstat)) failed. Values are
➥ 12716041 and -4.
There are 2 rows in 2 pages for object "testtable".
CHECKDB found 0 allocation errors and 3 consistency errors in table
➥ 'testtable' (object ID 87671360).
CHECKDB found 0 allocation errors and 4 consistency errors in database
➥ 'AdventureWorks'.
repair_allow_data_loss is the minimum repair level for the errors found by
➥ DBCC CHECKDB (AdventureWorks).
DBCC execution completed. If DBCC printed error messages, contact your
➥ system administrator.
```

There are a few things to note here. Near the end of the output is the line
repair_allow_data_loss is the minimum repair level... This essentially means
that corruption was found on a clustered index (or a heap). As we'll see in the next
chapter, these items are the data pages themselves, so removing them will result in
data loss, hence the warning.

Looking further up in the output, we can see error messages coming from Object
ID 87671360, index ID 0, and index ID 2. Tables without a clustered index are referred
to as a *heap*. Index ID 0 refers to a base data page from a heap table. Index ID 1 refers
to a clustered index page, and index ID 2 and above refer to pages from nonclustered
indexes. When interpreting the DBCC output, seeing corruptions only from index IDs
2 and above is somewhat good news; it means that the only corruption is on nonclustered index pages. In such cases, recovery is quite straightforward; we can simply
rebuild the index(es), or proceed with the REPAIR_REBUILD option of DBCC, which

will reinstate the missing/corrupted rows in the nonclustered index (or rebuild it). Neither of these options will result in any data loss.

In our case, we have errors from index IDs less than 2. As a result, DBCC is suggesting that the repair_allow_data_loss option is the minimum repair level. This doesn't mean that we *should* run with this option. As the name implies, it will result in data loss, so we need to think through our options. We'll cover the recovery options shortly. Before doing so, let's look at a way of inspecting the extent of potential data loss.

12.4.2 Determining the extent of data loss with DBCC PAGE

One of the DBCC commands that we haven't spoken of yet is DBCC PAGE, an undocumented (and therefore unsupported) command. If a database page is accessible, DBCC PAGE can be used to inspect its contents. In certain corruption scenarios, this can be very useful in determining the extent of damage. Consider a case where a range of clustered index (data) pages are corrupted—for example, pages 98 through 118. By inspecting the pages either side of the corruption range, 97 and 119 in this case, we'll get a much better idea of the extent of damage.

Figure 12.6 shows the output of the DBCC PAGE command. Before running the command, we turn on trace flag 3604 to enable the output to be displayed to screen.

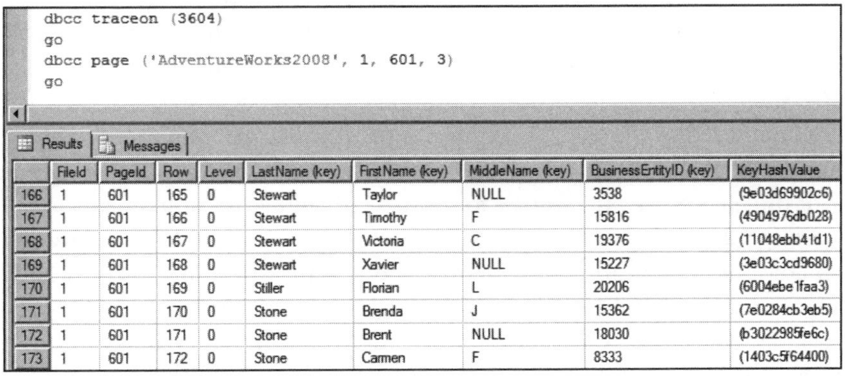

```
dbcc traceon (3604)
go
dbcc page ('AdventureWorks2008', 1, 601, 3)
go
```

	FieId	PageId	Row	Level	LastName (key)	FirstName (key)	MiddleName (key)	BusinessEntityID (key)	KeyHashValue
166	1	601	165	0	Stewart	Taylor	NULL	3538	(9e03d69902c6)
167	1	601	166	0	Stewart	Timothy	F	15816	(4904976db028)
168	1	601	167	0	Stewart	Victoria	C	19376	(11048ebb41d1)
169	1	601	168	0	Stewart	Xavier	NULL	15227	(3e03c3cd9680)
170	1	601	169	0	Stiller	Florian	L	20206	(6004ebe1faa3)
171	1	601	170	0	Stone	Brenda	J	15362	(7e0284cb3eb5)
172	1	601	171	0	Stone	Brent	NULL	18030	(b3022985fe6c)
173	1	601	172	0	Stone	Carmen	F	8333	(1403c5f64400)

Figure 12.6 Using the undocumented (and unsupported) DBCC PAGE command to inspect the contents of a database page

As figure 12.6 shows, DBCC PAGE[3] will return data from the page that we can use to determine the contents, and thus the potential data loss—an important factor in deciding on an appropriate recovery option.

12.4.3 Recovery options

To recap, validating the I/O system with SQLIOSIM before production implementation and ensuring page checksums are enabled are crucial steps in avoiding a scenario in which a large amount of data is corrupted before being discovered. SQLIOSIM will

---

[3] The four parameters for DBCC PAGE are database name, file number, page number, and print option. Print option 3 includes page header information and row details.

ensure the I/O system is valid and reliable for SQL Server use, and using page checksums in combination with regular event log monitoring helps you identify corrupted pages early, hopefully before the corruption becomes widespread.

Of course, neither of these best practices is a guarantee that we'll never have to deal with corrupted data, so knowing the available recovery options is an important step in preparing for the unexpected. Let's walk through the major physical corruption recovery options, beginning with corrupted nonclustered indexes.

REBUILDING NONCLUSTERED INDEXES

As we saw earlier, if the only corruption found was in nonclustered indexes (index ID 2 and above), then we can use the REPAIR_REBUILD option, or we can simply re-create the index. If the corruption is on a clustered index, we're not as lucky, and the restoration of a recent backup becomes our best option. Fortunately, we're able to restore individual pages.

PAGE RESTORE

The importance of regular, validated backups can't be overstated, particularly in corruption situations. In some cases, the only way out of a corruption scenario is to restore a backup. The only thing worse than discovering corruption is to then discover the backups are invalid (or don't exist!). Performing regular backups with the WITH CHECKSUM clause, together with regular monitoring for page checksum failures, provides the best chance of detecting corruption early and having reliable backups for recovery. Depending on the scale of corruption, the availability of recent backups may enable the use of the page restore technique.

In chapter 10 we looked at online restores, an option available in the Enterprise edition of SQL Server, to restore individual filegroups. Online restores are also available at the page level, enabling us to restore individual corrupted pages.

Listing 12.1 shows an example script to restore two pages. Like a filegroup restore, we follow the first restore with one or more transaction log restores, which apply changes made to the pages since the full backup was taken. After the first two restores, we take an additional transaction log backup to ensure all changes to the pages are captured and restored. Finally, we perform all restores with the exception of the last using the WITH NORECOVERY option to enable subsequent restores to occur.

Listing 12.1   Page restore

```
-- Restore an individual page from a full backup file
-- Restore in NORECOVERY mode to allow subsequent t-log roll forwards

RESTORE DATABASE [AdventureWorks2008]
    PAGE='1:676, 1:800'
    FROM DISK = 'G:\SQL Backup\AdventureWorks.bak'
    WITH NORECOVERY;

RESTORE LOG [AdventureWorks2008]
    FROM DISK = 'G:\SQL Backup\AdventureWorks-Trn.bak'
    WITH NORECOVERY;
```

```
BACKUP LOG [AdventureWorks2008]
   TO DISK = 'G:\SQL Backup\AdventureWorks_20080718_0915_log.bak'

RESTORE LOG [AdventureWorks2008]
   FROM DISK = 'G:\SQL Backup\AdventureWorks_20080718_0915_log.bak'
   WITH RECOVERY;
GO
```

Note that page restore is still possible in the non-Enterprise editions of SQL Server, but the database can't be online during the restore process. Further, page restores aren't possible for the transaction log and certain pages of the database: the GAM and SGAM pages, page 0 (the file boot page), and page 1:9 (the database boot page). Finally, as with other online restores, an unbroken sequence of transaction log backups is required.

Of course, if the full backup used for the restore also contains corruption on the page, then that's obviously of no help. Again, active event log monitoring with page checksums in place is crucial in avoiding this situation by identifying corruption as soon as possible.

If a valid backup isn't available for recovery, then as a last resort, the REPAIR_ALLOW_DATA_LOSS option can be used, after acknowledging that data *will* be lost as a result.

REPAIR_ALLOW_DATA_LOSS

Before running the REPAIR_ALLOW_DATA_LOSS command, it's worth either making a backup of the database or creating a snapshot. If the repair doesn't yield the required results, then the database can be restored or reverted to the snapshot. Alternatively (or as well as), the repair can be performed in a user-defined transaction, with a rollback statement undoing the repair if appropriate.

If the repair operation completes with the desired result, you should run DBCC CHECKCONSTRAINTS, particularly if the repaired object was a table involved in foreign key relationships or had other check constraints in place. Additional business logic checking should be performed where possible to make sure the effects of the repair won't cause unexpected problems at a later point.

> **What CHECKDB can't repair**
> The REPAIR_ALLOW_DATA_LOSS option isn't capable of repairing certain types of corruptions (or it doesn't make sense to try), notably the PFS (Page Free Space) page, critical system tables, and corrupted column range values. In such cases, backups will be required for recovery purposes.

After any unexpected recovery situation that results from corruption, perform a root cause analysis, discussed next, as soon as possible.

12.4.4 *Root cause analysis*

In most cases, corruption will most likely be the result of a faulty I/O component. We've already covered the importance of using SQLIOSIM to validate the I/O system before a server is implemented in production. If it passes validation, that doesn't preclude it from future problems; it just means that the I/O system is valid *at that moment*.

Following a corruption event, it's absolutely crucial that you perform a thorough analysis of the events leading up to the error. The usual suspects come into play here, such as Windows event logs, SQL Server error logs, and I/O software logs. If you suspect an I/O problem but can't pinpoint it, consider rerunning SQLIOSIM. If any weakness exists in the I/O, SQLIOSIM will more than likely find it.

A thorough post-restore root-cause analysis is essential in limiting the likelihood of further corruption events. Finally, if the required backups weren't available as part of the recovery process, now would be a good time to ensure this situation is addressed!

12.5 *Best practice considerations: DBCC validation*

A well-configured server with reliable I/O components should rarely experience physical data corruption. That being said, it's important to prepare for corruption and have a recovery plan ready to go that minimizes downtime and data loss.

- Backups, backups, backups! There are certain corruptions that simply can't be repaired, and those that can often result in data loss. Backups, for obvious reasons, are crucial.

- Ensure the Page Checksum option is left enabled for databases, and ensure both the SQL Server logs and the suspect_pages table in the MSDB database are monitored for any sign of checksum failure.

- Use the SQLIOSIM tool to validate the I/O hardware before production implementation. Once in production, should the I/O be suspected of causing corruption, consider rerunning SQLIOSIM to assist in pinpointing any weaknesses.

- If you're running CHECKDB during periods of substantial user activity (which should be avoided if possible), consider the disk space that will be used by the internal snapshot. DBCC checks can be executed against user-defined snapshots, providing you with control over the placement of snapshot files, and therefore disk usage, during the DBCC check.

- To assist in scheduling maintenance activities, be familiar with the average time taken for CHECKDB operations for each database. If a particular CHECKDB operation is taking much longer than normal, this may be a sign that it's found corruption.

- To assist in sizing the tempdb database, run the CHECKDB operation with ESTIMATEONLY for all databases to ensure there's enough tempdb space.

- Run DBCC checks as frequently as possible based on the criticality of the data. If the impact of running the check is causing too much production impact, use the PHYSICAL_ONLY option, or try lower-impact measures such as running CHECKTABLE or FILEGROUP checks spread across several nights.

- Consider running CHECKDB on restored backups. Automating this process (restore and CHECKDB) on a backup verification server (or test environment) will enable regular and ongoing validation of both the backup/restore process and the data integrity, as well as allowing you to implement an automatic production data refresh process for testing purposes.

- When a database is upgraded from SQL Server 2000, run CHECKDB with the DATA_PURITY option to enable checks for invalid data values.

- Use REPAIR_ALLOW_DATA_LOSS as a last resort option. Consider all backup restore options before this is used.

- Given the possibility of REPAIR_ALLOW_DATA_LOSS invalidating data constraints, run DBCC CHECKCONSTRAINTS along with other business logic validation following the repair.

- Prior to running REPAIR_ALLOW_DATA_LOSS, make a backup or snapshot of the database for rollback purposes if appropriate. Alternatively, execute the repair in a user transaction, which enables the effects of the repair to be rolled back if required.

- Follow up all corruption events with a root cause analysis to identify the cause of the corruption and to prevent it from reoccurring.

Additional information on the best practices covered in this chapter can be found online at http://www.sqlCrunch.com/DBCC.

We've made several references in this chapter to clustered and nonclustered indexes. We'll cover these in detail in the next chapter.

Index design and maintenance 13

In this chapter, we'll cover

- Designing indexes
- Filtered indexes and indexed views
- Analyzing index usage
- Index maintenance
- Statistics maintenance

Well-designed indexes reduce the time needed to access required data, but designed and used incorrectly, they slow query performance, lengthen maintenance routines, and increase database size and storage costs. The ability to successfully design and maintain indexes is an important DBA skill that requires a good understanding of how SQL Server uses indexes along with a solid grasp of index-analysis and maintenance techniques.

In this chapter, we'll begin with an overview of SQL Server indexes and cover strategies for successful index design. We'll then focus on a number of index-analysis techniques aimed at identifying indexes to add, drop, and defragment. We'll close the chapter with coverage of the tools and techniques involved in maintaining indexes and statistics, a crucial component of any database maintenance strategy.

13.1   *An introduction to indexes*

Like the index at the end of this book, indexes within a database enable fast access to table contents. With each table in a SQL Server 2008 database supporting up to 1000 indexes, fast access can be enabled for a wide variety of lookups. However, as you'll soon see, poor index selection and maintenance can have the opposite effect, with reduced performance a common outcome.

It's possible (and common) for tables to be created without any indexes. Such tables are known as *heaps*. Before continuing, let's take a brief look at heaps.

13.1.1   *Heaps*

Consider the script in listing 13.1, which creates a simple table and inserts five rows.

Listing 13.1   Creating a heap table

```
-- Create a heap table and seed with data
CREATE TABLE dbo.client (
    clientCode int
    , surname nvarchar(100)
    , firstName nvarchar(100)
    , SSN char(12)
    , DOB datetime
)
GO

INSERT INTO dbo.client (
    clientCode
    , surname
    , firstName
    , SSN
    , DOB
)
VALUES (1, 'Smith', 'John', '111-622-3033', '18 Jun 1974')
, (2, 'Jones', 'Harry', '121-221-3933', '01 Mar 1964')
, (3, 'Brown', 'Bill', '113-262-3223', '19 Apr 1949')
, (4, 'Dean', 'Sally', '191-422-3775', '26 Dec 1979')
, (5, 'White', 'Linda', '118-252-2243', '01 Jan 1998')
GO
```

Heap tables, such as the one created in listing 13.1, store their data in no particular physical order. For various reasons that will become apparent throughout this chapter, we recommend that all[1] tables be created with a physical order, achieved by creating a *clustered index*.

13.1.2   *Clustered indexes*

A clustered index is added to a table using the create clustered index command, as per the following example:

```
CREATE CLUSTERED INDEX cixClientSSN ON dbo.client(SSN)
GO
```

---

[1] A possible exception is small, temporary tables or those used for inserts only.

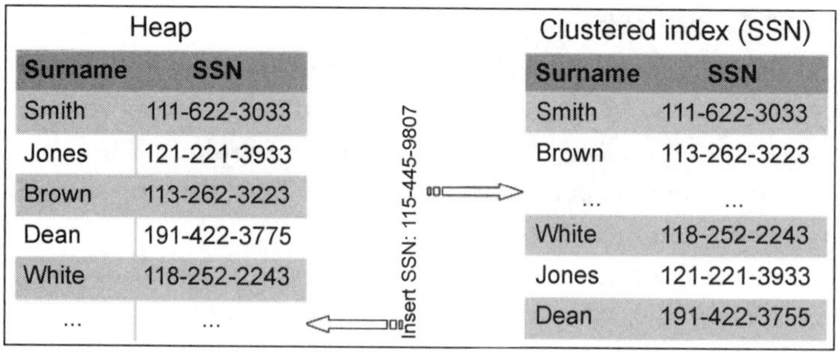

Figure 13.1   Inserting a row into a table with a clustered index will physically position the row based on the value of the column in the clustered index key, in this case SSN.

After you create the clustered index on the Social Security number (SSN) column, the data within the client table is physically ordered by SSN. The table can now be considered a *clustered table*. In addition to reordering the existing rows in the table, new rows will be inserted in order, based on the SSN value being inserted. Figure 13.1 illustrates the difference between inserting a record into the client table as a heap compared to a version with a clustered index on SSN.

Unlike nonclustered indexes, which we'll cover shortly, a table can have only one clustered index; that is, you can physically order the rows in a table in only one way. In order to enable fast access to the data within a table based on the value of other column(s), we can create additional (up to 999) nonclustered indexes.

More than just an index

Despite the name, a clustered index is more than just an index. It also contains the table data itself, which is stored at the leaf level of the index. By default, a primary key constraint will be created as a clustered index, thereby physically ordering the table rows based on the value of the primary key column(s).

Take our client table above (and assume it was populated with millions of rows). If we wanted to access a client, and we had their SSN, we would issue a query similar to this:

```
SELECT *
FROM dbo.client
WHERE SSN = '111-622-3033'
```

Given the client table is physically ordered by SSN, SQL Server can very quickly access the required record(s). Let's assume now that we wanted to find a client based on their date of birth and surname, as per the following query:

```
SELECT *
FROM dbo.client
WHERE
    DOB = '18 Jun 1974'
    AND surname = 'Smith'
```

In this case, since the table is ordered by SSN and there are no other indexes in place, SQL Server is forced to scan through the table a row at a time, looking for matching records. On small tables, the performance overhead involved in such a scan wouldn't be noticed. However, as the table grows, so too does the performance hit. To address this, we can create additional *nonclustered* indexes.

13.1.3 *Nonclustered indexes*

A nonclustered index is created using the `create nonclustered index` command, as per the following example;

```
CREATE NONCLUSTERED INDEX ixClientDOBSurname ON dbo.client(DOB, surname)
GO
```

What we've done here is create an index on the combination[2] of the DOB and Surname columns. In doing so, a separate physical index structure containing, and ordered by, DOB and Surname is created and maintained in line with the table. Each time a row is inserted, updated, or deleted from the client table, the corresponding updates are made to the nonclustered index. When running a query such as the one above that selects data based on the DOB/Surname combination, the index is used, or looked up, with the leaf level of the matching index entries pointing to the appropriate records in the table.

A good way of understanding the difference between clustered and nonclustered indexes is thinking about a paper-based phone book, ordered by surname. If you're looking for the address of someone whose surname is White, you'd immediately flip to the back of the book and adjust your search from there. In this sense, the phone book can be considered to be clustered on Surname.

On the other hand, if all you had was a phone number and you needed the matching address, your only choice would be to scan every page of the book, an immensely time-consuming process! If there was a section added to the rear of the book containing ordered phone numbers with a corresponding name, you could then flip to the appropriate page to retrieve the address. This extra section of ordered phone numbers can be considered a nonclustered index.

Taking this example further, let's imagine email addresses were added as additional contact information. If all we had was someone's email address, and we wanted their street address (or phone number), we'd be back to scanning through the book from start to finish. As we did with phone numbers, we could build another section at the back of the book containing ordered email addresses with a corresponding name to enable fast lookup to the section of the book containing the contact details. Figure 13.2 illustrates this concept further.

As per database tables, each time we add indexes to the rear of our phone book, two things happen. First, the size of the book increases, and second, we have additional information to maintain. If anyone changes their name, phone number, or email address, as well as updating the appropriate page within the book, we'd have to update one (or both) of the additional indexes. The additional size and maintenance

---

[2] An index created on more than one column is referred to as a *composite* index.

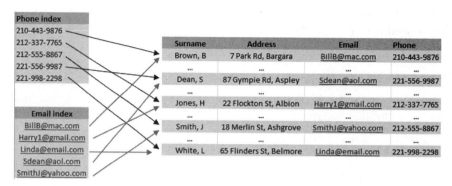

Figure 13.2   A hypothetical enhanced paper-based phone book with additional indexes allowing lookups based on phone numbers and email addresses

overhead are important considerations when creating nonclustered indexes. Later in this chapter, we'll examine ways of measuring the frequency of their use in order to determine the usefulness of their existence when considered against their size and maintenance overhead.

Before we complete our brief overview of clustered and nonclustered indexes, let's examine their internal structure a little further.

> **Full-text indexes**
>
> In addition to the index types covered in this book, SQL Server includes support for *full-text* indexes. Unlike the basic partial-text matching offered by the LIKE command, full-text indexes enable optimized and comprehensive searching against large volumes of unstructured data, including linguistic searching based on the installed language set.

13.1.4 *Index structure*

One of the important aspects of nonclustered indexes we've yet to cover is how they link to the records in the base table. The section of the nonclustered index that points to the record in the base table is known as a *row locator*. If the base table is a heap (no clustered index) the row locator is a pointer to the appropriate table row, identified with a *row ID*. The row ID consists of the file ID, the page number, and the row number on the page. If a table contains a clustered index, a nonclustered index's row locator is the row's clustered index key.

Indexes within SQL Server (both clustered and nonclustered) are implemented as *B-trees*. An index *seek* starts at the top, or root node, of the tree and traverses through intermediate levels before arriving at the leaf nodes. In a clustered index, the leaf nodes contain the actual table data. In a nonclustered index, the leaf nodes contain the row locators. Figure 13.3 illustrates this structure further.

With SQL Server including the clustered index key value in the row locator of nonclustered indexes, two important design points emerge. First, the *width*, or size, of the

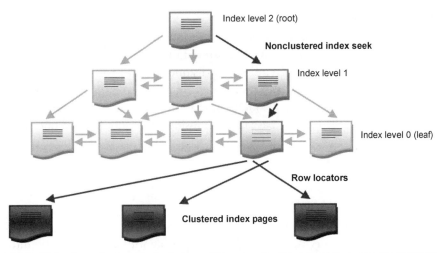

Figure 13.3 A nonclustered index lookup will traverse the B-tree until it reaches the leaf node, at which point the row locator is used to locate the data page in the clustered index.

clustered index directly affects the size of each nonclustered index. For example, a single integer-based column is much narrower or smaller than four char(100)-based columns. It follows that from both storage efficiency and lookup performance perspectives, clustered indexes should be as small and as narrow as possible.

The other design point to emerge is that the clustered index should be created before the nonclustered indexes. Think about what would happen if a table was created as a heap with nonclustered indexes. As we covered previously, each nonclustered index would use the heap's row ID as its row locator. If a clustered index was then created on the table, each of the nonclustered indexes would need to be updated to include the clustered index key in place of the row ID.

Finally, an important property of a clustered index is whether it's created with a *unique* constraint. A nonclustered index's row locator must point to a single row, so if the clustered index is not unique, which row will the row locator point to? In addressing this issue, SQL Server will make nonunique clustered indexes unique by adding a hidden *uniqueifier* value, which distinguishes rows with the same clustered index value.

The use of the row locator to link a nonclustered index row to its corresponding heap or clustered index row is typically referred to as a *bookmark lookup*; however, in SQL Server 2008, a bookmark lookup operation no longer exists and has been replaced with *clustered index seeks, RID lookups,* and *key lookups.*[3] Which of these is used is determined by the presence (or absence) of a clustered index and whether SQL Server chooses to use an index or scan the table. Let's explore this a little further with a look at the key lookup process.

---

[3] Despite this, the term *bookmark lookup* is still commonly used to represent the process of locating table data based on an index key value.

13.1.5 *Key lookup*

When SQL Server uses a nonclustered index to fulfill a query request, it uses a key lookup to retrieve the data from the clustered index (and a RID lookup in the case of a heap). When a nonclustered index returns one (or few) rows, this is an efficient and fast operation. However, as the number of matching rows increases, the combined cost of the index seek plus key lookup operations increases to the point where it may be quicker to simply scan the base table. Consider the following two queries:

```
-- Query A
SELECT * FROM client WHERE SSN = '191-422-3775'

-- Query B
SELECT * FROM client WHERE surname = 'Smith'
```

In Query A, an index lookup on SSN will return a single row, assuming each client has a unique SSN. In Query B, we're looking for people with a surname of Smith. Assuming the client table has millions of rows, this query could return thousands of matching rows.

Let's assume that the client table has two nonclustered indexes to support each of the above queries—one on SSN and the other on surname—with a clustered index on clientCode. In the first query, the SSN index seek would return one row, with a single key lookup required on the clustered index to return the remaining columns. Contrast this with the second query, which may return thousands of instances of Smith, each of which requires a key lookup. Because the base table is clustered on client-Code, each of the resultant Smith key lookups will be fulfilled from different physical parts of the table, requiring thousands of random I/O operations.

Depending on the number of rows to be returned, it may be much faster to ignore the index and sequentially scan the table's clustered index. Despite reading more rows, the overall cost of a single, large, sequential I/O operation may be less than thousands of individual random I/Os.[4]

A couple of interesting points emerge from this. The first is the possibility of including additional columns in the nonclustered index to avoid the key lookup. For example, rather than select *, we specify a limited number of query columns, each of which is added to the nonclustered index definition. By doing so, the query request is satisfied from the contents of the nonclustered index alone, avoiding the need for key lookups to the clustered index. Such a technique is possible with both covering indexes and included columns, both of which we'll cover in more detail later in the chapter.

Second, how does SQL Server know how many key lookups will be involved in fulfilling a query request? How does it decide that it's more efficient to do a table/clustered index scan? Enter statistics.

---

[4]   It's common for nonclustered indexes requiring key lookups to be ignored in favor of clustered index scans if more than 1 percent or 2 percent (sometimes less) of the table's rows are estimated to match the query. Such is the cost placed on random I/O.

13.1.6 *Statistics*

When indexes are first created, SQL Server calculates and stores statistical information on the column values in the index. When evaluating how a query will be executed, that is, whether to use an index or not, SQL Server uses the statistics to estimate the likely cost of using the index compared to other alternatives.

The *selectivity* of an index seek is used to define the estimated percentage of matched rows compared to the total number of rows in the table. Broadly speaking, the overall selectivity of an index can be defined as follows:

```
index selectivity = number of distinct index keys / table row count
```

The selectivity of an index will range from 0 to 1, or the equivalent value expressed as a percentage. Looking at the extreme ends of the selectivity scale, a unique index represents the best possible selectivity of 1, or 100 percent; every row has a unique (distinct) value. Primary key indexes are perfectly selective. In contrast, an index on a column where every row has the same value (approaching 0 percent selectivity) is obviously of limited/zero value.

By keeping statistics on the distribution of column values in the index, the selectivity of the query can be estimated. As an example, if there are 1020 Smiths and 2 Zatorskys in a surname index, a search on Zatorsky is far more selective than a search on Smith and therefore is more likely to use an index lookup. As you'll see later in the chapter, you can use the `DBCC SHOW_STATISTICS` command to inspect the index statistics used by SQL Server.

An important aspect of statistics is whether they remain up to date. Consider an example where an index starts out being highly selective. A query that performs an *equals* search on such an indexed column would obviously perform very well. But if a large volume of rows was added to the table with the same indexed column value, the selectivity would lower, potentially dramatically, depending on the volume of rows added and the contents of the indexed column. At this point, the same query, using the same index, may then perform very poorly. To counter situations such as this, SQL Server has a number of settings for automatically updating statistics. We'll explore these settings and other important aspects of statistics later in the chapter.

With this background in mind, let's move on to look at the index design process.

13.2 *Index design*

A good database design is made in conjunction with, and is conscious of, application data access logic. For example, in order to design indexes for a particular table, the database designer must know how users will be accessing the table from the application(s). If an application allows searching for data on a particular column or set of columns, then this needs to be considered from an indexing point of view. That's not to suggest that the application completely dictates index design. The reverse is often true; sometimes unrealistic application access must be modified in order to prevent user-generated activity that causes database performance problems.

In this section, we'll concentrate on generic index design strategies, beginning with the type of columns suitable for a clustered index. We'll then look at an area we touched on in our introduction, covering indexes and included columns, before concluding the section with coverage of a new feature in SQL Server 2008, *filtered indexes*, and how they compare with indexed views.

Let's begin with an important step in table design: selecting a clustered index.

13.2.1 *Selecting a clustered index*

When a table is created with a primary key constraint, as per the following example, a unique clustered index is automatically created on the column(s) in the primary key, unless specified otherwise.

```
-- Creates a clustered index by default on the clientCode primary key
CREATE TABLE dbo.client (
    clientCode int PRIMARY KEY
    , surname nvarchar(100)
    , firstName nvarchar(100)
    , SSN char(11)
    , DOB datetime
)
GO
```

In this example, the clientCode column will be used as the primary key of the table as well as the unique clustered index. Defining the column as the primary key means an explicit CREATE CLUSTERED INDEX command is not required. Should we wish to create the clustered index on a different column, SSN for example, we could create the table as follows:

```
-- Create a clustered index on a nonprimary key column
CREATE TABLE dbo.client (
    clientCode int PRIMARY KEY NONCLUSTERED
    , surname nvarchar(100)
    , firstName nvarchar(100)
    , SSN char(11)
    , DOB datetime
)
GO

CREATE UNIQUE CLUSTERED INDEX cixClientSSN ON dbo.client(SSN)
GO
```

Created in this manner, the client table will contain two indexes: a unique nonclustered index for the primary key constraint and a unique clustered index for the SSN column.

So, generally speaking, which types of columns make the best candidates for a clustered index? In answering this, let's recap some points from earlier in the chapter:

- The clustered index key is contained in the leaf node of each nonclustered index as the row locator. If the clustered index changes from one column to another, each nonclustered index needs to be updated in order to maintain the linkage from the nonclustered index to the base table. Further, if the column value of the clustered index changes, similar updates are required in each of the nonclustered indexes.

- The width of the clustered index directly affects the size of each nonclustered index. Again, this is a consequence of including the clustered index key in the leaf node of each nonclustered index.
- If a clustered index is not unique, SQL Server will make it so by adding a hidden uniqueifier column to the table for inclusion in the index.

It follows that the best candidates for a clustered index are columns that

- *Change infrequently (ideally not at all)*—A stable column value avoids the need to maintain nonclustered index row locators.
- *Are narrow*—They limit the size of each nonclustered index.
- *Are unique*—They avoid the need for a uniqueifier.

With these attributes in mind, a common pattern for table design is to create what's called a *surrogate key*, using the IDENTITY property as per this example:

```
-- Use the IDENTITY property to create a clustered primary key column
CREATE TABLE dbo.client (
    clientKey int IDENTITY (1,1) PRIMARY KEY
    , surname nvarchar(100)
    , firstName nvarchar(100)
    , SSN char(11)
    , DOB datetime
)
GO
```

By adding the IDENTITY (1,1) property to the clientKey column definition, SQL Server will populate this column's value with an automatically incrementing number for each new row, starting at 1 for the first row and increasing upward by 1 for each new row.

Using the IDENTITY property to create a surrogate key in this manner meets the desired attributes for a clustered index. It's an arbitrary number used purely to identify the record, and therefore it has no reason to be modified. It's narrow: a single integer-based column will occupy only 4 bytes. Finally, it's unique; SQL Server will automatically take care of the uniqueness, courtesy of the IDENTITY property.

In our client table example, the other candidate for a clustered index, as well as the primary key, is the Social Security number. It's reasonably narrow (11 bytes), unlikely to change, and unique. In fact, if we made SSN the unique clustered primary key, we'd have no need for the identity-based clientKey column. But there's one big problem here. It's unique for those *who have* an SSN. What about those who don't have one or those who can't recall it? If the SSN was the primary key value, the lack of an SSN would prevent a row from being inserted into the table.[5] For this reason, the best primary keys/unique clustered indexes tend to be artificial or surrogate keys that lack

---

[5] As an Australian without a U.S. Social Security number, I've witnessed this firsthand.

meaning and use system-generated uniqueness features such as the identity column. Of course, there are exceptions to this rule, and this is a commonly argued point among database design professionals.

The other consideration for a clustered index is column(s) involved in frequent range scans and queries that require sorted data.

GUIDs and clustered indexes

A common database design practice is to use globally unique identifier (GUID) columns as primary keys, which by default will also be the table's clustered index unless specified otherwise. Not only are GUIDs wide (16 bytes), they're randomly generated. Given such tables are clustered on the GUID column, newly inserted rows will be randomly positioned throughout the table, leading to page splits and subsequent fragmentation. This is a particular concern for tables with a high volume of data inserts. SQL Server 2005 introduced the `NewSequentialID()` function, which partially offsets this problem by generating GUIDs in a sequential manner. Removing the "randomness" from the GUID values helps in reducing both page splits and fragmentation.

RANGE SCANS AND SORT OPERATIONS

Earlier in the chapter we covered the case where nonclustered indexes are sometimes ignored if the estimated number of rows to be returned exceeds a certain percentage. The reason for this is the accumulated cost of the individual key/RID lookup and random I/O operations for each row.

For tables that are frequently used in range-scanning operations, clustering on the column(s) used in the range scan can provide a big performance boost. As an example, consider a sales table with an orderDate column and frequent queries such as this one:

```
-- Range Scan - Potential for a clustered index on orderDate?
SELECT *
FROM dbo.sales
WHERE orderDate BETWEEN '1 Jan 2008' AND '1 Feb 2008'
```

Depending on the statistics, a nonclustered index seek on orderDate will more than likely be ignored because of the number of key lookups involved. However, a clustered index on orderDate would be ideal; using the clustered index, SQL Server would quickly locate the first order and then use sequential I/O to return all remaining orders for the date range.

Finally, queries that select large volumes of sorted (ORDER BY) data often benefit from clustered indexes on the column used in the ORDER BY clause. With the data already sorted in the clustered index, the sort operation is avoided, boosting performance.

Often, a number of attributes come together to make a column an ideal clustered index candidate. Take, for example, the previous query, which selects orders based on a date range; if that query also required orders to be sorted, then we could avoid both key lookups *and* sort operations by clustering on orderDate.

AdventureWorks database

Some of the examples used throughout this chapter are based on the Adventure-Works database, available for download from codeplex.com, Microsoft's open source project-hosting website. CodePlex contains a huge amount of Microsoft and community-based code samples and databases, including a 2008 version of the Adventure-Works database containing FileStream data.

As with most recommendations throughout this book, the process for choosing the best clustered index is obviously dependent on the specifics of each database table and knowledge of how applications use the table. That being said, the above recommendations hold true in most cases. In a similar manner, there are a number of common techniques used in designing nonclustered indexes.

13.2.2 *Improving nonclustered index efficiency*

As we've covered throughout this chapter, the accumulated cost of random I/O involved in key/RID lookups often leads to nonclustered indexes being ignored in favor of sequential I/O with clustered index scans. To illustrate this and explore options for avoiding the key lookup process, let's walk through a number of examples using the Person.Contact table in the sample AdventureWorks database. In demonstrating how SQL Server uses different indexes for different queries, we'll view the graphical execution plans, which use different icons, as shown in figure 13.4, to represent different actions (lookups, scans, seeks, and so forth).

Seek vs. scan

Several important terms are used when discussing index usage. An *index seek* is used when the query optimizer chooses to navigate through the levels of a clustered or nonclustered index B-tree to quickly reach the appropriate leaf level pages. In contrast, an *index scan*, as the name suggests, scans the leaf level, left to right, one page at a time.

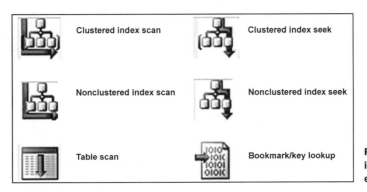

Figure 13.4 Common icons used in graphical execution plans

The Person.Contact table, as defined below (abbreviated table definition), contains approximately 20,000 rows. For the purposes of this test, we'll create a nonunique, nonclustered index on the LastName column:

```
-- Create a contact table with a nonclustered index on LastName
CREATE TABLE [Person].[Contact](
    [ContactID] [int] IDENTITY(1,1) PRIMARY KEY CLUSTERED
    , [Title] [nvarchar](8) NULL
    , [FirstName] [dbo].[Name] NOT NULL
    , [LastName] [dbo].[Name] NOT NULL
    , [EmailAddress] [nvarchar](50) NULL
)
GO

CREATE NONCLUSTERED INDEX [ixContactLastName] ON [Person].[Contact]
    ([LastName] ASC)
GO
```

For our first example, let's run a query to return all contacts with a LastName starting with *C*:

```
-- Statistics indicate too many rows for an index lookup
SELECT *
FROM Person.Contact
WHERE LastName like 'C%'
```

Despite the presence of a nonclustered index on LastName, which in theory could be used for this query, SQL Server correctly ignores it in favor of a clustered index scan. If we execute this query in SQL Server Management Studio using the Include Actual Execution Plan option (Ctrl+M, or select from the Query menu), we can see the graphical representation of the query execution, as shown in figure 13.5.

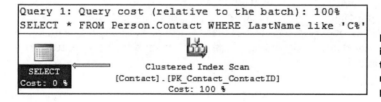

Figure 13.5   A clustered index scan is favored for this query in place of a nonclustered index seek plus key lookup.

No great surprises here; SQL Server is performing a clustered index scan to retrieve the results. Using an index hint, let's rerun this query and force SQL Server to use the ixContactLastName index:

```
-- Force the index lookup with an index hint
SELECT *
FROM Person.Contact WITH (index=ixContactLastName)
WHERE LastName like 'C%'
```

Looking at the graphical execution plan, we can confirm that the index is being used, as per figure 13.6.

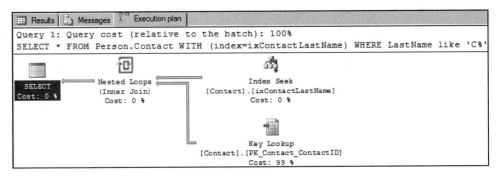

Figure 13.6 Adding an index hint to the previous query results in an index seek plus key lookup.

On a small database such as AdventureWorks, the performance difference between these two methods is negligible; both complete in under a second. To better understand how much slower the index lookup method is, we can use the SET STATISTICS IO option, which returns disk usage statistics[6] alongside the query results. Consider the script in listing 13.2.

Listing 13.2 Comparing query execution methods

```
-- Compare the Disk I/O with and without an index lookup
SET STATISTICS IO ON
GO

DBCC DROPCLEANBUFFERS
GO

SELECT *
FROM Person.Contact
WHERE LastName like 'C%'

DBCC DROPCLEANBUFFERS

SELECT *
FROM Person.Contact with (index=ixContactLastName)
WHERE LastName like 'C%'
GO
```

This script will run the query with and without the index hint. Before each query, we'll clear the buffer cache using DBCC DROPCLEANBUFFERS to eliminate the memory cache effects. The STATISTICS IO option will produce, for each query, the number of logical, physical, and read-ahead pages, defined as follows:

- *Logical Reads*—Represents the number of pages read from the data cache.
- *Physical Reads*—If the required page is not in cache, it will be read from disk. It follows that this value will be the same or less than the Logical Reads counter.

---

[6] Not to be confused with index statistics, query statistics refer to disk usage, such as the number of pages read from buffer or physical disk reads.

```
Results    Messages    Execution plan
DBCC execution completed. If DBCC printed error messages, contact your system administrator.

(1386 row(s) affected)
Table 'Contact'. Scan count 1, logical reads 569, physical reads 1, read-ahead reads 567, lo

(1 row(s) affected)
DBCC execution completed. If DBCC printed error messages, contact your system administrator.

(1386 row(s) affected)
Table 'Contact'. Scan count 1, logical reads 3326, physical reads 11, read-ahead reads 500,

(1 row(s) affected)
```

Figure 13.7   Forcing a nonclustered index seek plus key lookup significantly increases the number of pages read.

- *Read Ahead Reads*—The SQL Server storage engine uses a performance optimization technique called Read Ahead, which anticipates a query's future page needs and prefetches those pages from disk into the data cache. In doing so, the pages are available in cache when required, avoiding the need for the query to wait on future physical page reads.

So with these definitions in mind, let's look at the STATISTICS IO output in figure 13.7.

These statistics make for some very interesting reading. Note the big increase in logical reads (3326 versus 569) for the second query, which contains the (index= ixContactLastName) hint. Why such a big increase? A quick check of sys.dm_ db_index_physical_stats, covered in more detail later in the chapter, reveals there are only 570 pages in the table/clustered index. This is consistent with the statistics from the query that used the clustered index scan. So how can the query using the nonclustered index read so many more pages? The answer lies in the key lookup.

What's actually occurring here is that a number of clustered index pages are being read more than once. In addition to reading the nonclustered index pages for matching records, each key lookup reads pages from the clustered index to compete the query. In this case, a number of the key lookups are rereading the same clustered index page. Clearly a single clustered index scan is more efficient, and SQL Server was right to ignore the nonclustered index.

Let's move on to look at an example where SQL Server uses the nonclustered index without any index hints:

```
SELECT *
FROM Person.Contact
WHERE LastName like 'Carter%'
```

The graphical execution plan for this query is shown in figure 13.8, and it confirms the index is being used.

We can see that of the overall query cost, 98 percent is the key lookup. Eliminating this step will derive a further performance increase. You'll note that in our queries so far we've been using select *; what if we reduced the required columns for the query

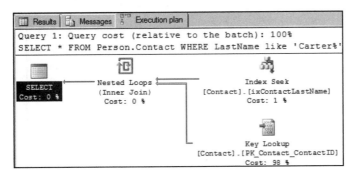

Figure 13.8 **This particular query uses the nonclustered index without any hints. Note the major cost of the query is the key lookup at 98 percent.**

to only those actually required and included them in the index? Such an index is called a *covering index.*

COVERING INDEXES

Let's assume we actually need only FirstName, LastName, and EmailAddress. If we created a composite index containing these three columns, the key lookup wouldn't be required. Let's modify the index to include the columns and rerun the query:

```
-- Create a covering index
DROP INDEX [ixContactLastName] ON [Person].[Contact]
GO
CREATE NONCLUSTERED INDEX [ixContactLastName] ON [Person].[Contact]
(
    [LastName] ASC
    , [FirstName] ASC
    , [EmailAddress] ASC
)
GO

SELECT LastName, FirstName, EmailAddress
FROM Person.Contact
WHERE LastName LIKE 'Carter%'
```

The execution plan from the query with the new index is shown in figure 13.9.

As you can see, the query is now satisfied from the contents of the nonclustered index alone. No key lookups are necessary, as all of the required columns are contained in the nonclustered index. In some ways, this index can be considered a mini, alternatively clustered version of the table.

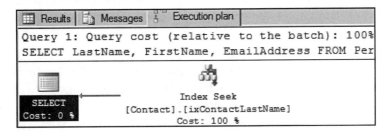

Figure 13.9 **Covering the index eliminates the key lookup, significantly improving query performance.**

```
DBCC DROPCLEANBUFFERS
GO


SELECT *
FROM Person.Contact
WHERE LastName like 'Carter%'
GO


DBCC DROPCLEANBUFFERS
GO


SELECT LastName, FirstName, EmailAddress
FROM Person.Contact
WHERE LastName like 'Carter%'
GO
```

| Results | Messages | Execution plan |

```
DBCC execution completed. If DBCC printed error messages, contact your system administr

(76 row(s) affected)
Table 'Contact'. Scan count 1, logical reads 279, physical reads 2, read-ahead reads 66

(1 row(s) affected)
DBCC execution completed. If DBCC printed error messages, contact your system administr

(76 row(s) affected)
Table 'Contact'. Scan count 1, logical reads 5, physical reads 1, read-ahead reads 2, 1

(1 row(s) affected)
```

Figure 13.10   By listing the required columns in the `select` clause and including them in the nonclustered index, the key lookups are eliminated, with logical reads dropping from 279 to 5.

Confirming the improvement from a disk-statistics perspective, the logical reads drop significantly, from 279 to 5, as shown in figure 13.10.

Including additional columns in the nonclustered index to avoid the key lookup process makes it a *covering index*. While this is an excellent performance-tuning technique, the one downside is that the additional columns are included at all levels of the index (root, all intermediate levels, and the leaf level). In our query above, given that we're not using the additional columns as predicates, that is, where clause conditions, they're not required at any level of the index other than the leaf level to avoid the key lookup. In small indexes, this is not really an issue. However, for very large indexes, the additional space taken up by the additional columns at each index level not only increases the index size but makes the index seek process less efficient. The included columns feature, introduced in SQL Server 2005, enhances covering indexes in several ways.

INCLUDED COLUMNS

While they're a relatively simple and very effective performance-tuning mechanism, covering indexes are not without their limitations; there can be a maximum of 16 columns in a composite index with a maximum combined size of 900 bytes. Further, columns of certain data types, including n/varchar(max), n/varbinary(max), n/text, XML, and image cannot be specified as index key columns.

Recognizing the value of covering indexes, SQL Server 2005 and above circumvent the size and data type limitations through indexes with included columns. Such indexes allow additional columns to be added to the leaf level of nonclustered indexes. In doing so, the additional columns are not counted in the 16 column and 900 byte maximum, and additional data types are allowed for these columns (n/varchar(max), n/varbinary(max), and XML). Consider the following `create index` statement:

```
-- Include columns at the leaf level of the index
CREATE NONCLUSTERED INDEX ixContactLastName
ON Person.Contact (LastName)
INCLUDE (FirstName, EmailAddress)
```

Notice the additional `INCLUDE` clause at the end of the statement; this index will offer all the benefits of the previous covering index. Further, if appropriate, we could add columns with data types not supported in traditional indexes, and we wouldn't be restricted by the 16-column maximum.

When deciding whether to place a column in the index definition as a key column or as an included column, the determining factor is whether the column will be used as a predicate, that is, a search condition in the `where` clause of a query. If a column is added purely to avoid the key lookup because of inclusion in the `select` list, then it makes sense for it to be an included column. Alternatively, a column used for filtering/searching purposes should be included as a key column in the index definition.

Let's take our previous example of a surname search. If a common search condition was on the combination of surname and first name, then it would make sense for both columns to be included in the index as key columns for more efficient lookups when seeking through the intermediate index levels. If the email address column is used purely as return information, that is, in the query's `select` list, but not as a predicate (`where` clause condition), then it makes sense for it to be an included column. Such an index definition would look like this:

```
CREATE NONCLUSTERED INDEX ixContactLastName
ON Person.Contact (LastName, FirstName)
INCLUDE (EmailAddress)
```

In summary, included column indexes retain the power of covering indexes while minimizing the index size and therefore maximizing lookup efficiency.

Before closing our section on nonclustered index design, let's spend some time covering an important new indexing feature included in SQL Server 2008: *filtered indexes*.

FILTERED INDEXES

New in 2008

Filtered indexes are one of my favorite new features in SQL Server 2008. Before we investigate their many advantages, consider the following table used to store customer details, including a country code:

```
CREATE TABLE [Person].[Customer](
   [CustomerID] [int] IDENTITY(1,1) PRIMARY KEY CLUSTERED
```

```
    , [Title] [nvarchar](8) NULL
    , [FirstName] [nvarchar](100) NOT NULL
    , [LastName] [nvarchar](100) NOT NULL
    , [EmailAddress] [nvarchar](100) NULL
    , [CountryCode] char(2) NULL
)
GO
```

Let's imagine this table is part of a database used around the globe on a 24/7 basis. The Customer table is used predominantly by a follow-the-sun call center, where customer details are accessed by call center staff from the same country or region as the calling customers.

Creating a nonclustered index on this table similar to the one earlier in the chapter where we included FirstName, LastName, and EmailAddress will enable lookups on customer name to return the required details. If this was a very large table, the size of the corresponding nonclustered indexes would also be large. As we'll see later in the chapter, maintaining large indexes that are in use 24/7 presents some interesting challenges.

In our example here, a traditional (full table) index would be created similar to what we've already seen earlier in the chapter; columns would be defined as key or included index columns, ideally as part of a covering index. All is fine so far, but wouldn't it be good if we could have separate versions of the index for specific countries? That would enable, for example, the Australian version of the index to be rebuilt when it's midnight in Australia and few, if any, Australian users are being accessed. Such an index design would reduce the impact on sections of users that are unlikely to be accessed at the time of the index maintenance.

Consider the following two index-creation statements:

```
-- Create 2 filtered indexes on the Customer table
CREATE NONCLUSTERED INDEX ixCustomerAustralia
ON Person.Customer (LastName, FirstName)
INCLUDE (EmailAddress)
WHERE CountryCode = 'AU'
GO

CREATE NONCLUSTERED INDEX  ixCustomerUnitedKingdom
ON Person.Customer (LastName, FirstName)
INCLUDE (EmailAddress)
WHERE CountryCode = 'UK'
GO
```

The indexes we've created here are similar to ones from earlier in the chapter with one notable exception: they have a predicate (where clause filter) as part of their definition. When a search is performed using a matching predicate and index keys, the query optimizer will consider using the index, subject to the usual considerations. For example, the ixCustomerAustralia index could be used for a query that includes the CountryCode = 'AU' predicate such as this:

```
SELECT FirstName, LastName, EmailAddress
FROM Person.Customer
WHERE
```

```
LastName = 'Colledge'
AND FirstName like 'Rod%'
AND CountryCode = 'AU'
```

Such indexes, known as *filtered indexes*, enable a whole range of benefits. Let's cover the major ones:

- *Segregated maintenance*—As we've discussed, creating multiple smaller versions of a single larger index enables maintenance routines such as index rebuilds to be scheduled in isolation from other versions of the index that may be receiving heavy usage.

- *Smaller, faster indexes*—Filtering an index makes it smaller and therefore faster. Best of all, covered filtered indexes support optimized lookups for specialized purposes. Consider a very large product table with a ProductCategory column; filtered indexes could be created for product categories, which include the appropriate columns specific to that category. When combined with application logic, such indexes enable fast, optimized lookups for sections of data within a table.

- *Creating unique indexes on nullable columns*—Consider the Social Security number (SSN) column from earlier in the chapter; to support storing records for non-U.S. residents, we couldn't define the column as NOT NULL. This would mean that a percentage of the records would have a NULL SSN, but those that do have one should be unique. By creating a filtered unique nonclustered index, we can achieve both of these goals by defining the index with a WHERE SSN IS NOT NULL predicate.

- *More accurate statistics*—Unless created with the FULLSCAN option (covered later in the chapter), statistics work by sampling a subset of the index. In a filtered index, all of the sampled statistics are specific to the filter; therefore they are more accurate compared to an index that keeps statistics on all table data, some of which may never be used for index lookups.

- *Lower storage costs*—The ability to exclude unwanted data from indexes enables the size, and therefore storage costs, to be reduced.

Some of the advantages of filtered indexes could be achieved in earlier versions of SQL Server using indexed views. While similar, there are important differences and restrictions to be aware of when choosing one method over the other.

13.2.3 Indexed views

A traditional, nonindexed view provides a filter over one or more tables. Used for various purposes, views are an excellent mechanism for abstracting table join complexity and securing data. Indexed views, introduced in SQL Server 2000, materialize the results of the view. Think of an indexed view as another table with its own data, the difference being the data is sourced from one or more other tables. Indexed views are sometimes referred to as *virtual tables*.

To illustrate the power of indexed views, let's consider a modified example from SQL Server Books Online, where sales data is summarized by product and date. The original query, run against the base tables, is shown in listing 13.3.

> **Listing 13.3   Sorted and grouped sales orders**

```
-- Return orders grouped by date and product name
SELECT
    o.OrderDate
    , p.Name as productName
    , sum(UnitPrice * OrderQty * (1.00-UnitPriceDiscount)) as revenue
    , count_big(*) as salesQty
FROM Sales.SalesOrderDetail as od
    INNER JOIN Sales.SalesOrderHeader as o
      ON od.SalesOrderID = o.SalesOrderID
    INNER JOIN Production.Product as p
      ON od.ProductID = p.ProductID
WHERE o.OrderDate between '1 July 2001' and '31 July 2001'
GROUP BY o.OrderDate, p.Name
ORDER BY o.OrderDate, p.Name
```

What we're doing here is selecting the total sales (dollar total and count) for sales from July 2001, grouped by date and product. The I/O statistics for this query are as follows:

> Table Worktable: Scan count 0, logical reads 0, physical reads 0, read-ahead reads 0

> Table SalesOrderDetail: Scan count 184, logical reads 861, physical reads 1, read-ahead reads 8

> Table SalesOrderHeader: Scan count 1, logical reads 703, physical reads 1, read-ahead reads 699

> Table Product: Scan count 1, logical reads 5, physical reads 1, read-ahead reads 0

The AdventureWorks database is quite small, and as a result, the query completes in only a few seconds. On a much larger, real-world database, the query would take substantially longer, with a corresponding user impact. Consider the execution plan for this query, as shown in figure 13.11.

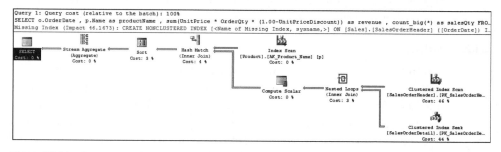

Figure 13.11   Query execution plan to return grouped, sorted sales data by date and product

The join, grouping, and sorting logic in this query are all contributing factors to its complexity and disk I/O usage. If this query was run once a day and after hours, then perhaps it wouldn't be much of a problem, but consider the user impact if this query was run by many users throughout the day.

Using indexed views, we can materialize the results of this query, as shown in listing 13.4.

Listing 13.4 Creating an indexed view

```
-- Create an indexed view
CREATE VIEW Sales.OrdersView
WITH SCHEMABINDING
AS
    SELECT
        o.OrderDate
        , p.Name as productName
        , sum(UnitPrice * OrderQty * (1.00-UnitPriceDiscount)) as revenue
        , count_big(*) as salesQty
    FROM Sales.SalesOrderDetail as od
        INNER JOIN Sales.SalesOrderHeader as o
          ON od.SalesOrderID = o.SalesOrderID
        INNER JOIN Production.Product as p
          ON od.ProductID = p.ProductID
    GROUP BY o.OrderDate, p.Name
GO


--Create an index on the view
CREATE UNIQUE CLUSTERED INDEX ixv_productSales
    ON Sales.OrdersView (OrderDate, productName);
GO
```

Notice the `WITH SCHEMABINDING` used when creating the view. This essentially ties the view to the table definition, preventing structural table changes while the view exists. Further, creating the unique clustered index in the second half of the script is what materializes the results of the view to disk. Once materialized, the same query that we ran before can be run again, *without needing to reference the indexed view.*[7] The difference can be seen in the I/O statistics and dramatically simpler query execution plan, as shown in figure 13.12.

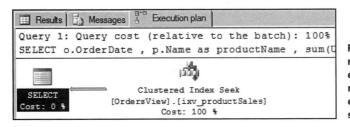

Figure 13.12 Indexed views result in dramatically simpler execution plans and reduced resource usage. Compare this execution plan with the plan shown in figure 13.11.

---

[7] This assumes the Enterprise edition is being used. Non-Enterprise editions require an explicit reference to the indexed view with the `NOEXPAND` hint.

Essentially, what we've done in creating the indexed view is store, or *materialize,* the results such that the base tables no longer need to be queried to return the results, thereby avoiding the (expensive) aggregation process to calculate revenue and sales volume. The I/O statistics for the query using the indexed view are as follows:

> Table OrdersView: Scan count 1, logical reads 5, physical reads 1, read-ahead reads 2

That's a total of 5 logical reads, compared to 1500-plus before the indexed view was created. You can imagine the accumulated positive performance impact of the indexed view if the query was run repeatedly throughout the day.

Once an indexed view is materialized with the unique clustered index, additional nonclustered indexes can be created on it; however, the same performance impact and index maintenance considerations apply as per a standard table.

Used correctly, indexed views are incredibly powerful, but there are several downsides and considerations. The primary one is the overhead in maintaining the view; that is, every time a record in one of the view's source tables is modified, the corresponding updates are required in the indexed view, including re-aggregating results if appropriate. The maintenance overhead for updates on the base tables may outweigh the read performance benefits; thus, indexed views are best used on tables with infrequent updates.

The other major consideration for creating indexed views is their constraints and base table requirements. Books Online contains a complete description of these constraints. The major ones are as follows:

- Schema binding on the base tables prevents any schema changes to the underlying tables while the indexed view exists.
- The index that materializes the view, that is, the initial clustered index, must be unique; hence, there must be a unique column, or combination of columns, in the view.
- The indexed view cannot include n/text or image columns.

The indexed view that we created in the previous example for sales data grouped by product and date was one of many possible implementations. A simpler example of an indexed view follows:

```
-- Create an indexed view
CREATE VIEW Person.AustralianCustomers
WITH SCHEMABINDING
AS
SELECT CustomerID, LastName, FirstName, EmailAddress
FROM Person.Customer
WHERE CountryCode = 'AU'
go

CREATE UNIQUE CLUSTERED INDEX ixv_AustralianCustomers
    ON Person.AustralianCustomers(CustomerID);
GO
```

If you recall our example from earlier in the chapter when we looked at filtered indexes, this essentially achieves the same thing. So which is the better method to use?

INDEXED VIEWS VS. FILTERED INDEXES

We can use both filtered indexes and indexed views to achieve fast lookups for subsets of data within a table. The method chosen is based in part on the constraints and limitations of each method. We've covered some of the indexed view restrictions (schema binding, no n/text or image columns, and so forth). When it comes to filtered indexes, the major restriction is the fact that, like full table indexes, they can be defined on only a single table. In contrast, as you saw in our example with sales data, an indexed view can be created across many tables joined together.

Additional restrictions apply to the predicates for a filtered index. In our earlier example, we created filtered indexes with simple conditions such as `where Country-Code = 'AU'`. More complex predicates such as string comparisons using the `LIKE` operator are not permitted in filtered indexes, nor are computed columns.

Data type conversion is not permitted on the left-hand side of a filtered index predicate, for example, a table containing a varbinary(4) column named col1, with a filter predicate such as `where col1 = 10`. In this case, the filtered index would fail because col1 requires an implicit binary-to-integer conversion.[8]

In summary, filtered indexes are best used against single tables with simple predicates where the row volume of the index is a small percentage of the total table row count. In contrast, indexed views are a powerful solution for multi-table join scenarios with aggregate calculations and more complex predicates on tables that are infrequently updated. Perhaps the major determining factor is the edition of SQL Server used. While indexed views can be created in any edition of SQL Server, they'll be automatically considered for use only in the Enterprise edition. In other editions, they need to be explicitly referenced with the `NOEXPAND` query hint.

With these index design points in mind, let's now look at processes and techniques for analyzing indexes to determine their usage and subsequent maintenance requirements.

13.3   *Index analysis*

An unfortunate, all-too-common indexing approach is to carpet bomb the database with indexes in the hope that performance will (eventually) improve. Not only will such an approach fail, but it usually ends in tears with the accumulated performance and maintenance costs of unnecessary indexes eventually having a paralyzing effect. Fortunately, there is a much more effective approach, made all the easier using several index-related Dynamic Management Views (DMVs).

In this section, we'll approach index analysis from three angles, identifying indexes to drop, add, and defragment. Let's begin with a look at using DMVs to identify indexes that are candidates for removal.

---

[8]   Changing the filtered index predicate to `where col1 = convert(varbinary(4), 10)` would be valid.

> ### Dynamic Management Views
>
> Dynamic Management Views return server state information useful in diagnosing server health and tuning performance. The values returned by some DMVs, including the ones in this section, are reset when the SQL Server instance restarts. Before making any decisions that are based on DMV results, consider when the instance was last restarted to ensure the DMV results are representative of the full range of database access patterns, for example, daily, weekly, and monthly reports. Taking a database offline, or using the AUTOCLOSE option, will also reset certain DMV values. Links to various DMV scripts and further details are available at http://www.sqlCrunch.com/index.

13.3.1 *Identifying indexes to drop/disable*

Indexes that are either not used or used infrequently not only consume additional space, but they also lengthen maintenance routines and slow performance, given the need to keep them updated in line with the base table data. As an example, consider an index on a FirstName column in a very large customer table and a query such as select * from customers where FirstName = 'John'. A lack of understanding as to why SQL Server is unlikely to use such an index may cause a junior DBA to create it in the hope that it may improve performance. Usually, such indexes are left in place without any follow-up analysis as to whether or not the index is being used.

Before we look at techniques for removing indexes, let's cover a very important DMV, sys.dm_db_index_usage_stats, to help us in this task.

SYS.DM_DB_INDEX_USAGE_STATS

As the name implies, the sys.dm_db_index_usage_stats DMV returns information on how indexes are being used. For each index, counts are kept on the number of times the index has been scanned, updated, and used for lookup or seek purposes, since the SQL instance was last restarted.

A full description of all of the columns returned by this DMV is available in Books Online. Let's cover the important ones:

- *user_seeks*—Each time an index is used for seek purposes, that is, navigating through levels of its B-tree, this counter is incremented. A high value here usually represents an effective index.
- *user_scans*—When a index is scanned at the leaf level (as opposed to seeking through the B-tree), this counter is incremented.
- *user_lookups*—Each time a nonclustered index is used for a lookup into a heap or clustered index, this counter is incremented.
- *user_updates*—Insert, update, and delete operations on a table must maintain the appropriate indexes. Every insert and delete operation will have a corresponding action for each nonclustered index, with updates effecting certain indexes, depending on the columns that have changed. Each time an index is maintained for any of these actions, this counter is incremented.

In addition to these columns, sys.dm_db_index_usage_stats returns many others, including the last date and time for each of the actions covered previously. The major value of this DMV is using it to identify indexes that are rarely used but have a high maintenance overhead. Such indexes are candidates for removal, and we'll walk through a script that uses this DMV shortly.

UNUSED INDEXES

Like many other DMVs, sys.dm_db_index_usage_stats holds index usage stats only since the SQL instance was last started. One of the implications that can be drawn from this is that any index that does not appear in this list has not been used since the instance was started. If the instance has been online for long enough to cover the full range of access patterns—for example, daily, weekly and monthly reports—and the database is not using the AUTOCLOSE option (or has been taken offline), then an index not appearing in this DMV is unlikely to be used at all.

The script in listing 13.5 uses *sys*.dm_db_index_usage_stats along with a number of system tables to return indexes not used since the last instance restart.

Listing 13.5   Indexes not used since last instance restart

```
-- Identify unused indexes (since last restart)
SELECT
    sc.name + '.' + object_name(i.object_id) as objectName
    , i.name as indexName
    , i.type_desc as indexType
FROM sys.indexes i
    INNER JOIN sys.objects o on o.object_id = i.object_id
    INNER JOIN sys.schemas sc on o.schema_id = sc.schema_id
WHERE
    objectproperty(i.object_id,'IsUserTable') = 1
    AND i.index_id not in (
        SELECT s.index_id
        FROM sys.dm_db_index_usage_stats s
        WHERE
            s.object_id = i.object_id
            AND i.index_id = s.index_id
            AND database_id = db_id()
    )
ORDER BY objectName, indexName ASC
```

This script uses sys.indexes, sys.objects, and sys.schemas to return index information followed by a simple not in clause to exclude those indexes in the DMV. The end result includes indexes not used since the SQL instance last started.

We also need to identify indexes whose maintenance cost outweighs their value.

HIGH-MAINTENANCE/LOW-VALUE INDEXES

In our next script, shown in listing 13.6, let's use the count values returned from sys.dm_db_index_usage_stats to compare the update count to the use count, that is, their maintenance-versus-usage ratio.

Listing 13.6 High-maintenance/low-value indexes

```
-- Identify high maintenance indexes with low usage
SELECT
    sc.name + '.' + object_name(i.object_id) as objectName
    , i.name as indexName
    , user_seeks
    , user_scans
    , user_lookups
    , (user_seeks + user_scans + user_lookups) as indexReads
    , user_updates as indexWrites
    , user_updates - (user_seeks + user_scans + user_lookups) as usageDiff
FROM sys.dm_db_index_usage_stats s
    INNER JOIN sys.indexes i on i.index_id = s.index_id
    INNER JOIN sys.objects o on o.object_id = i.object_id
    INNER JOIN sys.schemas sc on o.schema_id = sc.schema_id
WHERE
    database_id = db_id()
    AND objectproperty(s.object_id,'IsUserTable') = 1
    AND i.object_id = s.object_id
    AND i.type_desc = 'NONCLUSTERED'
ORDER BY
    usageDiff DESC
```

By ordering the results descending on the usageDiff column, this script identifies indexes with the biggest differential between their read and write counts. In the extreme cases where indexReads is zero, the index is being maintained for no read benefits at all. Note that the previous script filters for nonclustered indexes. We can remove this condition to display information on the base table/clustered index as well, including the last accessed stats to display when a table was last used in any capacity.

The result of this script, run against the AdventureWorks database, is shown in figure 13.13. Note that negative values for usageDiff represent cases where the index has been used for read purposes more than for updates.

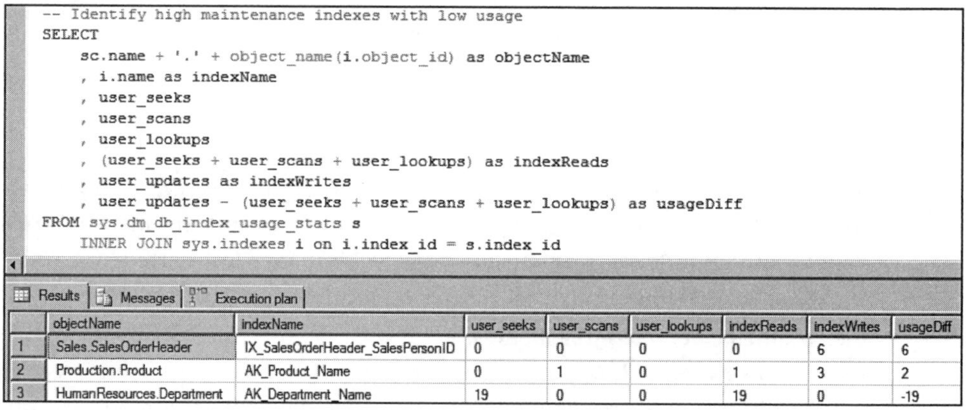

	objectName	indexName	user_seeks	user_scans	user_lookups	indexReads	indexWrites	usageDiff
1	Sales.SalesOrderHeader	IX_SalesOrderHeader_SalesPersonID	0	0	0	0	6	6
2	Production.Product	AK_Product_Name	0	1	0	1	3	2
3	HumanResources.Department	AK_Department_Name	19	0	0	19	0	-19

Figure 13.13 Large differences between the update and usage counts are indicative of high-maintenance/low-value indexes.

It's also possible for some indexes, while valuable and frequently used, to be duplicated or overlapping.

DUPLICATE AND OVERLAPPING INDEXES

A duplicate index, that is, an index with the same columns, defined in the same order, presents a very easy and clear case for removal. In a similar manner, an index that shares the same leading columns can also be considered a duplicate of another index. For example, Index B on lastName, firstName is really a duplicate of Index A on lastName, firstName, dateOfBirth. A number of links to scripts for detecting duplicate and overlapping indexes have been placed on the book's companion website, available at www.sqlCrunch.com/index.

Before dropping duplicate indexes, you should take care to ensure that no existing T-SQL or stored procedure code uses the index(es) as part of an index hint. Dropping such indexes without updating referencing code will obviously result in errors when the (now nonexistent) indexes are referenced.

In this section, we've identified indexes that are candidates for removal. In SQL Server 2005 and above, indexes can be disabled as well as removed or dropped, an important consideration and one that we'll cover when we look at index maintenance later in the chapter. For now, let's look at index analysis from a different perspective: identifying indexes that don't exist.

13.3.2 *Identifying indexes to add*

The analysis and potential removal of duplicate, unused, or infrequently used indexes can be periodically scheduled as a weekly or monthly maintenance task. In contrast, the addition of indexes is usually the result of a performance-tuning exercise, often started to investigate the sudden or gradual performance decline in one or more queries.

When a query is submitted to SQL Server for execution, the query optimizer determines the ideal index structures for executing the query. If such indexes exist, they're used; otherwise, a suboptimal plan is created with the details of the missing/ideal indexes stored for later reference. Such details can be accessed using one of two methods: the XML query plan and Dynamic Management Views.

> **Indexes on foreign keys**
>
> A common performance problem is related to the absence of foreign key indexes. In almost all cases, an index on a foreign key column will improve performance. For example, in an orders table, there is typically a foreign key to a customers table, with a very common query being something like `select * from orders where customerId = 623901`. In this example, an index on the customerId foreign key would most likely be beneficial.

XML QUERY PLANS

In its simplest form, the missing-indexes feature can be used for individual queries by inspecting the `<MissingIndexes>` element of the XML execution plan of a query executed in SQL Server Management Studio. As an example, let's imagine an application change was recently made to support searching AdventureWorks orders by a partial string match on the PurchaseOrderNumber column. Such a query would look like this:

```
-- Generate a missing index event
SELECT OrderDate, CustomerID, SubTotal, SalesPersonID
FROM Sales.SalesOrderHeader
WHERE PurchaseOrderNumber like 'PO166%'
```

With no clustered or nonclustered index on the PurchaseOrderNumber column, this query is forced to use a clustered index scan. Let's execute the query after running SET STATISTICS XML ON. The results are shown in figure 13.14.

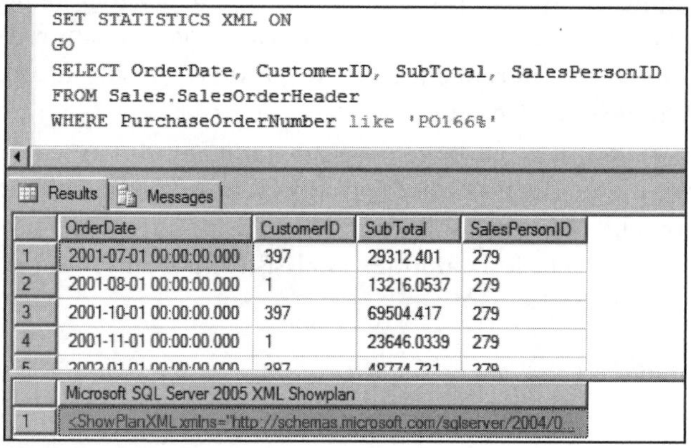

Figure 13.14   Query results with XML statistics

Note the XML that's returned below the result set. Clicking on the XML will open the graphical query execution plan. Right-click the resultant plan and choose Show Execution Plan XML. An example of the resultant XML is shown in figure 13.15.

The part of the XML plan we're interested in is highlighted. The <MissingIndexes> element contains the details of the ideal index that the query optimizer identified as being missing. In this particular case, the suggested index contains the PurchaseOrderNumber column as an index key with the other columns as included

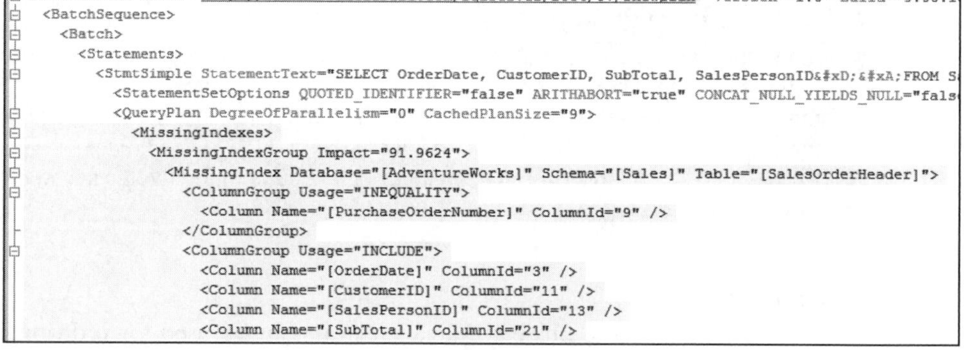

Figure 13.15   XML statistics with missing indexes highlighted

columns. Further, the `Impact` attribute of the `<MissingIndexGroup>` element esti-mates a 91.9624 percent improvement in query performance if this index is in place.

Using this information, the `create` statement for the suggested index would be created as follows:

```
CREATE NONCLUSTERED INDEX ixSalesOrderHeader_PurchaseOrderNumber
ON Sales.SalesOrderHeader(PurchaseOrderNumber)
INCLUDE (OrderDate, CustomerID, SubTotal, SalesPersonID)
```

Rerunning the query with the above index in place changes the execution plan from a clustered index scan to a nonclustered index seek without the need for key lookups (courtesy of the included columns). Running the query with `SET STATISTICS IO ON` confirms the reduction of page reads and the estimated 91 percent improve-ment suggested in the XML we saw earlier.

Now, this does not mean we should run out and immediately add this index. The recommendation for this particular example is made in isolation from the rest of the workload on the server. If this was a one-off ad hoc query, then adding this index would likely result in a net decrease in performance, given its maintenance require-ments and the fact that it would be used infrequently. However, if this is a common query, then perhaps it's a candidate for addition.

SET STATISTICS XML ON

In SQL Server versions prior to 2005, query execution plans could be viewed in text or graphical format. Graphical plans are nice, except when they span more than one screen and you need to send them to someone for analysis. On the other hand, text plans are sometimes difficult to read, especially complex plans. XML plans offer the best of both worlds. They can be saved as XML files for distribution, and when viewed in SQL Server Management studio, they're shown graphically with a right-click option for displaying the XML. Further, the XML can be inspected for details on missing in-dexes and viewing the compiled-versus-runtime parameter values for assistance in diagnosing parameter-sniffing problems, which we'll cover in chapter 17.

In essence, XML query plans allow us to access missing index information for a partic-ular query. While this is valuable, what would be really nice would be the ability to look back on previous production workload to identify all of the missing indexes. This is possible using the sys.dm_db_missing_index DMVs.

SYS.DM_DB_MISSING_INDEX DMVs

As we discussed earlier, when the query optimizer uses a suboptimal query plan, it records the details of the missing indexes that it believes are optimal for the query. In addition to viewing these details for a particular query using the XML plans, we can access these details for all queries[9] since the SQL instance last restarted through the sys.dm_db_missing_index DMVs. There are four DMVs in this group:

---

[9]   Up to 500 missing index groups are maintained by these DMVs.

- *sys.dm_db_missing_index_details*—This DMV returns one record for each missing index and contains columns for suggested key and included columns. Each missing index is identified with an index_handle.
- *sys.dm_db_missing_index_groups* —This DMV acts as a mapping between sys.dm_db_missing_index_details and sys.dm_db_missing_index_group_stats. It contains two columns: index_handle and group_handle.
- *sys.dm_db_missing_index_group_stats*—Each time the same index is identified by the query optimizer as missing, its potential value grows. This DMV stores the accumulated statistics on the index's potential value. Identified with group_handle, the accumulated stats can be traced back to the details of the missing index via the sys.dm_db_missing_index_groups DMV.
- *sys.dm_db_missing_index_columns*—This dynamic management function takes an index_handle as a parameter and returns the missing index's columns in a table format with a column indicating the suggested index column type.

To understand how each of these DMVs operates, let's use our example query from earlier:

```
SELECT OrderDate, CustomerID, SubTotal, SalesPersonID
FROM Sales.SalesOrderHeader
WHERE PurchaseOrderNumber like 'PO166%'
```

After restarting our SQL instance to clear the contents of the DMVs, we'll run this query, along with inspecting the results of the four DMVs. There are a couple of points to note about what we've done here. First, like the sys.dm_db_index_usage_stats DMV, these DMVs are cleared with each instance restart, so any decision based on their content should be made after the instance has been up and running for a period of time that covers the full range of activity. Second, the value of the sys.dm_db_missing_index_group_stats DMV is that it accumulates statistics on the potential value of a missing index after repeat misses. In our case, we've missed the index only once since the instance was started, so the figures shown for this DMV are for a single miss. So with these points in mind, let's examine the output from the DMVs, shown in figure 13.16.

First, you'll note that the equality column for sys.dm_db_missing_index_details is empty. This is because there are no equality predicates in our query, for example, where x=10. We used like, so this appears as an inequality column. Second, note that sys.dm_db_missing_index_columns is a function that takes an index_handle as an input and returns index columns in a tabular fashion along with the column usage (equality, inequality, include). In contrast, sys.dm_db_missing_index_details returns one row per missing index.

The real value of these DMVs is when the instance has been up and running for a period of time. This allows us to take advantage of the accumulated statistics from the sys.dm_db_missing_index_group_stats DMV. Books Online has a complete description of the columns returned from this DMV, but there are a few that stand out:

- *avg_total_user_cost*—This column represents the reduction in query cost if the suggested index was present.

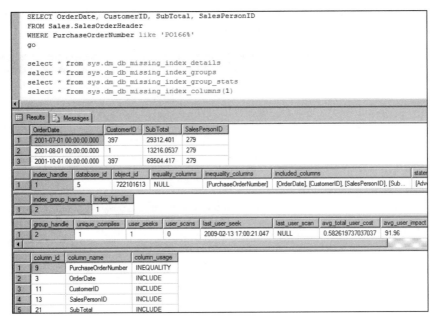

Figure 13.16 Missing index information returned from various DMVs

- *avg_user_impact*—This represents the estimated percentage improvement of the query with the index present.
- *user_seeks and user_scans*—Each time the query is executed without the suggested index, these values increment to represent the number of times the index could have been used in either a seek or scan capacity.

When selecting from the sys.dm_db_missing_index_group_stats DMV, we can order by the above columns to show the indexes with the greatest potential for improvement. To simulate this, we can rerun our `SalesOrderHeader` query multiple times and then query the DMV ordering by the above columns. Listing 13.7 shows the code for this. Note the `GO 10` command after the `SalesOrderHeader` query, used to execute the query 10 times. In addition to this query, we execute another query on the DatabaseLog table, which also generates a missing index event. This allows us to view multiple missing indexes ordered by potential value.

Listing 13.7 Simulating activity to view missing indexes by priority

```
-- Simulate a weighted query workload by using GO 10 for 1 statement
SELECT OrderDate, CustomerID, SubTotal, SalesPersonID
FROM Sales.SalesOrderHeader
WHERE PurchaseOrderNumber like 'PO166%'
GO 10

SELECT DatabaseUser, TSQL
FROM dbo.DatabaseLog
WHERE Event = 'ALTER_TABLE'
GO
```

Listing 13.8 shows the code to view the missing index information generated by the above two queries, weighted by potential value.

Listing 13.8   Missing index DMV query with potential weighting

```
-- View missing indexes Weighted by potential value
SELECT
      sc.name + '.' + OBJECT_NAME(details.object_id)
    , details.equality_columns
    , details.inequality_columns
    , details.included_columns
    , stats.avg_total_user_cost
    , stats.user_seeks
    , stats.avg_user_impact
    , stats.avg_total_user_cost * stats.avg_user_impact
      * (stats.user_seeks + stats.user_scans) as potential
FROM sys.dm_db_missing_index_group_stats stats
    INNER JOIN sys.dm_db_missing_index_groups groups
      ON stats.group_handle = groups.index_group_handle
    INNER JOIN sys.dm_db_missing_index_details details
      ON details.index_handle = groups.index_handle
    INNER JOIN sys.objects o
      ON o.object_id = details.object_id
    INNER JOIN sys.schemas sc
      ON o.schema_id = sc.schema_id
ORDER BY potential desc
```

The calculated potential column takes into account the columns from the sys.dm_db_missing_index_group_stats that we covered earlier. By executing the query on the SalesOrderHeader table 10 times (using the GO 10 command), the potential value of the missing index on this table is increased by virtue of the user_seeks column, together with the avg_total_user_cost and avg_user_impact columns. The output from the query in listing 13.8 is shown in figure 13.17.

The potential value for the missing indexes is calculated by multiplying the sum of seeks/scans against the user cost and impact columns. Because the SalesOrderHeader

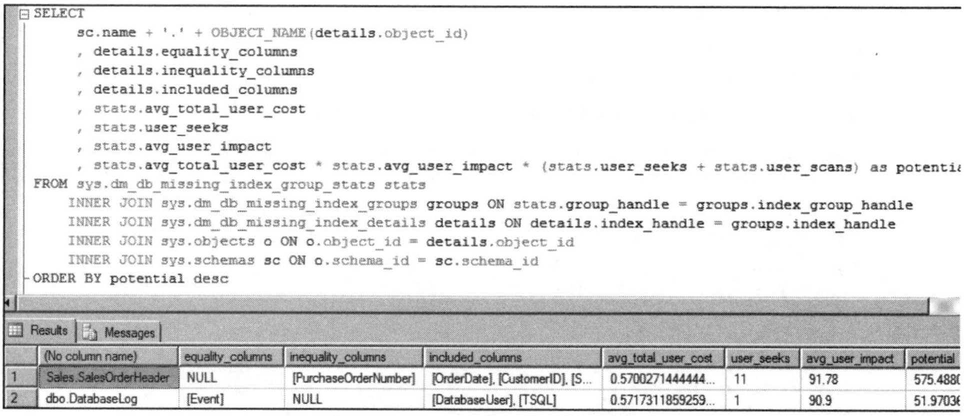

Figure 13.17   Missing index DMV query with weighting potential

query was executed 11 times, its potential weighting is greater compared to a single execution of the query on the DatabaseLog table.

The full value of the missing index DMVs can be exploited as part of a regular maintenance routine. For example, weekly checks on index usage to remove duplicate/unused indexes could be combined with checks on the potential for missing indexes using a query similar to the previous one.

Despite the power of the missing index DMVs, there are some limitations, all of which are listed in Books Online. The major ones are as follows:

- A maximum of 500 missing indexes will be kept.
- The DMVs will be cleared when the SQL instance is restarted or the table definition changes.
- While the missing indexes report the columns to include (key and included columns), they don't suggest a column order for the index.
- Certain index types, including filtered indexes, clustered indexes, and indexed views, are not suggested.

The Database Engine Tuning Advisor, covered next, addresses some of these shortcomings.

DATABASE ENGINE TUNING ADVISOR

The *Database Engine Tuning Advisor,* accessible in the Performance Tools folder of the Microsoft SQL Server 2008 program group, analyzes workload from either a T-SQL file or SQL Trace file/table. T-SQL files are typically used to analyze a limited set of commands, whereas SQL traces, covered in more detail in chapter 14, are used to analyze workload over a period of time, for example, a 24-hour period covering typical production activity.

Once the workload input has been specified, options can be configured to limit the scope of recommendations that the tuning advisor will consider. Figure 13.18 shows the broad range of options available for consideration.

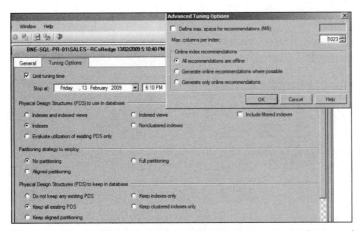

Figure 13.18   The Database Engine Tuning Advisor can be used to examine a workload and suggest various index types to improve performance.

As shown in figure 13.18, the analysis options are far greater than what can be achieved using the missing index DMVs that we covered earlier. Further, the analysis can be based on a wide range of production activity captured in a trace file (or table) for future analysis. In the next chapter, we'll provide more coverage of using SQL Server Profiler to capture production database activity.

Once the workload input has been selected and a target database chosen, analysis can begin. When the analysis is complete, recommendations can be viewed, an example of which is shown in figure 13.19.

One of the clear advantages of using the tuning advisor over other index analysis methods is the ease with which the recommendations can be turned into actual T-SQL code for implementation. As shown in figure 13.19, you can click the Definition column to display the appropriate T-SQL code to effect the recommendation. Further, the tool can be used for recommendations on indexes to drop as well as those to add.

As per the recommendations from the missing index DMVs, you should carefully consider indexes suggested by the tuning advisor before implementing them. Among others, considerations include these:

- Is the workload sufficient to cover the full range of production activity?
- Can the suggested recommendations be load/volume tested before production implementation?

A common theme throughout this book is ensuring the existence of a volume test environment where configuration changes can be verified for performance impact before implementing them in production. For suggested index changes, this is crucial.

So far in this section we've covered techniques to identify indexes to add and delete. What's missing is a technique to identify the fragmentation levels of existing indexes that are being used.

13.3.3 *Identifying index fragmentation*

Indexes, like any other storage object, become fragmented over time through the course of normal insert, delete, and update activity. Identifying the level of fragmentation is a crucial component of a targeted maintenance plan. Later in the chapter we'll look at prioritizing index maintenance based on the level of fragmentation. In this

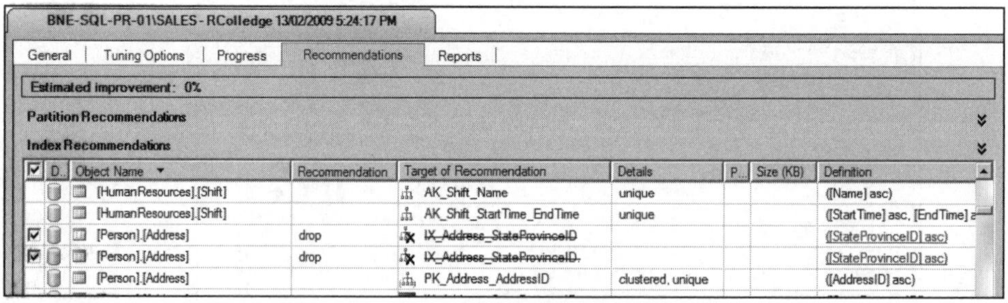

Figure 13.19   Database Engine Tuning Advisor recommendations are shown after workload analysis is complete.

section, our focus is on identifying fragmentation levels, achieved using the `sys.dm_db_index_physical_stats` dynamic management function.

One of the columns returned from this DMF is avg_fragmentation_in_percent. This indicates the percentage of pages that are out of order, meaning the logical and physical ordering of index pages no longer match, incurring additional disk activity when scanning/seeking. As you'll see later in the chapter, rebuilding or defragmenting an index repositions physical pages to be adjacent to and in line with the logical order.

The code displayed in listing 13.9 uses the `sys.dm_db_index_physical_stats` function to return index fragmentation levels for all tables and indexes in the AdventureWorks database.

Listing 13.9 Displaying index fragmentation

```
-- View index fragmentation ordered by fragmentation level
SELECT stats.index_id, name, avg_fragmentation_in_percent
FROM sys.dm_db_index_physical_stats(
   DB_ID(N'AdventureWorks'), NULL, NULL, NULL, NULL
) as stats
    INNER JOIN sys.indexes AS b
        ON stats.object_id = b.object_id AND stats.index_id = b.index_id
ORDER BY avg_fragmentation_in_percent DESC
```

The output of this command, as shown in figure 13.20, is one row for each index in the database, with the avg_fragmentation_in_percent column ordered descending to list the most fragmented indexes first. This list will include clustered indexes, which indicates the level of fragmentation of the table itself.

In previous versions of SQL Server, we used the `DBCC SHOWCONTIG` command to retrieve, among other things, the logical scan fragmentation value for a given index. While this command is still available, the `sys.dm_db_index_physical_stats` function is the preferred method. One of the limitations with `DBCC SHOWCONTIG` is its lack of accuracy when analyzing storage spanning multiple files. In contrast, the `sys.dm_db_index_physical_stats` function has no such limitations and is therefore the recommended method for index fragmentation analysis.

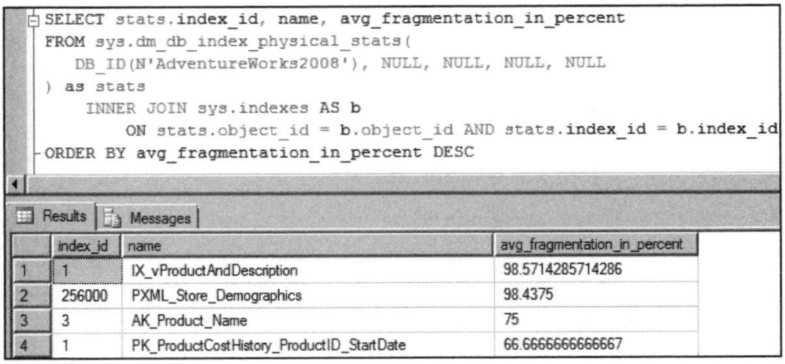

```
SELECT stats.index_id, name, avg_fragmentation_in_percent
FROM sys.dm_db_index_physical_stats(
   DB_ID(N'AdventureWorks2008'), NULL, NULL, NULL, NULL
) as stats
    INNER JOIN sys.indexes AS b
        ON stats.object_id = b.object_id AND stats.index_id = b.index_id
ORDER BY avg_fragmentation_in_percent DESC
```

Results | Messages

	index_id	name	avg_fragmentation_in_percent
1	1	IX_vProductAndDescription	98.5714285714286
2	256000	PXML_Store_Demographics	98.4375
3	3	AK_Product_Name	75
4	1	PK_ProductCostHistory_ProductID_StartDate	66.6666666666667

Figure 13.20 Index fragmentation levels for AdventureWorks tables

> **Automating index analysis and** REBUILD/REORGANIZE
>
> A common database maintenance technique involves an automated script that uses the sys.dm_db_index_physical_stats function to analyze index fragmentation levels and perform the appropriate action, for example, REORGANIZE if fragmentation between 5 percent and 30 percent and REBUILD if greater than 30 percent. A script to perform this is provided in SQL Server Books Online under the sys.dm_db_index_physical_stats topic.

Having covered a number of important index-analysis techniques, let's move on now to the actual index-maintenance tasks required to keep our databases performing well.

13.4   Index maintenance

The maintenance actions outlined in this section are directly associated with the corresponding analysis activities from the previous section. We'll begin with dropping unused or duplicated indexes before looking at removing index fragmentation.

13.4.1   Dropping and disabling indexes

In the previous section, we covered the use of the sys.dm_db_index_usage_stats DMV along with a number of system tables to identify indexes that are not used, used rarely, or duplicated. Once identified, the indexes are candidates for removal. The question is, how should they be removed? An index can be easily dropped using the DROP INDEX command as per this example:

```
DROP INDEX tablename.indexname
```

If the index was dropped as a result of being identified as a duplicate or suspected as being of low value, then it's possible that certain unexpected errors or performance problems eventuate from the index being dropped. For example, a query may still be referencing the index with an index hint, or a rare (but important) report is executed that relies on the (now missing) index. In such cases, if the definition of the index was not saved, that is, the index type, columns, and column order, then it may take some time to restore the index to its previous state.

In SQL Server 2005, the ALTER INDEX command was enhanced with a DISABLE option. Disabling an index has the following effects:

- If nonclustered, the data is removed from the index but the index metadata definition remains.
- User access to the index is not permitted.
- The query optimizer will not consider the index.
- If a clustered index is disabled, access to the table is prevented until the index is re-enabled via either the REBUILD or the CREATE WITH DROP_EXISTING command, both of which are covered shortly.

When it comes to removing a duplicated or low-value index, disabling the index allows its definition to be retained should the index need to be reinstated, without the

> ### Disk space and disabling indexes
>
> When you use the index REBUILD option (covered shortly), additional temporary disk space is required for storing the old and new copies of the index. One of the advantages of disabling an index before rebuilding it is the reduction in disk space required for the rebuild operation. The estimated overhead of rebuilding a disabled index is approximately 20 percent on top of the index size. The disadvantage of disabling an index is that it's unavailable for use until the rebuild is complete. This technique may be appropriate if disk space is limited and the temporary unavailability of the index is permitted.

maintenance overhead of keeping it. An index can be disabled using the ALTER INDEX command as follows:

```
-- Disable an index
ALTER INDEX ixSalesOrderHeader_PurchaseOrderNumber
ON Sales.SalesOrderHeader
DISABLE
GO
```

The other major use for disabling indexes is during data warehouse loads. The classic load process is *drop indexes, load data, reinstate indexes*. The problem with this approach is that the definition of the indexes needs to be known when adding them back, complicating the process somewhat, particularly when the table or index definition changes and the change is not added to the drop/re-create process. In such cases, the index creation may fail or add back an old, poorly performing version of the index. By disabling an index rather than dropping it, the index definition is not required when re-enabling it, simplifying the re-creation process.

To re-enable a disabled index, use the ALTER INDEX REBUILD or CREATE INDEX WITH DROP EXISTING command, which we'll cover shortly.

13.4.2 Removing fragmentation

In the section "Identifying index fragmentation," we discussed index fragmentation levels and a Books Online script for maintaining indexes based on the fragmentation percentage. In this section, we'll cover a number of different techniques for maintaining an index and the implications these have on fragmentation, user access, statistics, and transaction log usage.

ALTER INDEX REORGANIZE

The ALTER INDEX REORGANIZE option is the replacement for DBCC INDEXDEFRAG used in earlier SQL Server versions. Reorganizing an index removes fragmentation by reordering the leaf level of clustered and nonclustered indexes by aligning the physical order with the logical order. An example follows:

```
-- Reorganize (Defragment) an index
ALTER INDEX IX_SalesOrderHeader_SalesPersonID
ON Sales.SalesOrderHeader
REORGANIZE
```

The REORGANIZE method is ideal as a low-impact, online method for removing light to medium levels of fragmentation from an index. In most cases, an index with a 5- to 30-percent fragmentation level (as reported by the avg_fragmentation_in_percent column in the sys.dm_index_physical_stats function) can be defragmented using this method, without any major user impact.

On the downside, REORGANIZE will not remove fragmentation from the nonleaf (intermediate) levels, nor will it update statistics. For that, we need a more thorough approach, available through ALTER INDEX REBUILD.

ALTER INDEX REBUILD

ALTER INDEX REBUILD is the replacement for DBCC DBREINDEX used in earlier versions of SQL Server. This command essentially drops and re-creates the index, with a number of important differences.

First, the REBUILD method reads and rebuilds every page, and consequently, its statistics, covered in more detail later in the chapter, are updated *in full*. Second, all levels of the index are rebuilt, meaning a greater performance boost and disk space reduction compared to the REORGANIZE method. An example REBUILD command follows:

```
-- Rebuild an index (Online mode)
ALTER INDEX ALL
ON Sales.SalesOrderHeader
REBUILD WITH (ONLINE = ON)
```

You'll note a few differences (and similarities) between this command and REORGANIZE. First, it uses the same ALTER INDEX command, but in this case ALL is used in place of a specific index in the earlier example. ALL is supported for both REBUILD and REORGANIZE as a means to operate on all of the specified table indexes rather than a specific index.

The other option specified in the above example is ONLINE = ON. Available in the Enterprise edition of SQL Server, this option rebuilds the index in a manner that allows continued user access to the index during the rebuild operation. Thus, it's ideal for rebuilding indexes in 24/7 environments.

Drop/re-create vs. REBUILD

While REBUILD will essentially achieve the same thing as dropping and re-creating an index, it offers a number of important advantages. First, the ONLINE option can be used, which allows continued user access. Second, dropping and re-creating a clustered index will cause all nonclustered indexes to be rebuilt *twice*; the clustered index key is included in the leaf level of each nonclustered index. When the clustered index is dropped, the table is converted to a heap, with the nonclustered indexes changing their leaf-level row locators to a row ID containing the file, page, and row number. When the clustered index is re-created, the row ID changes back to the clustered index key. When the REBUILD option is used, all of this is avoided, with the clustered index key remaining unchanged throughout.

Table 13.1 summarizes the appropriate index-maintenance technique based on the fragmentation level. Although indexes of any fragmentation level will benefit from the REBUILD method, in order to limit the transaction log usage (and subsequent effects on database mirroring and/or log shipping), it's recommended that only indexes with greater than 30 percent fragmentation use REBUILD, with tables having fragmentation levels lower than this value using REORGANIZE. The 30 percent level is a general recommendation only and is subject to the local nuances of the database and its environment. The overall goal is to strike a balance between transaction log size, user impact, and increased index performance.

Table 13.1 Fragmentation levels and options

Index fragmentation	Maintenance technique
5%–30%	ALTER INDEX REORGANIZE
30% +	ALTER INDEX REBUILD

An alternative to REBUILD is CREATE WITH DROP_EXISTING.

CREATE WITH DROP_EXISTING

The CREATE WITH DROP_EXISTING command, an example of which follows, allows the index definition to be modified as part of the re-creation process, for example, adding additional columns or moving the index to another filegroup.

```
-- Rebuild an index with an altered definition
CREATE CLUSTERED INDEX cixClientSSN
ON dbo.client(SSN, DOB)
WITH (DROP_EXISTING = ON)
```

Using CREATE WITH DROP_EXISTING is particularly useful for rebuilding clustered indexes on tables with one or more nonclustered indexes. Unlike a traditional drop/re-create, which rebuilds the nonclustered indexes twice, nonclustered indexes are rebuilt only once using this option—or not at all if the index definition remains the same. On the downside, CREATE WITH DROP EXISTING operates on a single index at a time, in contrast to the ALL option of the REBUILD/REORGANIZE commands covered earlier.

Each of the index-maintenance techniques we've covered thus far can be executed with a large number of optional parameters, all of which are documented in SQL Server Books Online. Before we close this section, let's cover some frequently used ones.

INDEX OPTIONS

In chapter 7 we covered a number of server-level settings including MAXDOP and FILL-FACTOR, both of which can be specified at a statement level for index creation/modification. Let's recap these options and cover some other commonly used ones

- *FILLFACTOR*—When building an index, FILLFACTOR determines how full (as a percentage) each index page will be *for existing data*. By default, FILLFACTOR is 0 (which is equivalent to 100), which means index pages will fill to capacity. This has two implications: with a higher page fill rate, fewer pages need to be read, but on the downside, a high update rate will result in more page splits and fragmentation. For tables with a high update rate, a lower fill factor *may* increase performance and reduce fragmentation, although the trade-off is that the index (and therefore the database) will occupy more space because each page is less than 100 percent full.

- *PAD_INDEX*—FILLFACTOR applies at the leaf level of index pages only. When the PAD_INDEX option is set to ON, the FILLFACTOR setting is applied to intermediate index levels as well.
- *MAXDOP*—This option allows the number of CPUs to be limited to (or increased from) the default server setting; for example, if the default server MAXDOP setting is set to 1 to prevent parallel queries, MAXDOP = 0 can be specified to maximize the performance of the index operation.
- *SORT_IN_TEMPDB*—By default, the temporary disk space used during index rebuild operations comes from the user database containing the index. This option directs the operation to use the tempdb database, which may improve rebuild performance, particularly when tempdb is located on dedicated disks. When using this option, take care to ensure tempdb has sufficient disk space available.
- *DATA_COMPRESSION*—As covered in chapter 9, individual tables and indexes can be compressed, using either the ROW or PAGE method.

An example of using these options as part of an index rebuild follows:

```
-- Rebuild an index with various custom options
ALTER INDEX IX_SalesOrderHeader_CustomerID
ON Sales.SalesOrderHeader
REBUILD WITH (
    FILLFACTOR = 80
    , PAD_INDEX = ON
    , MAXDOP = 0
    , SORT_IN_TEMPDB = ON
    , DATA_COMPRESSION = PAGE
)
```

In closing the chapter, let's look at management techniques for statistics.

13.5   *Managing statistics*

Earlier in the chapter we looked at the important role played by statistics in providing the query optimizer with information on the selectivity of an index and the likely value it therefore has for use in a given query. In addition to maintaining statistics on index selectivity, statistics are created and maintained for nonindexed columns as well. In this section we'll take a further look at index statistics and introduce *column statistics*.

13.5.1 *Index statistics*

The default statistics configuration enables SQL Server to automatically create and update statistics on all indexed columns. This setting reduces maintenance requirements and ensures SQL Server makes accurate decisions when creating query execution plans.

In cases where the index has multiple columns, statistics are also kept for the combination of column prefixes, for example, an index on LastName, FirstName, DOB will keep statistics on (LastName), (LastName + FirstName), and (LastName + FirstName + DOB). This enables the most accurate estimate to be made on the index's selectivity when evaluating a query containing predicates on one or more of these columns.

In a case where LastName and DOB are specified (but not FirstName), the selectivity would be based on LastName alone. For this reason, if the most selective column is always supplied as a search predicate, and other index columns are not, then it makes sense for the most selective column to be placed first in the index column order.

Updating statistics after an index rebuild

When an index is rebuilt using one of the various options (REBUILD, CREATE WITH DROP EXISTING, or DROP/CREATE), the statistics are updated *in full*. A common mistake made when creating maintenance plans is to run the UPDATE STATISTICS command after an index rebuild. When run with the default parameters, UPDATE STATISTICS creates statistics based on a sample of rows. When run in this manner, the full statistics from the index rebuild are replaced with less-accurate statistics.

In almost all cases, the default database settings for statistics (Auto Create Statistics and Auto Update Statistics) should remain in place. These settings, accessible via the Database Properties page as shown in figure 13.21, ensure that SQL Server automatically manages both the creation and update of statistics information.

When the query optimizer compiles a query plan requiring statistics, the statistics are automatically updated if they are detected as being out of date. Statistics are deemed as being out of date for a variety of reasons, primarily when a certain percentage of rows have been modified since the statistics were last updated. In such an event,

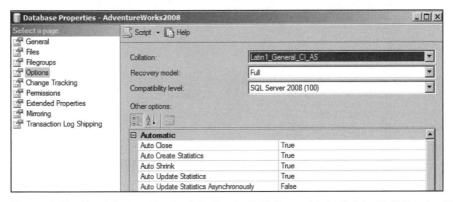

Figure 13.21   The default setting for Auto Create Statistics and Auto Update Statistics should remain in place for almost all database implementations.

the statistics are updated *in line*; that is, the query compilation pauses, waiting for the statistics update to complete. Such events, which can be confirmed using a SQL Profiler trace containing the `Auto Stats` event, may lead to occasional, unpredictable query performance, a situation that sometimes leads to DBAs switching off the automatic statistic options in a bid for more predictable query performance.

While automatic statistic events may result in an occasional query execution delay, the benefit of automatic statistics maintenance must be considered, particularly its advantage of avoiding poor query plans based on old statistics. The alternative of hand-crafting customized statistics is simply far too time consuming and inaccurate for all but the most specialized of cases.

Fortunately, a compromise setting was introduced in SQL Server 2005. The Auto Update Statistics Asynchronously option, set using the database property shown earlier in figure 13.21, will trigger automatic statistic update events *asynchronously*; that is, a query compilation will not wait on the new statistics and will proceed with the old, with subsequent queries benefiting from the newly updated statistics. Using this setting is a trade-off between the most accurate query plan and predictable query performance.

In addition to creating and maintaining indexed column statistics, SQL Server creates and maintains statistics on nonindexed columns. Such statistics are called *column statistics*.

13.5.2   *Column statistics*

Along with index statistics, you can view column statistics in SQL Server Management Studio, as shown in figure 13.22. Column statistics are named with a _WA_Sys prefix.

So why and how are column statistics useful? We know that unless an appropriate index exists on a query's predicate column(s), the statistics are not used for evaluating the usage of an index, *because there is no index*. The answer lies in the query optimizer needing an accurate indication of the likely number of rows that will be returned

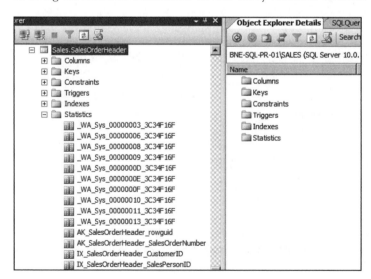

Figure 13.22   Automatically created column statistics are prefixed with _WA_Sys_.

from a query in order to select the best query plan, in particular, the appropriate join logic. For example, consider this query:

```
-- Statistics on large + red products may help to optimize the join ...
SELECT orders.*
FROM dbo.product
    INNER JOIN dbo.orders on product.productId = orders.productId
WHERE
    product.color = 'red'
    AND product.size = 'large'
```

Assuming there are no indexes on the color and/or size columns, what good is it to maintain statistics on them? How many rows SQL Server *thinks* will be returned after applying the filter condition on the products table determines the type of join operation that will be used, that is, hash join, nested loop, or merge. Join logic is beyond the scope of this book, but suffice to say that nested loop joins perform very well *or* very poorly depending on the row count from one side of the join. By having accurate statistics on the columns, the query optimizer is given the best chance to choose the best join technique.

For nonindexed columns, statistics are maintained only for singular column values. In the previous example, statistics would be automatically created and maintained on the color column but not the combination of color and size. Consider a case where the table contained a million records with red products but only two with large red products. The quality of the compiled execution plan depends on whether the query optimizer has the required statistics. Depending on the selectivity of color, compared to color and size, it may be worthwhile to manually create multicolumn statistics, as per the following example:

```
-- Create custom column statistics
CREATE STATISTICS Product_Color_Size
ON dbo.product (color, size)
WITH FULLSCAN
```

In addition to the CREATE STATISTICS command shown above, SQL Server provides a number of other commands enabling manual control over statistics.

13.5.3 *Manually creating/updating statistics*

Assuming the automatic statistics options are in place, there are a few cases that call for manual intervention. As we've just discussed, creating multicolumn statistics on combinations of certain nonindexed columns is one such case. Another may be where the default sampling frequency is inadequate and is producing inaccurate plans.[10]

SQL Server Books Online provides a full description of the statistics management commands, summarized briefly as follows:

- *DROP STATISTICS*—This command enables a specified statistics set to be dropped, whether created manually or automatically. Index statistics, however, cannot be dropped.

---

[10] Indexes on monotonically increasing values such as IDENTITY columns is a common example where high insert rates cause a large number of rows to fall outside the known statistics range.

- *CREATE STATISTICS*—This command can be used to create statistics for a supplied column or set of columns. If you're using the default automatic statistics settings, this command is typically used only to create multicolumn statistics, an example of which you saw earlier. New to SQL Server 2008 is the ability to create filtered statistics, which, similar to filtered indexes, maintain statistics for a subset of data.
- *sp_createstats*—This command creates single-column statistics for all eligible columns in all user tables in the database in which the command in executed.
- *UPDATE STATISTICS*—Updates statistics for a given statistics name. Again, if the automatic statistics settings are in place, this command is typically used only when statistics are suspected of being out of date. Running this command enables a more frequent refresh compared to the automatic default.
- *sp_updatestats*—This command runs UPDATE STATISTICS against all user tables using the ALL keyword, therefore updating all statistics maintained for each user table.

With the exception of DROP STATISTICS, all of the above commands take an optional parameter for the sampling rate. Without specifying a value, SQL Server estimates the appropriate number of rows to inspect, with the goal of striking a balance between useful statistics and low impact. In all cases, the FULLSCAN (or 100 percent) option can be used to sample every row, thereby achieving maximum accuracy.

As we covered earlier, rebuilding an index will update the statistics with the equivalent of a manual full scan. A common reason for performing a full index rebuild is to ensure the statistics are kept at their most accurate. However, as we also discussed, unnecessary index rebuilds create a lot of transaction log data, in turn causing potential issues with log shipping and mirroring solutions. If indexes are being rebuilt for the express purpose of maintaining statistics, that is, fragmentation levels are not of concern, then manually running UPDATE STATISTICS using the FULLSCAN option is perhaps a better choice; statistics will be updated in full, without the overhead of the index rebuild.

In closing the chapter, let's see how to inspect the statistics information kept by SQL Server.

13.5.4 *Inspecting statistics*

The DBCC SHOW_STATISTICS command can be used to view the statistics information for a given index, as per the example shown in figure 13.23.

DBCC SHOW_STATISTICS provides a great deal of information useful in inspecting the statistics for a given index. The output is grouped into three sections, referred to as STAT_HEADER, DENSITY_VECTOR, and HISTOGRAM:

- *STAT_HEADER*—Contains information including the date and time of the last stats update, number of rows sampled versus table rows, and any filtering conditions.
- *DENSITY_VECTOR*—Contains the length and selectivity of each column prefix. As discussed previously, stats are kept for all depth levels of the index.

```
DBCC SHOW_STATISTICS ("Person.Contact", ixContactLastName)
```

Results | Messages

	Name	Updated	Rows	Rows Sampled	Steps	Density	Average key length	String Index
1	ixContactLastName	Feb 13 2009 3:38PM	19972	19972	200	0.4936212	15.2126	YES

	All density	Average Length	Columns
1	0.0008291874	11.2126	LastName
2	5.00701E-05	15.2126	LastName, ContactID

	RANGE_HI_KEY	RANGE_ROWS	EQ_ROWS	DISTINCT_RANGE_ROWS	AVG_RANGE_ROWS
160	Simmons	15	109	11	1.363636
161	Smith	21	103	10	2.1
162	Srini	23	62	14	1.642857
163	Stewart	21	93	16	1.3125
164	Suarez	30	105	9	3.333333
165	Subram	0	85	0	1
166	Sun	15	72	4	3.75

Figure 13.23 `DBCC SHOW_STATISTICS` is used to inspect statistics information, including the histogram, date and time of the last update, and column information.

- *HISTOGRAM*—The histogram is the most descriptive section of output, containing the actual sampled values and associated statistics such as the number of records that match the sampled value.

We've covered a lot of ground in this chapter but still only scratched the surface of the inner workings of indexes and statistics. SQL Server Books Online contains a wealth of information for gaining a deeper and broader understanding of the crucial role played by indexes and statistics.

13.6 Best practice considerations: index design and maintenance

Poor index design and maintenance strategies are a significant contributor to reduced database performance. Classic index-related problems include too many indexes, high fragmentation levels, and missing indexes. Fortunately, SQL Server includes a number of tools and processes for improving index design and maintenance.

- With the possible exception of small temporary tables, or those used for insert activity only, all tables should be created with a physical order, achieved through the use of a clustered index. Clustered tables enable fragmentation to be controlled without user outage and enable fast lookups when querying on the clustered key(s).
- Given that the clustered index key is included in each nonclustered index as the row locator, from a size and performance perspective, wide-clustered index keys should be avoided in favor of narrower ones. The ideal clustered index key is narrow, unique, and holds no intrinsic business value, therefore avoiding updates and the subsequent need to maintain nonclustered index row locators. For these reasons, identity-based columns are often used for clustered surrogate primary keys.
- When creating tables, creating the clustered index *before* nonclustered indexes will prevent the need for nonclustered index rebuilds.

- A common database design practice is to use globally unique identifier (GUID) columns as primary keys, which by default will also be the table's clustered index unless specified otherwise. Not only are GUIDs wide (16 bytes), they're randomly generated. Given such tables are clustered on the GUID column, newly inserted rows will be randomly positioned throughout the table, leading to page splits and subsequent fragmentation. This is a particular concern for tables with a high volume of data inserts. SQL Server 2005 introduced the NewSequentialID() function, which partially offsets this problem by generating GUIDs in a sequential manner. Removing the "randomness" from the GUID values helps in reducing both page splits and fragmentation.

- Columns frequently used for range scans and sort operations are good candidates for a clustered index, for example, an order date column used to return orders within a date range. A clustered index on this column may avoid the need for both scan and sort operations.

- Look for opportunities to cover queries using either additional nonclustered keys or included columns. Covered indexes avoid the need for key/RID lookup operations, improving performance substantially and increasing the likelihood of a nonclustered index being used.

- Filtered indexes are excellent for creating small and fast indexes on tables with subsets of data accessed using simple predicates commonly supplied during searches. They also enable segregated index maintenance, more accurate statistics, and the ability to create unique indexes on columns containing null values (but whose not-null values are unique). However, if most of a table's rows would be included in the filtered index, a full table index is most likely a better option.

- Indexed views achieve similar benefits to filtered indexes but enable more complex predicates and can span more than one table. They are ideal when using aggregate functions, but because of the cost of maintaining the data in line with the base tables, they are best used when the base table(s) are infrequently modified. The maintenance costs of maintaining indexed views on heavily modified tables may outweigh the benefits and should therefore be carefully considered and measured before production implementation.

- Loading up a database with indexes in the hope that performance will eventually improve is a flawed and dangerous approach. A measured approach using views and functions such as sys.dm_db_index_usage_stats and the sys.dm_db_missing_index group offers a much better *qualitative* approach as part of an ongoing, proactive maintenance regime.

- Consider all foreign keys as index candidates. Table lookups based on a foreign key column are very common, as are performance problems stemming from the lack of indexes on these columns.

- For multicolumn indexes, placing the most selective column first usually results in the best performance, particularly when using *like* searches. In cases where doing so makes the index unusable, for example, when the column is rarely supplied as a search condition, then this is obviously not appropriate.

- For very large join operations in specialist situations—for example, a data conversion process—consider the possibility of clustering each table on the join column. Doing so permits a merge join and can result in substantial performance gains.

- Use the sys.dm_db_index_usage_stats DMV to determine the maintenance cost of an index compared to its usage benefits. This DMV is best used as part of a regular index-analysis maintenance routine. Bear in mind that the values reported by this DMV are applicable only since the last instance restart, so decisions based on its output should take this into consideration.

- Identify and remove duplicate and/or overlapping indexes, but consider the possibility that they may be referenced in T-SQL code as index hints. Before dropping such indexes, script their definition or use the DISABLE function.

- Using the SET STATISTICS XML ON command enables the query execution plan to be captured in XML format. This enables plan portability for support and analysis purposes, while also allowing inspection of missing indexes as reported by the query optimizer.

- Using the sys.dm_db_missing_index DMVs allows retrospective inspection of all missing indexes as reported by the query optimizer since the last instance restart. By using the cumulative statistics in the index_group_stats DMV, missing indexes can be prioritized in order of potential value and considered as candidates for addition. Like the index usage inspection, this can be part of a regular maintenance routine.

- The Database Engine Tuning Advisor overcomes some of the limitations of the missing index DMVs such as the maximum of 500 stored missing indexes and their inability to suggest clustered/filtered indexes and indexed views. Further, its input can be a profiler trace of actual production activity, captured over the appropriate timeframe.

- For all index additions/removals, measuring the performance impact in a volume test environment before production implementation is crucial in avoiding unexpected problems.

- The sys.dm_db_index_physical_stats function can be used to identify an index's fragmentation level and should be used in place of the older, limited functionality offered by DBCC SHOWCONTIG.

- For operations such as large data loads where indexes are dropped and re-created around the load, disabling indexes rather than dropping them enables the index re-creation step to be much simpler by excluding the need to store the index definition. A disabled index retains its metadata, so a simple rebuild command is sufficient to restore the index.

- Use the ALTER INDEX REORGANIZE command in place of the older DBCC INDEXDEFRAG command to correct index fragmentation levels of up to 30 percent.

- Use the ALTER INDEX REBUILD command in place of the older DBCC DBREINDEX command to correct index fragmentation of greater than 30 percent.

- Avoid unnecessary index rebuilds. Unnecessary index rebuilds deliver limited benefits while increasing transaction log usage and potential user impact. Increased transaction log usage is of prime concern with database-mirroring solutions, particularly when in high-safety (synchronous) mode.

- If you rebuild indexes only in order to maintain accurate statistics, consider the statistics maintenance commands with the FULLSCAN or Sample 100 options.

- The ONLINE = ON option of ALTER INDEX REBUILD is available in the Enterprise edition of SQL Server, making it the ideal choice for low user impact index maintenance in 24/7 environments or those with limited maintenance windows.

- Using CREATE WITH DROP_EXISTING is an ideal alternative to dropping and re-creating clustered indexes with a different structure. Dropping and re-creating a clustered index incurs a double rebuild impact on existing nonclustered indexes, a process avoided by using the DROP_EXISTING command.

- Avoid the classic mistake of updating statistics following an index rebuild. An index rebuild automatically performs a full statistics update, so performing another one is at best unnecessary, and at worst lowers statistics accuracy by replacing full statistics with a sampled set.

- A lower fill factor (80–90 percent) may be appropriate for indexes on tables with high amounts of update activity. While a lower fill factor reduces fragmentation and page splits, it also increases index size and page reads, so the performance improvement (or decrease) should be carefully measured in a volume-testing environment before production implementation.

- The SORT_IN_TEMPDB option may improve index rebuild performance if the tempdb database is located on dedicated disks. If you're using this option, be sure to capacity plan the disk space requirements for tempdb to prevent index rebuilds failing from lack of disk space. Again, the best way to plan this is by using a volume-test environment configured identically to the production environment.

- Leave the default automatic statistics settings in place. If you're attempting to avoid occasional query execution delay due to automatic statistics operations, consider the asynchronous statistics mode as an alternative to disabling automatic statistic settings.

- Following a SQL Server upgrade, a full statistics update on all indexes and columns is recommended to enable the enhanced query optimizer in SQL Server 2008 to take full advantage of the most accurate statistics.

- In cases where combinations of nonindexed columns are frequently supplied as search predicates, for example, ProductType and Color, creating multicolumn statistics on the column combination can improve performance by enabling SQL Server to better estimate the likely row count and therefore choose the most appropriate join type. Doing so avoids the need to supply join hints in an attempt at optimizing performance.

- In cases where calculations across multiple nonindexed columns are used as a predicate, for example, `where price + tax > 1000`, consider creating this as a calculated column. This will enable SQL Server to create statistics on the column for more accurate query plans.

- In cases where indexes exist on columns with monotonically increasing values, for example, IDENTITY columns, and the table receives a large volume of inserts, the most recently inserted rows will fall outside the statistics histogram. In cases where the lack of statistics on the new rows is causing inaccurate query plans, consider manually updating statistics on a more frequent basis than that performed by the automatic statistics process.

Additional information on the best practices covered in this chapter can be found online at http://www.sqlCrunch.com/index.

In the next chapter we'll cover a number of techniques for automating some of the index maintenance tasks we've covered in this chapter.

14

Monitoring and automation

This chapter is dedicated to the *production DBA*, whose role, among other things, includes monitoring SQL Server instances for abnormal activity, managing the response to failure conditions, and carrying out a number of proactive maintenance tasks. In large organizations, such DBAs are typically located within, or accessible to, a *command center*, whose role is to perform similar tasks for all supported infrastructure and applications on a 24/7 basis.

We'll begin this chapter with coverage of a range of monitoring tools including Activity Monitor, SQL Server Profiler, and Performance Monitor. With a vast range of monitoring tools available, choosing the right tool for the job is an important skill; in addition to covering how these tools are used, we'll touch on how they should not be used.

Our focus will then shift to the importance of automation and its role in reducing errors and achieving more within the limited hours of a day. We'll cover maintenance plans and SQL Server Agent jobs before looking at setting up alerts for error and performance conditions.

14.1 Activity Monitor

New in 2008

In SQL Server 2005, we accessed *Activity Monitor* in SQL Server Management Studio by expanding Management and choosing Activity Monitor. This allowed us to view running processes as well as locks by process or object.

While beneficial, there was a limit to the level of detail that could be obtained using this tool, with typical follow-up investigations involving queries against various DMVs and/or system tables. In response to this, the new Activity Monitor in SQL Server 2008, as shown in figure 14.1, has been completely overhauled to help DBAs quickly see performance hot spots and related information.

Apart from the obvious visual differences, the way to access Activity Monitor has also changed. Rather than opening it via the Management section of SQL Server Management Studio, you either right-click the instance name and choose Activity Monitor or click the Activity Monitor icon on the standard toolbar.

Arguably the greatest feature of the new Activity Monitor is the ability to spot abnormal activity at a glance using the four included graphs. You can change the default graph refresh rate of 10 seconds by right-clicking any of the four graphs and selecting the appropriate refresh interval. The menu also allows you to pause or resume the display.

Let's explore this new tool further by examining the four expandable panes that appear below the graphs: Processes, Resource Waits, Data File I/O, and Recent Expensive Queries.

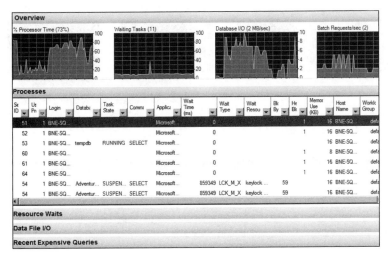

Figure 14.1 Visually similar to the Resource Monitor in Windows Vista and Server 2008, the new Activity Monitor included in SQL Server 2008 offers a rich view of system activity.

14.1.1 Processes

Expanding the Processes pane, as shown earlier in figure 14.1, provides information on currently running processes similar to the old Activity Monitor, including the ability to sort columns in ascending or descending order. Certain new columns are visible, such as Workload Group, a property of Resource Governor, which we'll cover in chapter 16.

Perhaps the most powerful new feature accessible through this pane is the ability to right-click a process and choose Trace Process in SQL Server Profiler. As the name suggests, this will open SQL Server Profiler with a filter on the selected session ID (SPID), allowing an in-depth, live analysis of the process activity. We'll cover SQL Server Profiler shortly.

The next pane in Activity Monitor is Resource Waits.

14.1.2 Resource Waits

As shown in figure 14.2, clicking the Resource Waits pane shows the latest information from several DMVs, including sys.dm_os_wait_stats, which we'll cover in detail in chapter 17. Note the Wait Category column. The categories in this column represent a system-level grouping of the various wait types a process can encounter.

During periods of widespread poor response, this view is ideal for spotting resource bottlenecks that may be contributing to a large number of waits. We'll cover this further in chapter 17 when we focus on performance tuning from a waits perspective.

The next pane in Activity Monitor is Data File I/O.

14.1.3 Data File I/O

Information from the sys.dm_io_virtual_file_stats dynamic management function is used to populate the results of the Data File I/O pane, as shown in figure 14.3. Providing a summary of I/O, broken down by database and file, this view includes MB/sec Read and Written and the average response time in ms for each file.

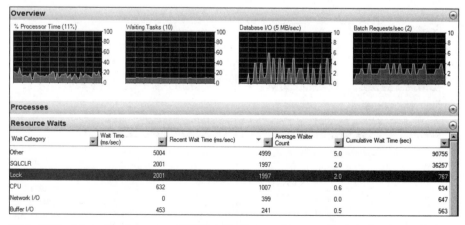

Figure 14.2   Information from several DMVs including sys.dm_os_wait_stats dmv is used in displaying the outstanding wait types, grouped by category.

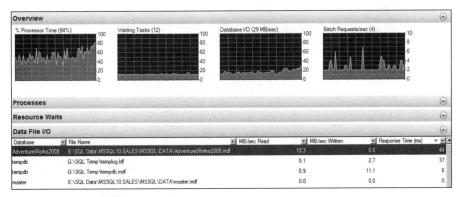

Figure 14.3   The Data File I/O pane displays various statistics for each database file.

In chapter 9 we covered the importance of database object separation, for example, placing data, logs, and tempdb on dedicated disks. Apart from better performance, one of the other benefits of doing so is that by using the Data File I/O pane of the new Activity Monitor, it's easy to spot high disk usage and response times across all of the database objects, enabling a more targeted disk I/O performance-tuning exercise.

The last pane in Activity Monitor is Recent Expensive Queries, which draws its information from the sys.dm_exec_query_stats DMV.

14.1.4   *Recent Expensive Queries*

In addition to viewing the text of recently completed expensive queries, we can sort the results in ascending or descending order by CPU usage, physical/logical reads/ sec, duration, plan count, and executions/min. A powerful feature of this particular pane is the ability to right-click any of the queries and view the graphical execution plan, as shown in figure 14.4.

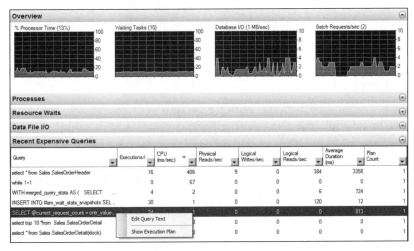

Figure 14.4   Right-clicking any of the queries shown in the Recent Expensive Queries pane allows the graphical execution plan of the query to be displayed.

All of the Activity Monitor views and graphs are based on information from one or more dynamic management views or functions, so in that sense, there was nothing stopping us from getting this information in SQL Server 2005. The nice thing is having all of the work done for us, in an easy-to-use interface.

> **SQL Server Management Studio startup option**
> One of the options I suspect many DBAs will use is automatically opening Activity Monitor on startup of SQL Server Management Studio. You can set this by selecting Open Object Explorer and Activity Monitor in the General page of the Tools > Options menu in SQL Server Management Studio.

Activity Monitor provides an excellent, high-level overview of system activity. For a more detailed statement-level view, you can use *SQL Server Profiler.*

14.2   *SQL Server Profiler*

Prior to SQL Server 2005 (and the introduction of DMVs), SQL Server Profiler was one of the few tools that could be used to gain visibility of SQL Server activity and was therefore used for a broad range of performance and debugging purposes. As you'll soon see, Profiler remains an extremely versatile tool; however, it's often used for the wrong reasons, creating significant performance problems as a result.

In chapter 17 we'll introduce a performance-tuning methodology called *waits and queues,* which uses a combination of DMVs and Performance Monitor counters to narrow the scope of a performance-tuning exercise by focusing on the largest system bottlenecks. Such an approach is far more effective than a Profiler-only approach, frequently used in years gone by and still used by some.

In this section, we'll focus on using Profiler for alternate purposes, namely workload replay and deadlocked/blocked process analysis. We'll also cover the important difference between a Profiler trace and a server trace. Before we get to that, let's begin with perhaps the most common use for Profiler: workload analysis.

14.2.1   *Workload analysis*

A common task in a performance-tuning exercise is analyzing the *cost* of the queries that make up an application's workload. For example, if CPU is a significant system bottleneck, you need to establish which queries consume the most CPU. Profiler enables such analysis through its ability to capture, or *trace,* the execution of queries along with their associated cost metrics, that is, disk reads and writes, CPU usage, and duration.

As we've just explained, using Profiler as the *only* performance-tuning tool ignores much more effective options; however, for the purposes of introducing Profiler, let's proceed on that basis with a simple example.

SQL Server Profiler can be accessed through the Performance Tools folder of the SQL Server program group. After opening Profiler and choosing File > New Trace,

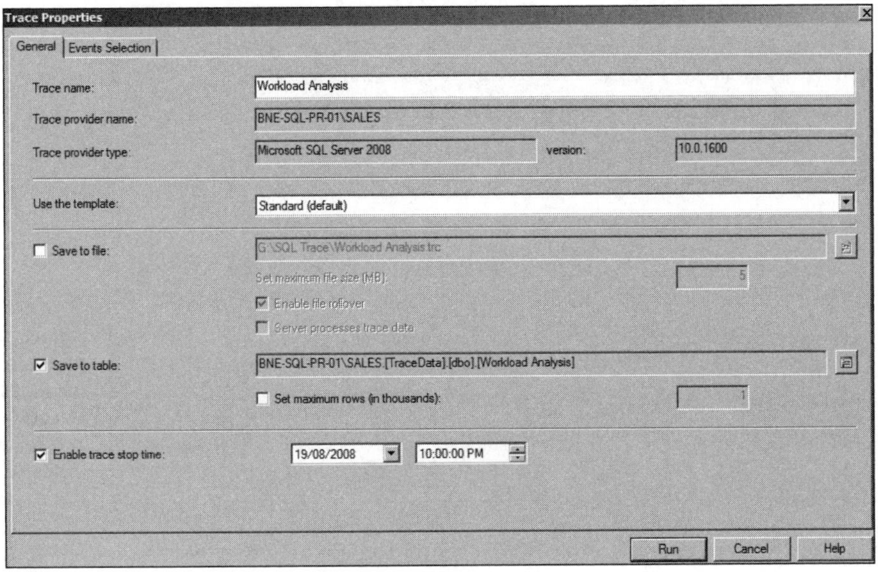

Figure 14.5   The General Tab of a Profiler Trace Properties window enables us to select the trace location along with a template and stop time.

you're prompted with the Connect to Server dialog box, which enables you to select a SQL instance to trace. After connecting to an instance, you're presented with the Trace Properties window, as shown in figure 14.5.

After giving the trace a name, you can choose to base the trace on a template, which is used to define the included columns and events on the Events Selection tab, which we'll cover shortly. By default, the output of the trace is displayed to screen only. For this example, we'll choose to save the results to a table for reasons that will become apparent shortly.

After entering an optional stop time (a trace can also be manually stopped), click the Events Selection tab, as shown in figure 14.6, to choose the included events and event columns.

For the purposes of this example, we'll limit the included events to the RPC:Completed and SQL:BatchCompleted events. These events represent the completion of T-SQL batches and stored procedures and include the associated cost metrics. The Column Filters button enables us to apply filters, such as limiting the trace to include events for a particular user or database, or queries exceeding a particular duration or cost. As mentioned earlier, when we launch SQL Profiler via the Activity Monitor's Processors pane, a filter is automatically applied for the selected SPID.

Finally, selecting the Show All Events and Show All Columns check boxes enables the inclusion of additional events and columns from the full list, rather than the limited set derived from the selected template on the General tab.

Once you're ready, click Run, and the trace begins and database activity matching the selected events and filters is displayed on screen. For this example, a small number

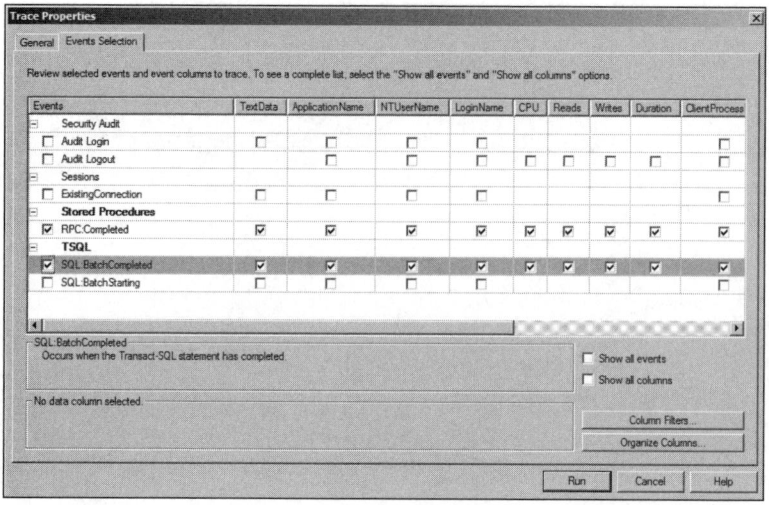

Figure 14.6   The Events Selection tab enables the selection of events and columns for inclusion in the trace results.

of queries were executed in Management Studio after the trace was started, the result of which is shown in figure 14.7.

A quick inspection of the Profiler trace screen reveals that the values of the Duration, CPU, and Reads columns for the last row are clearly greater than the rest of the captured values. Clicking on this record displays the query text in the lower section of the Profiler window.

For a simple example such as this, you can visually browse the small number of captured events. However, when a real trace is run and captured over a period of time representing peak production activity, the number of captured events typically runs into the thousands (or more). Not only does this prevent a visual analysis of activity,

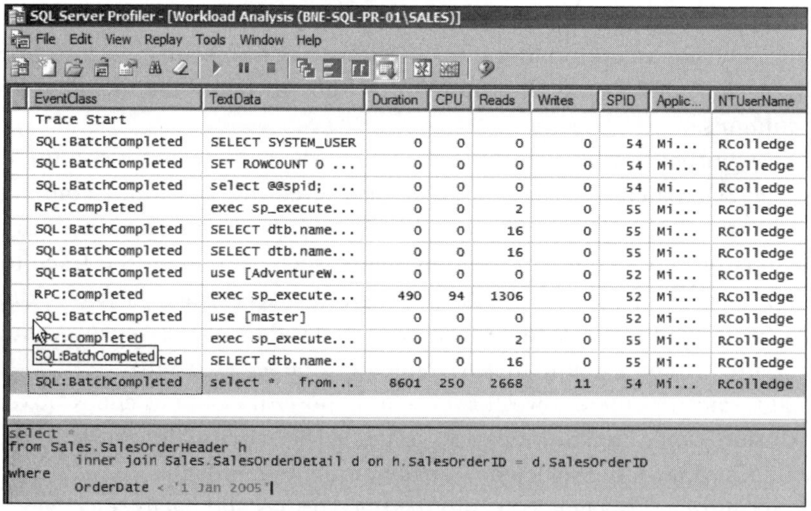

Figure 14.7   The output of a Profiler trace is shown on screen as well as saved to file and table if these options were chosen.

but it can also cause significant performance problems. In addressing this, you can use a *server-side trace*.

14.2.2 *Server-side trace*

Using SQL Server Profiler to trace database activity is frequently referred to as *client-side tracing*, that is, events are streamed from the server, over the network, to the Profiler application. Even if the Profiler application is being run on the SQL Server itself, this is still considered a client-side trace.

One of the worrisome aspects of client-side tracing with SQL Profiler is that under certain conditions, events can be dropped, therefore invalidating event sequencing and performance analysis. Further, depending on the server load, the overhead of streaming events can impact server performance, in some cases quite dramatically.

SQL Server Profiler is a GUI-based client interface to SQL Trace, the event-tracing service within the database engine. As an alternative to using SQL Profiler, we can create a server-side trace using a number of SQL Trace system stored procedures and in doing so avoid both the performance problems and dropped events commonly associated with client-side traces.

A good example of a server-side trace is the SQL Server default trace, a lightweight, always-on trace recording selected events, primarily configuration changes. As shown in figure 14.8, the Configuration Changes History standard report, accessed by right-clicking a server instance and choosing Reports, uses this trace to display the date and time of recent configuration changes. The log files created by this trace (named log_1.trc, log_2.trc, and so forth) are stored in the default MSSQL\LOG directory and can be opened in SQL Profiler for inspection if required.

As we said earlier, one of the nice things about SQL Profiler is the ease with which a trace can be created and executed, particularly when compared to the alternative of creating T-SQL scripts using the SQL Trace procedures. Fortunately, one of the options available within SQL Profiler is the ability to script a trace definition, which can then be used in creating a server-side trace. Creating a trace in this manner, we get the best of both worlds: using the Profiler GUI to create our traces, yet running the trace as a server-side trace, thereby avoiding the performance overhead and dropped events associated with client-side traces.

Configuration Changes History

on BNE-SQL-PR-01\SALES at 11/10/2008 12:30:30 AM

Microsoft® SQL Server 2008

This report provides a history of all sp_configure and Trace Flag changes recorded by the Default Trace.

Configuration Changes History (Since 6/10/2008 9:46:54 PM).

Shows changes in server configuration and flags.

Configuration Option	Old Value	New Value	Time	User
blocked process threshold (s)	0	20	10/10/2008 11:23:51 PM	BNE-SQL-PR-01\RColledge
show advanced options	1	1	10/10/2008 11:23:51 PM	BNE-SQL-PR-01\RColledge
Trace Flag (3604)	--	on	6/10/2008 9:47:14 PM	BNE-SQL-PR-01\RColledge
Trace Flag (3604)	--	on	6/10/2008 9:46:54 PM	BNE-SQL-PR-01\RColledge

Figure 14.8 One of the many available standard reports

```
/****************************************************/
/* Created by: SQL Server 2008 Profiler             */
/* Date: 10/10/2008   09:36:00 PM        */
/****************************************************/


-- Create a Queue
declare @rc int
declare @TraceID int
declare @maxfilesize bigint
declare @DateTime datetime

set @DateTime = '2008-10-10 22:33:53.000'
set @maxfilesize = 5

-- Please replace the text InsertFileNameHere, with an appropriate
-- filename prefixed by a path, e.g., c:\MyFolder\MyTrace. The .trc extension
-- will be appended to the filename automatically. If you are writing from
-- remote server to local drive, please use UNC path and make sure server has
-- write access to your network share

exec @rc = sp_trace_create @TraceID output, 0, N'InsertFileNameHere', @maxfilesize, @Datetime
if (@rc != 0) goto error

-- Client side File and Table cannot be scripted

-- Set the events
declare @on bit
set @on = 1
exec sp_trace_setevent @TraceID, 10, 15, @on
exec sp_trace_setevent @TraceID, 10, 16, @on
exec sp_trace_setevent @TraceID, 10, 1, @on
```

Figure 14.9   A Profiler trace can be scripted to file for execution as a server-side trace. Before doing so, we must specify the trace file location, as per the highlighted text.

A Profiler trace can be exported to a file using the File > Export menu item after the trace has been defined with the required events, columns, and filters. The resultant T-SQL code, an example of which is shown in figure 14.9, can then be executed against the required instance, which creates the server-side trace. Once the trace is created, we can use the sp_trace_setstatus and fn_trace_getinfo commands, as documented in Books Online, to control and inspect the trace status.

As per figure 14.9, we specify the trace file location by editing the sp_trace_create parameters in the script produced by SQL Server Profiler.

One of the important aspects of a server-side trace is that events *cannot* be dropped; that is, system throughput may slow if writing the trace file becomes a bottleneck. While the overhead in writing a server-side trace file is significantly lower than the Profiler equivalent, it's an important consideration nonetheless. Therefore the trace file should be treated in a similar manner to a transaction log file, that is, located on a dedicated, high-speed disk that's local to the server instance—not a network file share.

With the importance of client-side versus server-side traces in mind, let's continue and look at a number of alternate uses for SQL Server Profiler, starting with the ability to replay a trace.

14.2.3 *Trace replay*

Trace replay refers to the process whereby a captured trace file is replayed against a database to regenerate the commands as they occurred when the trace was captured. Such a process is typically used for both debugging and load generation.

Capturing a trace that will be used for replay purposes requires particular events and columns to be included. The easiest way to do this is by using SQL Profiler's TSQL_Replay template when entering the details in the Trace Properties window, as shown earlier in figure 14.5. Selecting this template will ensure all of the necessary events and columns are included for replay.

When the trace has captured the required events, you can invoke replay by opening the trace file or table in SQL Profiler and selecting Start from the Replay menu. The resultant screen, as shown in figure 14.10, enables various options during replay.

Understanding the replay options is crucial in understanding some of the limitations of using it:

- *Replay Server* allows the selection of the server instance where the trace file will be replayed. Notice there is no mention of which database to replay the trace against. The database with the same name (and database ID) should exist on the replay instance, which is *usually* an instance separate from where the trace was captured. If so, the replay instance should also include the same logins, passwords, users, and default databases applicable to the captured trace.

- *Save to File/Table* enables the results of the replay to be captured to a file or table. The captured results include the full output of the replayed commands. For example, a select command that returns 10 rows will result in 10 rows in the trace replay output file/table. The resultant output can be potentially huge and should therefore be chosen with caution; however, used correctly, this option is invaluable for debugging purposes.

- *Number of Replay Threads* enables the degree of concurrency to be set for replay purposes. A high number of threads will consume more resources but will result in a faster replay.

- *Replay Events in the Order They Were Traced* will do exactly that and is the option to use when reconstructing an event for debugging purposes.

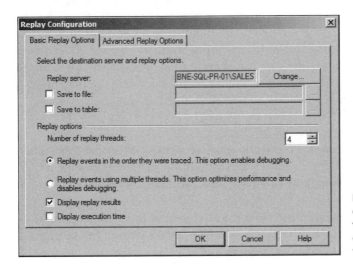

Figure 14.10 Trace replay options include saving results to file and/or table and controlling replay concurrency with multiple threads.

- *Replay Events Using Multiple Threads* is the high-performance replay mode that disables debugging. Events are replayed using multiple threads, with each thread ordering events *for a* given SPID; for example, SPID 55 will have its events replayed in the correct order, but its events may be replayed before SPID 68, even though SPID 68's events occurred first.

- *Display Replay Results* shows the results of the replay on screen. The same warnings apply here as for the Save to File/Table options we covered earlier.

For the purposes of debugging complex application problems, SQL Profiler's trace replay is undoubtedly a powerful tool, particularly when debugging in a live production environment is not an option. In such cases, a production database backup is typically restored in a testing environment followed by the replay of a trace captured while the problem was reproduced in production. Once captured, the trace can be replayed in a testing environment multiple times, optionally preceded by a database restore before each replay. Debug options such as Run to Cursor and Toggle Breakpoint enable classic debugging by replaying the trace to a certain point, inspecting the output, and then iteratively moving through the remaining events as required.

Despite its strengths, there are a number of limitations with trace replay that you need to understand. SQL Server Books Online documents all of them, but the major limitation is its lack of support for traces containing certain data types and activity; for example, a trace containing transactional replication, GUID operations, or Bulk Copy Process (BCP) actions on n/text or image columns cannot be replayed. Further, the logins and users referenced in the trace must exist on the target instance with the same permissions, passwords, default database, and database ID.

Another common use for replaying trace files is simulating load for change and/or configuration-testing purposes. Capturing a trace during a peak load period allows performance to be observed in a test environment under different configuration settings; however, despite the ability to increase the number of threads during playback, a trace replay cannot *exactly* reproduce the timing and sequencing of events as they occurred during the capture of the trace. Using the Replay Events in the Order They Were Traced option will guarantee event sequencing but will not simulate concurrent activity. Conversely, using Replay Events Using Multiple Threads will generate simultaneous event replay but at the expense of event sequencing across all SPIDs.

One of the things preventing exact event reproduction is the inability to use multiple replay machines, a limitation addressed in the RML utilities.

14.2.4 *RML utilities*

For many years, Microsoft Product Support Services (PSS) used a collection of private tools for assisting in the diagnosis and resolution of customer support issues. Now known as the replay markup language (RML) utilities, PSS released them to the general public in 2004.

Available as a free download from the Microsoft website, the RML utilities, comprising *ReadTrace, Reporter,* and *OStress,* are used both for diagnosing performance problems and constructing stress-test scenarios.

READTRACE AND REPORTER

When we defined our Profiler trace earlier in figure 14.5, we chose to save the results to a database table. Doing so allows the results of the trace to be examined in a variety of ways once the trace is closed. For example, we could run the following query against the specified table to determine the top 10 expensive queries from a disk-usage perspective:

```
-- Top 10 most expensive queries from a disk usage perspective
SELECT TOP 10 TextData, CPU, (Reads + Writes) as DiskTotal, Duration
FROM dbo.[Workload Analysis]
ORDER BY DiskTotal DESC
```

Queries such as the above are among the many possible ways in which the results can be analyzed. Further, as we saw in chapter 13, we can use the saved results as input for the Database Engine Tuning Advisor, which will analyze the trace contents and make various recommendations.

One of the limitations of using Profiler for workload analysis such as this is that query executions that are the same with the exception of the literal values are difficult to analyze together as a group. Take these two queries, for example:

```
SELECT * FROM [authors] WHERE [lastName] = 'Smith'

SELECT * FROM "authors" WHERE "lastName" = 'Brown'
```

These are really different versions of the same query, so grouping them together for the purpose of obtaining the *aggregate* cost of the query is beneficial; however, without a significant amount of string-manipulation logic, this would be difficult to achieve. ReadTrace performs such grouping analysis automatically.

Executed at the command line with a number of input parameters including a trace file name, ReadTrace

- Creates a new database, by default named *PerfAnalysis*, in a specified SQL Server instance
- Analyzes and aggregates information contained within the trace file and stores the results in the PerfAnalysis database
- Produces .RML files, which can be used as input for the OStress utility, which we'll discuss shortly
- Launches the Reporter utility, which graphically summarizes the results captured in the PerfAnalysis database

The first step in using ReadTrace is capturing a trace file. In order for ReadTrace to work and provide the most beneficial analysis, we need to include a number of events and columns in the trace. The help file that's supplied with the RML utilities documents all the required events and columns.

Once the trace file has been captured, the ReadTrace utility can be executed against it, an example of which follows:

```
Readtrace -IG:\Trace\SalesTrace_1.trc -o"c:\temp\rml" -SBNE-SQL-PR-01\SALES
```

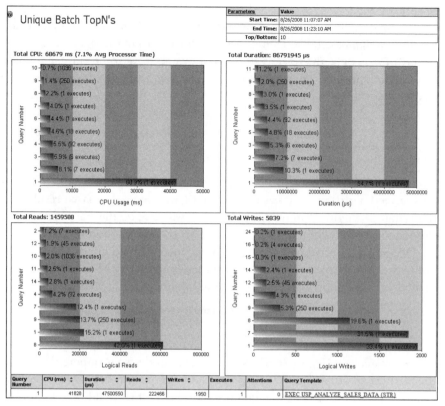

Figure 14.11   Figure One of the many reports available in the RML Reporter utility. This one breaks down resource usage by query.

Once processing is complete, the Reporter utility automatically opens and displays the results of the analysis. The example report shown in figure 14.11 demonstrates one of the clear advantages of using the ReadTrace/Reporter utilities over manual analysis of SQL Profiler results stored in a table. Note the {STR} value in the Query Template column at the very bottom of the report for Query 1. The ReadTrace utility analyzes and aggregates different executions of the same query/stored procedure as a group by stripping out literal values such as stored procedure parameter values. In the example shown, {STR} represents RML's understanding of this as a parameter value. Thus, the total cost of all executions of this stored procedure will be automatically calculated.

In addition to viewing the results of ReadTrace analysis via the Reporter utility, you can directly query the PerfAnalysis database for more advanced analysis.

Finally, one of the major benefits of ReadTrace is the .RML files it creates once processing is complete. The OStress utility can use these files for both replay and stress-testing purposes.

OStress

When covering the SQL Profiler trace replay option earlier in the chapter, we discussed one of its limitations: the inability to use multiple machines for replay purposes, thereby limiting the scale of the load that can be achieved. In contrast, OStress has no such limitation.

Like ReadTrace, OStress is a command-line utility. It's used to execute a command or series of commands against a supplied instance and database. Its input can be a single inline query, a query file, or an .RML file produced by the ReadTrace utility. Consider the following example:

```
ostress –o"c:\temp\o" –SBNE-SQL-PR-01\SALES –dOrders –iStress.sql –n10 –r25
```

The end result of running the above command will be to spawn 10 threads (-n parameter), each of which will execute the contents of the Stress.sql file against the Orders database 25 times (-r parameter), for a total of 250 executions. Further, this could potentially run on multiple machines simultaneously, each of which is stressing the same database. You can imagine the scale of stress that could be achieved!

The -i parameter also accepts RML files as input, and the -Q parameter is used for a single inline query. If an RML file is used, -m replay can be used to instruct OStress to use replay mode instead of stress mode. In replay mode, events are replayed in the sequence in which they were captured. In contrast, stress mode replays events as fast as possible for maximum stress.

> ## LoadRunner and Test Load Agent
>
> When used for stress-testing purposes, Profiler's trace replay and the RML utilities share a common attribute: they generate load at a database level only. In order to obtain confidence in the ability of all levels of an application's infrastructure to withstand the expected production load, such utilities are insufficient. In addressing this deficiency, developers frequently use application load-generation tools such as LoadRunner and Visual Studio Team System: Test Load Agent.

In addition to load generation and debugging, SQL Server Profiler can also be used in diagnosing deadlocks.

14.2.5 Deadlock diagnosis

Troubleshooting deadlocks isn't the nicest (or easiest) task for a DBA; however, SQL Profiler makes it much simpler. In demonstrating this, consider listing 14.1, which contains a simple T-SQL batch file. When a second instance of this batch file is executed within 10 seconds of the first (from a separate connection/query window), a deadlock will occur, with the second query chosen as the deadlock victim and killed by SQL Server.

> ### Listing 14.1 T-SQL code to generate a deadlock

```
-- T-SQL to simulate a deadlock. Run this from 2 separate query windows
-- The 2nd will deadlock if executed within 10 seconds of the 1st

SET TRANSACTION ISOLATION LEVEL SERIALIZABLE -- hold share lock till end
```

```
BEGIN TRANSACTION
    SELECT * FROM HumanResources.Department

    WAITFOR DELAY '00:00:10.000' -- delay for 2nd transaction to start

    UPDATE HumanResources.Department
    SET Name = 'Production'
    WHERE DepartmentID=7

COMMIT TRANSACTION
```

What's happening here is that the shared lock on the HumanResources.Department table is being held until the end of the transaction, courtesy of the Serializable isolation level chosen at the start of the batch. When the update command runs later in the transaction, the locks need to be upgraded to an exclusive lock. However, in the meantime, another instance of this batch has run, which also has a shared lock on the HumanResources.Department table and also needs to upgrade its locks. Both transactions will wait on each other forever. SQL Server detects this situation as a deadlock and chooses to kill one of the transactions to enable the other to complete.

When creating a Profiler trace, one of the events we can capture is the deadlock graph, found under the Locks category when the Show All Events check box is checked. We saw this check box earlier in figure 14.6. When we select the deadlock event, an additional tab becomes available in the Trace Properties window, which enables the deadlock graph(s) to be saved to a file.

With this event selected and the trace running, executing the above code from two separate connections will generate a deadlock graph event and a deadlock results file. Opening the file in SQL Server Management Studio (by double-clicking it) will reveal the graph shown in figure 14.12.

You'll notice in the above image the blue X through the left-hand query. This was the chosen deadlock victim. Hovering the mouse over the query will reveal the query text. The item in the middle of the graph represents the resource that the two queries deadlocked over.

The ability to easily capture deadlock information using Profiler makes the process of identifying the application or database code causing the deadlocks significantly easier.

Figure 14.12 The deadlock graph event can be included in a trace to visually represent the deadlock, including details such as the deadlock victim and resource.

> ### Deadlock trace flags
>
> An alternative to using Profiler to capture deadlock information is using trace flags. Both 1204 and 1222 will return the resources, commands, and locks involved in a deadlock. 1222 will return the information in an XML format. In both cases, the trace flags write the information to the SQL Server error log, enabling alerts to be set up on the events, a process we'll cover later in the chapter. As with all trace flags, these flags can be enabled using either `DBCC TRACEON` or the `-T` command-line startup option. Full details of these methods are contained in SQL Server Books Online.

Not only can Profiler detect deadlocks, it can also be used to detect blocked processes.

14.2.6 Blocked process report

When a process attempts to lock a resource that's currently locked by another process, it waits for the lock to be released, and it's known for the duration of the wait as a *blocked process*. Unlike deadlocks, blocked processes are perfectly normal; however, depending on the frequency and duration of the waits, blocked processes can significantly contribute to poor application performance. Consider the code in listing 14.2.

Listing 14.2   T-SQL code to generate a block

```
-- T-SQL to simulate lengthly locking period
BEGIN TRANSACTION
    SELECT * FROM HumanResources.Department(xlock)
    WAITFOR DELAY '00:00:50.000' -- hold lock for 50 seconds
COMMIT TRANSACTION
```

What we're doing here is simulating a long-running transaction that holds locks for the duration of the transaction, in this case an exclusive lock on the department table for 50 seconds. Similar to our deadlock example earlier, we'll run this batch from two separate connections. With the first execution holding an exclusive lock on the department table, the second execution will be blocked, waiting for the first to complete.

In helping to diagnose blocked processes such as the one that we're simulating here, we can set the Blocked Process Threshold server configuration setting. As shown listing 14.3, this setting takes a parameter representing the number of seconds a process can be blocked before an alert is raised. Let's configure this value to 20 seconds.

Listing 14.3   Setting the Blocked Process Threshold

```
-- Set the Blocked Process Threshold to 20 seconds
EXEC sp_configure 'show advanced options', 1
GO
RECONFIGURE
GO

EXEC sp_configure 'blocked process threshold', 20
GO
RECONFIGURE
GO
```

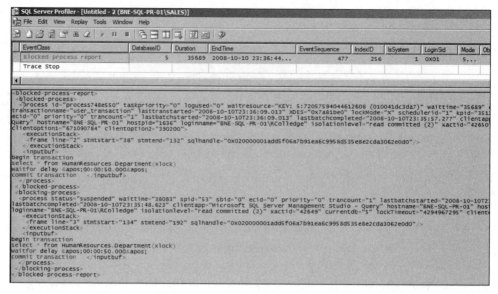

Figure 14.13   You can use the Blocked Process Report event in combination with the Blocked Process Threshold setting to capture blocking events exceeding a certain duration.

With this setting in place, we can create a SQL Server Profiler trace that profiles the Blocked Process Report event (found in the Errors and Warnings category). After running the T-SQL batch from two separate connections, our Profiler trace will capture the Blocked Process Report event, as shown in figure 14.13. The XML contained within the report provides details on both the blocking and blocked processes, including the T-SQL, client application, and login name.

A common characteristic of poorly designed database applications is frequent and lengthy process blocking, largely due to inappropriate locking levels and transaction length. In combination with the Blocked Process Threshold setting, SQL Server Profiler's Blocked Process Report event offers an effective and easily implemented method of detecting and analyzing such blocking events.

In closing our coverage of SQL Server Profiler, let's look at how we can enhance the collected events with Performance Monitor data.

14.2.7 *Correlating traces with performance logs*

Correlating different perspectives of the same event almost always leads to a deeper understanding of any situation. In SQL Server monitoring, one of the opportunities we have for doing that is importing Performance Monitor data into a Profiler trace, as shown in figure 14.14.

After opening a saved Profiler trace file (or table), you can choose the File > Import Performance Data menu option to select a Performance Monitor log file to import. You can then select the appropriate counters from the log for inclusion.

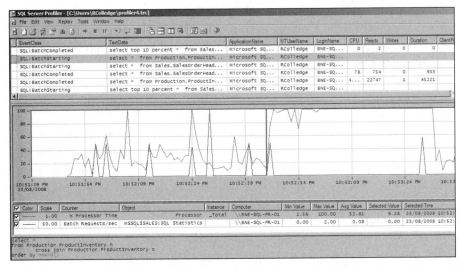

Figure 14.14   Profiler allows Performance Monitor logs to be imported, and this permits correlation of Profiler events with the corresponding Performance Monitor counters of interest.

Once the log file is imported, clicking a particular traced command in the top half of the window will move the red bar to the appropriate spot in the Performance Monitor log (and vice versa). In the example shown in figure 14.14, you can see a spike in CPU usage just over halfway through the displayed time frame. Clicking on the start of the spike will select the appropriate command in the trace results, with the full command shown at the bottom of the screen. In this example, you can see the cause of the CPU spike: a cross join between two tables with a random ordering clause.

In addition to enhancing our Profiler traces, Performance Monitor data is invaluable in gaining a deeper understanding of SQL Server activity, as well as enabling baseline analysis, both of which we'll cover next.

14.3   Performance Monitor

Performance Monitor enables the graphical display and logging of counters representing aspects of system performance, such as CPU Usage % and Memory Paging. SQL Server exposes its own counters, such as Buffer Cache Hit Ratio, to Performance Monitor through the sys.dm_os_performance_counters DMV.

In chapter 17, we'll cover the use of Performance Monitor as part of a targeted performance-tuning methodology. In this chapter, our focus will be twofold: a broad overview of viewing and capturing counters and using the collected values for baseline analysis. Let's begin with a look at the process of viewing and capturing counters.

14.3.1   Viewing counters in real time

In Windows Vista and Server 2008, Performance Monitor is one component of the Reliability and Performance Monitor tool. As with versions in older operating systems, counters can be viewed in real time as well as being captured for later analysis.

After you open Reliability and Performance Monitor, the % Processor Time counter from the Processor object is automatically tracked in real time with a 1-second refresh interval. Additional counters can be added to the graph by clicking the green + icon on the toolbar.

Counters are added by first navigating thorough *objects*, which categorize the counters into *groups*. For example, in figure 14.15, the Batch Request/Sec counter is found within the SQL Statistics object.

Viewing counters in real time is frequently used for detecting abnormal values at a glance for a small number of key performance counters on critical SQL Server instances. Depending on the refresh interval and window width, only approximately 30–90 seconds of the most recent activity will be displayed at any given moment. For longer-term analysis, we can create *data collector sets*.

Data collector sets, like the equivalent counter logs in previous versions of Performance Monitor, are created to capture performance counters to a log file. The log files can then be opened for retrospective performance troubleshooting, for example, importing into Profiler as we saw earlier, and baseline analysis.

14.3.2 *Baseline analysis*

A *baseline* is a record of the average values of a number of key system metrics such as % CPU Usage over a period of time in which performance is reported as being normal. Initial baselines are often recorded shortly after a system enters production and serve as a reference point for future comparison.

As we'll discuss shortly, one of the recommended DBA tasks is the ongoing capture and analysis of performance counters in order to compare current performance characteristics to a known baseline. In doing so, performance trends can be detected and used for capacity-planning purposes.

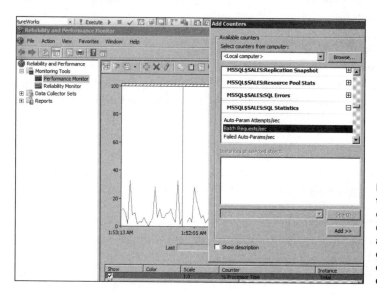

Figure 14.15   In addition to the % Processor Time counter, which is displayed automatically, additional performance counters can be added by clicking the green + icon on the toolbar.

The baseline analysis technique is particularly powerful when combined with a stress-testing exercise to establish the system *breaking point.* For example, the RML utilities allow us to use the OStress tool to load the system with transactions until response time degrades to an unacceptable level. Once that level is established, a baseline analysis exercise becomes much more meaningful. Imagine being able to confidently say to management, "We know the system will break when we reach 500 batches per second, and based on my observations of recent usage, we'll reach that point in 12 weeks." Figure 14.16 illustrates the combination of baseline analysis and a benchmarking exercise that establishes a system breaking point.

When capturing performance counters for both the initial baseline and ongoing analysis, there are a number of important considerations, particularly around the sampling frequency, logging timeframes, and included metrics:

- Counter values should be captured during times that include peak usage periods. Limiting the capture of counters to periods of low usage (sometimes done to reduce server load) will miss the most important points of the day.
- Depending on how the data collector set is created, the default sample interval ranges from 1 second to 15 seconds. While a 1-second sample interval is likely to add slightly more server load, the resultant data provides a much better performance resolution. In contrast, a 15-second interval is likely to miss (or obscure) some important periods of activity.
- Finally, in considering which counters to include, there are two schools of thought. One advocates including lots of counters in order to have a detailed picture if and when one is required. The other argues for only a few key metrics in order to reduce the monitoring-induced load on the server. In almost all cases, the best approach is in between these two, with site-specific conditions usually having an important bearing.

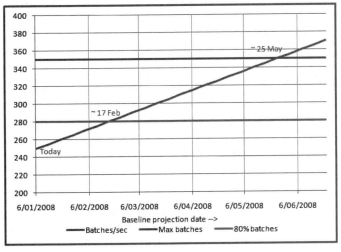

Figure 14.16 In combination with a benchmark that establishes a system's breaking point, baseline analysis enables early warning of likely performance-degradation points.

Appendix C contains a list of commonly captured Performance Monitor counters, and in chapter 17, we'll focus on a performance-tuning methodology that measures various counters in combination with a number of wait types.

The focus of the chapter thus far has been on monitoring tools and reports. As any experienced DBA knows, spending all day manually monitoring a large number of server instances is both mind numbing and only moderately successful, if at all possible. Together with good configuration settings and proactive management, an *exception-based* management approach is required for large environments, and fortunately there are a number of automation and alert techniques that we can employ to do most of the monitoring for us, freeing up time for more important and/or rewarding tasks.

14.4   *Task automation and alerts*

A common attribute among all successful database-monitoring regimes is a strong automation and alerting component. A DBA may be able to manually manage and monitor a handful of instances with moderate success, but as the number of instances increases, actions become more and more reactive, eventually culminating in complete chaos.

Automation delivers a crucial advantage to a DBA. It enables more things to be achieved with fewer mistakes in a given amount of time, therefore enabling a DBA to pick and choose the things to spend time on, be it research, design, or reading the newspaper. Either way, having the luxury to choose is a valuable asset.

Throughout this book, we've spoken a lot about the importance of a number of administration tasks such as backups, integrity checks, and index/statistics maintenance. What we've yet to address is a mechanism for the automation of such tasks. Let's do that right now, beginning with SQL Server maintenance plans.

14.4.1   *Maintenance plans*

A SQL Server maintenance plan allows the creation and scheduling of maintenance tasks through either a wizard-driven interface or using the Maintenance Plan *design surface*.

Right-clicking Maintenance Plans under Management in SQL Server Management Studio allows you to select the Maintenance Plan Wizard option. The purpose of this wizard is to create and schedule tasks covering the major administration items such as backups, DBCC checks, and index maintenance. The steps in this wizard enable the selection and scheduling of common maintenance tasks, as shown in figure 14.17.

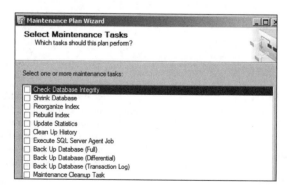

Figure 14.17   The Maintenance Plan Wizard automates the creation and scheduling of important maintenance tasks.

Despite the ease of use of the Maintenance Plan Wizard, it lacks a certain level of flexibility, particularly in executing custom T-SQL tasks and flow control, both of which are catered to in the Maintenance Plan design surface.

As with the Maintenance Plan Wizard, the design surface is accessed by right-clicking Maintenance Plans under the Management node in SQL Server Management Studio. Selecting New Maintenance Plan prompts you for a maintenance plan name before opening the design surface, as shown in figure 14.18.

Let's walk through the major components of a maintenance plan design, beginning with connections.

CONNECTIONS

As shown in figure 14.18, the toolbar on top of the design surface includes a Manage Connections button. By default, each plan is created with a local server connection, which each task uses as the default connection. Additional connections can be created to remote server instances as required, with each connection defined with either Windows integrated security or a SQL Server username and password.

SUBPLANS AND SCHEDULES

Each maintenance plan is defined with one or more *subplans*, with each subplan having its own tasks and schedule. For example, we can have a weekday schedule containing differential backups and index reorganization with a weekly subplan containing full backups and index rebuilds.

In our example in figure 14.18, we have two subplans, one called Weekday and the other Weekend. The design surface shown is for the Weekend subplan, which is set to

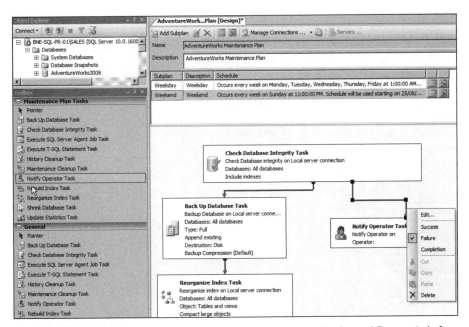

Figure 14.18 The Maintenance Plan design surface allows the selection and flow control of common database maintenance tasks.

run at 11:00 p.m. every Sunday. The Weekday subplan operates Monday through Friday at 1:00 a.m. and has its own design surface and task definition. You can create additional subplans as required by clicking the Add Subplan button on the toolbar.

TASKS AND PRECEDENCE

For each subplan, you can click and drag tasks onto the design surface using the Maintenance Plan Tasks toolbox. Tasks available for selection include Back Up Database, Rebuild Index, Reorganize Index, and Check Database Integrity.

Once a task has been added, you can access and customize its properties by double-clicking it. For example, the properties of the Back Up Database Task, as shown in figure 14.19, permit the selection of which databases to back up, the backup location, compression settings, and so forth. One of the nice things about the task properties window is being able to click the View T-SQL button to view how the selected options will be implemented by SQL Server when the OK button is clicked. An alternative to clicking OK is to save (and optionally customize) the displayed T-SQL script for later execution.

When multiple tasks are added, precedence constraints can be added between the tasks to control the execution flow. For example, in the design surface shown earlier in figure 14.18, we set the Failure action of the Check Database Integrity Task (DBCC CHECKDB) to execute the Notify Operator Task, with a successful Integrity check flowing down the left-hand side to execute the Back Up Database and Reorganize Index Tasks. You can add and modify precedence constraints by clicking a task and dragging the green arrow to the appropriate destination task. Once it's connected, you can change the constraint to Error, Completion, or Success by right-clicking the green arrow and selecting the appropriate action.

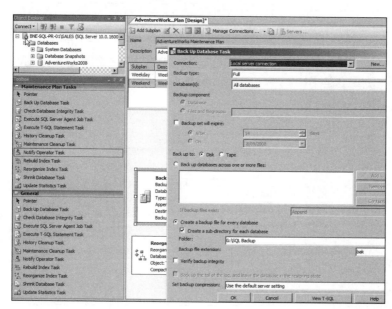

Figure 14.19   Each task added to the design surface can be customized as required. In this example, the Back Up Database Task is customized to back up all databases.

In addition to the classic maintenance tasks such as backups, integrity checks, and index-related maintenance, plans can be highly customized through the use of tasks such as Execute SQL Server Agent Job and Execute T-SQL Statement. Further, the Maintenance Cleanup and History Cleanup Tasks can be added to control the deletion of old backup files, SQL Server Agent history, and Maintenance Plan reports. These tasks allow a retention period to be specified, which is particularly useful in automatically deleting old disk-based backup files.

Despite the power and flexibility of maintenance plans, some limitations prevent or restrict their use in certain environments. For example, despite the existence of both the Rebuild Index and Reorganize Index Tasks, there's no option to rebuild only if fragmentation exceeds a certain level. As explained in the previous chapter, conditional index maintenance of this sort is important both from a maintenance duration perspective and for controlling the size of the transaction log, particularly when using synchronous database mirroring.

For maximum control over job scheduling and automation, we can use SQL Server Agent jobs.

14.4.2 *SQL Server Agent*

SQL Server Agent is a component of SQL Server responsible for the scheduled execution of tasks defined within jobs. Creating a maintenance plan will automatically create SQL Server Agent jobs to execute the tasks contained within the subplans. In our earlier example shown in figure 14.18, two SQL Server Agent jobs will be created to support the maintenance plan:[1] AdventureWorks Maintenance Plan.Weekday and AdventureWorks Maintenance Plan.Weekend.

SQL Server Agent jobs can be manually created in SQL Server Management Studio by right-clicking Jobs under SQL Server Agent and choosing New Job. The resultant window allows the specification of a job name and schedule, along with a series of steps, each of which can be defined with success and failure conditions to control the flow of job execution. Each SQL Server Agent job step is created as a particular *type*; the available types include T-SQL, Operating System, and Integration Services Package.

In chapter 8, we created a SQL Server Agent job with a PowerShell step to automate the evaluation of a policy against a SQL Server 2005 instance. In terms of more traditional database maintenance, common uses for SQL Server Agent jobs include conditional index maintenance, as discussed earlier, and running DBCC checks with options such as ALL_ERRORMSGS, an option not available for selection when using the Check Database Integrity Task in Maintenance Plan Tasks.

In addition to its ability to automate jobs such as backups and index maintenance, SQL Server Agent can be used to generate alerts, an essential component of a successful monitoring regime.

---

[1] In addition to scheduled execution via SQL Agent, a maintenance plan can be executed manually by right-clicking it and selecting Execute.

14.4.3 *Event alerts*

Let's consider some of the undesirable things that may happen to a SQL Server instance at any point throughout the day:

- A SQL Server Agent job fails.
- A performance counter, for example, Batches/sec, approaches a critical level where performance is known to degrade.
- A critical error is raised and written to the SQL Server error log.
- Disk drives fill to capacity.
- Critical error messages appear in the Windows event log.

As you can imagine, the above list is only a very small selection of all of the possible things that could go wrong, at any time of the day. The problem is magnified when you consider each of these things could occur on any number of the SQL Server instances being managed; consider a site with hundreds of SQL Server instances, which is not uncommon. The point to be made here is that in the absence of an alerting system that automatically detects a variety of events and alerts the appropriate people, the administration technique is either entirely reactive or very inefficient (most likely both).

Fortunately, there are a number of proven techniques for automated monitoring and alerting for SQL Server. Without considering third-party products, the frequently used ones are System Center Operations Manager and SQL Server Agent.

MICROSOFT SYSTEM CENTER OPERATIONS MANAGER

Previously known (and commonly referred to) as Microsoft Operations Manager, or MOM, this product is frequently deployed in organizations with large amounts of server infrastructure under management. When deployed with the optional SQL Server Management Pack, MOM enables the automation of a number of proactive (and reactive) maintenance tasks, including the following:

- Regular connectivity checks to any number of SQL Server instances
- Disk and database space monitoring
- Monitoring and alerts for SQL Agent job failures (or those taking too long to complete)
- Replication and database-mirroring health checks
- Blocked process checks
- SQL Service status checks

The strength of the MOM product offering is the ability to use it not only for SQL Server monitoring but for a wide variety of other Microsoft-based infrastructure features such as Exchange, IIS, BizTalk, and the Windows Server operating system. Thus, it's a widely used option for large Microsoft-centric enterprise environments.

The scope of this book does not allow for coverage of SQL Server monitoring with MOM, so let's turn our attention to how we can use SQL Server Agent to achieve our monitoring and alerting goals.

SQL SERVER AGENT ALERTS

The starting point for enabling alerts in SQL Server Agent is through the creation of an *operator*. Operators can be created in SQL Server Management Studio by right-clicking Operators under SQL Server Agent and selecting New Operator. Depending on the required notification method, each operator can be created with a net send, email or pager address.

Email alerts are enabled in SQL Server through the use of Database Mail, enabled in SQL Server Management Studio by right-clicking Database Mail under Management and selecting Configure Database Mail. The Database Mail Configuration Wizard then walks you through the required settings, one screen of which is shown in figure 14.20.

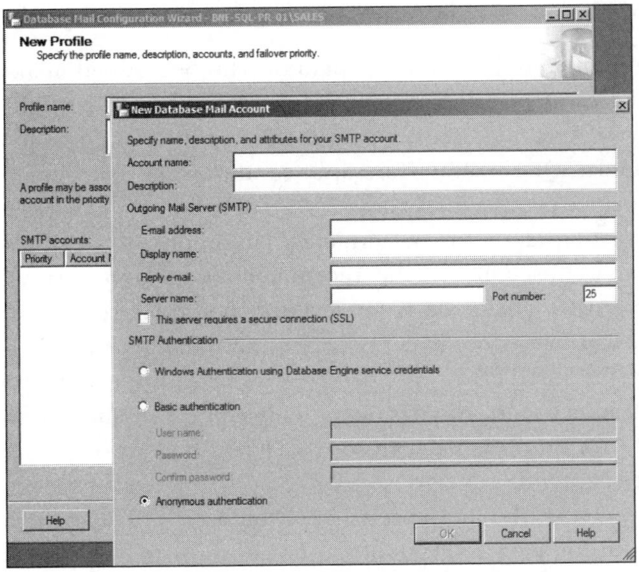

Figure 14.20 The Database Mail Configuration Wizard configures the SQL Server instance for sending email and therefore enables you to set up email alerts for job failures and various other events.

Creating operators with the appropriate notification method enables various benefits such as the ability to produce notifications on job failures. For example, as shown in figure 14.21, the Notifications page of the Archive Sales Data SQL Server Agent job is configured to notify Rod Colledge (via email) when the job fails.

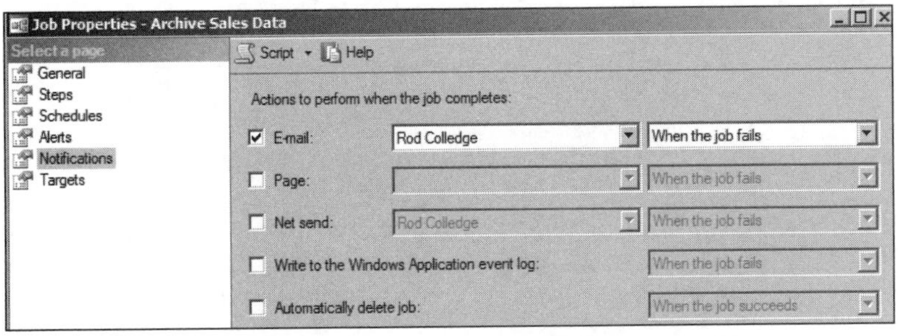

Figure 14.21 After creating operators, you can use them for various purposes such as notification of SQL Server Agent job failures.

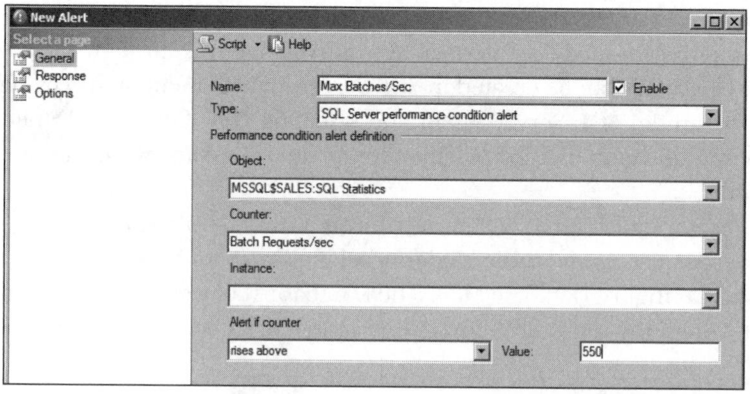

Figure 14.22 You can create alerts for SQL Server events such as deadlocks or for performance counter thresholds such as this one for Batch Requests/sec.

In addition to being notified of job failures, operators can be notified of alert conditions. An alert can be created in SQL Server Management Studio by right-clicking Alerts under SQL Server Agent and selecting New Alert. In the example shown in figure 14.22, we've created a SQL Server performance condition alert for when the Batch Requests/sec performance counter rises above 550.

In addition to creating alerts for performance conditions, you can also create alerts for SQL Server events. One of the recommended tasks for each installed instance of SQL Server is to create alerts for severity 16 and above errors. You can achieve this using the SQL Server event alert type, as shown in figure 14.23.

In addition to severity-based errors, you can create alerts for specific error events. For example, for a deadlock alert, you'd enter 1205 in the Error Number box. Alternatively, you can use error numbers 34050 through 34053 for alerts on policy failures, a topic we covered in chapter 8.

As shown in figure 14.24, the Response page of the Alert properties enables the selection of an operator for alert notification via the appropriate method in addition to providing the option to execute a SQL Server Agent job in response to the alert. In the above example, in addition to alerting an operator, we may decide to execute a SQL Server Agent job that stops nonessential services such as ad hoc reports.

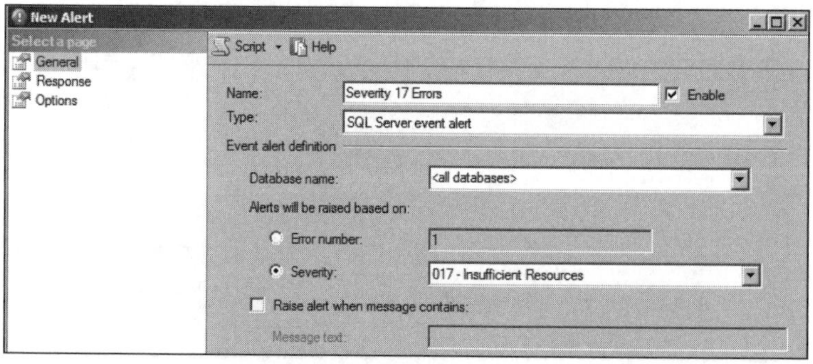

Figure 14.23   An alert definition for level 17 errors. Error levels 16 thru 25 should have individual alerts created.

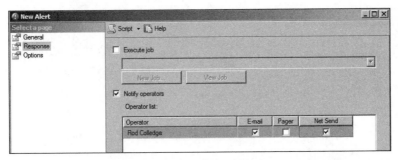

Figure 14.24   The Response page of an alert enables the selection of operators to notify along with a notification method. In addition to this, we can choose to execute a SQL Server Agent job.

Finally, the Options page, shown in figure 14.25, enables additional options such as the delay between alerts and whether to include the error text in the alert condition.

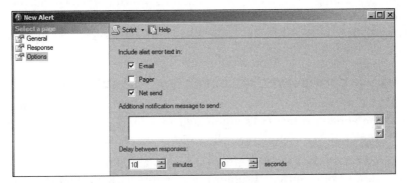

Figure 14.25   The Options page of an alert enables alert delays and error text inclusion.

Setting up alerts is a basic yet crucial administration technique. Despite this, it's often overlooked, as is the next task, monitoring error logs.

14.4.4   *Error logs*

Like Windows, SQL Server maintains logs that you can browse for details on both informational and error events. Accessed via Management Studio under the Management > SQL Server Logs path, the Log File Viewer can be opened by double-clicking one of the listed logs.

SQL Server will start a new log each time the instance is started, and by default it will maintain six[2] archived logs before overwriting the oldest. Not only does the log file viewer permit viewing of SQL Server information, it also allows the Windows event logs to be viewed through the same interface.

In addition to error events, the SQL Server logs contain valuable diagnostic information, particularly around the startup time. For example, in figure 14.26, you can see the NUMA node configuration is recorded to the log when the instance starts.

---

[2]   This value is configurable up to 99.

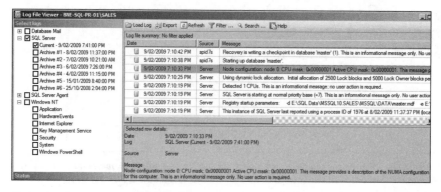

Figure 14.26   The SQL Server Log File Viewer enables visibility of a number of logs, including the SQL Server error log and the Windows event logs.

In addition to creating alerts for error conditions, browsing the SQL Server logs for abnormal entries is a basic administration task and one that should ideally be performed on a daily basis. In appendix B, we'll walk through a suggested DBA work plan, which lists recommended daily, weekly, and monthly tasks.

14.5 *Best practice considerations: monitoring and automation*

A good DBA knows the tools at his or her disposal and selects the right tool for the job, with mundane and repetitive tasks automated to achieve more and reduce errors, thereby freeing up time for more rewarding and enjoyable tasks.

- Wherever possible, use server-side traces configured to write to local dedicated disks instead of client-side Profiler traces, particularly for high-volume and/or long-running traces. Use Profiler's Export menu to create server-side scripts once the required events, columns, and filters have been chosen.

- Use Profiler for specialized tasks such as deadlock and blocked process monitoring, rather than as a primary performance analysis and tuning tool. Dynamic management views are far more effective in this regard, particularly when used as part of a waits and queues analysis technique, covered in chapter 17.

- The RML utilities (ReadTrace, OStress) are ideal for database load testing and evaluating the performance impact of proposed changes. Such tools, however, cannot be used for load testing all aspects of an application infrastructure. Tools such as Visual Studio Team System: Test Load Agent and LoadRunner are ideal for this purpose.

- Recording a baseline of system performance under typical operating conditions and performance response times is crucial in understanding normal system behavior. Such understanding is invaluable when troubleshooting performance problems as it allows abnormal performance measurements to stand out, thereby narrowing the scope of a performance troubleshooting exercise.

- A performance baseline is typically created using Performance Monitor to record a number of key metrics over a period of time representing typical system usage. A one-second sampling interval should be used for this recording (unless the log size and/or performance impact become too great).

- Consider including application metrics in the baseline, for example, number of users and user response time. Such metrics enhance the value of the baseline by providing a richer end-to-end performance picture and enable projection of likely database performance under future application-load scenarios. Depending on the application, such metrics may be exposed as Performance Monitor counters in a manner similar to how SQL Server exposes its own internal metrics.

- Maintaining a load-test environment, ideally configured identically to production, allows the impact of proposed production changes to be measured before production implementation. It also permits *benchmark testing*, which is crucial in understanding a system's breaking point and essential for capacity-planning purposes.

- Regular performance baseline analysis allows emerging performance trends to be understood, for example, the growth in batches/sec over a number of months. When combined with benchmark testing to establish a known breaking point, such analysis enables performance projections as part of a capacity-planning exercise.

- Ensure counters such as user connections and logins/logouts per second are kept in the baseline. Most counter values tend to rise in unison with the number of connected users, so these are valuable counters for cross-referencing purposes.

- While maintenance plans are easy to create and use, beware of their limitations, for example, the inability to set threshold levels for index rebuild/reorganize. Although you could use the T-SQL task here, SQL Server Agent jobs provide more flexibility with the ability to create additional job step types such as Powershell.

- Consider the use of backup devices for more flexibility when scripting backup jobs for implementation as SQL Server Agent jobs. Rather than using script jobs containing hard-coded directory paths, the use of backup devices enables portability of backup scripts, with each environment's backup devices configured for the appropriate drive letters and directory paths.

- Ensure the appropriate alerts are enabled either using SQL Server Agent operators or through the use of MOM or something similar. At a minimum, alerts should be established for job failures, severity 16+ errors, deadlocks, and peak performance conditions.

- When using trace flags in a production environment, using the –T startup option is preferred over the DBCC TRACEON command. Having the trace flag invoked on startup ensures that all statements run with the same trace flag setting.

Additional links and information on the best practices covered in this chapter can be found online at http://www.sqlcrunch.com/automation-monitoring.

In the next chapter, we'll expand on our coverage of automation by focusing on a new feature introduced in SQL Server 2008 that automates the collection of performance and management data for storage and later analysis.

Data Collector and MDW

In this chapter, we'll cover

- Data collection overview
- Setup and configuration
- Data collection
- Reporting

New in 2008

Automating and scheduling the collection, storage, and archival of SQL Server performance and management information is a task that most DBAs recognize as being of value, particularly for baseline analysis purposes. Until SQL Server 2008, such a task required third-party products or a custom-developed process. As a result, its implementation was often avoided, delayed, or half-baked. Fortunately, Microsoft recognized the value of such a process and included an out-of-the-box, customizable data collection process in SQL Server 2008.

Commonly referred to as the *Data Collector*, it comprises a number of key components, all of which work together to provide automated data collection and management services for participating server instances.

We'll begin this chapter with a general overview of the data collection platform before looking at the setup and initial configuration process. We'll then move on to cover the Data Collector configuration process and look at some important considerations for using a centralized management data warehouse (MDW). We'll conclude the chapter with the major benefit of the data collection platform, reporting against the collected data.

15.1 Component overview

The data collection platform comprises three key components: the *Data Collector, collection sets,* and the *management data warehouse.* These components work together to enable information to be automatically collected and stored for later analysis and reporting. Before we focus on the setup, administration, and benefits of this platform, let's walk through an overview of the key components.

15.1.1 Data Collector

The Data Collector component controls the collection and upload of information from a SQL Server instance to the management data warehouse using a combination of SQL Server Agent jobs and SQL Server Integration Services (SSIS) packages. The information collected is defined in the data collection sets.

15.1.2 Data collection sets

A data collection set is comprised of information relating to a particular aspect of a SQL Server instance. Three system data collection sets are included with SQL Server 2008: *Disk Usage, Query Statistics*, and *Server Activity.*

DISK USAGE

This collection set records disk usage statistics for each database on the instance where the data collection set is located. By collecting this information on a regular basis, you can report on information such as the average data file growth per day.

QUERY STATISTICS

One of the limitations of DMVs such as sys.dm_exec_query_stats is that the information they contain is lost each time SQL Server restarts. The Query Statistics collection set overcomes this limitation by regularly collecting and storing this information, enabling retrospective analysis of query information such as Top N queries by CPU from any period of time in which the collection data is available.

SERVER ACTIVITY

In the previous chapter we spoke about setting up Performance Monitor to record counters to log files for later analysis. When enabled, this collection set does that for us automatically, enabling reporting on counter values across periods of the collected data so that we can easily compare current performance to previous points.

In addition to these system collection sets, we can define custom collection sets, an example of which we'll cover a little later. The data collected by the collection sets is uploaded by the Data Collector component to the management data warehouse.

15.1.3 Management data warehouse

When created by the setup wizard, the management data warehouse, commonly known as the MDW, is created with all of the necessary data structures to store uploaded data

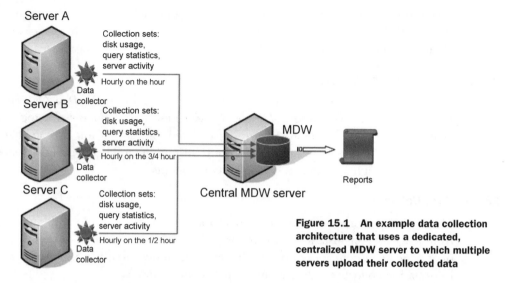

Figure 15.1   An example data collection architecture that uses a dedicated, centralized MDW server to which multiple servers upload their collected data

from the data collection sets of participating servers. Each server is individually configured for data collection, and one of the steps in this process is choosing the MDW location where the collected data will be loaded.

Once the data collection sets begin loading, the MDW becomes the source for a number of included (and very powerful) reports, which we'll cover shortly. Figure 15.1 shows the major components of the data collection platform working together.

With this overview in mind, let's proceed by looking at the initial setup and configuration steps.

15.2   Setup and configuration

We use SQL Server Management Studio to begin the process of configuring the data collection platform for a SQL Server 2008 instance,[1] with the first step being the selection (or creation) of the MDW.

15.2.1   MDW selection or creation

Right-clicking Data Collection under the Management node in SQL Server Management Studio allows you to select the Configure Management Data Warehouse menu option, which starts the Configure Management Data Warehouse Wizard. The first wizard step presents two options, as shown in figure 15.2: Create or Upgrade a Management Data Warehouse and Set Up Data Collection. According to the provided option descriptions, if an MDW database does not yet exist, you can select the first option to create an MDW for subsequent server instances to use. Alternatively, the second option allows you to select an existing MDW.

---

[1]   SQL Server 2005 instances (and earlier) cannot be configured for data collection.

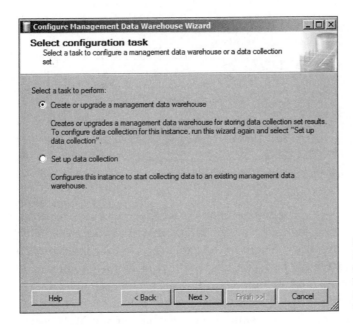

Figure 15.2   Right-clicking Data Collection and choosing Configure Management Data Warehouse starts the Configure Management Data Warehouse Wizard.

Although it's possible for each instance to host its own local MDW database, choosing to create it on a centralized, dedicated server (as per the example shown earlier in figure 15.1) provides a number of advantages, particularly in large environments containing many server instances that will be configured for data collection. Among others, the major benefits of a single centralized MDW database include the following:

- *Centralized administration*—A single MDW database enables simpler administration for actions such as backups and disk space monitoring. Depending on the configured collection sets and upload frequencies, the volume of uploaded data can grow very quickly, so having a single administration point is very beneficial in this regard.
- *Single report source*—A centralized MDW enables a custom enterprise reporting solution to be configured against a single-source MDW database.
- *Minimal performance impact*—Offloading the MDW overhead from each of the uploading servers minimizes (and centralizes) the performance overhead of the data collection platform.

For the purposes of this example, let's imagine our MDW is yet to be created. Thus, we'll select the first option shown in figure 15.2. The next screen, as shown in figure 15.3, permits the creation of a new MDW by clicking the New button and entering the name, location, and size details. As with the creation of any database, we must consider the initial size and growth factors; an MDW can grow very quickly,[2] so avoiding frequent autogrow operations is a vital performance consideration.

---

[2]   ~ 300MB per uploading server per day, depending on collection sets and upload frequency

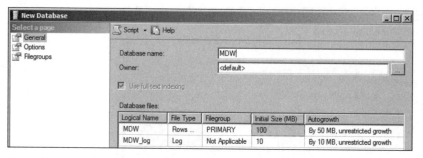

Figure 15.3   The Configure Management Data Warehouse Wizard permits the creation of a new MDW database.

The next and final step in the initial setup wizard is configuring the MDW security, which involves mapping logins to one of three MDW database roles: mdw_admin, mdw_reader, and mdw_writer. These roles enable control over the two main uses of the MDW: loading data into it and reporting on the data within. Should a central MDW database instance be used by multiple uploading instances, each uploading instance's SQL Agent account would need to be defined as a member of the mdw_writer role, unless the account already has sysadmin membership on the MDW instance. The mdw_reader role is used for accounts requiring reporting access, and the mdw_admin role is a superset of both the reader and writer roles.

Once the MDW database has been created, the next step is to set up data collection. In a central MDW installation, the data collection setup process is repeated on each SQL Server instance, each of which would be configured to upload to the recently created MDW database.

15.2.2   *Data collection setup*

Setting up data collection involves accessing the same wizard we used to create the MDW database. Right-click Data Collection and choose Configure Management Data Warehouse; however, this time select Setup Data Collection from the step shown earlier in figure 15.2.

The next step, as shown in figure 15.4, allows you to select the MDW database you've just created, along with a cache directory. One of the properties of each data

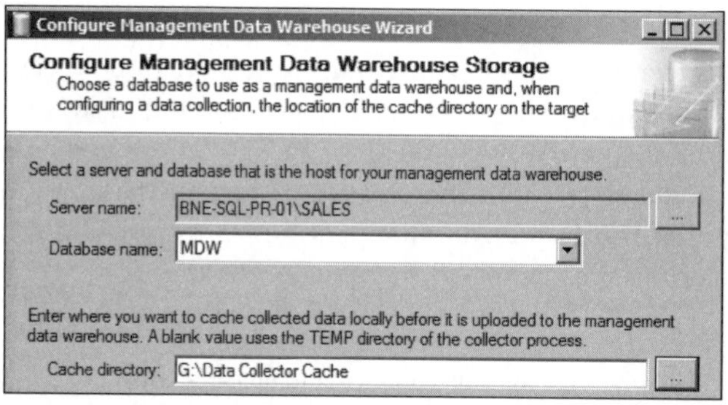

Figure 15.4   After selecting Set Up Data Collection from the Configure Management Data Warehouse Wizard, you can select an MDW database and specify a cache directory for cached collection sets.

collection set is whether its data is cached before being uploaded to the MDW. As we'll discuss shortly, caching collected data before upload reduces the cost of the collection process, particularly for large and/or frequently collected data sets.

If the cache directory is not specified, cached data collection sets will use the directory specified in the %TEMP% or %TMP% system variables. For more control over disk usage, specifying a custom directory is recommended, ideally on a disk separate from data/transaction log files. Further, the SQL Agent service account will need read/write permissions to the specified cache directory.

Once you enter these settings, the wizard completes and creates the necessary components to begin collecting and uploading to the selected MDW. Without any further action, the system data collection sets will remain configured with default settings determining the upload frequency, cache method, and data retention period.

To gain a deeper understanding of the data collection platform, let's look at the properties of the default data collection sets and how they can be customized.

15.3 *Data collection*

Once configured for data collection, a SQL Server instance is enabled with three default system collection sets and the ability to define custom sets if required. In both cases, there are a number of important considerations about upload frequencies/methods and retention periods. All of these properties can be accessed and modified in SQL Server Management Studio under the Management > Data Collection folder by right-clicking on a collection set and choosing Properties.

15.3.1 *Upload method and frequency*

Each data collection set has its own data collection and upload method, with the two options being Non-cached and Cached. As the name suggests, the cached method collects and caches data locally before uploading to the MDW. In contrast, the non-cached method collects and uploads at the same time, using the same schedule.

Non-cached mode is typically used for lightweight and/or infrequent collection sets such as Disk Usage. In contrast, both the Query Statistics and Server Activity sets should (and do) use cached mode because their collected content is greater and occurs more frequently.

Non-cached mode collects and uploads on the same schedule, which can be specified via the General page of the collection set's Properties window by clicking the Pick or New button. In figure 15.5, the Server Activity collection set is defined with the cached upload method. Earlier in the section (figure 15.4) we covered the initial configuration of the data collection platform, part of which was selecting a cache directory. This directory is used by each data collection set using cached mode.

When cached mode is selected, the Uploads page of the collection set's Properties window lets you select or create an upload schedule, as per figure 15.6. The collection schedule is specified using the General page, as shown in figure 15.5, by entering a value in the Collection Frequency (sec) column.

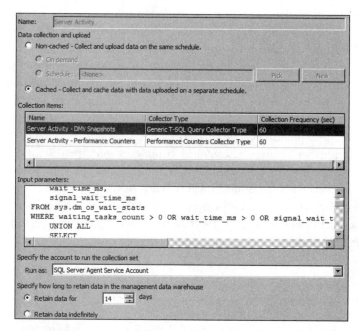

Figure 15.5   The Properties window of each collection set lets you configure the upload mode and schedule as well as the data retention period.

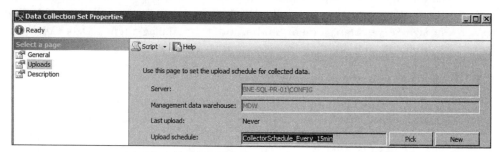

Figure 15.6   The Uploads page of the collection set's Properties window is used to set an upload schedule for a cached collection set.

Staggered upload with cached mode

When a large number of servers are frequently collecting and uploading large collection sets, the collective data volume may overwhelm the centralized MDW server. Cached mode allows each uploading server to collect and upload on a staggered schedule, thereby reducing the impact on the MDW server. For example, one server may upload hourly on the hour, with the next server uploading at 15 minutes past the hour, and so forth.

Once the upload mode and schedules are defined for each collection set, SQL Server Agent jobs are used to execute the collection and upload to the MDW. For a cached mode collection set, two agent jobs will be used: one for the collection and another

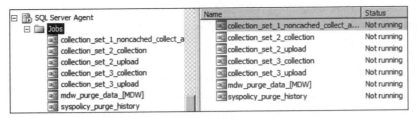

Figure 15.7 SQL Server Agent jobs are used to execute the collection and upload steps of each collection set. You can rename the jobs for easier identification.

for the upload. In contrast, a non-cached collection set will have a single job for both collection and upload.

The names given to the SQL Server Agent jobs are based on their collection set number, as shown in figure 15.7. The jobs can be renamed in order to easily identify the correlation between a SQL Server Agent job and the collection set it's servicing. For example, the collection_set_2_collection/upload jobs can be renamed to Server Activity Collection and Server Activity Upload.

Before changing the collection mode and/or collection and upload schedules, make sure you understand the performance impacts of doing so, particularly in a production environment with a large number of servers uploading to a central MDW database. The reporting benefits of scheduling frequent uploads need to be balanced against the performance impact on the MDW server that the data is being loaded to. Staggering the uploads can certainly help in reducing the load impact on the MDW database.

In addition to the upload mode and schedule for each instance, another important consideration is the backup of the MDW database.

15.3.2 *Backup considerations*

In a production environment using the data collection platform, there are a number of additional backup considerations, summarized as follows:

- *MDW database*—Depending on the collection sets and upload frequency, the MDW database can expect to receive approximately 300MB of uploaded data *per server per day*. It's easy to see how this database can grow very rapidly. Therefore, you need to carefully consider doing backups and monitoring disk space on the MDW server as well as archiving, which we'll cover shortly.
- *MDW recovery model*—By default, the MDW database is created with the simple recovery model. In a production environment, you need to change this to the full recovery model, unless you can accept the possibility of losing data collected since the last full backup.
- *MSDB database*—Each uploading instance's collection sets, upload schedules, and log histories are defined and stored in the MSDB database of each instance. Regardless of whether the data collection platform is used, this database should be backed up; however, with an active collection configuration, the need to back up this database becomes even more important.

To assist with containing the growth of the MDW database, each collection set is defined with a retention period, which we'll discuss next.

15.3.3 *Retention period*

As we've just discussed, the MDW database will grow by approximately 300MB per server per day. This obviously makes containing the growth of this database very important, particularly in a large enterprise environment with a central MDW database and many uploading servers. Fortunately, as we saw in figure 15.5, each collection set is defined with a retention period, specified as a number of days.

When the data collection upload job executes, previous data from the collection set that's older than the retention period is removed from the database. It follows that for a given number of uploading servers, the MDW database will grow to a certain size and then stabilize. The retention period of each collection set should be based on a number of factors such as the reporting requirements and available disk space.

Typically, things don't always run according to plan, with a variety of potential problems preventing the successful collection and upload of a collection set's data. Fortunately, the logging component allows you to inspect the history and detail of each set's activity.

15.3.4 *Logging*

Right-clicking a collection set (or data collection) and selecting View Logs brings up the Log File Viewer, which, as shown in figure 15.8, presents a detailed history of the collection and upload process.

As mentioned earlier, in addition to the default system data collection sets, you can create custom collection sets.

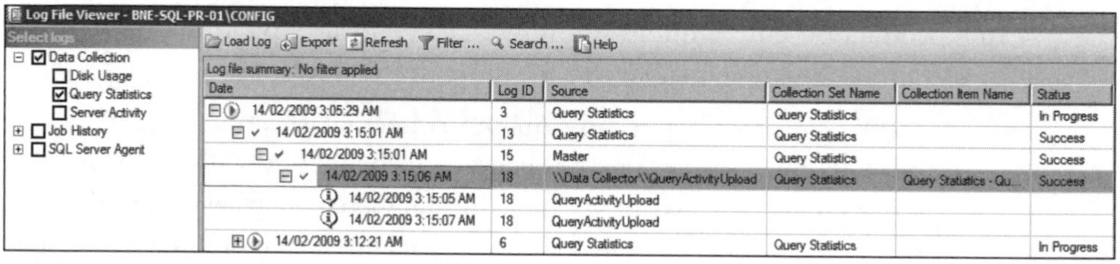

Figure 15.8   Selecting View Logs after right-clicking a collection set allows the detailed inspection of recent collection and upload activities.

15.4   *Custom collection sets*

You can define additional collection sets that draw information from a number of different sources, using one of three collector types: T-SQL Query, SQL Trace, and Performance Counter. A fourth collector type, Query Activity, collects the same information as the Query Statistics system collection set.

Creating custom collection sets requires the use of a number of stored procedures including sp_syscollector_create_collection_set and sp_syscollector_create_collection _item. Unfortunately, you cannot create custom collection sets using the Management Studio interface. However, once they are created, you can manage their upload configuration and schedule using Management Studio as with the system collection sets.

You can create custom collection sets for a variety of purposes, including the following:

- *Longer-term storage of DMVs* such as the missing index DMVs. As we covered in chapter 13, these DMVs are limited to the last 500 missing indexes reported by the query optimizer, so storing a regular snapshot of these DMVs in the MDW can overcome this limitation.
- *Creating a customized compliance solution* with policy-based management, for example, uploading the results of policy checks from multiple servers to the central MDW for a centralized compliance-reporting solution.
- *Collecting customized Performance Monitor counters* as part of a broader baseline. Despite the Server Activity system collection set including a number of performance counters, additional counters not included in this set may be required.

A full description of the process and procedures for creating a custom collection set is found in SQL Server Books Online. A brief example in listing 15.1 demonstrates the T-SQL code for creating a custom set called Performance Baseline, which includes a number of performance counters.

Listing 15.1 Creating a custom collection set for performance counters

```
-- Create a Custom Collection Set containing three Performance Counters
use msdb;

declare @collection_set_id_1 int
declare @collection_set_uid_2 uniqueidentifier

exec [dbo].[sp_syscollector_create_collection_set]
 @name=N'Performance Baseline'
 , @collection_mode=0
 , @description=N'Custom Performance Counters'
 , @target=N''
 , @logging_level=0
 , @days_until_expiration=5
 , @proxy_name=N''
 , @schedule_name=N'CollectorSchedule_Every_5min'
 , @collection_set_id=@collection_set_id_1 OUTPUT
 , @collection_set_uid=@collection_set_uid_2 OUTPUT

declare @collector_type_uid_3 uniqueidentifier
select @collector_type_uid_3 = collector_type_uid
from [dbo].[syscollector_collector_types]
Where name = N'Performance Counters Collector Type'

declare @collection_item_id_4 int
exec [dbo].[sp_syscollector_create_collection_item]
 @name=N'PerfCounters'
 , @parameters=
```

```
'<ns:PerformanceCountersCollector xmlns:ns="DataCollectorType">

  <PerformanceCounters Objects="$(INSTANCE):Buffer Manager" Counters="Page
➥ life expectancy" />

  <PerformanceCounters Objects="$(INSTANCE):General Statistics"
➥ Counters="User Connections" />

  <PerformanceCounters Objects="LogicalDisk" Counters="Avg. Disk sec/Read"
➥ Instances="*" />

</ns:PerformanceCountersCollector>'
 , @collection_item_id=@collection_item_id_4 OUTPUT
 , @frequency=5
 , @collection_set_id=@collection_set_id_1
 , @collector_type_uid=@collector_type_uid_3
```

Once the custom set is created using the code in listing 15.1, it will appear in Management Studio as a new collection set, at which point you can configure its upload settings in the same manner as we covered earlier for system data collection sets.

Finally, the benefit of collecting and uploading data is, of course, to enable reporting on it, and in that regard a number of powerful reports are included to work with the system collection sets.

15.5 Reporting

In closing our coverage of the data collection platform, let's take a look at the standard reports. Each of these can be accessed in SQL Server Management Studio by right-clicking Data Collection and choosing Reports > Management Data Warehouse. The data shown in the resultant report will be filtered for the server from which the report was run. Let's start with the Disk Usage Summary report.

15.5.1 Disk Usage Summary

The initial view of the Disk Usage Summary report, as shown in figure 15.9, presents a view of each database's disk usage within the instance.

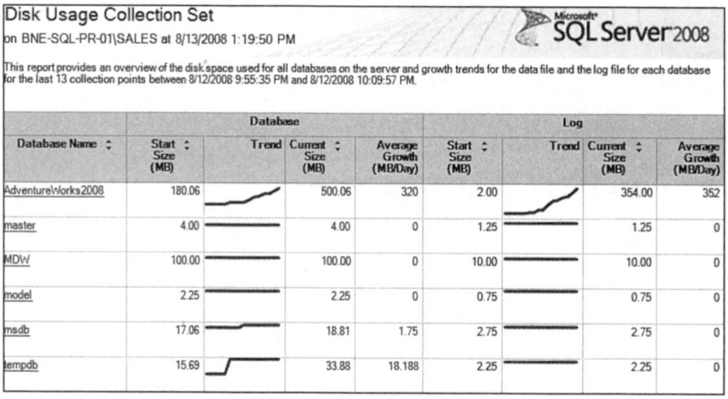

Disk Usage Collection Set
on BNE-SQL-PR-01\SALES at 8/13/2008 1:19:50 PM

This report provides an overview of the disk space used for all databases on the server and growth trends for the data file and the log file for each database for the last 13 collection points between 8/12/2008 9:55:35 PM and 8/12/2008 10:09:57 PM.

	Database				Log			
Database Name	Start Size (MB)	Trend	Current Size (MB)	Average Growth (MB/Day)	Start Size (MB)	Trend	Current Size (MB)	Average Growth (MB/Day)
AdventureWorks2008	180.06		500.06	320	2.00		354.00	352
master	4.00		4.00	0	1.25		1.25	0
MDW	100.00		100.00	0	10.00		10.00	0
model	2.25		2.25	0	0.75		0.75	0
msdb	17.06		18.81	1.75	2.75		2.75	0
tempdb	15.69		33.88	18.188	2.25		2.25	0

Figure 15.9 The Disk Usage report includes trend lines and average growth per day for both data and log files.

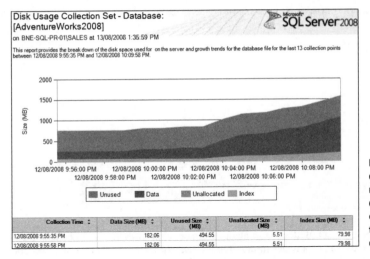

Figure 15.10 Drilling down from the Disk Usage report provides further detail on disk usage, in this case, for the data file of the AdventureWorks2008 database.

The value of this report is enhanced through the ability to click on the blue trend lines to drill down into more detail. For example, clicking on the AdventureWorks2008 database trend line opens another report, as shown in figure 15.10.

The clear visibility of historical disk usage enabled by the Disk Usage reports makes capacity planning in SQL Server 2008 much simpler than in SQL Server 2005 and earlier, which required a custom process and/or a third-party product.

Next up, let's examine the Query Statistics History report.

15.5.2 Query Statistics History

The Query Statistics History report permits analysis of the most expensive queries (by duration, CPU, or disk usage). As with the Server Activity report, you can select a particular period in which to filter the report using the timeline navigation, as shown in figure 15.11.

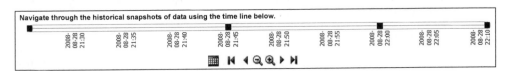

Figure 15.11 The timeline at the top of certain reports allows the report to be filtered for a time period.

A section of the Query Statistics report is shown in figure 15.12.

The value of this report is enhanced by the ability to drill down into the details of each query. For example, clicking on one of the queries brings up another report, as shown in figure 15.13. Among other details, this report shows aggregated query statistics and the full query text.

Additional drill-through actions from this report provide further detail, all the way down to viewing the individual graphical execution plans.

The final report we'll examine is the Server Activity History report.

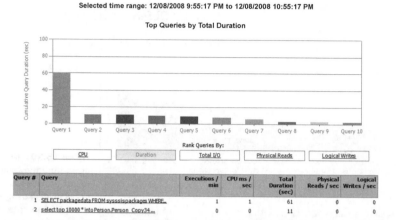

Figure 15.12 The Query Statistics report allows the most expensive queries to be identified for a time period. Clicking on the query provides further details, such as the full query text and execution plan.

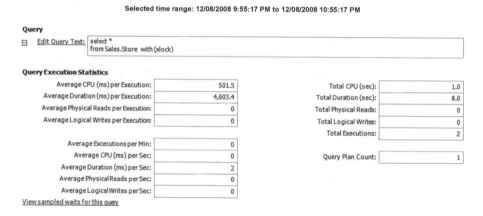

Figure 15.13 Drilling through from the Query Statistics report shows additional query details such as execution count and average duration per execution.

15.5.3 *Server Activity History*

As shown in figure 15.14, the Server Activity History report provides a wealth of information for a selected time period, including resource usage, wait types, and performance counter values.

Like the other reports we've looked at, the Server Activity report enables drill-through action into more detail, such as clicking on the Disk I/O Usage graph line and viewing the details of each disk, as shown in figure 15.15.

Bear in mind that all of the reports shown here are standard, out-of-the-box reports that work with the standard system collection sets. Thus, the ability to derive a deeper understanding of system usage not only is very simple but comes with a relatively low administration overhead.

In addition to these standard reports, you can create custom reports as well.

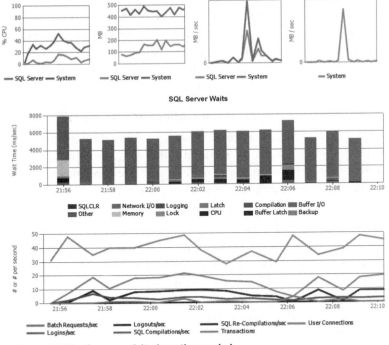

Figure 15.14   Server activity for a time period

Selected time range: 12/08/2008 9:55:17 PM to 12/08/2008 10:10:17 PM

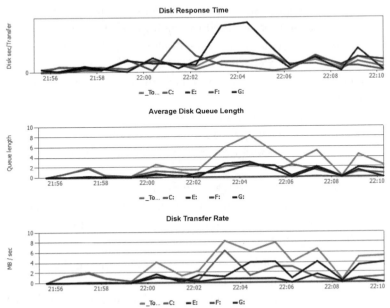

Figure 15.15   Drilling through from the Server Activity report enables a deeper analysis, in this case viewing each disk's response time, queue length, and transfer rate.

15.5.4 *Custom reports*

SQL Server Books Online contains a description of the tables within the MDW database. These tables can be directly queried as part of a custom report for a custom collection set or to enhance the standard reports, for example, to include data from multiple instances side by side. Further possibilities for customization exist, for example, to create Analysis Services cubes off the collected data.

15.6 *Best practice considerations: Data Collector and MDW*

The data collection platform is a significant leap forward in deriving maximum value from the vast amount of information contained within a SQL Server instance, opening up a whole range of new reporting options unavailable in previous versions of SQL Server without customized solutions or third-party products.

- When using the data collection platform, creating a centralized MDW database (ideally on a dedicated server) is preferable to creating an MDW on each instance configured with data collection. The benefits of a centralized MDW include a single administration and reporting point and offloading the impact of the data collection load process to the dedicated MDW server.
- When configuring multiple server instances to upload to a central MDW, the uploads should ideally be staggered to reduce the impact of multiple servers uploading data at the same time.
- After creating the MDW database, consider setting its recovery model to full, and ensure the database is adequately sized to avoid frequent autogrow operations.
- For large data collection sets, or sets configured with a high collection frequency, use the cached mode to reduce the impact on the network and server.
- For maximum performance, the cache directory should ideally be set to a dedicated disk that is separate from the database data and transaction log disks. Further, the SQL Server Agent service account will need read/write access to this directory.
- Before changing the collection mode and/or collection and upload schedules, you need to understand the performance impacts of doing so, particularly in a production environment with a large number of servers uploading to a central MDW database.
- Ensure the MDW database and transaction log are backed up as per any other production database. Further, since the MSDB database contains the data collection configuration for each uploading instance, ensure this database is backed up on each participating instance.

Additional links and information on the best practices covered in this chapter can be found online at http://www.sqlcrunch.com/datacollector.

The data collection platform is one of many new features introduced in SQL Server 2008. In the next chapter, we'll look at another one: Resource Governor.

Resource Governor

16

New in 2008

Throughout this book, we've looked at a number of performance-management tools used for *observation* and/or *simulation purposes*. What's missing from those tools is a mechanism to control resource usage based on the connection source, now possible using *Resource Governor*, introduced in the Enterprise Edition of SQL Server 2008.

In this chapter, we'll begin with an overview of Resource Governor before concentrating on its major components: the *classifier function*, *workload groups*, and *resource pools*. We'll conclude the chapter with an example implementation using T-SQL script and cover some of the monitoring techniques used.

16.1   *Resource Governor overview*

A common (and unfortunate) situation that DBAs often encounter in production systems is a single runaway query that flatlines server performance to the detriment of all users. Unless the offending query can be identified and killed, users are effectively at the mercy of the query completing. To make matters worse, there's nothing stopping the same query from occurring over and over again, with the end result being an unpredictable experience for end users and a frustrating one for DBAs.

In previous versions of SQL Server, resources could be constrained at an instance level with configuration settings such as CPU affinity and maximum memory, but such settings are coarse grained and don't apply to individual users or applications. Thus, instances that host groups of users or applications with varying resource usage present a challenge for a DBA whose goal is to provide a stable, predictable environment for *all* users.

A classic example of this is a SQL Server instance used for both reporting and data entry. In such a case, performance for data entry users may be fine until someone decides to run a large report, at which time data entry performance grinds to a halt. Resource Governor is purpose built to address problems of this type.

16.1.1   *Resource Governor benefits*

Put simply, Resource Governor enables resource sharing and segregation between groups of users or applications based on their connection source. For example, we could assign our data entry group minimum CPU and memory resources, effectively *shielding* them from the impact of a large report query.

As you'll see shortly, Resource Governor is not only relatively easy to set up and use, but it's also very effective in limiting the performance impact of one group on others. That being said, there are a number of considerations before using it, as well as several limitations.

16.1.2   *Resource Governor limitations*

As a brand-new feature in SQL Server 2008, Resource Governor comes with a number of limitations that will presumably be removed in subsequent SQL Server versions as the feature matures:

- Resource constraints are limited to memory and CPU. Network and disk I/O resources cannot be constrained in SQL Server 2008.
- Reporting Services, Analysis Services, and Integration Services resource usage cannot be constrained. In this version, resource constraints apply to core database engine usage only.
- Resource Governor constraints are defined *within (and apply within)* a SQL Server instance; resource constraints do not apply across instances on a multi-instance server.[1]

---

[1]   Resource segregation across instances can be achieved with CPU affinity and min/max memory settings.

Further, Resource Governor is most effective when resource usage is well defined and consistent across a number of distinct groups, for example, data entry and reports. In cases where particular data entry transactions dominate resource usage, Resource Governor may not be effective, unless there is a method of identifying and classifying the source of such transactions.

Before we dive into the details of Resource Governor, let's briefly define the major components.

16.1.3 *Resource Governor components*

Resource Governor tracks and allocates CPU and memory resources using three major components: *resource pools, workload groups,* and a *classifier function*:

- A *resource pool* is created to define the minimum and maximum usage of a server's CPU and memory resources. A resource pool can be used by one or more workload groups.
- Connections to a SQL Server instance are classified into a workload group by the classifier function. The workload group is mapped to a resource pool defining the minimum and maximum resource consumption available to the connection. The resource group also serves as a monitoring and aggregation point for resource consumption and as a method of applying a uniform resource usage policy, for example, a MAXDOP setting specific to each group.
- The classifier function, invoked upon connection to a SQL Server instance, defines which resource group the connection is assigned to. Connections can be classified based on the username, application name, host name, or role membership.

Workload groups and resource pools are either user defined or system based. There are two system groups and pools: internal and default. The internal group and pool are used for SQL Server processes, whereas the default group and pool are used for connections that are not otherwise classified into a user-defined group and pool.

Figure 16.1 illustrates the above components working together to define resource usage limits for an incoming connection to a SQL Server 2008 instance.

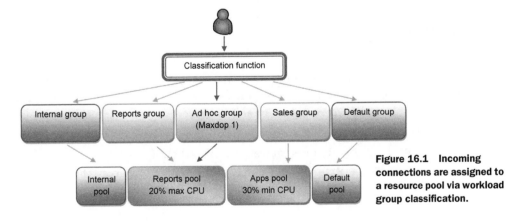

Figure 16.1 Incoming connections are assigned to a resource pool via workload group classification.

With this overview in mind, let's consider the components in more detail, beginning with the classifier function.

16.2   *Classifier function*

When a user or application connects to a SQL Server instance, the logon process includes two major steps before the session is established: authentication, followed by the firing of any logon triggers. When Resource Governor is enabled, a third step is included for classifying the connection using the classifier function. The process is summarized in figure 16.2.

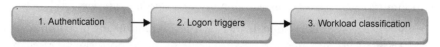

Figure 16.2   The logon process with Resource Governor enabled consists of authentication, logon triggers, and workload classification.

Given the integration of the classifier function within the logon process, the efficiency of the function becomes a crucial consideration. Poorly written functions have the potential for logins to time out if the execution time of the function exceeds the login timeout setting of the connecting application. Therefore, the classifier function should be tested, ideally under load, before production implementation.

As with workload groups and resource pools, the best classifier functions are those that are relatively simple in nature. Consider the example in listing 16.1.

Listing 16.1   Example classifier function

```
-- Create a Classifier Function
CREATE FUNCTION fn_rg_classifier() RETURNS SYSNAME
WITH SCHEMABINDING
AS
BEGIN
    DECLARE @grp_name AS SYSNAME
      IF (IS_SRVROLEMEMBER('sysadmin') = 1)
         SET @grp_name = 'rgDBAGroup'
      IF (APP_NAME() LIKE '%REPORT SERVER%')
         SET @grp_name = 'rgReportGroup'
    RETURN @grp_name
END
GO
```

The classifier function presented here is an example of a relatively simple function putting little overhead on the logon process. It uses the SUSR_NAME() and APP_NAME() functions to classify incoming connections based on the username or application name. The full list of supported functions for classification purposes is as follows:

- *HOST_NAME ()* — Returns values such as MarketingPC4
- *APP_NAME ()* — Returns values such as Microsoft SQL Server Management Studio - Query

- *SUSER_NAME()* and *SUSER_SNAME()*—Returns values such as BNESales\RColledge
- *IS_SRVROLEMEMBER()*—Used to evaluate server role membership, for example, if IS_SRVROLEMEMBER ('sysadmin') = 1
- *IS_MEMBER()*—Used to evaluate database role membership, for example, if IS_MEMBER ('db_owner') = 1

When designing a classifier function, you need to consider the following aspects of its effect on a Resource Governor implementation:

- A connection not explicitly classified will be assigned to the default workload group (and therefore the default resource pool). With this in mind, the function logic should address only connections that should be targeted for a nondefault workload group.
- Connections made using the dedicated administrator connection (DAC) are not subject to workload group classification. Using the DAC is one method of fixing a poorly written classifier function that's denying connections based on logon timeouts. For this reason, enabling the DAC is recommended when using Resource Governor.
- When Resource Governor is disabled, the classifier function is not executed as part of the logon process; all connections are automatically set to use the default workload group, whose settings are returned to their default values along with the values of the default resource pool.

Finally, you need to consider the security of the functions being used (or misused) for classification. One example of this, which also applies to logon triggers (covered in chapter 6), is spoofing the value of the supplied application name in an application's connection string. An example of this is shown in figure 16.3.

The Application Name attribute of the connection string is returned by the SQL Server APP_NAME() function. It follows that a user with access to the application's connection string and knowledge of the classification function's logic can potentially circumvent the intended result of the classification function (or logon trigger). Therefore, you must consider the security of the connection string details and the possible use of a more secure classification function.

```
<add key="ConnectionString" value="Integrated Security=SSPI;
    Persist Security Info=False;Initial Catalog=SalesDB;Data Source=SalesServer;
    Packet Size=4096;Application Name=Net SqlClient Data Provider"/>
```

```
<add key="ConnectionString" value="Integrated Security=SSPI;
    Persist Security Info=False;Initial Catalog=SalesDB;Data Source=SalesServer;
    Packet Size=4096;Application Name=Accounting Application"/>
```

Figure 16.3 A developer with access to the connection string can spoof the application name to circumvent logon triggers and workload classification.

Let's now focus on the purpose of the classifier function: to assign connections to a workload group.

16.3 *Workload groups*

Classifying incoming database connections into a workload group offers a number of benefits, including the following:

- Connections that share a similar property, for example, Application Name, can be grouped together for purposes of applying resource usage boundaries via a specific resource pool.

- Application of resource usage constraints, such as a custom MAXDOP setting, can be made at a workload group level, thereby enabling more control over resources in mixed-purpose environments.

- Resource usage can be monitored at a group level, enabling a deeper understanding and visibility of current, aggregate, minimum, and maximum resource usage for a given group.

As covered earlier, there are two preexisting system workload groups, default and internal. The default group is used for any connections not classified into a user-defined group or classified into a group that no longer exists. The internal group, used for internal SQL Server operations, can be monitored, but connections cannot be classified into this group, nor can the group be modified in any way.

In addition to these system workload groups, user-defined groups can be created using the CREATE WORKLOAD GROUP T-SQL command. To gain a deeper understanding of workload groups, let's examine the syntax of this command before discussing its optional arguments:

```
CREATE WORKLOAD GROUP group_name
[ WITH
     ( [ IMPORTANCE = { LOW | MEDIUM | HIGH } ]
          [ [ , ] REQUEST_MAX_MEMORY_GRANT_PERCENT = value ]
          [ [ , ] REQUEST_MAX_CPU_TIME_SEC = value ]
          [ [ , ] REQUEST_MEMORY_GRANT_TIMEOUT_SEC = value ]
          [ [ , ] MAX_DOP = value ]
          [ [ , ] GROUP_MAX_REQUESTS = value ] )
  ]
[ USING { pool_name | "default" } ]
```

- *IMPORTANCE*—When multiple workload groups are set to use the same resource pool, the IMPORTANCE argument enables tasks from one group to be weighted ahead of others; for example, if a Miscellaneous Query resource pool is used by two workload groups called AdHoc and Admin, assigning a high importance to the Admin group will place its access to resources before that of the AdHoc group. A high importance should not be confused with priority access to system resources; that is, importance is a simple weighting mechanism to establish order among multiple groups in the same resource pool.

- *REQUEST_MAX_MEMORY_GRANT_PERCENT* — This argument enables the specification of the largest allowable percentage of resource pool memory that can be assigned to a single request from the group; for example, a `value` of 10 would permit a maximum of 50MB of memory to be assigned to a query from a pool with a 500MB memory size. A query that exceeds this value will be met with an error message similar to that shown in figure 16.4.

- `REQUEST_MAX_CPU_TIME_SEC`—Similar to the `MAX_MEMORY_GRANT` argument, this argument applies to the maximum CPU seconds; however, rather than cancel the query, Resource Governor will allow the query to continue and will generate an alert. We'll examine Resource Governor alerts and monitoring in more detail later in this chapter.

- `REQUEST_MEMORY_GRANT_TIMEOUT_SEC`—This argument represents the maximum amount of time in seconds that a query from the group will wait for a memory grant. After the time period expires, rather than the query failing, it will receive the minimum memory grant, which may result in lower-than-expected performance.

- `MAX_DOP`—A workload group can be configured with its own default `MAXDOP` level. Doing so allows commands from a group to use a `MAXDOP` setting that may differ from the server default, without specifying an explicit `MAXDOP` setting. If a query from the group is executed that *does* specify a `MAXDOP` value, it will be used, so long as the value does not exceed the group's `MAXDOP` setting. This argument presents some interesting possibilities; for example, Microsoft Report Builder provides no option to specify a `MAXDOP` value to assign to the queries it generates. Thus, the only option is to use a server default `MAXDOP` setting to control the parallelism of its queries; however, changing the server default may introduce unwanted results in other areas. Using Resource Governor, we can classify Report Builder queries into a workload group with its own `MAXDOP` setting.

- `GROUP_MAX_REQUESTS`—This argument allows a limit to be applied to the number of simultaneous requests that can execute from the workload group. However, in some cases, the SQL engine may allow this limit to be exceeded if doing so prevents a blocking or deadlock scenario from occurring.

- `USING`—This argument links a workload group to a resource pool. If this argument is excluded, the default pool is used.

As with classifier functions, you should be careful when creating workload groups. The group and pool names are returned in any error messages, potentially exposing information that could be used maliciously. Figure 16.4 contains an example of an error message that includes the group/pool names.

```
Results    Messages
Msg 8657, Level 17, State 1, Line 3
Could not get the memory grant of 1280 KB because it exceeds the maximum configuration limit in
workload group 'RG_Reporting' (256) and resource pool 'RP_Reporting' (257).  Contact the server
administrator to increase the memory usage limit.
```

Figure 16.4 Carefully consider the names assigned to workload groups and resource pools because the names are returned in error messages, as shown in this example.

Finally, a user connection classified into a workload group remains in the group for the life of the connection, regardless of whether the classifier function is changed while the connection is active.

As you've just seen, one of the major roles for a workload group is to define a connection's resource pool.

16.4   *Resource pools*

We come now to the final component of Resource Governor, the resource pool, created using the T-SQL command shown below. As you can see, the command is fairly simple, with arguments for min and max values for CPU and memory, the two resources under our control in SQL Server 2008.

```
CREATE RESOURCE POOL pool_name
[ WITH
    ( [ MIN_CPU_PERCENT = value ]
      [ [ , ] MAX_CPU_PERCENT = value ]
      [ [ , ] MIN_MEMORY_PERCENT = value ]
      [ [ , ] MAX_MEMORY_PERCENT = value ] )
]
```

There are two system pools, *default* and *internal,* and as with workload groups, the internal pool is for system usage only, and its resource limits cannot be modified. Given the importance of internal SQL Server system processes, its resource usage is not constrained, regardless of the resources reserved in other pools. In contrast, the default pool *can* be modified, with multiple user-defined workload groups in addition to the default workload group able to use it.

Before we look at what min and max actually mean in the context of resource pool usage (there's more to it than you may think), let's first define some important terms: *effective maximum percentage* and *shared percentage.* In doing so, let's look at an example of the two resource pools defined in table 16.1. The values in this table can represent either CPU or memory; the terms apply in both cases.

Table 16.1   Example pool configuration—internal pool excluded

Pool name	Min %	Max %
Default	0	100
Pool A	30	100
Pool B	60	75

Have a look at Pool A; its *maximum* value is specified as 100 percent; however, Pool B is configured with a *minimum* of 60 percent. It follows that Pool A could never receive more than 40 percent, hence the term *effective maximum.* In a similar vein, Pool B is configured with a maximum of 75 percent, but given Pool A's minimum value of 30 percent, it will never receive more than 70 percent.

The minimums of pools A and B added together total 90 percent; therefore, only 10 percent is left for pools to use over their minimum values. The 10 percent value is referred to as the *total shared percentage* and is used in calculating the effective maximum values. Essentially, effective maximums decrease as minimum values increase.

A poorly configured pool design with large minimum values may have the unwanted effect of starving resources from certain pools. The important point to take from this is that the best resource pool designs are usually the simplest, and like other configuration settings, they should be changed only for a good reason after a well-considered analysis. Later in the chapter we'll look at a plan of attack for deciding how to size these values. Table 16.2 includes the effective maximum values based on the pool design from table 16.1.

Table 16.2 Pool configuration with effective maximum values included

Pool name	Min %	Max %	Effective max %
Default	0	100	10
Pool A	30	100	40
Pool B	60	75	70

With these points in mind, let's look at further ramifications of minimum resource values on CPU and memory.

16.4.1 Effective minimum: memory considerations

You must take special care when configuring a resource pool with a minimum memory percentage. When SQL Server starts, the memory minimums for each pool are reserved up front, regardless of whether the memory is required, or even if there are no active workload groups using the pool. It follows that in a case where there are a number of unused pools with configured minimum memory values, there is potentially a large amount of memory that's unable to be accessed by pools that actually need it. In contrast, CPU limits are more fluid.

16.4.2 Effective minimum: CPU considerations

Consider figure 16.5, which shows the CPU usage of two resource pools in Performance Monitor.

What we're looking at here is a running query in the RP_Reporting pool (represented by the line that starts near 100 percent and drops down to around 15 percent). This pool is configured with a maximum CPU usage of 15 percent. In the left half of the screen, it's clearly using much more than that, in some cases 100 percent. About halfway across, we see the emergence of a query running in the RP_Sales pool (represented by the line that starts at 0 percent and increases to around 80 percent). At this point, the original query's CPU usage is throttled back dramatically, to around the 15 percent average value.

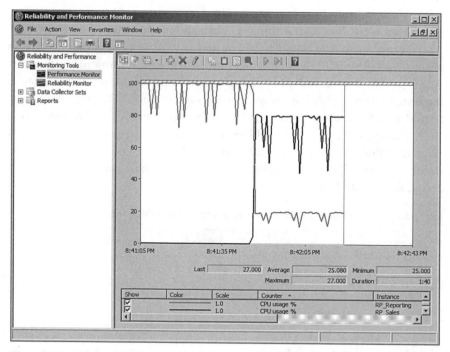

Figure 16.5   Resource Governor throttles resource usage based on contention from other processes.

What's actually happening here is that Resource Governor is smart enough to figure out that there's no CPU contention, so it lets the first query use as much of the resource as it needs. As soon as a second query comes along, CPU contention occurs, at which point resource limits are applied.

Perhaps the most important point to learn from this is in regard to appropriate load testing. For example, testing the impact of a 30 percent CPU pool maximum is pointless unless there is something else running that throttles the pool's CPU usage down to 30 percent.

Finally, note that the resource values are to be interpreted as *averages*, not hard and fast limits; that is, monitoring will occasionally show limits being exceeded, while the average values should be maintained.

With this background, let's walk through a script to set up a Resource Governor scheme from start to finish.

16.5   *Resource Governor in action*

Now that you have a solid understanding of the components that make up Resource Governor, let's walk through an example of its implementation. Let's imagine we have a database used for both a production point-of-sales application and as a source for a reporting system. Our goal is to constrain the CPU and memory resources consumed by the reporting system in order to reduce the impact on the point-of-sales system when large reports are executed.

Let's walk through the T-SQL code for creating the necessary components, beginning with the creation of the workload groups, as shown in listing 16.2.

Listing 16.2 Creating workload groups

```
-- Create 2 Workload Groups
USE MASTER
GO

CREATE WORKLOAD GROUP RG_Reporting
GO
CREATE WORKLOAD GROUP RG_Sales
GO
```

Despite the various options available, we create our workload groups with all of the default settings. Next up, we'll create the classifier function used to assign incoming connections to the appropriate group. After the function is created, we'll configure Resource Governor to use it, as shown in listing 16.3.

Listing 16.3 Classifier function

```
-- Create a Classifier Function
CREATE FUNCTION ClassifierFn_Basic() RETURNS SYSNAME WITH SCHEMABINDING AS
 BEGIN
    DECLARE @ResGroup AS SYSNAME
    IF (SUSER_NAME() = 'reporting')
       SET @ResGroup = 'RG_Reporting'
    IF (SUSER_NAME() = 'sales')
       SET @ResGroup = 'RG_Sales'
    RETURN @ResGroup
END
GO

-- Configure Resource Governor to use the new function
ALTER RESOURCE GOVERNOR WITH (CLASSIFIER_FUNCTION=dbo.ClassifierFn_Basic)
GO
```

In this example, our classifier function uses the login name via the SUSER_NAME() function as the basis for classification. As we explained earlier, this could be based on the application, host, or role membership using the appropriate function.

Our final step is to create the resource pools and assign them to the appropriate workload groups, as per listing 16.4.

Listing 16.4 Assigning resource pools to workload groups

```
-- Create a new Resource Pool
CREATE RESOURCE POOL RP_Sales WITH (
    MIN_CPU_PERCENT = 40
    , MAX_CPU_PERCENT = 60
    , MIN_MEMORY_PERCENT = 40
    , MAX_MEMORY_PERCENT = 60
)
GO
```

```
-- Configure a Workload Group to use the new Resource Pool
ALTER WORKLOAD GROUP RG_Sales USING RP_Sales
GO

-- Create a new Resource Pool
CREATE RESOURCE POOL RP_Reporting WITH (
    MIN_CPU_PERCENT = 5
    , MAX_CPU_PERCENT = 15
    , MIN_MEMORY_PERCENT = 5
    , MAX_MEMORY_PERCENT = 15
)
GO

-- Configure a Workload Group to use the new Resource Pool
ALTER WORKLOAD GROUP RG_Reporting USING RP_Reporting
GO
```

In the above example, we've created resource pools with minimum and maximum CPU and memory values. At this point, the only step left is to reconfigure the Resource Governor to enable the new settings. We can do this using the following command:

```
-- Reconfigure the Resource Governor to enable the new settings
ALTER RESOURCE GOVERNOR RECONFIGURE
GO
```

Once the above T-SQL has been executed, we can confirm our settings using SQL Server Management Studio by right-clicking Resource Governor and choosing Properties. The resultant screen, as shown in figure 16.6, allows us to modify the settings should we wish to do so.

Finally, should we wish to disable Resource Governor, we can do so using the following command:

```
-- Disable the Resource Governor
ALTER RESOURCE GOVERNOR DISABLE
GO
```

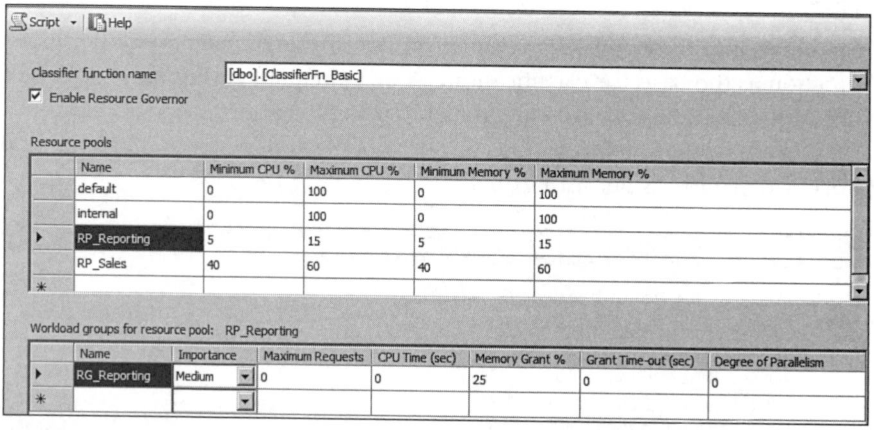

Figure 16.6   You can use the properties window of Resource Governor to select the classifier function and view or edit the resource pools and workload groups settings.

To complete our coverage of Resource Governor, let's review some of the monitoring options available.

16.6 Monitoring resource usage

Workload groups and resource pools can be monitored using three methods: Performance Monitor, events, and Dynamic Management Views.

16.6.1 Performance Monitor

Performance Monitor is the primary mechanism for monitoring Resource Governor usage in SQL Server 2008. Two performance objects are available: SQLServer:Workload Group Stats and SQLServer:Resource Pool Stats.

We saw an example of using the CPU Usage % counter from the SQLServer: Resource Pool Stats earlier in figure 16.5. SQL Server Books Online documents all of the counters for these objects, but let's briefly have a look at some of the counters available for SQLServer:Workload Group Stats:

- *Queued Requests*—If you're using the GROUP_MAX_REQUESTS argument in the workload group definition, this value may be non-zero if throttling has occurred.
- *Active Requests*—This counter represents the number of requests currently executing in the group.
- *CPU Usage %*—This shows the total CPU usage percentage used by all executing requests in the group.
- *Max Request CPU Time*—This is the maximum CPU time used by requests currently executing in the group.
- *Active Parallel Threads*—This indicates the number of executing parallel threads.

Resource Governor also fires events that can be captured and used for alerting.

16.6.2 Events

In chapter 14, we examined the power of establishing alerts for certain events. Resource Governor introduces three new events:

- *CPU Threshold Exceeded*—As we discussed earlier, when a query exceeds its CPU threshold, this event will fire, rather than the query being canceled.
- *PreConnect:Starting and PreConnect:Completed*—When a Resource Governor classifier function or logon trigger starts and finishes, these events will fire.

Finally, we have three DMVs for monitoring purposes.

16.6.3 DMVs

The following DMVs are available for inspecting Resource Governor configurations and statistics:

- *sys.dm_resource_governor_configuration*—This DMV returns the Resource Governor configuration state. Figure 16.6, shown earlier, returns similar information through Management Studio.

- *sys.dm_resource_governor_workload_groups*—This DMV is used to return work-load group configuration and statistics.
- *sys.dm_resource_governor_resource_pools*—This DMV is used to return resource pool configuration and statistics.

In closing this section, let's consider how we can use these monitoring tools to help establish the ideal resource boundaries for resource pools.

16.6.4 *Establishing resource boundaries*

Earlier in our coverage, we spoke about the danger of running complex Resource Governor schemes with numerous configured minimum resource values, particularly for memory. We also covered the fact that Resource Governor is best used in SQL instances where there are well-defined groups of usage patterns, for example, reports versus data entry. If you decide to proceed with Resource Governor, perhaps the best way of evaluating the most appropriate resource usage limits is by using the supplied monitoring tools and the following approach:

1 Create the user-defined workload groups as planned, but assign all of them to the default resource pool configured with min/max values of 0/100.
2 Run the database instance for a period of time long enough to cover the typical usage cycle.
3 Once the test is complete, use the monitoring tools covered previously to determine how resources are used by each of the workload groups; that is, determining the average, minimum, and maximum values of memory and CPU will help you to shape the appropriate minimum and maximum values to apply, as well as estimate the impact of such values.
4 In a load-testing environment, establish resource pools for each of the workload groups, based on information gathered from step 3.
5 Load test the system, ensuring enough load is generated for all resource groups to enable appropriate contention in order to observe the performance impact once Resource Governor CPU throttling kicks in.
6 Adjust and refine the pool and/or workload group parameters until the desired result is achieved.
7 Apply the results to production, ensuring the dedicated administrator connection is available.

Such an approach enables more realistic starting values to be used, while also producing a deeper understanding of resource usage for each of the workload groups.

16.7   *Best practice considerations: Resource Governor*

Prior to SQL Server 2008, the only mechanisms available for controlling resource usage were coarse-grain settings such as CPU Affinity and Query Governor Cost Limit. The introduction of Resource Governor in the Enterprise edition of SQL Server 2008 now enables much finer control over resource usage, but like any feature, system performance may suffer if it's used incorrectly.

- Resource Governor is most effective when resource usage is well defined and consistent across a number of distinct groups, for example, data entry and reports. In cases where certain data entry transactions dominate resource usage, Resource Governor may not be effective, unless there is a method of identifying and classifying the source of such transactions.

- Classifier functions should be small, simple, and execute quickly to ensure logins do not time out waiting for the function to execute. The function should be tested, ideally under load, before production implementation.

- Workload groups and resource pools should be as simple as possible, and you should take care when assigning minimum values, particularly for memory. Complex pools and groups run the risk of wasted memory and less-than-expected resource availability.

- When setting minimum resource values, consider the effective maximums that will apply to other pools as a result.

- Minimum memory values are reserved up front, regardless of the usage frequency of the pool. Therefore, take particular care when setting memory minimums.

- Before assigning resource pool boundaries, assign groups to the default pool with 0/100 min/max values and observe the resource usage over time. Understanding how groups use resources will lead to more realistic resource settings.

- Consider the security of classification functions; for example, APP_NAME() can be spoofed by someone with access to a connection string to circumvent logon triggers and workload group classification.

- The names of Resource Governor groups and pools should not contain sensitive information, given their inclusion in error messages presented to the user.

- The dedicated administrator connection (DAC) should be enabled, which assists in troubleshooting the classifier function.

- When load testing the impact of a max CPU pool setting, ensure there is sufficient CPU contention such that the CPU maximum value is actually applied. If there is no concurrent activity to cause contention, the maximum limit will not be applied.

Additional links and information on the best practices covered in this chapter can be found online at http://www.sqlcrunch.com/resourcegovernor.

In the next and final chapter, we'll bring together a number of topics that we've covered throughout the book by introducing a performance-tuning methodology called *waits and queues*.

17

Waits and queues:
a performance-tuning
methodology

In this chapter, we'll cover

- SQLOS
- Wait analysis
- Common performance problems
- Correlating waits and queues

Performance tuning, particularly performance troubleshooting, can be tough work. With entire books (and careers) dedicated to this topic, what can we possibly hope to achieve in a single chapter? Rather than attempt to provide a root cause analysis for a wide variety of potential performance problems, the goal of this chapter is to introduce you to a performance-tuning methodology called *waits and queues*.

Tom Davidson's excellent whitepaper SQL *Server 2005 Waits and Queues* is a must read for anyone interested in SQL Server performance tuning. Equally applicable to SQL Server 2008, it argues the case for a targeted approach to performance tuning by determining the resources that processes are spending the most time *waiting* on. Knowing this enables the analysis of a smaller subset of *queues*, therefore eliminating inconsequential data from the analysis-and-troubleshooting process.

In this chapter, we'll begin with an overview of the SQL Operating System (SQLOS) with a particular focus on its scheduling mechanism, part of which is the use of a waiter list for processes waiting on resources to become available. We'll then focus on the analysis of this waiter list as part of a targeted performance-tuning process using the waits and queues methodology. We'll spend the rest of the chapter on common performance problems and how waits and queues metrics can assist in the diagnosis of such problems.

17.1 *SQLOS schedulers*

SQL Server is a large and complex product with many interconnected components requiring access to common services such as memory allocation and process scheduling. In order to reduce the complexity of each of these components, the SQL Server architecture includes a layer responsible for providing common services.

In SQL Server 2000, this layer, known as the *User Mode Scheduler (UMS)*, was quite thin and had limited responsibilities. Therefore, the ability of the various SQL Server components to take maximum advantage of emerging hardware architecture such as NUMA and hot-add memory was limited. In addressing this, Microsoft rewrote this layer in the SQL Server 2005 release and renamed it the SQL Operating System (SQLOS). Figure 17.1 illustrates SQLOS in relation to other components.

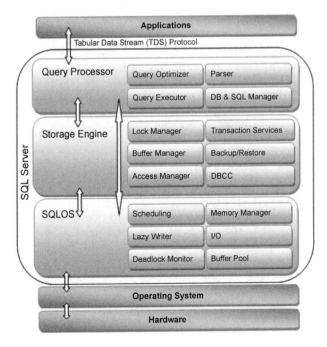

Figure 17.1 Shown here are some (but not all) of the SQL Server components. The SQLOS layer provides common services to a number of components.

While some of the SQLOS services could be provided by the Windows operating system directly, SQL Server includes them in SQLOS to maximize performance and scalability. Scheduling is a good example of such a service; SQL Server knows its scheduling requirements much better than Windows does. Thus, SQLOS, like the UMS before it, implements scheduling itself.

User requests are scheduled for execution by SQLOS using *schedulers*. SQLOS creates one scheduler for each CPU core that the SQL Server instance has access to. For example, an instance with access to two quad core CPUs would have eight active schedulers. Each of these schedulers executes user requests, or SPIDs, as per the example shown in figure 17.2.

When a running process requires a resource that isn't available, for example, a page that's not found in cache, it's moved to the wait list until its resource is available, at which point it's moved to the runnable queue until the CPU becomes available to complete the request. A process moves through the three states until the request is complete, at which point it enters the sleeping state.

From a performance-tuning perspective, what's very beneficial is the ability to measure the wait list over time, in order to determine which resources are waited on the most. Once this is established, performance tuning becomes a more targeted process by concentrating on the resource bottlenecks. Such a process is commonly called the w*aits and queues methodology*.

Let's drill down into the various means of analyzing the wait list as part of a performance tuning/troubleshooting process.

17.2 *Wait analysis*

Prior to SQL Server 2005, the only means of obtaining information on wait statistics was through the use of the undocumented DBCC SQLPERF(waitstat) command. Fortunately, SQL Server 2005 (and 2008) provides a number of fully documented DMVs for this purpose, making them a central component of *wait analysis*.

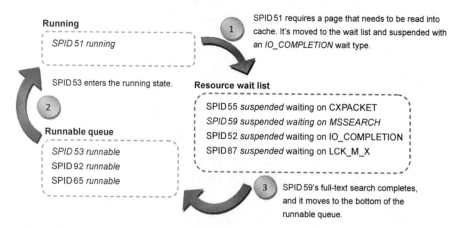

Figure 17.2   SQLOS uses one scheduler per CPU core. Each scheduler processes SPIDs, which move among the running, suspended, and runnable states/queues.

Let's look at wait analysis from two perspectives: at a server level using the sys.dm_os_wait_stats DMV and at an individual process level using extended events. This section will focus on measuring waits. In the next section, we'll look at the association of particular wait types with common performance problems.

17.2.1 sys.dm_os_wait_stats

As we mentioned earlier, when a session requires a resource that's not available, it's moved to the wait list until the resource becomes available. SQLOS aggregates each occurrence of such waits by the wait type and exposes the results through the sys.dm_os_wait_stats DMV. The columns returned by this DMV are as follows:

- *wait_type*—SQL Server Books Online documents over 200 wait types returned by this DMV. There are three categories of wait types: resource waits, queue waits, and external waits. Queue waits are used for background tasks such as deadlock monitoring, whereas external waits are used for (among other things) linked server queries and extended stored procedures. In this chapter, our focus will be on resource waits such as disk I/O and locks.
- *waiting_tasks_count*—This column represents the total number of individual waits recorded for each wait type.
- *wait_time_ms*—This represents the total amount of time spent waiting on each wait type.
- *max_wait_time_ms*—This is the maximum amount of time spent for a single occurrence of each wait type.
- *signal_wait_time_ms*—This represents the time difference between the end of each wait and when the task enters the runnable state, that is, how long tasks spend in the runnable state. This column is important in a performance-tuning exercise because a high signal wait time is indicative of CPU bottlenecks.

As with other DMVs, the results returned by sys.dm_os_wait_stats are applicable only since the last server restart or when the results are manually reset using DBCC SQLPERF ("sys.dm_os_wait_stats", CLEAR). Further, the results are aggregated across the whole server, that is, the wait statistics for individual statements are not available via this DMV.

The sys.dm_os_wait_stats DMV makes server-level wait analysis very simple; at any time this DMV can be inspected and ordered as required. For example, figure 17.3 shows the use of this DMV to return the top 10 wait types in descending order by the total wait time. As we move throughout this chapter, we'll examine these wait types and how they can be correlated with other performance-monitoring data.

Despite the obvious usefulness of this DMV, the one limitation is that it returns *all* wait types, including system background tasks such as LAZYWRITER_SLEEP, which are not relevant in a performance-analysis/tuning process. Further, we need to manually analyze and rank the returned values in order to determine the most significant waits. In addressing these issues, we can use the track_waitstats and get_waitstats stored procedures.

```
select top 10
    [wait_type]
    , [waiting_tasks_count]
    , [wait_time_ms]
    , [max_wait_time_ms]
    , [signal_wait_time_ms]
from sys.dm_os_wait_stats
order by [wait_time_ms] desc
```

Results | Messages

	wait_type	waiting_tasks_count	wait_time_ms	max_wait_time_ms	signal_wait_time_ms
1	SQLTRACE_BUFFER_FLUSH	729717	2918897546	5265	4546
2	LAZYWRITER_SLEEP	4180712	2918203093	2468	327703
3	PAGEIOLATCH_SH	378602241	2425698750	13515	4983421
4	RESOURCE_SEMAPHORE_QUERY_COMPILE	380587	1181076734	177796	269406
5	OLEDB	224060460	364494250	1269562	0
6	BACKUPBUFFER	53000065	269705171	2046	1300593
7	PAGEIOLATCH_EX	16102091	131712031	12015	260734
8	SOS_SCHEDULER_YIELD	938994068	126788343	6453	126481296
9	LCK_M_IX	4240	117155734	300625	1296
10	BACKUPIO	24708788	83245859	5906	239687

Figure 17.3   You can use the output from the sys.dm_os_wait_stats DMV to determine the largest resource waits at a server level.

17.2.2 Track/get waitstats

The track_waitstats and get_waitstats stored procedures were written by Microsoft's Tom Davidson for internal use in diagnosing SQL Server performance issues for customer databases. While not officially supported, the code for these stored procedures is publicly available and widely used as part of performance-tuning/troubleshooting exercises.

Originally written to work with DBCC SQLPERF(waitstats), they've since been rewritten for the sys.dm_os_wait_stats DMV and renamed to track_waitstats_2005 and get_waitstats_2005. Working with both SQL Server 2005 and 2008, these stored procedures operate as follows:

- The track_waitstats_2005[1] stored procedure is executed with parameters that specify how many times to sample the sys.dm_os_wait_stats DMV and the interval between each sample. The results are saved to a table called *waitstats* for later analysis by the get_waitstats_2005 procedure.

- The get_waitstats_2005[2] procedure queries the waitstats table and returns aggregated results that exclude irrelevant wait types. Further, as shown in figure 17.4, the results are broken down by resource waits (wait time minus signal wait time) and signal waits, enabling a quick assessment of CPU pressure.

One of the (many) nice things about these procedures is that they can be called with parameter values that automatically clear the wait statistics, which is helpful in situations in which the monitoring is to be performed while reproducing a known problem. When you clear the waitstats before the event is reproduced, the waits will more accurately represent the waits causing the problem.

---

[1] See http://www.microsoft.com/technet/scriptcenter/scripts/sql/sql2005/waitstats/sql05vb049.mspx?mfr=true.
[2] See http://www.microsoft.com/technet/scriptcenter/scripts/sql/sql2005/perf/sql05vb021.mspx?mfr=true.

```
exec get_waitstats_2005
```

Results	Messages							
	start time	end time		duration (hh:mm:ss:ms)	report format	report order		
1	2008-09-01 13:30:42.993	2008-09-01 13:39:43.210		00:09:00:217	all	resource		

	wait_type	waiting_tasks_count	Resource wt (T1-T0)	res_wt_%	Signal wt (T2-T1)	sig_wt_%	Total wt (T2-T0)	wt_%
1	***total***	0	2213680	100.0	287201	100.0	2500881	100.0
2	PAGEIOLATCH_SH	177933	1107016	50.0	4437	1.5	1111453	44.4
3	SQLTRACE_BUFFER_FLUSH	135	540015	24.4	0	0.0	540015	21.6
4	RESOURCE_SEMAPHORE_QUERY_COMPILE	362	285921	12.9	250	0.1	286171	11.4
5	OLEDB	48752	138062	6.2	0	0.0	138062	5.5
6	PAGEIOLATCH_EX	9608	78281	3.5	265	0.1	78546	3.1
7	ASYNC_NETWORK_IO	54626	28438	1.3	16062	5.6	44500	1.8
8	WRITELOG	5867	19093	0.9	1453	0.5	20546	0.8
9	RESOURCE_SEMAPHORE	331	8265	0.4	0	0.0	8265	0.3
10	LCK_M_IX	4	6984	0.3	0	0.0	6984	0.3

	total waits	total signal=CPU waits	CPU resource waits % = signal waits / total waits	now
1	2500881	287201	11.0	2008-09-01 13:39:43.210

Figure 17.4 The results from `get_waitstats_2005` indicate the resources with the highest amount of waits. Irrelevant wait types are excluded.

As mentioned earlier, the wait statistics returned by sys.dm_os_wait_stats are at a server level and represent the cumulative wait statistics from all sessions. While other DMVs, such as sys.dm_os_waiting_tasks, include session-level wait information, the records exist in this DMV *only for the period of the wait*. Therefore, attempting retrospective wait analysis on a particular session is not possible, unless the information from this DMV is sampled (and saved) on a frequent basis when the session is active. Depending on the length of the session, this may be difficult to do. SQL Server 2008 offers a new alternative in this regard, using the sqlos.wait_info extended event.

17.2.3 *sqlos.wait_info extended event*

In SQL Server versions prior to 2008, events such as RPC:Completed can be traced using SQL Server Profiler or a server-side trace. SQL Server 2008 introduces a new event-handling system called *extended events*, which enables the ability to trace a whole new range of events in addition to those previously available. Extended events enable a complementary troubleshooting technique, which is particularly useful when dealing with difficult-to-diagnose performance problems.

SQL Server Books Online lists a number of possible examples of how extended events can be used. In the context of this chapter, let's look at an example where we'll create an extended event to examine wait information for a particular process. Consider the T-SQL code in listing 17.1, which creates an extended event of type sqlos.wait_info for SPID 53 and logs its wait type information to file.

Listing 17.1 sqlos.wait_info extended event

```
-- Create an extended event to log SPID 53's wait info to file
CREATE EVENT SESSION sessionWaits ON SERVER
ADD EVENT sqlos.wait_info
    (WHERE sqlserver.session_id = 53 AND duration > 0)

ADD TARGET package0.asynchronous_file_target
    (SET FILENAME = 'E:\SQL Data\waitStats.xel'
```

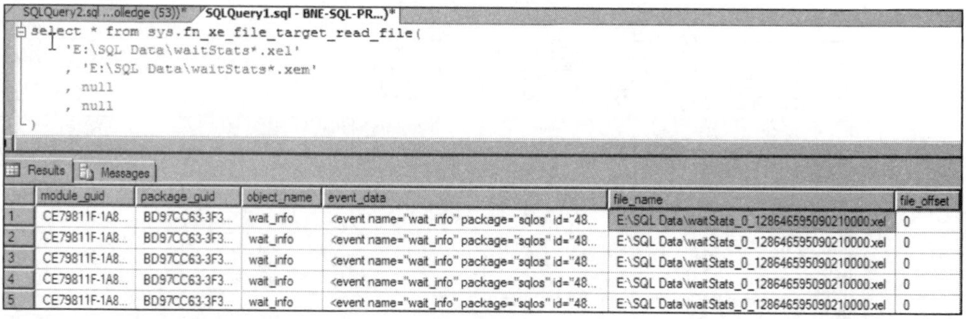

Figure 17.5   The extended event log file contains XML data (event_data). In our example, the XML would contain information on the wait types for SPID 53.

```
, METADATAFILE = 'E:\SQL Data\waitStats.xem');
```

```
ALTER EVENT SESSION sessionWaits ON SERVER STATE = START
```

The above code creates an extended event based on waits from SPID 53 with a non-zero duration. Once the event is created, any waits from this SPID will be logged to the specified file. We can read the event log file using the `sys.fn_xe_file_target_read_file` function, as shown in figure 17.5.

The wait type information that we're interested in is buried within the event_data XML. We can access this more easily using the code shown in listing 17.2.

Listing 17.2   Viewing wait type information using `sys.fn_xe_file_target_read_file`

```
-- Retrieve logged Extended Event information from file
CREATE TABLE xeResults (
    event_data XML
)
GO

INSERT INTO xeResults (event_data)
SELECT CAST(event_data as xml) AS event_data
FROM sys.fn_xe_file_target_read_file(
    'E:\SQL Data\waitStats*.xel'
    , 'E:\SQL Data\waitStats*.xem'
    , null
    , null
)
GO

SELECT
    event_data.value('(/event/data/text)[1]','nvarchar(50)') as 'wait_type'
    , event_data.value('(/event/data/value)[3]','int') as 'duration'
    , event_data.value('(/event/data/value)[6]','int') as 'signal_duration'
FROM xeResults
GO
```

Essentially what we're doing here is loading the XML into a table and reading the appropriate section to obtain the information we require. The result of this code is shown in figure 17.6.

```
select
    event_data.value('(/event/data/text)[1]','nvarchar(50)') as 'wait_type'
    , event_data.value('(/event/data/value)[3]','int') as 'duration'
    , event_data.value('(/event/data/value)[6]','int') as 'signal_duration'
from xeResults
```

Results | Messages

wait_type	duration	signal_duration
PAGEIOLATCH_SH	50	0
PAGEIOLATCH_SH	14	0
PAGEIOLATCH_SH	12	0
SOS_SCHEDULER_YIELD	3	3
SOS_SCHEDULER_YIELD	2	2

Figure 17.6 We can inspect the event_data column to obtain the wait information produced by the extended event created on sqlos.wait_info.

In this particular case, the main wait type for the SPID was PAGEIOLATCH_SH, which we'll cover shortly. While this is a simple example, it illustrates the ease with which extended events can be created in obtaining a clearer view of system activity, in this case, enabling retrospective wait type analysis on a completed session from a particular SPID. SQL Server Books Online contains a complete description of all extended events, including further details on sqlos.wait_info.

> **system_health extended event**
>
> SQL Server includes an "always on" extended event called system_health, which, among other things, captures the text and session ID of severity 20+ errors, deadlocks, and sessions with extra-long lock/latch wait times. Links and further details including a script to reveal the contents of the captured events are available at http://www.sqlCrunch.com/performance.

Let's turn our attention now to how the information gathered from wait analysis can be combined with Performance Monitor counters and other sources in diagnosing common performance problems.

17.3 Common performance problems

The rapid advance of technology together with falling component prices has meant a lot of database design and administration problems can be buried beneath a pile of memory and fast multicore CPUs. In some cases, this may be a valid option; however, throwing hardware at a problem is usually the least effective means of improving performance, with the greatest performance gains usually coming from good design and maintenance strategies.

In this section, we'll address a number of common performance problems and the wait types and performance counters applicable to each. We'll start with procedure cache bloating before moving on to CPU pressure, index-related memory pressure, disk bottlenecks, and blocking.

17.3.1 *Procedure cache bloating*

In chapter 7 we covered the various SQL Server components that utilize system memory, with the two largest components being the *data cache* and the *procedure cache*. The data cache is used for storing data read from disk, and the procedure cache is used for query compilation and execution plans.

Each time a query is submitted for processing, SQL Server assesses the contents of the procedure cache for an existing plan that can be reused. If none is found, SQL Server generates a new plan, storing it in the procedure cache for (possible) later reuse.

Reusing existing plans is a key performance-tuning goal for two reasons: first, we reduce the CPU overhead in compiling new plans, and second, the size of the procedure cache is kept as small as possible. A smaller procedure cache enables a larger data cache, effectively boosting RAM and reducing disk I/O.

The most effective way of controlling the growth of the procedure cache is reducing the incidence of unparameterized ad hoc queries.

AD HOC QUERIES

A common attribute among poorly performing SQL Server systems with a large procedure cache is the volume of ad hoc SQL that's submitted for execution. For example, consider the following queries:[3]

```
DBCC FREEPROCCACHE
GO
SELECT * FROM Production.Product WHERE ProductNumber = 'FW-5160'
GO
SELECT * FROM Production.Product WHERE ProductNumber = 'HN-1220'
GO
SELECT * FROM Production.Product WHERE ProductNumber = 'BE-2908'
GO
```

All three of these queries are exactly the same with the exception of the `ProductNumber` parameter. Using the `sys.dm_exec_cached_plans` and `sys.dm_exec_sql_text` views and functions, let's inspect the procedure cache to see how SQL Server has cached these queries. Figure 17.7 displays the results.

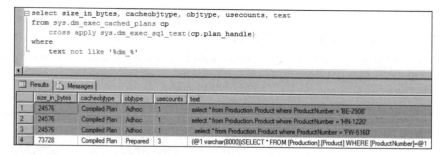

Figure 17.7   Unparameterized SQL results in multiple ad hoc compiled plans.

---

[3]   In the following examples, we'll run `DBCC FREEPROCCACHE` before each set of queries to clear the contents of the procedure cache, enabling the cache usage to be easily understood.

As per figure 17.7, SQL Server has stored one ad hoc compiled plan for each query, each of which is 24K in size, totaling ~73K. No real problems there, but let's imagine these queries were executed from a point-of-sales system used by a thousand users, each of which executed a thousand such queries a day. That's a million executions, each of which would have a 24K compiled plan totaling about 24GB of procedure cache!

There are a few things to point out here. First, as we covered in chapter 7, the procedure cache in a 32-bit system is limited to the 2–3GB address space, with AWE-mapped memory above 4GB accessible only to the data cache. This places a natural limit on the amount of space consumed by the procedure cache in a 32-bit system; however, a 64-bit system has no such limitations (which is both good and bad, and we'll come back to this shortly). Further, SQL Server ages plans out of cache to free up memory when required, based on the number of times the plan is reused and the compilation cost; that is, frequently used expensive plans will remain in cache longer than single-use low-cost plans.

The other point to note about figure 17.7 is the fourth row, which lists a *Prepared* plan with three usecounts. This is an example of SQL Server's *simple parameterization*, a topic we'll come back to shortly.

Arguably the most effective way to address the problem we just examined is through the use of stored procedures.

STORED PROCEDURES

Consider the code in listing 17.3, which creates a stored procedure used to search products and then executes it three times for the same product numbers as used earlier.

> **Listing 17.3   Stored procedure for parameterized product search**

```
-- Parameterized Stored Procedure to control cache bloat
CREATE PROCEDURE dbo.uspSearchProducts
    @ProductNumber nvarchar(25)
AS
BEGIN
    SET NOCOUNT ON

    SELECT *
    FROM Production.Product
    WHERE ProductNumber = @ProductNumber
END
GO

DBCC FREEPROCCACHE
GO
EXEC dbo.uspSearchProducts 'FW-5160'
GO
EXEC dbo.uspSearchProducts 'HN-1220'
GO
EXEC dbo.uspSearchProducts 'BE-2908'
GO
```

Figure 17.8 shows the results of reexamining the procedure cache. We have a single plan for the stored procedure with three usecounts and, more importantly, no ad hoc

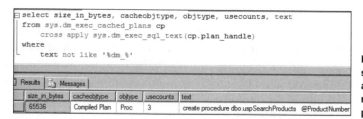

```
select size_in_bytes, cacheobjtype, objtype, usecounts, text
from sys.dm_exec_cached_plans cp
    cross apply sys.dm_exec_sql_text(cp.plan_handle)
where
    text not like '%dm_%'
```

size_in_bytes	cacheobjtype	objtype	usecounts	text
65536	Compiled Plan	Proc	3	create procedure dbo.uspSearchProducts @ProductNumber

Figure 17.8 Parameterized stored procedure executions avoid ad hoc plans, resulting in a smaller procedure cache.

plans. Compare this with the results in figure 17.7, where we ended up with three ad hoc plans, each of which has a single usecount. Each execution of the stored procedure effectively saves 24K of procedure cache; one can imagine the accumulated memory saving if this was executed thousands of times each day.

Depending on the parameter values passed into a stored procedure, caching the execution plan for subsequent reuse may be undesirable. Consider a stored procedure for a surname search. If the first execution of the procedure received a parameter for SMITH, the compiled plan would more than likely use a table scan. A subsequent execution using ZATORSKY would therefore also use a table scan, but an index seek would probably be preferred. Similar issues occur in reverse, and this is frequently called the *parameter-sniffing problem*.

In cases where stored procedures receive a wide variety of parameter values, and therefore plan reuse may not be desirable, one of the options for avoiding this issue is to create the procedure with the WITH RECOMPILE option, which will ensure the plan is not cached for reuse. That is, each execution will recompile for the supplied parameter value(s), incurring additional compilation costs in order to derive the best possible plan for each execution. Alternatively, the procedure can be defined without this option, but an individual execution can supply it, for example, EXEC dbo.uspSearchProducts 'AB-123' WITH RECOMPILE.

SET STATISTICS XML ON

The SET STATISTICS XML ON command, as covered in chapter 13, is ideal in diagnosing undesirable parameter-sniffing problems. For a given stored procedure execution, the <ParameterList> element includes both the *compiled* parameter(s) and the *runtime* parameter(s). If a given procedure appears to be executing slower than expected, you can compare the compiled and runtime parameters, which may reveal significant differences resulting in inappropriate index usage.

In dealing with ad hoc/parameterization problems such as we've just covered, the nature of the application usually determines the available options for improvement. For example, while an in-house-developed application could be modified to use stored procedures, an off-the-shelf vendor-supplied application cannot. In dealing with these cases, we have a number of options including *Forced Parameterization* and *Optimize for Ad Hoc Workloads*.

FORCED PARAMETERIZATION

In figure 17.7, shown earlier, we inspected the procedure cache after executing three SQL statements and found that three ad hoc plans with single usecounts were created in addition to a single prepared plan with three usecounts. This is an example of SQL Server's *simple parameterization* mechanism. This mechanism has detected that the three statements are essentially the same, with the only difference being the product number parameters, and therefore share the prepared plan. The three ad hoc plans are referred to as *shell plans* and point to the full prepared plan. The shells are saved for later executions of exactly the same statement, which reuses the same prepared plan. The key word here is *exactly*; a single character difference, for example, an extra space, is enough to cause a new plan to be created.

Simple parameterization is exactly that. There are many conditions in which simple parameterization cannot be used. For example, consider the three queries in listing 17.4.

Listing 17.4 Queries that cannot be parameterized with simple parameterization

```
DBCC FREEPROCCACHE
GO
SELECT * FROM Production.Product WHERE left(ProductNumber, 3) = 'FW-'
GO
SELECT * FROM Production.Product WHERE left(ProductNumber, 3) = 'HN-'
GO
SELECT * FROM Production.Product WHERE left(ProductNumber, 3) = 'BE-'
GO
```

The use of the `left` function means these three commands cannot be parameterized using simple parameterization. Let's inspect the procedure cache to see how SQL Server has cached these queries. Figure 17.9 displays the results. In this case, there is no prepared plan, with each ad hoc compiled plan containing the full plan; notice that the size of each plan is larger than the shell plans from the earlier simple parameterization example in figure 17.7. If queries such as these were executed many times per day, we would have an even worse problem than the one described earlier.

In SQL Server 2005, an option called *Forced Parameterization* was introduced, which is more aggressive in its parameterization. Each database contains a Parameterization

```
select size_in_bytes, cacheobjtype, objtype, usecounts, text
from sys.dm_exec_cached_plans cp
    cross apply sys.dm_exec_sql_text(cp.plan_handle)
where
    text not like '%dm_%'
```

	size_in_bytes	cacheobjtype	objtype	usecounts	text
1	81920	Compiled Plan	Adhoc	1	select * from Production.Product where left(ProductNumber, 3) = 'BE-'
2	57344	Compiled Plan	Adhoc	1	select * from Production.Product where left(ProductNumber, 3) = 'HN-'
3	57344	Compiled Plan	Adhoc	1	select * from Production.Product where left(ProductNumber, 3) = 'FW-'

Figure 17.9 Queries of moderate complexity cannot be parameterized using simple parameterization.

```
select size_in_bytes, cacheobjtype, objtype, usecounts, text
from sys.dm_exec_cached_plans cp
    cross apply sys.dm_exec_sql_text(cp.plan_handle)
where
    text not like '%dm_%'
```

Results | Messages

	size_in_bytes	cacheobjtype	objtype	usecounts	text
1	24576	Compiled Plan	Adhoc	1	select * from Production.Product where left(ProductNumber, 3) = 'BE-'
2	24576	Compiled Plan	Adhoc	1	select * from Production.Product where left(ProductNumber, 3) = 'HN-'
3	24576	Compiled Plan	Adhoc	1	select * from Production.Product where left(ProductNumber, 3) = 'FW-'
4	98304	Compiled Plan	Prepared	3	(@0 int,@1 varchar(8000))select * from Production . Product where left (ProductNumber , @0) = @1

Figure 17.10   After we enabled the Forced Parameterization option, the same three queries are parameterized.

property, which by default is set to Simple. Setting this value to Forced, through either Management Studio or using the ALTER DATABASE [dbname] SET PARAMETERIZATION FORCED command, will parameterize queries more frequently. For example, after enabling this property, rerunning the three queries from listing 17.4 will reveal a procedure cache, as shown in figure 17.10.

In this case, the three ad hoc plans are created as shell plans with a link to the full prepared plan. Subsequent queries of the same form will also benefit from reusing the prepared plan, thereby reducing compilation and plan cache size, which in turn enables more efficient use of both RAM and CPU resources.

Of course, modifying any configuration setting is not without a possible downside. SQL Server Books Online documents all of the considerations for using this option, the primary one being the possibility of reusing an inappropriate plan, with reduced performance a common outcome. However, for applications in which modifying code to use stored procedures is not an option, forced parameterization presents an opportunity for reducing compilation overhead and procedure cache size. Before enabling this option on a production system, a full load test with an appropriate workload should be observed in a testing environment to measure the positive (or negative) impact.

Optimization hints

In order to derive the best execution plan, SQL Server supports a number of query hints, fully described in SQL Server Books Online under "Query Hints." In addition to Forced Parameterization and WITH RECOMPILE, several other options exist, such as OPTIMIZE FOR and USE PLAN. OPTIMIZE FOR directs the query optimizer to use a specified value for a given parameter during query optimization (but uses the real value during execution). USE PLAN forces the query optimizer to use a specified XML query plan for a given query, which is useful in situations in which other options are not successful and complete control is required. Finally, Plan Guides are useful in situations in which the SQL or stored procedures cannot be modified, which is typical of third-party applications. Plan Guides direct the optimizer to add specified query hints to queries it optimizes of a particular format.

Despite the (possible) plan reuse, both forced and simple parameterization still cache the ad hoc plans, which for systems containing a very large number of single-use ad hoc queries presents a real problem in containing procedure cache size. In addressing this issue, SQL Server 2008 introduces *Optimize for Ad Hoc Workloads*.

OPTIMIZE FOR AD HOC WORKLOADS

New in 2008

In the worst examples, single-use unparameterized ad hoc plans can consume a very significant percentage of memory. For 64-bit instances, this is a particular problem, as the procedure cache has full access to all of the instance's memory. As a result, a very large procedure cache directly impacts the size of the data cache, leading to more and more disk I/O and significant cache churn.

Perhaps the most frustrating part of this for a DBA is that the ad hoc plans may never be used more than once. Forced parameterization may help in this regard but comes with some downsides, as we just covered.

DBCC FREEPROCCACHE vs. FREESYSTEMCACHE

In order to prevent ad hoc plans from bloating the procedure cache, some DBAs manually execute (or schedule) the DBCC FREEPROCCACHE command, which empties the procedure cache. Often seen as a hack, not only does this throw out the "bad" plans, it also throws out the good (and possibly expensive) plans with high reuse from all databases in the instance. Two alternatives to this method are running DBCC FLUSH-PROCINDB (which removes plans only for a specified database) and DBCC FREESYS-TEMCACHE('SQL Plans'), which clears out the ad hoc and prepared plans, leaving stored procedure plans in place.

The Optimize for Ad Hoc Workloads option is designed for exactly these situations. Enabled at a server level, this option detects ad hoc SQL and stores a simple stub in place of a plan. Should the same query be run a second time, the stub is upgraded to a full plan. As a result, the memory footprint of single-use ad hoc SQL is dramatically reduced.

After executing sp_configure 'Optimize for ad hoc workloads', 1 and putting our database back into the simple parameterization mode, we reran our three queries from listing 17.4. After executing these queries, we inspected the procedure cache, the results of which are shown in figure 17.11.

```
select size_in_bytes, cacheobjtype, objtype, usecounts, text, query_plan
from sys.dm_exec_cached_plans cp
    cross apply sys.dm_exec_sql_text(cp.plan_handle)
    cross apply sys.dm_exec_query_plan(cp.plan_handle)
where
    text not like '%dm_%'
```

	size_in_bytes	cacheobjtype	objtype	usecounts	text	query_plan
1	336	Compiled Plan Stub	Adhoc	1	select * from Production.Product where left(ProductNumber, 3) = 'BE-'	NULL
2	336	Compiled Plan Stub	Adhoc	1	select * from Production.Product where left(ProductNumber, 3) = 'HN-'	NULL
3	336	Compiled Plan Stub	Adhoc	1	select * from Production.Product where left(ProductNumber, 3) = 'FW-'	NULL

Figure 17.11 After we enabled the Optimize for Ad Hoc Workloads option, ad hoc queries are stubbed and have no saved query plan.

There are a few things to point out here. First, note the cacheobjtype column for the three queries. Instead of Compiled Plan, we have Compiled Plan Stub. Second, note the size_in_bytes value (336 bytes vs. ~ 57,000/82,000 bytes in figure 17.9). Third, the join to the sys.dm_exec_query_plan function reveals the absence of a stored query plan.

What's happening here is that SQL Server detects these queries as ad hoc and not parameterized and therefore does not store a plan; however, it stores the stub in order to detect subsequent executions of the queries. For example, let's reexecute the first query from listing 17.4 and take another look at the procedure cache. The results are shown in figure 17.12.

Note the difference in the size_in_bytes, cacheobjtype, usecounts, and query_plan columns for the first query that we reexecuted. By saving the stub from the first execution, SQL Server is able to detect subsequent executions as duplicates of the first. Thus, it upgrades the plan from a stub to a full plan on the second execution, with the third (and subsequent) executions able to reuse the saved plan.

For environments containing large amounts of single-use ad hoc SQL, the Optimize for Ad Hoc Workloads option is a *very* significant new feature. Not only does it dramatically reduce the size of the procedure cache, but it still enables plan reuse in cases where identical ad hoc queries are executed many times, therefore also reducing CPU-related compilation pressure.

In closing our section on procedure cache usage, let's look at a number of techniques for measuring the cache contents and plan reuse.

MEASURING PROCEDURE CACHE USAGE

The T-SQL code in listing 17.5 summarizes the contents of the sys.dm_exec_cached_plans DMV. It lists the number of plans for each object type (ad hoc, prepared, proc, and so forth) along with the number of megabytes consumed by such plans and the average plan reuse count.

Listing 17.5 Summary of procedure cache

```
-- Summary of Procedure Cache Contents
    SELECT
        objtype as [Object Type]
        , count(*) as [Plan Count]
```

```
select size_in_bytes, cacheobjtype, objtype, usecounts, text, query_plan
from sys.dm_exec_cached_plans cp
    cross apply sys.dm_exec_sql_text(cp.plan_handle)
    cross apply sys.dm_exec_query_plan(cp.plan_handle)
where
    text not like '%dm_%'
```

	size_in_bytes	cacheobjtype	objtype	usecounts	text	query_plan
1	57344	Compiled Plan	Adhoc	2	select '' from Production.Product where left(ProductNumber, 3) = 'FW-'	<ShowPlanXML xmlns="http:
2	336	Compiled Plan Stub	Adhoc	1	select '' from Production.Product where left(ProductNumber, 3) = 'BE-'	NULL
3	336	Compiled Plan Stub	Adhoc	1	select '' from Production.Product where left(ProductNumber, 3) = 'HN-'	NULL

Figure 17.12 Rerunning an ad hoc query converts the stub into a full plan.

```
    , sum(cast(size_in_bytes as bigint))/1024/1024 as [Total Size (mb)]
    , avg(usecounts) as [Avg. Use Count]
FROM sys.dm_exec_cached_plans
GROUP BY objtype
```

Procedure caches suffering from a high volume of ad hoc SQL typically have a dispro-portionate volume of ad hoc/prepared plans with a low average use count. Listing 17.6 determines the size in megabytes of such queries with a single-use count.

Listing 17.6 Size of single-use ad hoc plans

```
-- Procedure Cache space consumed by AhHoc Plans
    SELECT SUM(CAST(size_in_bytes AS bigint))/1024/1024 AS
        [Size of single use adhoc sql plans]
    FROM sys.dm_exec_cached_plans
    WHERE
        objtype IN ('Prepared', 'Adhoc')
        AND usecounts = 1
```

From a waits perspective, the RESOURCE_SEMAPHORE_QUERY_COMPILE wait type is a good indication of the presence of query compilation pressure. SQL Server 2005 intro-duced a throttling limit to the number of concurrent query compilations that can occur at any given moment. By doing so, it avoids situations where a sudden (and large) amount of memory is consumed for compilation purposes. A high incidence of this wait type may indicate that query plans are not being reused, a common problem with frequently executed unparameterized SQL.

Another method for determining plan reuse is measuring the following Perfor-mance Monitor counters:

- SQL Server SQL Statistics:SQL Compilations/Sec
- SQL Server SQL Statistics:SQL Re-Compilations/Sec
- SQL Server SQL Statistics:Batch Requests/Sec

With these counter values, we can measure plan reuse as follows:

```
Initial Compilations = SQL Compilations/Sec - SQL Recompilation/Sec
Plan Reuse = (Batch Req/sec - Initial Compilations) / Batch Req/sec
```

In other words, of the batch requests coming in per second, how many of them are resulting in query compilations? Ideally, in an OLTP system, this should be less than 10 percent, that is, a 90 percent or greater plan reuse. A value significantly less than this may indicate a high degree of compilations, and when observed in conjunction with significant RESOURCE_SEMAPHORE_QUERY_COMPILE waits, it's a reasonable sign that query parameterization may well be an issue, resulting in higher CPU and mem-ory consumption.

Poor plan reuse not only has a direct impact on available RAM, but it also affects CPU usage courtesy of higher amounts of compilations. In the next section, we'll address CPU pressure from a general perspective.

17.3.2   *CPU pressure*

How do you measure CPU pressure for a SQL Server system? While classic Performance Monitor counters such as Processor:% Processor Time and System:Processor Queue Length provide a general overview, they are insufficient on their own to use in forming the correct conclusion. For that, we need to look a little further, with signal waits a critical consideration.

SIGNAL WAITS

Earlier in the chapter, we looked at how SQLOS uses schedulers (figure 17.2) in allocating CPU time with processes (SPIDs) moving between three states: running, suspended, and runnable. There can be only a single SPID in the running status of a given scheduler at any one time, with the runnable queue containing SPIDs that are ready to run. The classic analogy used when discussing this model is the supermarket checkout line; that is, SPIDs in the runnable queue can be considered in the same manner as people lining up in the checkout queue: they have their groceries and are ready to leave, pending the availability of the checkout operator.

As we saw earlier, the sys.dm_os_wait_stats DMV includes a signal_wait_time_ms column, which indicates the amount of time, in total, processes spent in the runnable status for each wait type. Calculating the sum total of the signal wait time for all wait types as a percentage of the overall wait time gives a good indication of the depth of the runnable queue and therefore an indication of CPU pressure, from a SQL Server perspective.

When calculating the signal wait percentage, you should consider excluding certain wait types, LAZYWRITER_SLEEP, for example. Earlier in the chapter, we looked at the get/track_waitstats procedures, which take care of this automatically. A similar script is included toward the end of this section, in listing 17.7.

Generally speaking, a signal wait percentage of more than 25 percent may indicate CPU pressure, particularly in combination with a sustained high value for Processor:% Processor Time (> 80 percent). However, in some cases, CPU percentage may be well below 100 percent even though there is still significant CPU pressure. In such cases, the SOS_SCHEDULER_YIELD wait type is more than likely in the mix.

SOS_SCHEDULER_YIELD

As we covered earlier, a single SQLOS scheduler is created for each CPU core that a SQL Server instance has access to. When a request is sent to SQL Server for execution, it's assigned to a scheduler for execution and remains on that scheduler until complete. Despite SQL Server using various mechanisms for balancing load across the available schedulers, various situations may lead to a disproportionate load being assigned to a single scheduler.

Consider the following example: at a given point, all schedulers are equally busy, and two large CPU bound queries are submitted for execution. If they land on the same scheduler, they must remain on that scheduler until complete, even if load drops off the others. When multiple CPU bound tasks are executing on one scheduler, they *yield* to each other in order to ensure each task receives equal amounts of CPU time. In our example, the two large CPU bound tasks would be yielding to each other, despite the availability of a number of idle schedulers.[4] In this case, the total CPU percentage (as reported by Performance Monitor) may be well below 100 percent, even though there is significant contention on some CPU cores.

Of course, if a system is completely CPU bound (all CPU cores), then the yielding process, exposed with the SOS_SCHEDULER_YIELD wait type, would be occurring on all schedulers. The important point is that the yielding process may be occurring on only some schedulers, even when overall CPU usage appears low. This makes the SOS_SCHEDULER_YIELD wait type an important consideration in an overall assessment of CPU pressure.

> **sys.dm_os_schedulers**
> Scheduler details can be inspected with the sys.dm_os_schedulers DMV. Querying this DMV will reveal one scheduler per CPU core that the instance has access to, a number of system schedulers, and one for the dedicated administrator connection (DAC). Included columns reveal a number of scheduler-level details such as the number of tasks and yield count.

In closing this section on CPU pressure, let's look at some DMV queries that can be used in supplementing information from the waits and queues analysis.

DMV QUERIES

The two DMV queries in this section identify signal wait percentage and top CPU consumers.

Listing 17.7 can be used to detect signal waits and resource waits as a percentage of the total wait time. As discussed previously, a high signal wait time usually indicates CPU pressure.

Listing 17.7 Signal wait time

```
-- Wait Analysis; Signal vs. Resource Waits
SELECT
    SUM(wait_time_ms - signal_wait_time_ms) as [ResourceWaitTotal]
    , CAST(100.0 * sum(wait_time_ms - signal_wait_time_ms)
        / SUM(wait_time_ms) as numeric(20, 2)) AS [ResourceWait%]
    , SUM(signal_wait_time_ms) AS [SignalWaitTotal]
    , CAST (100.0 * sum(signal_wait_time_ms)
        / SUM (wait_time_ms) AS numeric(20, 2)) AS [SignalWait%]
FROM sys.dm_os_wait_stats
WHERE
    wait_type not in (
        'CLR_SEMAPHORE'
        , 'LAZYWRITER_SLEEP'
        , 'RESOURCE_QUEUE'
        , 'SLEEP_TASK'
```

---

[4] In this case restarting one of the processes would more than likely position it on an idle scheduler.

```
    , 'SLEEP_SYSTEMTASK'
    , 'WAITFOR'
)
```

Notice that the script excludes a number of wait types not relevant to a performance-tuning process. The get/track_waitstats stored procedures we covered earlier perform the same exclusions.

Listing 17.8 lists the top 50 queries ordered by CPU time. It includes the execution_count column to indicate how many times this query has been executed. Frequently executed queries with large CPU consumption are targets for optimization.

Listing 17.8   Top 50 queries by CPU consumption

```
-- Top 50 Queries by CPU Consumption
SELECT TOP 50
    queryStats.total_worker_time/queryStats.execution_count AS [Avg CPU
    ➡ Time]
    , queryStats.execution_count
    , SUBSTRING(queryText.text,queryStats.statement_start_offset/2,
      (CASE WHEN queryStats.statement_end_offset = -1
        THEN len(convert(nvarchar(max), queryText.text)) * 2
        ELSE queryStats.statement_end_offset end -
            queryStats.statement_start_offset) / 2)
AS query_text
    , dbname=db_name(queryText.dbid)
FROM sys.dm_exec_query_stats queryStats
    CROSS APPLY sys.dm_exec_sql_text(queryStats.sql_handle) AS queryText
ORDER BY
    [Avg CPU Time] DESC
```

One of the things that will become obvious as we move throughout this section is that common design problems affect a number of resources. For example, poor index selection and maintenance can have a dramatic impact on both memory and disk I/O.

17.3.3   *Index-related memory pressure*

As we covered in chapter 13, the correct selection and maintenance of indexes are crucial from a query-performance perspective. Numerous unused indexes have a large maintenance overhead, and missing or poorly maintained indexes have a double impact on resources: additional disk I/O and a reduction in the available buffer cache.

From a performance-monitoring perspective, the following performance counters are of interest in assessing the impact of poor index design and maintenance:

- *SQL Server:Buffer Manager – Page Life Expectancy*—This counter indicates the average time (in seconds) that data pages remain in memory. A common occurrence is for this value to drop suddenly in response to a large query that requires a lot of disk access, flushing data pages from memory to make way for the required data from disk. Missing indexes are a common contributor to this type of event. A system with adequate memory and good indexing should see this value in excess of 500 seconds, without frequent sudden drops during normal activity.

- *SQL Server:Buffer Manager – Buffer Cache Hit Ratio*—This counter indicates the percentage of time required pages are found in the buffer cache. The higher the value, the better, as memory access is obviously much faster than disk access. Once a SQL instance has been up and running for a period of time covering typical activity, values lower than 95 percent indicate memory pressure, one cause of which may be additional disk I/O required to fulfill queries without the appropriate indexes.

- *SQL Server:Access Methods – Full Scans/Sec*—This counter represents the number of full table (or index) scans per second. There are no benchmark numbers to compare this value against. In some cases, a table (or index) scan is actually preferred over an index lookup, as we discussed in chapter 13; however, one thing to look out for here is a sudden increase in this value, possibly indicating that an index is no longer being used. As with many other counters, baseline analysis is critical in being able to accurately detect a significant increase/decrease.

- *SQL Server:Access Methods – Index Searches/Sec*—Similar to Full Scans/Sec (but in the opposite direction), sudden *decreases* in this value may indicate an index is no longer being used.

- *SQL Server:Access Methods – Page Splits/Sec*—When a record is inserted into an index, it must be inserted *in order*. If the data page is full, the page splits in order to maintain the appropriate order. A high value for this counter may warrant the consideration of a lower fill factor, as covered in chapter 13.

In chapter 13, we covered a number of DMV-related queries that can be used to detect missing, unused, and duplicate/overlapping indexes. We won't duplicate coverage here.

In addition to increased memory pressure, poor index selection and maintenance have a direct and measurable impact on disk I/O.

17.3.4 Disk bottlenecks

Throughout this book we've covered a number of best practices pertaining to the layout of data and transaction log files, tempdb configuration, and sizing files to avoid autogrow operations. We've also covered the importance of striping data across multiple disks (spindles) and using RAID volumes for both performance and redundancy. With these things in mind, let's explore the waits and queues of significance in a disk bottleneck.

WAITS

A classic performance-tuning dictum is *there will always be a bottleneck somewhere*, the idea being to address/reduce each bottleneck until performance is acceptable. As the slowest component, the bottleneck is usually on disk, on both high- and low-performing systems. The following wait types usually occupy the top two wait-list positions (after excluding system background waits) on systems experiencing disk bottlenecks:

- *PAGEIOLATCH*—As pages are read into the buffer cache from disk, SQL Server uses a series of latches (lightweight locks) on the buffer pages as they are filled with data and released to the requesting process. Both PAGEIOLATCH_SH and

PAGEIOLATCH_EX are used as part of this process, and the appearance of these wait types in the top wait positions may be an indication of a disk I/O bottleneck, particularly when seen in combination with high disk sec/transfer counters, which we'll cover shortly.

- *ASYNC/IO_COMPLETION*—Both ASYNC_IO_COMPLETION and IO_COMPLETION indicate waits on disk I/O, with the async version typically associated with operations such as backups and restores.

- *WRITELOG*—This wait type is associated with writes to the transaction log. As covered throughout this book, locating transaction logs on dedicated disk volumes, preferably with a large battery-backed write cache, is essential in any high-volume database solution.

A top ranking of these waits necessitates the inspection of a number of related queues.

QUEUES

The classic disk-related Performance Monitor counters are *PhysicalDisk:Avg. Disk Sec/Read* and *PhysicalDisk:Avg. Disk Sec/Write*, with the commonly accepted ranges for performance as follows:

- *< 10ms*—Good
- *10–20ms*—Average/typical performance
- *20–50ms*—Slow
- *> 50ms*—Very slow, needs immediate attention

These counters measure the time in milliseconds for a read or write operation to disk and should be measured for each of the applicable disk volumes. For high-throughput applications, you need to pay particular attention to these counters for the transaction log disk, which should be well under 10ms.

As we covered earlier in the book, you should use the SQLIO and SQLIOSIM tools before commissioning any SQL Server system for production use to verify both the throughput and validity of the I/O system and compare the results to published vendor performance expectations. In addition to these counters, additional counters of interest are as follows:

- *Physical Disk:% Disk Time*—This counter measures the percentage of time the disk was busy servicing reads and writes. The generally accepted idea is that more than 50 percent may represent a bottleneck for the measured disk.

- *Physical Disk:Avg./Current Disk Queue Length*—A sustained value of more than 2 indicates the disk is struggling to service its queue. When measuring these counters, you need to consider the number of disks in the array. For example, a volume with 10 disks could reasonably service a queue of up to 20.

- *Physical Disk:Avg. Disk Reads & Writes /Sec*—As with the disk queue-length counters, you need to measure these counters in awareness of the disk volume's underlying disk count. Values approaching 90 percent of the disk's published read/writes per second capacity may indicate an approaching bottleneck.

Bear in mind that during disk-bound operations such as backups and restores, it's perfectly normal and reasonable to see sustained disk activity, with cause for concern centered on the speed or duration of the operation. For example, backing up a terabyte database to disk will obviously bottleneck on disk; however, the performance can be maximized by using dedicated backup disks, multiple backup files, and so forth.

In closing our brief look at disk I/O, let's examine a couple of DMV queries.

DMV QUERIES

The two DMV queries in this section identify queries with the largest I/O usage and database files with the highest stall rates.

Listing 17.9 lists the top 50 queries ordered by I/O usage.

Listing 17.9 Top 50 queries by I/O usage

```
-- Top 50 Queries by I/O Consumption
SELECT TOP 50
    (total_logical_reads + total_logical_writes) / execution_count AS [Avg
    ➥ IO]
    , substring (qt.text,qs.statement_start_offset/2, (
        CASE WHEN qs.statement_end_offset = -1
        THEN len(convert(nvarchar(max), qt.text)) * 2
        ELSE qs.statement_end_offset end - qs.statement_start_offset)/2
    ) AS query_text
    , qt.dbid
    , qt.objectid
FROM sys.dm_exec_query_stats qs
    CROSS APPLY sys.dm_exec_sql_text (qs.sql_handle) AS qt
ORDER BY [Avg IO] DESC
```

Listing 17.10 uses the sys.dm_io_virtual_file_stats function to inspect the *stall rate* of disk I/O per file. A stall occurs when a process waits for I/O to complete. By determining which files are stalling the most, opportunities arise for rebalancing I/O. A good example of this is multiple high-transaction-rate databases using the same physical disk(s). By segregating their database files on separate disks, you should be able to improve the throughput (and reduce the stall rate).

Listing 17.10 Database file I/O stalls

```
-- Identify database files with the highest stall rate
SELECT
    db_name(database_id)
    , file_id
    , io_stall_read_ms
    , num_of_reads
    , cast(io_stall_read_ms/(1.0+num_of_reads) as numeric(10,1)) as
      'avg_read_stall_ms'
    , io_stall_write_ms
    , num_of_writes
    , cast(io_stall_write_ms/(1.0+num_of_writes) as numeric(10,1)) as
      'avg_write_stall_ms'
    , io_stall_read_ms + io_stall_write_ms as io_stalls
```

```
        , num_of_reads + num_of_writes as total_io
        , cast((io_stall_read_ms+io_stall_write_ms)/(1.0+num_of_reads +
          num_of_writes) as numeric(10,1)) as 'avg_io_stall_ms'
FROM sys.dm_io_virtual_file_stats(null,null)
WHERE database_id > 4
ORDER BY
        database_id, avg_io_stall_ms DESC
```

As we covered in chapter 14, the Data File I/O pane in the new Activity Monitor presents some of this information in graphical form.

In closing this section on common performance problems, let's turn our attention to blocking.

17.3.5 Blocking

A *block* occurs when one query wants to access data that is locked by another. Despite blocks and locks being normal, fundamental components of any relational database management system, they present a significant problem in poorly designed databases and transactions.

In chapter 14, we covered the use of SQL Server Profiler in determining the presence of deadlocks and blocks exceeding a particular threshold. In this section, we'll cover blocking from a waits perspective.

LCK_* WAITS

SQL Server Books Online lists all of the wait types that may be encountered, including an impressive collection beginning with *LCK_*. All of these represent a wait on a particular lock being released. For example, a transaction with a *shared* lock on a row will block a separate transaction that requires an *exclusive* lock on the same row. In this case, the registered wait type will be LCK_M_X.

When the volume of locks and subsequent blocks increases, overall transaction throughput decreases, often accompanied by a reduction in Performance Monitor counters such as SQL Server SQL Statistics:Batch Requests/Sec. To the untrained eye, a severe blocking problem is often met with confusion; users complain of poor performance, but a quick check of the classic Performance Monitor counters (CPU, disk, and so forth) reveals little in the way of server load. When the blocking transaction completes, activity returns to normal.

A fundamental component of a good database design is short transaction length with the appropriate isolation level (and usually with an optimistic locking mode). Such topics are beyond the scope of this book: however, should you identify blocking as a top wait type, the sys.dm_db_index_operational_stats function can assist you in investigating the problem further.

SYS.SM_DB_INDEX_OPERATIONAL_STATS

One of the purposes of the sys.dm_db_index_operational_stats function is to determine the tables and indexes with the highest occurrence of row lock waits, as shown in listing 17.11.

Listing 17.11   Tables/indexes with high lock waits

```
-- Identify tables and indexes with the highest number of row lock waits
SELECT
    db_name(db_id())
    , object_name(s.object_id) as objectname
    , i.name as indexname
    , row_lock_count
    , row_lock_wait_count
    , cast (100.0 * row_lock_wait_count /
        (1 + row_lock_count) as numeric(15,2)) as [block %]
    , row_lock_wait_in_ms
    , cast (1.0 * row_lock_wait_in_ms /
        (1 + row_lock_wait_count) as numeric(15,2)) as [avg row lock waits in
        ➡ ms]
FROM sys.dm_db_index_operational_stats (db_id(), NULL, NULL, NULL) s
    INNER JOIN sys.indexes i on s.object_id = i.object_id
    AND s.index_id = i.index_id
WHERE objectproperty(s.object_id,'IsUserTable') = 1
ORDER BY row_lock_wait_count desc
```

In combination with the SQL Profiler blocked process report event, this script can be used to identify the source of common blocking problems. The *avg row lock waits in ms* column, as the name suggests, returns the average lock wait time. This value can be used in estimating which value to set for the sp_configure 'blocked process threshold' value, although it should be noted that the sp_configure value is set in seconds, whereas the value returned from the above script is in milliseconds.

In closing the chapter, let's summarize the waits, queues, and DMV scripts that we've covered thus far into resource categories.

17.4   *Waits, queues, and DMV cross-reference*

Figure 17.13 groups together relevant wait types, Performance Monitor counters, and DMVs by the appropriate resource bottleneck. This is certainly not an exhaustive list, but it's a reasonable starting point for further analysis.

17.5   *Best practice considerations: performance tuning*

Performance tuning is a specialist skill. In this chapter, we've briefly covered a number of common problems in addition to looking at the waits and queues methodology for a targeted tuning approach. I encourage you to visit http://www.sqlCrunch.com/ performance for links that provide broader and deeper coverage on this most important area.

- A good performance-tuning strategy considers input from multiple sources before drawing any conclusions. In this chapter, we've consider input from waits, queues, and DMVs in assisting in the diagnosis of common performance problems.
- The waits and queues methodology permits a targeted approach to performance tuning by narrowing the target to the biggest pain points identified using the sys.dm_os_wait_stats DMV.

Category	Waits	Queues	DMVs/DMFs	Additional notes and ideal values
CPU	Signal Wait % SOS_SCHEDULER_YIELD CXPACKET	% Processor Time % User Time % Privileged Time Interrupts/sec Processor Queue Length Context Switches/sec	sys.dm_os_wait_stats sys.dm_exec_query_stats sys.dm_exec_sql_text sys.dm_exec_cached_plans sys.dm_os_schedulers	Signal waits < 25%. High % privileged time may indicate hardware/driver issue. If Context Switches/sec > 20,000, *consider* fibre mode. CXPACKET waits on OLTP systems < 5%. *Consider* MAXDOP 1 and index analysis.
Memory	PAGEIOLATCH_*	Page Life Expectancy Buffer Cache Hit Ratio Pages/sec Page Faults/sec Memory Grants Pending CheckPoint Pages/sec Lazy Writes/sec Readahead Pages/sec	sys.dm_os_wait_stats sys.dm_os_memory_clerks	Page Life Expectancy > 500. Sudden page life drops may indicate poor indexing.
Disk IO	PAGEIOLATCH_* ASYNC/IO_COMPLETION WRITELOG LOGMGR	Disk Seconds/Read and Write Disk Reads and Writes/sec % Disk Time Current and Avg. Disk Queue Length Log Flush Wait Time Log Flush Waits/sec Average Latch Wait Time Latch Waits/sec Total Latch Wait Time	sys.dm_os_wait_stats sys.dm_exec_query_stats sys.dm_exec_sql_text sys.dm_io_virtual_file_stats	Ensure storage tested with SQLIO/SIM before production implementation. Disk Layout best practices including tempdb separation. autogrow/shrink and t-log separation. Disk Sec/read and write <20 ms. Transaction log disk < 10ms. Disk queue length < 2 per disk in volume.
Network	NET_WAITFOR_PACKET	Bytes Received/sec Bytes Sent/sec Output Q length Dropped/Discarded Packets	sys.dm_os_wait_stats	Consider number of application round trips. Switched gigabit network connections.
Blocking	LCK_*	Lock Waits/sec Lock Wait Time	sys.dm_os_wait_stats sys.dm_db_index_operational_stats	Consider SQL Profiler's blocked process report and deadlock graphs. Check transaction length, isolation levels and optimistic locking.
Indexing	Refer disk and memory waits	Forwarded Records/sec Full Scans/sec Index Searches/sec Pages Splits/sec	sys.dm_os_wait_stats sys.dm_db_index_operational_stats	Page Life Expectancy > 500. Sudden page life drops may indicate poor indexing.
Compilation	RESOURCE_SEMAPHORE_ QUERY_COMPILE	SQL Compilations/sec SQL Recompilations/sec Batch Requests/sec Auto Param Attempts/sec Failed Auto Param Attempts/sec Cache Hit Ratio (Plan Cache)	sys.dm_os_wait_stats sys.dm_exec_cached_plans sys.dm_exec_sql_text	Parameterized queries with sp_executesql. Consider forced parameterization (after acknowledging possible downsides). Consider "optimize for ad hoc workloads" (after acknowledging possible downsides). Pay attention to large plan cache on 64-bit systems. Plan reuse on an OLTP system should be > 90%.

Figure 17.13   Performance-tuning information sources by resource category

- A good baseline and regular baseline analysis should form part of an overall performance-tuning exercise. The values for many of the counters discussed throughout this chapter are meaningless unless seen in the context of a known value recorded during times of acceptable performance. Knowing these values is key in detecting emerging trends that can be arrested before the problem becomes widespread.

- Wherever possible, use stored procedures (or parameterized sp_executesql) instead of dynamically executed SQL using `exec`. Parameterizing SQL avoids the common procedure bloat issue whereby valuable memory (and CPU resources) is wasted on single-use ad hoc SQL; further, dynamic SQL opens up the possibilities of SQL injection attacks that we covered in chapter 6.

- In situations where direct control over application code is not possible, consider using the Forced Parameterization or the Optimize for Ad Hoc Workload option. As with all other configuration recommendations throughout this book, such changes should be made after observation in a testing environment with an appropriate workload simulation.

- In cases where a small number of queries are causing compilation issues, and the queries themselves cannot be changed, such as in a vendor-supplied application, consider using plan guides (not covered in this book) in place of Forced Parameterization.

- The excellent Microsoft whitepaper titled *Batch Compilation, Recompilation and Plan Caching Issues* is a must read in understanding the (many) issues for consideration in increasing plan usage. One such recommendation is ensuring objects are fully qualified, for example, `select * from dbo.table` rather than `select * from table`.

- For stored procedures that take a wide variety of parameter values, consider creating the procedure with the `WITH RECOMPILE` option to avoid parameter-sniffing issues whereby ongoing performance is dictated by the parameters used in the first execution. While ongoing compilation will be higher, the resultant plans are typically more accurate. In cases where the additional compilation overhead is accepted in return for improved (and consistent) performance, such an option is certainly worth considering.

Additional links and information on the best practices covered in this chapter can be found online at http://www.sqlcrunch.com/performance.

Appendix A:
Top 25 DBA worst practices

While there may be some disagreement on *best* practices, there is usually no argument on *worst* practices, some of which are listed below (in no particular order):

1   Not considering service-level agreements (SLAs) when designing a database environment and/or not considering the need for scheduled downtime for various maintenance activities, such as the installation of service packs.

2   Defining "disaster" too narrowly and not simulating/practicing a disaster recovery (DR) plan. Having a DR plan is fine, but how do you know it will work (and several people can follow it) when required?

3   Designing a storage system from a capacity perspective alone.

4   Assuming a storage area network (SAN) will meet/exceed performance requirements. Just because SANs are (typically) expensive, it does not mean the storage design process can be skipped.

5   Failing to track-align disk partitions and/or formatting them with the default allocation unit size (4K).

6   Using RAID 5 volumes for write-intensive applications.

7   Failing to validate an I/O subsystem for performance and validity before production implementation.

8   Virtualizing/consolidating SQL Server instances and databases without consideration of the scalability, licensing, support, administration, and performance profile implications.

9   Installing service packs, cumulative updates, or hotfixes without reading the release notes and/or not installing them in a test environment first.

10 Installing *all* SQL Server features on the off chance they may be needed at some point in the future. Doing so increases the attack surface area and results in running unnecessary services that may reduce performance.

11   Installing multi-instance clusters without considering the resource implications of failover situations.

12   Creating logins/jobs with elevated privileges. Implementing least privilege can be tough work, but it's essential in locking down a system for maximum security.

13   Changing configuration values from their default settings without adequate research and/or a detailed change log.

14   Placing data and transaction logs on the same physical disk(s).

15   Storing backups on the same disk as the database files.

16   Relying on autogrow for file sizing, and leaving the tempdb database at its default size.

17   Not making backups and/or not checking their validity and/or not practicing and documenting various recovery situations. All of these are equally bad.

18   Leaving the database in the full recovery model without taking transaction log backups.

19   Implementing database mirroring in high-safety (synchronous) mode without considering network latency and/or transaction log usage from index maintenance.

20   Not running regular DBCC checks.

21   Running REPAIR_ALLOW_DATA_LOSS as the primary/default recovery response, and not following up corruption events with a root-cause analysis.

22   Not evaluating index usage and/or fragmentation levels as part of an index-maintenance routine.

23   Updating statistics using the default sampling rate after a full index rebuild.

24   Using SQL Profiler in place of server-side traces, and using it as the primary performance analysis/tuning technique.

25   Doing manual administration with SQL Server Management Studio. For maximum efficiency and minimal errors, tasks should be scripted and automated, and you should employ appropriate monitoring and alerting mechanisms such as MOM or SQL Agent operators and alerts.

Appendix B:
Suggested DBA work plan

The tasks presented here are general DBA tasks that are appropriate in most instances. Obviously each environment will have specific tasks, and depending on the automation techniques and monitoring software, the implementation and monitoring of these tasks will differ. For that reason, implementation and monitoring commentary have been excluded. The goal of this section is to suggest a starting point in developing a site-specific DBA task list.

B.1 Daily tasks

- Check for successful backup completion, including tape archives if using the "disk then tape" backup methodology.
- Confirm SQL Server Agent jobs completed successfully.
- Check free disk space on all disks, including system drives and SQL Server data, log, tempdb, and backup disks.
- Check the free space of each database's data and transaction log files and expand if necessary to avoid autogrow operations.
- Check SQL Server errors logs and Windows event logs.
- Confirm DBCC checks executed without error by opening and inspecting the appropriate log files. Depending on the DBCC check frequency, this may be a weekly task.
- Check site-specific tasks as appropriate, such as the success of archive batch jobs.
- Check technology-specific tasks as appropriate, such as log shipping or database mirroring status/health.
- Throughout the day, monitor long-running queries and general performance of critical servers using a dashboard of key Performance Monitor counters.

- Stay up to date with SQL Server via magazine/website articles, blogs (using a good RSS reader), and other general-research methods. Good managers understand the importance of allocating time to this task.

B.2   Weekly tasks

- Collate and update Performance Monitor log information for baseline analysis purposes, looking for emerging trends among counter values. This information will feed into the monthly capacity-planning task.
- Review recent wait statistics and include them alongside the Performance Monitor counter information in the performance baseline.
- Execute index and statistics maintenance jobs (during periods of low activity) as appropriate. For systems with large enough maintenance windows, this may be a simple rebuild of all indexes (while being aware of the impact on log shipping/database mirroring) or a more targeted approach that selects the appropriate technique (reorganize/rebuild) based on the fragmentation level.
- Record disk usage trends and note them for the monthly capacity-planning exercise.
- Review server configuration for unauthorized configuration changes. Policy-based management is purpose built for this task.

B.3   Monthly tasks

- Review and update documentation and scripts as appropriate, ensuring their accuracy and suitability for use in disaster-recovery situations.
- Review and plan the implementation of any service packs and/or hotfixes as appropriate.
- Conduct capacity planning using the inputs from the weekly baseline-analysis and disk-usage tasks. In addition to using this as a chance to identify upcoming budgetary requirements, this task may also serve as an opportunity to consolidate databases and/or instances for a better performance/resource usage balance.
- Conduct "fire drills" to practice recovering from various failure conditions. Ideally these drills are random and unannounced and involve simulated corruption (preferably not on production databases!) to ensure all staff are capable of recovering from a wide variety of possible failure conditions. The more these events are simulated and practiced, the quicker the recovery in the event of a real disaster.

Appendix C:
Common Performance
Monitor counters

There are literally hundreds of counters that *could* be captured. The capture purpose (for example, troubleshooting or baseline analysis) usually determines which ones are included. Provided here is a list of common counters by category. Each counter is preceded by the object, for example, Processor:%Processor Time indicates the %Processor Time counter in the `Processor` object. The descriptions for all of these counters can be found in the Performance Monitor tool itself.

C.1   CPU

- Processor:%Processor Time
- Processor:Interrups/Sec
- System:Processor Queue Length
- System:Context Switches/Sec

C.2   Memory

- Memory:Pages/Sec
- Memory:Page Faults/Sec
- SQL Server Memory Manager:Memory Grants Pending
- SQL Server Buffer Manager:Buffer Cache Hit Ratio
- SQL Server Buffer Manager:Page Life Expectancy

C.3   Disk

- Physical Disk:Current Disk Queue Length
- Physical Disk:Avg. Disk Queue Length

- Physical Disk:Avg. Disk Sec/Read
- Physical Disk:Avg. Disk Sec/Write
- SQL Server Databases:Log Flush Wait Time
- SQL Server Databases:Log Flush Waits/Sec

C.4   Network

- Network Interface:Bytes Received/Sec
- Network Interface:Bytes Sent/Sec

C.5   SQL Server

- SQL Server Access Method:Forwarded Records/Sec
- SQL Server Access Method:Full Scans/Sec
- SQL Server Access Method:Index Searches/Sec
- SQL Server Access Method:Pages Splits/Sec
- SQL Server Buffer Manager:CheckPoint Pages/Sec
- SQL Server Buffer Manager:Lazy Writes/Sec
- SQL Server Buffer Manager:Readahead Pages/Sec
- SQL Server Plan Cache:Cache Hit Ratio
- SQL Server Databases:Log Growths
- SQL Server Databases:Transactions/Sec
- SQL Server General Statistics:Logins/Sec
- SQL Server General Statistics:Logouts/Sec
- SQL Server General Statistics:User Connections
- SQL Server Latches:Average Latch Wait Time (ms)
- SQL Server Latches:Latch Waits/Sec
- SQL Server Latches:Total Latch Wait Time
- SQL Server Locks:Lock Waits/Sec
- SQL Server Locks:Lock Wait Time (ms)
- SQL Server SQL Statistics:SQL Compilations/Sec
- SQL Server SQL Statistics:SQL ReCompilations/Sec
- SQL Server SQL Statistics:Batch Requests/Sec
- SQL Server SQL Statistics:Auto Param Attempts/Sec
- SQL Server SQL Statistics:Failed Auto Params/Sec

Appendix D:
Top 10 Management
Studio enhancements

1 IntelliSense, plus T-SQL collapse/expand regions.

2 Want quick information on a column's data type and nullability? Enable the Quick Info feature by selecting Edit > IntelliSense > Quick Info (or Ctrl+K, Ctrl+I). After this, simply mouse over a column in a query for pop-up information, including its nullability and data type.

3 Have you ever accidentally dropped a production table when you thought you were connected to a test server? When connecting to a new server, click Options and under the Connection Properties tab, select a custom color. Whenever a query window is opened against this server, the status bar at the bottom will display the chosen color (for example, bright red for production!).

4 Right-clicking a process within the new Activity Monitor allows the process to be tracked in Profiler with an automatic filter applied for the SPID. Further, you can automatically open Activity Monitor on startup of Management Studio by choosing Open Object Explorer and Activity Monitor in the General page of the Tools > Options menu in SQL Server Management Studio.

5 The missing index DMV information is displayed in the graphical execution plan output. Right-click it and choose Missing Index Details to display the T-SQL to create the index.

6 T-SQL Debugger (accessed by clicking the green arrow next to the ! Execute icon), with associated Step Into/Over, Breakpoints, Locals, and Call Stacks, is fantastic for tracking variable values as they pass through multiple procedures, triggers, and so forth.

7 The ability to run a query against multiple servers. Open a query window against a registered servers group. Query results will contain an extra column for the server name.

8 The Tools > Options menu (SQL Server Object Explorer section) allows you to specify the number of rows for Edit/Select Top N; for example, setting Edit Top <n> Rows Command to 12 will change the right-click menu option for a table to Edit Top 12 Rows.

9 Powershell integration. For a DBA who is responsible for managing a large number of servers, Powershell is an essential tool. Those who learn it will be one step ahead of most DBAs.

10 Right-clicking a selection of results in the query output window lets you select Copy with Headers, which allows the results to be pasted into another application with the corresponding column names.

Appendix E:
Date/time data types in SQL Server 2008

SQL Server 2008 introduces a number of new data types. In chapter 9 we covered one of these, FILESTREAM. In addition to a couple of geospatial types (GEOGRAPHY and GEOMETRY), the major new types are HIERARCHYID, used for storing data representing positions in a hierarchical structure (for example, an organizational chart), and four date-related types: DATE, TIME, DATETIME2, and DATETIMEOFFSET. Let's spend a little time exploring the new date data types, beginning with DATE.

E.1   DATE

In SQL Server 2005 and earlier, there was no way of storing a date without a time component (unless stored as a string). Further, the earliest date that could be stored was 1 Jan 1753. Fortunately, SQL Server 2008 introduces the DATE type, and as the name suggests, it stores only the date without a time component.

Consuming just 3 bytes (compared to 8 bytes for DATETIME), DATE types are stored in the format YYYY-MM-DD and permit dates from 0001-01-01 through to 9999-12-32.

E.2   TIME

One of the limitations of the old DATETIME data type (which is still available) is the precision of the time component. Accurate to .333 second, the DATETIME type lacked granularity for certain applications, an issue addressed by the TIME type.

In addition to supporting the ability to store just the time component (without a corresponding date), the TIME data type, consuming between 3 and 5 bytes, is accurate to 100 nanoseconds and permits the storage of time values from 00:00:00.0000000 through 23:59:59:9999999.

E.3   *DATETIME2*

With a storage footprint of between 6 and 8 bytes, DATETIME2 combines the advantages of the DATE and TIME types, enhancing DATETIME by allowing dates from 0001 and times accurate to 100 nanoseconds.

E.4   *DATETIMEOFFSET*

DATETIMEOFFSET further enhances the DATETIME2 type by accommodating a time zone offset component. With a storage size of between 8 and 10 bytes, DATETIMEOFF-SET types are ideal for multinational database applications.

To further illustrate these data types, let's cast a string in both the old datetime formats (DATETIME and SMALLDATETIME) as well as the four new types covered above:

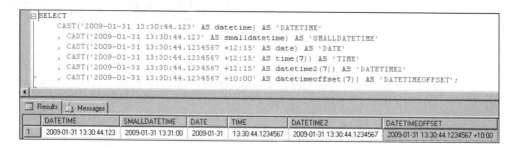

index

Symbols

/3GB 129–131
/PAE 130–131
##MS_PolicyTsqlExecution-
    Login## 164
% Disk Time 410
% Processor Time 406
%TMP% 365

Numerics

32-bit memory management 131
64-bit memory management 131

A

abnormal activity 331
acceptable data loss 229
Active Directory 151
active transaction 197
active/active 84
active/passive 84
Activity Monitor 171, 331–334
ad hoc queries 398
Address Windowing Extensions
    (AWE) 44, 129
addressable memory 44
administration cost 184
advanced cluster completion 87
advanced cluster preparation 87
advanced installation. See install-
    ing SQL Server 2008
AdventureWorks database 291
AES encryption algorithm 121
aggregate query cost 341
alerts 354

alias 101
allocation bitmap 171
allocation contention 171, 174
allocation errors (DBCC) 265
allocation unit 33, 35
  size 181
ALTER DATABASE 204
ALTER DATABASE SET
    PARTNER 246
ALTER RESOURCE
    GOVERNOR 386
Analysis Services 154, 376
antivirus software 92, 127
application design 12
application failure 68
application performance 12
application reconnection
    logic 245
application roles 110
APP_NAME() 117, 378
archive filegroup 176
asynchronous database mirror-
    ing. See database mirroring
asynchronous statistics
    update 322
ASYNC_IO_COMPLETION 410
ATA 16
at-rest encryption 119
attach database (upgrade
    technique) 72
audit 112
audit action groups 112, 147
auditing
  C2 111
  database audit
    specification 113
  implementing 111–119

server audit specification 112
  SQL Server audit 111–115
  support per SQL edition 7
authentication mode 65
  Mixed Mode 98
  Windows authentication
    mode 97
auto create statistics 321
auto stats event 322
auto update statistics 321
autoclose 157, 191, 304–305
autogrow 363
autogrowth 154, 172
automatic failover
    (mirroring) 243
automatic failover support 230
automation 331, 350–358
autosense (networking) 50
AutoShrink 157, 191
availability target 226, 229
average disk queue length 372
average latency (SQLIO) 40
avg row lock waits in ms 413
Avg. Disk Reads & Writes /
    Sec 410
Avg. Disk Sec/Read 410
Avg. Disk Sec/Write 410
Avg./Current Disk Queue
    Length 410
AWE. See Address Windowing
    Extensions

B

background services 144
backup
  checksum 210

backup *(continued)*
  compression 221–223, 232
  compression default 221
  convenience 223
  COPY_ONLY backup 203–204
  dedicated disks 170
  design 195, 199, 221
  destination, disk vs. tape 207
  devices 225, 359
  differential backup 199–200,
    351
  disk 170
  duration 184
  filegroup backup 214
  frequency 154, 201
  full backup 196–198
  hard-coded filename 225
  maintenance plans 352
  MDW database 367
  mirroring 210
  multiple files 199
  portability 221
  retention policy 209
  rotation policy 209
  scheduling 223
  snapshot backups 209, 217
  strategy 195, 219, 223
  support per SQL edition 7
  tail log backups 202
  transaction log 198, 200–203
  upgrade technique 72
  verification 195, 231
  verification servers 224
  window 210
  WITH COMPRESSION 221
  WITH COPY_ONLY 237
  WITH NORECOVERY 202
  WITH NO_TRUNCATE 202
BACKUP DATABASE 197
BACKUP DATABASE MIRROR
  TO 210
BACKUP DATABASE WITH
  CHECKSUM 210
BACKUP DATABASE WITH
  COMPRESSION 221
BACKUP DATABASE WITH
  DIFFERENTIAL 199
backup domain controller
  (BDC) 61
BACKUP LOG 200
BACKUP LOG WITH
  NORECOVERY 203, 215
BACKUP LOG WITH
  NO_TRUNCATE 202
BACKUP WITH
  COPY_ONLY 204
backups, SATA disk 17
backwards compatibility 68

bandwidth requirements 17
base backup 200
baseline analysis 38, 53, 57,
  348–350, 360
batch process 53
batch request/sec 372, 348,
  405
battery-backed cache 37
BCDEdit 129
BCM. *See* Bulk Changed Map
BCP. *See* Bulk Copy Process
BDC. *See* backup domain controller
BEGIN TRANSACTION WITH
  MARK 211
benchmarking. *See* baseline analysis
best practices
  backup and recovery 223
  Data Collector and MDW 374
  data management 190
  database mirroring 256
  DBCC validation 278
  failover clustering 91
  high availability 256
  indexes 325
  installing and upgrading SQL
    Server 75
  log shipping 256
  monitoring and
    automation 358
  physical server design 56
  policy-based management 166
  Resource Governor 388
  security 124
  SQL Server configuration 145
  storage system sizing 30
binary large object (BLOB)
  storage in the database 178
  storage in the filesystem 179
  See also FileStream
bit mask (NUMA node) 49
BitLocker 127
BLOB. *See* binary large object
block replication 24
blocked process report 345, 413
blocked process threshold 345
blocking 263, 412
BOL. *See* SQL Server Books
  Online
bookmark lookup 285
boost SQL Server priority 135
boot time 28
boot.ini 129
bottleneck 12
  disk 32
  RAM 47
  SSD implications 29

breaking point. *See* baseline analysis
brute-force attack 97
b-trees 178, 284
budgetary constraints 3, 21
buffer cache 180, 184–185, 189,
  197
Buffer Cache Hit Ratio 409
buffer overflow bug 101
buffer pool 269
bug 75
BUILTIN\Administrators 66,
  104
Bulk Changed Map (BCM) 206
Bulk Copy Process (BCP) 206,
  340
bulk insert 206
bulk load 242
bulk update 41
Bulk_Logged recovery
  model 206, 232, 239
bus bandwidth 17

C

cache (storage) 37
  bloat. *See* procedure cache
  churn 403
  efficiency 34
calculating required disk
  quantity 15
capacity-centric design 18
capacity planning 172–173, 191,
  370, 371
CDC. *See* Change Data Capture
cell erasure (SSD) 29
cell-level encryption 119, 123
central management servers 159
central point of failure 228, 230
centralized computing 51
certificate 120
change control 148
Change Data Capture
  (CDC) 117–119
  support per SQL edition 7
change log 128, 145, 257
character large object
  (CLOB) 177
check constraints 268
checklist (installation) 59
checkpoint 38, 41, 140, 197, 204
checksum 210, 269
classifier function (Resource
  Governor) 378–379
cleanup tasks (maintenance
  plans) 353
client redirection logic 227

client-side trace 337
CLOB. *See* character large object
CLR. *See* Common Language Runtime
CLRIntegrationEnabled 152
cluadmin.msc 91–92
cluster management tool 91
cluster security policy 90
clustered index 281–284, 288–291
clustering. *See* failover clustering
cmdlets 164
codeplex.com 291
collation 60, 64, 247
column prefix 185
column statistics 322–323
command center 330
command prompt installation 67
commodity servers 32
Common Language Runtime (CLR) 152
Compact edition 8
compatibility level 69
composite index 295–296
composite keys 283
compressed backups 221–223
compression (NTFS) 5, 35
   rate 186, 222
   See also data compression, backup compression
compute constrained systems 30
computed columns 267
condition (policy-based management) 152
conditional index maintenance 353
configuration changes history report 337
configurationfile.ini 66
connection properties (Management Studio) 160
connection string 62, 71, 379
connection strings (passwords) 98
consistency errors (DBCC) 265
constraining resources 376
context switches/sec 136
CONTINUE_AFTER_ERROR 210
controller cards 36
controlling object placement 175
copy database wizard 73
copy on write 217
COPY_ONLY backup 203–204
Core i7 43
corrupt backup 226

corrupted page 241
corruption 260
   logical 268
   physical 268
   root cause analysis 278
cost savings 221
cost threshold for parallelism 139
counter logs 348
covering indexes 286, 295–296
CPU
   affinity 137, 376
   affinity mask 49
   boost SQL Server priority 135
   cache 43
   clock speed 43
   compilation pressure. *See* procedure cache
   cost threshold for parallelism 139
   fiber mode 136
   hot-add 46
   hyperthreading 42
   Itanium 44
   kernel mode 136
   lightweight pooling 136
   max worker threads 69, 135–136
   multicore 42
   Opteron 44
   overhead (compression) 184
   parallelism 137
   support per SQL edition 45
   thread pooling 135
   threads 134
   throttling with Resource Governor 384
   user mode 136
   x64 44
   x86 44
   Xeon 45
CREATE DATABASE AS SNAPSHOT 218
CREATE EVENT SESSION 395
CREATE RESOURCE POOL 385
CREATE STATISTICS 324
CREATE WORKLOAD GROUP 385
credentials 105
credit card details (encryption) 120
cumulative updates 74, 223
custom reports 374
custom statistics 322

D

DAC. *See* dedicated administrator connection
daily tasks 419
damaged database 203
DAS. *See* direct-attached storage
data
   corruption 241
   distribution. *See* replication
   encryption 119–123
   integrity 23
   latency 230
   loss 195, 202, 242
data access pattern 175
data cache 130, 140
data center 19
Data Collector
   cache directory 365
   component overview 361
   custom collection sets 368
   default collection sets 361
   logging 368
   new in 2008 5
   scheduling uploads 365
   setup and configuration 362–365
   support per SQL edition 7
data collector sets (Performance Monitor) 348
data compression 164, 183–189
   support per SQL edition 6
Data Dude 256
data file configuration
   AutoClose 191
   autogrowth 172
   AutoShrink 191
   instant initialization 174
   multiple files 171
   proportional fill 174
   sizing files 172
   volume separation 169
data file I/O 332
data type conversion 303
data warehousing 117, 317
database administrator (DBA) 11
   development DBA 10
   production DBA 10, 330
   responsibilities 10
   work plan 419
database audit specification 112
database consistency check. *See* DBCC
database console commands. *See* DBCC
database design 29

database encryption key
    (DEK) 121
Database Engine Tuning
    Advisor 313–314, 341
Database Exposure Survey
    2007 101
database integrity 260, 352
Database Mail 7, 125, 152, 155,
    355
database migration 67, 172
database mirroring overview 228
  automatic corruption
      recovery 270
  automatic failover 243
  configure security 248
  design considerations 246
  encryption 249
  endpoint 239, 249
  failover 239
  failure scenarios 246
  FileStream limitations 182
  forced service 239, 241, 245
  high performance mode 239,
      241
  high safety mode 239–240,
      242
  initializing 247
  log sequence number
      (LSN) 240
  log stream compression 241
  manual failover 245, 254
  mirror database 238
  mirror instance 238
  mirroring multiple
      databases 255
  monitor 250
  monitoring stored
      procedures 251
  network latency 243
  performance counters 252
  principal database 238
  principal instance 238
  recovery model 247
  redo queue 238–241
  restrictions 239
  resuming 254
  send queue 238–239
  snapshots 259
  SQL logins 247
  status 250
  support per SQL edition 6
  suspending 253
  TCP port 249
  terminology 238
  thresholds 252
  timeout 244
  witness 239

database ownership chain 127
database roles 108–110
database snapshots 182,
    217–221, 239
DatabaseMailEnabled 152
DATETIME data types 425
David Litchfield 101
DBA. See database administrator
DBCC
  auditing 113
  commands categorized 261
  database snapshot 263
  false positives 263
  I/O load 14
  interpreting output 274
  page restore 276
  REPAIR_ALLOW_DATA_
      LOSS 273, 277
  REPAIR_REBUILD 274
  source (database
      snapshots) 221
  transactional consistency 263
  user defined snapshots 273
DBCC CHECKALLOC 262, 267
DBCC CHECKCATALOG 262,
    267
DBCC CHECKCONSTRAINTS
    268
DBCC CHECKDB 262
  ALL_ERRORMSGS 264
  controlling user impact 270
  DATA_PURITY 265
  described 262
  ESTIMATE_ONLY 264
  EXTENDED_LOGICAL_
      CHECKS 264
  last successful execution 272
  MAXDOP 272
  NOINDEX 264
  NO_INFOMSGS 264
  repair options 264
  TABLOCK 264
  WITH PHYSICAL_ONLY 265,
      271
DBCC
      CHECKFILEGROUP 267,
      272
DBCC CHECKIDENT 268
DBCC CHECKTABLE 262, 267,
    272
DBCC DBREINDEX 318
DBCC DROPCLEANBUFFERS
    188–189, 293
DBCC FREEPROCCACHE 403
DBCC
      FREESYSTEMCACHE 403
DBCC INDEXDEFRAG 317

DBCC PAGE 272, 275
DBCC SHOWCONTIG 315
DBCC SHOW_STATISTICS 287,
    324
DBCC SQLPERF 392–394
DBCC TRACEON 272, 345
DBCC UPDATEUSAGE 70
dbcreator 111
db_datareader 111
db_datawriter 111
dbi_dbccLastKnownGood 272
DCM. See Differential Changed
    Map
DDL triggers 115–116, 153
deadlock 343–344
  graph 344
  trace flags 345
  victim 344
debugging 334, 338, 340
decentralized computing 51
decision support system
    (DSS) 13
dedicated administrator connec-
    tion (DAC) 136, 143, 379
dedicated disks 170
default filegroup 176, 214
default instance 62–63
default schema 110
default trace 154, 337
DEK. See database encryption key
density_vector 324
design surface 350
detach database 172
detach database (upgrade
    technique) 72
detecting corruption 268
Developer edition 8
development environments 205
DHCP. See Dynamic Host Config-
    uration Protocol
differential backup 199–200
Differential Changed Map
    (DCM) 203
direct-attached storage
    (DAS) 22, 169
directory locations 66
dirty pages 140, 197
dirty reads 142
disabling indexes 316
disaster recovery (DR) 23, 174
  planning 206
  SAN options 24, 27
  simulation 223
  time 229
  virtualization 55
disconnect users 234

disk
  backups 207
  configuration 32
  controller 172
  controller cards 22
  drive anatomy 32
  enclosures 22
  failure 18, 36
  fragmentation 33, 168, 173
  head 32
  mirroring 20
  performance 185
  quantity 25
  queue 18, 36
  response time 372
  space requirements
    (installation) 63
  transfer rate 372
  usage report 361, 370
  utilization 20, 25
disk management tool 35
disk reads per second 14
disk then tape backups 208
disk writes per second 14
diskpar.exe 34
diskpart.exe 34
display replay results 340
distributed partitioned views 7
distributed transactions 240
DML triggers 115
documentation 162, 206, 223
domain accounts 60
domain administrator 60
double caching 37
downtime 68, 74
DR. *See* disaster recovery
drive letters (mount points) 171
drivers 38, 268
DROP DATABASE 219
DROP STATISTICS 323
dropped events 337–338
dropping indexes 316
DSS. *See* decision support system
dual channel SCSI 16
Dynamic Host Configuration
  Protocol (DHCP) 82
Dynamic Management View
  (DMV) 304
dynamic ports 100

E

ECC. *See* error-correcting code
editions of SQL Server
  Compact 8
  Developer 8
  Enterprise 5

  Express 8
  Standard 7
  Web 8
  Workgroup 7
effective maximum percentage
  (Resource Governor) 382
EFS 127
EKM. *See* Extensible Key Management
encryption 5
  See also cell level encryption,
    TDE, data encryption,
    backup encryption, *and* SSL
endpoint 239, 249
enterprise DBA 148
Enterprise edition 5
environment destruction 231
error logs 357
error-correcting code (ECC) 46
ESX Server. *See* virtualization
ETL. *See* extract, transform, load
event alert 356
event sequencing 337, 340
EVENTDATA function 115
event tracing 337
exception-based
  management 150, 350
exclusive lock 344
ExecuteSql() 162
ExecuteWql() 162
execution plan 291, 321
expensive queries 333
exporting policies (policy-based
  management) 158
Express edition 8
extended events 395
Extensible Key Management
  (EKM) 127
extent 35, 206, 265–266
external waits 393
extract, transform, load
  (ETL) 117

F

facet (policy-based
  management) 151
failback settings. *See* failover clustering
failover
  database mirroring 243
  log shipping 237
Failover Cluster Configuration
  Program (FCCP) 82
failover clustering
  advantages and limitations 80

  architecture 79
  cluster network priority 92
  failover rules 85
  FCCP certification 82
  high availability 227
  iSCSI storage 24
  multi-instance clusters 84
  N + 1/M clusters 85
  quorum models 82–83
  resource groups 80
  single instance clusters 84
  validation test 81
failover partner (SNAC) 244
failure rate (tape) 207
failure tolerance (RAID) 21
false positive (DBCC) 263
fault tolerance 36, 169
faulty hardware 260
fiber mode 136
fibre channel 17, 22
file header 266
file I/O streaming access
  (filestream) 180
file system (blob storage) 179
filegroup backup 214
filegroups 175–177
  dbcc checks 272
  default filegroup 176
  primary filegroup 176
  secondary filegroup 176
FileStream
  allocation unit size 181
  DBCC checks 263
  described 180–183
  installing 66
  limitations 182
fill factor 141, 319, 409
filtered indexes 297–299
  compared to indexed
    views 303
filtered statistics 324
fine-grained auditing 111
fire drill 206
firewall 61
  perimeter configuration 100
  ports 100
  Windows firewall 101
firmware 38, 268
five nines 229
fixed database roles 111
fixed server roles 111
flash storage. *See* solid-state disk
fn_trace_getinfo 338
follow the sun 298
forced
  parameterization 401–403
forced service 239, 241
foreign keys 268, 307

foreign keys (DBCC) 277
fragmentation 35, 168, 173
fragmentation (indexes) 314
free list 140
FTP utility 127
full backup 196–198
full duplex 17
full recovery model 205, 232, 239
full scan 324
Full Scans/Sec 409
full table index 298
full text indexes 284

G

GAM. *See* global allocation map
get_waitstats 394
GFS. *See* grandfather-father-son
global allocation map (GAM) 266
globally unique identifier (GUID) 117, 290, 340
grandfather-father-son (GFS) tape rotation policy 209
GRANT CONNECT 249
granular auditing 111
graphical execution plan 291, 333
group policy editor 130
GROUP_MAX_REQUESTS 381
growth patterns 173
GUID. *See* globally unique identifier

H

hard error 244
hardening (disk writes) 38
hardware components 31
hardware NUMA. *See* non-uniform memory access
hardware security module (HSM) 127
hash join 323
HBA. *See* host bus adapter
heap 274, 281, 284
heartbeat (mirroring) 244
heat generation 28
hidden snapshot (dbcc) 273
high availability 226
  options compared 229
high performance database mirroring. *See* database mirroring
high-performance mode 239
high-safety mode 239
histogram 325

host bus adapter (HBA) 22
HOST_NAME() 378
hot spots 331
hot standby 238
hot-add CPU 46
hot-add RAM 46
hotfix 74, 223
HP Integrity Superdome 45
HP ProLiant DL585 36
HSM. *See* hardware security module
hubs (networking) 50
Hyper-V. *See* virtualization
hypervisors. *See* virtualization

I

I/O
  capacity 36
  delay messages 154, 162
  driver 38
  failure 36
  firmware 38
  generation 38
  integrity (SQLIOSIM) 41
  IOPS 38
  latency 38
  load balancing (multipathing) 37
  profile 26
  thread (NUMA) 49
  throughput 38
I/O per second (IOPS) 15
IANA registration database 100
IDE. *See* ATA
identity columns 289, 323
identity spoofing 98, 379
image data type 178
inaccessible database 203
included columns 286, 296–297
increaseuserva 129
incremental servicing model 74
index scan 175, 291
Index Searches/Sec 409
index seek 291
indexed views 299–303
  compared to filtered indexes 303
  DBCC checks 263
  support per SQL edition 7
indexes
  analysis 303–316
  bookmark lookup 285
  clustered index 281–283, 288–291
  composite index 296
  conditional maintenance 353
  covering indexes 286, 295–296

create with drop existing 319
data compression 320
design 287–303
disabling 316
dropping 316
duplicate and overlapping indexes 307
dynamic management views 303
fill factor 141, 319
filtered indexes 297–299
fragmentation 314–316, 319
full table index 298
full text indexes 284
heap 281
hint 292
identifying indexes to add 307–314
identifying indexes to drop/disable 304–307
included columns 286, 297
key lookup 286
leaf node 284
maintenance 316–320
maintenance plans 352
nonclustered index 283–284, 291
online operations 318
PAD_INDEX 320
predicate 298
range scan 290
rebuild 242, 318
reorganize 317, 351
seek 284
selectivity 287
sort 290
sort in tempdb 320
SSD implications 29
statistics 320–322
structure 284–285
support per SQL edition 7
information storage explosion 183
infrastructure solution 231
in-place upgrade 70
input verification (SQL injection) 124
installation center 62
installation checklist 59
installing SQL Server 2008
  command prompt installation 67
  GUI installation 62–67
  installing a clustered instance 86–91
  pre-installation checklist 59–62
instance ID 62

instant initialization 60, 173–174
integrated installation. *See* installing SQL Server 2008
Integration Services 376
integrity 38
intent-based management 150
interleaved NUMA. *See* non-uniform memory access
Internet Protocol Security (IPSec) 102
internet SCSI (iSCSI) 23
Invoke-PolicyEvaluation cmdlet 165
IO_COMPLETION 410
IOPS. *See* I/O per second
IPAll 100
IPSec. *See* Internet Protocol Security
IPv6 81
IsAlive 85
iSCSI. *See* internet SCSI
IS_MEMBER() 379
isolation level 344
IS_SRVROLEMEMBER() 379

J

job failover 230
join logic 323

K

kernel mode 136
key column 297
key lookup 286, 291, 294

L

LAN. *See* local area network
lane (PCI) 36
large object (LOB) 177
latency 38
LazyWriter 41, 49, 140
LAZYWRITER_SLEEP 393
LCK_* waits 412
.ldf file 169
leaf node (index) 284
least privilege 103–111, 149
license terms 63
licensing 56
lightweight pooling 136
linked servers 127
load balancing (I/O) 37
load generation 338
load testing
    high availability 256
    LoadRunner 343

OStress 342
Resource Governor considerations 384
Visual Studio Team System 343
LoadRunner 343
LOB. *See* large object
local administrator 60
local administrator privilege 103
local area network (LAN) 243
local server groups 160
lock pages in memory 60, 130–132
locks (configuration setting) 142
log chain 200, 203, 219
    validation 231
log sequence number (LSN) 119, 198, 240
log shipping
    backup verification 224
    disconnect users 234
    failover and role reversal 237
    monitoring instance 236
    no recovery mode 234
    overview 227
    pre–SQL Server 2000 230
    recovery model 205
    restore frequency 236
    script configuration 236
    standby mode 234
    status report 236
    transaction latency 231
    usage scenarios 231
    warm standby 236
log stream compression 241
logical corruption 268
logical integrity 262
logical reads 293, 333
logical unit number (LUN) 22
    configuring for SQL Server 26
    replication 23
    snapping and cloning 209
    zoning 27
logical write 16
login failover 230
login timeout 378
logins/sec 372
logon triggers 116–117, 378
long-running transactions 205
LooksAlive 85
lossless compression 183
lossy compression 183
LSN. *See* log sequence number
LUN. *See* logical unit number

M

magnetic erase 127
maintenance plans 314, 350–353
maintenance window 53, 74, 270
Majority Node Set (MNS) 82
man-in-the-middle attacks 98
MAN. *See* metropolitan area network
management data warehouse (MDW) 361
    advantages of centralizing 363
    autogrow operations 363
    backup considerations 367
    configure MDW wizard 362
    database roles 364
    mdw_admin 364
    mdw_reader 364
    mdw_writer 364
    retention period 368
manual failover, (log shipping) 237
manual failover (mirroring) 245
master boot record (MBR) 33
master database 239
master key 120
max worker threads 69, 135–136
MAXDOP. *See* Maximum Degree of Parallelism
Maximum Degree of Parallelism (MAXDOP) 154, 137–139, 187, 320, 381
max_wait_time_ms 393
MBR. *See* master boot record
.mdf file 169
MDW. *See* management data warehouse
mdw_admin 364
mdw_reader 364
mdw_writer 364
media cost 196
media failure 208
memory bus. *See* non-uniform memory access
memory sniffing 122
merge join 323
metropolitan area network (MAN) 243
Microsoft assessment and planning toolkit 51
Microsoft Baseline Security Analyzer (MBSA) 153
Microsoft iSCSI Software Initiator 24
Microsoft Multipath I/O (MPIO) 36

Microsoft product support services (PSS) 340
Microsoft Source Code Analyzer for SQL Injection 124
Microsoft Virtual Server. *See* virtualization
migrating databases 67
mirror commit overhead 253
mirror database 238
mirror instance 238
mirroring backups 210
mirroring session 240
missing index 314
missingindexes XML element 307
MissingIndexGroup XML element 309
mission-critical database 231
mixed extent 266
Mixed Mode authentication 65, 98
MNS. *See* Majority Node Set
model database 169, 173, 204, 239
monitoring instance 236
monitoring regime 350
monitoring tools 330
monthly tasks 420
mount points 171
MPIO. *See* Microsoft Multipath I/O
msdb database 166, 239, 367
MSDTC 91
multi-server queries 160
multi-file backups 199
multipathing 36
multiple column statistics 321
multiple data files 171
multiple standby destinations 230
MySQL 148

N

named instances 62–63, 100
namespace 110
NAS. *See* network-attached storage
Native Command Queuing (NCQ) 16
natural key 289
NCQ. *See* Native Command Queuing
.ndf file 169
nested loop join 323
net send 355
NetBIOS 61

.NET framework 62
network
    autosense 50
    bandwidth 50, 241
    configuring 50
    data transmission 122
    hubs 50
    latency 243
    NIC teaming 24, 50, 92
    quality 247
    saturation 255
    switches 50
    traffic 50
network-constrained systems 30
network protocols
    AppleTalk 99
    Banyan Vines 99
    Multiprotocol 99
    Named Pipes 99
    NWLink IPX/SPX 99
    shared memory 99
    TCP/IP 99
    VIA 99
network-attached storage (NAS) 23
NewSequentialID() 290
NIC teaming 50
no majority. *See* failover clustering
NO_CHECKSUM 210
node and disk majority. *See* failover clustering
node and file share majority. *See* failover clustering
noexpand 303
nonclustered index 262, 283–284, 290–291
non-uniform memory access (NUMA) 47–50, 146, 357
notify operator task (maintenance plans) 352
NTFS compression 35, 183
NUMA. *See* non-uniform memory access
nvarchar(max) data type 178

O

object placement 175
offline 305
offsetting partitions 33
offsite recovery point 231
offsite rotation (backup tape) 207
off-the-shelf components 32
OLAP. *See* online analytical processing

OLTP. *See* online transaction processing
on demand (policy-based management) 153
on schedule (policy-based management) 153
on-call rotation 148
online analytical processing (OLAP) 13, 138
online backups 197
ONLINE index operations 318
online piecemeal restore 72, 212–217
online transaction processing (OLTP) 13, 138, 145
operating costs 52
operations staff 148
operator 355
Opteron 45
Optimization hints 402
OPTIMIZE FOR 402
Optimize for Ad Hoc Workloads 403–404
Oracle 148
ORIGINAL_LOGON 117
OStress 342, 349
out-of-the-box settings 148
owner-qualified object reference 415

P

P2V. *See* physical to virtual
pad_index 320
PAE. *See* Physical Address Extensions
page 140, 266
    checksums 269
    compression 185
    dictionary 185
    file 145
page free space (PFS) 266
Page Life Expectancy 408
page restore 276
Page Splits/Sec 409
PAGEIOLATCH 409
pager alert 355
PAGE_VERIFY 210
parallel ATA. *See* ATA
parallel queries 137
parallelism 44, 381
parameter sniffing 309, 400
parity 20
partitioning 164
partition offset. *See* track-aligning partitions
partitioned tables 177

partitioning 6
password complexity 60, 97
  policies 97
password expiration 60
  policies 97
Paul Randal 198
PCI Express (PCI-E) 36
PCI-E. *See* PCI Express
PDC. *See* primary domain controller
peak latency (SQLIO) 40
peak usage period 349
peer-to-peer transactional
  replication 259
pending reboots 61
PerfAnalysis database 341
perform volume maintenance
  tasks 60, 174
performance baseline 27
performance-centric design 18
performance condition
  alert 356
Performance Monitor 14, 27,
  346–350, 387
  counters 421
performance requirements 32
performance trends 348
performance tuning 12
permissions management 110
PFS. *See* Page Free Space
Physical Address Extensions
  (PAE) 129
physical corruption 268
physical integrity 262
physical reads 293, 37, 333
physical security 120, 127
physical to virtual (P2V) 54
physical write 16
piecemeal restore 175
plan cache 44
plan count 333
Plan Guides 402
plan reuse. *See* procedure cache
platter 32
point-in-time recovery 205, 207,
  209, 217
policy (policy-based
  management) 153
policy compliance 153
policy failure alerts 156
PolicyAdministratorRole 164
policy-based management 51
  ##MS_PolicyTsqlExecution-
    Login## 164
  alerts 356
  central management
    servers 161
  conditions 152

creating new policies 157
evaluating policies 155
evaluation modes 153
exporting policies 158
facet 151
importing policies 153
new in 2008 4
policies 153
policy state 154
PolicyAdministratorRole 164
Powershell 164
predefined policies 154
target 151
poor maintenance practice 226
port 1433 100
port scanners 101
possible owner. *See* failover clustering
power consumption 28
power failure 37, 244
Powershell 147, 164–166
precedence constraint (maintenance plans) 352
predefined policies (policy-based
  management) 153
preferred owner. *See* failover clustering
preinstallation checklist 59
prepared plans 401
preserved on import (policy-
  based management) 154
preventing corruption 268
primary data file 169
primary domain controller
  (PDC) 61
primary filegroup 175–176
primary key 282, 288
principal 107
principal database 238
principal instance 238
principals (proxy) 106
private network 92
proactive maintenance 150, 173,
  191, 227
procedure cache
  AWE setting 130
  bloating 398–405
processadmin 111
processes 332
Processor Queue Length 406
product key 63
production DBA 330
proportional fill 174
proxies 106
public certification authority
  certificates 102
public network 92
pure NUMA. *See* non-uniform
  memory access

Q

query governor cost limit 143,
  388
query importance 380
query optimizer 307, 321
query statistics (report) 361, 371
query wait 142
queue depth (HBA
  configuration) 27
queue depth (SQLIO) 39
queue wait 393
quorum, failover clustering 82

R

RAID. *See* redundant array of
  inexpensive disks
RAM
  32-bit memory
    management 131
  64-bit memory
    management 131
  controlling usage with
    Resource Governor 383
  ECC RAM 46
  hot-add 46
  lock pages in memory 60,
    130–132
  maximum memory
    setting 132–134
  minimum memory
    setting 132–134
  page file 145
  query wait 142
  support per SQL edition 46
random I/O 13, 170, 286, 291
random read performance
  (SSD) 29
random write performance
  (SSD) 29
range scan 290
rate of database change (differential backups) 199
reactive administration 3
reactive work environment 227
read ahead 41, 294
read cache 37
read/write percentage 27
reading a database mirror (database snapshots) 220
readtrace 341–342
rebuilding indexes 318
recompilation 400
reconfigure server (policy-based
  management) 161
recovering state 200
recovery interval 140

recovery model
  bulk_logged 206, 232, 239
  full 149, 205, 232, 239
  MDW database 367
  simple 204
recovery point 196
redo queue 239–241
reduced maintenance
    requirements 205
reducing backup impact 221
Redundant Array of Inexpensive
    Disks (RAID) 19
  hardware RAID 22
  RAID 0 19
  RAID 1 20
  RAID 10 21
  RAID 5 20
  RAID controller 33
  software RAID 22
  stripe size 33
refresh rate 331
registered servers 159
registry 62
regulatory requirements 183
Reliability and Performance
    Monitor 347
remote memory. See non-uni-
    form memory access
reorganize indexes 317
REPAIR_ALLOW_DATA_LOSS
    277
replay events, in order 339
replay events, multiple
    threads 340
replay markup language
    (RML) 343
replay server 339
replay threads 339
replaying a trace 338
replication 227, 340
replication (upgrade
    technique) 73
Report Builder 381
Reporter (RML utility) 342
reporting database 271
reporting database (database
    snapshots) 220
Reporting Services 154, 376
reporting solution 230–231
reports
  custom reports 374
  disk usage summary 370
  query statistics history 371
  server activity history 372
REQUEST_MAX_CPU_TIME_
    SEC 381
REQUEST_MAX_MEMORY_
    GRANT_PERCENT 380

REQUEST_MEMORY_GRANT_
    TIMEOUT_SEC 381
resource arbitration 80
resource crunch 85
resource flexibility 54
Resource Governor 376
  Activity Monitor 332
  benefits and limitations 376
  classifier function 377–379
  CPU considerations 383
  effective maximum and
      minimums 382
  establishing resource
      boundaries 388
  load testing 384
  memory considerations 383
  monitoring 387
  new in 2008 4
  resource pools 377, 382–384
  workload groups 377,
      380–382
resource pools (Resource
    Governor) 382–384
resource segregation 376
resource starvation 383
resource throttling 383
resource waits 393
RESOURCE_SEMAPHORE_
    QUERY_COMPILE 405
response time 38
restoration time 195
restore
  complexity 202
  differential backup
      restore 200
  FROM
      DATABASE_SNAPSHOT
      219
  full backup restore 198
  online piecemeal restore 72,
      212–217
  page restore 276
  STOPBEFOREMARK 211
  support per SQL edition 6
  synchronized restores 211
  transaction log restore 202
  WITH NORECOVERY 200
  WITH RECOVERY 202
  WITH STOPAT 202
RESTORE DATABASE 198
RESTORE DATABASE FROM
    DATABASE
    SNAPSHOT 219
RESTORE DATABASE WITH
    NORECOVERY 200
RESTORE DATABASE WITH
    PARTIAL 215

RESTORE LOG WITH
    NORECOVERY 203, 237
RESTORE LOG WITH
    RECOVERY 203, 237
RESTORE LOG WITH
    STOPAT 203
RESTORE LOG WITH
    STOPBEFOREMARK 211
restoring compressed
    backups 221
retrospective performance
    troubleshooting 348
ribbon cable 16
RID. See row id
role reversal, log shipping 237
role-based security 107–111
roll back 198, 200
roll forward 198, 200
rollback (DBCC) 277
ROLLBACK (DDL Trigger) 116
rollback point 217, 232
rolling back database changes
    (database snapshots) 220
root cause analysis 278
row compression 185
row id (RID) 284
  lookup 291
row locator 284
ROWGUIDCOL 181
RPC:Completed 335
run as 107
run to cursor 340
runaway query 376
runnable queue 392

S

SA account 65, 97
sampling frequency 349
sampling frequency
    (statistics) 323
SAN. See storage area network
SAS. See Serial Attached SCSI
SATA. See Serial ATA
scalability 44
schedulers 392
schema 110
schema binding 301
schema comparison tools 256
SCOM. See Systems Center Oper-
    ations Manager
script configuration 236
scripting a trace definition 337
SCSI. See Small Computer Sys-
    tems Interface
secondary data file 169
secondary filegroups 176, 217
sector 32

securable 107
secure environment 95
Secure Sockets Layer (SSL) 102
security breach 226
security identifier (SID) 247, 257
security notifications 127
security token 97
seek (index) 284
seek latency 17, 28
selectivity 287, 321
self-managing features 148
self-signed certificates 98, 102
send queue 239
separation of powers 104
sequential I/O 13, 170, 286, 291
Serial ATA (SATA) 16, 170
Serial Attached SCSI (SAS) 17, 170
serializable isolation level 344
server activity (report) 361, 372
server audit specification 112
server components 31
server consolidation 51–56, 62
server load 349
Server Message Block (SMB) 61
server replacement policy 56
server-side trace 337
server sizing 29
server sprawl 51
Server Virtualization Validation Program (SVVP) 55
service accounts 249, 59, 64, 104
service broker 263
service level agreement (SLA) 12, 38, 195, 202, 221, 223, 229, 256
service packs 223
  application outage 74
  installation considerations 74
  named instance 62
services (stopping unnecessary) 144
SET PARTNER FAILOVER 254
SET PARTNER FORCE_SERVICE_ALLOW _DATA_LOSS 255
SET PARTNER RESUME 254
SET PARTNER SUSPEND 253
SET STATISTICS IO 309
SET STATISTICS XML 309
set warnings thresholds (mirroring) 253
setup support files 63
setup support rules 63
SGAM. See shared global allocation map

shared global allocation map (SGAM) 266
shared lock 344
shared nothing 79
shared percentage (Resource Governor) 382
shared scalable databases 259
shared storage 80, 228
shell plans 401
shock resistance 28
show execution plan XML 308
SID. See security identifier
side-by-side upgrade techniques 71
  attach/detach 72
  backup and restore 72
  transaction log backup/restore 72
  transactional replication 73
signal waits 394, 406
signal_wait_time_ms 393
simple parameterization 401
simple recovery model 204
single-column statistics 324
single-user mode 104
sizing database files 168
SLA. See service level agreement
sliding window (disk backups) 208
sliding windows (partitioning) 177
Small Computer Systems Interface (SCSI) 16, 170
SMB. See Server Message Block
SMO. See SQL Server Management Objects
SNAC. See SQL Server Native Client
snapshot backups (SAN) 24
snapshot. See database snapshots
soft error 244
soft NUMA. See non-uniform memory access
solid-state disks (SSD) 17, 28–30
  array 29
sort space 44
SOS_SCHEDULER_YIELD 406
source control 256
sparse file 217
sp_createstats 324
sp_dbcmptlevel 69
sp_dbmmonitoraddmonitoring 252
sp_dbmmonitorchangealert 253
sp_dbmmonitorchangemonitoring 252
sp_dbmmonitordropalert 253
sp_dbmmonitordropmonitoring 252

sp_dbmmonitorhelpalert 253
sp_dbmmonitorhelpmonitoring 252
sp_dbmmonitorresults 252
sp_dbmmonitorupdate 251
specialization 148
sp_estimate_data_compression_savings 186–187
spindle-based storage 28
split brain 82
split I/O 35
split mirror backup (SAN) 27
sp_setapprole 110
sp_spaceused 70
sp_syscollector_create_collection_item 369
sp_syscollector_create_collection_set 368
sp_trace_create 338
sp_trace_setstatus 338
sp_updatestats 324
SQL Agent job steps 107
SQL compilatons/sec 372, 405
SQL injection 123–124
SQL Mail 125
SQL Operating System (SQLOS) 391
SQL recompilations/sec 372, 405
SQL Server Agent 356–357
  automating jobs 356
  event alerts 355
  job permissions 105
  Powershell job type 166
SQL Server Books Online (BOL) 9
SQL Server Browser 100
SQL Server Configuration Manager
  FileStream configuration 180
  network configuration 99
  service accounts 105
SQL Server features
  new in SQL Server 2008 4
  support per SQL edition 5
SQL Server log 270, 357
SQL Server Management Objects (SMO) 147
SQL Server management pack 354
SQL Server Management Studio 423
SQL Server Native Client (SNAC) 244
SQL Server network name 87
SQL Server Profiler 314, 332, 334–347
SQL slammer worm 101

SQL Trace 337
SQL trace file 313
SQL:BatchCompleted 335
SQLIO 38, 61
SQLIOSIM 41, 61, 268, 278
SQLOS. *See* SQL Operating System
sqlos.wait_info 395
SQLskills.com 198
SSD. *See* solid state disk
SSIS package subsystem 106
SSL. *See* Secure Sockets Layer
staggered uploads (MDW) 367
standard configuration 150
Standard edition 7
standard server build 56
standby mode 234
startup option 104, 345
StarWind iSCSI software 24
stat_header 324
static ports 100
statistics 320–325, 287
    asynchronous statistics
        update 322
    auto create statistics 321
    auto update statistics 321
    column statistics 322–323
    create statistics 324
    DBCC
        SHOW_STATISTICS 324
    density vector 324
    drop statistics 323
    filtered indexes 299
    fullscan 324
    histogram 325
    sp_createstats 324
    sp_updatestats 324
    stat header 324
    update statistics 321, 324
    updating post upgrade 69
STATISTICS IO 293
STATISTICS XML 308
status bar (Management
    Studio) 160
STOPAT 202
storage
    bottlenecks 12
    cost 199
    design 30
    formats 16
    infrastructure 22
    management 23
    requirements 27
storage allocation 23
storage area network (SAN) 22
    administrator 25
    configuring for SQL Server 25
    monitoring tools 27

performance testing 27
storage cache 27, 37
storage controller 36
storage virtualization 27
stored procedures 399
streaming events 337
streaming performance
    (FileStream) 180
stress testing 349
stripe size 33
striping 20, 26, 36
subplan. *See* maintenance plans
support lifecycle 74–75
surface area configuration 98,
    152, 154
surrogate key 289
SUSER_NAME() 379
SUSER_SNAME() 379
suspect_pages table 210
SVVP. *See* Server Virtualization
    Validation Program
switch speed (networking) 50
symmetric key 120
Symmetric MultiProcessor
    (SMP) 48
synchronized backups 211
synchronized restores 211
synchronous database mirroring.
    See database mirroring
synonyms 220
sys.database_mirroring 252
sys.database_mirroring_
    endpoints 252
sys.database_mirroring_witnesses
    252
sys.dm_database_encryption_
    keys 121
sys.dm_db_index_operational_
    stats 188
sys.dm_db_index_physical_stats
    315–316
sys.dm_db_index_usage_stats
    188, 304–305
sys.dm_db_missing_index
    DMVs 309–313
sys.dm_exec_cached_plans 398,
    404
sys.dm_exec_query_plan 404
sys.dm_exec_query_stats 333,
    361
sys.dm_exec_sql_text 398
sys.dm_io_virtual_file_stats 332,
    411
sys.dm_os_memory_clerks 48
sys.dm_os_performance_
    counters 347
sys.dm_os_schedulers 407
sys.dm_os_waiting_tasks 395

sys.dm_os_wait_stats 332, 393
sys.dm_resource_governor_
    configuration 387
sys.dm_resource_governor_
    resource_pools 388
sys.dm_resource_governor_
    workload_groups 388
sys.fn_cdc_map_time_to_lsn 119
sys.fn_xe_file_target_read_file
    396
sys.indexes 305
sys.objects 305
sys.schemas 305
sys.sm_db_index_operational_
    stats 412
sys.sp_cdc_enable_table 126
sysadmin lock-out 104
system cache 180
system database backup 223
system databases 239
system failures 154
system objects 176
system tables 169
system_health extended
    event 397
Systems Center Operations Manager (SCOM) 125, 148, 354

T

table lock (DBCC) 263
table name policy 155
table scan 40, 175, 286
tail log backups 202
tape archive 208
tape backups 207
tape drivers 211
tape rotation policy 209
tape software 211
target (policy-based
    management) 151
TCO. *See* total cost of ownership
TDE. *See* Transparent Data
    Encryption
tempdb 122
    allocation contention 171,
        266
    consolidation
        considerations 53
    dedicated disks 170
    multiple data files 171
    presizing files 173
    RAID level 19
    single vs. multi-instance 53
    sizing for DBCC 278
    sort_in_tempdb option 320
    space required for DBCC 264

test data 256
test environments 205
Test Load Agent (Visual Studio Team System) 343
testing strategy (database snapshots) 220
text data type 178
third-party backup compression tools 208, 221
thread pooling 135
threads 134
timestamp 117
toggle breakpoint 340
total cost of ownership (TCO) 24
TPC. *See* Transaction Processing Performance Council
TPC-C 45
trace
  definition 337
  file 313
  filter 335
  flag 3604 275
  flags 345
  process 332
  properties 335
  replay 338
  template 335
track 32
track-aligning partitions 33
track_waitstats 394
transaction
  performance 238
  profile 38
  rate 37
  response time 26, 242
  safety 238
  throughput 16, 241
transaction (DBCC) 277
transaction duration 37
transaction latency 231, 242
transaction log
  backup frequency 201
  backups 198, 200
  bottleneck 37
  Bulk_Logged backup 206
  checkpoint 140
  dedicated disks 16
  described 197
  growth 198
  log chain 200
  log sequence number (LSN) 198
  LUN configuration 26
  marking WITH MARK 211
  purpose and usage 200
  recovery interval 140
  restore 202

roll back 140
roll forward 140
tail log backups 202
volume separation 170
transaction log backup 200–203
transaction log marks 211
transaction performance targets 229
Transaction Processing Performance Council (TPC) 18
transactional consistency (BLOBs) 182
transactional replication 340
transactionally consistent 179, 197, 273
transactions/sec 372
Transparent Data Encryption (TDE) 102, 120–123, 182, 223
  support per SQL edition 7
triple DES 120
trustworthy computing initiative 124
TSQL_Replay template 339
tuning advisor. *See* Database Engine Tuning Advisor

U

Ultra320 SCSI 17
UMS. *See* User Mode Scheduler
unattended installation 67
unexpected outage 226
uniform extent 266
unique constraint 285
UNIQUEIDENTIFIER 181
uniqueifier 285
unpredictable performance 376
unrestored log 253
unsent log 253
UPDATE STATISTICS 321, 324
Upgrade Advisor 68
upgrade solution 232
upgrade technical reference guide 68
upgrading to SQL Server 2008
  in-place upgrade 70
  side-by-side upgrade 71–73
  Upgrade Advisor 68–70
  upgrade technical reference guide 68
UPS 37
usable life (SSD) 29
USE PLAN 402
usecount 400
user connections 143
user connections (report) 372
user mode 136

User Mode Scheduler (UMS) 391
user objects 169
user/schema separation 110
user_lookups. *See* sys.dm_db_index_usage_stats
user_scans. *See* sys.dm_db_index_usage_stats
user_seeks. *See* sys.dm_db_index_usage_stats
user_updates. *See* sys.dm_db_index_usage_stats

V

varbinary(max) data type 178
varchar(max) data type 178
VDI. *See* Virtual Device Interface
vendor support 74
very large database (VLDB) 212
Virtual Device Interface (VDI) 23
virtual LAN (VLAN) 92
virtual machines (VM) 53
virtual server 79
virtualization 51–56, 70
virtualized RAID 15, 19
virtualized storage 169
virus scanners 41
Visual Studio Team System Database Edition 256
VLAN. *See* virtual LAN
VLDB. *See* very large database
VM. *See* virtual machines
VMWare. *See* virtualization
volume separation 169
volume test environment 314
V-RAID. *See* virtualized RAID

W

wait category 332
wait list 392
waiting_tasks_count 393
waits 372
  observing with Activity Monitor 332
  observing with sys.dm_os_wait_stats 393
waits and queues tuning methodology 392
wait_time_ms 393
wait_type 393

WAN. *See* wide area network
warm standby 236, 238
_WA_Sys 322
Web edition 8
weekly tasks 420
wide area network (WAN) 243
Windows administrator 104
Windows authentication 65, 97,
     160
Windows authentication
     mode 97
Windows event log 162, 270, 357
Windows installer 62
Windows Management Instru-
     mentation (WMI) 61, 162
Windows Server 2008 61
     clustering improvements 81
WITH RECOMPILE 400

WMI Query Language
     (WQL) 162
WMI. *See* Windows Management
     Instrumentation
worker threads 255
Workgroup edition 7
working relationship 26
workload analysis 334
workload classification 14
workload groups (Resource
     Governor) 380–382
worst practices 417
WQL. *See* WMI Query Language
write balancing (SSD) 29
write burst 37
write cache 37, 172
write ordering 28
write overhead (RAID) 21

write performance 37
WRITELOG 410

X

Xeon 45
XML indexes 264
XML policy files 158
xp_cmdshell 105, 125, 152
XPCmdShellEnabled 152

Z

ZBR. *See* zoned-bit recording
zero data loss 238, 242
zero padding files 174
zoned-bit recording (ZBR) 32
zoning 27